VISUAL QUICKSTART GUIDE

FrameMaker 4

FOR WINDOWS

Jann Tolman

Peachpit Press *Berkeley, California*

Visual QuickStart Guide
FrameMaker 4 for Windows
Jann Tolman

Peachpit Press, Inc.
2414 Sixth Street
Berkeley, CA 94710
(510) 548-4393
(510) 548-5991 (fax)

Screen captures created with Collage Complete, Inner Media.

The text face is BerkeleyOS; Futura, Futura Light, and Futura Extra Bold are used for most heads and other type.

ISBN: 1-56609-097-0
0 9 8 7 6 5 4 3 2 1

Printed and bound in the United States of America

Printed on recycled paper

Contents

Contents

Getting Started

■ FrameMaker bests

Here are a few of my favorite things about FrameMaker.

■ **A single, fully WYSIWYG screen** for formatting, editing, graphics, tables, and equations. I love not having to switch screens or views to do different things.

■ **The Designer windows** (Paragraph Designer, Character Designer, and Table Designer). In other desktop publishing applications, "Styles" are sort of frosting on the cake. In FrameMaker, the Designer windows are used to create formats ("styles") *and* as a general work area. They're not frosting, they're the cake. Don't be afraid to play around and see how they work. They're not hard, honest! Chapter 5 tells all.

■ **Tables** are particularly intuitive in FrameMaker. You don't have to change modules or invoke an editor, and you can see exactly what you're getting as you work. You can even put graphics in them.

■ **Cross references! Hypertext! Smart Quotes! Variables!** I don't know where to stop... Welcome to FrameMaker.

Take advantage of FrameMaker

If you take advantage of features such as the Designer windows and the format catalogs, you will be able to produce crisp, beautiful, and incredibly consistent *documents without ever having to repeat any formatting work. This is FrameMaker's great offering. When you have made something look the way you want it to, you never have to do that work again. You can reuse layouts and formats for paragraphs, tables, characters, pages, cross references, and variables. Other people can use your formats in their documents, and you can use theirs.*

FrameMaker can seem like a bit of a bear when you begin because it does so much, but it has very consistent ways of working. You'll be surprised at how quickly you feel at home using it.

I hope this book will help you.

■ Notation in this book

Menu choices

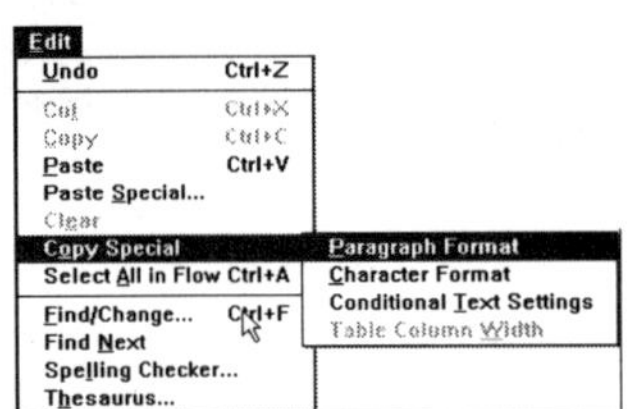

A menu path.

When I want to tell you where to find something in the Main menuing system—the menu bar that's always at the top of the screen—I use this symbol, ➜, to show the menu path you take to find the item. For example, I'll write **Edit ➜ Copy Special ➜ Paragraph Format** to refer to the selection sequence shown in the margin.

Mouse actions

This	Means do this
Click	Press and quickly release the *left* mouse button.
Double-click	Click the left mouse button twice rapidly without moving the mouse.
Right-click	Press and quickly release the right mouse button.
Shift-click or Ctrl-click	Hold down the shift key or the Ctrl key and click the left mouse button.
Press-and-drag	Hold down the left mouse button as you move the mouse.

Keyboard shortcuts

I note my favorite keyboard shortcuts throughout this book. They are always **in this typeface**.Often, they are at the end of the sentence in square brackets. [**like this**] A hyphen between the keys means you press the keys all together. Spaces between means you just type them in sequence—no need to hold anything down.

This	Means do this
Alt f i f	Type the Alt key, and lowercase letters **f**, **i**, and **f** in succession. No need to hold down one key while the next is typed.
Ctrl-s	Hold down the Ctrl key while you type **s**.

■ Starting FrameMaker

You have the usual Windows choices:

The FrameMaker icon.

- Double-click the FrameMaker icon.
- In File Manager, double-click on MAKER.EXE, or highlight MAKER.EXE and choose Run from the File menu.

Starting FrameMaker by clicking on a FrameMaker file icon

You can also start FrameMaker by double-clicking on the icon of any FrameMaker file if you have associated the filename extension with FrameMaker. To begin with, choose and consistently use an extension for your FrameMaker files.

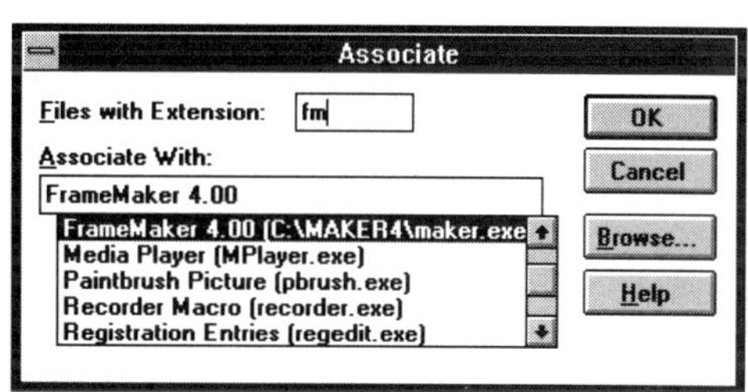

In Windows File Manager, choose **File→Associate** *to display this dialog box.*

▼

Using .DOC as the extension for your FrameMaker files may cause problems because so many other applications use this. Try something more distinctive, like .FM, if you're going to have File Manager associate the extension with FrameMaker.

▲

- Go to Windows File Manager and choose **File→Associate** to associate the file extension you use for FrameMaker files with MAKER.EXE in the directory where FrameMaker is installed. Those of you who are upgrading from FrameMaker 3 will need to use different extensions for the two versions if you are Associating both versions. Be sure that you associate the MAKER.EXE that is in the latest FrameMaker directory.

Note If FrameMaker is already running when you double-click on a FrameMaker file icon, you will get a pop-up error window.

■ The FrameMaker screen

This is the FrameMaker screen with a file open full size. The QuickAccess bar, the Formatting bar, rulers, and borders are turned on.

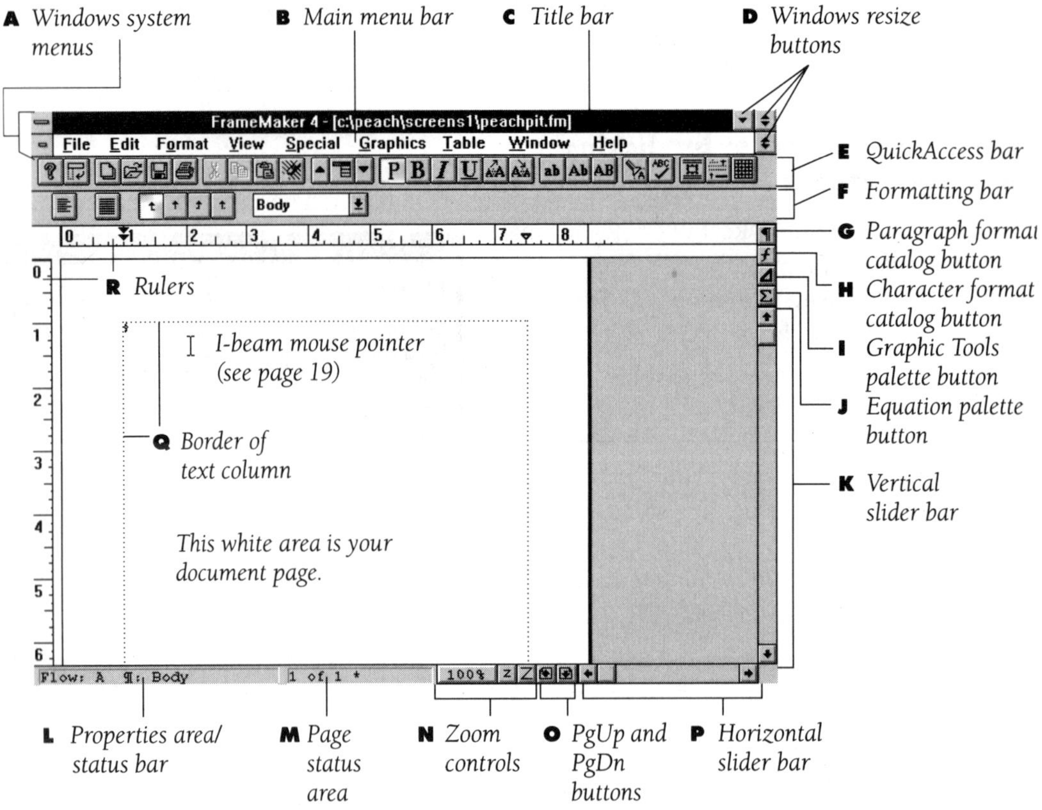

A *Windows system menus*
B *Main menu bar*
C *Title bar*
D *Windows resize buttons*
E *QuickAccess bar*
F *Formatting bar*
G *Paragraph format catalog button*
H *Character format catalog button*
I *Graphic Tools palette button*
J *Equation palette button*
K *Vertical slider bar*
L *Properties area/ status bar*
M *Page status area*
N *Zoom controls*
O *PgUp and PgDn buttons*
P *Horizontal slider bar*
Q *Border of text column*
R *Rulers*

I-beam mouse pointer *(see page 19)*

This white area is your document page.

Other familiar FrameMaker screens On the left below is a screen with no Formatting bar and the QuickAccess bar in vertical position. On the right is a screen with a document at reduced size (use the [button] button). The QuickAccess and Formatting bars are off. (See page 25 for how to turn them on and off.)

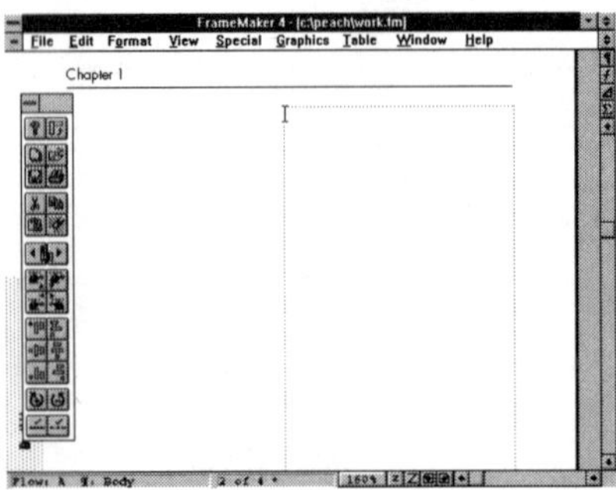

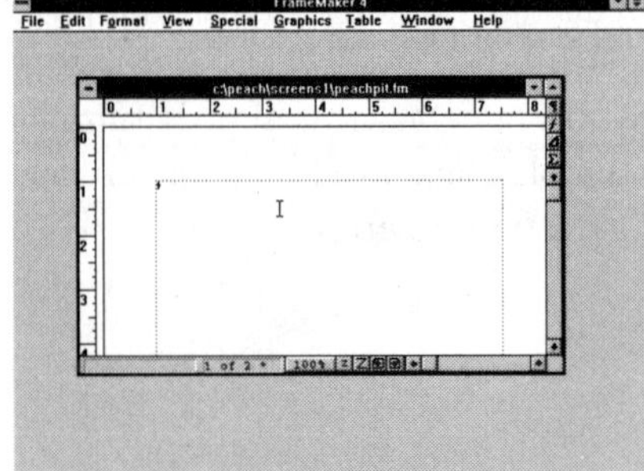

Key to the FrameMaker screen

A Windows system menus The bottom one is for the displayed document. The top one is for FrameMaker. Click to get a menu for moving, switching, or closing windows. Double-click on the document button to close the document (same as **File ➔Close**).

B Main menu bar Click on any one of these items to get a menu of choices. See Chapter 2 for a run-through of what choices are available in each item.

C Title bar Shows the name of the displayed file, including the path. When you Save, you write to this file. If **No Name** appears here, you opened the file using the New command, and must SaveAs to create a new file.

D Windows resize buttons These are the standard Windows controls: make the window fill the screen, shrink partway down, or turn into an icon. The top two are for the FrameMaker window, the bottom one is for your document window.

E Quick Access bar This is optional, but handy: four "pages" of buttons for text, graphics, and table editing, plus some basic commands that are always visible. See pages 7 and 8.

F Formatting bar Apply paragraph formats and set paragraph alignment, line spacing, and tab types. Again, optional, but handy. Its use is described on pages 9 and 10.

G Paragraph format catalog button

Click this to display a list of available paragraph formats. You can create these with Paragraph Designer (page 93) or the Formatting bar (page 94), or import them from another document (page 107).

H Character format catalog button

Click this to display a list of available character formats. You can create these with Character Designer (100) or import them from another document (page 107).

I Graphic Tools palette button Click this to display a moveable graphics/drawing toolbox, including buttons for creating text columns (page 215), text lines (page 68), and frames (page203). See Chapter 12 on drawing and editing graphics in FrameMaker.

J Equations palette button Click this to display FrameMaker's palette of elements for creating and evaluating equations. This is a breathtaking feature, but is beyond the scope of this book. Tell Peachpit Press you're waiting for the advanced FrameMaker book.

K Vertical slider bar Move forward and back by lines, pages, screens, or variable increments. See page 17.

L Properties area (status bar)

- If you have an insertion point (page 19) in text, this area shows the flow, the paragraph format name (tag), and the character format name of the text at that point.

```
Flow: A  ¶: Body   f: C-Ca
```

The paragraph tag of the current paragraph. *The character tag of the current text.*

- If you are drawing an object, it shows the height and width of the object.
- If you are moving an object, it shows the location of the upper left-hand corner of the object. See pages 257 to 265 for more on how to see and change the size and location of your object.

Key to the FrameMaker screen *(continued)*

M Page status area Click on this area once to display the Go to Page dialog box. For more information on Go to Page, see page 16.

This area shows you how many pages are in the file, and what page is displayed. If you have made a change since you last Saved the file, the asterisk appears, to remind you to save your work.

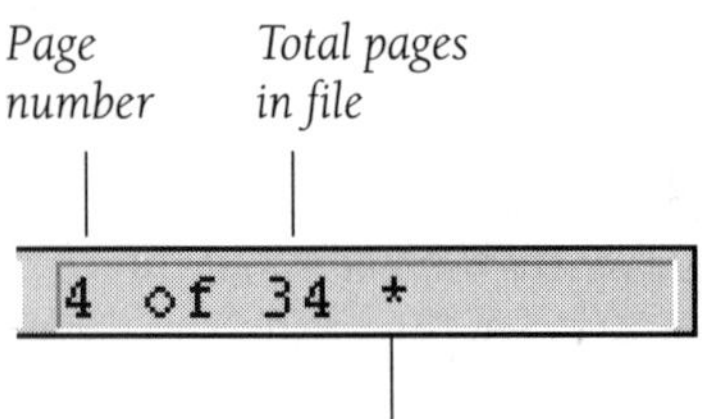

■ If the first page of the document is a number other than one, the bar looks like this:

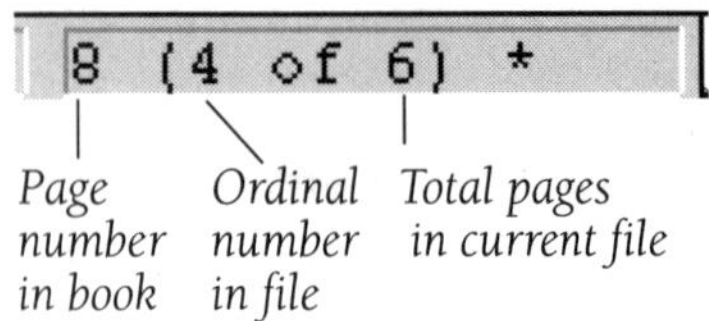

If you have combined several files into a book and the page numbering continues between files, this is what you see.

N Zoom controls Use these to adjust the display size of your document. This doesn't affect the type size, or the printing; just the display. The Zoom controls are explained beginning on page 12.

O PageUp/PageDown buttons Click on these to go to the next or previous page. See pages 16–17 for more on moving around in your document.

P Horizontal slider bar Lets you move sideways in the display.

Q Border of text column A text column is an area you can type into. What you see here is the *border* of a text column. See page 25 for displaying or hiding borders.

R Rulers The rulers help you position things when you're working.

■ Display/hide rulers from the View menu: **View →Rulers.** **[Alt v r]**

■ You can see and change tabs and indents on the ruler bar. Changes that you make here are for selected paragraphs only. You can set tabs in the Paragraph Designer. See page 113 for setting tabs, and page 112 for setting indents, using either technique.

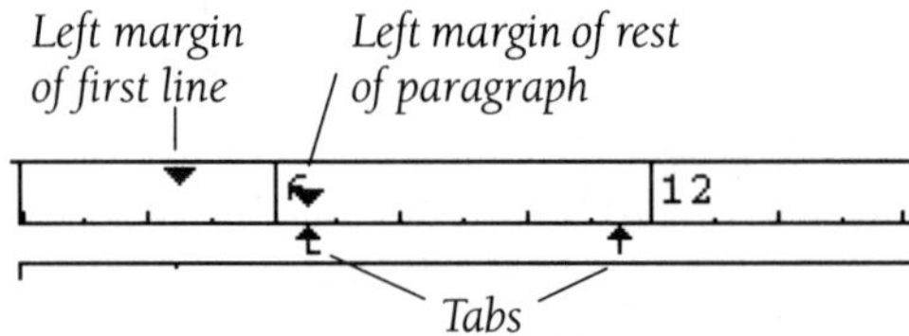

■ You can set the units that the ruler displays using **View →Options →Ruler**. The example above is set to display picas. See page 26 for more on setting units of measurement and other View Options.

■ The borders of selected objects are visible in the rulers when you point on the border of the object and hold down Ctrl and the left mouse button.

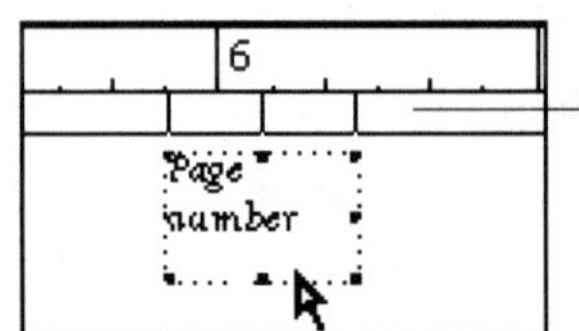

These three lines show the two sides and the center of the object. The side ruler shows the vertical boundaries.

■ The QuickAccess bar

Horizontal QuickAccess bar

Change the "page" of the bar

This part of the bar never changes

This part has four layers (or pages). You see page one here.

The same bar, vertical position

The QuickAccess bar works just the same whether it's vertical or horizontal. You can drag the vertical one around by its top. [Alt v q]

Left button	Right button
Help	Swing bar to horizontal
New file	Open file
Save	Print
Cut	Copy
Paste	Undo
Previous page	**Next page**
Plain text	Bold
Italic	Underline
1 point larger	1 point smaller
Lowercase	Anchored frame
Initial cap	Insert footnote
Uppercase	Insert table
Find/Change	Spelling checker

Page 1 Text editing

Left button	Right button
Previous page	**Next page**
Group	Ungroup
Bring to front	Send to back
Distribute	Reshape
Smooth	Unsmooth
Flip up/down	Flip right/left
Scale	Properties
Snap	Gravity

Page 2 Graphics

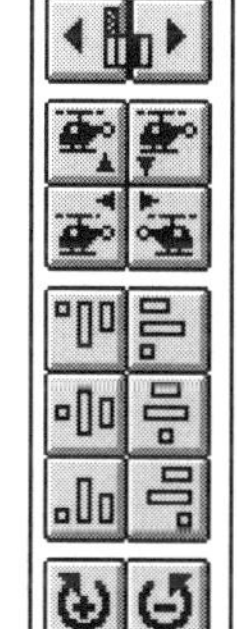

Left button	Right button
Previous page	**Next page**
Move up 1 pt	Move down 1 pt
Move 1 pt left	Move 1 pt right
Top align	Left align
Vertical center align	Horizontal center align
Bottom align	Right align
Rotate clockwise	Rotate counterclockwise
Set line to solid	Set line to dashed

Page 3 Graphics editing

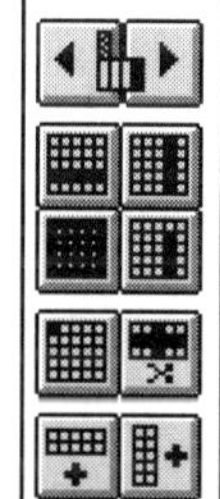

Left button	Right button
Previous page	**Next page**
Select row	Select column
Select table	Select column omitting hdr/footer
Insertion point to UL corner	Cut rows or cols omitting alert
Add rows below	Add columns to right
Top-align text	Straddle/unstraddle
Middle-align text	Shrinkwrap selected
Bottom-align text	Ruling and shading

Page 4 Table editing

Press-and-drag on this part to move the bar.

Using the QuickAccess bar

The buttons are the same whether the bar is vertical or horizontal.

Display or dismiss it	**View→QuickAccess Bar** The bar appears in either horizontal or vertical position, whichever you used last. [**Alt v q**]
Flip it *between vertical and horizontal*	Click this or this button.
Move it *(vertical bar only)*	Point on the top of the bar, hold down the left mouse button, and drag the bar where you want it. You can't move the bar when it's horizontal.
Change page	Click on one of the Change Page arrow buttons. The middle symbol shows you which page is currently displayed. 
Get help	Click this button.

Everything you can do with the QuickAccess bar can also be done using the Main menu and the various Designer windows and palettes. The QuickAccess bar is a convenience.

To understand how to use a QuickAccess button, look at the label on page 7 and then read the appropriate section of this book. The buttons are just another way to access the commands.

Bold, italic and underline: A modest proposal

Changes that you make using the buttons for Bold, Italic, Underline, and point size on page one of the QuickAccess bar are hard to find and hard to change because they have no format tag. You can't search for them by tag name, or automatically update them by changing the format definition. Eventually, I think you'll come to appreciate tagged formats, so be cautious about using these buttons at first. You can make character formats for bold, italic, and underline (page 106), and apply them from the catalog (page 99) or from the keyboard (page 91). It's as easy as the buttons, and you've got the advantage of a format tag.

Use all the rest of the QuickAccess bar to your heart's content—it's one of FrameMaker4's spiffy new offerings.

■ The Formatting bar

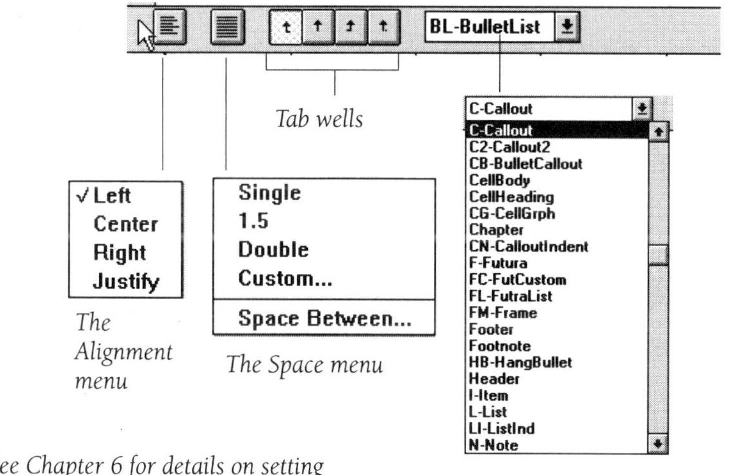

The Alignment menu

The Space menu

See Chapter 6 for details on setting paragraph properties.

The Paragraph format pop-up menu

The Alignment menu

Set the alignment for the paragraph containing the insertion point. This is exactly the same as choosing Alignment in the Paragraph Designer and then choosing Apply to Selection.

The Space menu

Set the space either between the lines of the paragraph containing the insertion point or between two selected paragraphs. This is exactly the same as setting the Line Spacing or Space Above/Space Below in the Paragraph Designer and choosing Apply to Selection. See "Space above and below paragraphs" on page 118.

Custom Set custom space between the lines. It also shows you what the value of "Single," etc. is in the selected paragraph.

Space Between Adjust the space between two paragraphs. You must have two paragraphs selected before you choose this. See page 66 for how to select two paragraphs.

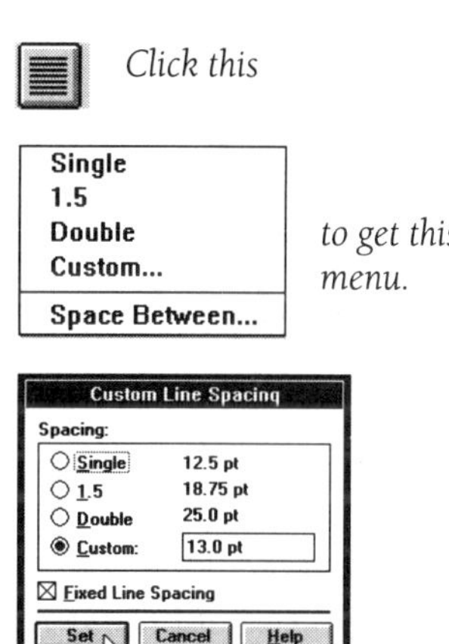

The Custom linespace menu.

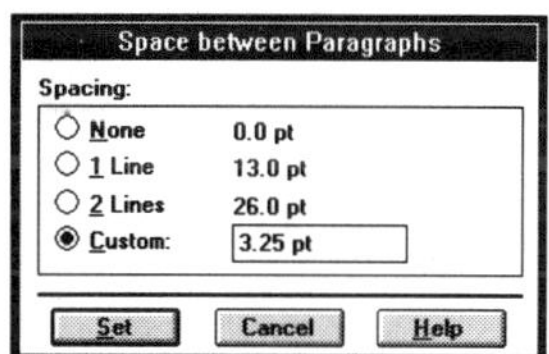

The Space Between menu.

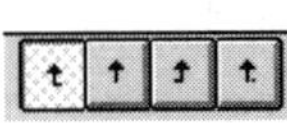

Click on one of these to and then click in the space below the ruler to create a left, center, right, or decimal tab.

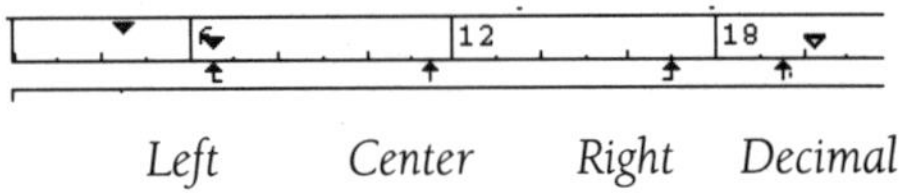

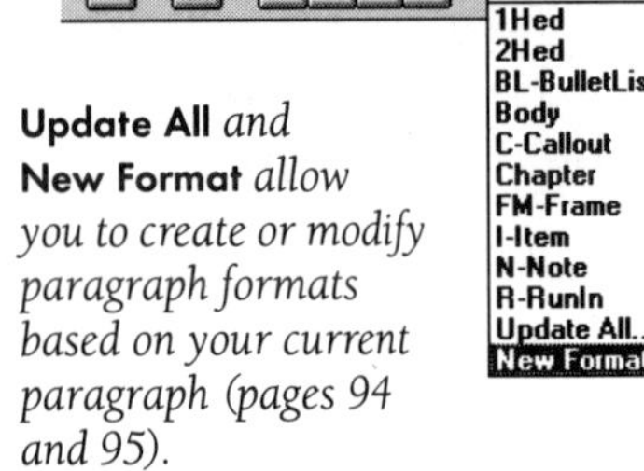

Update All *and* **New Format** *allow you to create or modify paragraph formats based on your current paragraph (pages 94 and 95).*

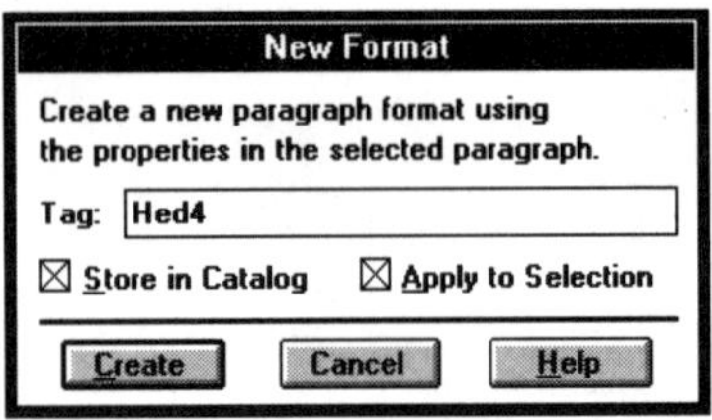

Click on New Format in the Formatting bar pop-up to display the New Format dialog box.

Using the Designers

If you are going to want a particular format more than once or twice it is well worth while to make a character format or a paragraph format using the Character Designer and the Paragraph Designer. If you change your mind later, you can change everything that has a particular format tag by changing the definition of the format. See Chapter 5 for how to use the Designers.

Tab buttons

(FrameMaker calls these "tab wells.") Another way to set tabs: click on one of these to choose the type of tab, then click in the ruler to place the tab. You can set tabs in the Paragraph Designer, too. See "Tabs" on page 113.

Paragraph Format pop-up menu

This is a catalog of available paragraph formats. Click on one of these to apply the format to the paragraph containing the insertion point. This is the same list that appears in the Paragraph Catalog that you pop up with the ¶ button, and the same one that appears in the Paragraph Designer. The difference is that this one includes Update All and New Format at the end of the list.

Update All Make a change to the alignment, spacing, or tabs, and then change the format definition and all occurrences of that format by clicking on this. See "Modifying a format to match your text" on page 95.

New Format Create a new paragraph format from the paragraph that contains your insertion point, including any changes you just made. See "Creating a new paragraph format from your text" on page 94.

A general note about the Formatting bar

Changes that you make with this bar apply only to the selected paragraphs unless you also apply Update All or New Format. These changes are called "overrides."

Anything you can do with the Formatting bar you can also do from the Paragraph Designer. I like to use the Paragraph Designer because all my other paragraph formatting choices are right there, too. And I almost always used named formats because it's so much easier to keep things consistent and current that way. Chapter 5 tells you all about using the Designers.

■ Using the menu bar

■ Click on any Main menu item to get a drop-down menu, then click on the item you want.

■ **or** press-and-drag on the menu item, and drag the highlight bar to your item. When you release the mouse button, the action happens.

■ **Three dots** after an item mean you will see another window displayed (like the Find/Change window, or the View Options window).

■ **A little triangle** on the right means there is another menu level. When you choose that item, the next menu is displayed.

■ **A checkmark** to the left means that the item is toggled on. If you select it again, you will turn it off.

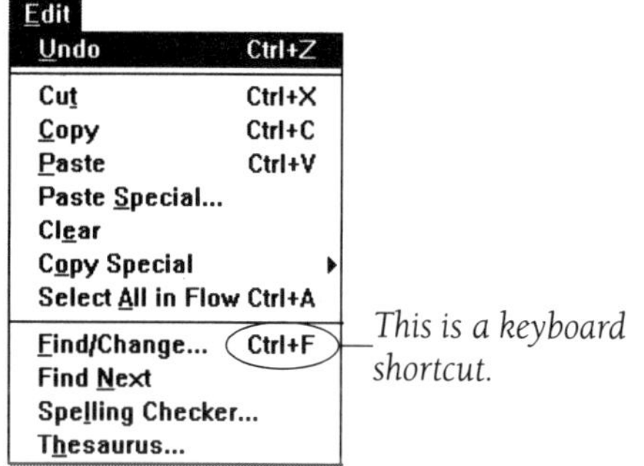

This is a keyboard shortcut.

Using keyboard shortcuts

■ Open any Main menu by typing **Alt** and the underlined letter. Then choose any item from the menu by typing the underlined letter. You don't have to hold **Alt** down, or press it again.

■ There are some shortcuts listed on the right side of some drop-down menus. **Ctrl+X**, for example, means hold down the **Ctrl** key while you type **x**. When the control key is used, it never matters whether you type an uppercase or a lower case letter. In other combinations, such as those with the **Alt** key, case may make a difference. My notation for **Ctrl+X** is **Ctrl-x**.

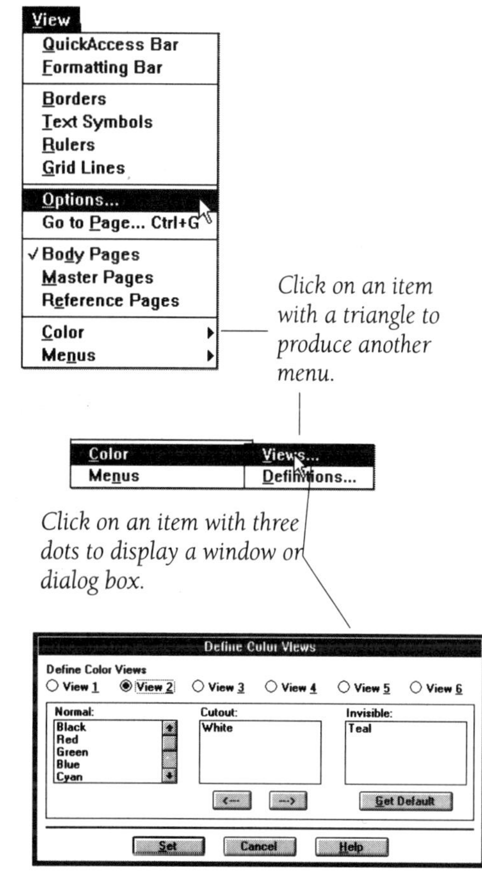

Click on an item with a triangle to produce another menu.

Click on an item with three dots to display a window or dialog box.

A note about Edit→Select All in This menu item changes, depending on what's selected. **Ctrl-a** always selects whatever is shown in this menu entry.

What's selected	What's in the Edit Menu
A paragraph (meaning you've got an insertion point)	Select All in Flow
A frame, or anything in a frame	Select All in Frame
Nothing; or an object not in a frame; or a text column on a page	Select all on Page

If you can see something, but can't select it, it's probably on a master page. Choose **View→Master Page** to go to the master page underlying the body page. [**Alt v m**]

■ Changing the magnification of the display

Press on the Zoom button [100%] and drag the highlight bar to the magnification you want.

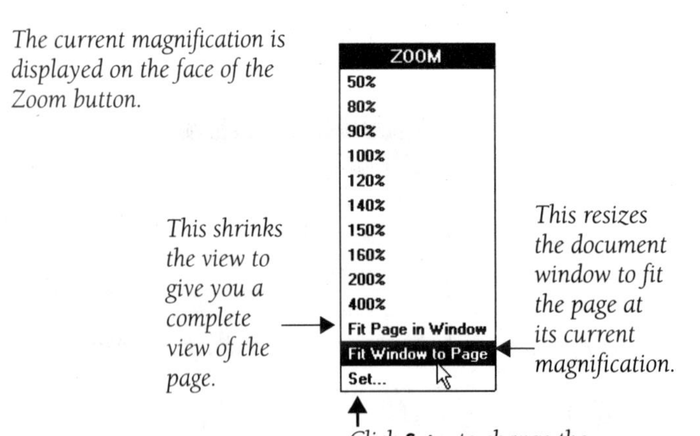

The current magnification is displayed on the face of the Zoom button.

This shrinks the view to give you a complete view of the page.

This resizes the document window to fit the page at its current magnification.

Click **Set...** *to change the choices you see in this menu.*

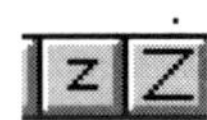

Zoom buttons

Click the small **z** *to Zoom out to the next smaller choice on the menu. Click the large* **Z** *to Zoom in to the next larger choice. The Zoom menu does not have to be open.*

▪ When you Zoom in or out, FrameMaker places any selected paragraph, object, frame, or text column at the center of the new view. A paragraph containing the insertion point is "selected."

Changing the choices in the Zoom menu

The Zoom menu can contain any ten sizes you want. In the Zoom menu, click on Set.... to display the Zoom Set menu. Replace any choices you don't want with any percents between 25 and 1600. (See page 14 if you're not sure how to type into text boxes like these.) Don't worry about the order. FrameMaker will display the numbers in ascending sequence.

▪ Your changes will be there next time you start FrameMaker. It "remembers." Click on the Get Defaults button to return to the choices that ship with FrameMaker.

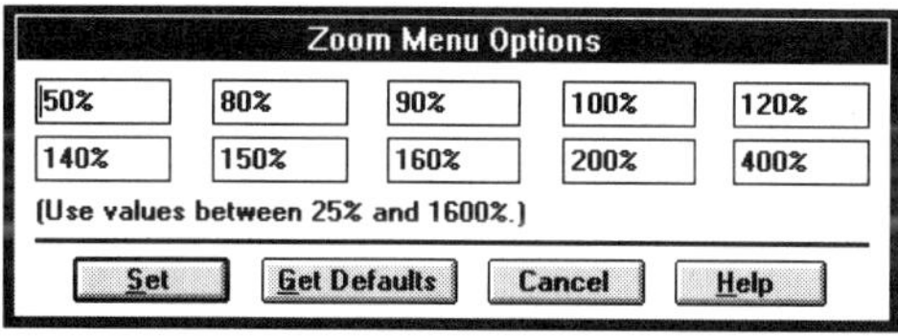

You can have any ten zoom sizes you want. Replace one that you don't want with a number you do want. FrameMaker automatically puts the numbers in order.

▪ Using windows and dialog boxes

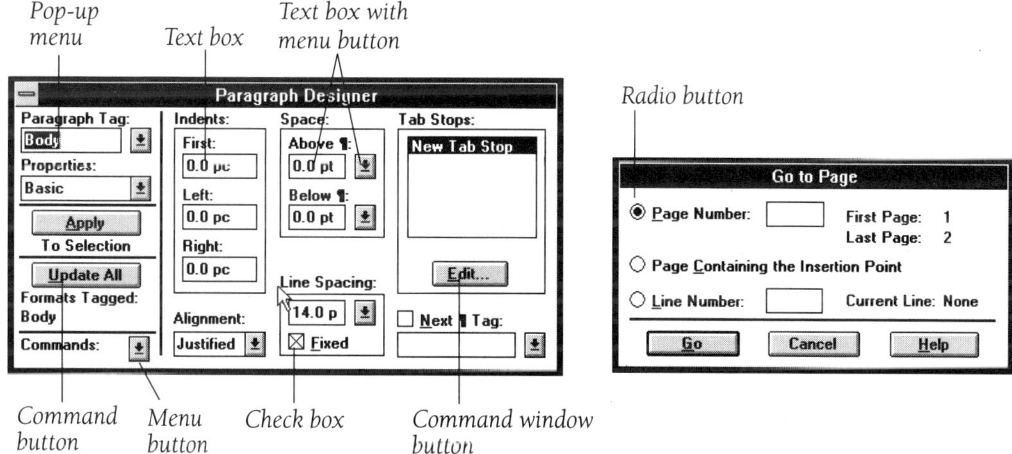

Press Tab to move the focus from one area of the window to the next. Shift-Tab moves the focus back. The "focus" is where you can work. Clicking on an area automatically brings the focus there.

The parts of a window or dialog box

Basic	*Pop-up menu*	Click anywhere on the box or button, and then click on the item you want; or press-and drag the highlight bar to the item you want. You can't type into a box that's attached to a button. The box shows which item is chosen. When the list is more than a few items it becomes a *scroll list.* (See page 15 for more about working in scroll lists.)
0.0 pc	*Text box*	Click once to get an insertion point and edit the old entry, or click twice to select the old entry. What you type will replace the highlighted entry. If the box contains display units and you want a different unit, see "Display Units," page 26. You don't have to type a unit at all if you are using the default unit.
0.0 pt	*Text box with button*	When the box is next to the button, but not attached, you have two choices: ■ **Type what you want in the box.** When you click in a box-with-button like this, the contents are highlighted. When you type, the old contents are replaced with your entry. Click twice to get an insertion point so you can edit the old entry. Press Home or End to go to the beginning or end of a long entry. ■ **Click on the button** to get a pop-up menu of choices.
Apply	*Command button*	Click on the button; the command happens.
Edit...	*Command window button*	Three dots on the button label mean that clicking on the button will display a window or dialog box.
	Radio buttons	Click on the button to select (left button in this illustration) an item; this unselects all other items in the group.
	Check boxes	Mostly, the check boxes just toggle between on ("do it") and off. In the Designer windows, however, clicking on a check box cycles it between three states. The gray is "As Is." It says to FrameMaker, "When you apply the other properties in this window, leave this property alone."

The menu button

This menu button ⊻ is a special case of the command button. Whenever you see it, you can click to get a pop-up menu.

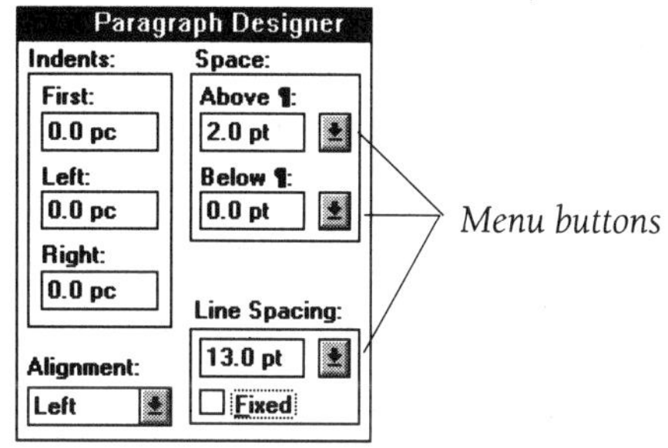

▼

The difference between windows and dialog boxes

Windows stay up while you work; they've got the Windows menu box ▭ in the upper left-hand corner. Dismiss a window by double-clicking on that corner.

Dialog boxes must be dismissed before you can click in the document window. You can always press Esc to get rid of a dialog box. If there's a Cancel or Done button, click that.

▲

About using scroll menus

Here are some ways to use a scroll menu:

- If the item you want is off the top or bottom of the list, hold down the left mouse button and push the mouse pointer against the top or bottom of the box. Don't let go of the mouse button until the item you want is highlighted.
- Type the first letter of the item you want repeatedly, until your item is highlighted.
- Move the highlight bar with the up and down arrow keys.
- Use the scroll bar. Click on an arrow to scroll the list one line. Drag the button to move quickly. Click on the gray area above or below the button to scroll one window at a time.

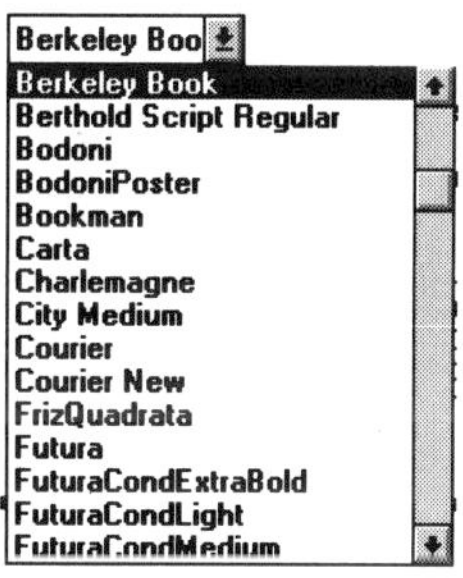

A scroll menu.

When the item you want is highlighted

Either click on the item or click on the menu button to close the list.

Cancelling a scroll menu: Click on the menu button ⊻ or click outside the window or dialog box. The list "un-pops."

■ Moving around in your document

You have several ways to move around in your Framemaker document: the scroll bar, the Go to Page box, the page buttons, and keyboard shortcuts.

The page buttons

Look on the bottom border of your window for the Page buttons.

Click on a button to go to the next or previous page. Shift-click to go to the first or last page of the file.

The Go to Page box

To get this box, click on the Page Status area, type **Ctrl-g**, or choose **View➔Go to Page**.

Type the number of the page you want in here.

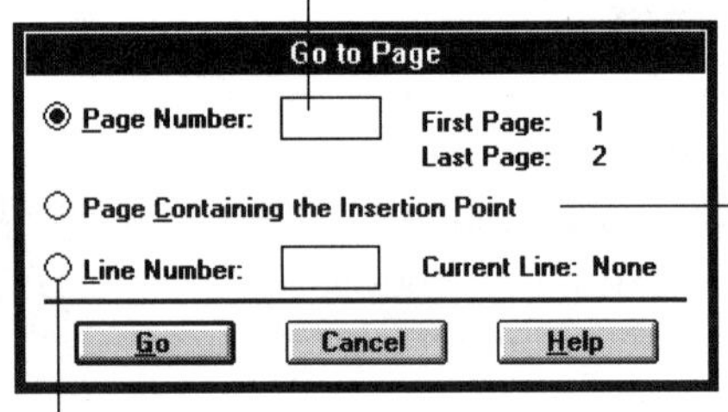

If you change pages but don't click on anything, your insertion point doesn't move. This is a quick way to get back to where you were last working.

You can go to an exact line anywhere in the file, if you know the number.

4 of 34 *

The quickest way to get the Go to Page dialog box is to click on the Page Status area.

Press-and-drag

Move up, down, and sideways on a page by holding down the left mouse button and moving the pointer against the side of the page you want to move to. Try to position the pointer outside of a text column or frame, so you don't select anything. If you do select text or objects as you move, just click in a blank area (outside all text columns or frames) to unselect everything. If you've not sure where a blank area is, turn on borders, **View➔Borders**. **[Alt v b]**

The slide bars

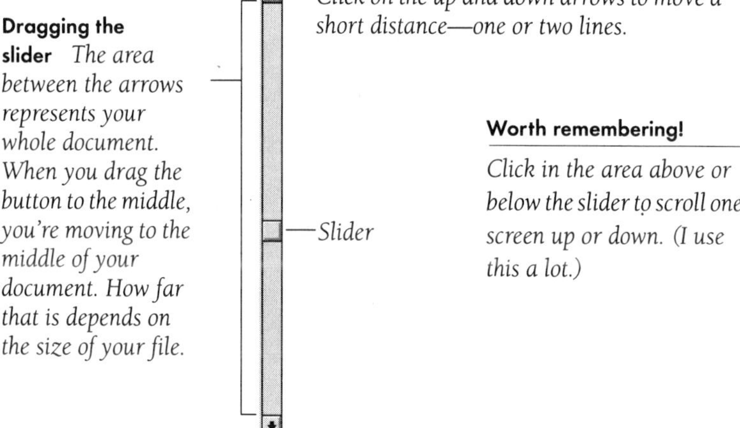

Worth remembering!

Click in the area above or below the slider to scroll one screen up or down. (I use this a lot.)

Keyboard shortcuts

Keyboard shortcuts let you move your insertion point through text with speed and agility. Here are my favorites.

To move this far	Use this shortcut
Beginning/end of word*	**Ctrl-→, Ctrl-←**
Beginning/end of line*	**Home, End**
Beginning/end of sentence*	**Ctrl-Home, Ctrl-End**
Beginning/end of paragraph*	**Ctrl-↑, Ctrl-↓**
Top/bottom of text column	**Ctrl-PgUp, Ctrl-PgDn**
Next/previous page	**PgUp, PgDn**
Beginning/end of flow	**Alt-Shift-PgUp, Alt-Shift-PgDn**

For these starred items, if you hold down Shift as well, you will select the text as you move the insertion point. For more on selecting, see page 66.

▼

Easy paging

Here's an easy way to scroll through pages when the page is larger than the screen: **Ctrl-PgDn** *and then* **down arrow key**. *Ctrl-PgDn takes you to the last line on the page. Then the down arrow key pops you to the top of the next page. Similarly, you can page backward with Ctrl-PgUp and the up arrow key. On a multiple-column page, this moves you smoothly through the columns, one after another.*

▲

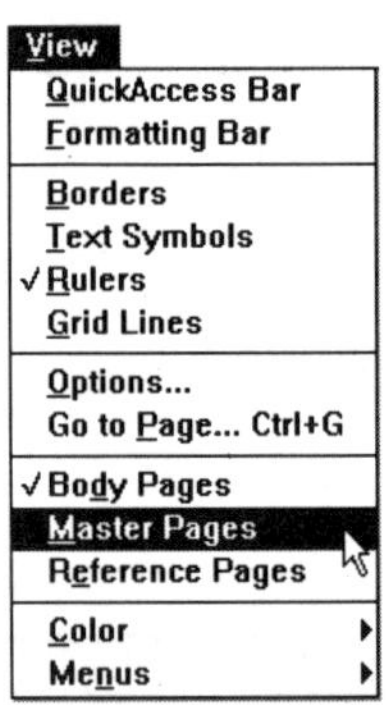

Move between body pages, master pages, and reference pages here.

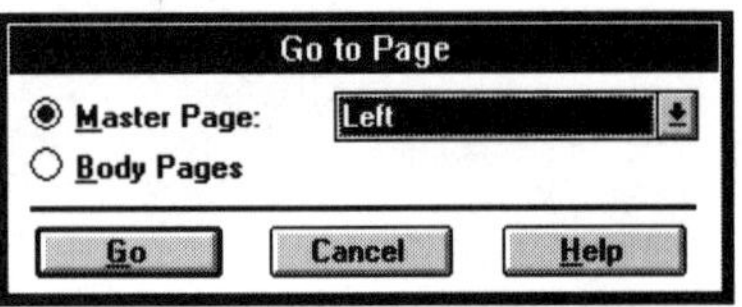

This is what the Go to Page dialog box looks like when you're on a master page. [**Ctrl-g**]

Displaying a master page

View→Master Pages [**Alt v m**] takes you the master page that goes with the current body page. When you are on a master page, **Ctrl-g** displays this special form of the Go to Page dialog box. Click on the Master Page menu button to see a list of master pages.

Displaying a reference page

View→Reference Pages [**Alt v e**] takes you to the first reference page. (Often there is only one.)

Returning to a body page

View→Body Pages [**Alt v d**] returns you to the body page for either a master page or a reference page.

FrameMaker 4 - [c:\peach\work.fm]
Edit Format View Special Graphics Table Window Help

To return the focus from a Designer window to your full-screen document without unselecting anything, click on the Title bar at the top of the document window.

A document window

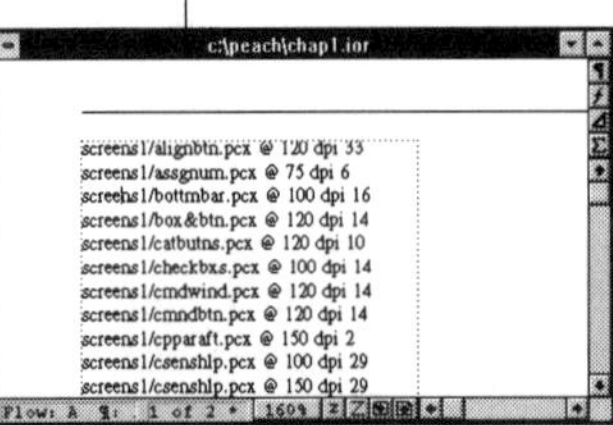

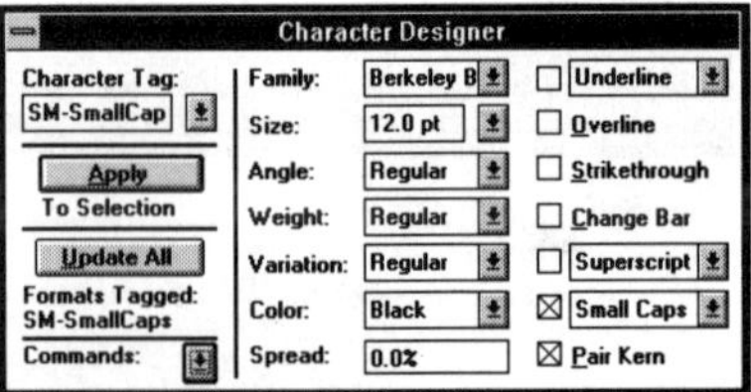

A Designer window

Types of windows: an active window—the window where the focus is—has a darker-colored bar at the top.

■ The insertion point and the active window

Where's the focus?

As you work in FrameMaker, there are two things you need to keep in mind: the active window and the insertion point. You can type only in an active window, and you can type only if you have an insertion point. Your document window must be active before you can save the document or display a different Designer window.

■ "Window" means a document window, a work window such as the Paragraph Designer, a dialog box, a palette, or a catalog.

To make a window active (to change the focus to that window) Click anywhere in a window to make it active. Clicking on the Title bar is safest, because you won't accidentally activate something. This is also known as "changing the focus" to that window.

The insertion point

You must have an insertion point to begin typing in a text column. Position the mouse pointer where you want to type. It should look like an I-beam. Click; you should see the blinking vertical line that is the insertion point. If you're trying to type and nothing happens, see "The insertion point" on page 63 for a whole discussion of why that might be, and what to do.

Position this I-beam pointer at the spot where you want to type or edit, and click to get the blinking vertical line that is your insertion point.

■ Mouse pointer shapes

Watch your mouse pointer! The shape of the mouse pointer tells you what's happening on the screen and what will happen if you click. It changes shape depending on whether it is over text, a graphic object border, an object handle, or a dialog box. Here's the list:

Shape	What it means
I	You're over a text column; click to get an insertion point; you can type or edit text.
	You're over an object border; click to select an object, or press-and-drag to move the object.
1. 2.	You're over a resize handle; press-and-drag to resize or reshape a selected object. **1.** Side: one direction only. **2.** Corner: both directions.
	Click to activate a command button or pop-up a menu.

■ Undo

To cancel the effects of your last command, click on the Undo button on the QuickAccess bar, or type **Ctrl-z**. **Edit→Undo** will accomplish this, too. You can un-paste, un-select, un-move, un-copy, and un-type, among other things. Undoing from the menu, the keyboard, and the QuickAccess bar are exactly the same.

Undoing Undo If you don't like what happened when you Undid, use Undo again. It Undoes the Undo, and things are back where they were. You don't have to use the same technique. If you used a keyboard shortcut the first time, you can use the QuickAccess button or **Edit→Undo** the second time. They're all the same.

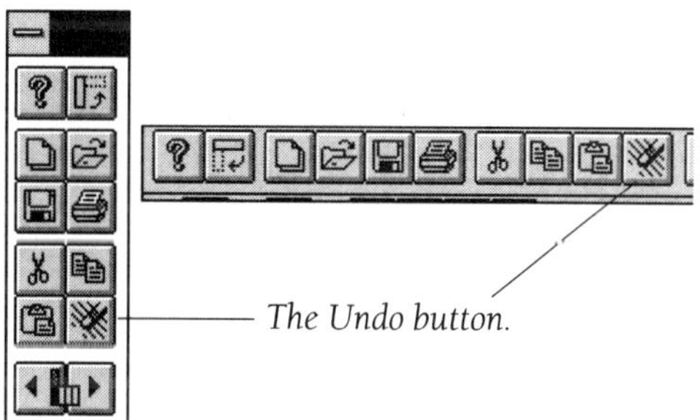

The Undo button.

■ Redrawing the page

Ctrl-l (*ell*) redraws the screen. Sometimes when you are editing, some material will seem to disappear off your screen. Don't panic; try Ctrl-l first. This also clears things up when there are leftover bits and pieces on your screen.

■ Preferences, options, and views

This section describes several things that you control about your work environment and how things behave. Most are specific to each document. You can have several documents open with different settings in each. The Preferences in the File menu are permanent: they apply to all documents.

Automatic backups and autosaves

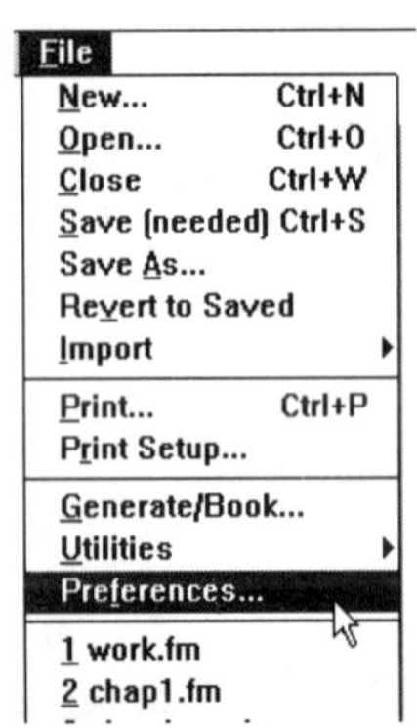

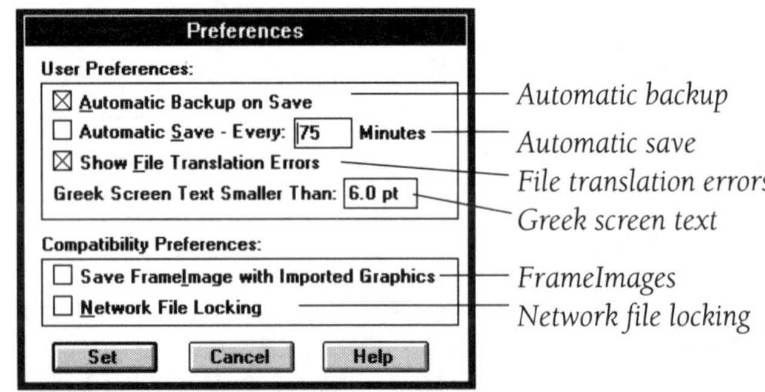

Adjust the settings to your liking, and click Set.

Automatic Backup on Save With this turned on, FrameMaker saves the previous version to a backup file each time you Save a file. The name of the backup file has "%" as the character just before the period: **filename.fm** becomes **filenam%.fm**.

Automatic save When this is turned on, FrameMaker automatically saves your file at the interval you specify in the box. This autosave file name has "$" right before the period: **filename.fm** becomes **filenam$.fm**. When you save your file manually (or revert to the last-saved version—see page 55), FrameMaker erases the autosave file.

☒ Automatic Save - Every: 15 Minutes

In the Preferences dialog box, turn autosave on or off here, and specify how often you want FrameMaker to automatically save your file.

Other FrameMaker Preferences

These are all choices in the **File→Preferences** dialog box shown on page 20. These settings are in effect for all open FrameMaker documents.

File translation errors If FrameMaker encounters any difficulty in opening a file—missing fonts, for example—it will describe these problems in a new window if you turn this feature on.

Greek screen text "Greek" in this context means that FrameMaker puts a gray bar on the screen for each line of type whose size is below the size you specify, rather than taking the time to form each tiny letter on the screen. This speeds up the display time, and is also handy when you are just checking the overall appearance of the page. Typical values for this box would be six, seven, or eight points. Greeking never affects printed output

FrameImages When this is on, FrameMaker adds a FrameImage to any graphic that you copy into your document. This image is viewable on all platforms (Mac, Unix, Windows) that Frame-Maker runs on. FrameImages let you move FrameMaker files between different platforms without worrying about whether your graphic file formats are compatible.

Network file locking When this is on, a user who opens a file that is already in use receives a pop-up warning box, identifying the current user of the file.

▼

Recover files If your system crashes, Frame-Maker tries to save your latest changes in a recover file. This file name has "#" right before the period: **filename.fm** becomes **filenam#.fm**.

▲

9-pt headline

Small, Greeked text with an un-Greeked headline.

Document-specific options

There are several areas on the Main menu where you set document views and preferences. Here's an overview. Each one is discussed in more detail in the next few pages on the referenced page.

Use this menu	To change these
Format→Document	■ Page and paragraph numbering. ■ Smart Quotes and Smart Spaces. ■ Size and position of superscripts, subscripts, and small caps. ■ Adjust page count on Save.
Format→Flow	■ Synchronization (how text lines up across columns). ■ Feathering (make text reach the bottom of the column).
Format→Headers & Footers	Contents of your header and footer lines.
Format→Change Bars	Turn automatic change bar on or off.
Format→Footnote Properties	The style and position of footnotes and their callouts (page 158).
View	Show/hide borders, text symbols, rulers, and visible grid.
View→Options	Set display units, graphics display, page display, visible grid, snap grid, rotate snap.
Graphics menu	Turn on Gravity and Snap.

All of these settings affect only the document you are working in when you set them. They are stored with the document and will be present next time you open that document, no matter what you have worked on in the meantime.

Format
Font
Size
Style
Characters
Paragraphs
Page Break...
Flow...
Pages
Headers & Footers
Document...
Change Bars...
Footnote Properties...

To display the Document Properties window [Alt o d]

Document Properties
Numbering:
1st Page #: 1 Page # Style: Numeric (4)
Restart Paragraph Numbering
Text:
Smart Quotes Smart Spaces
Allow Line Breaks After: / - \= \m
Before Saving & Printing: Delete Empty Pages
Superscript: Subscript: Small Caps:
Size: 80.0% 80.0% 80.0%
Offset: 40.0% 25.0%
Apply Cancel Help

Setting document properties Make the changes and settings you want, and click on Apply.

The Document Properties dialog box

Page and paragraph numbering

1st Page # If your file is part of a larger work, this is where you can make the first page be any number you wish.

Note If your file is part of a book, and the first page number will vary depending on the sizes of previous files, leave this box blank. See page 279 for how to set up files in a book. (A "book" is any multi-file document.)

Page # Style Use this menu to choose the *type* of page numbers you want: numeric, roman, etc.

Other page number issues: Format the *look* of the numbers by changing the definition of the Header or Footer paragraph format or by applying a character format to the page number symbol on the master pages. You can also apply any paragraph format you want to the header and footer. ▲ Change the *location* of the page number by working directly on the master page. See page 212 for more on working with headers and footers.

▼

A page numbering trick

What if you want page one to not be at the beginning of the file? Maybe you've got some front matter that comes first. In a large work, you usually put the front stuff in a separate file, but if you don't want to do that, set the first page number to a negative number in this box. Pick one that will make page one land where you need it to.

▲

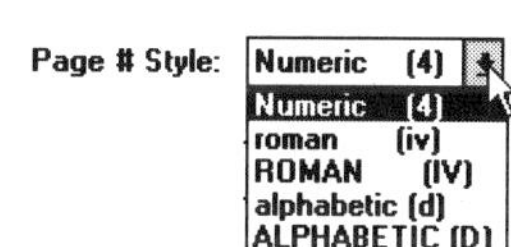

The Page # Style pop-up in the Document Properties dialog box.

Restart Paragraph Numbering This applies to autonumbered paragraphs in a multi-file document. Turn this off if you want chapter numbering, for example, to continue between files in a book. If you want all autonumbering to restart in each file, turn this on.

“ ” ‘ ’

Typographic quotation marks (FrameMaker's "Smart Quotes")

' "

Straight quotes, also used as inch and foot signs

Smart Quotes

When you turn Smart Quotes on, FrameMaker automatically uses the typographic single and double quotation marks. Turn to page 81 for a complete list of how to type quotation marks. "Straight quotes" are the same as the inch and foot signs. For most purposes, you will want Smart Quotes on. They're the standard in desktop publishing and typography.

Text:

☒ Smart Quotes ☒ Smart Spaces

Toggle Smart Quotes and Smart Spaces on/off in the Document Properties dialog box. [**Alt o d**]

Smart Spaces

When this is turned on, FrameMaker does not allow two spaces in a row. This may sound strange to those of you who are used to typewriters, but in desktop publishing, as in typography, two spaces after a period ruin the "texture" of the type. For most purposes, it is useful to keep Smart Spaces on, to correct accidental double spaces.

■ Smart Spaces doesn't remove double spaces that may already be present in text you import into FrameMaker. To do that, use the Spelling Checker (pages 179 to 185).

Allow Line Breaks after

Is it okay with you if lines break after an em dash or en space? Would you like to prevent all line breaks after hyphens that are a permanent part of a word? This is where you tell FrameMaker where it's okay to break a line. The example in the Document Properties window on page 23 looks a little strange because typing special characters in a dialog box requires using the codes in the chart on page A-321. FrameMaker ships with a set of line-ending characters that's perfectly usable for most purposes. Here's where you modify it if you want to.

Allow Line Breaks After: / \\ - \sm \m

This example tells FrameMaker that it's okay to break lines after a forward slash, a backslash (\\), a permanent hyphen, an em space (\sm) and an em dash (\m).

Preferences, options, and views

Before Saving and Printing

Sometimes you want empty pages at the end of a file to go away. Sometimes you want a file to always have an even number of pages, or an odd number of pages. Click this menu button to tell FrameMaker what to do with the end of your file.

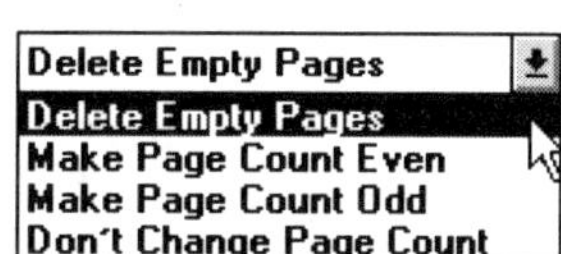

You can tell FrameMaker how to adjust the page count before printing or saving.

Superscripts, subscripts, and small caps

You can specify the size and baseline offset (in percent of the base size) of these elements. The values that you set here are for the whole file. If you change something here, it changes throughout the file.

"Size" is a percent of the default paragraph font size.

	Superscript:	Subscript:	Small Caps:
Size:	80.0%	80.0%	80.0%
Offset:	40.0%	25.0%	

A positive Offset number is up for superscripts and down for subscripts. You can use negative numbers for special purposes.

The View menu

From the View menu, you can affect several things about what you see on the screen. None of these choices affects printed output. View Borders, Text Symbols, Rulers, and Grid Lines are all toggles. Choose one to change it from on to off.

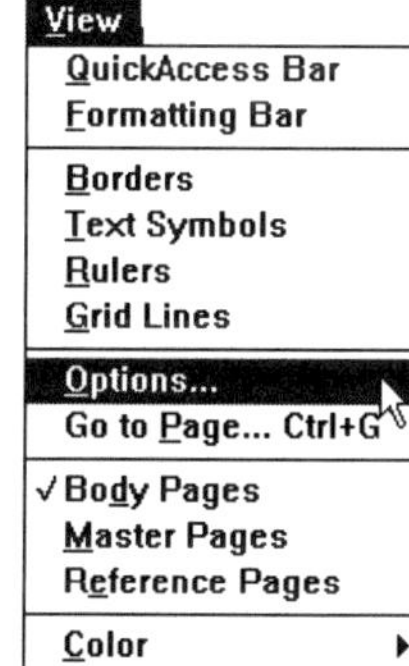

NOTE *The View menu is where you display or hide the Rulers, QuickAccess bar, and Formatting bar (see pages 6, 7, and 9).*

Borders are the dotted lines around text columns and frames. They're handy when you're working, but you'll probably want to turn them off to see what your work really looks like. [Alt v b]

A an empty text column with Borders turned on.

Text symbols When Text Symbols are turned on, the following symbols are displayed, so that you can see where these functional elements occur in text. They do not print. [Alt v t]

¶	End of paragraph	§	End of Flow
<	Forced ("hard") line return	>	Tab
⊥	Anchored frame or table anchor	T	Marker
⌐	Discretionary hyphenation	–	Suppressed hyphenation
|	Equation alignment point	␣	Nonbreaking space

Grid Lines This is a visible grid to help you align things. [Alt v g] There is also an invisible Snap grid.

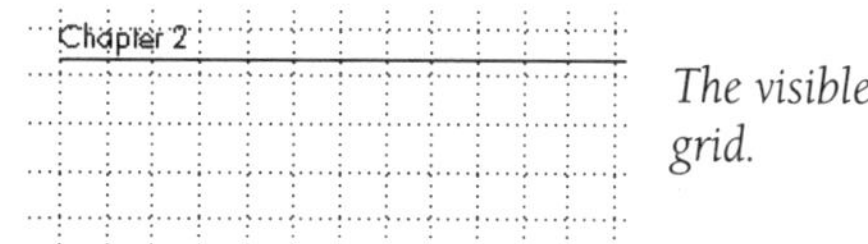

The visible grid.

View Options

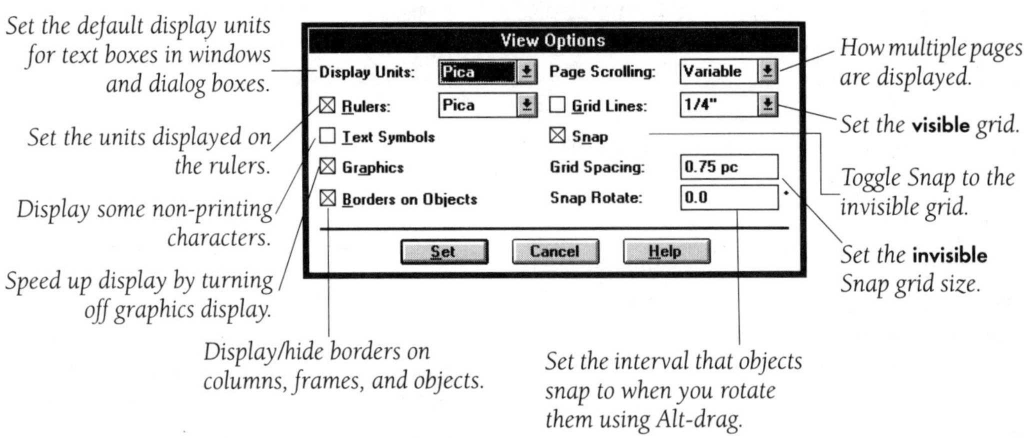

The View Options dialog box

Choose **View→Options** to display this dialog box. [**Alt v o**] Make the changes and settings you want, and click Set.

Display Units

When a text box requires a measurement, the default unit is displayed in the box. This is where you determine what that default unit is.

When you enter an amount, you don't have to enter the unit if you want to use the default. You can use any unit from this list:

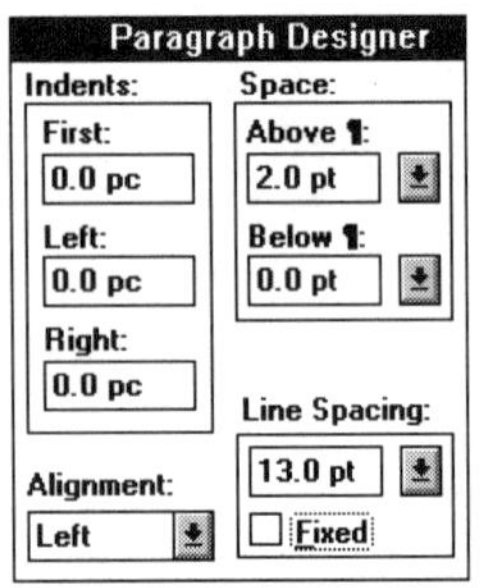

When you choose picas for the display unit, you get points (1/12th of a pica) in some places where it's appropriate, such as line spacing.

Type this	To get this
cm	Centimeters
mm	Millimeters
" *or* **in**	Inches
pc, **pi**, *or* **pica**	Picas
pt *or* **point**	Points
dd	Didots
cc *or* **cicero**	Ciceros

Rulers, Text Symbols, and Borders on Objects

The on/off settings you see here will always be the same as the checkmarks on the View menu, because they *are* the same. Use the pop-up menu next to Rulers to set the units that appear on your Rulers.

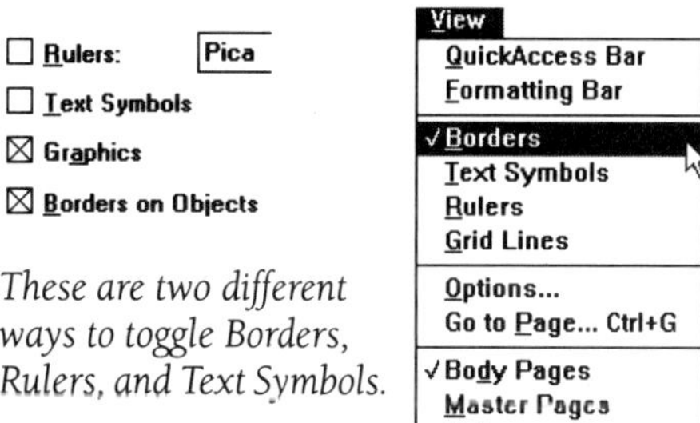

These are two different ways to toggle Borders, Rulers, and Text Symbols.

Graphics

When you turn Graphics off, FrameMaker displays all imported graphics as gray squares. This greatly speeds up the display of pages.

Page Scrolling

This determines how pages are displayed when there is room for more than one page on the screen.

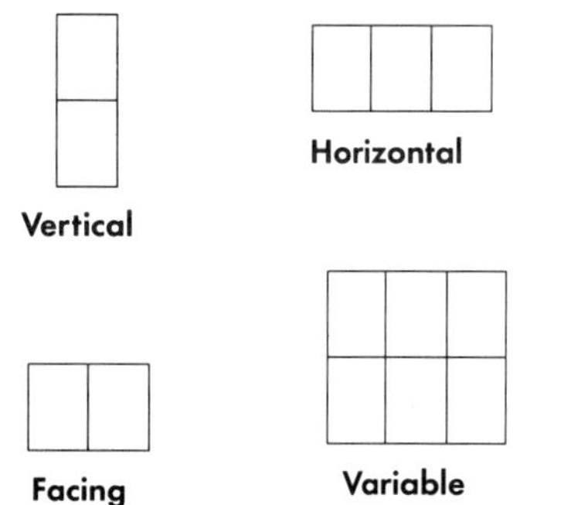

Page scrolling. Each rectangle represents a page displayed on your screen.

Grid Lines

This is the same on/off setting for the *visible* grid as **View➜Grid** (page 25), but this is where you set the distance between the lines in the grid.

Snap

This checkbox is the same as **Graphics➜Snap**. Turn Snap on/off. See Grid Spacing, below.

Grid Spacing

When you turn on Snap, objects jump to the nearest *invisible* snap grid as you move them. This is where you set the size of that grid. It is totally separate from the visible grid lines.

In the View Options dialog box

Page Scrolling: Variable
Grid Lines: 1/4" — *Visible grid*
Snap — *Snap*
Grid Spacing: 0.25 pc — *Invisible Snap grid*
Snap Rotate: 90.0 °

Snap rotate

To rotate an object manually, select it and hold down Alt as you drag one of the handles. Use this setting to specify the number of degrees that the object will Snap as it turns.

Toggle Gravity and Snap on and off.

The Graphics menu

Gravity and Snap are toggles. Click once to turn them on. Click again to turn them off. A check mark next to the item means it's on.

Gravity With gravity on, when you move an object close to another, the two objects join, as though drawn together by gravity—very useful for getting pieces to join when you're drawing objects.

Snap With Snap on, objects will snap to an invisible alignment grid as you move them. This makes is very easy to keep things lined up without having to do anything extra. Turn it off if you need to position an object at a point not on the grid. Set the size of the grid in **View➜Options** (page 26).

■ Getting help

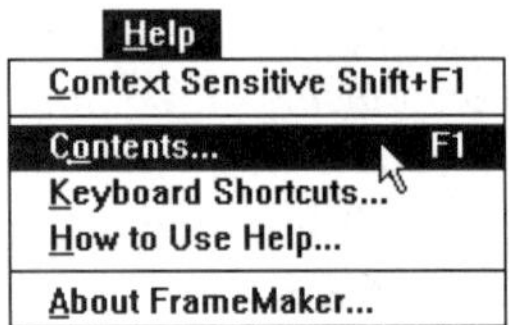

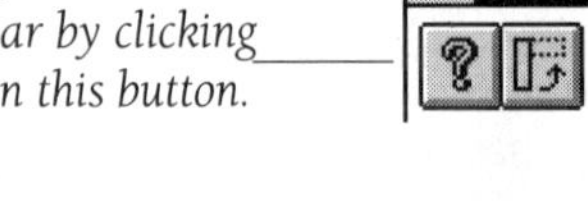

Get help on the QuickAccess bar by clicking on this button.

Many dialog boxes contain buttons like this. Click on the button and then click on the item in the dialog box that you want to know about.

Help on Help

Read HOW TO USE HELP for details on using help. FrameMaker's help is well-organized and easier to use than most.

The Help Main Menu

Press **F1** or choose **Help➜Contents** to display the Help Main Menu. That's your starting point.

Context-sensitive help

Press **Shift-F1** or click a help button in a dialog box to get the context-sensitive Help pointer: ↖?. Then position the pointer over the item you want to know about and click.

Special items

Check out the ONLINE MANUALS, the SYNTAX DESCRIPTIONS, and the SAMPLES AND CLIP ART. These are all items listed in the Help Main Menu, and they are all little gold mines of information.

A Menu Bar Preview

2

■ What's in this chapter

This chapter gives you a brief description of what areas each menu covers. There's a one-liner for each entry and highlights of special items.

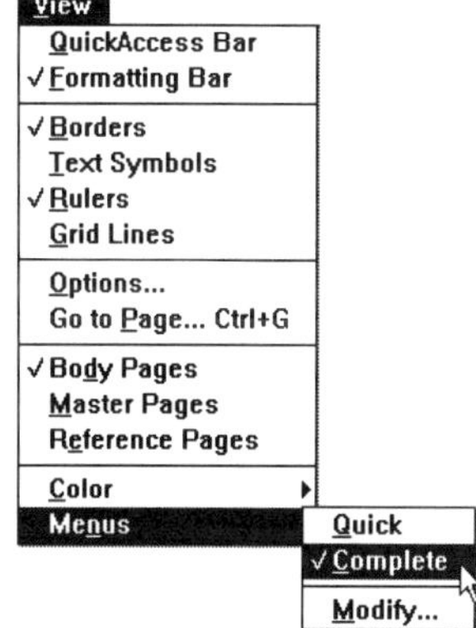

Choose complete menus or quick menus from the View menu.

■ Your choice of menus

FrameMaker offers you a choice of quick menus or complete menus. The quick menus give you only the most basic choices on the menus. They leave all the fancy stuff off. The idea behind this is that if you're a basic user, you don't want to be confused by a lot of choices you don't understand.

I recommend using the complete menus. You'll get used to the FrameMaker basics very quickly, and want to use more and more of the features FrameMaker offers. If you use the complete menus, they'll serve as a reminder of what tools you have available to you. If you use the quick menus, you won't know what you're missing!

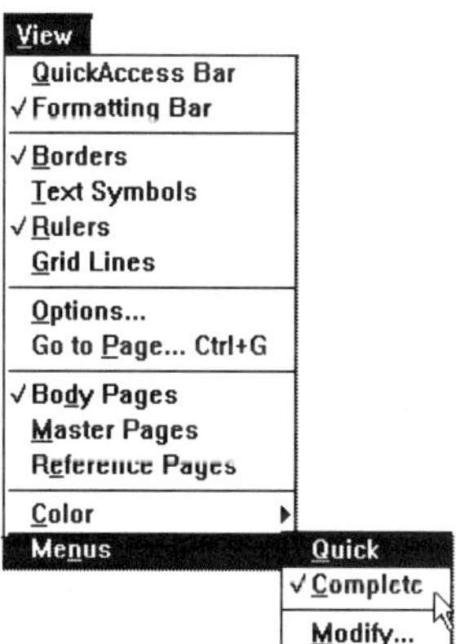

See page 40 for a note about modifying menus.

What's in this chapter

■ The File menu

	File	
Start a new file	New... Ctrl+N	
	Open... Ctrl+O	*Open an existing file*
Close the highlighted file	Close Ctrl+W	
	Save (not needed) Ctrl+S	*Save a file, same name*
Save a file with a new name	Save As...	
	Revert to Saved	*Go back to the last time you saved*
Import a file or format	Import ▸	
	Print... Ctrl+P	*Print a file*
Set up printing conditions	Print Setup...	
	Generate/Book...	*Generate books and files*
Document compare & Word Count	Utilities ▸	
	Preferences...	*Set preferences that apply to all FrameMaker files*
The last five files you opened are listed here. Click on one to open it. Very handy!	1 chap1.fm 2 chap3.fm 3 chap4.fm 4 chap5.fm 5 work.fm	
	Exit	*Close FrameMaker*

In general

The File menu is for things you do to a whole file: open, close, save, print, import, compare, and revert. This is also where you generate books, lists, and indexes, and where you set application-wide preferences.

File menu highlights

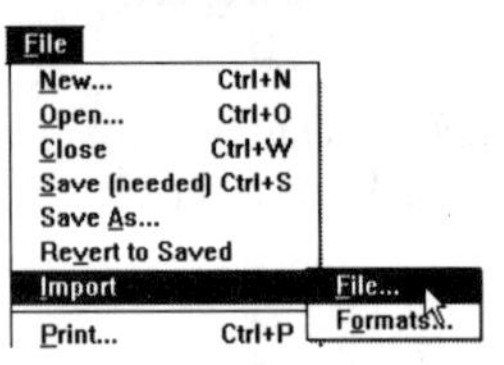

Import

Import a non-FrameMaker file (page 82) or import formats from another FrameMaker file (page 107). To import text or graphic material from another FrameMaker file, use cut and paste.

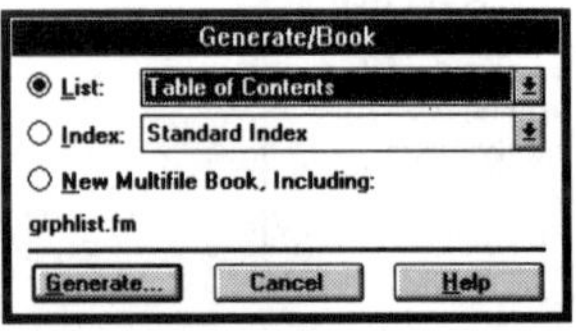

Generate/Book

Generate many different kinds of lists: lists of tables or illustrations, for example, or lists of first-level heads. Generate lists of fonts, or external cross-references. Start the process of creating a book here. You can generate many more types of files. See pages 55 and 278.

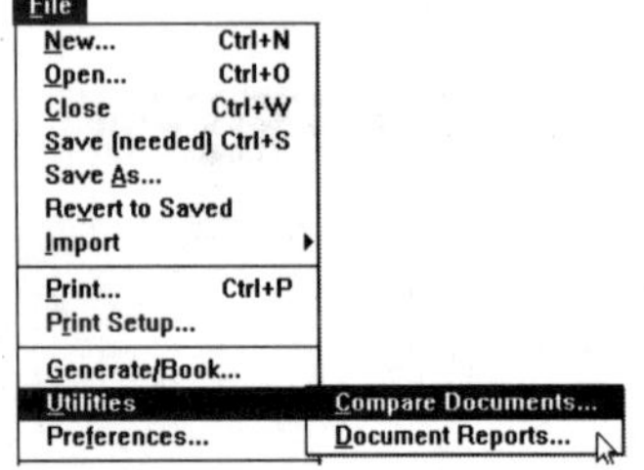

Utilities

FrameMaker currently ships with two utilities: Compare two documents, and a document report on the word count. Other document reports can be created using the Developer's Kit.

The Edit menu

Description	Edit menu	Description
Undo	Undo Ctrl+Z	
	Cut Ctrl+X	*Cut selected material to the clipboard*
Copy selected material to the clipboard	Copy Ctrl+C	
	Paste Ctrl+V	*Paste the contents of the clipboard*
Import from the clipboard	Paste Special...	
	Clear	*Delete without saving to the clipboard*
Copy formats, & more	Copy Special ▸	
	Select All in Flow Ctrl+A	*Select All in page, flow, or frame*
Find/change much more than just text	Find/Change... Ctrl+F	
	Find Next	*Find next item*
Check spelling and hyphenation	Spelling Checker...	
	Thesaurus...	*Choose the exact word you want from a list*

In general

The Edit menu is for working with the *content* of your text. When you want to copy it, delete it, move it, find it, spell check it, or find a better word, this is your menu.

Edit menu highlights

Copy Special

Copy the *format* of the selected paragraph [**Alt e o p**] or text [**Alt e o c**] using the appropriate Copy Special choice. Then apply that format to other selected text or paragraphs by pasting. This is even faster than applying a format tag. I use this a lot.

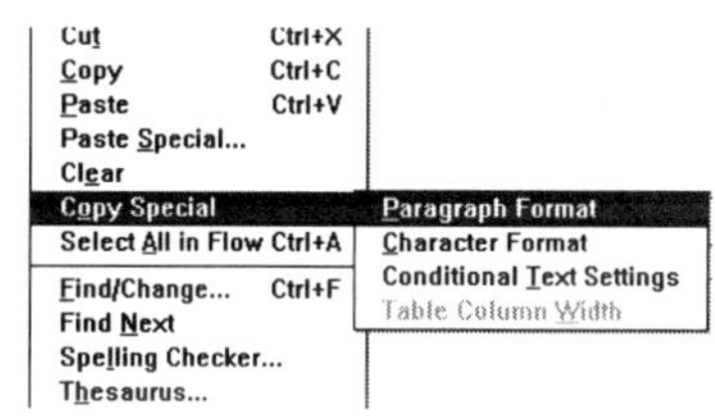

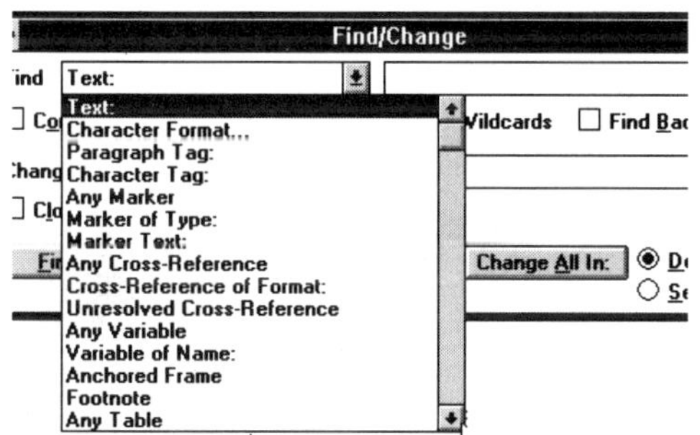

Find/change

FrameMaker has the most powerful and useful Find/Change feature I've ever seen. You can find text, tags, formats, tables, markers, cross-references, variables, footnotes, frames, conditional text, automatic hyphens, and anything that's on the clipboard. You can use wildcards and other controls to make your search exact, and then replace your target with text, a format, or the contents of the clipboard. This is a real power tool.

■ The Format menu

Choose a font for selected characters

Apply a font style to selected characters

Format paragraphs

Flow tag, Autoconnect, baseline synch

Add elements to your headers & footers

Set change bar properties; toggle on/off

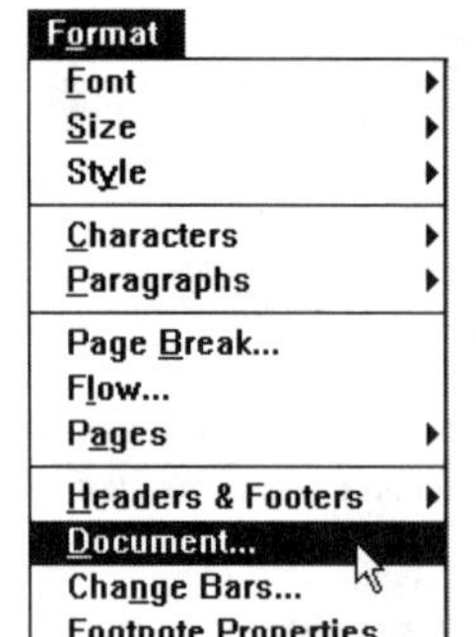

Choose font size for selected characters

Format characters

Choose Rt, Left, or Any Page, or Column

Page layout & master page usage

Set document defaults

Choose many footnote defaults & properties

In general

The Format menu is where you deal with how things *look*. Use this menu to control the appearance of characters, paragraphs, page layout, footnotes, and change bars. From the Document entry, you set page numbering, toggle Smart Quotes and Smart Spaces, specify where lines can end, adjust page count on Save, and format superscripts, subscripts, and small caps.

Format menu highlights

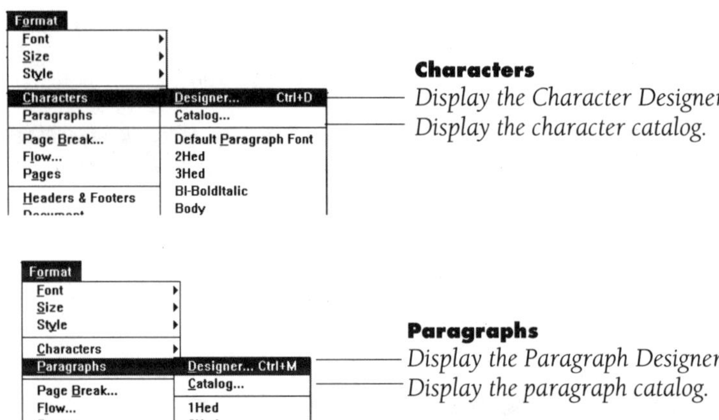

(There are buttons on the right side of every document window for displaying the catalogs. You don't need the Format menu.)

Pages
Use this menu to perform page layout tasks, and to apply master pages to body pages.

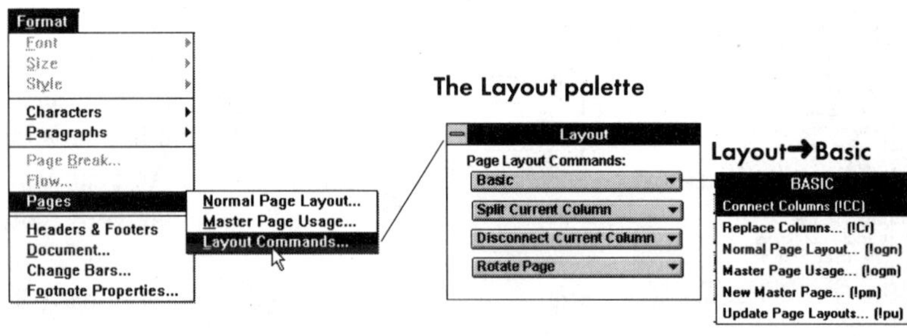

The View menu

Display/hide the QuickAccess bar

Display/hide borders

Display/hide rulers

Set screen defaults

Display body, master, or reference pages

Set Quick, Complete, or Custom menus

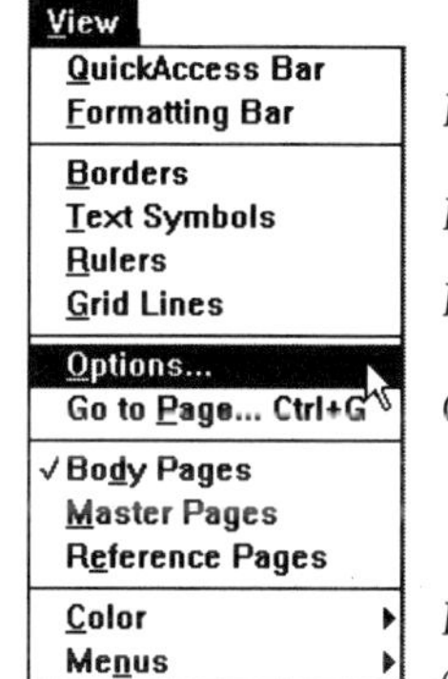

Display/hide the Formatting bar

Display/hide text symbols

Display/hide grid lines

Go to a specified page or line number

Define colors & control the display and printing of them

In general

The View menu is where you select what you see on the screen: rulers, borders, text symbols, visible grid, colors, and graphic display. It's also where you choose whether to see body, master, or reference pages.

View menu highlights

Options

The View Options are described on page 26. Set display, grid, and ruler units here, among other things.

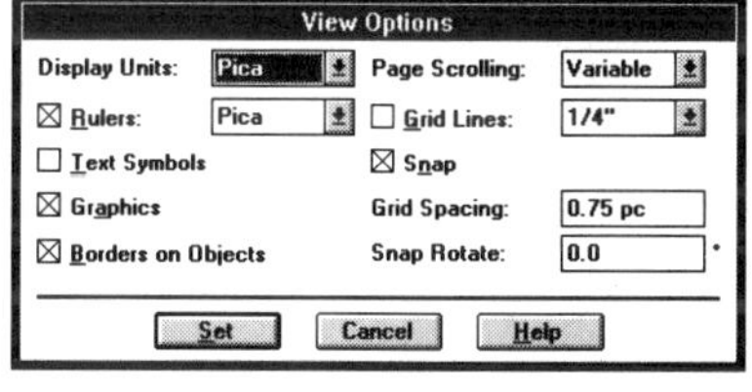

Borders turned on

When borders are turned on, you can see the edges of text columns, frames, and imported objects.§

Text Symbols turned on

› This sample shows you‹ a few of the text symbols.¶ §

Grid Lines turned on

Colors

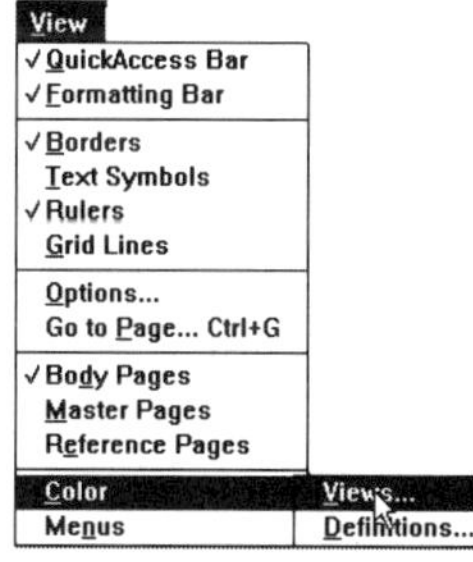

View➔Color➔Views....
Specify what spot colors will both display and print.

View➔Color➔Definitions...
Define your own colors, and modify existing definitions.

■ The Special menu

Insert or modify an anchored frame

Insert or modify a cross reference

Display the Marker window

Display the Conditional Text window

Delete one or more pages

Insert a footnote

Insert or modify a variable

Display the Equations palette

Add pages that text does not flow into

In general

The Special menu is where you add or modify all the special kinds of text that you have available in FrameMaker: footnotes, cross-references, variables, markers, equations, and conditional text. This is also where you add frames and pages, and where you delete pages.

Special menu highlights

To give you a clue, here are the dialog boxes for each entry on the Special menu. "Footnote" just inserts a footnote, so there's no box.

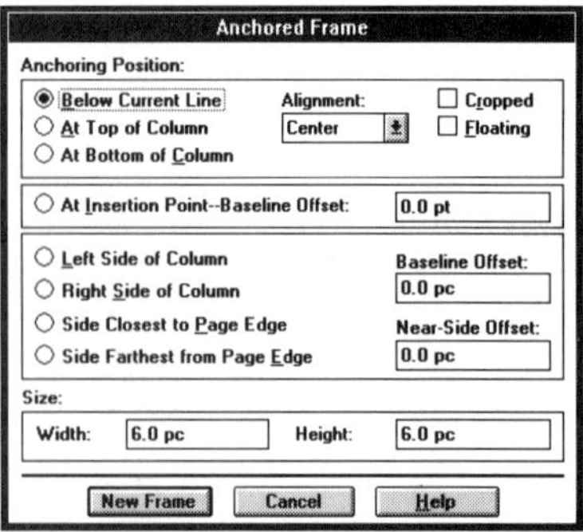

Anchored Frame...

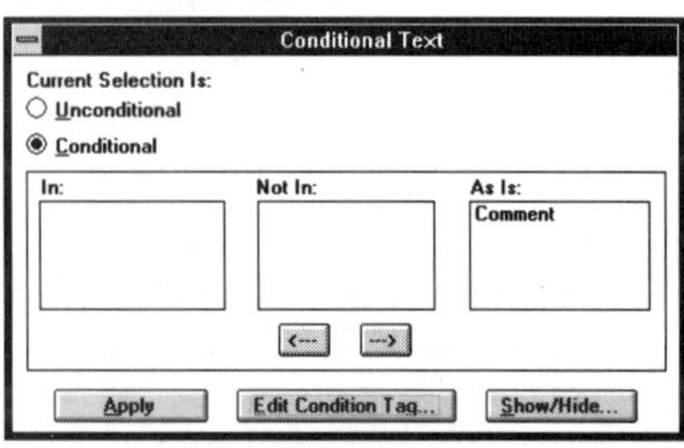

Conditional Text...

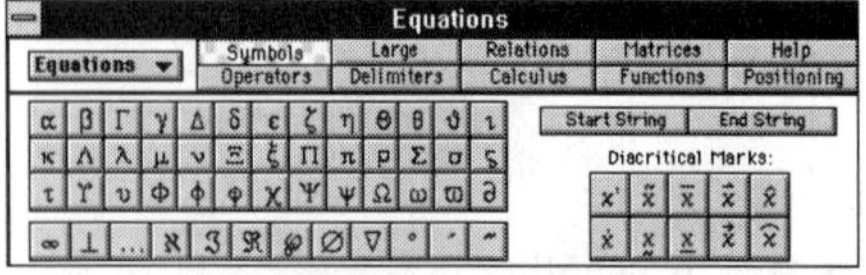

Equation... *(This is page 1 of 9)*

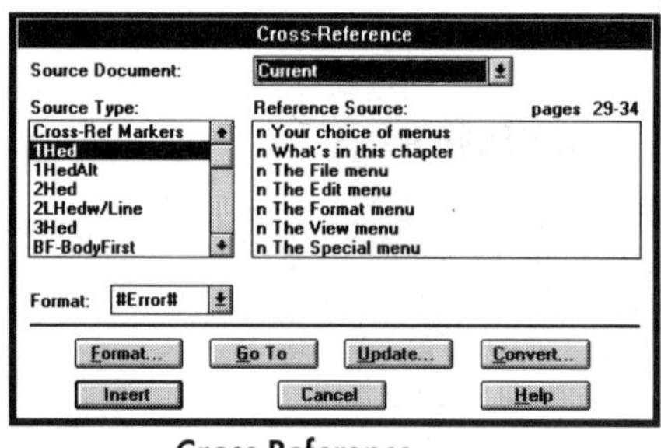

Cross Reference...

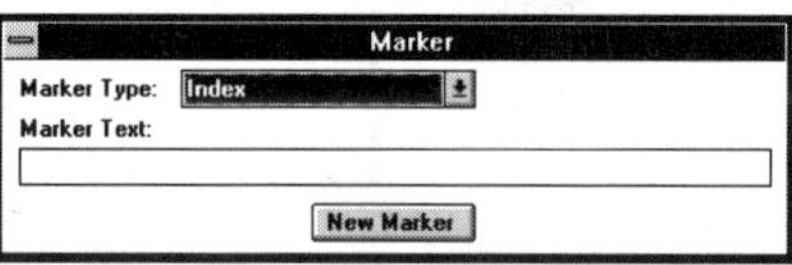

Marker...

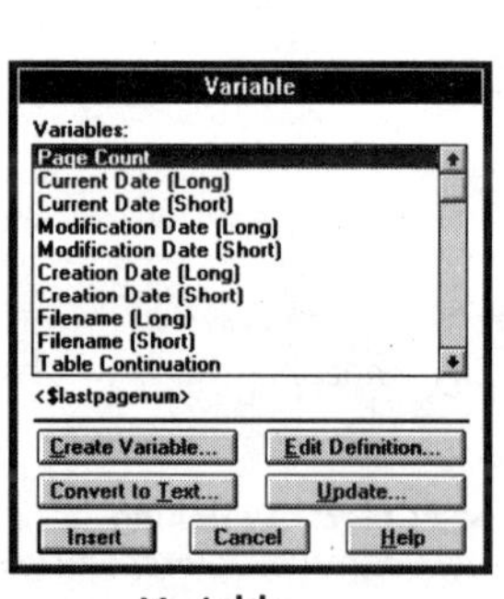

Variable...

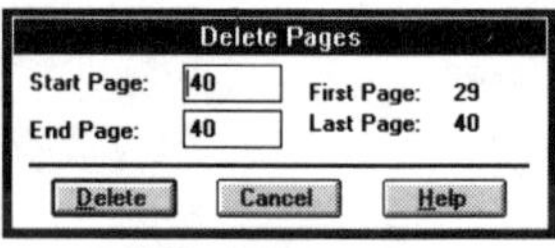

Delete Pages...

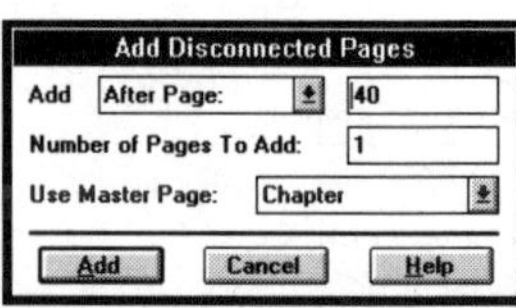

Add Disconnected Pages...

■ The Graphics menu

Description	Graphics menu	Description
Display the Graphics palette	Tools...	
	Group	Make a single object out of selected items
Split a grouped object into its components	Ungroup	
	Bring to Front	Put selected object on top of all others
Put selected object behind all others	Send to Back	
	Align...	Line up selected objects at sides or centers
Equalize space between edges or centers	Distribute...	
	Reshape	Put reshape handles on selected object
Change straight lines to curves	Smooth	
	Unsmooth	Make curved lines straight
Flip objects vertically	Flip Up/Down	
	Flip Left/Right	Flip objects horizontally
Turn objects	Rotate...	
	Scale...	Specify a new size in % or exact measure
Change the number of sides of an object	Set # Sides...	
	Object Properties...	Change the size, shape, or location of an item
Set how objects behind are printed	Overprint...	
	Gravity	"Magnetize" objects to help them join
Make objects align to the snap grid	✓Snap	

In general

The Graphics menu is where you perform all actions on graphic objects. Remember that a text column is a graphic object if you select it with control-click. Text lines created with A are graphic objects, too. See page 67 for information on text columns and text lines.

Graphics menu highlights

Note

Every command available on the Graphics menu is also available on pages two and three of the Quick-Access bar.

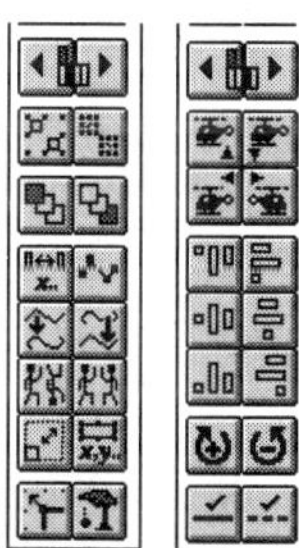

The graphics commands on pages two and three of the QuickAccess bar (page 7).

Tools

Clicking on this entry displays the Graphic Tools palette. You can also do this by clicking on the symbol on the right border of the screen, or by using the keyboard shortcuts, **Esc 1** (one) **w** or **Alt g t**.

The Graphic Tools palette

Snap

When you turn Snap on, objects will jump to the nearest point of the invisible Snap Grid as you drag them around. This is an easy way to make things line up precisely (including text columns). If you're trying to move something to a point that's not on the Snap Grid, turn Snap off.

■ The Table menu

Specify the size of table and insert it

Set row height; control where table breaks

Add rows and columns to your table

Combine several cells into one

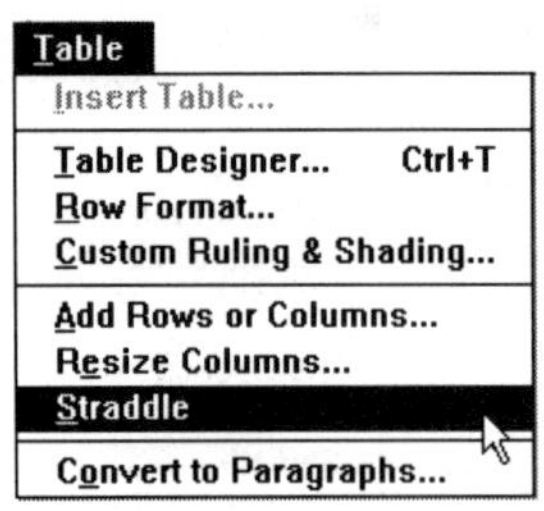

Display the Table Designer

Format selected table cells

Many ways to set column size

Convert tables to text, or text to tables

In general

The Table menu, together with the Table Designer, provides you with the commands you need to create and modify tables. The only other place you need to look is the last page of the Paragraph Designer, to change how a paragraph style is positioned in table cells. You can create virtually any kind of table, in a completely WYSIWYG environment, without changing screens or views. It's superb. Tables are also good for boxing text, and for positioning titles for graphics.

Table menu highlights

Table Designer

This is similar to the Paragraph Designer and the Character Designer. Use it as your work area for creating and modifying tables. It has three pages: Basic, Ruling, and Shading.

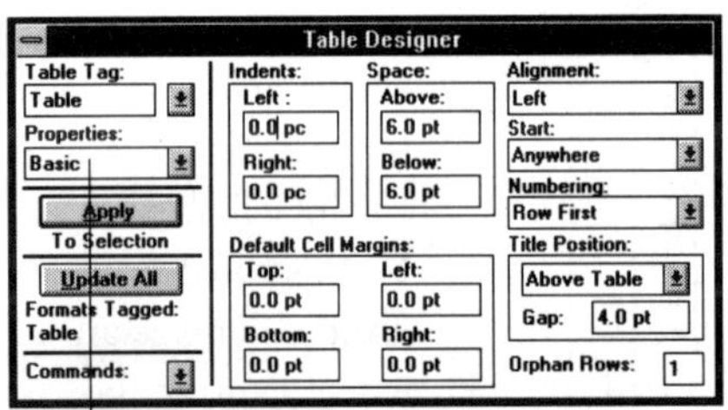

Change pages of the Designer

Ruling and Shading

This window is where you change the definitions of the line widths, and where you can see what is currently applied to your selected cells, as well as your tool for applying ruling and shading to selected portions of the table.

Change line definitions

See current settings for selected cells

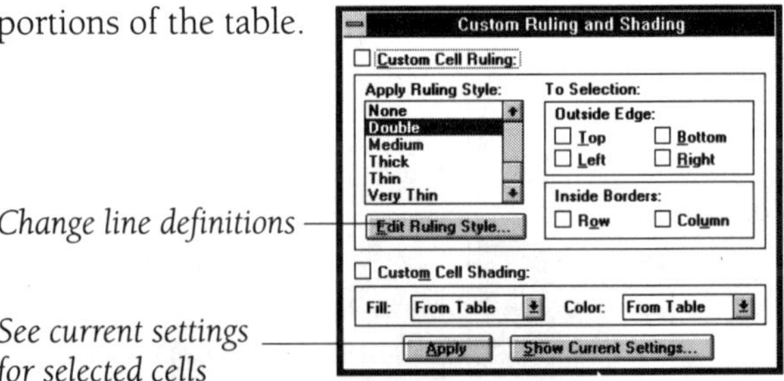

Convert to Paragraphs/ Convert to Table

This entry changes, depending on whether your selected text is in a table or not.

Select text that is in a table to see the Convert to Paragraphs entry, and display this window.

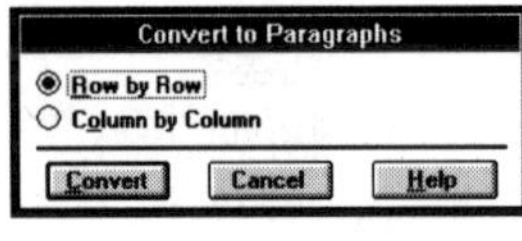

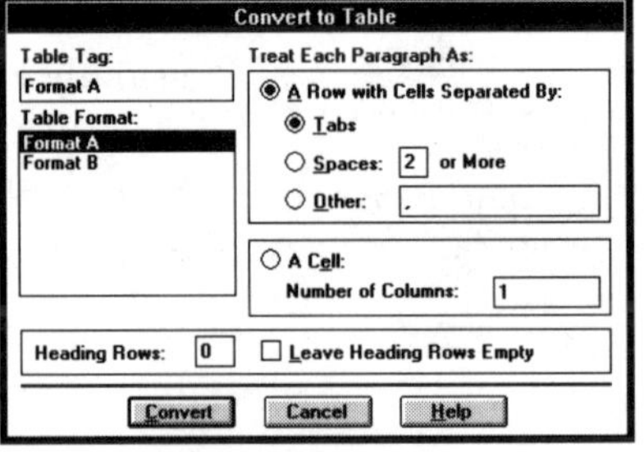

Select text that is not in a table to see the Convert to Table entry, and display this window.

■ The Window menu

Cascade or tile document windows if you have several documents open

Redraw the screen if it is scrambled, or something seems to be missing

Window
Cascade Shift+F4
Tile Shift+F5
Arrange Icons
Refresh Ctrl+L
✓1 c:\peach\chap5.fm
2 c:\peach\chap4.fm
3 c:\peach\chap3.fm
4 c:\peach\chap1.fm

Autoarrange document icons

Switch between open documents by clicking on a document name in this list

In general

The Cascade, Tile, and Arrange Icons functions are just like the equivalent functions in Windows 3.1, but the windows that you are Cascading, Tiling, or Arranging are all your open FrameMaker document windows.

Window menu highlights

It's magic!

(lowercase ell)

Refresh

This is important to know about! Every now and then your screen will have leftover stuff on it, or will become scrambled. Worse still, things will occasionally disappear, especially when you're cutting and pasting. Before you panic, press **Ctrl-l** (*lowercase ell*). If you didn't actually delete it, your material reappears, and any garbage is cleared away.

The open file list

The bottom part of the menu is a list of FrameMaker files that are currently open. To bring a document to the foreground and make it active (so you can work in it), just click on the name in this list. The keyboard shortcut is **Alt w** plus the number of the document. In this example, you could switch to CHAP4.FM by typing **Alt w 2**.

✓1 c:\peach\chap5.fm
2 c:\peach\chap4.fm
3 c:\peach\chap3.fm
4 c:\peach\chap1.fm

■ The Help menu

Get the Context-sensitive mouse pointer

Get the Main Keyboard Shortcuts menu

Version number, copyrights, disclaimers

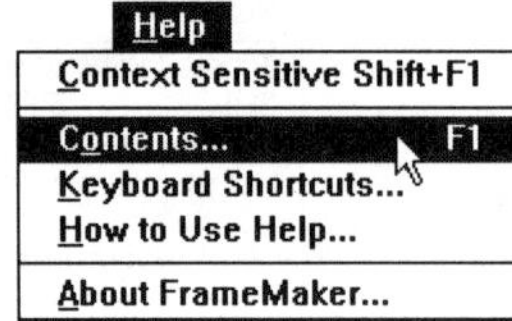

Display the Help Main Menu

Get help on Help

In general

Not a lot of surprises here. This is where you go for help. FrameMaker's help system is particularly well-organized and friendly. It's easier to use than most and very complete. You can choose regular or context-sensitive help.

Here's a secret!

How to print out help

If FrameMaker is in \MAKER4, then the help files are in \MAKER4\HELP\MAKER. *But in order to print one of these files, you must copy it to another directory.* When they're in their original directory, they are view-only documents, so that nobody can accidentally change them. The files have helpful names. Browse until you find the ones you want, and copy them to a different location. You can then open them and print them just like any other files. The Syntax help files are particularly good reference files.

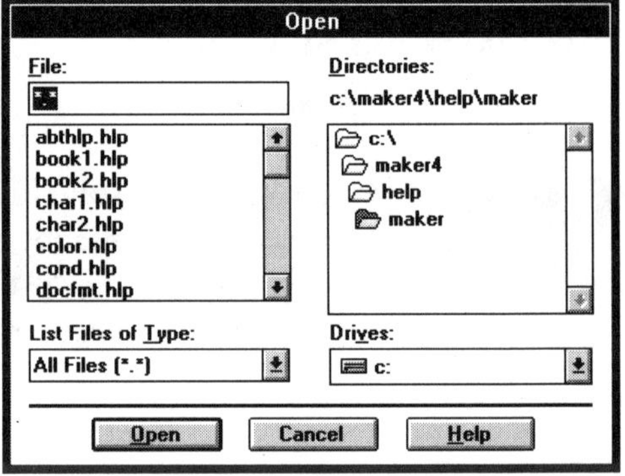

To edit the file or change the zoom setting, you must unlock the file. Click on it, and then type **Esc F l k**. The F must be capital, the "ell" and k are lower case.

About FrameMaker

Besides all the legal stuff, your registration number is in here, and a telephone number for Frame Corp. Click on More to find your exact version number.

■ The Quick menus

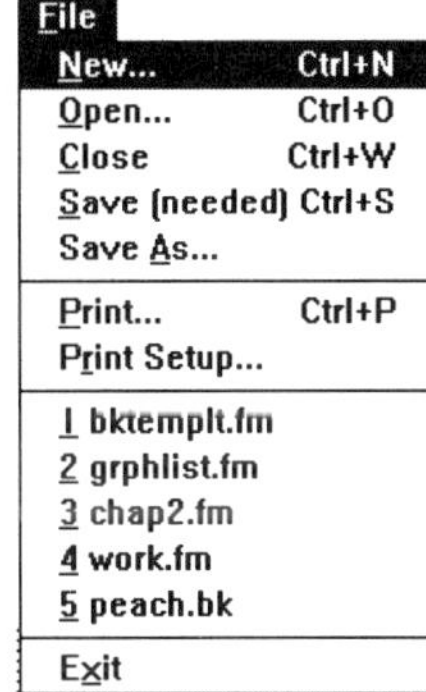

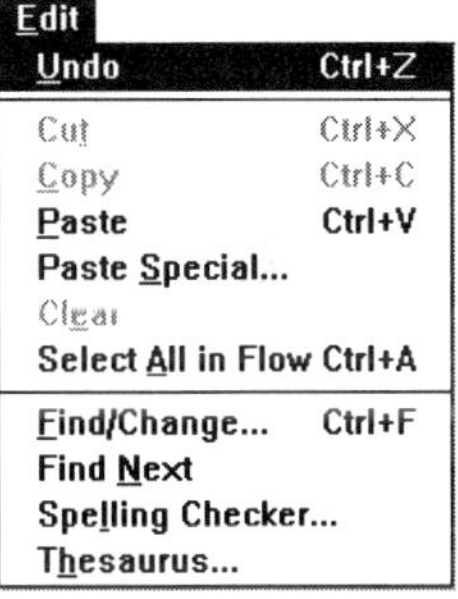

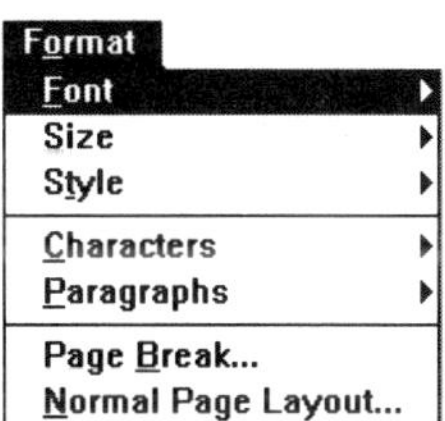

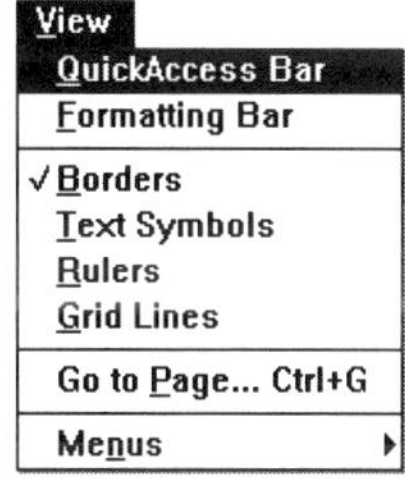

Choose **View➔Menus** *and then either Quick or Complete to display the menus you want.*

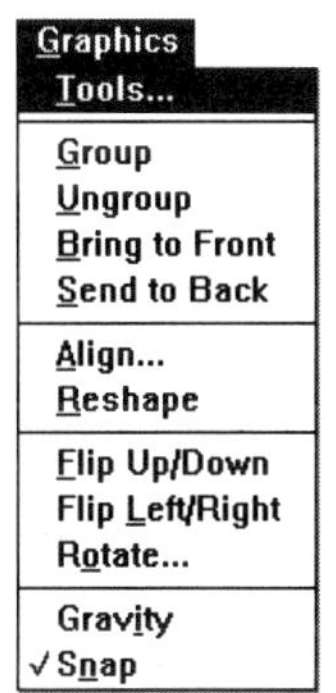

A quick note on the Quick menus

You'll notice that there are a lot of things you can't do from the Quick menus. Also, you can't use the normal **Alt** keyboard shortcuts for missing menu items. However, all the keyboard shortcuts that begin with **Esc** will work when Quick menus are in use. These shortcuts are listed in FrameMaker's *Quick Reference* and in the online help.

The ones I think you will need most if you use Quick menus are these. (But I still think you should just use the Complete menus!)

Go to	Keyboard Shortcut
master pages	**Esc v M**
reference pages	**Esc v R**
body pages	**Esc v B**

■ Custom menus

Yes! You can customize menus in FrameMaker 4.

■ If you use FrameMaker at work, this task would typically be done by your system administrator or one of your tech-people. It's not actually drop-dead easy.

■ Remember that if you customize your menus, they won't match the documentation any more. Still, there are a few things I'm planning to try as soon as I finish this book...

■ If you are among the truly intrepid or the technically adept, you will find instructions in the online manual, "Customizing Frame Products."

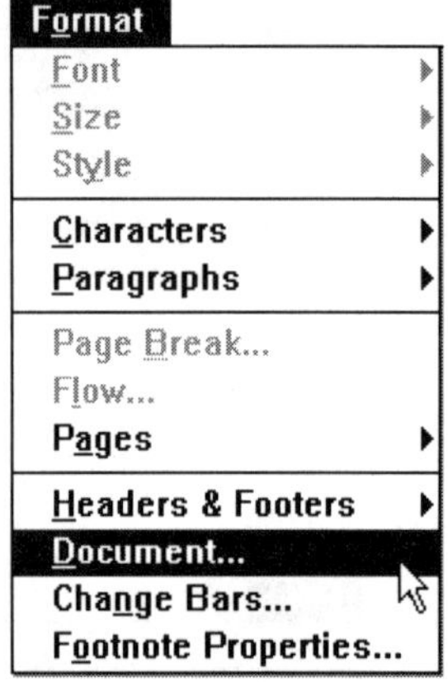

■ When the menu entry is gray

Don't you hate it? There's the very menu entry you need, and you can't choose it because it's gray. What to do, what to do? Here are some suggestions to help you.

When this is gray	Try this
File menu entries	Open or de-iconize a document
Most Format and Special entries, and some Edit entries	Put an insertion point in a paragraph
Most Edit entries	Select some text
Most Graphics entries	Select an object (including a text column)
Most Table entries	Select text or cells in a table
Paste and Paste Special	Copy or cut something

Dealing with Documents

3

■ What's in this chapter

There are a lot of things you do to a document as a whole, rather than to part of it:

- open
- save
- close
- print
- generate lists and indices
- revert to a previous version
- compare two documents
- import formats, text, or graphics

This chapter is where we talk about these document-as-a-whole operations.

There are a couple of things that are *not* in this chapter.

■ If you want to copy or move a file, you must go to Windows' File Manager or your favorite desktop utility.

■ Many of the document preferences are discussed in "Document-specific options" on page 22. There's also a check list at the end of this chapter (page 61).

File
New... Ctrl+N
Open... Ctrl+O
Close Ctrl+W
Save (not needed) Ctrl+S
Save As...
Revert to Saved
Import
Print... Ctrl+P
Print Setup...
Generate/Book...
Utilities
Preferences...
1 chap1.fm
2 chap3.fm
3 chap4.fm
4 chap5.fm
5 work.fm
Exit

Most of the topics in this chapter involve entries on the File menu.

■ Typing file names

In the Open and New file windows (pages 42 and 44), you can type a partial name and use wildcards to shorten the list of files displayed in a large directory.

Wildcard characters in file names

This	Means this	Examples
*	Any characters, any number	*.* = all files *.FM = all files with a .FM extension
?	Any one character (you can use more than one)	CHAP?.FM = CHAP1.FM and CHAP2.FM, but not CHAP01.FM

■ Opening files

An Open overview

Type a filename in this box, **or** *use wildcards to display a limited list of files (*.FM, for example).*

Display this window by choosing **File→Open** [**Ctrl-o**]

Instead of typing the filename, you can press Tab to move the focus to the scroll list, **or** *click in the list. Move the highlight bar with the up and down arrows,* **or** *type the first letter of the filename you want repeatedly until the file is highlighted,* **or** *use the scroll bar and click on the file name.*

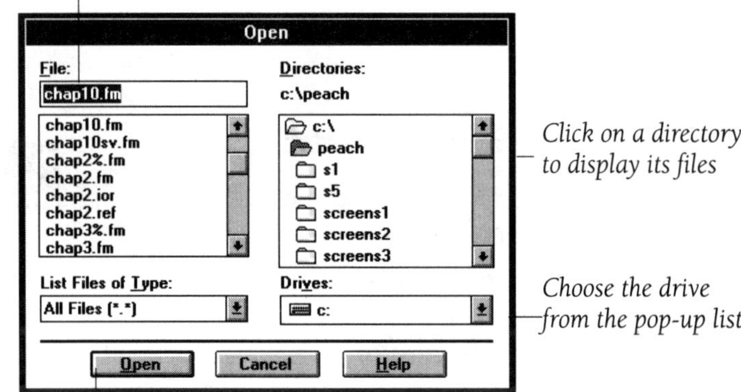

Click on a directory to display its files

Choose the drive from the pop-up list

When the file you want to open is highlighted or typed, press Enter, **or** *click Open.*

List Files of Type:

Click on this button to get the list shown here.

This choice determines what files will be displayed in the File list. FrameMaker assumes that you are going to give your FrameMaker files a .DOC extension, and there is no way to change this. I recommend using a more distinctive extension, since so many other applications also claim .DOC as an identifying extension. I just leave this set on "All Files (*.*)." You can always type wildcards in the name box.

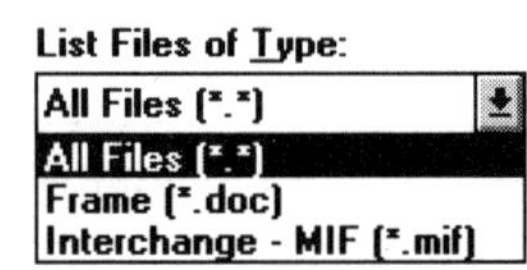

Your five most recently-opened files appear near the bottom of the File menu. [**Alt f** *filenumber*]

Utilities
Preferences...
1 chap1.fm
2 chap3.fm
3 chap4.fm
4 chap5.fm
5 work.fm
Exit

Opening a recently used file

If the file you want is one of the last five files you opened, you can click on File in the main menu bar, and then click on the name of the file you want from the list at the bottom of the menu. You can also type the number that appears next to the file name.

■ Opening a file

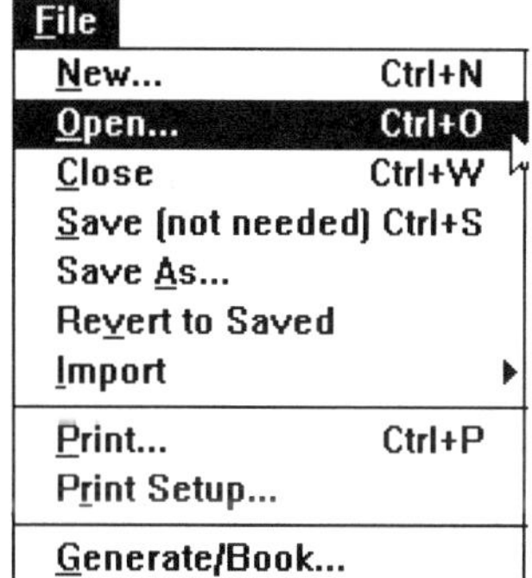

To open an existing FrameMaker file, follow these steps:

1. Choose **File→Open**. [**Ctrl-o**]
2. In the Open dialog box, change drive and directory, if necessary, to display the directory containing your file.
3. Select the file, using any of the techniques described in "Using windows and dialog boxes" on page 13.
4. Click Open.

Opening a file from another application

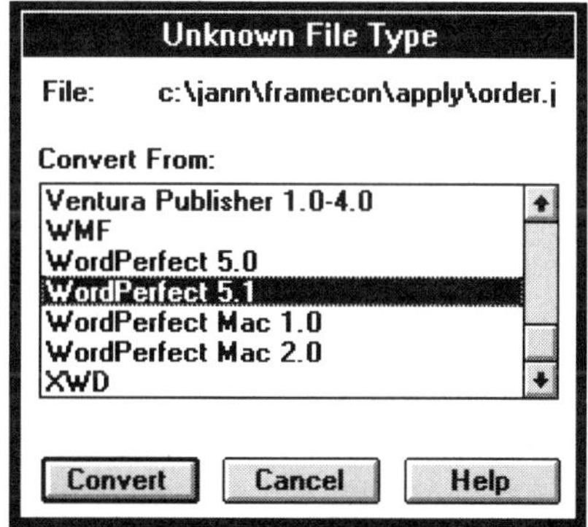

You can open a file created by another application if the correct filter has been installed.

1. Open it as you would any other file.
2. In the Unknown File Type dialog box, highlight the name of the file's application in the Convert From scroll list.
3. Click Convert.

If the list does not include the correct application, you can open the file as Text. You will be asked to specify the treatment of line endings.

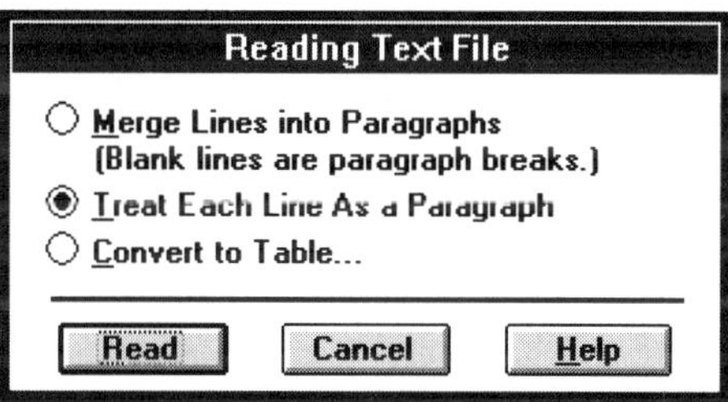

- If you want to keep the same line endings, choose Treat Each Line As a Paragraph.
- If you want FrameMaker to wrap the text, choose Merge Lines into Paragraphs.

▲ **There's help** This sounds simple enough, but converting documents between applications is generally a pretty hairy process. Documents frequently arrive in the new application in rather battered condition. FrameMaker has included an excellent document to help you with this.

1. Choose **Help→Online Manuals**
2. Choose **Using Frame Filters**.

■ Creating a new file

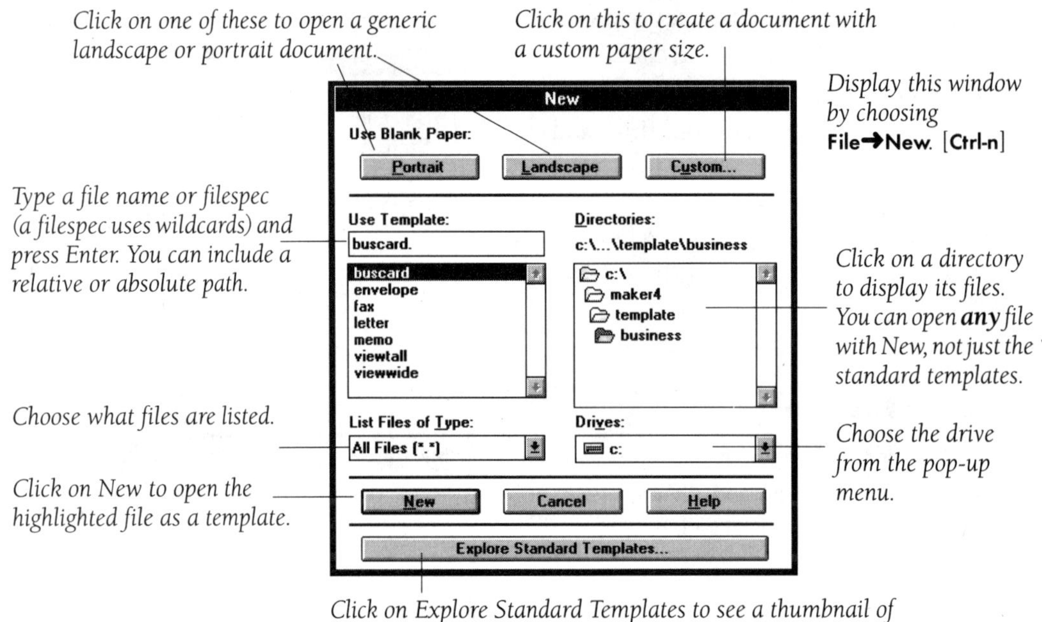

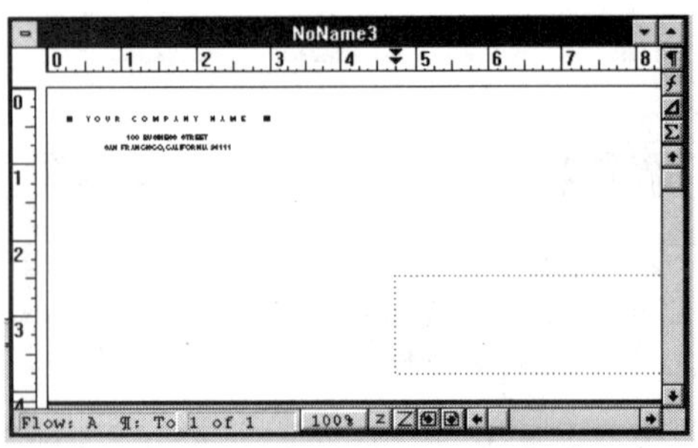

What happens when you use New?

- A new file window appears. The title bar says "No Name" and a number that shows how many new files you have opened in your current FrameMaker session. Click on the upper right-hand corner to make the window full screen.
- Choose Save As from the File menu [**Alt f a**] the first time you save, in order to give the file a name. (Save early and often—it's cheap insurance!)

What's a template?

A template is any document that has layout and design elements that would be useful to you. FrameMaker provides Standard Templates in several subdirectories of \MAKER4\TEMPLATE. You can create templates for types of work you do often, or your workplace may provide templates. Any document can serve as a template. Just open it using New, and give it a new name with Save As.

Using an existing document as a template

If you use an existing document as a template—a starting point—you get to re-use all the work that was done in that document: page layout; definitions of paragraph, character, table, and cross-reference formats, color definitions, variables, document defaults. The existing document can be specifically designated as a template and kept in a special directory, or it can be any document that's similar to the one you want to create.

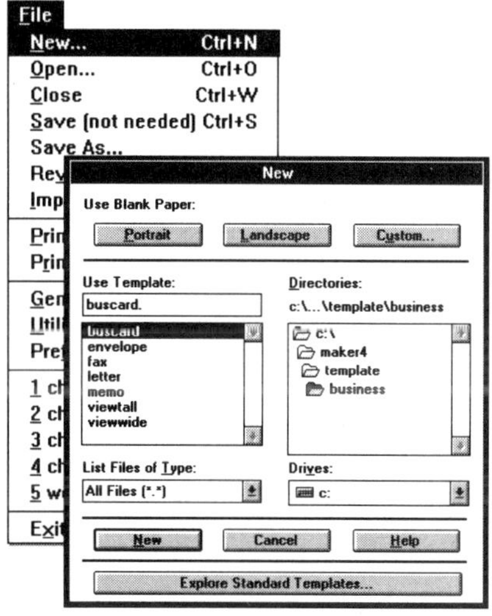

1. Choose **File➔New**. [**Ctrl-n**]
2. Change to the drive and directory where the existing file is located.
3. Click on the file name to select it, and click on New.
4. The file opens in a window labelled No Name plus a number. The number shows how many new files you have opened in the current FrameMaker session.

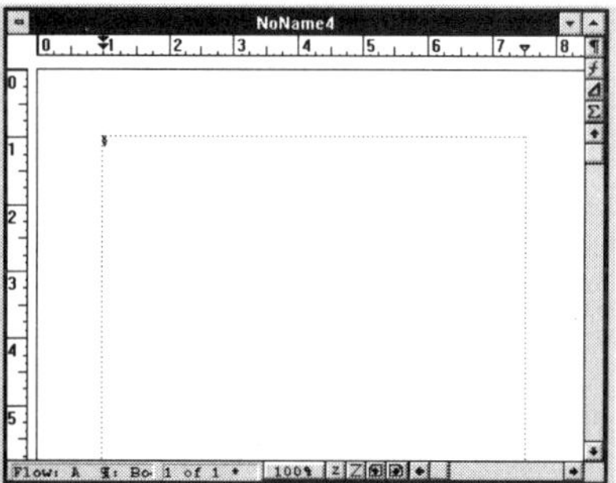

5. Choose **File➔Save As** [**Alt f a**] and save the file with its new name. Be sure to indicate the drive and directory, either by typing the full path name in the Save in File text box, or by navigating to the new location with Drives and Directories.
6. If you want to remove all of the old text, click anywhere in the text and then choose **File➔Select All in Flow**. [**Ctrl-a**] Press Delete. If there is more than one flow, as in a newsletter, do this for each flow.
7. You are now free to delete or modify the formats, layouts, and all other elements of the file, just as you would in any FrameMaker file. You will not affect anything in the "parent" file.

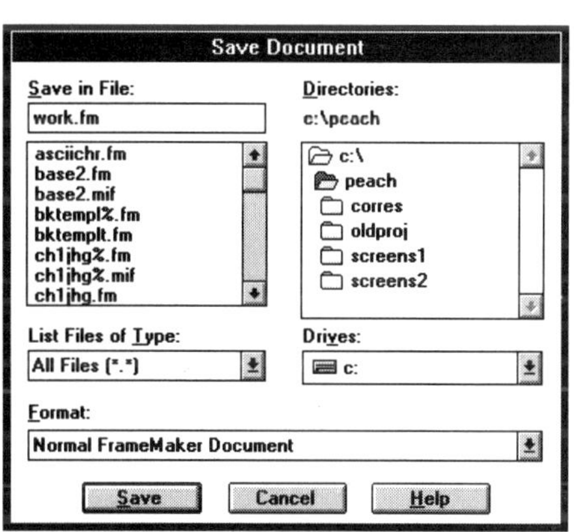

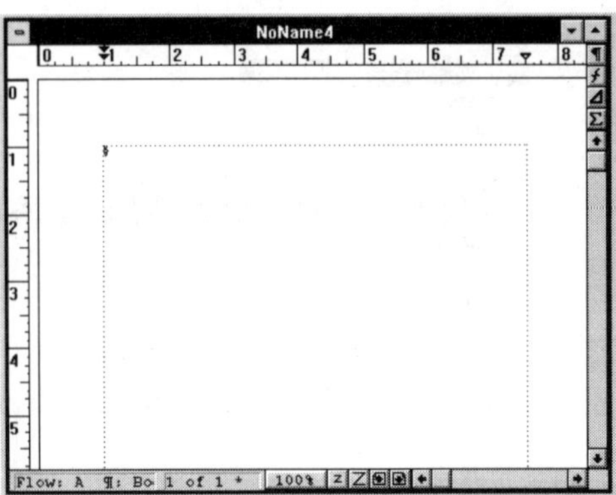

Opening a "plain" portrait or landscape document

When you click on Portrait or Landscape, you get a "No Name" file with the chosen orientation. It's complete with all the usual parts of a FrameMaker file: master and reference pages, catalogs of formats that you can use and modify, system variables, everything. See "The parts of a FrameMaker document" on page 57.

Opening a custom document

Click on Custom to get the Custom Blank Paper window. Choose your page size, margins, columns, and pagination, and click Create, or press **C**.

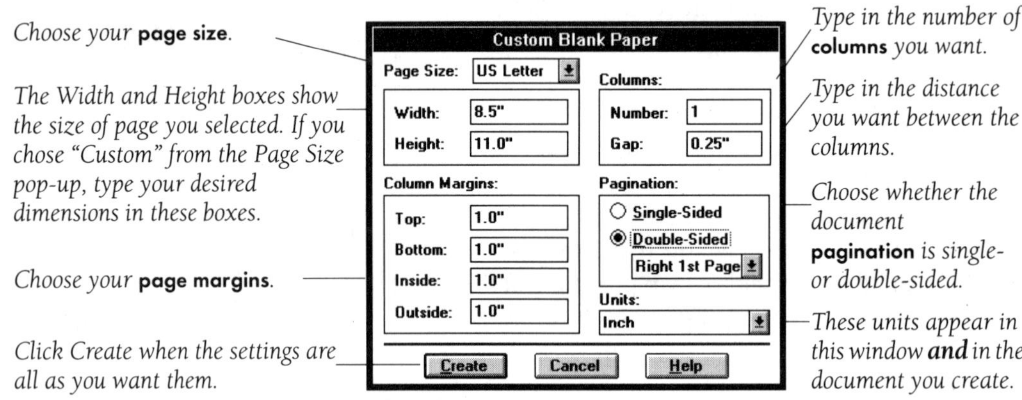

Choose your **page size**.

The Width and Height boxes show the size of page you selected. If you chose "Custom" from the Page Size pop-up, type your desired dimensions in these boxes.

Choose your **page margins**.

Click Create when the settings are all as you want them.

Type in the number of **columns** *you want.*

Type in the distance you want between the columns.

Choose whether the document **pagination** *is single- or double-sided.*

These units appear in this window ***and*** *in the document you create.*

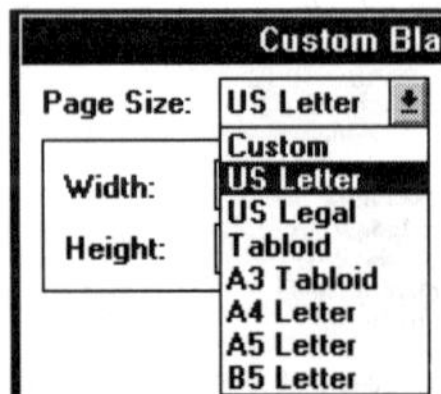

Page size

This pop-up menu gives you a choice of standard page sizes. If you want a custom size, click Custom and fill in the width and height of your page in the Width and Height text boxes.

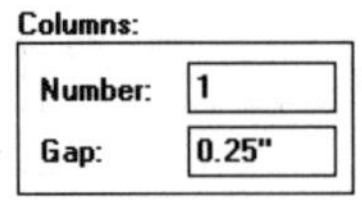

"Gap" is the distance between columns. It is meaningless when there is only one column.

Columns

FrameMaker creates either a Right master page (One-Sided) or Right and Left master pages (Double-Sided) with columns of equal width and the gap that you specify. You can modify these master pages by working on them directly. (See pages 210 to 220.)

Page margins

Specify the margins around the outside of the columns. If Double-Sided is checked, you can create off-center right and left pages. "Inside" is the side toward the binding, and "Outside" is the outer edge. If Single-Sided is checked, you are asked to specify Right and Left margins.

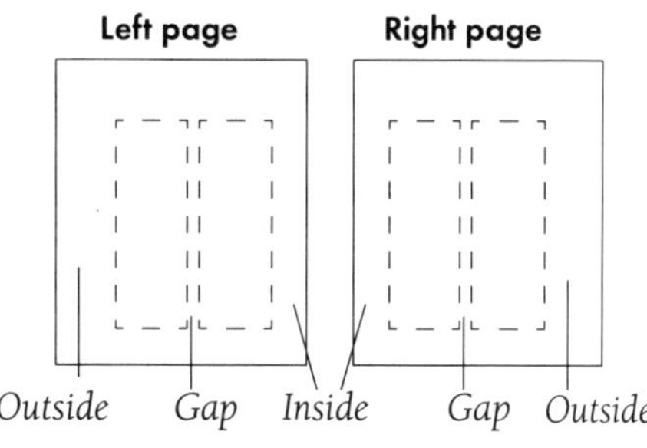

Pagination

For a single-sided document, FrameMaker creates only a Right master page—one "Normal" page. For double-sided documents, it creates two Normal pages, Right and Left. Choose Double-Sided if you want the right & left layouts to be different.

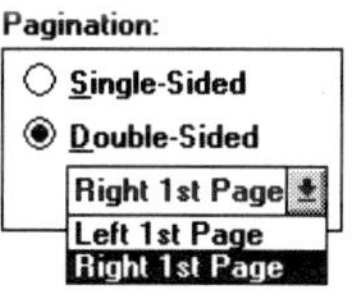

If your document is double-sided, you can choose whether the first page is a right or a left page.

Explore Standard Templates

Click the Explore Standard Templates bar at the bottom of the New dialog box to display this dialog box:

Click Create to get a document that has all the layout and format catalog elements you need to create a document in the sample style, but no text.

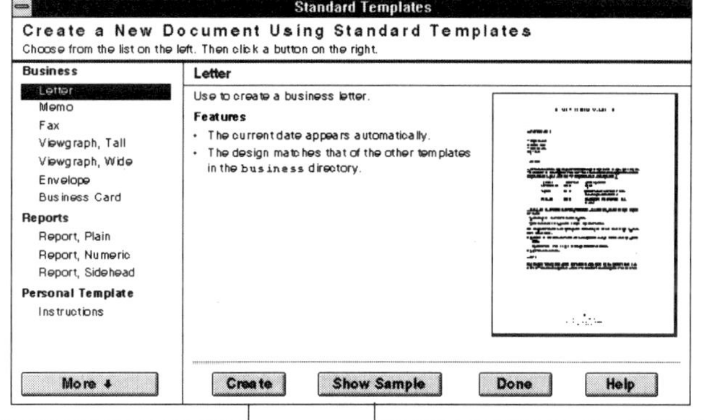

Click Show Sample to get all the same things that you get with Create, and sample text as well, so that you can see how each format looks.

■ Moving between open files

A list of open documents appears at the bottom of the Window menu. To make a different document active, click on it. The keyboard shortcut is **Alt w** *number.*

✓1 c:\peach\chap5.fm
2 c:\peach\chap4.fm
3 c:\peach\chap3.fm
4 c:\peach\chap1.fm

There is a list of open files at the bottom of the Window menu.

In this example, you can move to Chapter 1 by typing **Alt w 4** *in any of the other open files.*

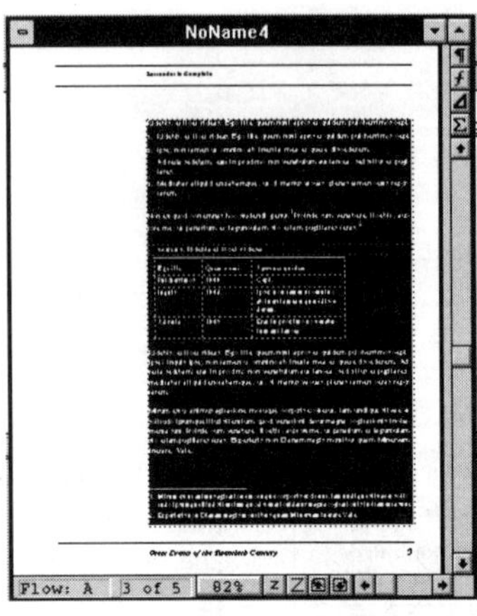

Use Ctrl-A to select all the text in a flow.

■ Clearing a file

When you create a file from a sample or template document that contains text, you may want to remove all of the old text once you have checked how the different formats look.

1. Place the insertion point anywhere in the text and choose **Edit ➔Select All in Flow** [**Ctrl-a**].
2. Press Delete (or **Edit ➔Clear**).

Note If your document has multiple flows, repeat this procedure for each flow.

If you need to remove material from the master pages, you must go to the master pages [**Alt v m**] to delete it.

The Save As dialog box

Type your new file name here.

Click here to display the directory where the file should be stored.

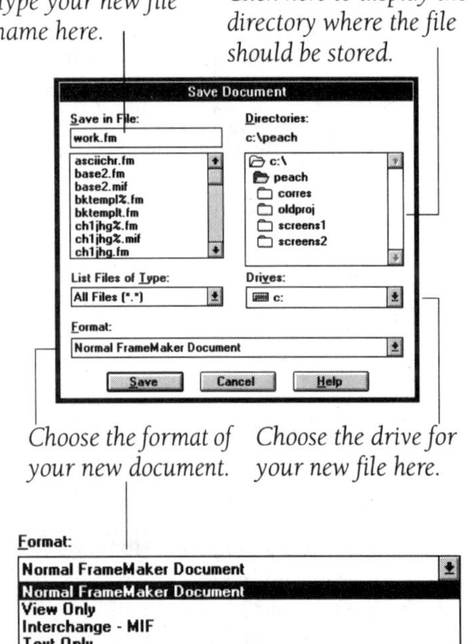

Choose the format of your new document.

Choose the drive for your new file here.

This is where you can choose to save a file as a text, MIF, view only, or RTF file.

■ Saving a file

Saving to the same name

Choose **Ctrl-s** or **File ➔Save** to write all the current changes in the active document window to disk, keeping the same file name. If your file says "No Name" and you try to save this way, FrameMaker displays the Save As window, so you can name the file.

Saving to a new name, location, or format

1. Click in the file you want to save.
2. Choose **File ➔Save As** [**Alt f a**].
3. Fill in the parts of the window you want to change: name, path, format. Click Save.

When you Save As, FrameMaker creates and opens a new document with the name you specify in the Save in File box. FrameMaker closes the document that you saved *from*, without saving any changes.

Saving automatically

1. Choose **File→Preferences**. [**Alt f f**]
2. Turn on Automatic Save-Every ☐ Minutes and type a value in the text box. Try something in the five to fifteen minutes range.

Preferences
User Preferences:
☒ Automatic Backup on Save
☐ Automatic Save - Every: 75 Minutes
☒ Show File Translation Errors
Greek Screen Text Smaller Than: 6.0 pt
Compatibility Preferences:
☐ Save FrameImage with Imported Graphics
☐ Network File Locking
Set Cancel Help

Saving all open files

1. Hold down Shift and click on File.
2. Click on Save All Open Files. [**Shift-Alt f s**]

■ Closing a file

1. Click in the file you want to close to move the focus to it.
2. Choose **File→Close**. [**Ctrl-w**]

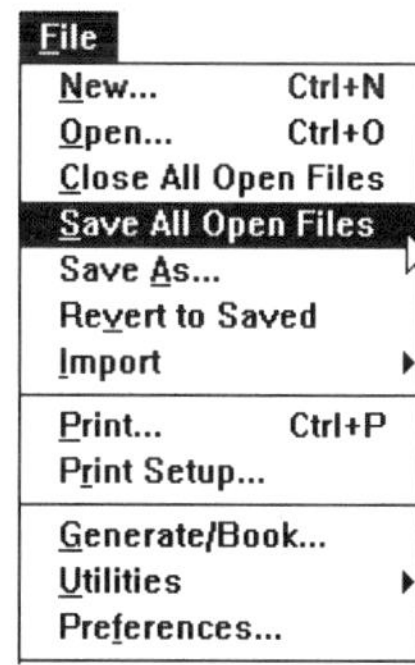

Hold down Shift when you click File to get this menu.

Closing all open files

1. Hold down Shift and click on File.
2. Click on Close All Open Files. [**Shift-Alt f c**]

■ Managing text files

Opening a text file

1. Choose the file in the Open dialog box [**Ctrl-o**], just as you would any FrameMkaer file, and click Open. FrameMaker display the Unknown File Type dialog box.
2. Click Text. Click Convert.
3. If you want the text to wrap to the column width, choose Merge Lines into Paragraphs. If you want to keep the line endings in the original file, choose Treat Each Line As a Paragraph.
4. Click Read.

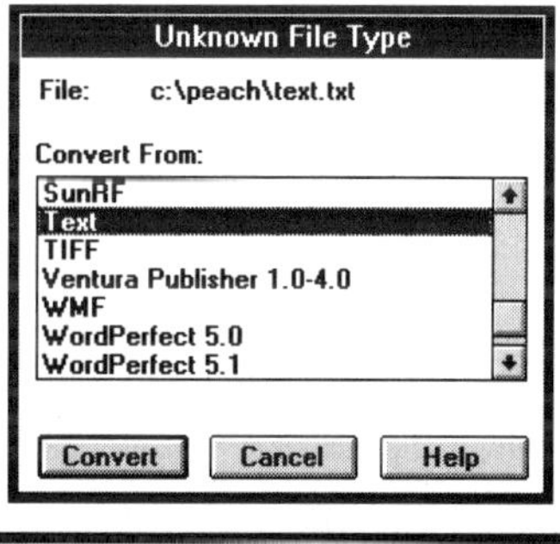

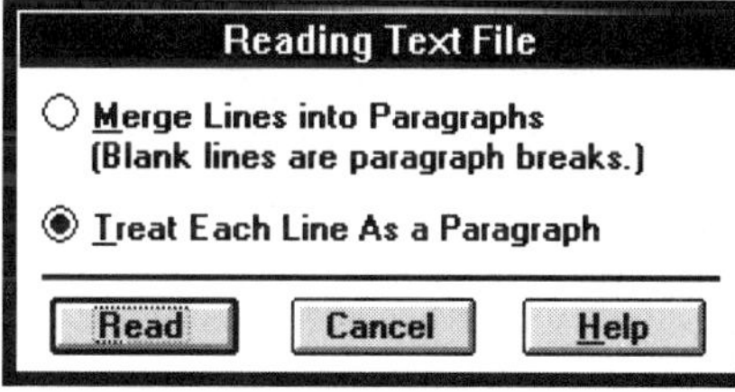

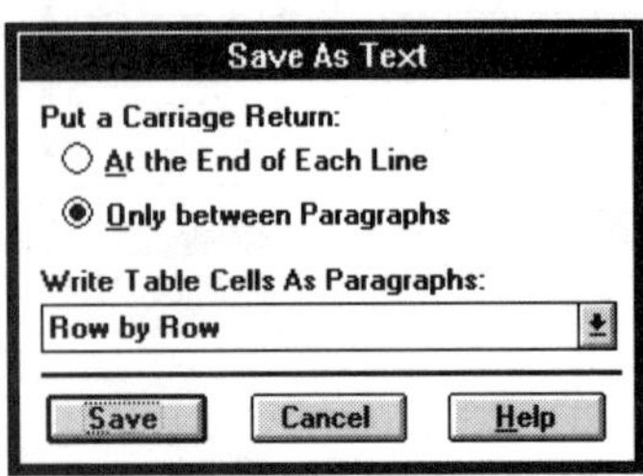

Format:
Normal FrameMaker Document
Normal FrameMaker Document
View Only
Interchange - MIF
Text Only ...
Rich Text Format (RTF)

In the Save Document dialog box, the Format pop-up menu allows you to save a document as MIF or text-only.

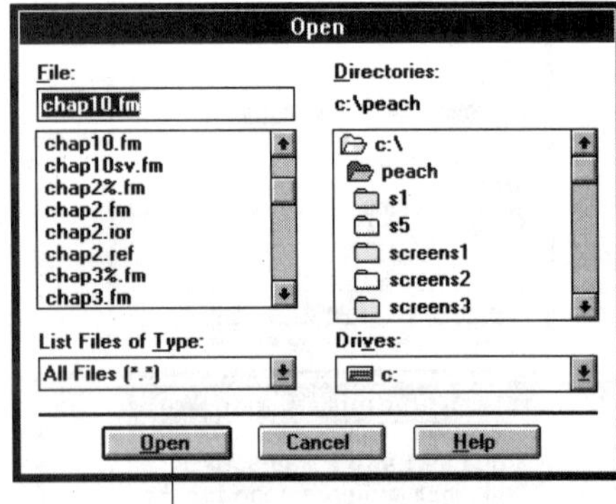

To edit a MIF file in FrameMaker, select the file, and then hold down Ctrl as you click Open.

Saving a file as text

You can save a file as text-only—no added coding or formatting. You need to do this if you are editing a dictionary for the Spelling Checker, for example, or the MAKER.INI file.

1. Choose **File→Save As**. [**Alt f a**]
2. Choose or type the name and location of the text file. Give it an identifying extension, such as TXT.
3. Click on the Format pop-up menu and choose Text Only.
4. In the Save As Text dialog box, choose whether the screen line endings become hard line returns or spaces. From the pop-up menu, select how to treat tables if there are any.
5. Click Save.

■ Managing MIF files

Saving a file as MIF (Maker Interchange Format) In FrameMaker 4, choose **File→Save As**. [**Alt f a**] Choose Interchange - MIF from the Format pop-up and click Save.

Opening a FrameMaker 4 file in FrameMaker 3 Save the file as MIF in FrameMaker 4. Open the MIF file as a normal FrameMaker file in FrameMaker 3.

Opening a MIF file as a normal FrameMaker file Open a MIF file as you would any FrameMaker file. You will see the original contents of the file, not the MIF code.

Opening the MIF file as MIF code Display the Open dialog box, select the MIF file, and hold down Ctrl as you click Open. You can now edit the MIF code in FrameMaker.

Saving an edited MIF file When you have opened a MIF file as text in FrameMaker in order to edit it, save it as Text when your edits are complete. See "Saving a file as text," above.

■ Printing

These are the printers that you have installed in Windows. Choose one.

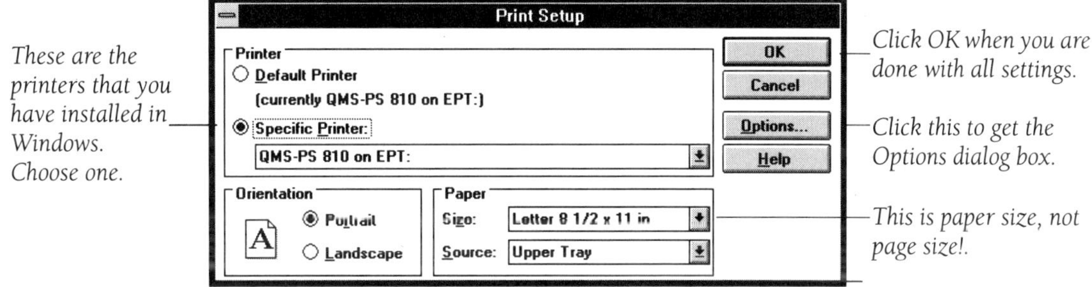

Click OK when you are done with all settings.

Click this to get the Options dialog box.

This is paper size, not page size!.

Choosing a printer

1. Choose **File→Printer Setup**. [Alt f r]
2. Choose a printer from the pop-up list of installed printers.
3. Make whatever other changes you need. Click OK.
4. All other settings in Setup, Options, and Advanced Options can be changed from the Print dialog box. Look on the next few pages for more details.

Printing a document

Print all of a document, or just a selected range of pages.

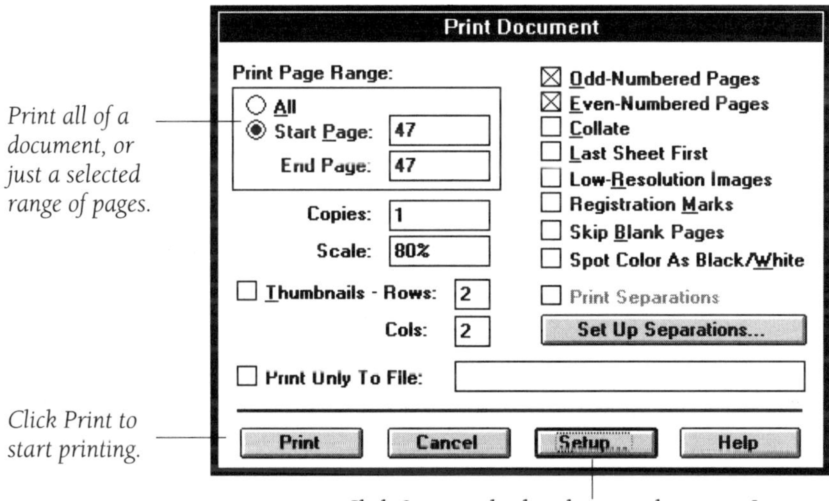

Choose **File→Print** to display this dialog box. The choices are discussed on the next page.

Click Print to start printing.

Click Setup to display the print document Setup dialog box. This one does not let you choose the printer. See page 54 for more on this Setup.

Item	Comments
Scale	Type in a percent to print at other than original size.
Thumbnails	Type in the number of rows and columns you want, to determine how many pages appear in miniature on each printed sheet.
Print only to file	Send your PostScript output to a file instead of a printer in order to print the file on a remote printer. Type the name for the output file here. Use a .PS extension. Be sure to select the correct printer in **Printer Setup** first.
Odd-Numbered & Even-Numbered pages	Normally you turn on both of these to print all the pages. To print double-spaced output on a non-duplex printer, you can print one side, and then turn the paper over and print the other side.
Collate	Turn this on to make FrameMaker print one complete set of pages before beginning the next set. Handy, but slower.
Last sheet first	Specify the order in which the sheets emerge from your printer.
Low-Resolution Images	If you turn this on, graphics are printed in low resolution; this speeds up printing. Useful for draft runs.
Registration Marks	Turn this on to print both registration marks and crop marks. Your page size must, of course, be smaller than the paper for the marks to show. cropmrk.fm Page 1 Saturday, Septem This is a very small page, printed with crop marks and registration marks. Choose **Registration Marks** in the Print Document dialog box to turn both of these on. *When you turn on Registration Marks, you get crop marks, too.*
Skip Blank Pages	Suppress printing of blank pages.
Spot Color as Back/White	This translates not only colors to black and white, but also anything that is gray (like the thumb tabs on this book). When this is off, colors print as shades of gray on a black and white printer.
Print Separations	When this is on, FrameMaker prints out separate sheets for each color that you specify in the Set Print Separations dialog box. Click Set Up Separations to choose which colors print as spot and as process.

Setting Up Separations

Each color that you specify in the Print As Process and Print As Spot boxes will print on a separate page when you turn on Print Separations in the Print dialog box. Talk to your commercial printer about an optimal use of color in your document.

To move colors Click on a color, then click on an arrow, or double-click on the color. **To move all colors**, click in a column, and then shift-click on an arrow.

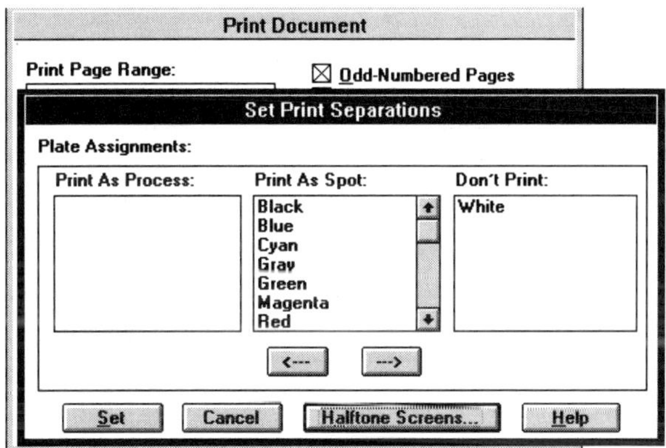

Halftone Screens If you are using process color, use the Halftone Screens dialog box to control the grids of dots. Your commercial printer, image shop, and printer manual can provide you with the information you need to make these decisions. They vary depending on the technology you are using.

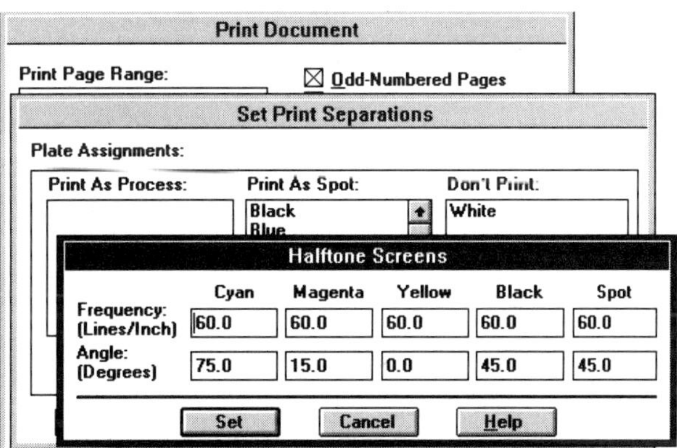

Printing several files at once

Put the files together in a book, and print the book. It doesn't matter whether the files actually *belong* together or not. A book is just a collection of files. See Chapter 13 for how to create a book, add files to it, and print them.

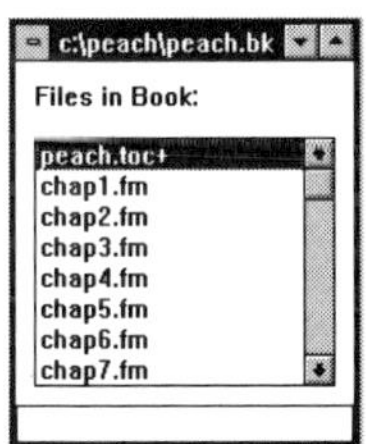

A book window (see Chapter 13).

▼

A warning

When you make changes in the Setup, Options, and Advanced Options Print dialog boxes (next page), the changes you make may not take effect the first time you print. FrameMaker says that this is a Windows problem.

The fix *Keep a little test file handy, and print it after making Setup and Options changes.*

▲

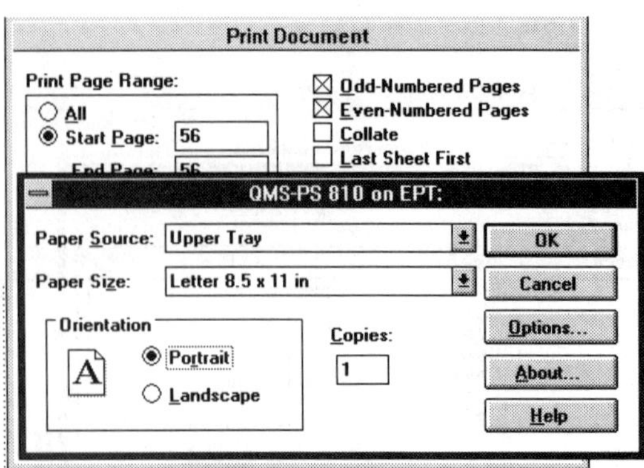

(Above) **File→Print→Setup**

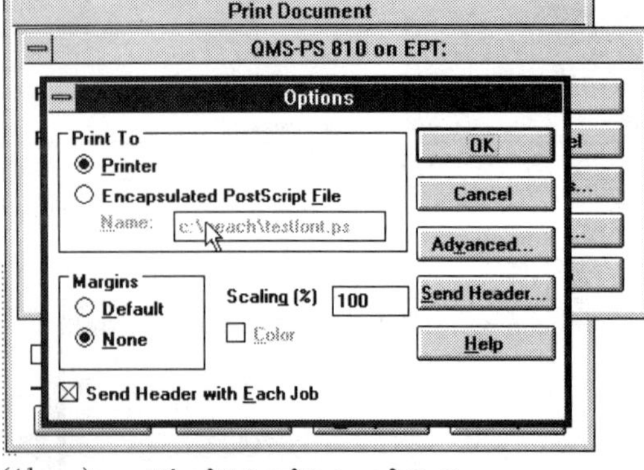

(Above) **File→Print→Setup→Options**

Print Document
QMS-PS 810 on EPT:
Options
Advanced Options
TrueType Fonts
Send to Printer as: Adobe Type 1
Use Printer Fonts for all TrueType Fonts
Use Substitution Table
Edit Substitution Table ...
Memory
Virtual Memory (KB): 324
Clear Memory per Page
Graphics
Resolution (DPI) 300
Halftone Frequency 60.0
Halftone Angle 45.0
Negative Image
Mirror
All Colors to Black
Compress Bitmaps
Conform to Adobe Document Structuring Convention
Print PostScript Error Information
OK
Cancel
Defaults
Help

File→Print→Setup→Options→Advanced

More print setups and options

Choose **File→Print** and click on the Setup button to get these choices.

Change the paper size or paper tray

The choices you see here depend on the printer you have chosen in **File→Print Setup**. These choices are instructions to your printer.

To change the print orientation (have your image aligned with the shorter or the longer dimension of the paper) click Setup and choose the orientation you want. You can also create a landscape-oriented document or rotate individual pages in a document using Frame-Maker's own layout features (pages 44, 214, and 220).

To create an Encapsulated PostScript file for inclusion as a graphic in an application that accepts PostScript graphics, go to Print Options and type in a name for the output file.

To create a file for output on a PostScript printer, use the Print Only To File option in the main Print dialog bo; do *not* use Encapsulated PostScript File for this purpose.

To print a negative or mirror image, go to Advanced Options [**Ctrl-p s o v**] and turn on Negative Image and/or Mirror.

To make all colors print as solid black, turn on All Colors to Black. All colors, including grays, print as solid black. When this is turned off, colors print as shades of gray.

Print PostScript Error Information If you turn on this option, your printer will output a description of any problems it encounters on a separate sheet of paper.

■ Abandoning your changes

■ If you decide you don't want to keep your current changes, you can revert to the last-saved version of your document by choosing **File→Revert to Saved** [**Alt f v**]. FrameMaker abandons the current changes and opens the last version of the file that you saved using **File→Save**.

■ If you have Automatic Save turned on [**File→Preferences**], you have another choice: open the autosaved file. It may be more recent than your manual save.

FrameMaker's file names

FILENAME.FM	File as you last saved it
FILENAM$.FM	Automatic Save file
FILENAM%.FM	Backup file *(This is never the last-saved; it is always the one before that.)*

■ Listing document elements

You can generate separate files containing information about what's in your document. Here are some examples:

■ List the **graphics** in a document that you have imported by reference.

■ List the **fonts** that are used in a document.

■ List all **cross-references** that refer to other documents (External Cross-References) or cross-references whose targets have been deleted or moved (Unresolved Cross-References).

■ List which **condition tags** are in use, and where they occur.

The difference between a list and an index

In a list (of fonts, for example), each item is listed as many times as it occurs, in order of occurrence. In an index, each item is listed only once, alphabetically, followed by a list of the pages where it occurs.

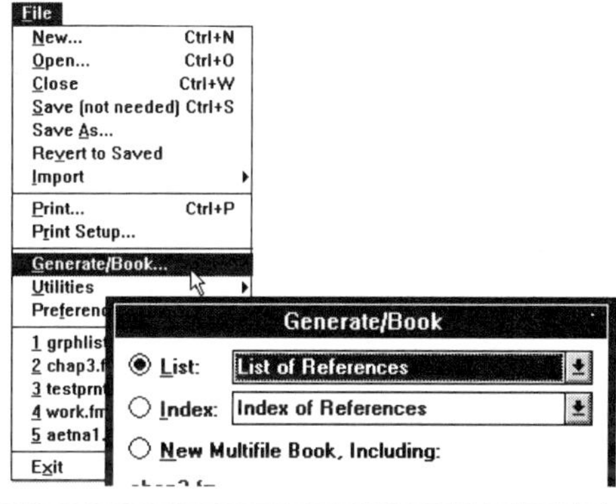

A list of fonts

Times @ 12.0 pt 1
FuturaExtraBold @ 9.0 pt 1
FuturaLight @ 9.0 pt 1
Berkeley Book @ 12.0 pt 1
Berkeley Book @ 12.0 pt 2
Times @ 12.0 pt 3
Berkeley Book @ 12.0 pt 3

An index of fonts from the same document

Berkeley Book @ 12.0 pt 1-3
FuturaExtraBold @ 9.0 pt 1
FuturaLight @ 9.0 pt 1
Times @ 12.0 pt 1, 3

To generate a List of References, *click on List and choose List of References from the pop-up menu.*

Then click on Generate.

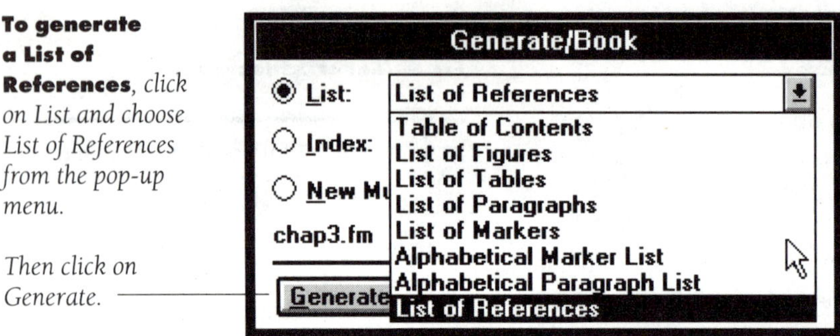

To generate an Index of References, *click on Index, and then choose Index of References from the pop-up menu.*

Set Up Index of References

Filename Suffix: IOR

Include References: Fonts

Don't Include: Condition Tags, External Cross-Refs, Imported Graphics, Unresolved Cross-Refs

<--- --->

Create Hypertext Links

Generate | Cancel | Help

Double-click on an item to move it from one box to the other. Shift-click on an arrow to move all the items.

When Include References contains the items you want, click Generate.

Create Hypertext Links *When you turn this on, you can Ctrl-Alt-click on an item in your generated list to go directly to that item in your document!*

Generating a list or an index of document elements

1. Choose **File➜Generate/Update**.
2. Click on List or Index. Choose List of References from either menu.
3. Click Generate.
4. In the Set Up dialog box, double-click on items to move them between the lists until you are including only the items you want. Shift-click on an arrow to move all the items in the indicated direction.
5. If you turn on **Create Hypertext Links**, the entries in the file that you generate will contain hypertext links to your document. This means that you can Ctrl-Alt-click on an item in the generated list to go directly to that occurrence of the item in the document that generated the list. (I hope you're impressed—I sure am.)
6. Click Generate.
7. FrameMaker generates a new file containing the information you requested. The new filename will be the same as the file that generated it except for the extension.

NAME.REF	List of References
NAME.IOR	Index of References

▲ You can format the contents of this generated file just as you would any other, and you can copy and paste its contents into any other file.

Seeing which paragraph tags are in use (another trick!)

Sometimes you may want to know just which paragraph formats are actually in use. (Perhaps you want to delete the unused ones.)

1. Choose **Special→Cross Reference...**.
2. In the Source Type box, click on a paragraph format. If it is in use, all the instances of it appear in the Reference Source box. Use the up and down arrow keys to move through the list of paragraph formats.

▲ You can go directly to a paragraph that displays in the Reference Source box by clicking on the paragraph and then clicking on Go To.

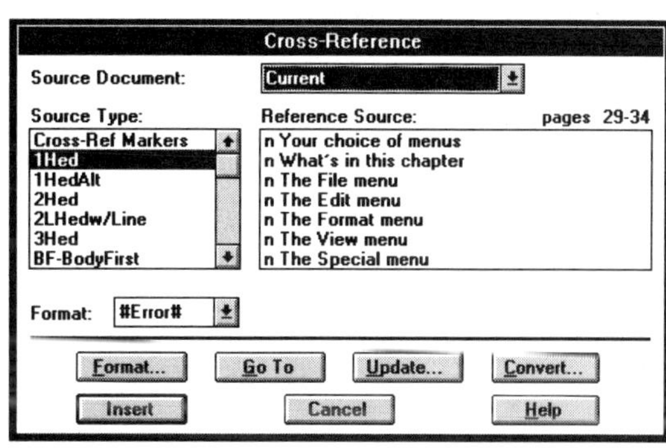

Choose **Special→Cross Reference...**. *Then highlight a paragraph tag on the left to see the first line of each occurrence of that tag on the right.*

■ The parts of a FrameMaker document

Just what do you get when you open a FrameMaker document, or a template? What do you save when you Save As? It's the same list for both, and here it is:

1. Any **text** that's in the document.
2. At least one **body page**.
3. At least one master page for a single-sided document, and at least two (a Right and a Left) **master pages** for a double-sided document.
4. One or more **reference pages**, and the elements on them.
5. All the **document defaults** that you set in various parts of the Format menu and the View menu, and View Options dialog box.
6. A catalog of **paragraph formats**, and another of **character formats**. All the formats that you create stay with the document. Every document has a few basic formats available, even if you just created it using New Portrait, Landscape, or Custom.

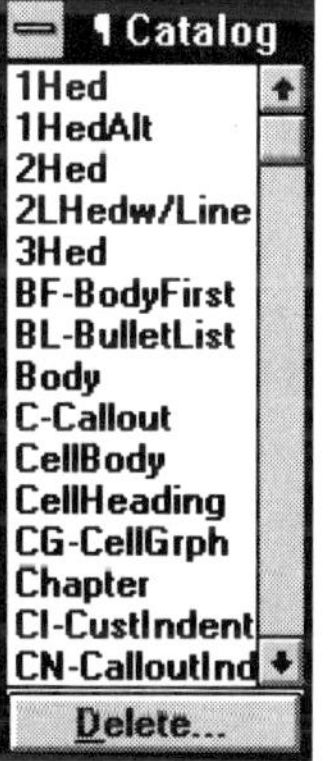

The Paragraph Catalog

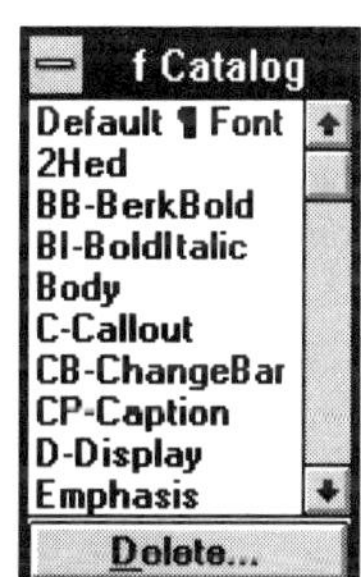

The Character Catalog

The parts of a FrameMaker document *(continued)*

7. Table format definitions.
8. System variables, and any user-defined variables that have been created in your current or source document.
9. Color definitions: basic, plus new ones defined by users. Color view definitions.

A master page [Alt v m]

Text and variables that will appear on all body pages using this master page.

Background text column (header).

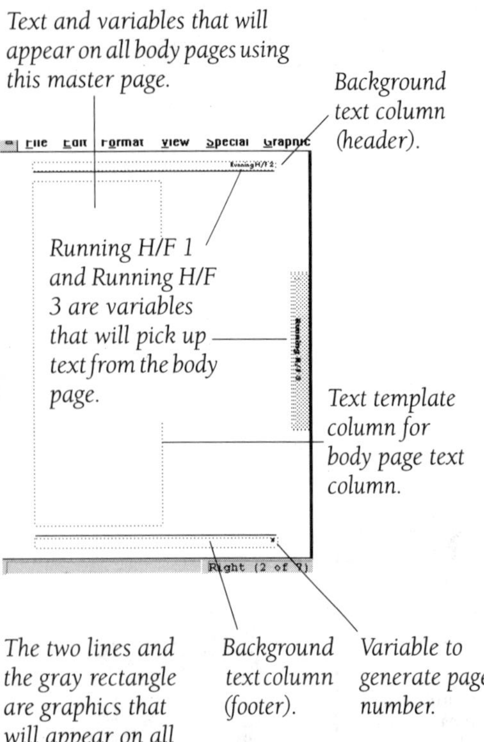

Running H/F 1 and Running H/F 3 are variables that will pick up text from the body page.

Text template column for body page text column.

The two lines and the gray rectangle are graphics that will appear on all body pages that use the master page.

Background text column (footer).

Variable to generate page number.

A reference page [Alt v e]

Above each frame is its name.

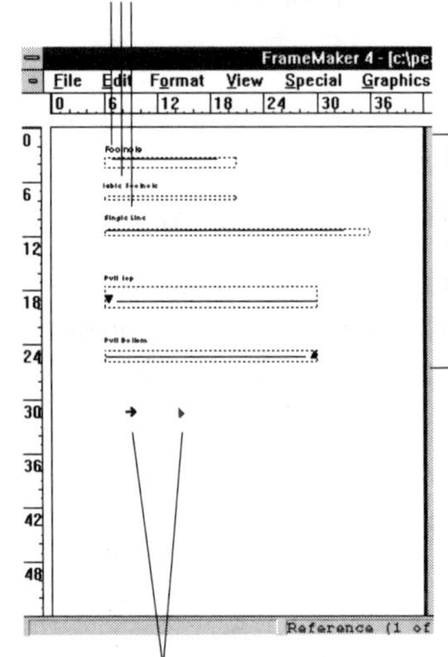

These are frames containing graphics that can appear above or below a paragraph. Look in the Advanced page of the Paragraph Designer at Frame Above ¶, and Frame Below ¶ to see how these are used.

These two graphic items are things that I store here for my own use. Reference pages can be storage for both you and FrameMaker.

Tip *Store often-used paragraphs on reference pages (you can have many), and cross-reference them in text instead of copying them. Then when you make a change to the original, all the cross-references are changed when you Update cross-references.*

The parts of a document

Thinking about master pages and reference pages

As you work with FrameMaker, it is useful to know how FrameMaker itself "thinks" about a file. To FrameMaker, there are three types of pages: body pages, master pages, and reference pages. A body page is what you normally see and type on when you're working in FrameMaker. You can see a master page by choosing **View ➔Master Pages [Alt v m]**, and you can see a reference page by choosing **View ➔Reference Pages** [**Alt v e**]. Return to the body pages with **View ➔Body Pages** [**Alt v d**].

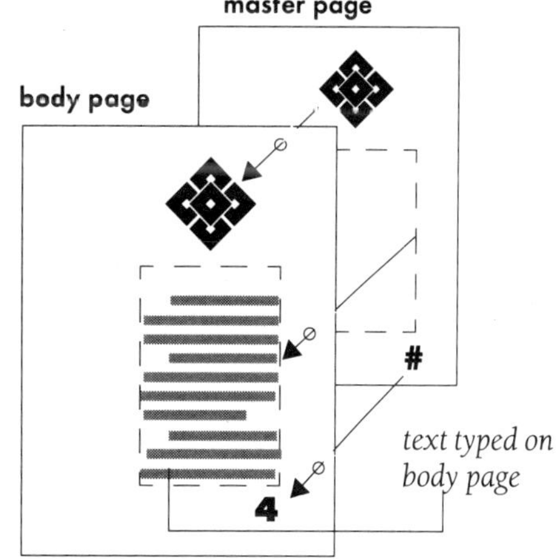

A master page with a text template column, page number variable, and graphic, produces a body page to which text is added.

Master pages

If you're FrameMaker, you think that every body page has a master page lying beneath it. Parts of the master page show through and are visible on the body page.

- A one-sided document has one master page, named Right, that underlies every body page. A two-sided document has two master pages, named Right and Left. You can edit these master pages, and create new ones. FrameMaker uses Right and Left by default, but you can assign any master page to any body page.
- **Text template columns** on the master page appear as dotted lines on the body page. They have a flow tag assigned (page 205), they are usually Autoconnected (page 205), and you type into them on the body pages. You can select a text column on a body page (Ctrl-click) and resize it or move it without affecting the master page.
- **Background text columns** on the master page contain text or variables for things like running headers and footers. You see their contents but not their borders on the body pages. They NEVER have a flow tag assigned. That's what makes them different. If you see text on a body page that you

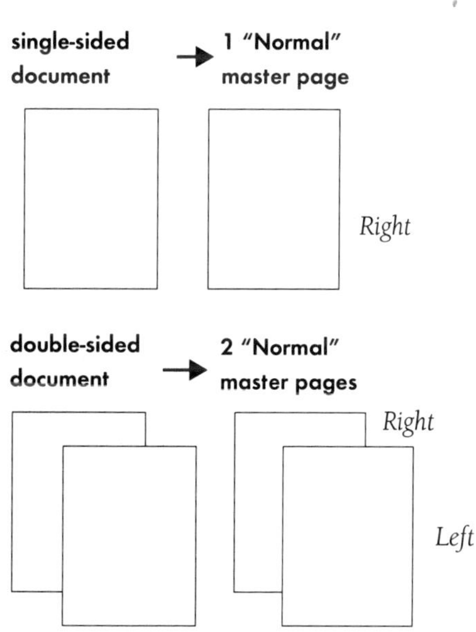

Master pages & reference pages

can't select or edit, it's probably on a master page in a background text column.

- **Graphics** on a master page appear on any body page that uses that master page.

Reference pages

FrameMaker thinks of these as a kind of storehouse, where it keeps pieces that it needs. You can store stuff here, too. It will never appear on a body page unless you copy it and paste it. You can put anything here that you might need in your text. This is also where you will put lines and graphics that appear above and below paragraphs. See "Rules and graphics above and below paragraphs" on page 146. (The paragraph at the side is an example!)

Master pages and you

It is possible to work in FrameMaker without ever thinking about a master page, or looking at one.

- If you begin by opening a document, template, or basic file whose layout suits you, you can forget about master pages.
- But when you need to modify layouts, or design special layouts that apply to more than one page, you will find yourself working on master pages.
- They're one more tool to help you do work only once, and not have to repeat anything.

■ Using a document as a template

When you create document defaults, paragraph formats, character formats, table formats, color definitions, color views, cross-reference formats, user variables, system variable format changes, conditions, and footnote and change bar definitions in a document, they are present in any copy of that document that you create by using New or Open, and then Save As. In other words, every document can be a template, and every template is really just a document. When you use an existing document as a source for a new document, the new document inherits from the source document all the elements that we've discussed in this section, "The parts of a FrameMaker document."

■ Checking document defaults

When you've got a document open, but before you begin entering or changing text, you may want to check these things:

Use this	To determine this
Format→Document	**1.** Are Smart Quotes and Smart Spaces turned on? Are the other items in the document formats set the way you want them? *page 24*
File→Import→Formats	**2.** Do you want to import formats from another document? *page 107*
Format→Change Bars Format→Footnote Properties	**3.** Are footnotes and change bars formatted to your liking? *pages158 and 186*
View→Options	**4.** Are the screen appearance options set the way you want them? *page 26*
View→Master Pages	**5.** Do you need to make changes to the layout of any of the master pages, or to other elements on the master pages? *pages 210 to 220*
View→Color→Views View→Color→Definitions	**6.** Do you need to define new colors, or change which ones are displayed and printed? *pages 300 to 302*
Graphics→Gravity Graphics→Snap	**7.** Do you want to change the way Gravity and Snap are set? *page 28*
Paragraph Designer →Pagination→Side Heed	**8.** Are you going to use Side Heads? If so, plan your side head spacing, and turn on Leave Room for Side Heads before you create other formats. *page 136*

■ If some of your document seems to be missing

Occasionally, you'll find that something you know is there seems to be missing. Here are a few troubleshooting tips:

Missing text

Turn on Borders [**Alt v b**] and look for a text column with a heavy black line across the bottom. If you find one, select it (Ctrl-click) and turn on Autoconnect in the Flow Properties dialog box. [**Alt o l** (*oh ell*)]

Now will I look to his remuneration. Remuneration. O that's the Latin word for three farthings. Three farthings, remuneration. What's the price of this inkle? One penny. No, I'll give you a remuneration. Why, it is a fairer name than French crown. I will never buy and

A heavy black line at the bottom of a text column means that there is undisplayed text.

Missing graphics

Choose **View➔Options** and make sure there is an **X** in the Graphics box. If View Graphics is turned off, all your graphics will seem to be gone.

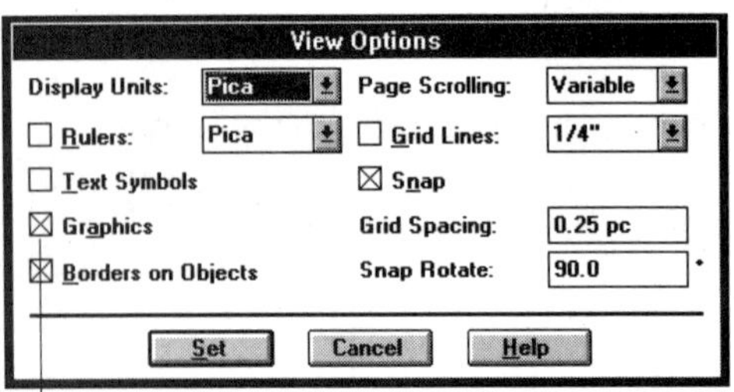

If your graphics seem to be missing, be sure the Graphics box has an **X** *in it.*

Missing text or graphics

- Your missing items may be in a color that's not in the current View. Choose **View➔Colors➔View** and choose a View in which there are no colors listed in the Invisible box.
- Maybe it's white. Draw a big selection border (Alt-Shift-drag) around the area where you think the missing elements might be. You will see the handles of the selected invisible object. Use the Graphic Tools palette for objects, or one of the Designers for text, to assign a color so you can see your missing items.

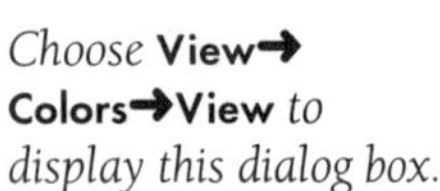

Choose **View➔ Colors➔View** *to display this dialog box.*

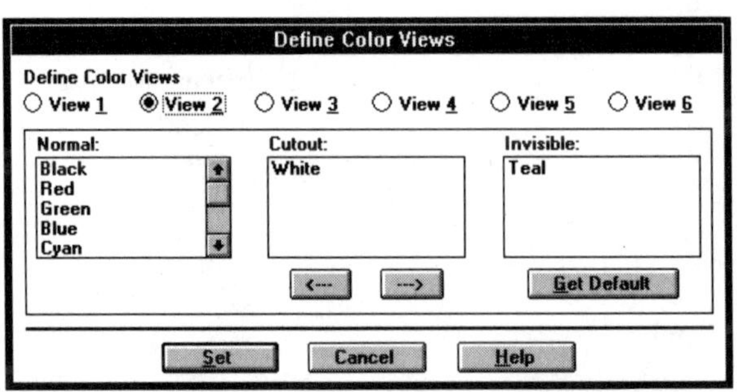

When this View is selected, no text or graphics with the Teal color property will be visible.

Creating and Editing Text

■ The insertion point

What to do if you don't have an insertion point

■ **Click in a text column** You can have an insertion point only in a text column. Turn on Borders [**Alt v b**] so you can see where the text columns are. Move your pointer until it becomes an I-beam and click where you want to edit.

■ If clicking doesn't work, double-click where you want the insertion point. This will change the focus to your document window, and unselect any graphic objects that might have been selected.

■ If your mouse pointer is inside a dotted line, and it isn't an I-beam shape, the dotted line is a frame rather than a text column. To put text in a frame, draw a text column in it (page 203).

■ **Are you trying to type in a blank area where there's no text?** Then you need to ask yourself: "Do I want the material I'm trying to enter to be *connected* to the previous text?" (As you edit the previous text, do you want this new text to move along with it?) *Unconnected* text will stay right where you put it, no matter what edits you make to other text. On the next page, you will find a variety of ways to get text to go where you want it to.

The all-important insertion point

The insertion point is a blinking vertical bar; you can't type, delete, paste, or select text without one. Normally, you just move the mouse pointer over a text column so that it becomes an I-beam, and click on the place where you want to work to get the insertion point. If this doesn't work, look at the list of suggestions in the left column.

I

This I-beam mouse pointer means you're over a text column.

te|xt

The blinking vertical line is your insertion point.

When Borders are turned on [**Alt v b**], *a text column appears as a dotted rectangle.*

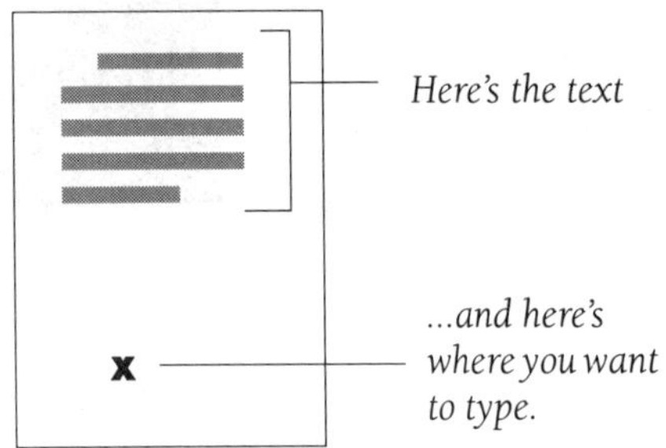

Go to the next page or column

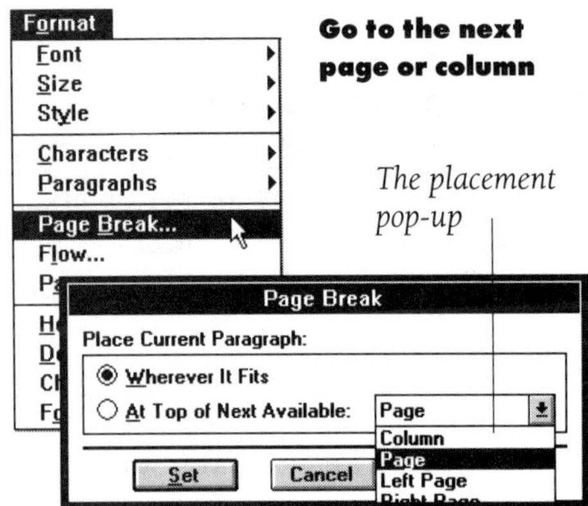

Or add indents or space above

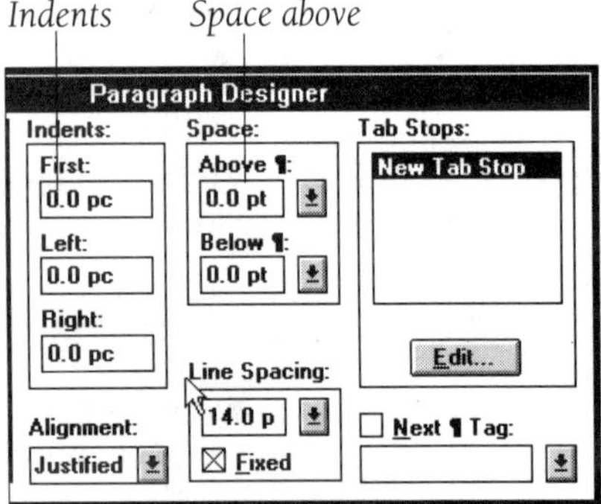

To enter connected text in a blank area, away from previous text

First, go to the end of the previous text. Click at the very end of the text. Type Return if necessary to get a new line. Then:

- To move the line to the next page or column, choose **Format→Page Break→At Top of Next Available**.
- **Or** add space above the line as necessary (page 118), and indents (page 112) to position your insertion point where you want it.
- **Or** insert an anchored frame (page 195). [**Alt s a**] Position and size it, and draw a text column in it where you want your text. This is the technique to use if you want to combine text and graphics, keep them together, and move the whole thing along with the rest of the text.

To enter unconnected text

- Draw a text column wherever you want it. [**Esc 1 t c**] It will stay right where you put it. Click in it and type.
- **Or** disconnect the column where you want to type from the previous column (page 219). [**Esc C P**] Now when you click in the column you will get an insertion point. Be aware that the previous column is now not only unconnected, but has Autoconnect turned off.
- **Or** type a *text line* (see next page).
- **Or** draw a frame, and then draw a text column inside it. If you have graphics, or more than one text block that you want to keep together, use this method. Remember that this unanchored frame will not move along with text.

Creating separate, disconnected text

Use one or more of these three techniques

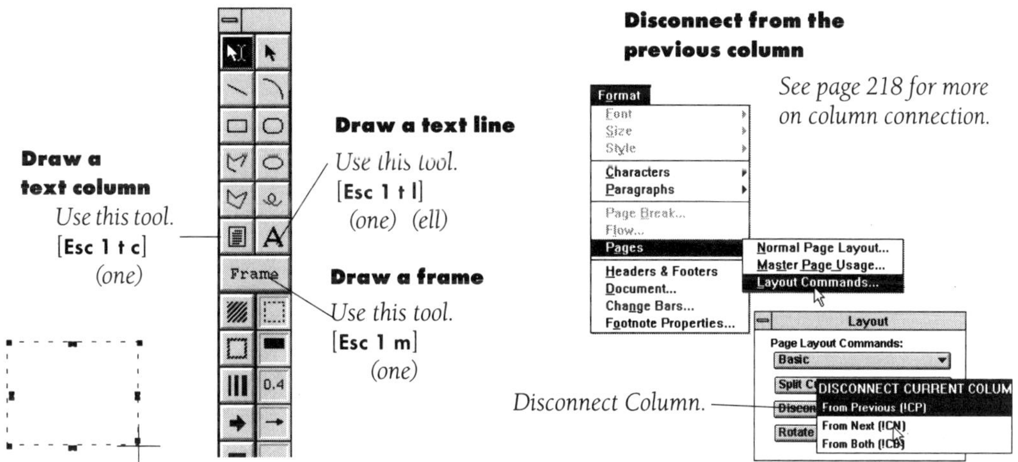

Note *This whole illustration is in an anchored frame to keep all the pieces together. Each chunk of text is in its own little text column to make it easy to position. The screen shots are imported.* [**Alt f i f**]

■ Entering text

When you have an insertion point in a text column (see above), you are ready to enter text. Here are some pointers:

■ As with all modern word-processing and desktop publishing programs, you press Enter only to end a paragraph, not to end a line.

■ **Understanding paragraphs** A paragraph definition (format) may include space or graphics above and/or below the paragraph. It may also automatically generate an autonumber or bullet. When you end a paragraph by typing Enter, you generate whatever space or graphics go at the end of the current paragraph, and at the beginning of the next paragraph, as well as any autonumbers or bullets.

▲ If you want to end a line but not a paragraph, type **Shift-Enter**. This is called a *hard line break*.

▼

Entering text

1 *Click in a text column and type.*

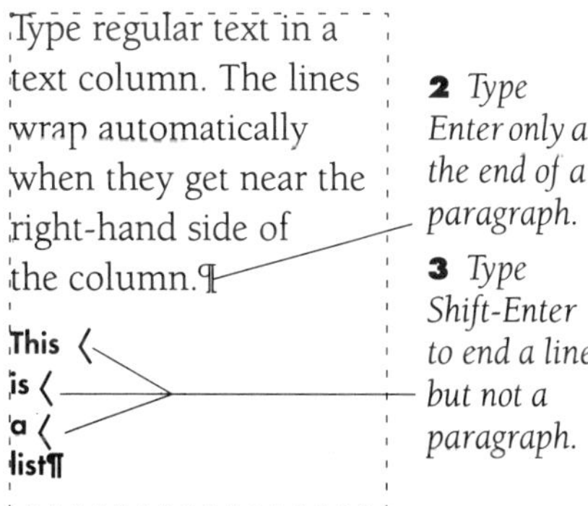

In the example above, text symbols are turned on. The ¶ symbol is the end of a paragraph, and the ⟨ symbol is a forced end of line (but not end of paragraph).

▲

■ Selecting

This is unselected text.

This is selected text.

There are a lot of handy tricks and shortcuts for selecting text. Here's a list of the most useful techniques. You select text in order to cut it, copy it, delete it, or format it.

To select this	Do this	To extend the selection
Exact range	■ Click at the beginning and drag to the end. ■ Click at the beginning and then shift-click at end. ■ Hold down **Shift** and press right or left arrows.	■ Shift-click. ■ **Shift-left/right arrow**.
Word or words	■ Double-click to select a word; drag to select additional words. ■ **Esc h w**.	■ Shift-click in the last word.
One or more paragraphs	■ Triple-click. ■ **Ctrl-Shift-up/down arrow**.	■ Drag to select additional paragraphs, or Shift-click in the last paragraph. ■ Repeat **Ctrl-Shift-up/down arrow**.
A line at a time	■ **Shift-Home** or **Shift-End** selects a line.	■ **Shift-Home/End** repeatedly selects previous/next line.
A sentence at a time	■ **Ctrl-Shift-End** to select forward. ■ **Ctrl-Shift-Home** to select backward.	■ Continue to hold down **Ctrl-Shift** and press **Home** or **End** repeatedly.
To top/bottom of column	■ **Shift-PgUp/PgDn**.	■ Does not repeat.
To end of flow	■ Click in text; **Ctrl-Shift-PgDn**.	■ Does not repeat.
Text column or text line	■ Ctrl-click.	■ Ctrl-click next one.
Object	■ Click near border of object.	■ Shift-click next object.
Unselect something	■ Click outside of all objects and text columns to unselect everything.	■ Shift-click to unselect an object while leaving others selected.

Selecting line endings

Watch out for the end of the line when you're selecting text. If the selection bar goes all the way to the end, you're selecting the line ending. If it doesn't, you're not. Are you going to be pasting this somewhere? Do you want to include the line return at the end? *Think ahead.*

▲ If you've accidentally selected the end of the line, the easiest way to unselect it is **Shift-left arrow**.

Line ending selected.

Line ending not selected.

If you select the line ending, you also select the paragraph properties, such as space above/below, indent, and alignment. If you don't select the line ending, you select only text, not paragraph properties.

Select All in...

- To select **all in flow**, click in the flow.
- To select **all on page**, click in the margin, outside all text columns and frames.
- To select **everything in a frame**, click on the border of the frame to select it.

▲ **Then** choose **File→Select All in**. [**Ctrl-a**]

▼

Extending your selection the easy way

- Hold down Shift and press the right or left arrow key to select/unselect a letter at a time.
- **Or** Shift-click in the exact place you want the selection to begin or end.

▲

■ Text columns and text lines

Text columns

- Text columns are what you normally type in. They are created automatically on the body pages by the master pages, and you can draw your own, as well (see top of page 65). They contain *text.*
- You can apply both paragraph formats and character formats to text in text columns. You cannot perform graphics operations (from the Graphics menu) on text. You can microposition selected text by using **Alt** and the arrow keys. (A slick trick—see page 131.)
- To select a text column, Ctrl-click on the border. The column itself is a *graphic object.*

Hint Turn on borders [**Alt v b**] to make them visible while you work. Then turn off borders to see what the page really looks like.

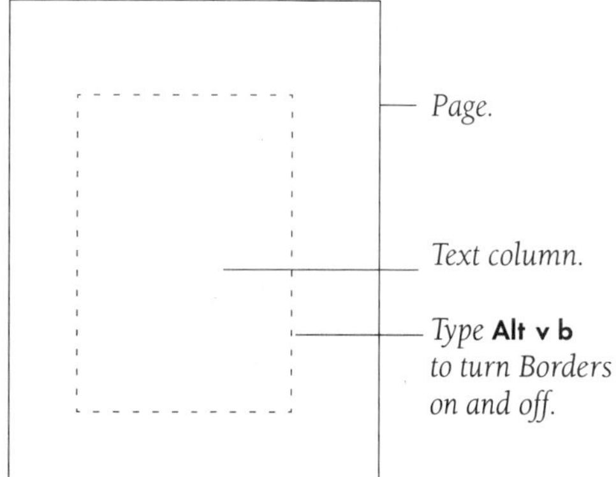

Type in the text columns created for you by the master page, or draw your own. See Chapter 10 for layout.

text line

A text line selected as a graphic object (Ctrl-click).

text line

A text line selected as text (press-and-drag).

Is the end of your text gone?

1. *Turn on Borders if they're not on already.* [**Alt v b**] *Look at the bottom of your last text column. Is it a solid dark line? Your column is not connected to another column and does not have Autoconnect turned on. Your text is there, but hidden.*
2. *Select the column and turn on Autoconnect* [**Alt o l** *(ell)* **a**]; **or** *connect the current column to the next column where you want the missing text to go (page 218).*

▲ *The keyboard shortcut for inserting a page break is either* **Alt o b a s**. *or* **Esc j P**. *I used it a lot in this book!*

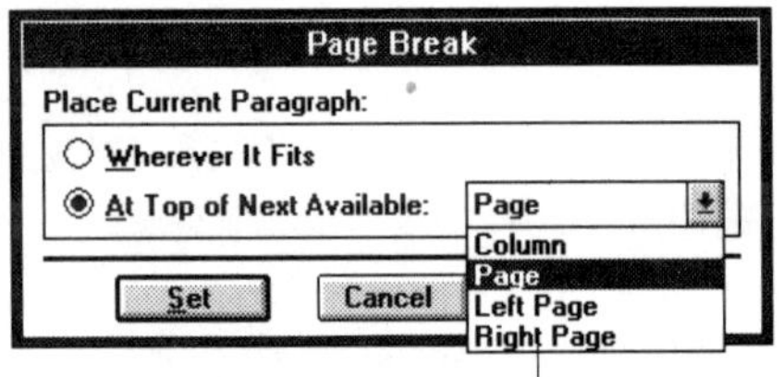

The pop-up list of choices

Text lines

■ **Creating a text line** Click on the Text Line tool [A] in the Graphics palette [**Esc 1** *(one)* **t l** *(ell)*]; click where you want the line to begin. Type. It doesn't have to be in a text column. *Text does not wrap. Each time you press Enter, you create a new text line.*

■ **Selecting as a graphic object** Ctrl-click on it. You can perform all Graphics menu operations on it. You can drag it around, and microposition it using **Alt** and the arrow keys (or **Alt-Shift-**arrows). See page 131 for micropositioning.

■ **Selecting the contents as text** Use any of the regular text selection techniques (page 66), and edit it like text (page 71).

■ **Formatting text in a text line** You can apply character formats to a text line, but not paragraph formats.

■ **Deleting a text line** *Always* select the line as an object (Ctrl-click) and delete it. If you just select and delete the text in the line you will leave an empty, invisible text line behind, that may get in your way later.

■ **Pasting a text line** You can select it as an object or as text and then paste it. If you're pasting it into text, select it as text.

■ Adding and deleting pages

Insert a page or column break (Add a connected page)

1. Click in the line that should be on the new page or column.
2. Choose **Format→Page Break**. [**Alt o b**]
3. In the Page Break dialog box, click the Page pop-up to choose where you want your text to begin: new column, any new page, or specifically a right or left page.
4. Click Set.

If the new page doesn't happen

If you try to apply a page break [**Esc j P**] and nothing happens:

- Check to see that your text column has Autoconnect turned on (pages 69 and 221).
- Display the Pagination page of the Paragraph Designer and see if the paragraph has Keep With Previous turned on (page 133).

Autoconnect is on.

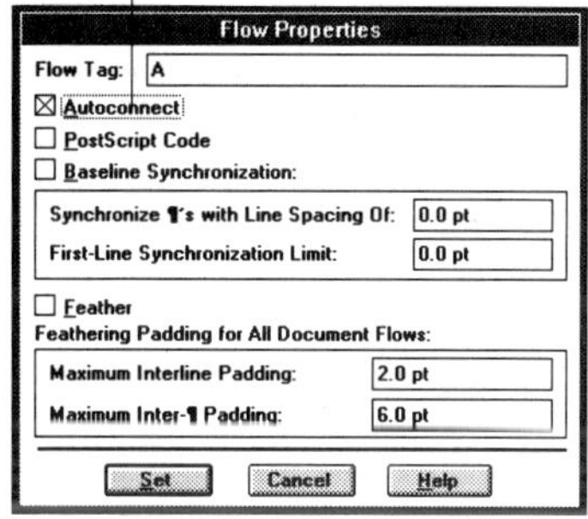

Removing a page break

1. Click in the top line of the page following the page break.
2. Choose **Format→Page Break**. [**Alt o b**]
3. Click Wherever It Fits. Click Set.

Here's where you control page breaks by keeping paragraphs together.

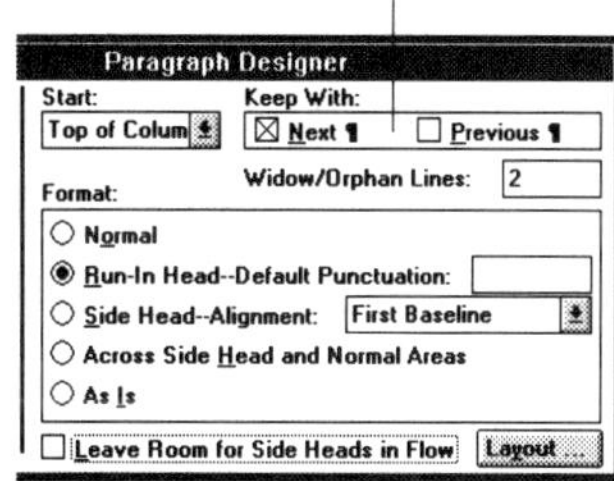

Automatic new pages

If Autoconnect is turned on for text columns on both your current body page and master page, FrameMaker adds new pages as necessary to accommodate your text. If you want to confirm that Autoconnect is on, do this:

1. Ctrl-click on the border of the text column to select it. (If necessary, turn Borders on with **Alt v b**.)
2. Choose **Format→Flow**. [**Alt o l**]

▲ See "How Autoconnect works" on page 221.

Put the new pages before or after the current page. *Type in the number of pages to add.*

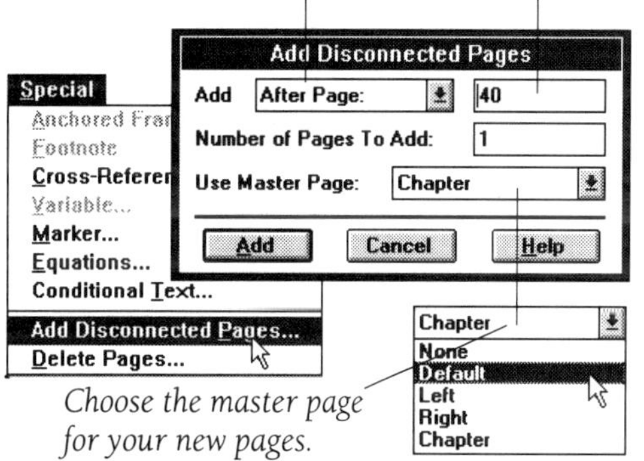

Choose the master page for your new pages.

Adding unconnected pages

1. Place your insertion point in a page that is to either precede or follow the pages you are adding.
2. Choose **Special→Add Disconnected Pages**.
3. In the Add Disconnected Pages dialog box, choose whether the new pages will come before or after the current page, and type how many pages to add in the text box.
4. Click on the Use Master Page pop-up to see a list of available master pages. Choose the one that you want for the majority of the new

Click OK on the warning stickup.

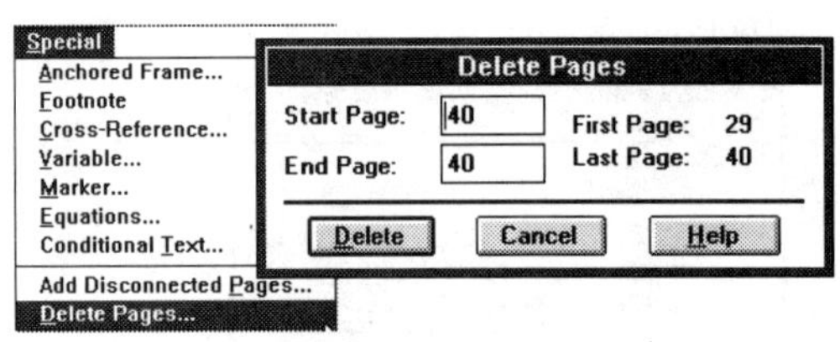

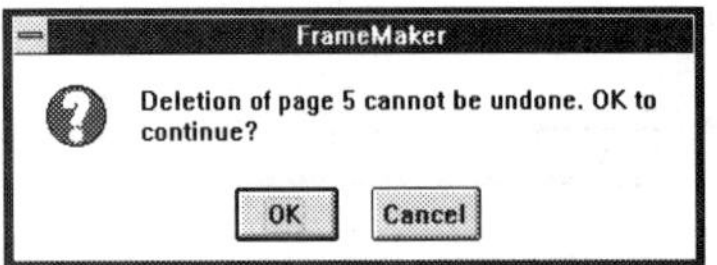

pages. You can always change the master page on individual body pages later.

5. Click Add. Click OK in the warning stickup.

▪ Text will flow around a disconnected page. As you add and delete text, the disconnected page stays right where it was, like an island. Under some circumstances, the page before the disconnected page may also become disconnected. In that case, you must reconnect it to the proper page. See “Connecting two columns” on page 218.

Deleting pages

1. Choose **Special→Delete Pages**. [**Alt s d**]
2. Type the start and end of the page range you're deleting into the appropriate text boxes. If you're deleting just one page, type that number in both boxes.
3. Click Delete. Click OK in the warning stickup.

Removing blank pages

You can make FrameMaker remove empty pages at the end of your document automatically, every time you save.

▪ Choose **Format→Document**. [**Alt o d**] In the Document Properties dialog box, be sure that the Before Saving & Printing pop-up reads Delete Empty Pages. This is the default.

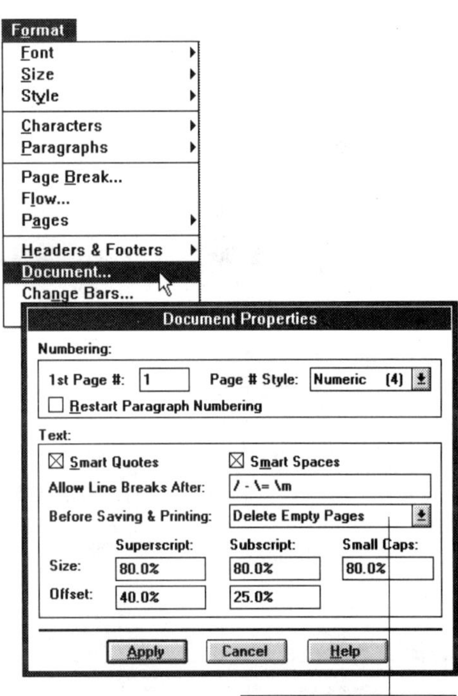

Adjust the page count automatically, each time you print or save, by making your choice here.

Making page count odd or even

You may want your document to always have an odd or even number of pages. You can make that happen automatically.

1. Choose **Format→Document**. [**Alt o d**]
2. Click on Before Saving & Printing.
3. Choose Make Page Count Even or Make Page Count Odd.
4. Click Apply.

■ Editing text

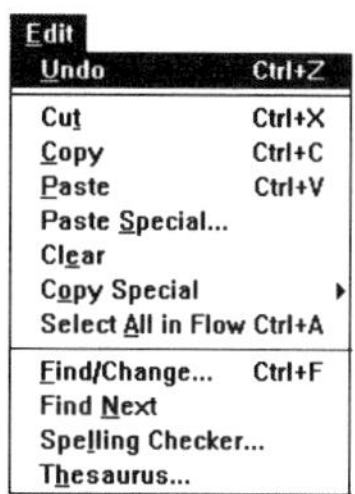

Below is a table of the most common text editing activities, and the different ways you can perform them in FrameMaker.

Cut, copy, and paste between FrameMaker documents exactly as you would within a single document.

A Table of Basic Text Editing Techniques

First select the text you want to edit, then follow the chart below.

To do this	From the Edit Menu	Keyboard Shortcut	QuickAccess Bar
Delete *without saving to Clipboard.*	Clear	Delete key	None
Cut *Place deleted text or graphics on Clipboard for pasting later.*	Cut	Ctrl-x	[scissors icon]
Copy *text or graphics to the Clipboard for pasting later.*	Copy	Ctrl-c	[copy icon]
Replace *selected text with new text.*	Paste *(Or just type new text.)*	Type or paste *The highlighted text is replaced by the new text.*	[paste icon]
Paste *contents of Clipboard at insertion point.*	Paste	Ctrl-v	[paste icon]

■ Quick copy

Copy text without using the Clipboard

1. Place the insertion point where you want the text to appear.
2. Hold down the Alt key and drag the I-beam pointer through the text you want to copy. The text appears at the insertion point! (This always seems slightly magical to me.)

A note about pasting

If you are pasting text that includes a final line ending, place your insertion point at the beginning of the line that will follow your pasted text. (See "Selecting line endings" on page 67.)

See page 71 for how to cut and paste.

Moving text

1. Select the text. (See page 66 for ways to select text.)
2. Cut it. [Ctrl-x]
3. Place the insertion point where you want the text to appear (see "A note about pasting" on the previous page) and paste. [Ctrl-v]

▼

Reversing two letters

1. Put the cursor in between the two reversed letters.
2. Press **Ctrl-F9**.

▲

Controlling hyphenation

On a case-by-case basis

▪ **Discretionary hyphens** [Ctrl-hyphen]
When you put one or more discretionary hyphens in a word, FrameMaker hyphenates the word only at those places (and only if needed).

▲ **Note** FrameMaker always obeys the hyphenation rules that are included in a paragraph format. You may need to go to the Advanced page of the Paragraph Designer and change the rules for hyphenating the paragraph in order to permit the hyphenation you want. See Chapter 85 for more on using the Paragraph Designer.

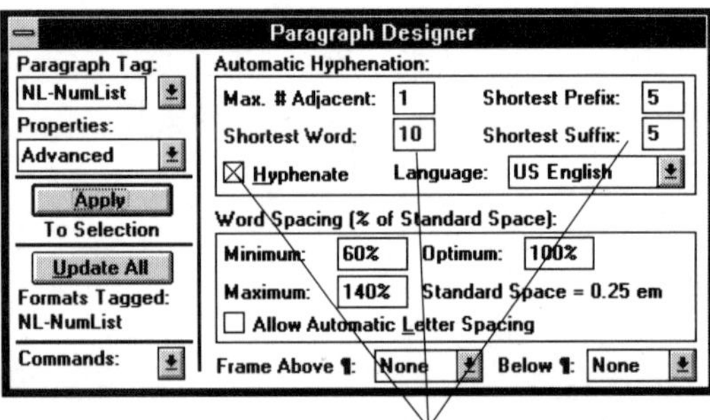

You may need to make changes here, and Apply to Selection to permit the hyphenation you want for a particular paragraph.

▪ **Suppress hyphenation** Putting a **Ctrl-hyphen** at the beginning of a word prevents that word from hyphenating.

▪ **Non-breaking hyphens** When a hyphen is a permanent part of a word, you can prevent FrameMaker from ending a line at that point by typing a non-breaking hyphen, **Esc hyphen h**, instead of a regular hyphen.

Controlling hyphenation *Continued*

In the document

- In the document format dialog box (**Format➔Document** or **Alt o d**), you can remove the hyphen from the Allow Line Breaks After box. Then a line will never break after a hyphen that is a permanent part of a word. This prevents line breaks in phone numbers, for example.

Document Properties
Numbering:
1st Page #: 1 Page # Style: Numeric (4)
☐ Restart Paragraph Numbering
Text:
☒ Smart Quotes ☒ Smart Spaces
Allow Line Breaks After: / - \= \m
Before Saving & Printing: Delete Empty Pages
Superscript: Subscript: Small Caps:
Size: 80.0% 80.0% 80.0%
Offset: 40.0% 25.0%
Apply Cancel Help

Remove the hyphen from this box to prevent hyphenation after permanent hyphens throughout the document.

In a paragraph format

In the Advanced page of the Paragraph Designer you can specify how you want paragraphs of that format to be hyphenated.

How many lines in a row can end with a hyphen?

What's the shortest word FrameMaker is allowed to hyphenate?

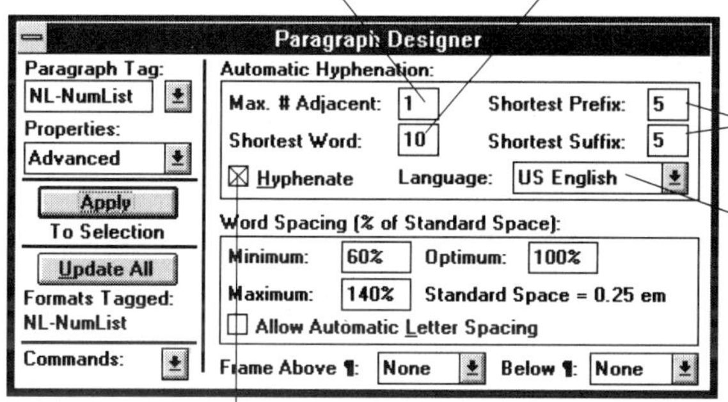

If you un-check Hyphenate, no words are hyphenated in the selected paragraphs, or in the format.

Controlling hyphenation from the Paragraph Designer

What's the minimum number of letters you want before (Prefix) or after (Suffix) a hyphen?

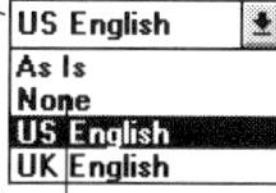

The **Language** *pop-up: Other languages are available from Frame Corp.*

Choose None to prevent all hyphenation and spellchecking. Useful for text such as computer code or other exotic material.

Applying the changes

To make your changes in the Paragraph Designer apply to all paragraphs having the displayed paragraph tag, click Update All. This changes the catalog definition as well. To apply the changes to only the selected paragraph or paragraphs, click Apply to Selection. See Chapter 5 for more on using the Paragraph Designer.

Remember *The paragraph containing the insertion point is a "selected" paragraph.*

Type the word to hyphenate here.

Click here to see the current hyphenation points.

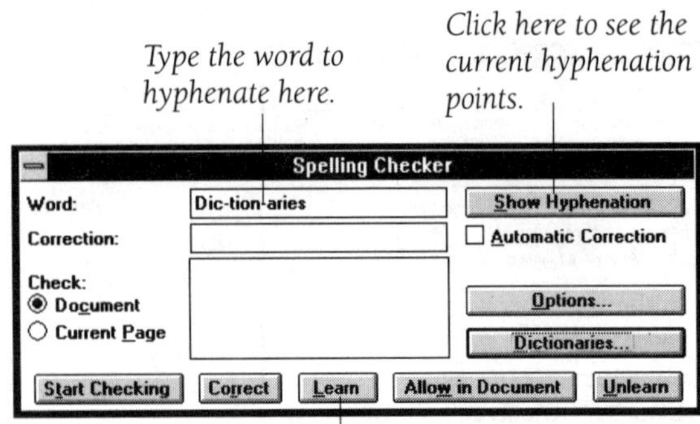

Click Learn when you've corrected the hyphenation.

Changing a word's hyphenation permanently

1. Display the Spelling Checker window: **Edit→Spelling Checker** or **Alt e l** (*ell*).
2. Type the word to change in the Word text box.
3. Click Show Hyphenation. [**Alt s**] FrameMaker displays the current hyphenation.
4. Add or remove hyphens in the Word box to show the correct hyphenation. A hyphen at the beginning of a word will suppress all hyphenation for that word.
5. Click Learn.
6. **To update other occurrences of the word in your document**: In the Spelling Checker window, click Dictionaries and turn on Rehyphenate Document. Click OK.

■ Controlling line breaks

Here are several ways to control pesky line breaks.

Here are several ways to control pesky line breaks.

Sometimes you don't like where a line is breaking—especially if it's in a conspicuous place, such as a headline. If you just end the line using the Enter key, you're likely to get unwanted results, like extra space, because you've ended the paragraph as well as the line. (See "Understanding Paragraphs" on page 65.) Here's a list of options for controlling line endings:

- **Type Shift-return** where you want the line to end. This is a "hard" line break. Soft line breaks are the ones the computer puts in to wrap lines.
- **Suppress or change hyphenation**, in any of the ways discussed on pages 72 to 74, if hyphenation is the problem.
- **Use a non-breaking space**. If you replace a regular word space with **Ctrl-Space** (a non-breaking space), FrameMaker can't break the line at the space. This will often improve the line break. You can connect as many words as you like this way.

Tip *If you use a hard line ending (Shift-Enter) in a line that is going to appear in a Table of Contents or other generated file, the line break will appear in that file. Instead, use a right indent or nonbreaking spaces to create the line break.*

■ **Change the right-hand indent**. With your insertion point in the paragraph you want to change, go to the Basic page of the Paragraph Designer. Change the right indent and click Apply To Selection. The new right indent will apply to the paragraph containing the insertion point.

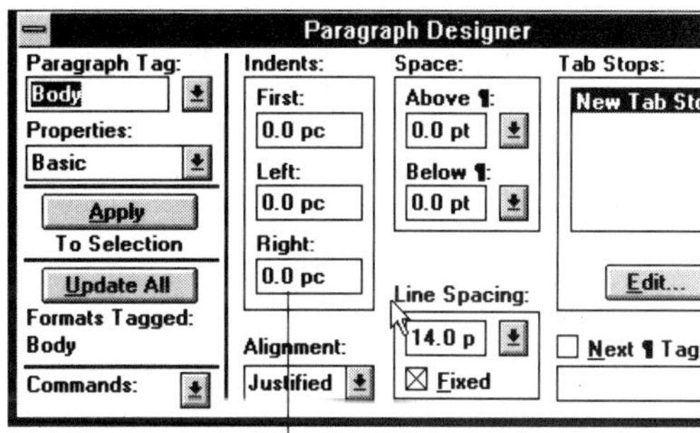

Type a right indent in this box, and click Apply To Selection.

■ **Modify "Allow Lines Breaks After"** FrameMaker does not allow a line break after a nonalphabetic character unless it appears in the Allow Line Breaks After box in the Document Properties dialog box.

1. Choose **Format→Document.**
2. In the Allow Line Breaks After box, list all the characters, and only the characters, that can come before a line break. Use the following special codes:

hyphen	-	em space	\sm
em dash	\m	en space	\sn
en dash	\=	slash	/
backslash	\\	ellipsis	\e

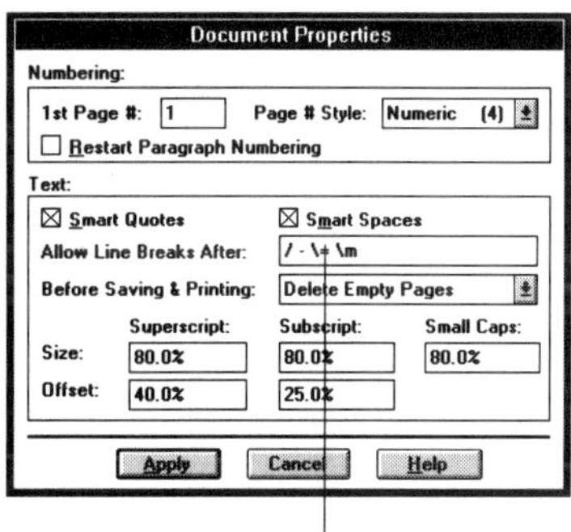

In this box, list nonalphabetic characters that can be followed by a soft line break.

■ Capitalization

FrameMaker offers some really handy ways to create, control, and change capitalization.

To change a specific word or words Select the words you want to change; then

Change to	QuickAccess bar	Keyboard
All lower case	ab	**Ctrl-Alt-l** *(ell)*
Initial cap	Ab	**Ctrl-Alt-c**
All caps	AB	**Ctrl-Alt-u**

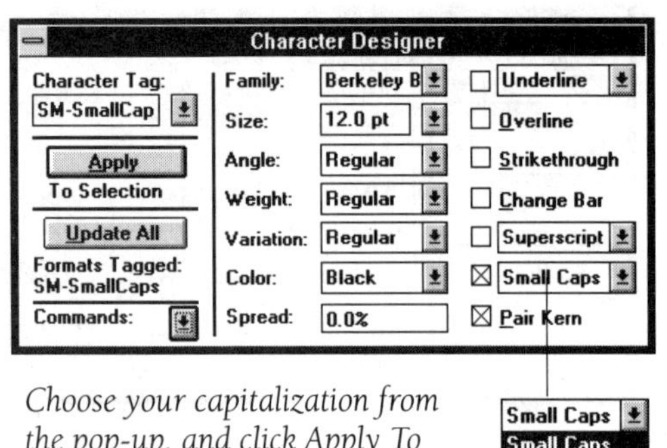

Choose your capitalization from the pop-up, and click Apply To Selection.

Upper case, lower case, and small caps—another way

1. Select the text to be changed.
2. Display the Character Designer. [**Ctrl-d**]
3. Choose Lowercase, Uppercase, or Small Caps from the pop-up, and
4. Click Apply to Selection.

Typing small caps

Type this	**Get This**
two words	TWO WORDS
Two Words	Two Words
TWO WORDS	TWO WORDS

Set the size of the small caps relative to the regular caps

■ **Setting the small caps size** in the **Format→Document** dialog box (page 25). Set the size as a percentage of the basic paragraph font size. The default is 80 percent, which works fine for most purposes.

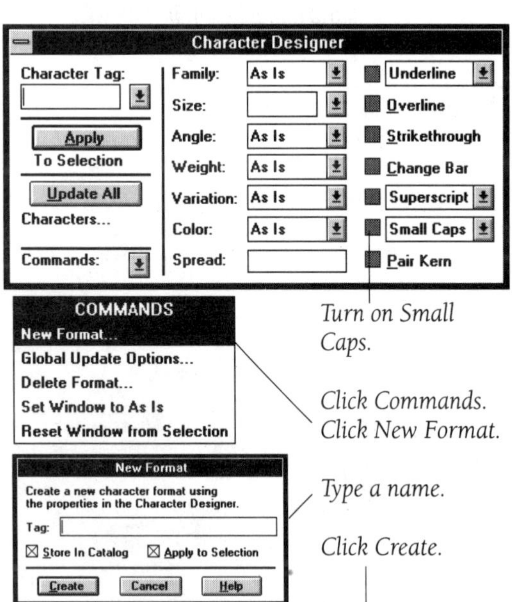

Turn on Small Caps.

Click Commands. Click New Format.

Type a name.

Click Create.

Making a small-caps character format

1. Display the Character Designer. [**Ctrl-d**]
2. Set it to As Is. [**Shift-F8**]
3. Turn on Small Caps.
4. Click Commands.
5. Click New Format.
6. Type a name, like SC-Small Caps.
7. Click Create.

You can now apply this format to selected text using **F8** and the first letter of the character tag.

■ Use this technique to create formats for any character or paragraph property that you use often.

■ Special characters

Accessing special characters

Appendix A in this book lists ANSI numbers, keyboard sequences, and hex code for the Symbol, Wingdings, and Zapf Dingbat fonts, as well as the full 255-character display for regular alphabetic fonts.

■ In regular text, use either the ANSI number or the keyboard sequence. Detailed instructions are given below.

■ To insert a special character into a dialog box, such as an autonumber, a variable or marker, or the Find/Change window, use either the special Dialog Box code or the hex code. Type the code, including the backslash, into the text box.

What's a special character?

A "special character" is any character that's not on the keyboard.

Inserting a character using the ANSI number

1. Turn on Num Lock.
2. Place the insertion point where you want the character.
3. Change the font, if necessary (page 80).
4. Hold down Alt and type the four-number ANSI code on the numeric keypad. (You *must* type the leading zeros.)
5. Return to the paragraph font by typing **F8 d Enter**.

Inserting a character using the keyboard sequence

1. Place the insertion point where you want the character.
2. Type the key sequence. You must do this before you apply the font.
3. Highlight the character and apply a special font—such as Zapf Dingbats—if necessary. See "Applying a font: three ways to do it" on page 80.

Using the character map

You can also copy characters from Windows' Character Map onto the Clipboard and paste them into your FrameMaker document. I consider this awfully clunky, so I am leaving you to get the details from your Windows manual, or Windows on-line help.

■ The Character Map can be useful for finding out the ANSI number or keystroke for the character you want.

Special characters and spaces

Here is a list of some often-needed characters in the regular font.

Char.	ANSI	Hex code	Keystroke	Name
	–	\x14	Esc space m Ctrl-Shift-space	em space
	–	\x13	Esc space n Ctrl-Alt-space	en space
	–	\x11	Esc space h Ctrl-space	nonbreaking space
	–	\x10	Esc space one	numeric space
	–	\x12	Esc space t	thin space
—	0151	\xd1	Ctrl-q Q	em dash
–	0150	\xf7	Ctrl-q P	en dash
•	0149	\xa5	Ctrl-q %	round bullet
. . .	0133	\xc9	Ctrl-q I *(Shift eye)*	ellipsis
™	0153	\xaa	Ctrl-q *	trademark serif
©	0169	\xa9	Ctrl-q)	copyright serif
®	0174	\xa8	Ctrl-q (	reg mark serif
¢	0162	\xa2	Ctrl-q "	cent sign
°	0176	\xfb	Ctrl-q {	degree sign
†	0134	\xa0	Ctrl-q space	dagger
‡	0135	\xe0	Ctrl-q ‘	double dagger
¼	0188	\xb9	Ctrl-q 9	
½	0189	\xba	Ctrl-q :	
¾	0190	\xbd	Ctrl-q =	

Use the hex code if you need to put the character in an autonumber, or in a variable or marker, or in the Find/Change window. In regular text, use the ANSI number or the Keyboard Sequence.

To use the hex code Type the characters, including the \ and the **x**.

A few popular Zapf Dingbats

Char.	ANSI	Hex	Key sequence
☎	0037	\x25	%
✔	0052	\x34	4
■	0110	\x6e	n
❑	0113	\x71	q
▲	0115	\x73	s
▼	0116	\x74	t
◆	0117	\x75	u
❖	0118	\x76	v
❦	0166	\xa6	Ctrl-q &
❧	0167	\xa7	Ctrl-q '
➔	0220	\xdc	Ctrl-q \
➤	0228	\xe4	Ctrl-q d
➧	0231	\xe7	Esc ' A

See Appendix A for a complete list.

Inserting characters

To use the ANSI numbers, change fonts first, then insert the number (page 77). To use the key sequence, type the keystrokes first and then change fonts. Use the hex codes in dialog boxes, such as autonumbers, markers, or Find.

Making a font format

If you use characters from special fonts like Symbol, Zapf Dingbats, and Wingdings, you will find it useful to have a character format for each font. In the example that follows, I will show you how to make a character format that applies a font, such as Zapf Dingbat, without changing the size or any other property. You can, of course, specify other properties if you want to.

1. Display the Character Designer. [**Ctrl-d**]
2. Set it to As Is. [**Shift-F8**]
3. Choose a font—Zapf Dingbats, for example—from the Family pop-up.
4. Click Commands.
5. Click New Format.
6. Type a name, like Z-ZapfDings.
7. Click Create.

Set the Character Designer to As Is. [**Shift-F8**]

Choose a font family.

Click Commands.

Click New Format.

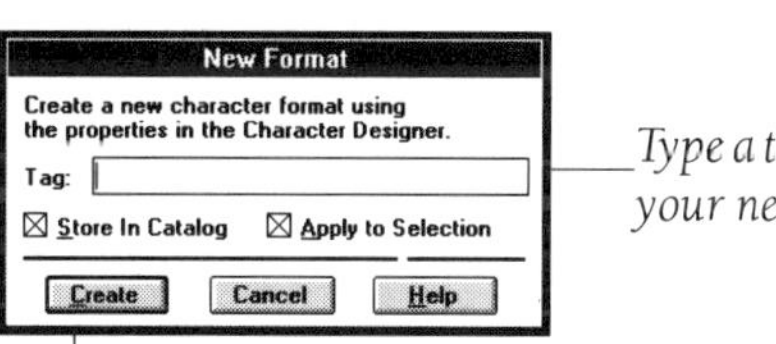

Type a tag name for your new format.

Click Create.

Special characters

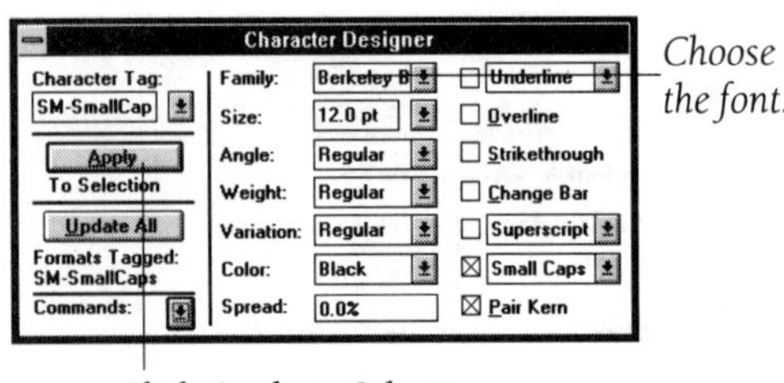

Choose the font.

Click Apply to Selection.

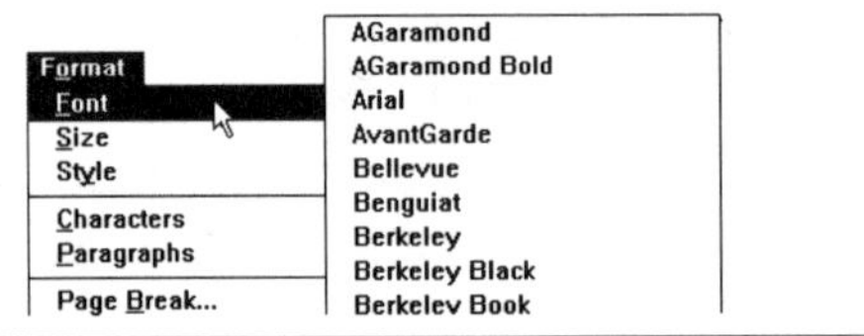

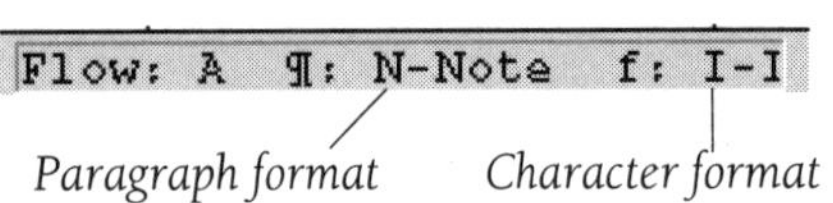

Paragraph format *Character format*

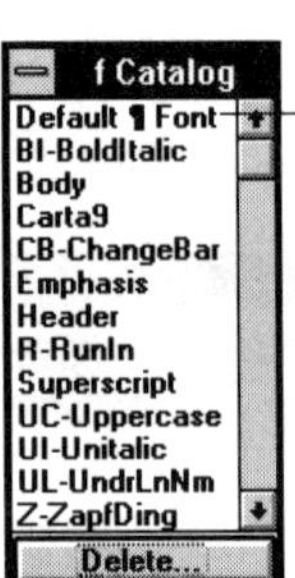

Apply Default ¶ Font to selected characters to remove special character formatting.

Apply any other format to selected characters to add the look you want.

The character catalog

Applying a font: three ways to do it

■ First highlight the characters to format, then

Use the Character Designer

1. Display the Character Designer. [**Ctrl-D**]
2. Choose the font from the Family pop-up.
3. Click Apply to Selection.

Use the Format menu

1. Choose **Format→Font**.
2. Click on the font name.

Apply a character format from the catalog *(The best way to work!)*

1. Press **F8** or **Ctrl-8**.
2. Press the first letter of the format name until the name appears in the Status Bar.
3. Press Enter.

▲ See Chapter 5, page 93, for how to create formats using the Character Designer.

Changing a font

1. Position the insertion point where you want the font to change.
2. Follow the instructions above for using the Character Designer or applying a format from the catalog. New characters that you type will appear in the new font.

Returning to the paragraph font

■ Click on Default ¶ Font in the character catalog. [**F8 d Enter**]

Removing a font format from characters

1. Highlight the characters.
2. Choose Default ¶ Font from the character catalog **or** press **F8 d Enter**.

Quotation marks

You type quotation marks differently depending on whether Smart Quotes are turned on or off. Here's how to type typographic (curved) quotation marks, and straight quotes.

Character	Smart Quotes on	Smart Quotes off
“	"	Ctrl-Alt-`
”	"	Ctrl-Alt-'
‘	'	`
’	'	'
'	Ctrl-'	Ctrl-'
"	Esc "	"

Typing accented characters

To type an accented character, type Esc plus one of the symbols in the table, plus the letter.

Type this	plus this	To get this	Example
Esc	' *Single quote*	´	Esc ' a = á
	`	`	Esc ` a = à
	^	ˆ	Esc ^ a = â
	~	˜	Esc ~ n = ñ
	%	¨	Esc % a = ä
	*	˚	Esc * a = å
	, *Comma*	¸ *Cedilla*	Esc , c = ç

All accented characters can also be accessed using their ANSI character numbers (Appendix A).

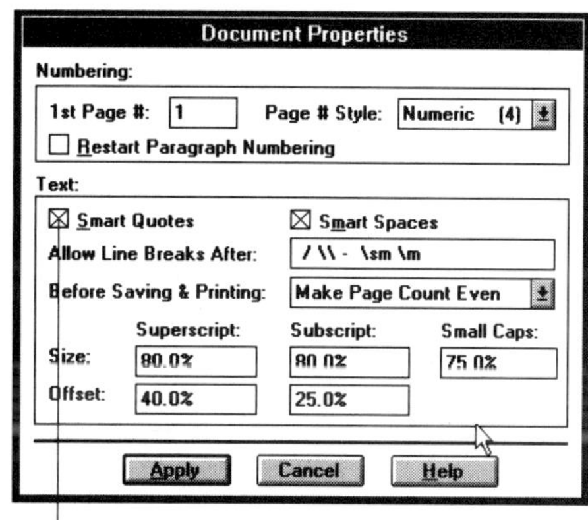

Here's where you turn Smart Quotes on and off. For most purposes, you will want them on. Choose **Format➔Document** *to display the Document Properties dialog box.*

■ Importing text and graphics

You can bring text and graphics into a FrameMaker file from other sources by importing (**File ➔Import➔File**), or by cutting and pasting.

■ You cannot import another FrameMaker file. Use copy and paste to move material between FrameMaker files, just as you would within a single file.

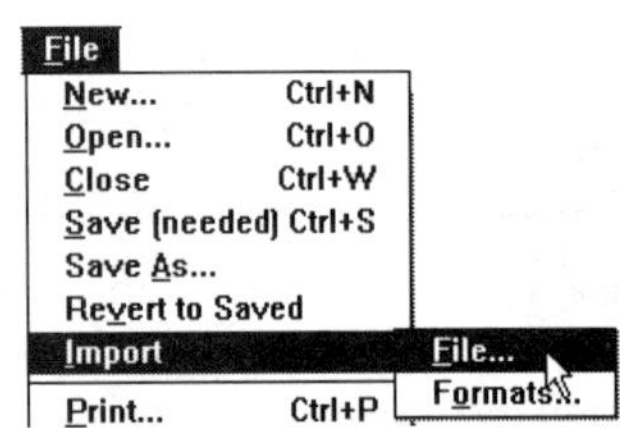

■ You can cut and paste between Windows applications. You can open a file in PageMaker 5, for instance, copy material onto the clipboard, and paste it into your FrameMaker file. You may need to do some cleanup afterward if the material includes complex formatting.

■ You can embed graphics from applications that support Object Linking and Embedding (page 270). Use Paste Special to place the graphic in FrameMaker. Then you can edit the object in the application that created it by double-clicking on the object in FrameMaker to open a window in the application.

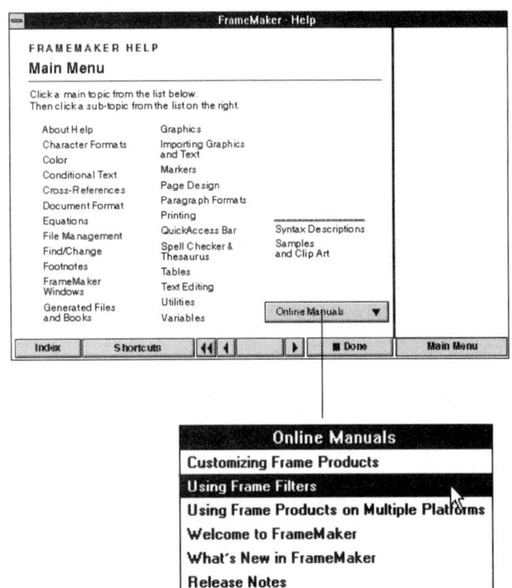

■ In many cases, you can open a file created by another application as a FrameMaker file. This is called "filtering." See Chapter 3, page 43.

■ Read the on-line manual "Using Frame Filters" for some really useful guidelines on importing documents from other applications, and for a list of included filters.

▲ The following few pages give detailed instructions on importing text files into FrameMaker. See pages 264 to 270 for how to import graphics.

Importing text

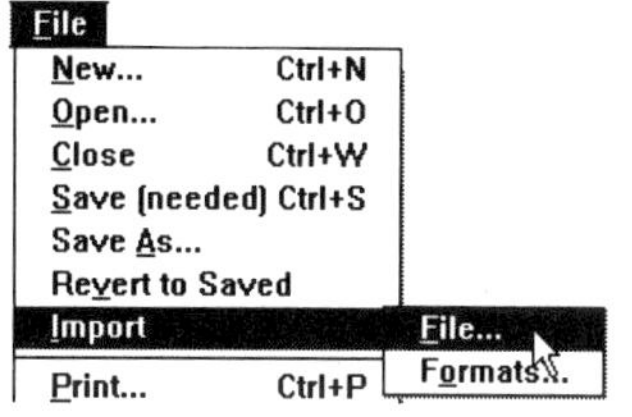

1. Position the insertion point where you want the imported text to appear.
2. Choose **File ➔Import ➔File** to display the import file dialog box.
3. Change the drive and directory to display the directory that include your file. Type the file name into the File text box or choose it from the scroll list.

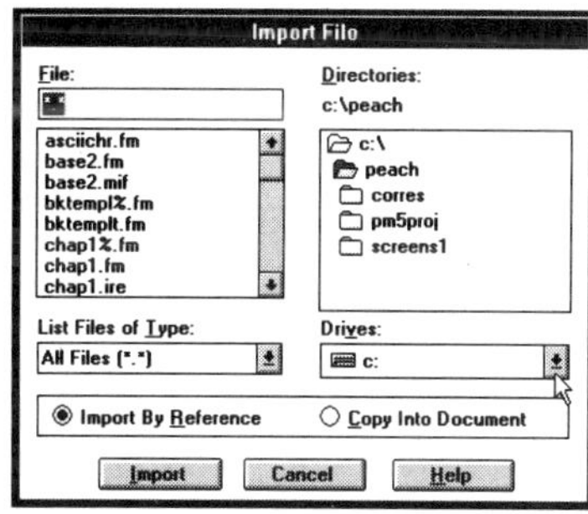

Note *Text files are always copied into the file. The Import By Reference choice applies only to graphics.*

4. Click Import. The File Type dialog box appears, with a file type highlighted.
5. Be sure the correct file type is highlighted, and click Convert. If your file type is Text, the Reading Text File dialog box appears.

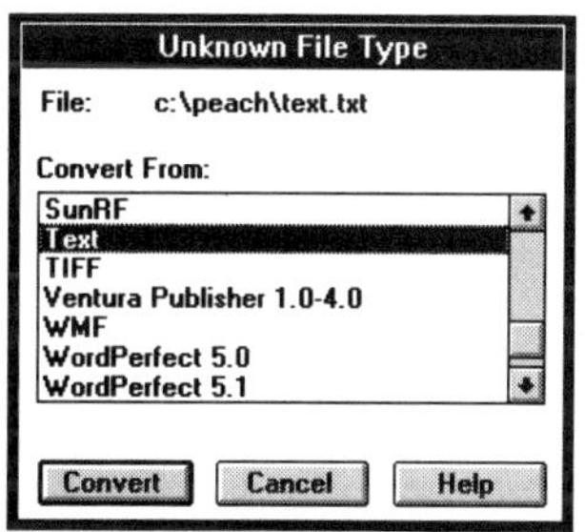

6. Choose **Merge Lines into Paragraphs** if you want your paragraphs to line wrap, i.e., to have "soft" line endings. Choose **Treat Each Line As a Paragraph** if you want to keep each line ending as is. Use this for lists and computer code. Use **Convert To Table** if you are importing material from a spreadsheet or database, and want it to be in a table.
7. Click Read.

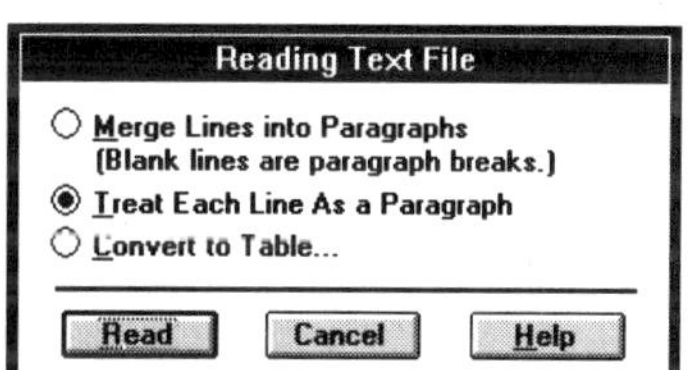

■ **A fix** The procedure described above is best used with plain text files. If you import a file from an application such as MS Word or WordPerfect, it is likely to appear on the following page in a separate flow. Here's how to fix it:

1. Ctrl-click in the text column where the material is to appear, to select the column.
2. Go to the next page, which contains your imported text. Ctrl-click to select the column. Connect the two columns. [**Esc CC**]
3. Click OK in the resulting query box. (The "invisible" column is the one that you chose first, on the previous page.)

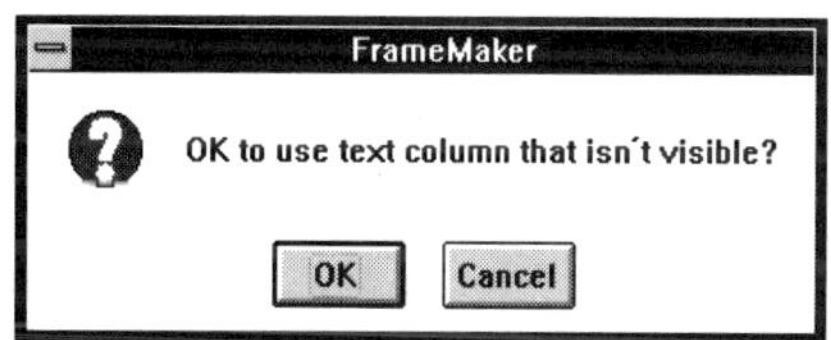

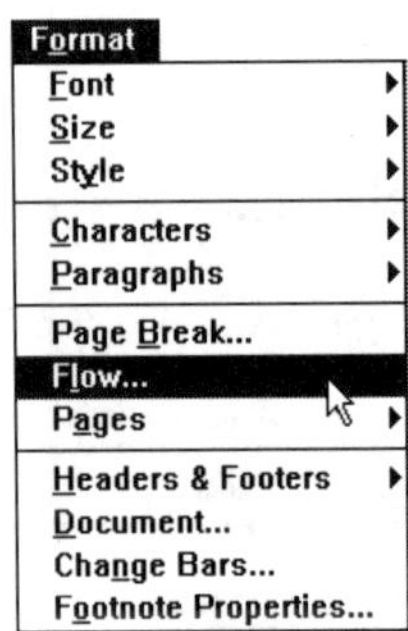

■ Including a PostScript file in your document

■ Encapsulated Postscript graphics files can be imported just as you would import any other graphics file. EPSF files created on the Macintosh will not preview on your screen, but will print correctly.

■ Importing or including PostScript code files requires some special handling.

1. Draw a separate text column where you want the graphic to appear. [**Esc 1** (*one*) **t c**]
2. Do one of the following:
   - Type PostScript code in it.
   - Import a file of raw PostScript code as a text file into it.
   - Cut and paste PostScript code into it.
   - Include the code by reference by typing #include '*filename*' where *filename* is the name of your PostScript file. You must use straight quotes.
3. Ctrl-click on the border of the column to select it.
4. Choose **Format→Flow.** [**Alt o l** (*ell*)]
5. In the Flow Properties dialog box, turn on PostScript Code; turn off Autoconnect.
6. **To edit included code**, you must turn off PostScript code in the Flow Properties box, and then turn it back on again to print.

Turn off Autoconnect. *Turn on PostScript Code.*

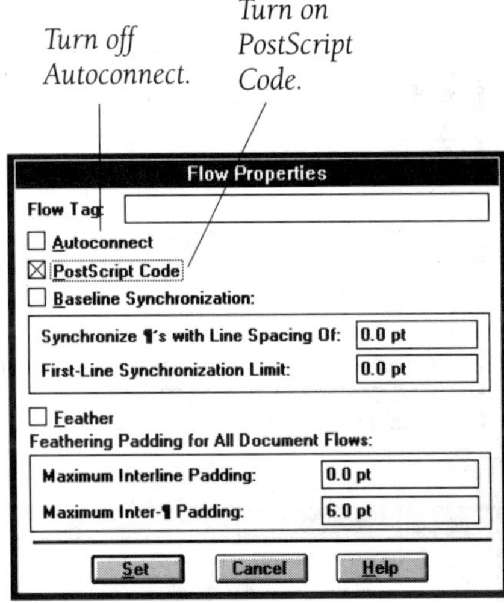

Special effects

In \MAKER4\SAMPLES\PSCRIPT, you will find a file called BIGRGB.PS. It allows you to fill a text column with type, and create a lot of special effects. If you open the file as a text file, you will find detailed instructions at the beginning of the file for using it.

Using the Designer Windows

5

■ What's in this chapter

This chapter is on the mechanics of using the Designer windows, the paragraph and character catalogs, and the Formatting bar.

The Designer windows—Paragraph Designer, Character Designer, and Table Designer—are an important work area in FrameMaker. They are where you create the formats that appear in the paragraph catalog and the character catalog. They are also a unified work area for making on-the-fly changes to selected text. This chapter discusses the Paragraph and Character Designers; the Table Designer is discussed in Chapter 11, Tables.

Every paragraph has a format tag This is a crucial concept in FrameMaker. A "tag" is a name for a set of properties. The properties of a paragraph format are listed in "What you can do with the Paragraph Designer" on page 87. The properties of a character format are listed in "What you can do with the Character Designer" on page 97. The default paragraph tag is Body.

■ Any time you press Enter, you create a new paragraph. The tag of the new paragraph is the same as the previous one unless you have specified a different "Next ¶ Tag" as part of the paragraph format definition. This sounds baffling until you understand it, but it's actually a slick trick. Take a look at "Automatic paragraph formats" on page 96.

What's in the next chapter

This chapter is about the mechanics of using FrameMaker's formatting tools. The next chapter is about typography, formatting, and designing with type.

Look on the Status Line to see the tag of the paragraph containing your insertion point.

Flow: A ¶: Body

The format tag of the current paragraph

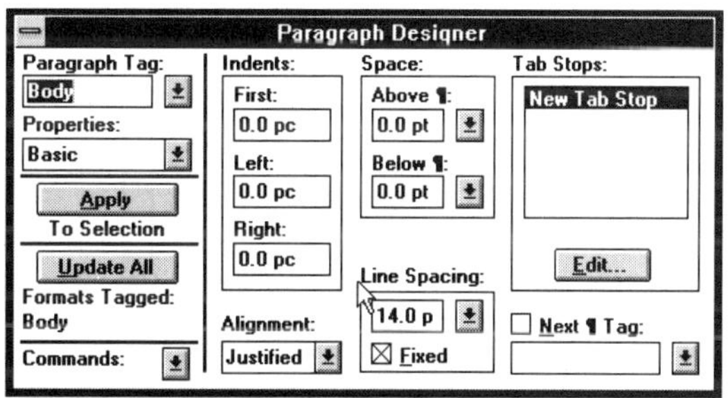

The Paragraph Designer displays the format tag and properties of the paragraph containing the insertion point. This is page 1 of 6 in the Paragraph Designer. They all tell you about your paragraph.

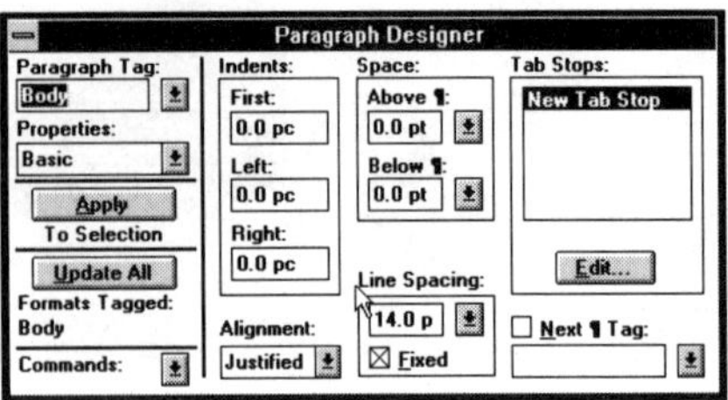

The Paragraph Designer

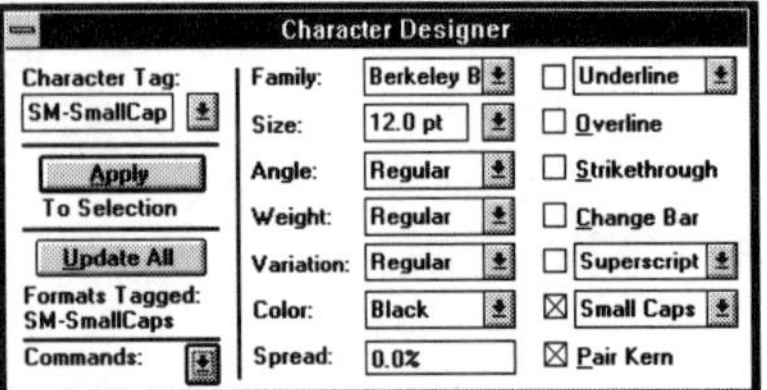

The Character Designer

■ What the Designer windows do for you

The Designer windows are at the very heart of using FrameMaker. You use them to create and modify the paragraph and character formats that make life so easy in FrameMaker, and you also use them to make individual, once-only adjustments to paragraphs and characters.

■ They're a compact work area where you can make many different kinds of changes from within one window. The Paragraph Designer is actually six windows—or "pages"—in one. That's because FrameMaker offers you so many kinds of control over paragraphs.

The paragraph catalog

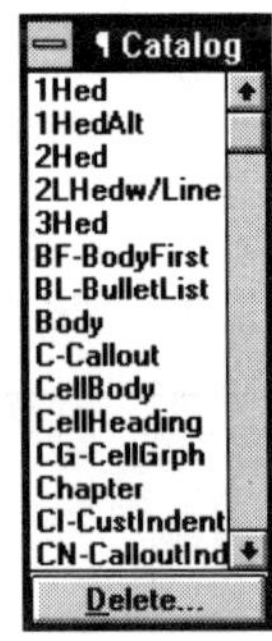

The character catalog

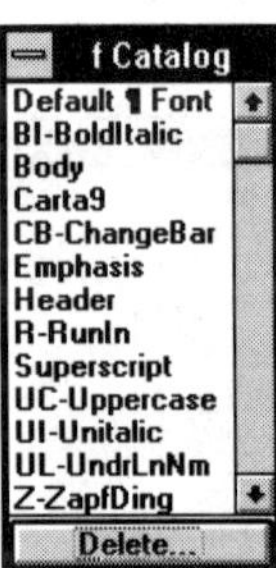

The Formatting bar

■ What formats do for you

Formats allow you to:

Keep your work consistent Paragraph and character formats ensure a consistent look for your design elements both within a document, and from one document to the next. A set of formats can be used in many documents, either by using a template containing the formats, or by importing formats. See "Using an existing document as a template" on page 45, and "Importing formats" on page 107.

Reuse your work Once a format is created, you don't have to do that work again. A single click or keystroke reproduces all that work.

Make changes easily You can make a change once, and then tell FrameMaker to apply that change to all formats having that format tag, or even to those having a different tag. Also, you can use Find/Change to find character and paragraph formats and change them selectively.

■ What you can do with the Paragraph Designer

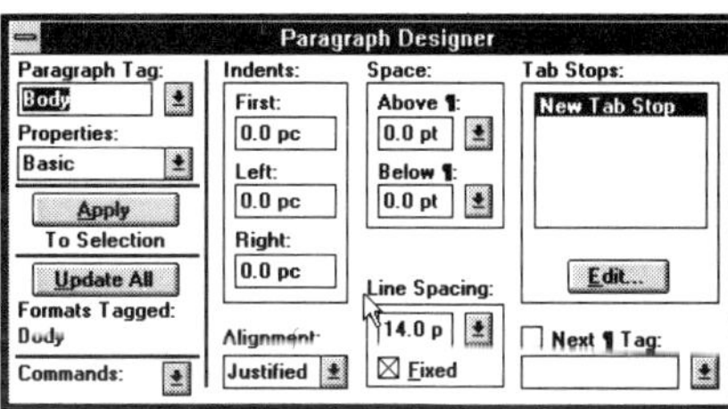

Page One: Basic

Left & right indents
Tab stops
Line spacing
Space above & below
Paragraph alignment
Next paragraph tag

Page Two: Default Font

Font family	Font size	Angle	Weight
Variation	Color	Spread	Underline
Overline	Superscript	Subscript	Change bar
Small caps	Uppercase	Lowercase	Kerning

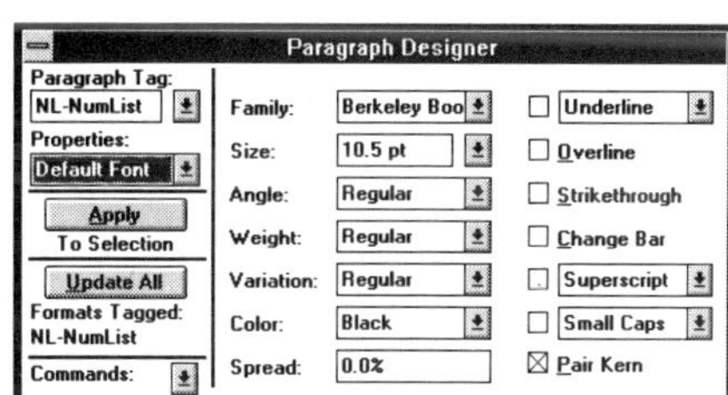

Page Three: Pagination

Keep lines together
Widows/orphans
Run-in heads
Side heads
Start at top of page or column
Start on left or right page

Page Four: Numbering

Automatic bullets
Automatic paragraph numbering

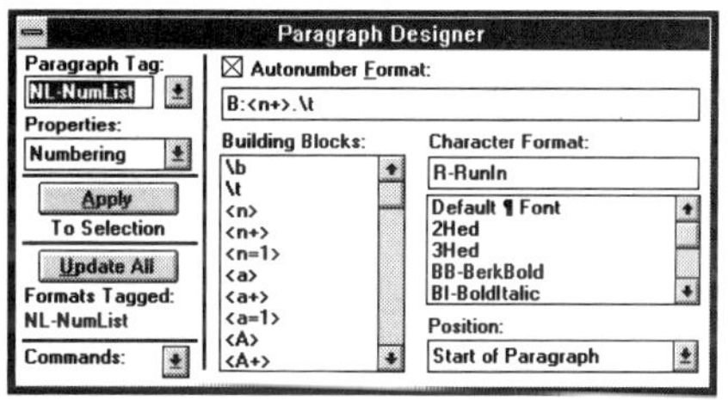

Page Five: Advanced

Hyphenation
Word & letter spacing
Graphics above & below the paragraph

Page Six: Table cells

How paragraphs having this format are positioned when they are in a table cell

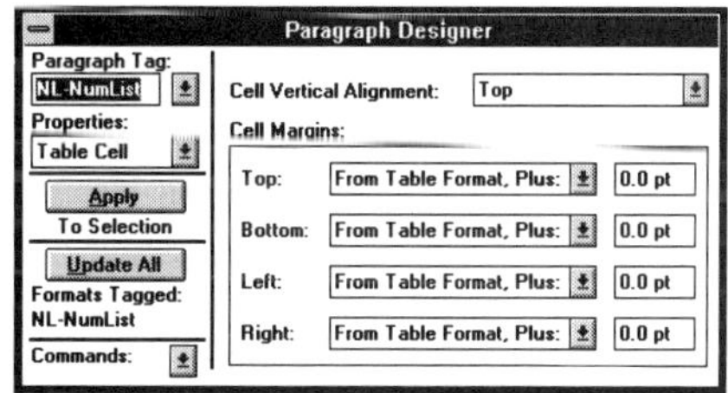

An overview of the Paragraph Designer

What you see here is page one, Basic. There are five more pages. (See "What you can do with the Paragraph Designer" on page 87.)

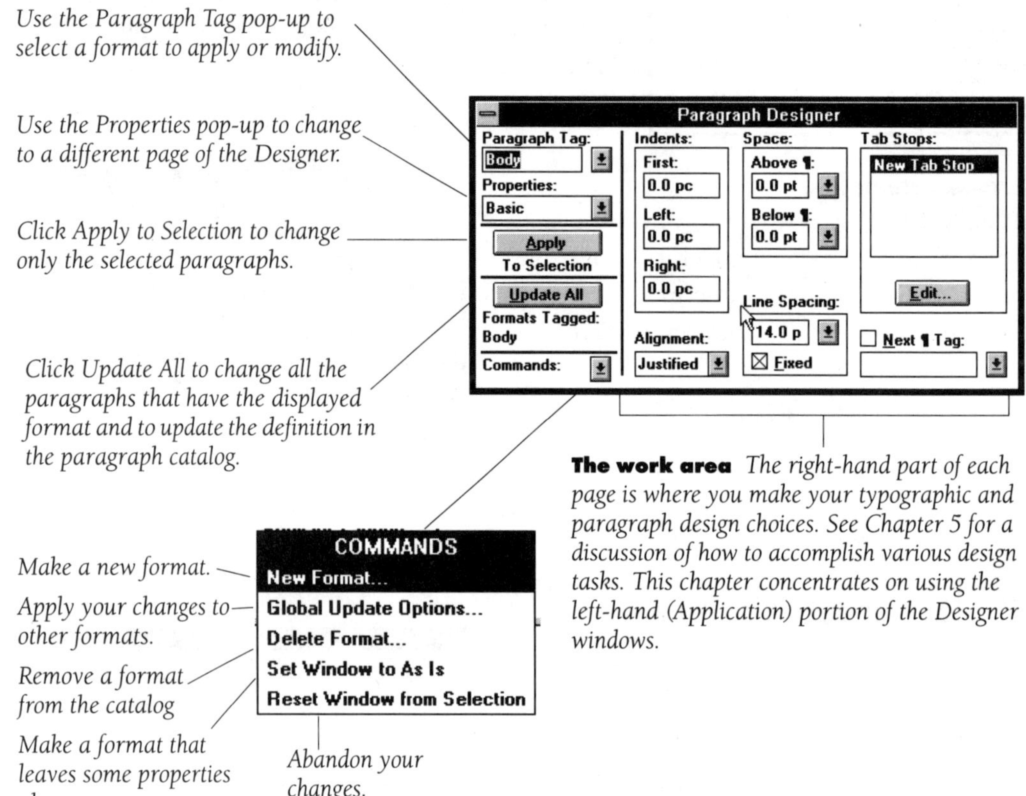

The work area *The right-hand part of each page is where you make your typographic and paragraph design choices. See Chapter 5 for a discussion of how to accomplish various design tasks. This chapter concentrates on using the left-hand (Application) portion of the Designer windows.*

Keeping focused

When you're working with the Designers, you're often going back and forth between the document and the Designer. When you return to the Designer, you must click on it to return the focus to it before you can type in a text box. The top bar is the safest place to click, because you won't select anything by accident.

Return the focus to the document *by clicking in the top bar of the document window if you want to keep text or graphics selected in the document.* [**Shift-F7**]

■ Using the Paragraph Designer

Paragraph formats always apply to whole paragraphs. Use character formats if you want to change only part of a paragraph. Any changes that you make in a Designer can be used

- to format the selected text
- or to create or modify a format definition
- or both.

Here are the basics of using the Paragraph Designer:

1. Display the Paragraph Designer:
   - I use the keyboard shortcut, **Ctrl-m**.
   - **Format→Paragraphs→Designer** displays it, too.
2. Put your insertion point in the paragraph you want to format. This *selects* that paragraph.
3. Click on the Properties pop-up to select the Designer page you want to work in.
4. Make the changes you want in the work area of the Designer.
5. Click Apply to Selection to apply the changes to the selected paragraphs,
   or click Update All to change every occurrence of the format in the file, and to update the catalog definition.
6. If you have changes to make that are on other pages of the Designer, use the Properties pop-up to go to another page, and repeat these steps.
   - If you make changes and then try to move to a new Designer page without applying them, you get the Apply Changes query box. You can apply your changes or abandon them. Don't Apply lets you move to the new page without making any changes. Cancel keeps you on the same page.

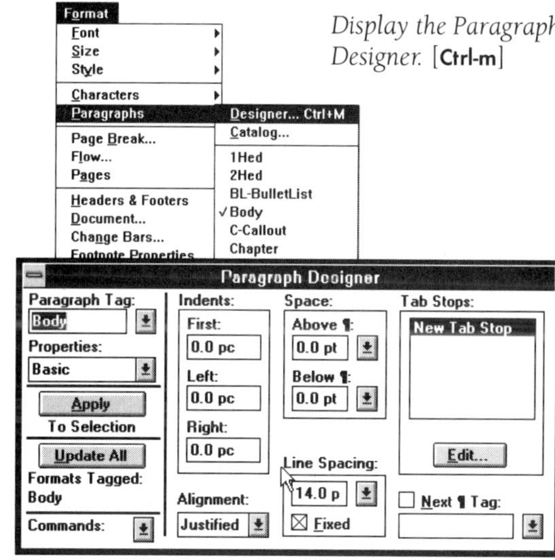

Display the Paragraph Designer. [**Ctrl-m**]

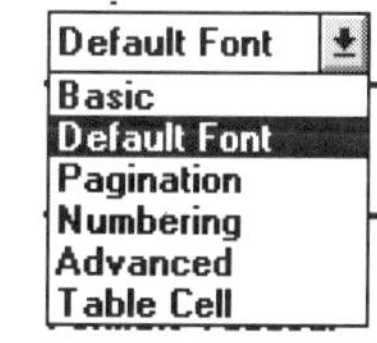

Use the Properties pop-up to move to a different page of the Designer.

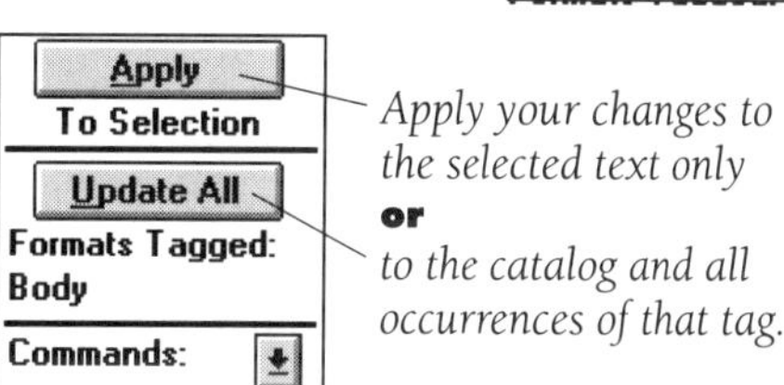

Apply your changes to the selected text only
or
to the catalog and all occurrences of that tag.

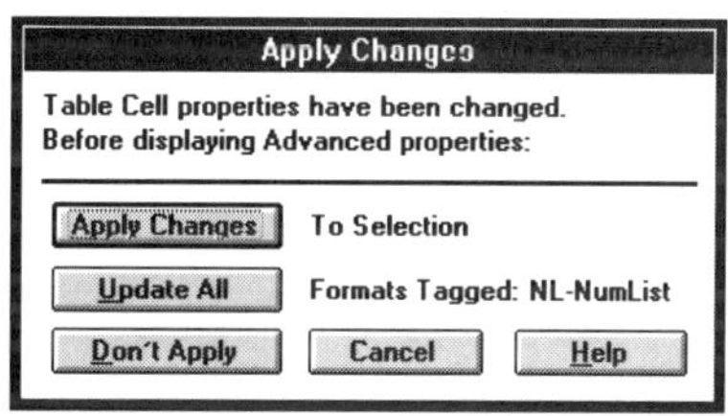

See Chapter 1, page 13, if you're not sure how to use the different kinds of text boxes, pop-ups, buttons, and windows.

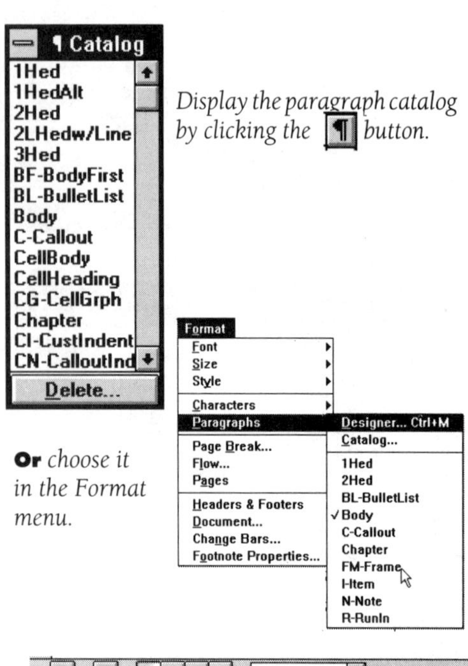

Display the paragraph catalog by clicking the ¶ button.

Or *choose it in the Format menu.*

Or *display it from the Formatting bar.*

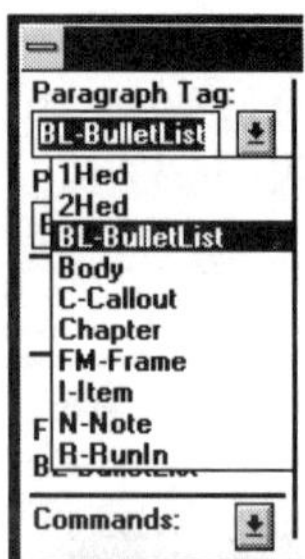

Or *click on the pop-up menu in the the Paragraph Designer. (This shows the left-hand side only.)*

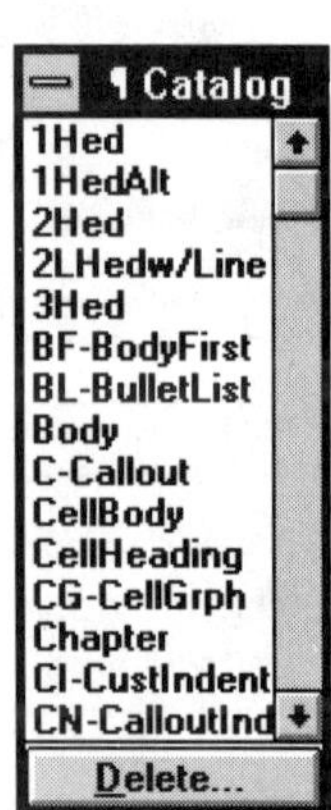

Select your paragraph(s), click on a format. It's that easy.

Displaying the paragraph catalog

FrameMaker stores a list of all available paragraph formats in a selection list called a catalog. Some of these formats come with the template you use to create the document; others you create yourself using the Paragraph Designer or Formatting bar.

Five ways to display a list of paragraph formats

- Click the ¶ button at the right of the document window.
- Click on the Paragraph Tag button in the Paragraph Designer.
- Choose **Format→Paragraphs→Catalog**.
- The same list of formats displays when you just choose **Format→Paragraphs**. The difference is that the catalog can stay up on the screen while you work. The list just stays up long enough for you to pick a format.
- Click on the BL-BulletList button in the Formatting bar.

Applying a paragraph format

1. Place your insertion point in the paragraph you want to change. (You have *selected* the paragraph.) **Or** select several paragraphs.
2. Display the paragraph catalog.
3. Click on the format you want to apply.

▲ If you are working from the Formatting bar, or the Format menu, or the main paragraph catalog (from the ¶ button), that's all you have to do. FrameMaker applies the format to the selected paragraphs as soon as you click.

▲ If you're using the list in the Paragraph Designer, you must click Apply To Selection.

- You can also apply a format using just the keyboard, described on page 91.

Using the keyboard to apply a paragraph format

(My favorite way!)

1. Select the paragraphs to format.
2. Press either **F9** or **Ctrl-9**.
3. Begin typing your format name until the name appears in the Status bar at the bottom of the window.
   Or just type the first letter of the format name repeatedly until the name appears in the Status bar.
4. Press Enter.

It's a lot easier to do than it is to describe.

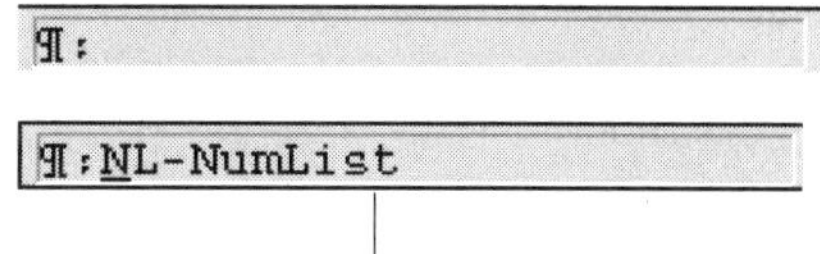

When you first press **F9**, *the Status bar becomes empty. Begin typing the format name you want until it appears in the Status bar; press Enter.*

Modifying a paragraph format definition

1. Display the format you want to change in the Paragraph Designer.
   • To display the catalog definition, choose it from the pop-up Paragraph Tag list, even if the name is already showing.
   • Select a paragraph that has the tag you want to modify. If the paragraph has overrides, they will become part of the modified definition.
2. Make whatever changes you want in the Designer.
3. Click Update All. *This changes the format definition in the catalog, and updates all occurrences of that format in the file.*
   • If FrameMaker detects overrides, you will be asked whether to remove them. See page 92 for a discussion of overrides.
4. Check the other pages of the Paragraph Designer to see if more changes need to be made to the format. Change one Designer page at a time and Update All before going on to the next.

Display the Designer.

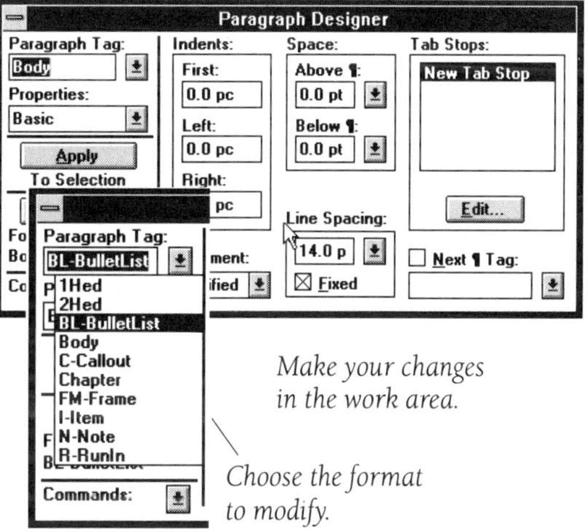

Make your changes in the work area.

Choose the format to modify.

Update All
Formats Tagged: NL-NumList

Click Update All.

See page 92 to read about overrides.

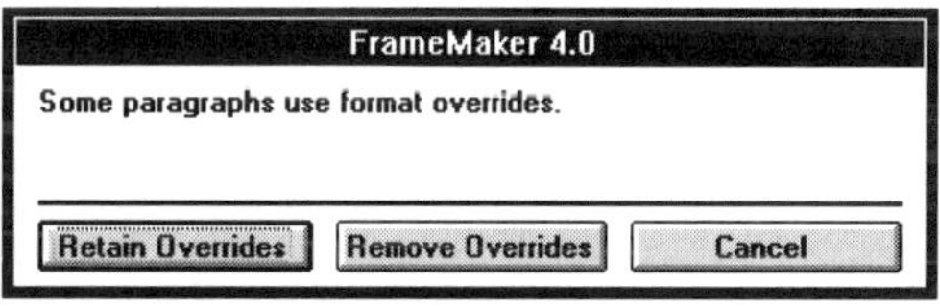

All you ever wanted to know about overrides

When you modify a format definition, FrameMaker looks to see if any occurrences of that format have overrides. If it finds any, it displays a query window, asking you if you want to keep or remove the overrides. What's an override? Read on.

You can—and often do—make format changes and apply them to a paragraph or selected text without changing the definition of the format. These changes are "overrides." Text with overrides has properties that no longer match the catalog definition of that format. When you use the Designers to format text, you create overrides when you use Apply to Selection, rather than Update All.

▪ Choosing to remove overrides guarantees that your work will be consistent. On the other hand, removing overrides may remove features that you need. Base your decision on your knowledge of the project. As always, FrameMaker gives you control.

▪ When your insertion point is in a paragraph that has overrides, the Designer window shows the properties of the selected paragraph or text, not the catalog definition of the format.

▪ When a paragraph has an override, an asterisk appears next to a tag name in the Status bar and the Tag pop-up of the Formatting bar.

▪ When you apply character formats to words within a paragraph, they are not considered overrides to the paragraph format *unless you include the last line ending when you select the text.*

▪ **Page breaks** are a special form of override. You create page breaks by specifying that a certain paragraph, or a paragraph format, should begin at the top of a page. (You can do this in the Pagination page of the Paragraph Designer or by selecting a paragraph and choosing **Format ➔Page Break**.) When you modify a format using Update All in the Formatting bar, you can choose to keep page breaks but not other overrides. When you use the Designer to modify a format, you choose to keep all overrides, or none.

You can't find the right answer until you ask the right question.	You can't find the right answer until you ask the right question.
This is how the paragraph looks with the original format applied.	*I changed the alignment using* **Esc j r**. *Now the paragraph has an* **override**.

Creating a new paragraph format

Type a new format name here.

Choose the Designer page here.

Paragraph Tag: C-Callout
Properties: Basic
Apply To Selection
Update All
Formats Tagged: C-Callout
Commands:

The Paragraph Designer

1. Display the Paragraph Designer. [**Ctrl-m**]
2. Choose a format from the Paragraph Tag pop-up that has some of the characteristics that you want your new format to have. **Or** place your insertion point in a similar paragraph.
   Note If the selected paragraph contains overrides—changes from the catalog definition—those modifications appear in the Designer until you reselect the format name from the Paragraph Tag pop-up. Then the catalog definition appears. You just need to decide which you want to work with: the catalog definition, or the modified one.
3. You can type a new name in the Paragraph Tag text box now, or you can wait and do it in step 6. If you do it now, you will avoid overwriting the old format by accident.
4. Make whatever changes you want to make on the current page of the Designer.
5. Click Commands. Click New Formats.
6. In the New Format dialog box, type the new name if you didn't type it in step 3.
7. Normally, you would turn on both Store in Catalog and Apply to Selection. Choose just Store in Catalog if you don't want to change the paragraph you're using as a starting point.
   ▲ If you only want to apply it to the selection, and not to the catalog, you may not need to create a new format. You can just Apply to Selection. (There *are* cases where you want to create a new name for a change and not apply it to the catalog, but they're not common.)
8. Click Create.
9. Use the Properties pop-up to go through the pages of the Designer, and make any other changes that you want. Be sure you have selected a paragraph with the new format, so that the name remains displayed.

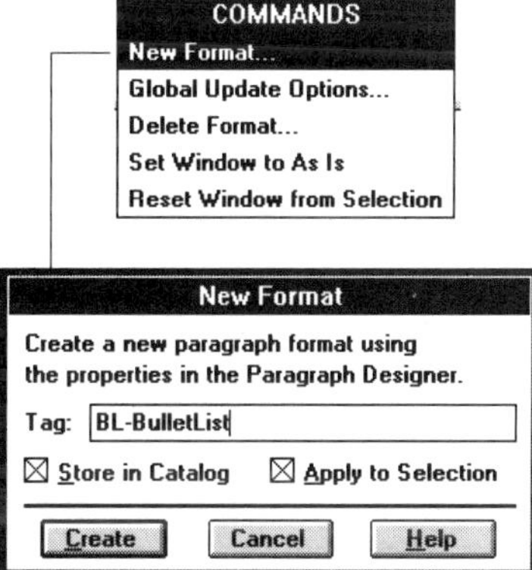

Normally, you store your new format in the catalog as well as applying it. As always, Frame-Maker gives you your choice.

Using the Paragraph Designer

▲ You must apply the changes on each page of the Designer before moving to the next page. Otherwise you get a warning.

▲ Choose Don't Apply to go to the next page of the Designer without applying any changes. Choose Cancel to stay on the same page and continue working.

A shortcut Instead of step 5, type the new name in the Tag text box and click on Apply to Selection. You get the New Format dialog box.

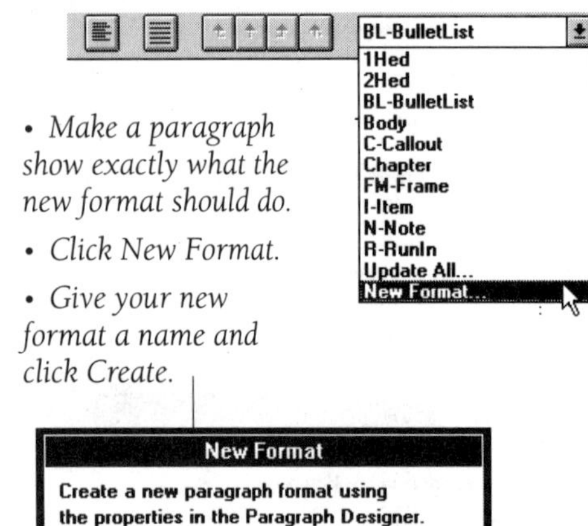

• *Make a paragraph show exactly what the new format should do.*

• *Click New Format.*

• *Give your new format a name and click Create.*

Creating a new paragraph format from your text

1. Format a paragraph so that it has exactly the properties you want the new format to have. Use any techniques you want—Paragraph Designer, Formatting bar, Format menu, QuickAccess bar.

   Hint When you apply font properties, such as family, size, and style, be sure you select the *whole* paragraph. Otherwise FrameMaker considers them character properties rather than paragraph properties. (See "Selecting line endings" on page 67.) Better still, apply font properties using the Default Font page of the Paragraph Designer.
2. Select the paragraph.
3. Display the Formatting bar. [**Alt v f**]
4. Choose New Format from the Paragraph Formats pop-up menu.
5. In the New Format dialog box, type in a name and turn on Store in Catalog and Apply to Selection.
6. Click Create.

Modifying a format to match your text

Use the Formatting bar This only works for paragraph formats.

1. Select a paragraph and format it so that looks exactly the way you want that format to be throughout the file. Change as many things as you want, using any of the techniques available. Apply each change to only that paragraph.
   Hint When you apply font characteristics, such as family, size, and style, be sure you select the whole paragraph, *including the last line ending*. Otherwise FrameMaker considers them character properties rather than paragraph properties. (See "Selecting line endings" on page 67.) Font changes that you make using the Default Font page of the Paragraph Designer are always part of the paragraph definition.
2. Display the Formatting bar. [**Alt v f**]
3. Click on the Paragraph Format pop-up menu in the Formatting bar.
4. Scroll down to Update All, and click on it. The Update Paragraph Format dialog box appears.
5. Now decide whether you want to preserve or remove overrides. (See "All you ever wanted to know about overrides" on page 92.) Removing overrides creates greater consistency, but may remove formatting that you want to keep. Character formats do not count as overrides to paragraphs.
6. Click Update.

▲ This applies *all* of your changes to the catalog definition and to every occurrence of the format in the file. This is how you can make changes that are on several different pages of the Paragraph Designer and then update everything all at once.

Modify formats *This is one way to modify a paragraph format. See "Modifying a paragraph format definition" on page 91 for using the Designer to modify a format.*

First, make your changes in a paragraph.

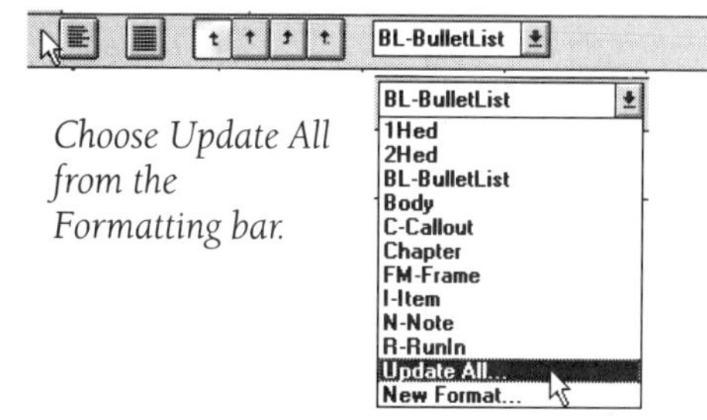

Choose Update All from the Formatting bar.

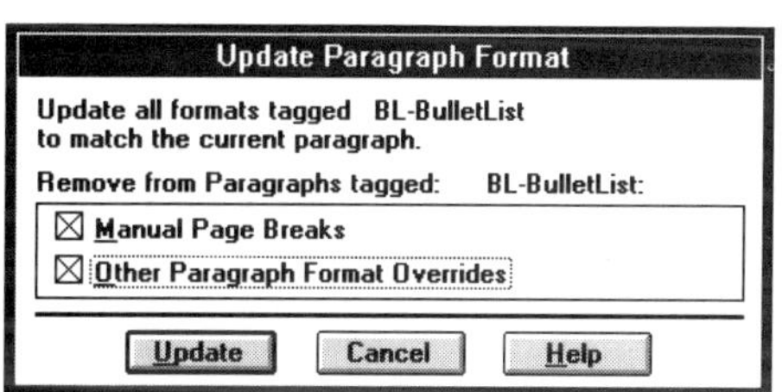

Click Update.

Removing overrides creates consistency.

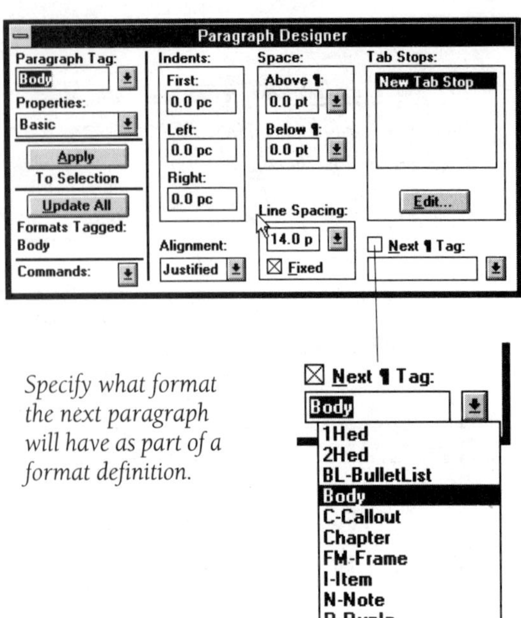

Specify what format the next paragraph will have as part of a format definition.

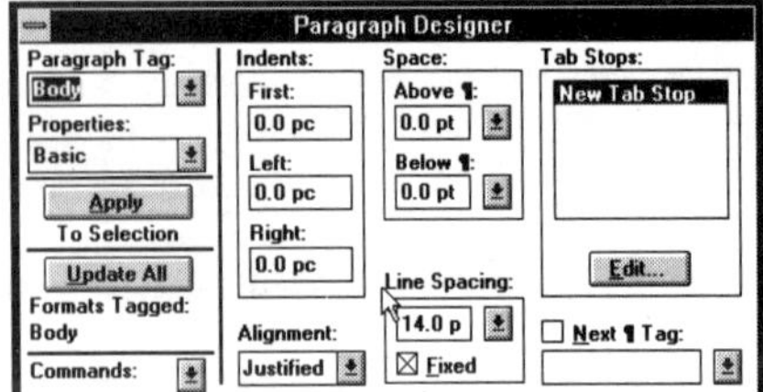

Automatic paragraph formats

There's one item over in the work area of the Paragraph Designer that's appropriate to discuss in this chapter: the Next ¶ Tag item. It's a slick trick for situations where one format is always followed by the same next format (a head followed by Body, for instance).

1. In the Basic page of the Paragraph Designer, choose the format of the first paragraph (Head, for example) from the Paragraph Tag list; **or** select a paragraph with that tag.
2. Turn on Next ¶ Tag.
3. Click on the Next ¶ Tag pop-up menu button to display the list of available paragraph formats.
4. Click on the name of the format that should follow (Body, for example).
5. Click Update All.

▲ Now, when you press Enter at the end of a paragraph with the first format, the new paragraph will automatically have the Next ¶ Tag format.

Finding out about a paragraph

A paragraph may have different properties than the basic format definition. To see the properties of a paragraph, select it by placing the insertion point in it, and then display the Paragraph Designer. Use PgUp and PgDn or the Properties pop-up to move through the different pages of the definition.

If you select more than one paragraph, the Designer will show you properties that are the same in all the paragraphs, and will display As Is or blank for properties that differ.

■ What you can do with the Character Designer

The Character Designer looks almost exactly like the Default Font page of the Paragraph Designer, but there's a big difference in how it works: things that you do in the Character Designer apply only to characters that are selected (highlighted). If you make the same choices in the Paragraph Designer they affect the entire paragraph.

Font family
Size
Angle
Weight
Variation
Color
Spread

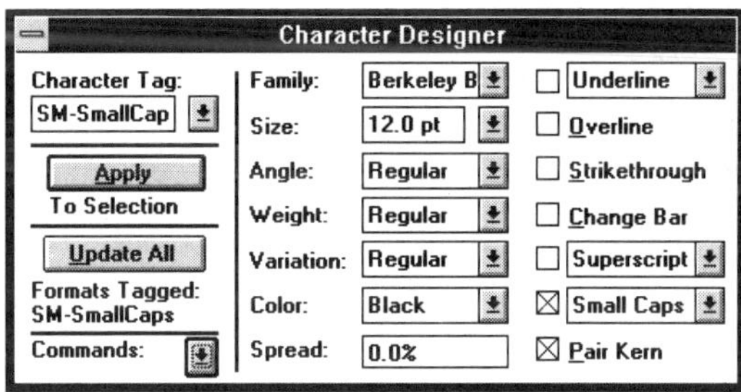

Underline
Overline
Strikethrough
Change bar
Superscript/Subscript
Small Caps, Upper & Lowercase
Kerning

An overview of the Character Designer

Use the Character Tag pop-up to select a format to apply or modify.

Click Apply to Selection to change only the selected characters.

Click Update All to change all the characters that have the displayed format and to update the definition in the character catalog.

Create a new format, apply changes to different formats, delete formats, reset Window.

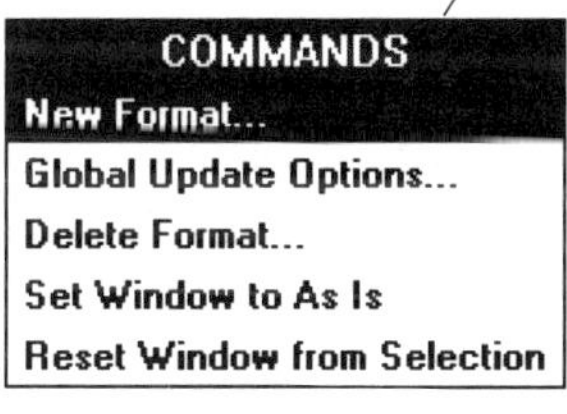

The work area *The right-hand part is where you make your typographic design choices. See Chapter 6 for a discussion of how to accomplish various design tasks. This chapter concentrates on using the left-hand portion of the Designer windows.*

■ Using the Character Designer

Display the Character Designer. [**Ctrl-d**]

Make your changes in the work area.

Apply to Selection *Apply your changes to the selected text only.*

Update All *Apply your changes to the catalog and all occurrences of that tag.*

Character formats apply only to highlighted (selected) text. Here is the overview on using the Character Designer:

1. Display the Character Designer:
   - I like the keyboard shortcut, **Ctrl-d**.
   - **Format→Characters→Designer** displays it, too.
2. Select the characters you want to format (see "Selecting" on page 66), or display the format you want to modify from the Character Tag pop-up.
3. Make the changes you want in the work area.
4. Click on Apply to Selection to apply the changes to the selected text, **or** on Update All to update the format definition and change every occurrence of this format in the file.

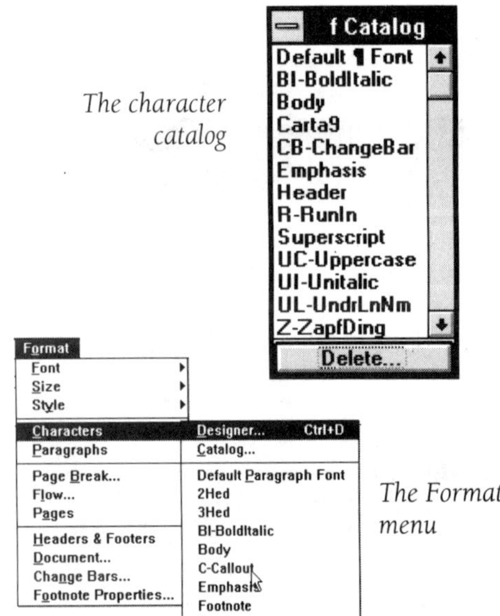

The character catalog

The Format menu

Displaying the character catalog

FrameMaker stores a list of all available character formats in the character catalog. Some of these come with the template you use to create the document; others you create using the Character Designer. Here are all the different ways to see a list of available character formats.

■ Click the *f* button at the right of the document window.

■ Click on the Character Tag pop-up in the Character Designer.

■ Choose **Format→Characters→Catalog**.

■ The same list of formats displays when you just choose **Format→Characters**. The difference is that the catalog can stay up on the screen while you work. The list just stays up long enough for you to pick a format.

Applying a character format

Formats in the character catalog apply only to characters that are highlighted (selected).

1. Select the characters you want to format.
2. Display the character catalog in any of the ways described on page 87.
3. Click on the format tag.

▪ *You can also apply a format using just the keyboard, described next.*

Here is **highlighted (selected)** text.

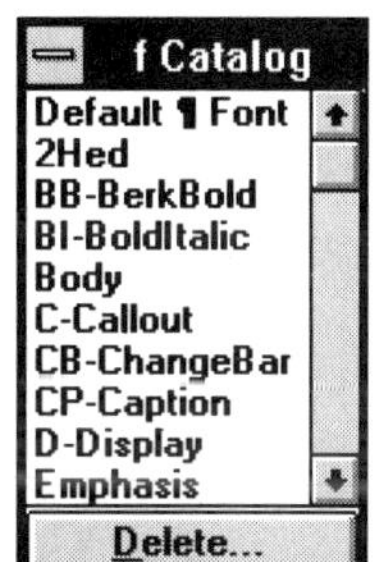

Select your text. Click on a format. It's done: you've applied the format to the text.

Using the keyboard to apply a character format

(My favorite way!)

1. Select the characters to format.
2. Press **F8** or **Ctrl-8** and begin typing your format name slowly until the name appears in the Status bar at the bottom of the window. (Or just type the first letter repeatedly until the name appears.)
3. Press Enter.

Note The character format name appears *after* the paragraph format name in the Status bar. If the paragraph tag name is long, you can't see the character tag name at first. After you press **F8** and a letter, you can see it all.

When you first press **F8**, *the status bar becomes empty. Begin typing the format name you want until it appears in the status bar; then press Enter.*

Removing a character format

1. Select the text from which you wish to remove a character format. The format doesn't have to have a tag—it can be something you applied from the Format menu, for example.
2. Apply Default ¶ Format from the character catalog, or press **F8 d Enter**.

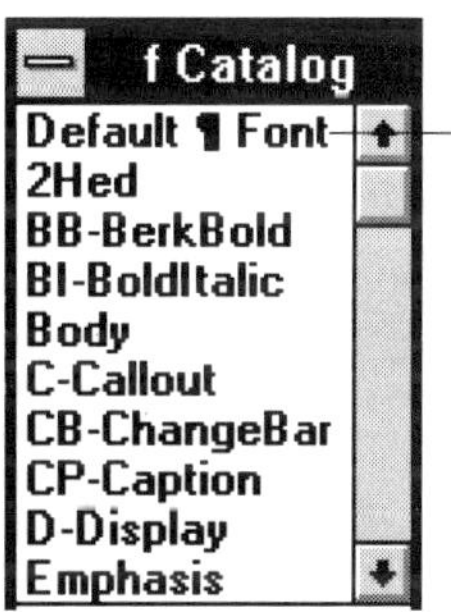

Click on Default ¶ Font to remove all character formatting from selected text.

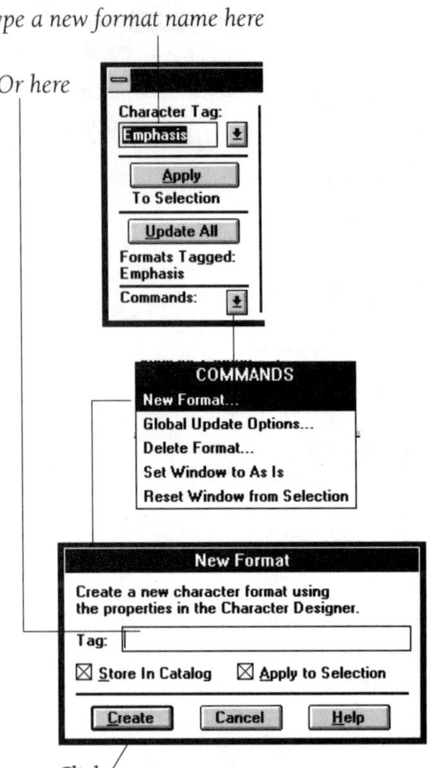

Creating a new character format

1. Display the Character Designer.
2. Choose a format from the Character Tag pop-up that is a good starting point for your new format. **Or** highlight the characters to be formatted.

   Note If the selected characters contain overrides—changes from the catalog definition—those modifications appear in the Designer. Reselect the format from the Character Tag pop-up if you want to display the catalog properties.
3. You can type a new name in the Character Tag text box now, or you can wait and do it in step 6. If you do it now, you will avoid overwriting the old format by accident.
4. Make whatever changes you want to make in the current page of the Designer.
5. Click Commands. Click New Format.
6. Type the new name in the Tag box if it's not already present from step 3.
7. To create a new format, turn on Store in Catalog. Turn on Apply to Selection if you want to apply the new format to selected text.
8. Click Create. Voilà.

A quicker way to make a new format

The steps above are the "official" way to create a new format. Here's a shortcut.

1. Select some text, and make your changes in the Designer, as in steps 1 and 2, above.
2. Type a new name in the Character Tag box.
3. Click Apply to Selection. The very same New Format dialog box appears that you get when you go the **Commands→New Format** route.
4. Choose Store in Catalog and/or Apply to Selection, and click Create.

Modifying a character format definition

Display the format to modify. *Make changes.*

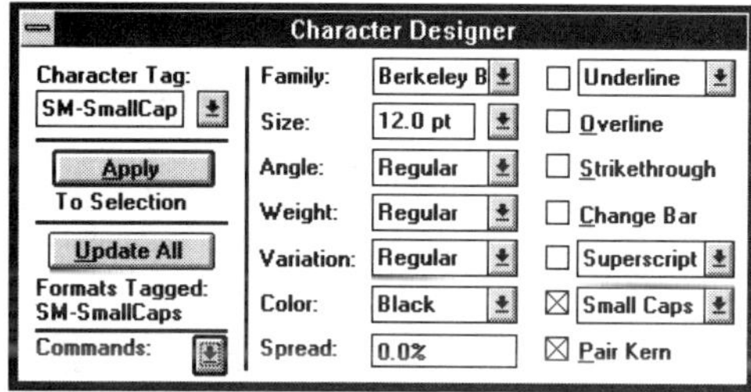

Click Update All.

1. Display the format you want to change in the Character Designer.
   • To display the catalog definition, choose it from the pop-up Character Tag list, even if the name is already showing,
   or select text that has the format you want to modify. Any overrides will be displayed in the Designer.
2. Make whatever changes you want in the Designer.
3. Click Update All. *This changes the format definition in the catalog, and updates all occurrences of that format in the file.*

▼

Overrides

When you click Update All, FrameMaker looks to see if there are any occurrences of that format that have overrides. If it finds any, it displays a query box so you can decide whether to keep or remove the overrides. See page for a description and discussion of overrides.

FrameMaker 4.0
Some paragraphs use format overrides.
Retain Overrides | Remove Overrides | Cancel

▲

Finding out about characters

If you have applied formatting to some characters in a paragraph, you cannot find out about that formatting by looking at the Default Font page of the Paragraph Designer. That shows you only paragraph properties. Instead, after you select the characters you want to know about, look in the Character Designer to find out the properties of those characters.

▪ If you select characters that are different for a property (some are bold and some are not, for example), FrameMaker displays As Is for that property.

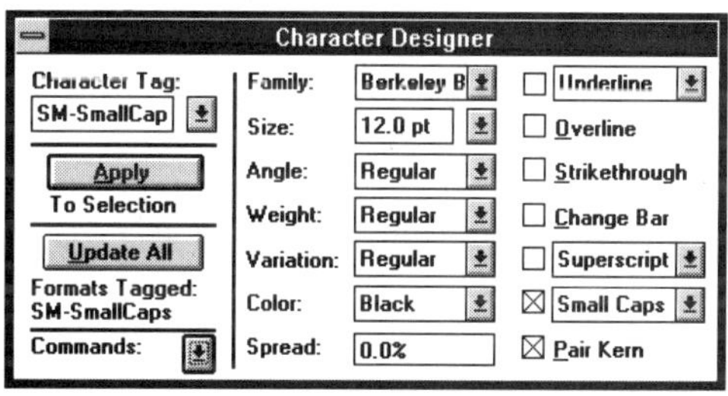

The Character Designer displays the properties of selected text, or of the insertion point.

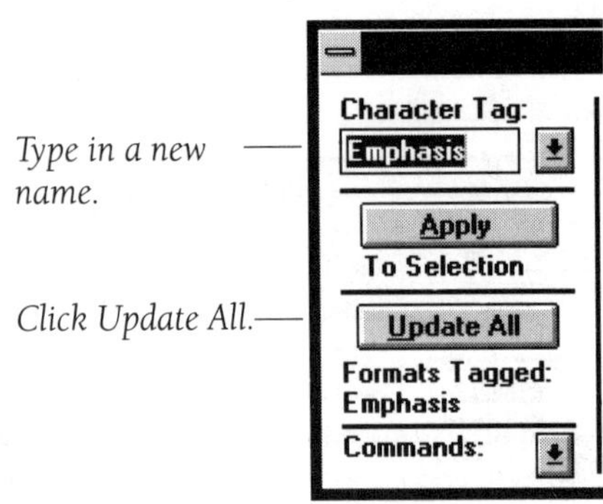

■ Managing formats

Renaming a format

1. Display the format in the Designer, either by choosing it from the Tag pop-up menu, or by selecting text that has that format.
2. Highlight the old tag name, and type in a new one.
3. Click Update All. The name is updated in the catalog and in all occurrences of the name in the file.

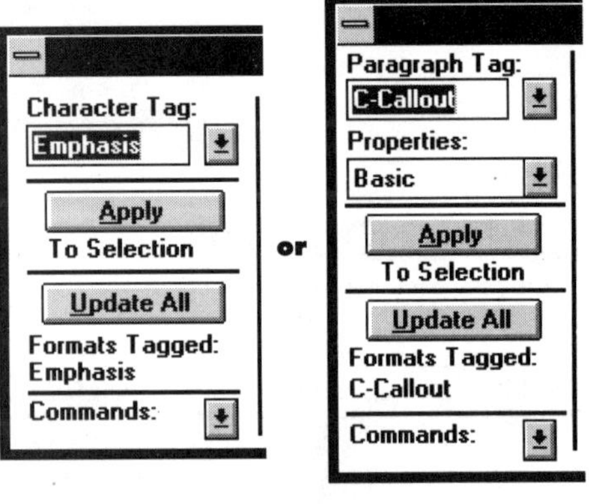

COMMANDS
New Format...
Global Update Options...
Delete Format...
Set Window to As Is
Reset Window from Selection

Click here to redisplay the properties of the selected paragraph or text item without making any changes.

Abandoning changes to a format

In either the Paragraph or the Character Designer, you can abandon changes to the format and redisplay the original properties.

Redisplaying the properties of the selected text Click on Commands. Click on Reset Window from Selection. The properties of the selected paragraph or text are displayed in the Designer.

Redisplaying the format definition properties Click on the Tag pop-up menu, and reselect the format name. The properties of the catalog definition are displayed in the Designer.

If the selected text has no format overrides, these two choices are the same.

Copying and pasting a format

This is one of my favorite slick tricks, and you can use it for either paragraph or character formats. When you're going to use a format several times, try this: first format a text item or a paragraph. Then *copy the format*. Now you can apply that format to as many other items as you want simply by pasting. It's even faster than applying a format with the keyboard. Here's how:

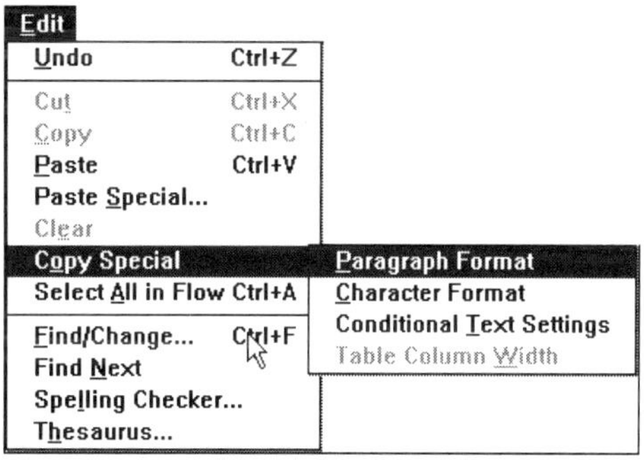

1. Select a paragraph or some characters. (Remember—the paragraph containing your insertion point is selected.)
2. Copy the format.
   - **Edit→Copy Special→Paragraph Format** if a paragraph is selected. [**Alt e o p**]
   - **Edit→Copy Special→Character Format** if characters are selected. [**Alt e o c**]

   ▲ The clipboard now contains the format—not the text—that you just copied. Until you put something else on the clipboard, you can apply that format to selected text just by pasting. [**Ctrl-v**] (But as always, paragraph formats apply only to paragraphs, and character formats only to selected characters.)
3. Select the paragraph or text that you want to apply the same format to.
4. Paste. [**Ctrl-v**]

Copy a format only and then apply it by pasting.

Edit
Undo Ctrl+Z
Cut Ctrl+X
Copy Ctrl+C
Paste Ctrl+V
Paste Special...
Clear
Copy Special
Select All in Flow Ctrl+A
Find/Change... Ctrl+F
Find Next
Spelling Checker...
Thesaurus...
Paragraph Format
Character Format
Conditional Text Settings
Table Column Width

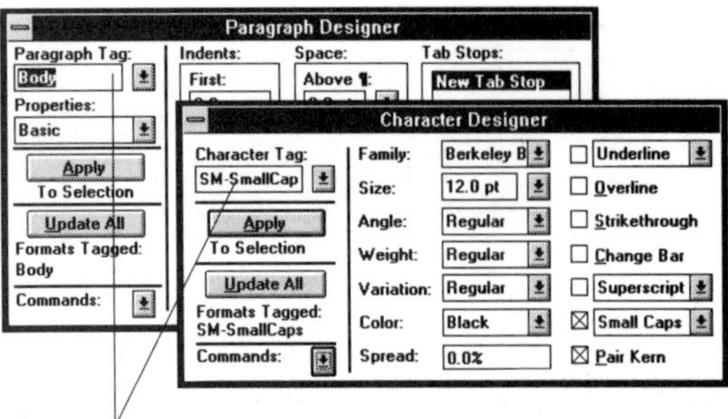

Select the format from the Tag pop-up, ***even if it's already displayed****, to be sure you're seeing the definition without overrides.*

Finding out about a format definition

Are you wondering just what's in a particular format definition?

1. Display the Paragraph or Character Designer, depending on which kind of format you're wondering about.
2. Choose the format you're interested in from the Character Tag pop-up list. Do this even if its name is already displayed, to be sure that you're seeing the definition without overrides.
3. You are now looking at the format definition. For a paragraph format, use PgUp and PgDn or the Properties pop-up to move through the different pages of the definition.

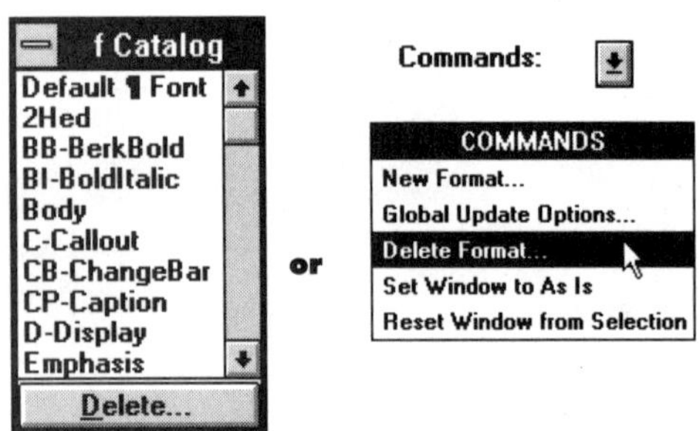

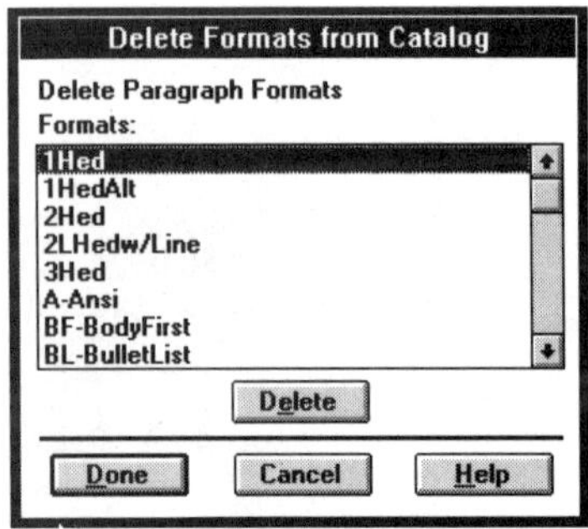

Deleting a format from the catalog

1. Display the character or paragraph catalog and click on Delete at the bottom.
   Or display the Character or Paragraph Designer and click on Commands. Then click on Delete Formats.
2. In the Delete Formats from Catalog dialog box, highlight the format to delete. (Type the first letter of the name, or use the scroll bar or the arrow keys, and click on it.)
3. Click on Delete. Repeat until you have deleted as many formats as you want to.
4. Click on Done.

Removing the format from the catalog does not affect any occurrences of it in the file.

Applying the properties of one format to another format

1. In either the Paragraph Designer or the Character Designer, click on the pop-up Tag list to display the list of formats.
2. Click on the format you want to apply (the source format). Its properties appear in the Designer page
3. Make whatever changes you want. If there are properties that you don't want to apply to the other format, change them to As Is, or delete them.
4. Delete the format name in the Tag box. If you don't do this, you will change the name of the target format, not just the properties.
5. Click Commands. Click Global Update Options.
6. If you're applying a paragraph format, choose All Properties or [Current] Properties Only, to determine whether you apply only the properties of the current page of the Designer, or the properties from all the pages.
7. Choose what to update:

   All Matching Tags in Selection Update the catalog and all paragraphs with the same tag. This is like Update All, except that in this dialog box you have the opportunity to specify that All Properties (from all pages of the Designer) will be applied. Normally Update All applies just the current page.

   All Tagged Apply the properties of the current format to the format you select from this pop-up list (the target format).

   All Paragraph and Catalog Entries Be careful! This makes *everything* have the properties of the current tag. You would typically use it only with most of the properties in the Designer set to As Is. You could use it to turn off hyphenation in a whole file, for example. (See next page.)
8. Click Update.

Display the Designer.

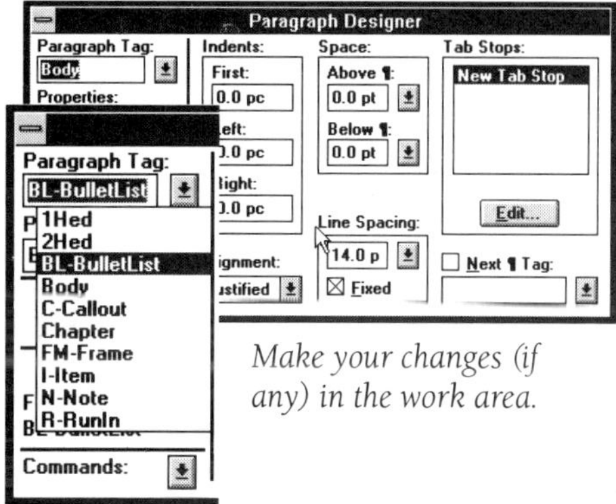

Make your changes (if any) in the work area.

Choose the format to apply (the source).

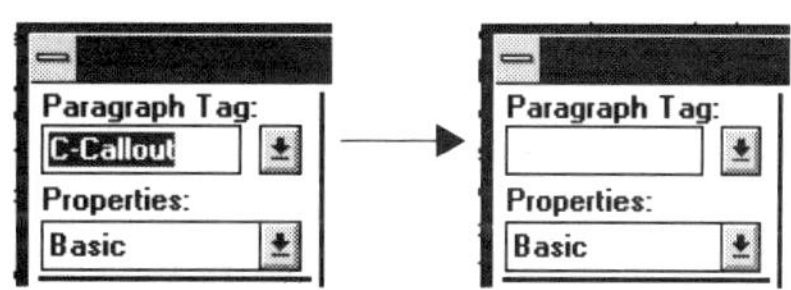

Delete the format name.

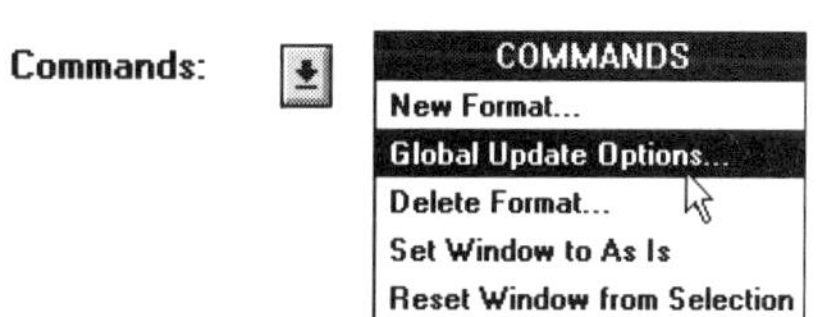

For paragraph formats only: choose to apply just the current page's properties, or all properties.

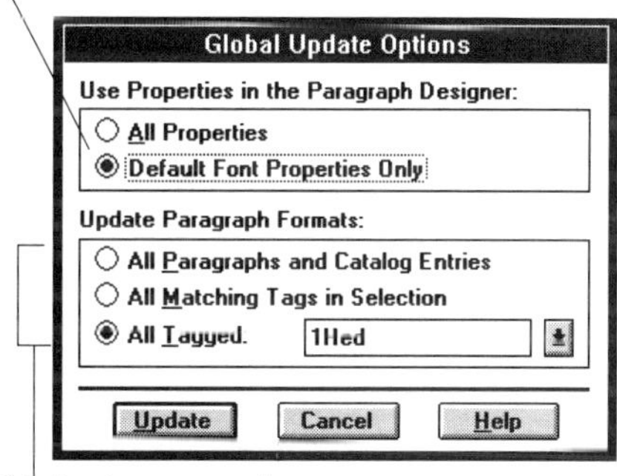

This is where you select what to apply the current properties to

Here Is highlighted (selected) text.

Some selected text.

Press **Ctrl-d** *to display the Character Designer.*

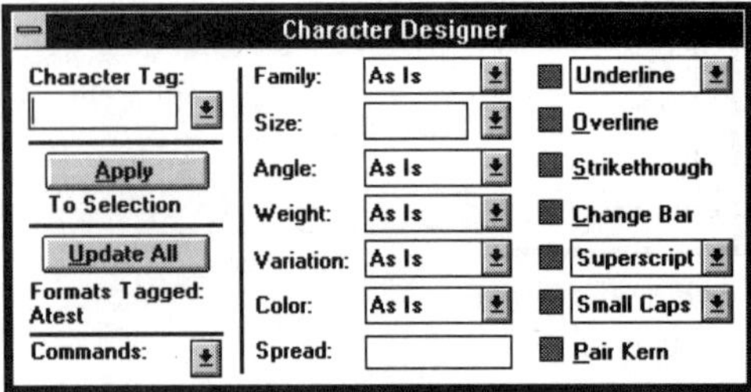

Press **F8** *to set the Designer to As Is.*

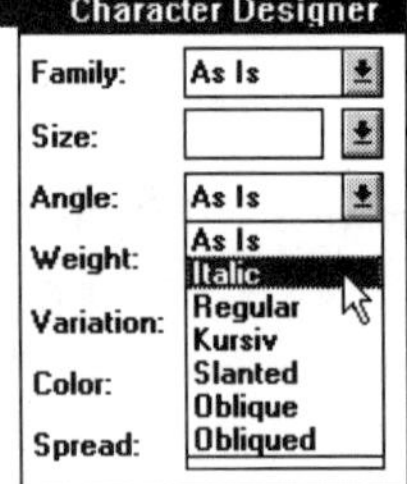

Click on Angle.
Click on Italic.

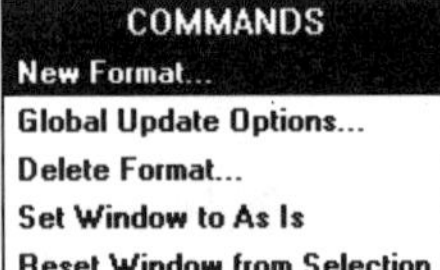

Click Commands.
Click New Format.

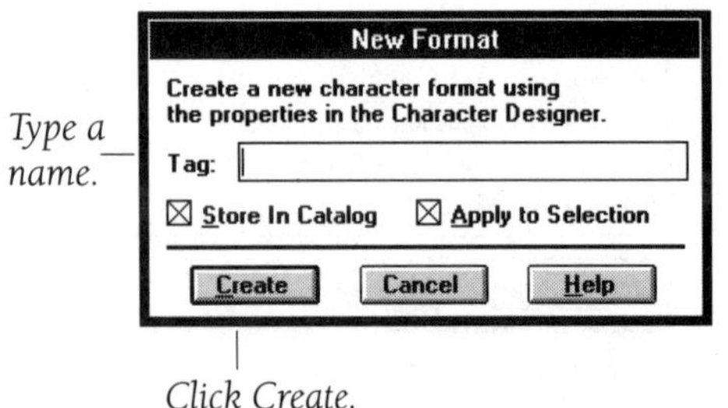

Type a name.

Click Create.

■ Using As Is

You can set all the properties of the Character Designer to As Is, and then create a format that applies only one or a few properties. When you set a property to As Is, the message to FrameMaker is "Leave this property alone when you apply the format."

1. Set the Character Designer to As Is by clicking on the Commands button, and then on Set Window to As Is. **Or** make sure the focus is on the Designer, and press **Shift-F8**.
2. Change just the properties you want to affect.
3. Click Command; click New Format. Type a name for your new format in the Tag text box.
4. Click Create.

■ The best way to explain this is by example. Here's how to create a format to italicize text while leaving all other properties alone.

A character format to italicize text

Here's how to create a character format that will italicize text without affecting anything else. It's exactly the same as applying Italic from the **Format→Style** menu, or from the QuickAccess bar, with one big difference: the text now has a format tag applied to it. Tagged characters are easy to find and change, and easy to keep consistent. You can change all occurrences of a tag by modifying the tag definition. (See "Modifying a character format definition" on page 101.)

1. Select the characters you want to italicize.
2. Display the Character Designer. [**Ctrl-d**]
3. Press **F8** to make all settings As Is.
4. Click on the Angle pop-up. Click on Italic.
5. Click on Commands. Click on New Format.
6. Type a name in the Tag text box, such as I-Italic.
7. Click Create.

■ Importing formats

In Chapter 3 we talked about using an existing document as a template for a new document (page 42). That's one way to use formats from an existing document.

You can also import the formats from another document into your current document by following these steps:

1. Open both documents: the source (the one with the formats you want to import) and the target (the one that needs the formats).
2. Place your insertion point in the target document.
3. Choose **File→Import→Formats** to display the Import Formats dialog box. [**Alt f i o**]
4. Choose the source file name from the Import from Document pop-up.
5. From the Import and Update list, choose which elements of the source file you want to import into the target file.
6. **Page breaks and overrides:** When a format has the same name in the target and source documents, you can choose to remove all overrides, or all except page breaks. This makes all occurrences of the format consistent. Or you can leave overrides, to preserve special formatting.
7. *Optional*. When a format tag exists in the target document, but not in the source, FrameMaker does not delete it from the catalog. This means you may have "leftover" formats after you Import. To avoid this, delete all formats from the Paragraph, Character, and Table format catalogs before you Import. When a format name is the same in both files, FrameMaker replaces the old definition in the target file with the new definition.
8. Click Import. FrameMaker adds the chosen formats from the source file to the target file.

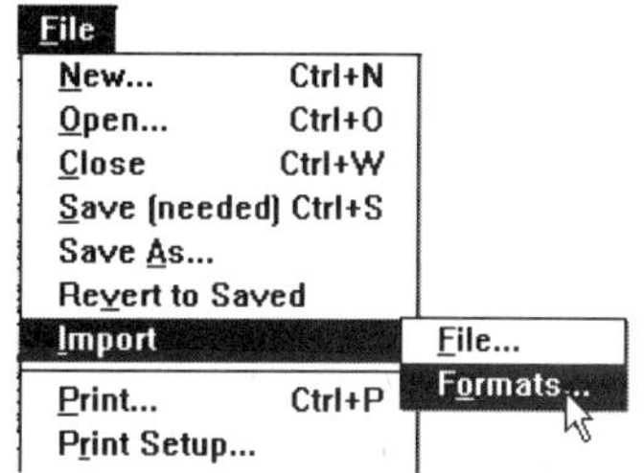

Choose your source file from this pop-up menu. The file must be open to appear in this list.

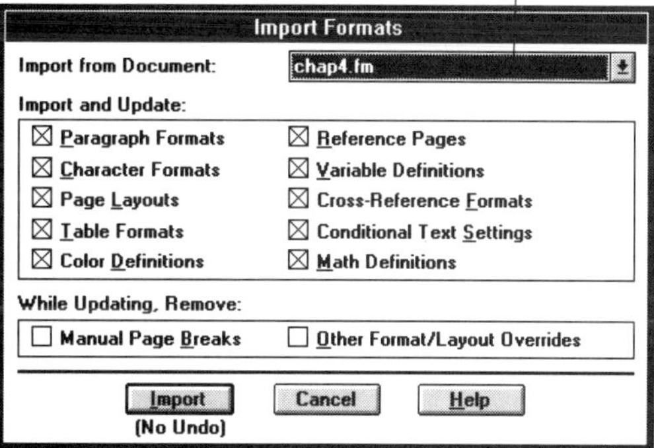

Choose which elements to import from the list. Choose whether Page Breaks and overrides will be removed in the target document when a format has the same name in both the source and target file.

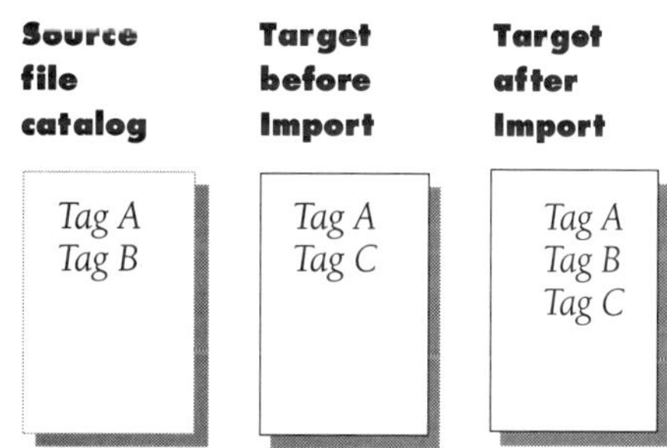

The catalogs: *After Import, Tag A in the target file has the definition from the source file.*

Design and Typography

■ What's in this chapter

This chapter is about *appearances*—how things look. Specifically, it's about making your paragraphs, and the individual characters in them, look the way you want them to. Page layout gets discussed in Chapter 10, and Chapter 12 talks about creating and importing graphics.

A note on formatting text

In FrameMaker, the easiest way to format text is to apply a format from the character or paragraph catalog. That process is described in Chapter 5. This chapter describes how to change format properties on a case-by-case basis, and how to put them into formats.

Formatting resources

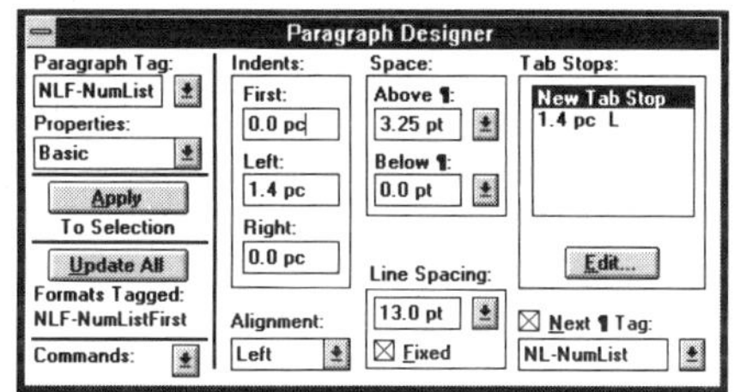

The Paragraph Designer

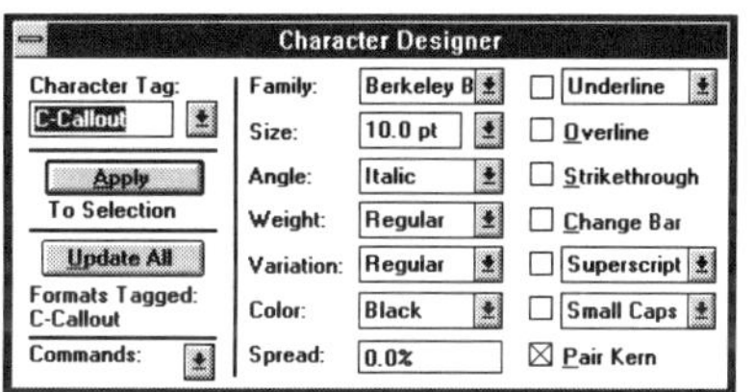

The Character Designer

The Formatting bar

The QuickAccess bar has some formatting functions, too, on page one.

■ Units of measurement

Throughout this chapter you will see instructions to type a measurement into text boxes.

- When you replace the original number, you don't need to type a unit if you want to use the displayed default unit.
- To use a different unit for one occurrence only, use the abbreviations in the table on page 26.
- Change the default unit for the whole document in the View Options dialog box (page 26).

The "properties" of a format are everything you see in this right-hand work area of the Designer.

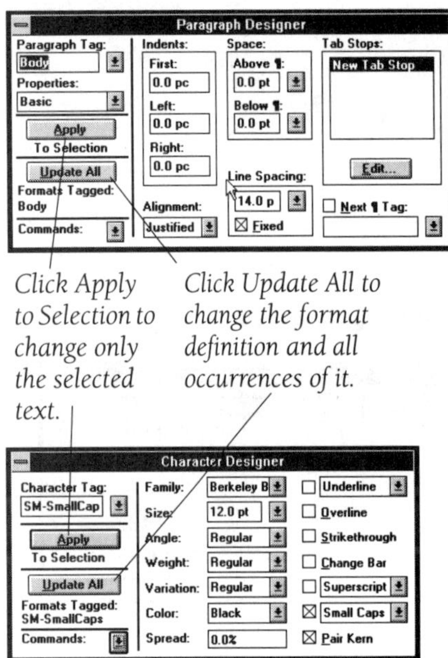

Click Apply to Selection to change only the selected text.

Click Update All to change the format definition and all occurrences of it.

This side of the Character Designer shows the properties of selected characters.

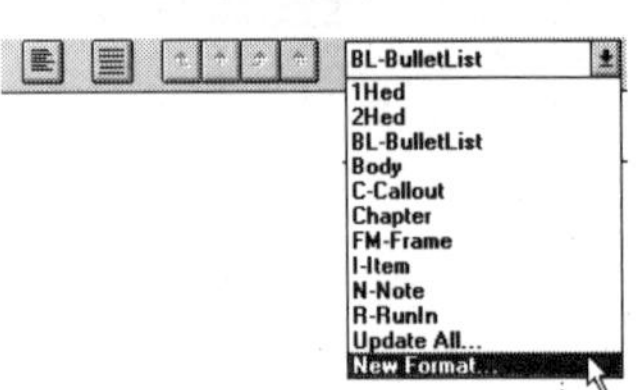

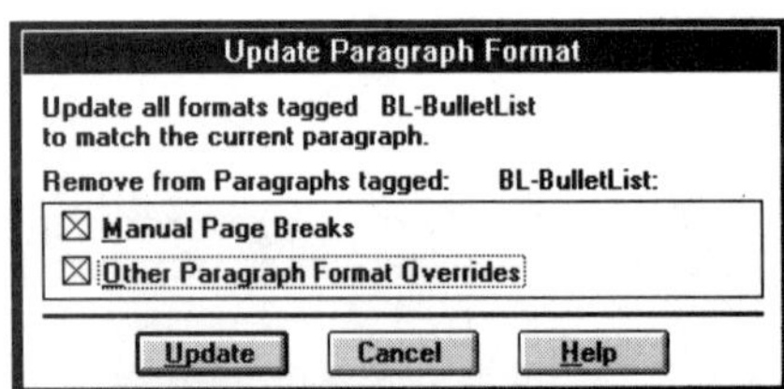

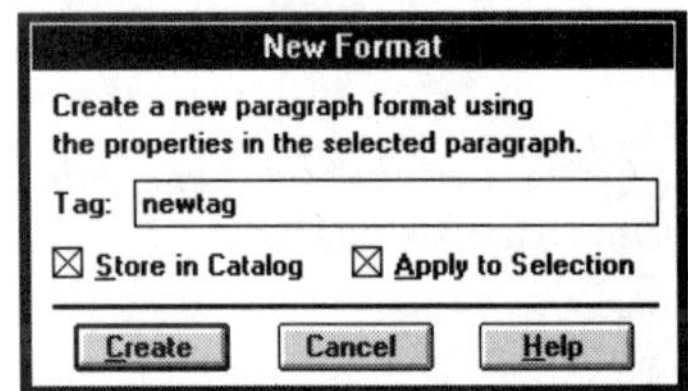

■ Applying your format changes

When you have made a formatting change, you always have the option of creating a new format or modifying the current paragraph or character format in addition to just modifying the current text. Here's a review of the techniques discussed at more length in Chapter 5.

Using the Paragraph or Character Designer

- Click Apply to Selection to apply the displayed properties to the currently selected paragraphs if you're working in the Paragraph Designer, or to the currently selected characters if you're working in the Character Designer.
- Click Update All to apply the displayed properties to the format definition, and to all occurrences of that format tag in the file.
- Type a new name in the Tag box, and click Apply to Selection to create a new format from the selected text, and store it in the catalog.

Using the Formatting bar

This works for paragraph formats only.

Make your format changes using the Formatting bar, the QuickAccess bar, or the Format menu.

- Display the Formatting bar [**Alt v f**] and select New Format or Update all from the paragraph formats pop-up. Make your choices in the resulting dialog box and click Update or Create.

▼

For more information...

Chapter 5 explains the above procedures in detail. This page is just a thumbnail sketch to remind you of your options as you use this chapter.

▲

■ The FrameMaker way to work

■ By using the Paragraph Designer and the Paragraph Designer to create tagged formats, you can increase both the speed with which you work, and the consistency of your work. the Designer windows are where you create tagged paragraph and character formats, as described in Chapter 5. They are also where you change individual characters and paragraphs, as described in this chapter.

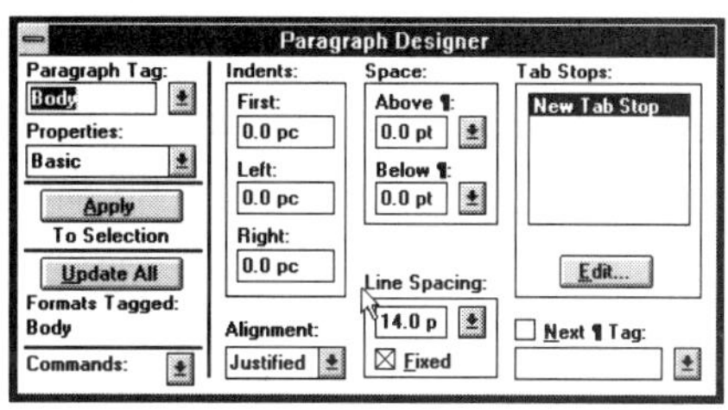

A sample paragraph format

This is a first-level head. Place your insertion point in text that you want to format.

1. Display the Basic page of the Paragraph Designer. [Ctrl-m]
2. Type a new format name in the Paragraph Tag box. (I'll use 1H-HeadOne for this example.)
3. Set Space Above to 14, Line Spacing to 28, Alignment to Left, and Next ¶ Tag to Body.
4. Click Commands. Click New Format.
5. Turn on Store in Catalog and Apply to Selection.
6. Click Create.
7. Press PgDn to display the next page of the Designer.
8. Set the Family to Helvetica, Size to 22 points, Weight to Bold, Spread to –2, and turn Pair Kern on.
9. Click Update All.
10. Continue through the pages of the Designer, setting the properties on each page and then clicking Update All until your paragraph format has exactly the properties you want.

Now you can create a first-level head by selecting a paragraph and pressing **F9 1**. (See page 91 for applying paragraph formats from the keyboard.)

A sample character format

Here's a sample character format that changes text to 9-point Helvetica Bold Narrow. On page 106, you will find instructions for creating a format that applies only italic.

1. Display the Character Designer. [Ctrl-d]
2. Set it to As Is. [Shift-F8]
3. Type a new format name in the Character Tag box. (Let's say E-Entry.)
4. Choose Helvetica from the Family pop-up.
5. Choose Bold from the Weight pop-up.
6. Choose 9 from the Size pop-up.
7. Choose Narrow from the Variation pop-up.
8. Click Commands. Click New Format.
9. Turn on Store in Catalog.
10. Click Create.

Now you can apply all these properties at once by pressing **F8 e** to apply this format. (See page 99 for applying character formats from the keyboard.)

■ Paragraph indents

Indent for the first line of the paragraph

Indent for the rest of the paragraph

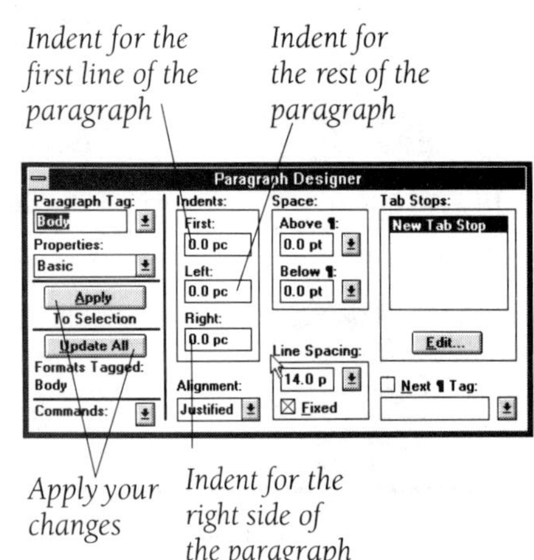

Apply your changes

Indent for the right side of the paragraph

Using the Paragraph Designer

1. Display the Paragraph Designer. [**Ctrl-m**]
2. Select one or more paragraphs to format, **or** select the format to change from the Paragraph Tag pop-up.
3. **Set the indent of the first line** Type an indent in the First text box.
4. **Set the indent of the rest of the paragraph** Type an indent in the Left text box. The Left and First indents are relative to the left side of the text column.
5. **Set a right indent** If you don't want the text to fill the width of the text column on the right, type a number in the Right text box for the distance from the text to the right side of the text column.
6. **Apply** Click Apply to Selection, Update All, or create a new format.

The numbers on the Ruler are the distance from the left side of the page.

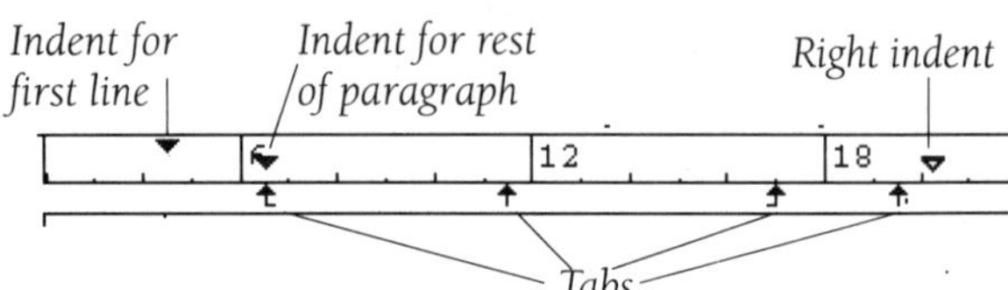

Using the Ruler

1. Display the Ruler. [**Alt v r**]
2. Select the paragraphs to change.
3. Place the mouse pointer on an indent symbol, hold down the left button, and drag the indent marker to a new position. The selected paragraphs show your changes.

▲ Using the Ruler lets you change indents in a visual, intuitive way. Use the Paragraph Designer if you want to use exact numbers.

■ Tabs

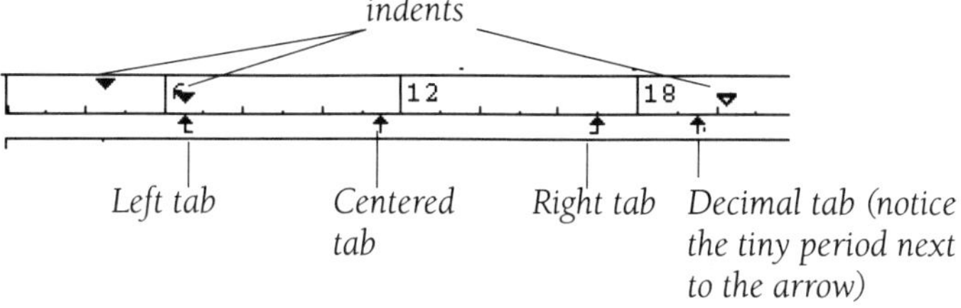

The numbers on the Ruler are the distance from the left side of the page.

How tabs work

■ When you press Tab *n* times, you go to the *n*th tab stop. If that tab stop is to the left of the insertion point, nothing happens. For example, press Tab four times to go to the fourth tab. (This is a bit different than many other applications, but it makes perfect sense once you understand it.)

■ You set tabs for each paragraph, or paragraph format.

■ The tabs are measured from the left side of the text column containing the paragraph.

Using the Paragraph Designer

This allows you to change the tabs in a single paragraph or in a format definition and all occurrences of the format.

1. *Page: Basic*. In the Tab Stops list, click on the tab you want to change. **Or** click on New Tab Stop to add a tab.
2. Click Edit.
3. In the Edit Tab Stop dialog box, make the changes you want.
4. Click Continue to return to the Designer.
5. **Apply** Click Apply to Selection, Update All, or create a new format.

▲ This box is almost like the one that you display by double-clicking on a tab stop in the Ruler (page 114). The only difference is that this one has a Continue button instead of an Edit button.

Click on a tab stop or on New Tab Stop

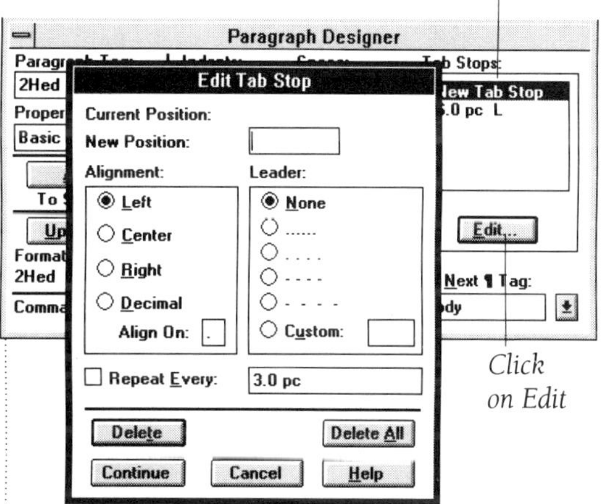

Click on Edit

Change the position, alignment, leader, or repeat, and click Continue. Then Apply the changes in the Paragraph Designer.

Tabs

Double-click on a tab in the Ruler to display this dialog box.

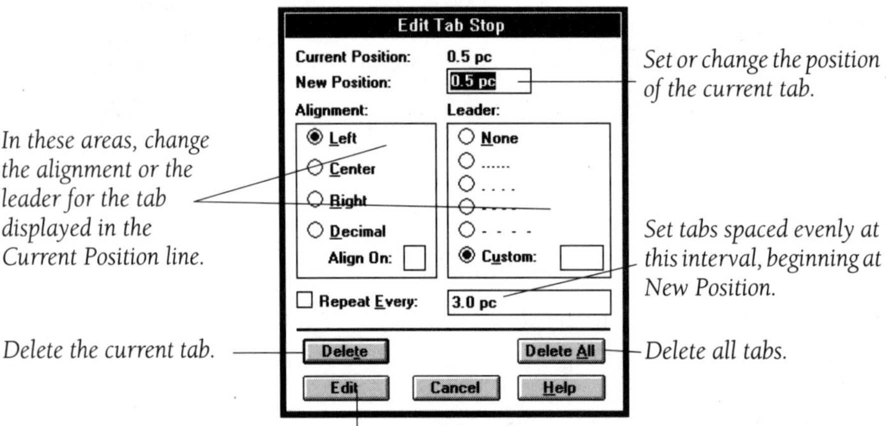

Click Edit when you have made all your changes.

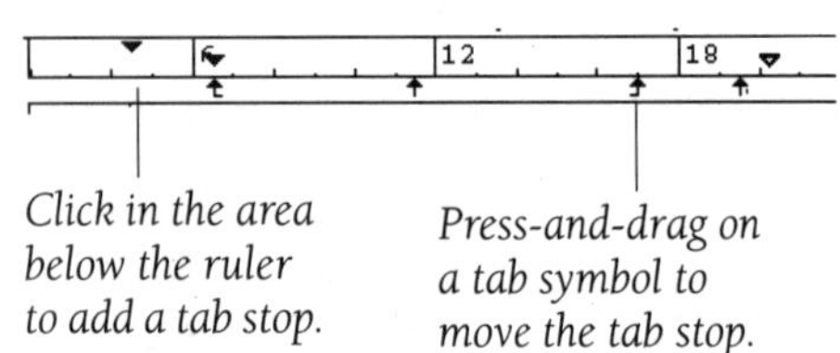

Click in the area below the ruler to add a tab stop.

Press-and-drag on a tab symbol to move the tab stop.

Tabs

Using the Ruler

Changes that you make using the Ruler apply only to the selected paragraphs unless you Update All from the Paragraph Designer (page 110) or the Formatting bar (page 95).

- **Add** Click at the bottom edge of the ruler to add a tab in that position. The alignment will be whatever is currently defined in the Edit Tab Stop dialog box.
- **Move** Press-and-drag on a tab stop in the Ruler, and drag it to a new position.
- **Delete** Drag a tab symbol away from the ruler to delete it.
- **Edit** Double-click on a tab stop to display the Edit Tab Stop dialog box. Make your changes and click Edit.

▲ **Making tab stops line up with the ruler marks** Turn on Snap in the Graphics menu. [**Alt g n**] Turn Snap off to be able to position the tab anywhere by dragging.

Using the Formatting bar and the Ruler

1. Display the Formatting bar [**Alt v f**] and the Ruler [**Alt v r**].
2. Select the paragraphs to format.
3. Click on the tab well for the alignment you want, and then click in the area below the Ruler at the position where you want the tab. That's it. Your tab is in place. You can edit tabs using any of the techniques described in "Using the Ruler" on page 114.

▲ To apply these changes to a format, see "Applying your format changes" on page 110.

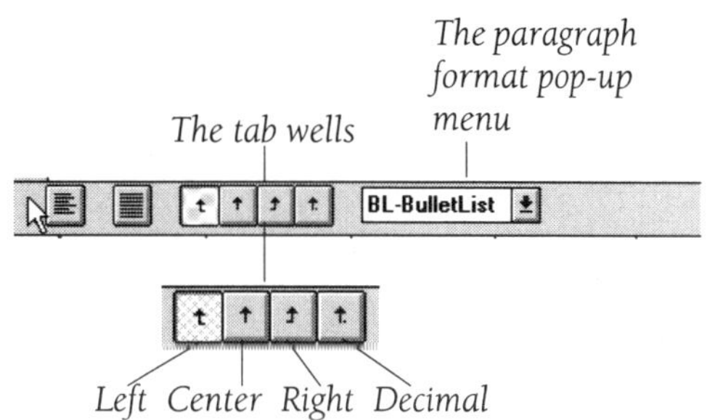

Notes on special tabs

Alignment character of a decimal tab

Your Decimal tab can align on any character, not just a period. In the Edit Tab Stop dialog box, type the character you want in the Align On text box.

14
14.0
14.00
414

These decimal tabs are aligned on the period.

Tabs with leaders

In the Edit Tab Stop dialog box, click one of the leader choices or type your own in the Custom text box. The leader character(s) fill the space from the insertion point to the tab position.

■ FrameMaker automatically lines the leader characters up vertically from line to line.

■ You can type more than one character, and can use the Dialog Box code (page A-322) for special spaces.

■ You can type any characters in the paragraph font as leader characters. You cannot change fonts. Use the hex code or the ANSI number to type characters not on the keyboard. See page77 for how to type special characters.

The leader here is a space and a period. Notice how FrameMaker lines the dots up.

Jan. 1-4. . . . . Quadrantids
Feb. 5-10. . . . . Alpha Aurigids

Set the leader tab here and a plain tab here to make a nice space between the end of the leader and the text.

A -+-+-+-+-+-+-+-+-+-+-+-+-+-+-+-+-+- B

Use a plus and a hyphen with a space before each to create this one.

A ______________________________________ B

Use the underscore in the Custom Leader box to create a solid line.

Tabs

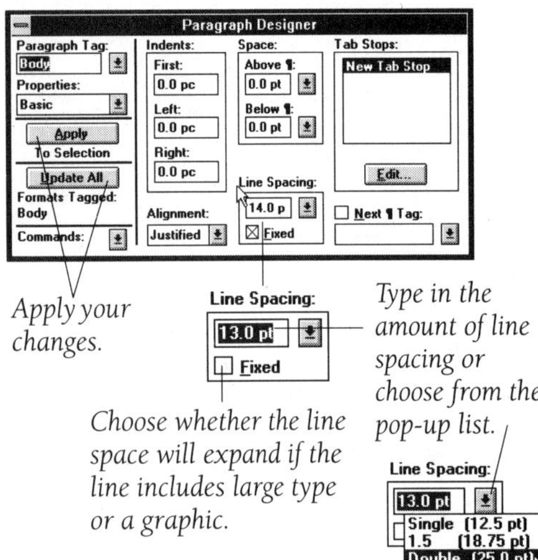

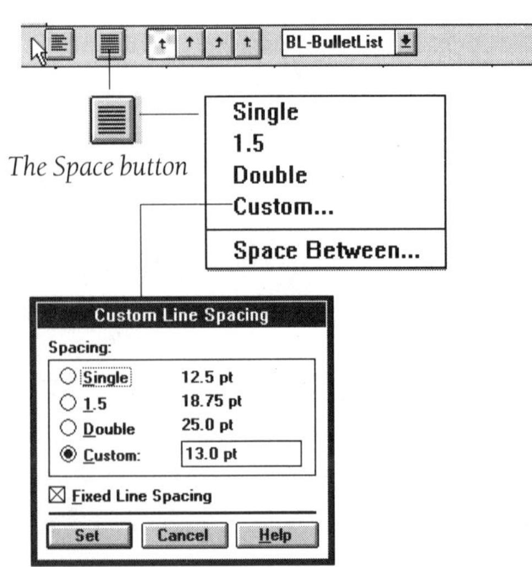

■ Line spacing

Using the Paragraph Designer

1. Select one or more paragraphs, **or** select the format to change from the Paragraph Tag pop-up in the Paragraph Designer.
2. Type the space you want from baseline to baseline within the paragraph in the Line Spacing box.
   Or click the pop-up button to choose Single, 1.5, or Double.
   • See "Some useful line space notes" on page 117.
3. Turn on Fixed to maintain even line spacing. Turn it off to allow the spacing to expand to accommodate large type or in-line graphics.
4. **Apply** Click Apply to Selection, Update All, or create a new format.

Using the Formatting bar

1. Display the Formatting bar. [**Alt v f**]
2. Select the paragraphs to change.
3. Click on the Space button. If you're doing things the desktop publishing way, click on Custom. Otherwise, click Single, 1.5, or Double. See "Some useful line space notes" on page 117.
4. In the Custom Line Spacing dialog box, type in the leading (line spacing) you want.
5. Click Set.

▲ To apply these changes to a format, see "Applying your format changes" on page 110.

A negative leading trick

This paragraph has a right indent of 4 pi and Space Below of –13 pt. The price at the end is a separate paragraph, flush right with no right indent and Space Above of –13 pt. $4.00

Negative line spacing

■ You can make two paragraphs occur on the same baseline to create special effects such as catalog entries. The first paragraph should have a negative Space Below equal to the Line Spacing. The second paragraph *must* have an equal amount of negative Space Above.

Some useful line space notes

■ Now that you're a desktop publisher, you have more choices than you did in the old typewriter days when it was only Single, 1.5, or Double. In typography (yes, that's what you're doing), space between lines is called *leading.*

■ FrameMaker's default leading is 120% of the type size, and it works fine for most things. You can't change the *default,* but you can, of course, change the leading.

■ For a more generous look, try increasing the leading by 1 or 2 (or even 3) points for text, and more for large type.

■ Changing the leading changes the "look" of your page. Play around with it when you're designing pages.

These are all 9 point type

9 points leading	If I were a woman, I would kiss as many of you as had beards that pleased me, complexions that liked me, and breaths that I defied not.
11 points leading	If I were a woman, I would kiss as many of you as had beards that pleased me, complexions that liked me, and breaths that I defied not.
13 points leading	If I were a woman, I would kiss as many of you as had beards that pleased me, complexions that liked me, and breaths that I defied not.

Making a draft version of a document

Even if you're using beautiful typographic line spacing, you may want to use 1.5 or Double spacing when you make a draft version, so that you have more space for proofing.

1. Make a copy of your file, or open it using New (page 45) and Save As a new name (page 48).
2. Place your cursor in any text and press **Ctrl-a** to select all the text in the flow.
3. Click on the Designer to select it, and set it to As Is. [**Shift-F8**]
4. From the Line Spacing pop-up, choose 1.5 or Double.
5. Click on Apply to Selection.
6. Repeat for each flow if you have a multi-flow document such as a newsletter.

▲ If you want to space only some of the text, then in step 2, choose one or more paragraphs whose formats you want to change. In step 5, choose **Commands➔Global Update Options➔All Matching Tags in Selection**.

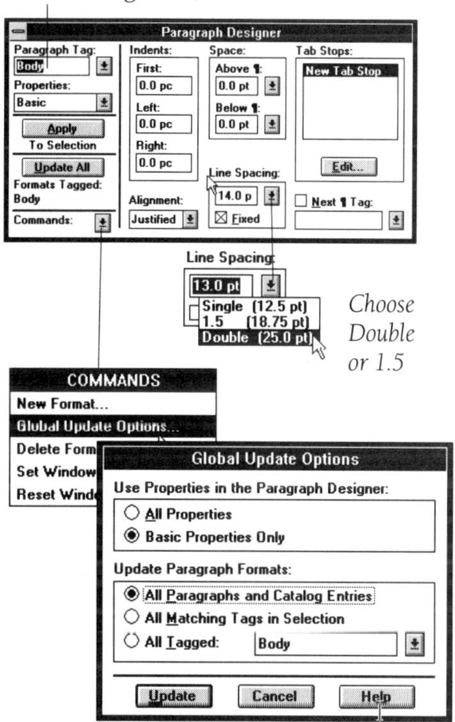

Choose Basic Properties Only and All Paragraphs and Catalog Entries (or just your body formats).

■ Space above and below paragraphs

When you press Enter, FrameMaker starts a new paragraph and adds space below the old one or above the new one. This space is part of the paragraph format definitions. *If both numbers—above and below—are defined, FrameMaker uses only the larger amount.*

At the top of a page FrameMaker ignores Space Above when a paragraph is at the top of a text column. If you really want the paragraph to start somewhere lower on the page, put another, empty, line above it, so that it's not first on the page anymore.

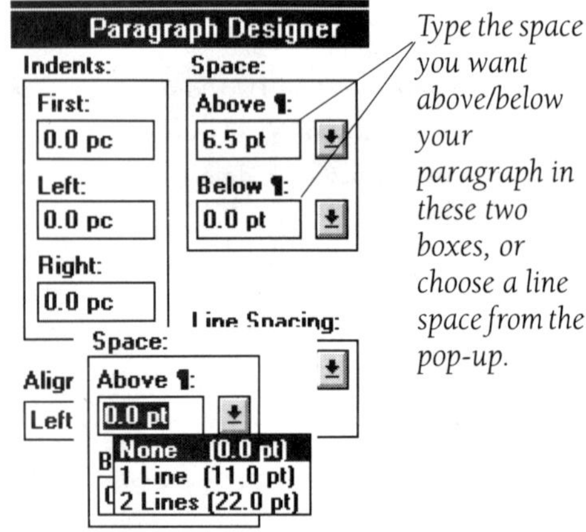

Type the space you want above/below your paragraph in these two boxes, or choose a line space from the pop-up.

Click the pop-up button to choose 0, 1, or 2 lines for either Above or Below.

Using the Paragraph Designer

1. Select one or more paragraphs, **or** select the format to change from the Paragraph Tab pop-up.
2. Space: Above is space between the selected paragraph and the one above. Space: Below is space between the current paragraph and the next paragraph. Type the space you want into the boxes, or choose from the pop-up list.
3. **Apply** Click Apply to Selection, Update All, or create a new format

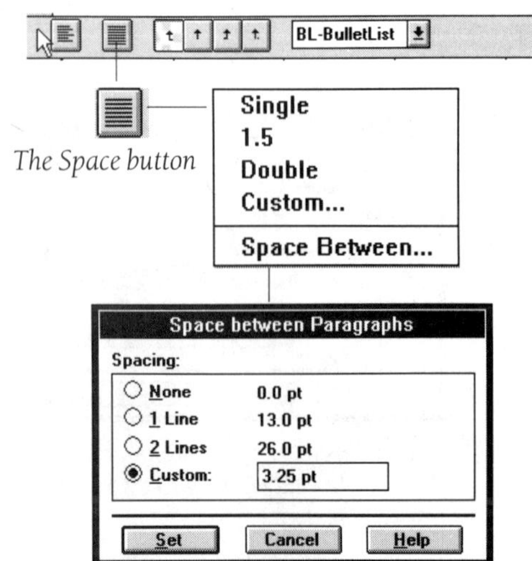

The Space button

Using the Formatting bar

1. Display the Formatting bar. [**Alt v f**]
2. Select two or more paragraphs.
3. Click on the Space button.
4. In the pop-up box, click on Space Between.
5. In the Space Between Paragraphs dialog box, type the space you want into the Custom line box, or choose None, 1, or 2 lines.
6. Click Set.

▲ To apply these changes to a format, see "Applying your format changes" on page 110.

■ Paragraph alignment

Alignment is also known in typography as "justification." Paragraphs are flush left, flush right, centered, or justified.

Using the Paragraph Designer

1. Select one or more paragraphs, **or** select the format to change from the Paragraph Tag pop-up in the Paragraph Designer.
2. Click on the Alignment pop-up button to display your choices.
3. Click on the alignment you want.
4. **Apply** Click Apply to Selection, Update All, or create a new format (see page 110).

▲ Choose **As Is** when you want to create a paragraph format that changes other things, but does not change the alignment.

Using the Formatting bar

1. Display the Formatting bar. [**Alt v f**]
2. Select the paragraphs to format.
3. Click on the Alignment button.
4. In the pop-up box, click on Left, Center, Right, or Justify.

▲ To apply these changes to a format, see "Applying your format changes" on page 110.

Flush left	**Centered**	**Flush right**
Life is just a dream; dream on.	Life is just a dream; dream on.	Life is just a dream; dream on.

Justified

Justified type aligns on both the left and right sides. The look is clean and formal. Flush left type is a more relaxed look. Take your pick.

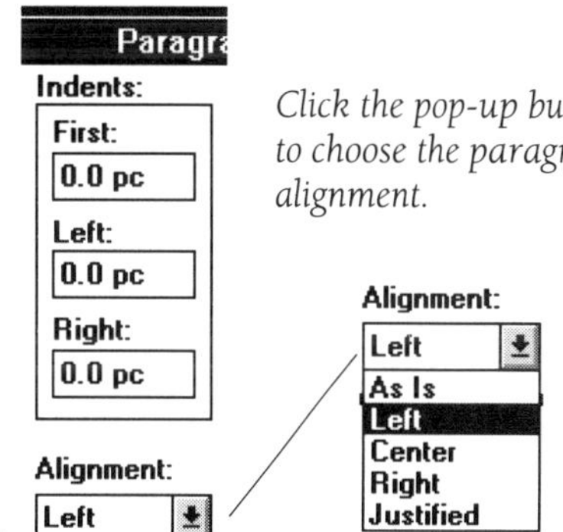

Click the pop-up button to choose the paragraph alignment.

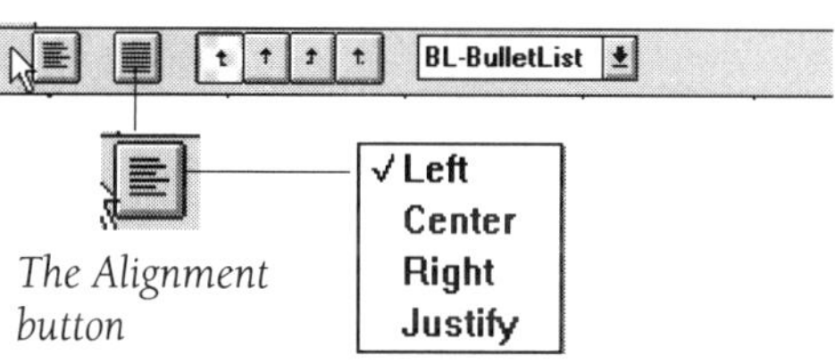

The Alignment button

Paragraph alignment

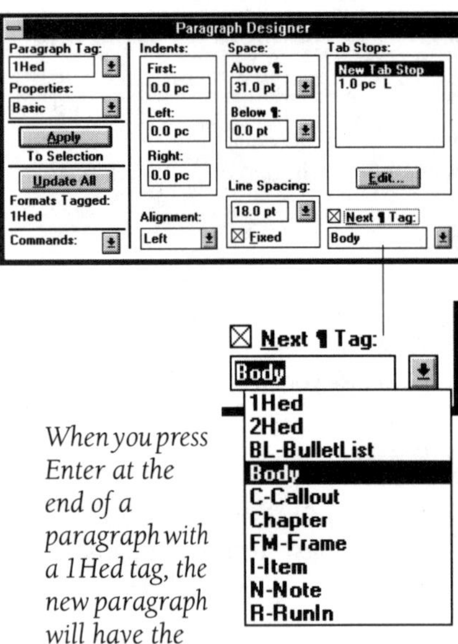

When you press Enter at the end of a paragraph with a 1Hed tag, the new paragraph will have the Body tag.

■ The format of the next paragraph

You can tell FrameMaker to give the next paragraph a different paragraph format automatically when you press Enter. (This is the feature that I also describe in Chapter 5 under "Automatic paragraph formats.")

1. Select the format to change from the Paragraph Tag pop-up in the Paragraph Designer.
2. Select the format for the following paragraph from the Next ¶ Tag pop-up list.
3. **Apply** Click Apply to Selection, Update All, or create a new format (see page 110).

▲ If you leave this blank, FrameMaker creates a new paragraph with the same tag as the previous one when you press Enter.

▲ After you have generated an automatically-tagged paragraph by pressing Enter, you can change the format tag to something else if you wish, just as you would change any paragraph format.

Planning the Next ¶ Tag

When you are creating formats for a document, think about the sequence in which things are likely to occur. If a paragraph with a 1-HeadOne tag is nearly always going to be followed by a B-Body tag, you can save a lot of work by having B-Body be the Next ¶ Tag of the 1-HeadOne format definition.

Another example of when to use Next ¶ Tag is autonumbered lists. You need one format that sets the numbering back to 1 for the first item in a list, and the rest will use the regular numbered list format that increments the number. You can have N-NumList be the Next ¶ Tag of NF-NumListFirst.

■ Font properties

"Font properties" include typeface (type family), type style (bold, italic, small caps, etc.), and type size.

Applying fonts to characters

■ Place the insertion point where you want the font change, **or** select the characters to format, then

Using the Character Designer

To change only part of a paragraph, or a character format

1. Choose the font from the Family pop-up.
2. Choose any other font properties such as weight, variation, etc.
3. **Apply** Click Apply to Selection, Update All, or create a new format.

Using the Format menu

1. Choose **Format→Font**.
2. Click on the font name.

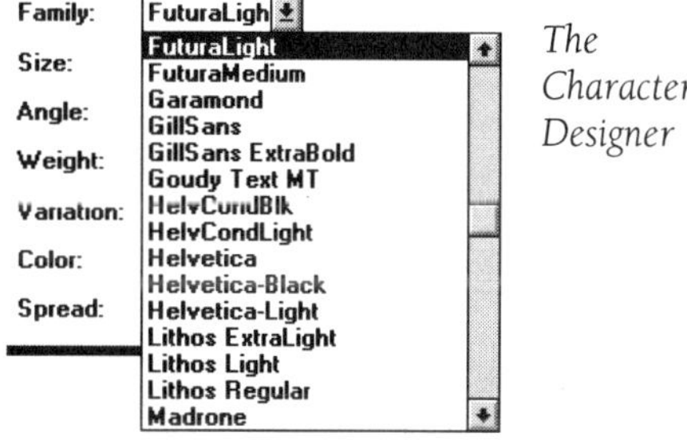

The Character Designer

The Format menu

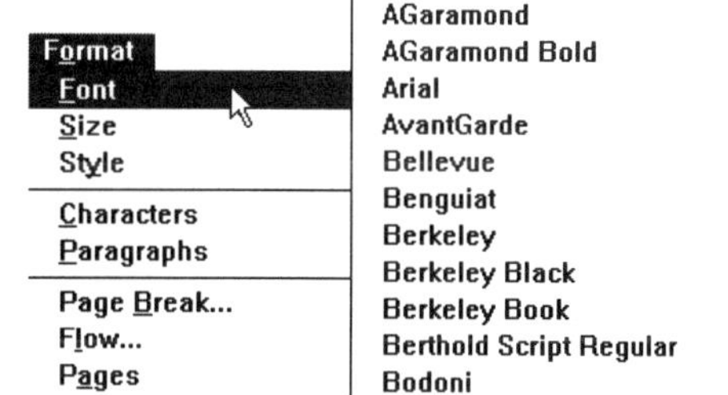

Applying fonts to paragraphs

■ Select the paragraphs to format, then

Using the Paragraph Designer

To change whole paragraphs, or a paragraph format

1. Display the Default Font page of the Paragraph Designer.
2. Choose the font from the Family pop-up.
3. Choose any other font properties such as weight, variation, etc.
4. **Apply** Click Apply to Selection, Update All, or create a new format.

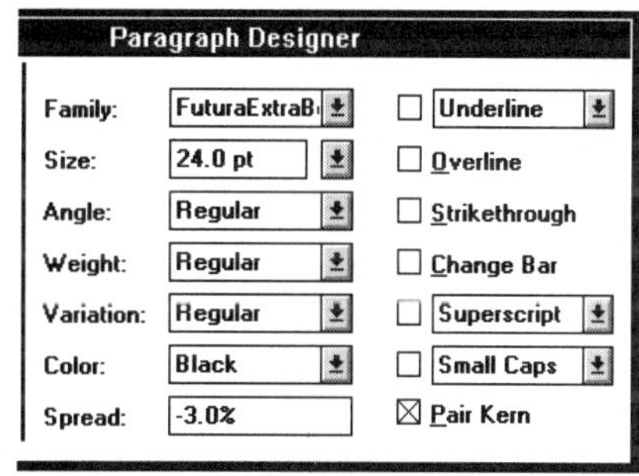

The Default Font page of the Paragraph Designer (right-hand side)

Font size

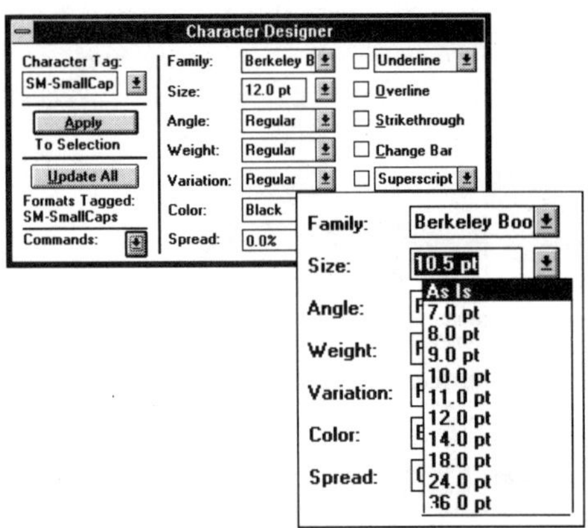

■ Select the paragraphs, characters, paragraph format, or character format to change.

Using the Character Designer

To change only part of a paragraph, or a character format

1. Choose a size from the Size pop-up **or** type any size from 2 to 400 points, to the nearest tenth of a point, in the Size text box.
2. **Apply** Click Apply to Selection, Update All, or create a new format.

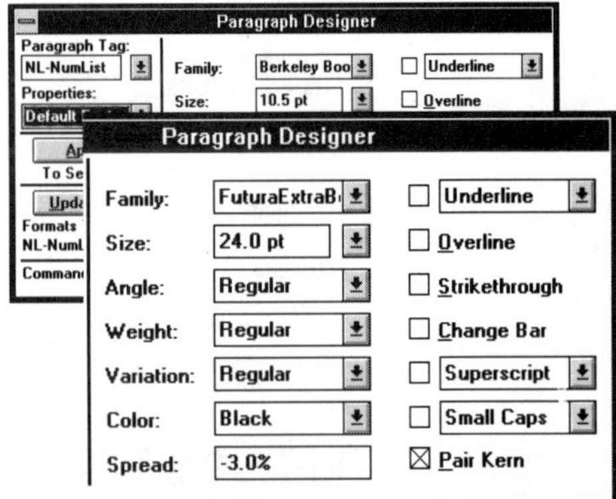

Using the Paragraph Designer

To change whole paragraphs, or a paragraph format

1. In the Default Font page, choose a size from the Size pop-up **or** type any size from 2 to 400 points, to the nearest tenth of a point, in the Size text box.
2. **Apply** Click Apply to Selection, Update All, or create a new format.

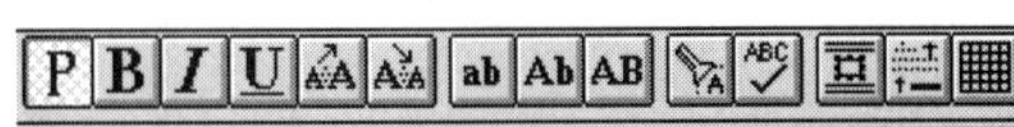

Using the QuickAccess bar

■ Click on [icon] to make selected text one point size larger.

■ Click on [icon] to make selected text one point size smaller.

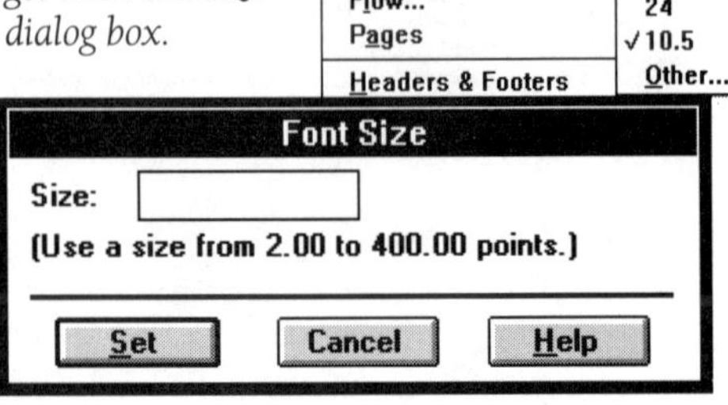

Click on Other to get this Font Size dialog box.

Using the Format menu

1. Choose **Format→Size**.
2. Click on a size or on Other (Type a size into the text box in the pop-up.)

KEYBOARD SHORTCUT: decrease 1 point **Esc c [**

increase 1 point **Esc c]**

Making characters bold, italic, or plain

■ Place the insertion point where you want the style change to begin, **or** select the characters to format, then

Using the Character Designer

To change only part of a paragraph, or a character format

1. Choose Italic or Regular from the Angle pop-up; choose Bold or Regular from the Weight pop-up.
2. **Apply** Click Apply to Selection, Update All, or create a new format.

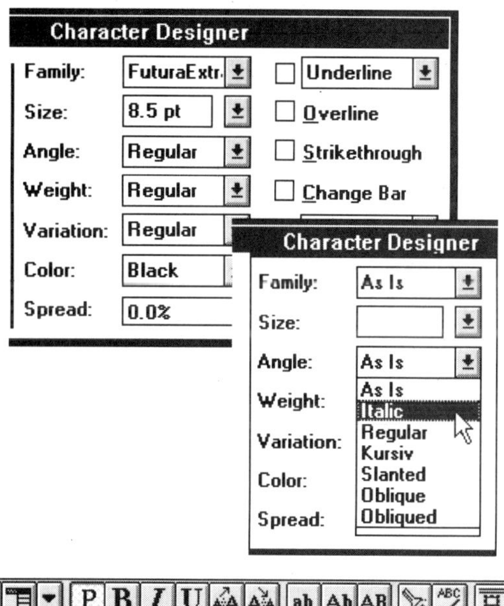

Using the QuickAccess bar

1. In the QuickAccess bar, click on bold B, italic I, or plain P.

Using the Format menu

1. Choose **Format➔Style**.
2. Click on Bold, Italic, or Plain.

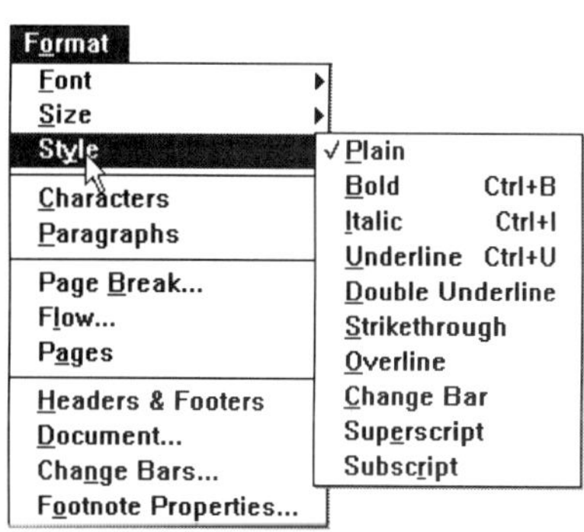

KEYBOARD SHORTCUT: Bold: **Ctrl-b** Italic: **Ctrl-i**

Changing bold or italic in paragraphs

■ Select the paragraphs to format, then

Using the Paragraph Designer

To change whole paragraphs, or a paragraph format

1. Choose Italic or Regular from the Angle pop-up; or choose Bold or Regular from the Weight pop-up.
2. **Apply** Click Apply to Selection, Update All, or create a new format.

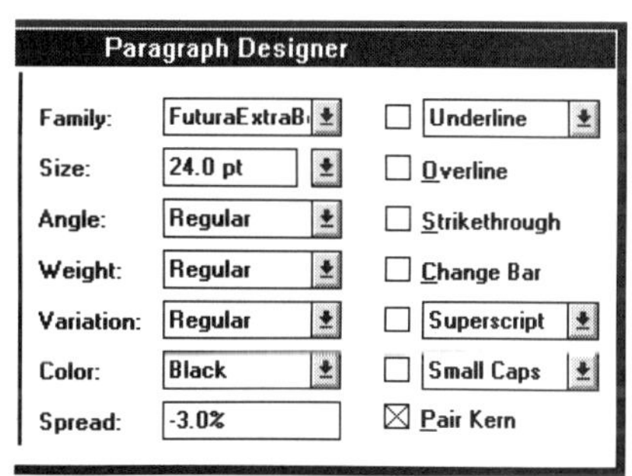

A note on "Plain"

"Plain" is not the same as Default ¶ Font. When you apply Plain from the Formatting bar or from the **Format➔Style** menu, you remove all bold and italic, even if the default paragraph font is bold or italic.

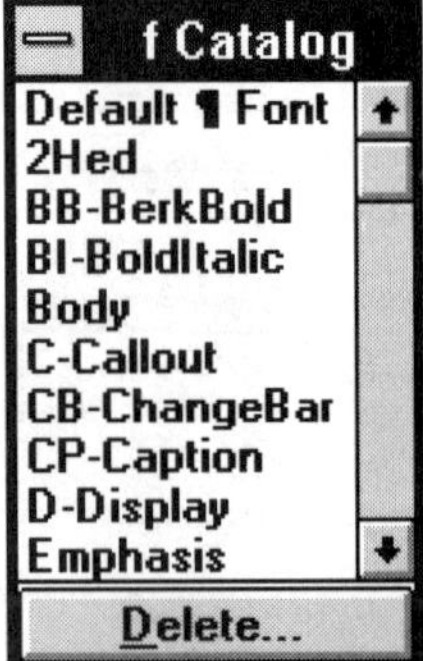

Remove character formats by applying Default ¶ Font to the selected characters. [**F8-d**]

Removing special font formatting

To restore the default paragraph font by removing special formatting:

From characters Select the characters and apply Default ¶ Font from the character catalog. [**F8 d** Return]

From paragraphs Sometimes you need to reapply the paragraph format after you apply Default ¶ Font in order to get your original type style back.

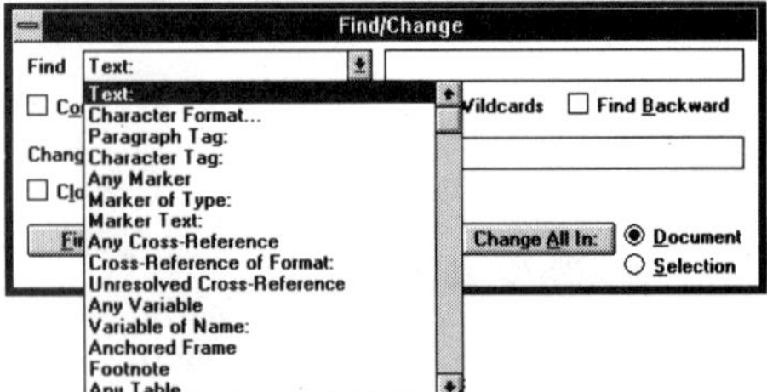

Hint: Use Find You can use Find to locate occurrences of a particular kind of formatting. [**Ctrl-f**] You can Find a paragraph tag, a character tag (page 173), or a character format (page 174). FrameMaker highlights an occurrence when it finds one, so all you have to do is apply Default ¶ Font. [**F8-d**]

What's a "variation"?

A variation is usually a wider or narrower version of a typeface. It is actually a different font, just as the bold and italic versions of a face are different fonts from regular. Variations are provided by the font manufacturer. They are not the electronic distortions of the font that some programs produce.

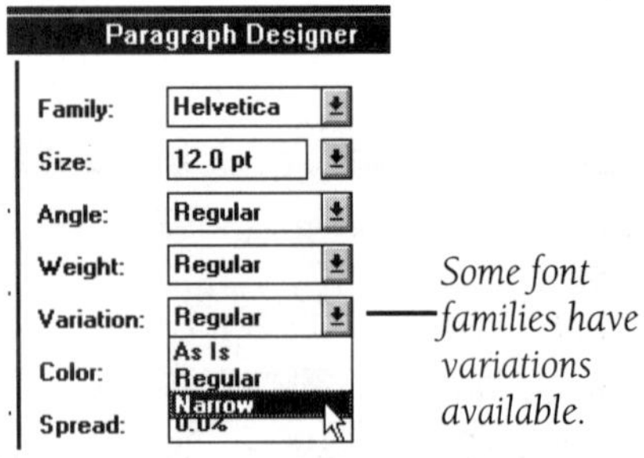

Some font families have variations available.

■ To choose a variation in either the Character Designer or the Paragraph Designer, display the typeface in the Family pop-up list, and then click on Variation and choose the variation from the list.

Underlining text

FrameMaker offers three types of underline:

Underline The offset and thickness of this "regular" underline are determined by the size and style of the text.

Numeric underline This is a thin underline whose thickness and offset never varies.

Double underline Two at once!

■ Select the text to underline, or click where you want to type underlined text.

Using the Character Designer *Regular, numeric, or double underlines; selected characters*

1. Choose an underline style from the Underline pop-up.
2. **Apply** Click Apply to Selection, Update All, or create a new format.

Using the Paragraph Designer *Regular, numeric, or double underlines; complete paragraphs*

1. In the Default Font page, choose the underline style from the Underline pop-up.
2. **Apply** Click Apply to Selection, Update All, or create a new format.

Using the QuickAccess bar *(Regular underlining; selected characters)*

■ In the QuickAccess bar, click on underline **U**.

Using the Format menu *(Regular and double underlines; selected characters)*

1. Choose **Format➔Style**.
2. Click on Underlining or Double Underlining.

KEYBOARD SHORTCUT: **Ctrl-u** *(regular underline only).*

Note All the underline styles crash into the descenders of letters. You cannot adjust this. However, underlining is not often used in typography and graphic design.

■ Try italic, or some other type style instead.

A trick You can draw a line under your text using the button in the graphics palette (page 254). The line will not move with the text, however, unless you put both text and line in an anchored frame (page 195). [**Alt s a**]

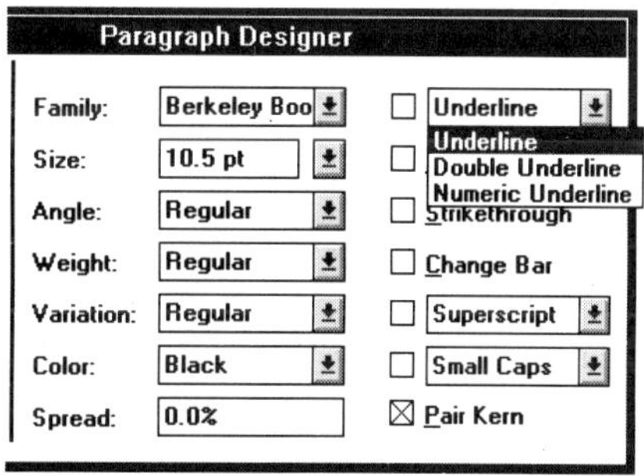

Choose an underline style here in both the Character and Paragraph Designers.

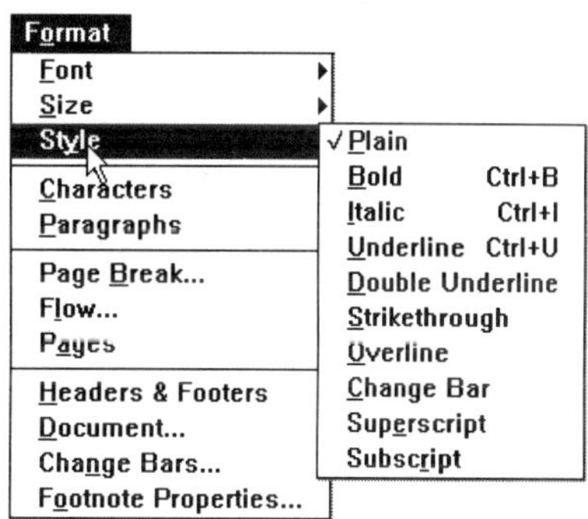

Font properties

Small Caps

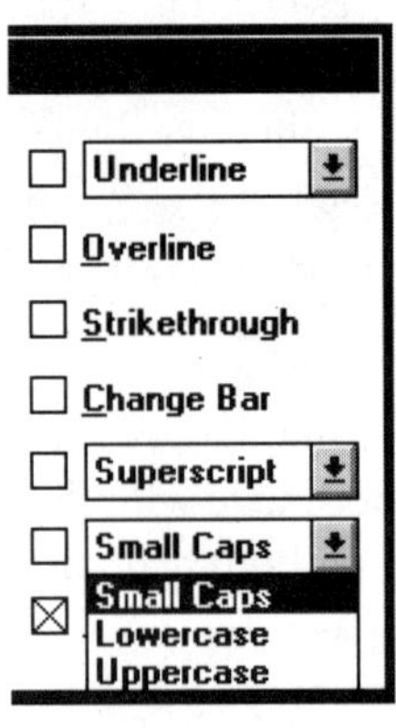

Choose Small Caps here, in both the Character and Paragraph Designers.

■ Place the insertion point where you want the small caps to begin, **or** select the characters to change, then

Using the Character Designer
To change selected characters or a character format

1. Click on the Small Caps box.
2. **Apply** Click Apply to Selection, Update All, or create a new format.

Using the Paragraph Designer
To change whole paragraphs, or a paragraph format

1. Click on the Small Caps box.
2. **Apply** Click Apply to Selection, Update All, or create a new format.

KEYBOARD SHORTCUT: **Esc c m**.

Typing small caps Type the letters that are to be small caps in lower case. Letters that you type in uppercase are unchanged by the small caps feature.

▲ See page76 for instructions on making a small caps format.

Typing small caps

Type this	**Get this**
two words	TWO WORDS
Two Words	Two Words
TWO WORDS	TWO WORDS

Managing size and leading

When large type is followed by small type, there is extra space following the large type. This space is a function of the leading assigned to the large type and ensures that the descenders of the large type don't crash into the type below. Sometimes, though, you need to reduce that space.

1. Select the large type and in the Paragraph Designer, give it a negative number for Space Below (Basic page).
2. Select the small type and give it the same negative number for Space Above.

Space Below = 0

Space Above = 0
(but the top line is 24-point type on 30 pts. leading)

Great
AND SMALL

Space Below = –9
Space Above = –9
(everything else is the same as the top example)

Superscripts and subscripts

■ Select the characters to be formatted, or place the insertion point where superscript or subscript begins, then

Using the Character Designer
To change selected characters, or a character format

1. Choose Superscript or Subscript from the pop-up and click on the check box.
2. **Apply** Click Apply to Selection, Update All, or create a new format.

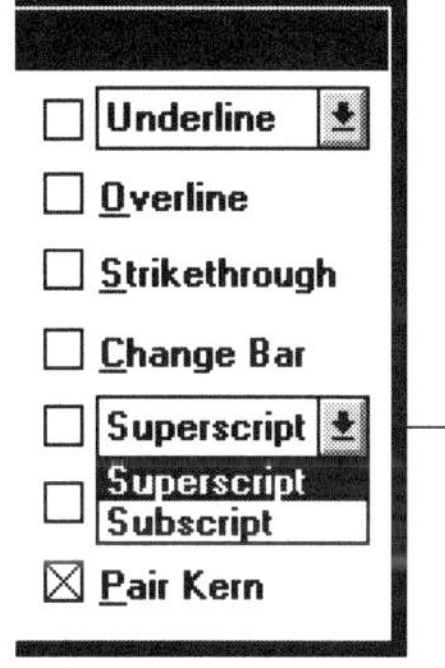

Choose Superscript or Subscript here, in both the Character and Paragraph Designers.

Using the Paragraph Designer
To change whole paragraphs, or a paragraph format

1. In the Default Font page, choose Superscript or Subscript from the pop-up and click on the check box.
2. **Apply** Click Apply to Selection, Update All, or create a new format.

Using the Format menu

Choose **Format→Style→Superscript/Subscript**.

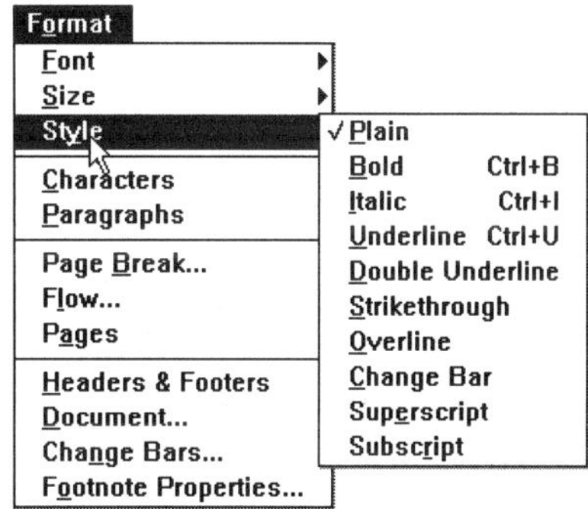

KEYBOARD SHORTCUTS:

Toggle superscript on/off **Esc c +**.

Toggle subscript on/off **Esc c -**.

■ To set the percent size and baseline offset of superscript and subscript character for the whole file, choose **Format→Document** (page 25).

A baseline trick

If you are not using actual superscripts or subscripts in your file, but would like to move certain characters—perhaps a bullet— off the baseline, do this:

1. Change the size and offset of either superscript or subscript. By default, a positive number moves characters up in the superscript and down in the subscript. You can reverse either of these directions by entering a negative number.
2. Optionally, change the size.
3. Apply superscript or subscript to the characters you want to change.

Overline and Strikethrough

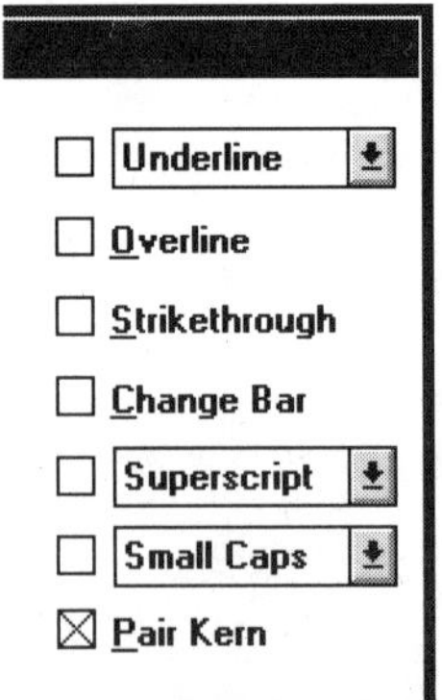

Choose Overline and Strikethrough here, in both the Character and Paragraph Designers.

■ Select the characters to be formatted, or place the insertion point where overline or strikethrough begins, then

Using the Character Designer
To change selected characters, or a character format

1. Click on either the Overline or Strike-through check box.
2. **Apply** Click Apply to Selection, Update All, or create a new format.

Using the Paragraph Designer
To change whole paragraphs, or a paragraph format

1. In the Default Font page, click on either the Overline or Strike-through check box.
2. **Apply** Click Apply to Selection, Update All, or create a new format.

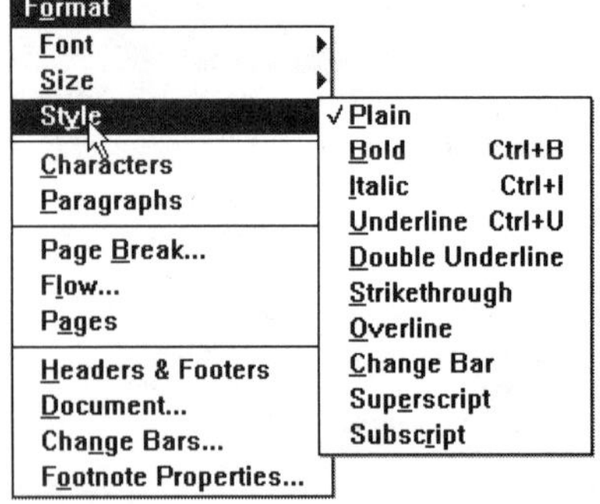

Using the Format menu

Choose **Format➔Style➔Overline/Strikethrough**.

Assigning color to text

Your type can be any color you want it to be!

Assigning color to selected characters or a paragraph

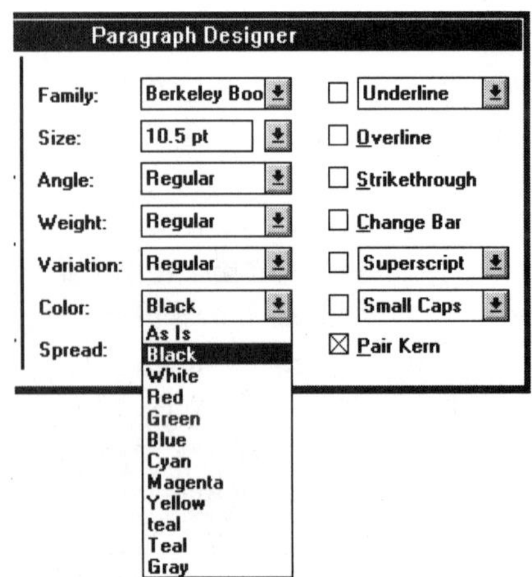

1. Display the Character Designer for characters, or the Paragraph Designer if you are assigning color to whole paragraphs or a paragraph format.
2. Select the characters, paragraphs or format to change.
3. Click on the Color pop-up to display a list of assigned colors. Click on the color you want.
4. **Apply** Click Apply to Selection, Update All, or create a new format.

Another way

Use the Color button on the Graphics palette to apply color to selected text (page 254).

Defining new colors

Choose **View→Color→Definitions**. You can define a new color using CMYK, RGB, HLS, or the Common Color Picker, You can also choose any Pantone® color.

Controlling display and printing of colors

Choose **View→Color→Views** to determine what colors will both print and display.

See Chapter 15 for more information on using color in your document.

View
✓QuickAccess Bar
✓Formatting Bar
✓Borders
Text Symbols
✓Rulers
Grid Lines
Options...
Go to Page... Ctrl+G
✓Body Pages
Master Pages
Reference Pages
Color — Views...
Menus — Definitions...

Where to go for local color.

■ Character spacing

Automatic kerning

"Kerning" is a delicate adjustment of spacing between characters. It makes the texture of your text more even. It's a nice subtlety that's available to you now that we have sophisticated desktop publishing software.

FAR AWAY

Kerned

FAR AWAY

Unkerned

■ Most fonts come with kern values as part of the font definition. All you have to do is turn kerning on in every paragraph definition (with the couple of exceptions in the next paragraph), and your type will automatically be kerned.

■ As a rule, you do not want to turn automatic kerning on for monospaced fonts—those typewriter-like faces whose characters are all the same width. Courier is the most common monospaced font. Kerned monospaced fonts look funny. If you have a format for a nonalphabetic font, such as Symbol or Wingdings, don't kern that, either.

Turn it on Click in the Pair Kern box to turn automatic kerning on in either the Character Designer or the Default Font page of the Paragraph Designer.

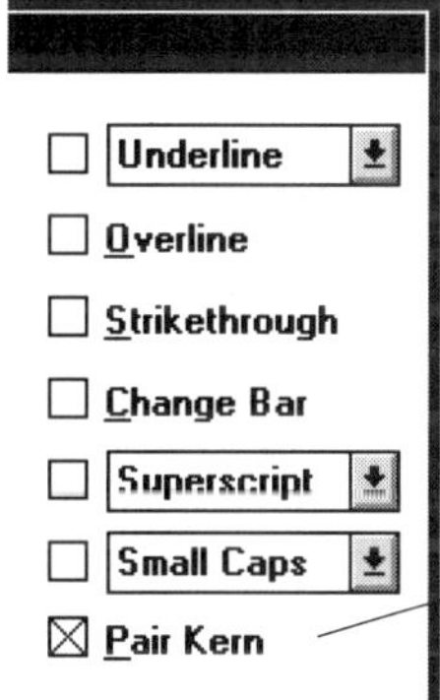

Turn on Pair Kerning here, in both the Character and Paragraph Designers.

Family:	FuturaExtraB
Size:	15.0 pt
Angle:	Regular
Weight:	Regular
Variation:	Regular
Color:	Black
Spread:	-2.0%

Here's where you control the "spread" between characters in both the Character and Paragraph Designers.

Spread: the spacing between characters

"Spread" will automatically tighten up the space between characters in a paragraph, or between selected characters, or spread them apart. A negative number in this box moves letters closer together, a positive number spreads them apart.

- Select the characters or paragraphs to be formatted, then

Using the Character Designer
To change selected characters or a character format

1. Type a positive or negative percent in the Spread box.
2. **Apply** Click Apply to Selection, Update All, or create a new format.

Using the Paragraph Designer
To change whole paragraphs, or a paragraph format

1. Type a positive or negative percent in the Spread box.
2. **Apply** Click Apply to Selection, Update All, or create a new format.

Tightening display type As type gets larger, it frequently needs to be tightened to look nice. The amount varies widely with the typeface. You want the letters to be close without touching. If you don't kern type that's over 40 points or so, it has that falling-apart kind of look. The chapter titles in this book are only 24 point type, and they have a –3% spread.

Spreading type for special effects Putting a large amount of space between letters can be a useful design tool.

Positive
S P R E A D

The word "SPREAD" has a Spread of 153%.

Hand-kerning text

Micropositioning This is another technique for altering the spacing between characters.

■ Use **Alt plus the arrow keys** to move a selected black of type to the right, left, up or down in very tiny increments. **Shift plus Alt and the arrow keys** moves it in somewhat larger increments.

Note To use this technique to hand kern to letters, select everything on the line to the right of the space you are kerning. Text within the selected area is not affected. The selected block is moved as a unit.

To kern here.

Towards

Select this

Towards

then press Alt-left arrow (or Shift-Alt-left arrow) until the space suits you.

Towards

■ Moving text off the baseline

There are several ways you can type text so that it is not on the baseline.

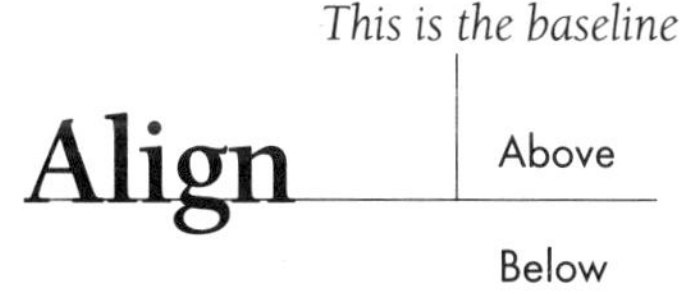

Micropositioning: Alt plus the arrow keys

1. Select the text to move.
2. Move the selected block of text by holding down Alt and pressing the up or down arrow keys.

   To move in larger increments, hold down Shift plus Alt as you press the arrow keys.

Use superscript or subscript

Select the text and apply superscript or subscript. You can apply the superscript and subscript properties to any text, not just "real" superscripts and subscripts.

▲ You can define superscript and subscript size and offset once for each file. Change the definition by choosing **Format→Document**. You can define the size and baseline to be anything you wish. Use a negative number for the baseline percent to reverse the direction.

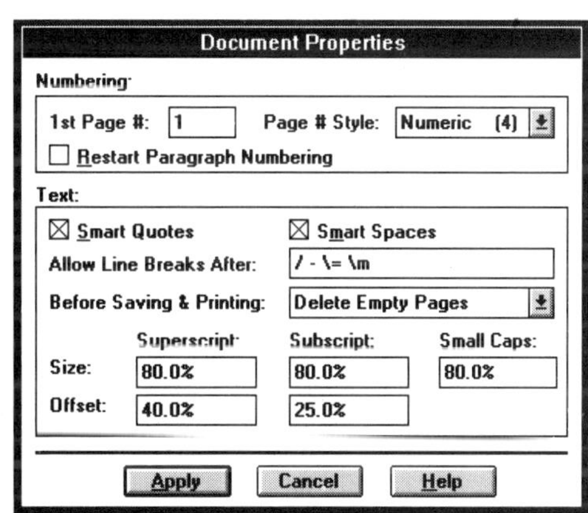

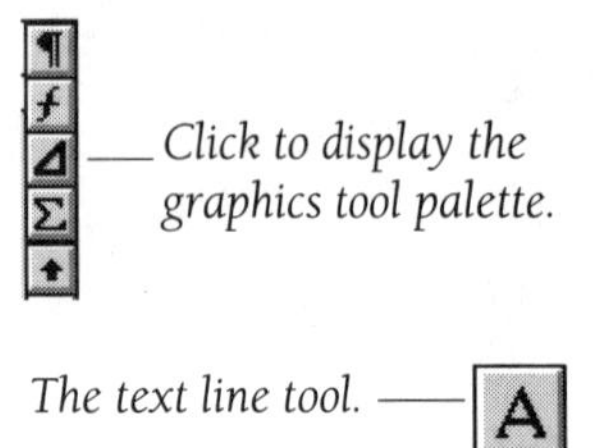

Click to display the graphics tool palette.

The text line tool.

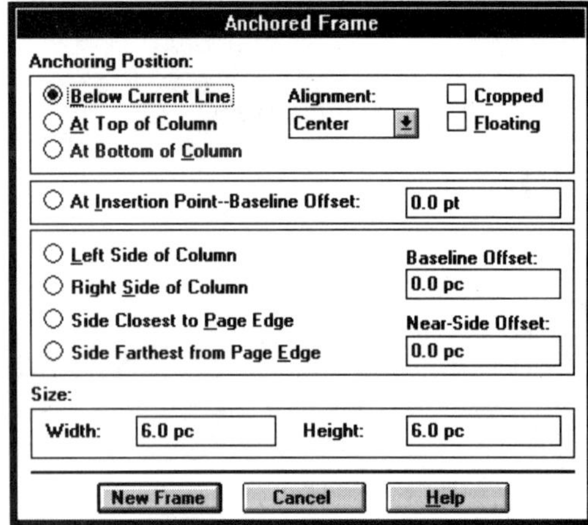

Moving text off the baseline *(cont.)*

Typing a text line

1. Display the graphics palette ( ), and choose the Text Line tool (A).
2. Click where you want your type to appear and type.

Formatting it Use character formats to change the appearance of your text line.

Moving it To select the text line, point on it while holding down Ctrl as you click. You can now microposition it by using Alt plus the arrow keys, or Shift-Alt and the arrow keys. *The text line will not flow along with your text unless you put it in an anchored frame.*

Typing text in an anchored frame

1. Put your insertion point where you want the text to occur.
2. Create an anchored frame at the insertion point. [**Alt s a**] Position and resize it.
3. Either type a text line [**Esc 1 t l**] in the frame, or draw a text column [**Esc 1 t c**] in the frame and type in it.

▲ See “Text lines” on page 68 for more on text lines.

■ Controlling paragraph and page breaks

Keeping paragraphs together

You can force a paragraph to stay either with the previous paragraph or with the next paragraph. This feature is often used in paragraph formats for heads, so that they don't get separated from their following paragraphs. It is also handy for preventing awkward page breaks on a case-by-case basis by keeping groups of paragraphs together.

Making it automatic

When you know that a particular type of paragraph should always be kept with the next or previous paragraph, make Keep With Next ¶ part of that paragraph's format:

1. Display the paragraph format.
2. In the Pagination page of the Paragraph Designer, turn on either Next or Previous.
3. Change other properties if necessary.
4. Click Update All, or create a new format.

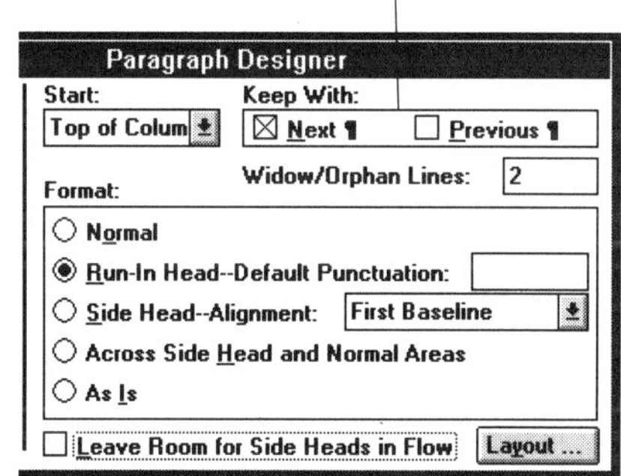

Here's where you control page breaks by keeping paragraphs together.

Keeping paragraphs together on a case-by-case basis

1. Select all but the last of the paragraphs that need to stay together.
2. In the Pagination page of the Paragraph Designer, turn on Keep with Next.
3. Apply to Selection.

Or Select all but the first of the paragraphs that need to stay together, and turn on Keep with Previous.

1 Paragraph one
2 Paragraph two
3 Paragraph three
4 Paragraph four

Select three paragraphs and apply Keep With Next. The four paragraphs are now a unit that cannot be separated by a page break.

Removing "Keeps" You can allow a page break in a group of paragraphs where Keep With has been turned on. Select the paragraphs and turn off both Keep With Next and Keep with Previous. Click Apply to Selection.

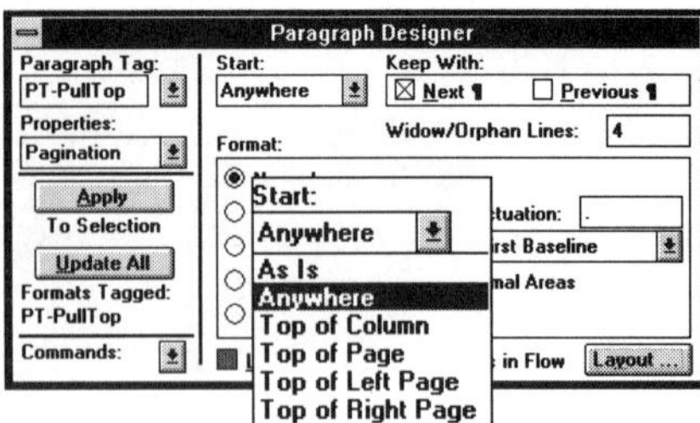

Creating new pages

When you apply one of the Start: Top of Page items from the Paragraph Designer Start pop-up menu to your current paragraph, you create a new page. If this doesn't seem to work, be sure that your text column has Autoconnect turned on. If necessary, use **Format➔Flow** [**Alt o l**] *to turn it on. You may want to turn it on for the master page column as well.*

■ *Another possibility: be sure the paragraph doesn't have Keep With Previous applied to it (page 133).* ▲

Positioning paragraphs where you want them

There are several techniques for placing paragraphs where you want them by creating page and column breaks.

Using the Paragraph Designer

1. Display the Pagination page of the Paragraph Designer. [**Ctrl-m**]
2. Place the insertion point in the paragraph you want to position.
3. Click on the Start pop-up and choose Top of Page, Top of Column, Top of Right Page, or Top of Left Page.
4. **Apply** Click Apply to Selection, Update All, or create a new format.

Using the Format menu

1. Place the insertion point in the paragraph you want to position.
2. Choose **Format➔Page Break**. [**Alt o b**]
3. From the pop-up in the Page Break dialog box, select the position for your paragraph.
4. Click Set.

Note If you tell a line to move to a new page and it doesn't go, then the text column it's in has Autoconnect turned off. Here's what to do:

1. Place the pointer near the border of the frame and Ctrl-click to select it. (Turn Borders on—**Alt v b**—if you can't see the text column.)
2. Choose **Format➔Flow**. [**Alt o l** (*ell*)]
3. Turn on Autoconnect.
4. Click Set.

▲ If you want FrameMaker to add pages automatically, check the text column on the master pages, and make sure that Autoconnect is turned on for those columns, too.

Using an anchored frame

Anchored frames are discussed in Chapter 9. This entry is really just to point you in that direction. You can position an anchored frame anywhere you want it in the column or the margins. You can then put any combination of text and graphics into it. Anchored frames flow along with the text, carrying their contents with them. Think of them as containers. They are a wonderful resource in FrameMaker. (This book is chock-a-block with frames!) I urge you to take at least a quick look at the chapter on frames, so that you have the power and flexibility of this tool available to you.

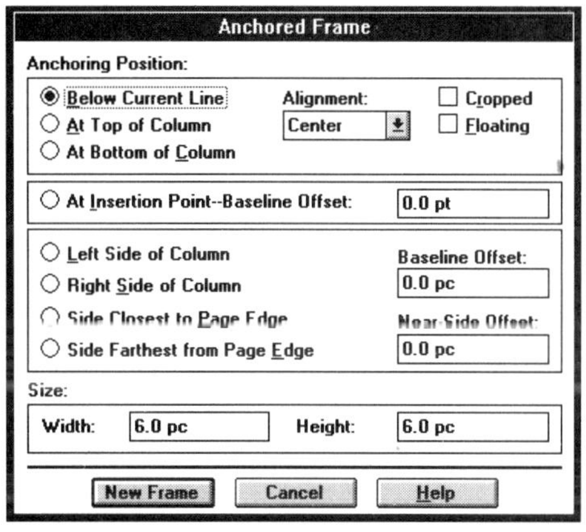

Display this with
Special→Anchored Frame. [Alt s a]

Preventing paragraph fragments (orphans and widows)

It's not very agreeable to see the first line of a paragraph at the bottom of a page by itself, or the last line of a paragraph at the top of a page. These days, both of these things get lumped under the heading of "orphans and widows." You can prevent them. Typically, this would be part of most of your paragraph formats, but you can use it at will as another way to prevent unfortunate page breaks.

I am a paragraph who is just here to provide a context for the poor, lonely line to follow.

I, alas, am an orphan

and I'm a widow.

I, again, am just here to provide context to the example and add to your understanding!

Orphans and widows

▪ The number you type in the Widow/Orphan box is the minimum number of lines at the bottom of a page *and* at the top of a page.

1. Select one or more paragraphs, **or** display the format to change from the Paragraph Tag pop-up in the Paragraph Designer.
2. In the Pagination page of the Paragraph Designer, type a number larger than one in the Widow/Orphan Lines box. Two is a good number.
3. **Apply** Click Apply to Selection, Update All, or create a new format.

Prevent them here.

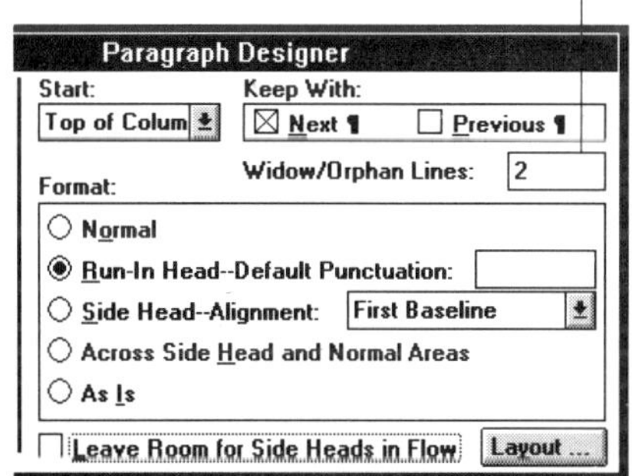

▲ You can prevent a paragraph from being split between two pages by giving it a large widow/orphan number.

■ Side heads

Side heads are a wonderful way to make text easy to read and scan. They're easy to do in FrameMaker 4.

Side head alignment styles

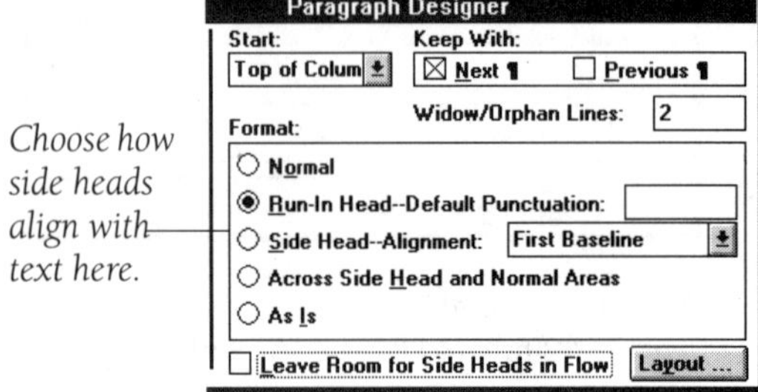

Side head Layout Side choices

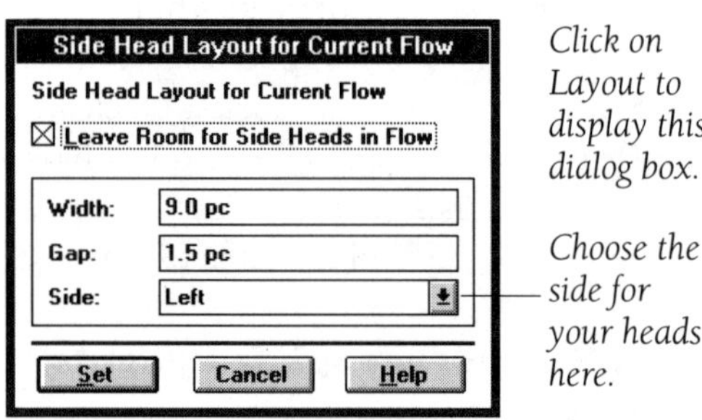

Side Head Top Aligned	*This is the main text column. Side heads are just that—at the side of the text. This is an example of* **First Baseline** *alignment.*
Another Side Head	*This is an example of the* **Last Baseline** *alignment style. Aren't you glad you have a choice?*

2 "You are old, Father William," the young man said. "And your hair has become very white. And yet you incessantly stand on your head. Do you think, at your age, it is right?"—**Top Edge** alignment style.

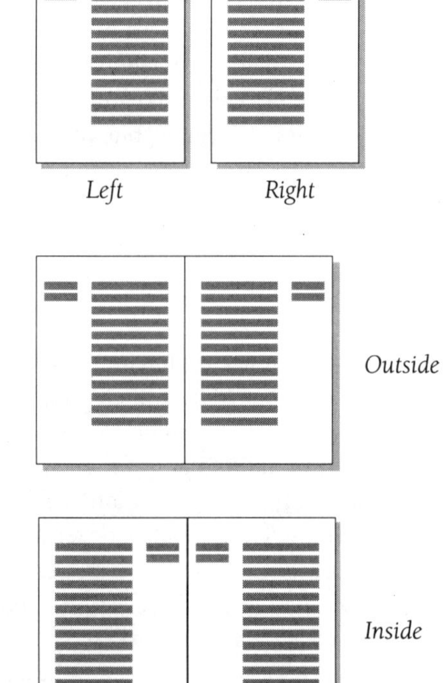

Turning on side heads

1. When you specify your text column widths, make the main text column wide enough to contain the side heads as well as the regular text.
2. Place your insertion point anywhere in the flow. If you are creating a document with several flows, you get to decide for each flow whether it will have side heads.
3. In the Pagination page of the Paragraph Designer, click on the Layout button.
4. **Width** Specify a width for the side head area.
5. **Gap** Specify the distance between the side head area and the normal text area.
6. **Side** Choose whether the side heads will be to the right, left, inside, or outside of the text.
7. Click Leave Room for Side Heads in Flow. Click Set.

▲ That's all. Every "Normal" format in the flow will now automatically leave room for side heads.

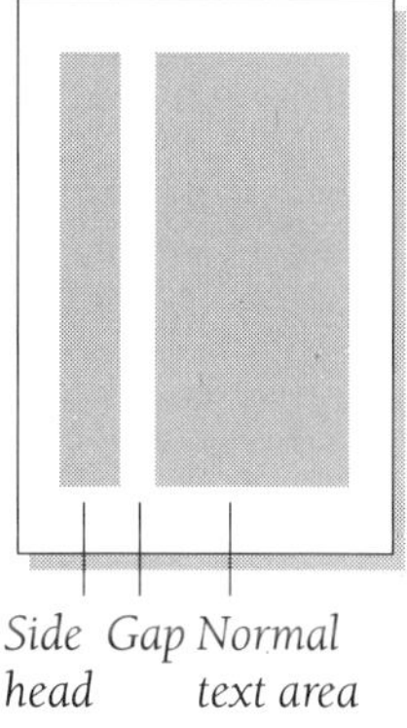

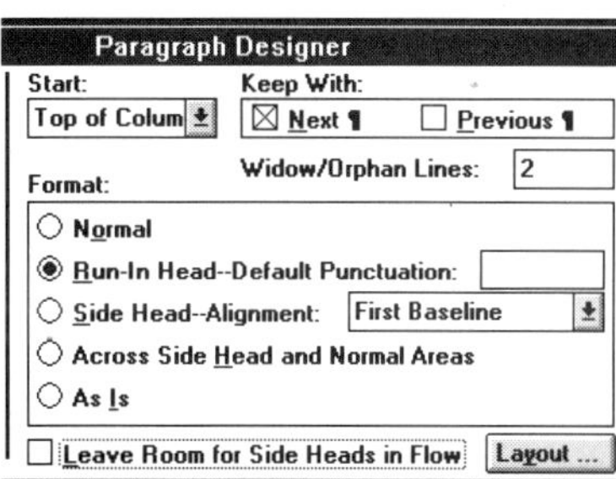

Using side heads

▪ When Side Heads have been turned on by choosing Leave Room for Side Heads in Flow, you define each paragraph format as being Normal (it occurs in the regular text area), Side Head (only in the side head area), or Across Side Head and Normal Area (it fills up both areas).

Alignment When you define a Side Head format, choose an alignment for it. See the illustration on page 136. You can define as many different side heads formats as you please.

Full-width formats Even when you have Leave Room for Side Heads turned on, you can have paragraphs or paragraph formats that ignore the side head area and fill the width of both areas. Display the format, or select the paragraphs, and turn on Across Side Head and Normal Area in the Pagination page of the Paragraph Designer.

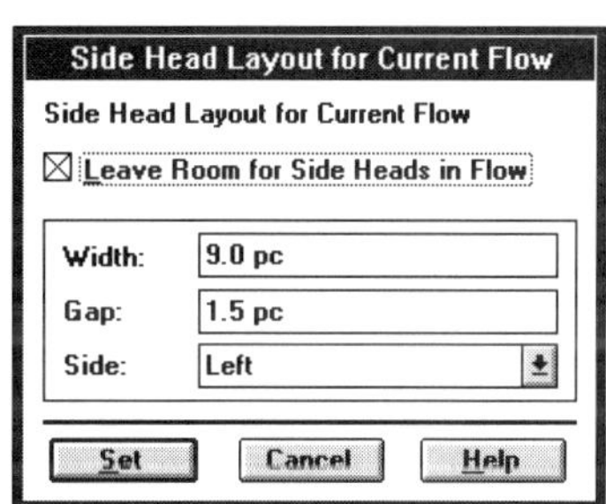

Turning off side heads To eliminate the side head space for the whole flow:

1. Place your insertion point in the flow with the side heads and turn off Leave Room in Flow for Side Heads.
2. Click Apply to Selection.

The side head area disappears, and all paragraph formats are relative to the left side of the text column.

▼

Run-in head—*This type of head "runs into" the rest of the paragraph. It's really a separate paragraph, though, so you can reference it easily.*

▲

■ Run-in heads

You don't have to make a run-in head be a separate paragraph. You have the option of just applying a character format. The disadvantage of that choice is that you can't refer to the run-in head in a table of contents, a list of paragraphs, or a running head or other variable. Here's how to have run-in heads that are separate paragraphs.

1. Display or create the format style that is to have the running head property.
2. In the Pagination page of the Paragraph Designer, turn on the Run-In Head–Default Punctuation radio button.
3. In the accompanying text box, type the characters or spaces that should automatically follow the running head. In the top example on the right, I used an em dash (**\m**).
   • You may have as many characters and spaces as you like, but they must be in the same font as the run-in head.
   • Use the special dialog box codes given on page A-322 for special characters and spaces **or** use the hex codes given in Appendix A.

Put the characters and spaces that should automatically follow your side head here. (You cannot leave this empty. You need at least a space.)

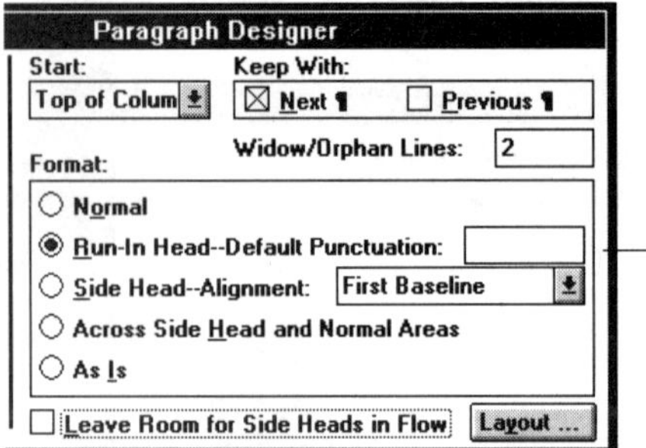

▲ A run-in head trick What if you want a character after the run-in head that's from a different font? Use two run-in heads in a row: one for each font. See the example at the side.

First run-in head *Second run-in head*

Run-in head ▲ *There are two run-in heads in front of this paragraph: one in Futura Extra Bold, and one in Zapf Dingbats. Each one automatically generates the next paragraph format.*

■ Bullets, autotext, and autonumbers

Autonumbering Create formats that automatically number paragraphs. You can autonumber lists, tables, figures, whatever. When you add or delete items in an autonumber series, FrameMaker automatically adjusts all the following numbers in the series! A real time- and tranquility-saver.

Bullets Create formats that automatically put plain or fancy bullets at the beginning of each paragraph—or at the end. Include whatever spacing, tabs, and character formatting you like.

Autotext Create formats that automatically add text to the beginning or end of a paragraph. You can combine the text with autonumber counters, or use it alone.

▼

All the triangles and squares that you see at the beginning of paragraphs in this book are automatically generated using the Autonumber feature. The numbered lists are all autonumbered, too.

▲

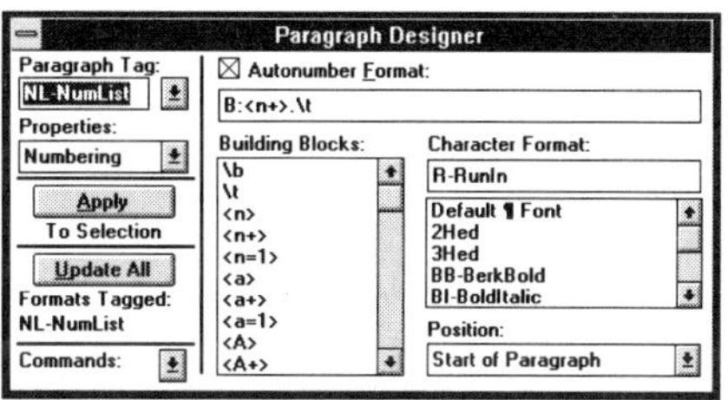

An autotext example

Note *The word "Note" at the beginning of this paragraph is autotext. The Autonumber Format box for this paragraph looks like this:*

Note\sm

The **\sm** *is an em space (page 142). I used a character format to change the font (page 140, steps 1 and 4).*

An autonumber overview

Create autonumbers on the Numbering page of the Paragraph Designer. See the next page for full details.

Put the text, tabs, spaces, and counters that will appear in your autotext in this text box.

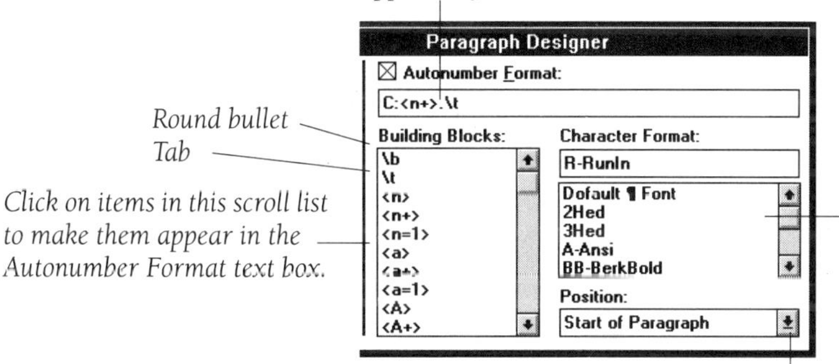

If your autotext needs a different font or size, choose the character format from this scroll list.

Choose whether the autotext is at the beginning or end of the paragraph.

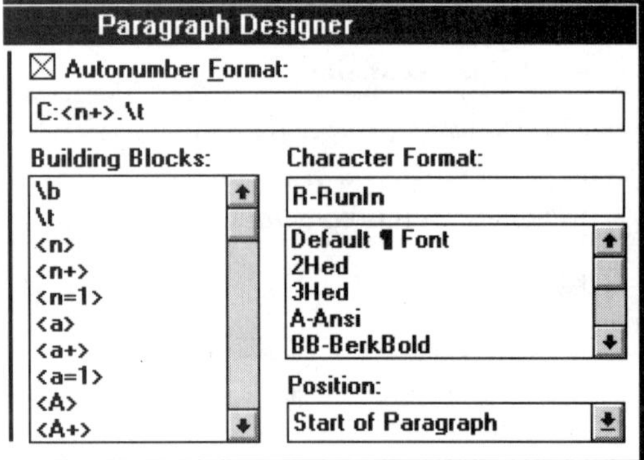

▼

If your autonumbers don't work

Are some of your autonumbers beginning over at one when they should continue a sequence? To be part of a series elsewhere in the flow, an autonumber must be

- *in a connected text column* **or**
- *in a text column in a frame anchored to a connected column.*

Turning Autoconnect won't fix the problem. You must connect the columns by hand. See page 218 for how to connect columns.

To see how your column are connected, put your insertion point in the last line of text in a column and press the down arrow. The insertion point moves to the next connected column.

▲

Creating an autonumber format

(Or automatic bullets, or autotext)

Autonumbers are a property of a paragraph. You add this property to a paragraph format as follows:

1. If you want to use a font other than the default font of the paragraph, or if you want a bullet from a special font, create a character format that gives the right font and font properties (page 111).
2. Display or create the paragraph format that should have the automatic bullet.
3. In the Numbering page of the Paragraph Designer, create the autonumber or autotext. Type the characters, tabs, and spaces in the Autonumber Format text box. Type the codes for counters, or click on building blocks from the scroll list. See "Autonumber building blocks" on page 141.
4. Choose a Character Format from the pop-up list. This format will apply to all the autotext, but not to the paragraph.
5. Choose Start of Paragraph or End of Paragraph from the Position pop-up.
6. **Apply** Click Apply to Selection, Update All, or create a new format.

▼

Position

Text created with the autonumber feature is positioned as follows:

Start of Paragraph Text is flush left on the first baseline of the paragraph. The First indent is observed.

End of Paragraph Text is flush right on the last baseline of the paragraph. The Right indent is observed.

To position text above or below a paragraph, see "Rules and graphics above and below paragraphs" on page 146.

▲

Autonumber building blocks

You can number paragraphs, lists, figures, tables, outlines, and anything else automatically. You use the counters from the Building Blocks scroll list. Combine the counters with text, spaces, and tabs in the Autonumber Format text box.

Use this counter	To get this kind of autonumber	Example
n	Arabic numbers	1 2 3 4
r	Lowercase Roman	i ii iii iv
R	Uppercase Roman	I II III IV
a	Lowercase alphabetic	a b c d
A	Uppercase alphabetic	A B C D

More about counters

In the table below, you can substitute any of the five types of counter for the "n."

Use this form	To accomplish this
<n+>	Increase the number by 1 each time the format is used
<n>	Keep the number the same
<n=1>	Set the number to one, or whatever is typed here. This is used to set number back to one for a new list.
< >	Keep the value the same and don't display it. This is used in multiple-counter numbers.
< =0>	Reset number and don't display it; used in multiple-counter numbers.

Building an autonumber

Type a combination of text, tabs, spaces, and counters into the Autonumber Format text box.

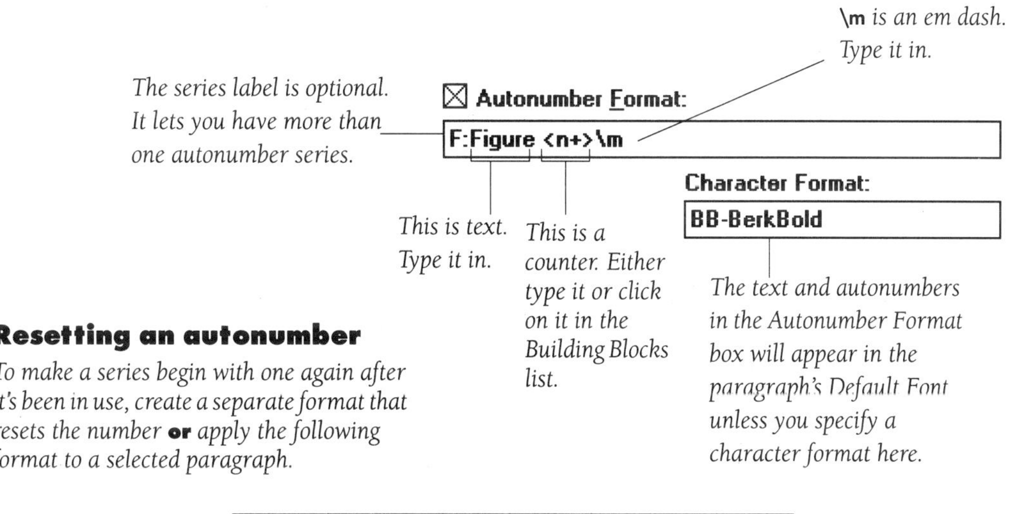

Resetting an autonumber

To make a series begin with one again after it's been in use, create a separate format that resets the number **or** *apply the following format to a selected paragraph.*

F:Figure <n=1>\m

This format resets the numbering to **1**. *It will produce "***Figure 1—** *" every time.*

s is the character you type in Zapf Dingbats to get the triangle. \sn is an en space.

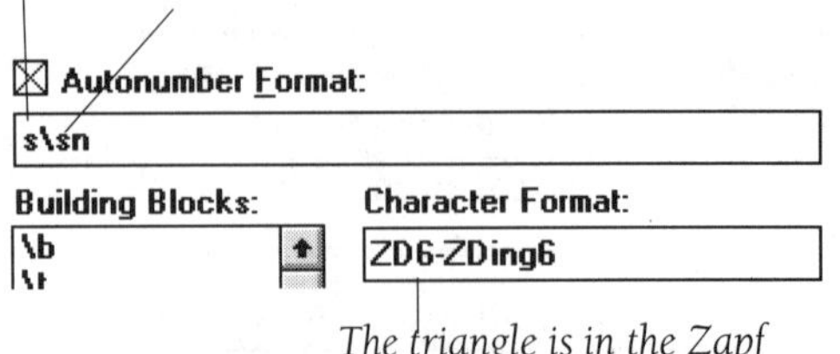

The triangle is in the Zapf Dingbat font, and I want it to be small (6 points).

▲ *Here's the autonumber format for these paragraphs that start with a triangle.*

▼

Special characters in autotext

You can put any character that's available on your system in the Autonumber Format box: use the hex code or the special dialog box code. See Appendix A for a complete listing.

▲

Bullets

▪ A plain round bullet is available in the Building Blocks list. You can have any kind of bullet you want as follows:

To use any character from another font

1. Find the hex number for that character. (The Zapf Dingbats, Wingdings, and Symbol fonts are listed in the back of this book.)
2. Type the hex number, beginning with the backslash, in the Autonumber Format box.
3. Choose a character format from the scroll list that will provide the font and size that you want. (You may need to create one.)

Some useful characters and spaces

Here are some characters and spaces you might want to use in your autonumbers. The bullet and tab are in the Building Blocks list. See Appendix A for a complete listing

Type this	To get this
\b	• bullet
\t	tab (like pressing the tab key)
\m	— em dash
\=	– en dash
\sm	em space
\sn	en space
`` \` ``	left double quote
`` \` ``	right double quote

Series label

A:Figure <n+>:\t

To have more than one series

Series labels What if you want to autonumber your chapters, tables, and your figures, and have some numbered lists besides? How does FrameMaker know which series you're in? *Use a different series label for each series.* The series label is a single letter followed by a colon. Put it at the beginning of the autonumber in the Autonumber Format box.

Multiple counters and outlines

You can use more than one counter in an autonumber. The two most common uses of this feature are outlines and compound autonumbers that include a chapter or part number plus the incremented number.

- In a multi-level autonumber, when a level increments, it sets the levels to the right—the lower levels—to zero. You can prevent this resetting by placing a blank counter, < >, in the position that should not reset.

A chapter, part, or section number

The number of this figure.

Figure 2-3:

The chapter autonumber:

A:Chapter <n+>

The figure autonumber:

A:Figure <n>-<n+>:

The <n> *in position one of series A just picks up the current value of position one in Series A. In this example, that value is created by the Chapter autonumber.*

Creating outlines

Here's an example of formats to create an outline. The indents are created using the Left and First Indent properties.

Format Name	Autonumber format definition
L1-Level1	<R+>.\t
L2-Level2	< ><A+>.\t
L3-Level3	< >< ><n+>.\t
L4-Level4	< >< >< ><a+>)\t

The table on the right shows what happens when you apply the format definitions from the table on the left in the given sequence. The indents are part of the paragraph definitions (specify them on the Basic page of the Paragraph Designer).

Use	Get
L1-Level1	I.
L2-Level2	A.
L3-Level3	1.
L4-Level4	a)
L4-Level4	b)
L3-L2vel3	2.
L2-Level2	B.
L1-Level1	II.
L2-Level2	A.
L3-Level3	1.
L4-Level4	a)

A compound autonumber example

Suppose you want figure and table numbers in your document to include chapter numbers. Furthermore, you have two levels of autonumbered heads that should include the chapter number. The autonumbered heads should not affect the numbering of tables and figures, and vice versa, but all numbering should restart in each chapter. Here's how you do it.

Paragraph format	**Entry in Autonumber Format box**	**Comments**
C-Chapter	A:Chapter <n+>	*A new chapter number resets all the other levels to one.*
F-FigureTitle	A:Figure <n>-<n+>:< >< >< >\t	*The Figure format will not cause table or head numbering to reset because of the < >s to the right.*
T-TableTitle	A:Table <n>< >-<n+>:< >< >\t	*The Table format will not affect figure or head numbering because of the < >s.*
H1-Head1	A:<n>< >< >.<n+>	*H1-Head 1 will not affect table or figure numbering, but it will reset H2-Head2 because there is no < > in the fifth, H2-Head2, position.*
H2-Head2	A:<n>< >< >.<n>.<n+>	*H2-Head2 prints both the chapter number and the H1-Head1 number without changing them (positions 1 and 4) while leaving the figure and title numbers unprinted and unchanged (positions 2 and 3).*

Here's how it works when you use these formats

If you use the paragraph formats defined above in the following sequence, here's what you get. (The two right-hand columns are a continuation of the two left-hand ones.)

Type this	**Get this**	**Type** *(cont.)*	**Get** *(cont.)*
C-Chapter	Chapter 1	C-Chapter	Chapter 2
H1-Head1	1.1	H1-Head1	2.1
H2-Head2	1.1.1	H2-Head2	2.1.1
H2-Head2	1.1.2	H2-Head2	2.1.2
F-FigureTitle	Figure 1-1:	F-FigureTitle	Figure 2-1:
T-TableTitle	Table 1-1:	T-TableTitle	Table 2-1:
T-TableTitle	Table 1-2:	T-TableTitle	Table 2-2:
H1-Head1	1.2	H1-Head1	2.2
H2-Head2	1.2.1	H2-Head2	2.2.1
H2-Head2	1.2.2	H2-Head2	2.2.2
T-TableTitle	Table 1-3:	T-TableTitle	Table 2-3:

■ Word spacing

You can give FrameMaker a minimum, maximum, and optimum word spacing range for each paragraph format. You can change the settings on a case-by-case basis by selecting one or more paragraphs and choosing Apply to Selection.

■ Giving a range of word spacing creates a more pleasant "texture" in body text than keeping the word spacing all one size. FrameMaker's default spacing is a minimum of 90% and a maximum of 110%. I prefer to use a minimum of 60% and a maximum of 150%. It's a matter of taste.

■ You can't change the Standard Space. It's just information about that particular font. Courier, for example, has an enormous standard word space. You can set the Optimum to less than 100%, if you don't need the letters to line up the way they do on a typewriter.

▲ Type in the Minimum, Maximum, and Optimum word space, as a percent of the standard space, and apply your changes (page 110).

Allow Automatic Letter Spacing If you turn this on, FrameMaker can add space between letters as well as between words to make a line fill its space. I keep this turned off. Spacing between letters can look pretty bad. Newspapers use this feature to help them set justified type in narrow columns. (They don't need to look pretty.)

"You are old, Father William," the young man said. "And your hair has become very white. And yet you incessantly stand

Minimum 70%, Maximum 140%, Optimum 100%

"You are old, Father William, the young man said. "And your hair has become very white. And yet you incessantly

Minimum 100%, Maximum 100%, Optimum 100%

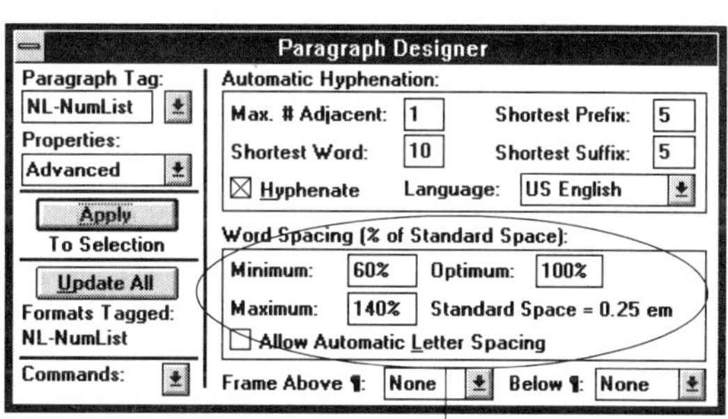

Set word spacing here.

▼

This is an example of a paragraph with a graphic above and below.

▲

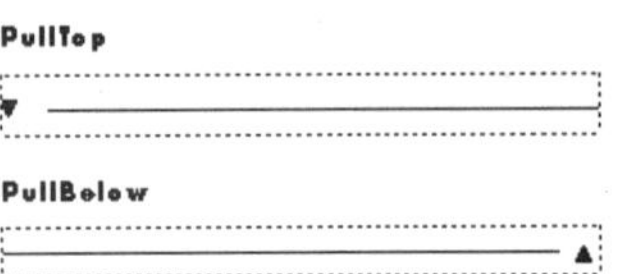

Here are the two named frames on the reference page. I used the Text Line tool to type the triangle from the Zapf Dingbats font, and the Line tool to draw the line.

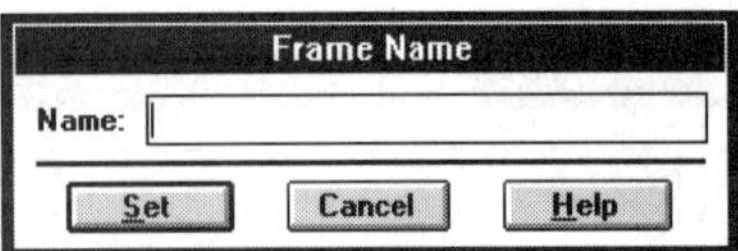

When you draw a frame on a reference page, you automatically get this box, prompting you for a name.

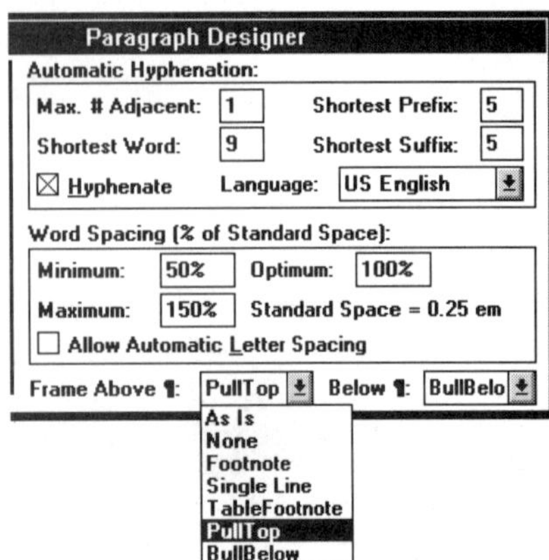

Here's where you add your reference page frames to your paragraph format. (Once you've drawn and named them on the reference page, they appear in this list.)

■ Rules and graphics above and below paragraphs

Autonumbering lets you automatically put characters on the first or last baseline of a paragraph. The Frame Above/Below feature lets you automatically put a frame above or below a paragraph. You can put text or graphics in the frame.

1. Go to a reference page. [**Alt v e**]
2. Draw a frame. [**Esc 1 m**] See Chapter 9 for more on drawing and editing frames.
3. At the prompt, give the frame an identifying name.
4. Choose the Text Line Tool [A] and type the name next to the frame.
5. Put into the frame the material you want to have automatically appear, using one or more of the following methods:
   • Use the graphics palette to draw lines or other objects.
   • Import graphics, just as you would into any other frame.
   • Draw a text column inside the frame and type text into it. [**Esc 1 t c**] Format it using paragraph and character formats.
   • Enter text with the Text Line Tool. Format it using character formats.
6. On the Advanced page of the Paragraph Designer, display the paragraph format to which you are adding the frame.
7. Choose the name of the frame you created on the reference page from the Frame Above or Frame Below pop-up list. You can place a frame in both places if you wish.
8. **Apply** Click Apply to Selection, Update All, or create a new format.

▲ Experiment with the height of the frame and the position of your material in it until it suits you.

■ Reverse type

In FrameMaker, you reverse type by creating white type on a black background. To keep this all together and make it move with the text, put it in an anchored frame (page 195).

Draw the background.

1. Draw a rectangle, a thick line, or any other shape to use as a background. Make it black or any color you like, if you're working with color.
2. Select the Text Line Tool. [**Esc 1 t l**] Select the character format you want (or apply it after you have typed the text).
3. Type your text.
4. Ctrl-click to select the text line as a graphic object. Drag the line halfway onto the background.
5. Apply white, or whatever foreground color you want to the text line, using the Color pop-up on the graphics palette (page 254), or the appropriate Designer (page 128).
6. Finish positioning the type in the background, using the positioning tools available to you in the Graphics menu and the QuickAccess bar. See Chapter 12 for more on editing graphics.

▲ *Optional* Select the background and the text line and Group them to make them a single unit. [**Alt g g**]

luna

Create your text. This is a text line. If you use a text column, be sure the fill is None.

Drag your text halfway over the background. Select it.

Make the text white (or whatever your foreground color is).

▼

Creating reverse type with tables

Set the fill of the table cell to 100% black using either the shading page of the Table Designer (page 247) or the Custom Ruling and Shading dialog box (page 246). Apply a color of White to the type, or use a format with a property of White (page 128).

▲

Position the type on the background.

Cross-References, Footnotes, and Variables

7

■ Cross-references

You can insert a cross-reference in your text that refers either to another spot in the current file, or to a spot in any other FrameMaker file on your system. You can reference the paragraph text, the autonumber of the paragraph, or the file name containing your reference point, as well as the page number.

Choose the document containing your referenced item.

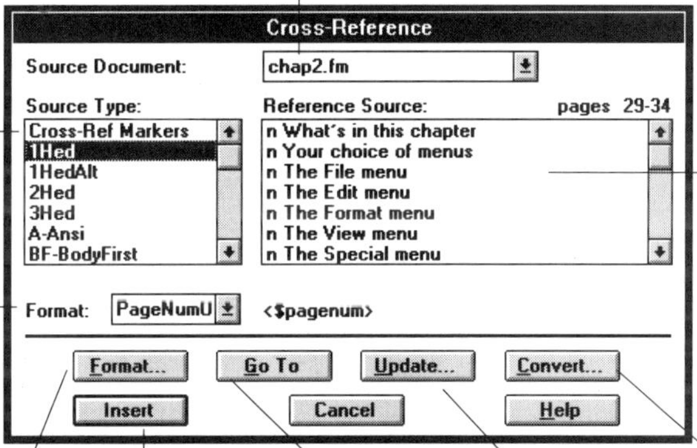

Choose the paragraph tag of your referenced item.

Choose a format (the form and content of your cross-reference).

Cross-Reference

Source Document: chap2.fm

Source Type: Cross-Ref Markers, 1Hed, 1HedAlt, 2Hed, 3Hed, A-Ansi, BF-BodyFirst

Reference Source: pages 29-34
n What's in this chapter
n Your choice of menus
n The File menu
n The Edit menu
n The Format menu
n The View menu
n The Special menu

Format: PageNumU <$pagenum>

Format... Go To Update... Convert...
Insert Cancel Help

This is a list of the first lines of all the occurrences of the tag you picked in the Source Type list in the document you picked from the Source Document list. Click on one to choose it.

Add a format to the Format list, or edit one.

When you have chosen the reference point and format of your cross-reference, click here to insert it.

Go directly to the selected Reference Source.

Make sure that all your cross-references are current.

Convert the selected cross-references to text

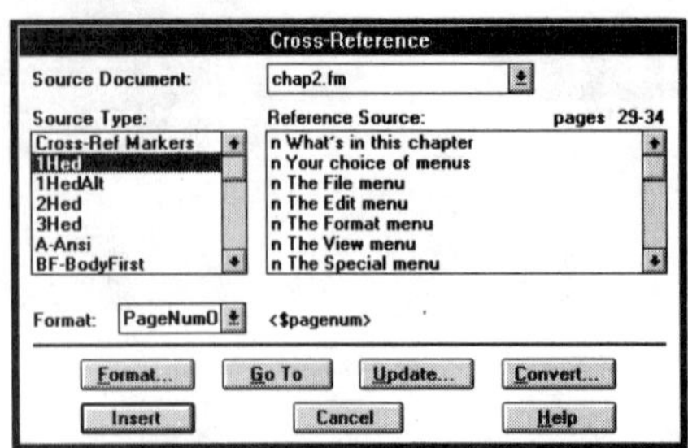

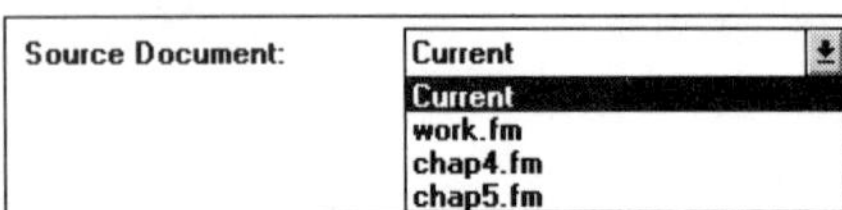

The Source Document contains the paragraph you are referencing.

Choose the format tag of the paragraph you are referencing.

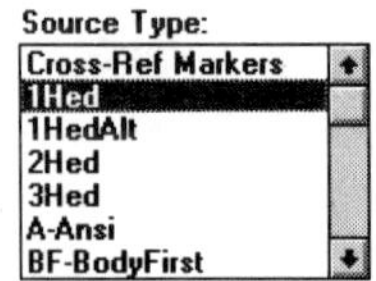

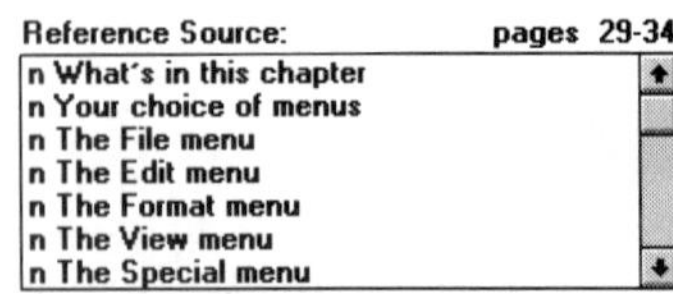

Pick the paragraph to reference.

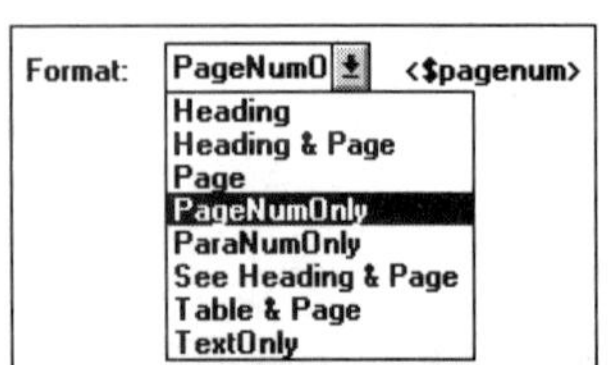

Choose a format that will give your cross-reference the form and content you want.

Inserting a cross-reference

1. In your current document, place your insertion point where you want the cross-reference to appear.
2. If you are referencing something in a document other than the current one, open that document. It is the “source document.”
3. Choose **Special→Cross-Reference** to display the Cross-Reference dialog box. [**Alt s c**]
4. **From the Source Document pop-up**, select the document—the Source Document—that contains the point you are referencing. If you are referencing a point in the current document, leave this set to Current.
5. **From the Source Type list**, choose the paragraph format of the item you are referencing. All paragraph format tags that occur in the Source Document are listed.
6. **In the Reference Source list**, you see all the occurrences of the Source Type paragraph format in the document you selected as the Source Document. Select the item you want to reference.
7. **In the Format list**, choose a format for your cross-reference. You can choose to see the page number, the text, or the paragraph number of the referenced item. You can make other choices as well. The list contains the formats that are defined for the current document. To the right of the list Frame-Maker displays the definition of the currently displayed format.
   • See Chapter 5 for an explanation of formats.
8. Click Insert. The reference that you identified using Source Document, Source Type, and Reference Source is displayed at the insertion point in the form that you specified with Format.

Cross-reference formats

The format determines the appearance and content of the cross-reference. FrameMaker gives you a number of building blocks. You combine these building blocks with character formats and text to create exactly the kind of cross-reference you want. Then you give it a name and Add it to the cross-reference catalog.

The Edit Cross-Reference Format dialog box

This is the format name that was selected when you clicked Edit. You can edit this format, or type a new name in here to create a new one.

If you want to edit an existing format, choose it from this list.

If you typed a new name in the Name box, click Add to add your new format to the catalog.

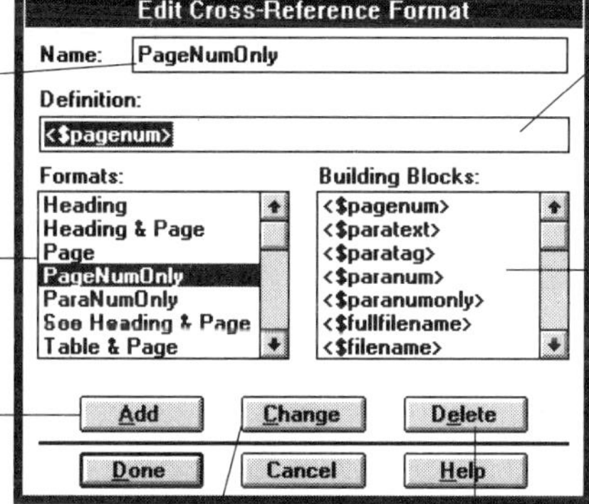

Type a combination of text, building blocks and character formats in here to define a format.

With your insertion point in the Definition box, click on any items you need from this list. Your whole catalog of character formats is at the bottom of the list.

If you are editing an existing format, click Change when you have completed your changes in the Definition box.

Click Delete to remove the displayed format name from the format catalog.

Creating or editing a cross-reference format

1. In the Cross-Reference dialog box, click Format.
2. In the Edit Cross-Reference Format dialog box, click on the name of the format you want to edit in the Format list, if it is not already displayed in the Name box.

   ▲ **Or** if you want to create a new format, replace the name in the Name box with a new name.

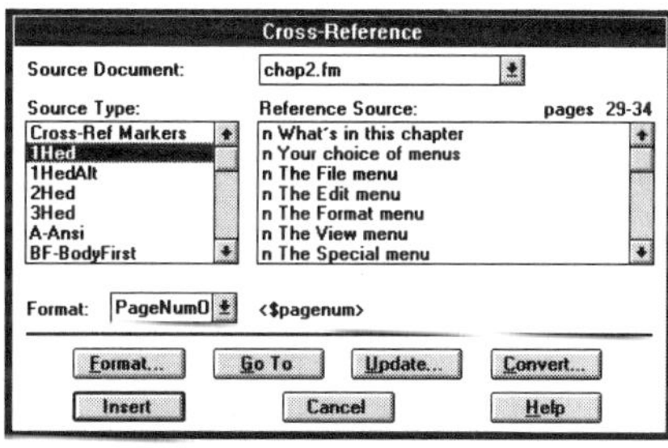

Click Format to display the Edit Cross-Reference Format dialog box.

3. Click in the Definition box to get an insertion point. Now you can type text, edit text, and insert or delete building blocks.

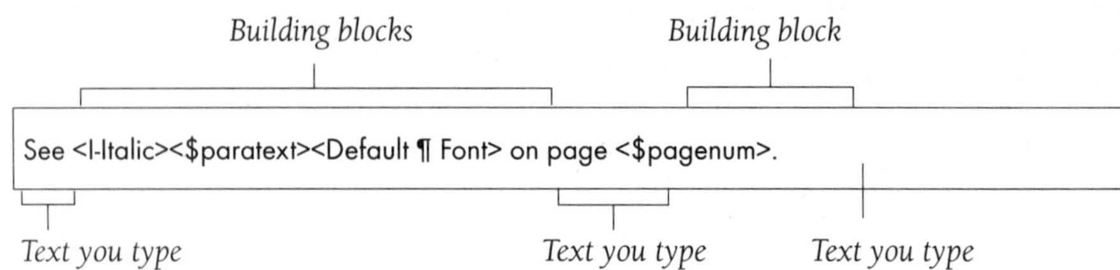

This would produce a cross-reference of the form See *Raising Rabbits* on page 144.

▲ **Insert a building block** by clicking on the item you want in the Building Blocks scroll list. Your whole character format catalog is available at the end of the list. The item you click appears at the insertion point in the Definition box.

The cross-reference building blocks

Here are the functional pieces—the building blocks—FrameMaker gives you to play with:

Building block	**Description**
<$pagenum>	The page number of your referenced item.
<$paratext>	The text of your referenced paragraph.
<$paratag>	The paragraph format tag name of your referenced paragraph.
<$paranum>	The autonumber of your referenced paragraph, including text typed in the Autonumber Format box for that format.
<$paranumonly>	Just the autonumber of your referenced paragraph, no additional text.
<$fullfilename>	The file name of the source document, including the path.
<$filename>	Just the file name of the source document, no path.
<$pagenum[paratag]> <$paratext[paratag]> <$paratag[paratag]> <$paranum[paratag]> <$paranumonly[paratag]>	When you include a paragraph tag in square brackets, FrameMaker looks backwards until it finds a paragraph with the format named in the square brackets, and then gives you the information you request—page number, paragraph text, paragraph tag, or autonumber—*for that paragraph* in your cross-reference.
Character format tags	Your whole catalog of character formats is at the bottom of the list.

▲ **Add character formats** to the format definition by clicking on them in the Building Block list. A format will affect text in your cross-reference until you insert another format, such as Default ¶ Format, from the list.

4. When your changes are complete, click Add if you are adding a new format, or Change if you are editing an existing one. You can create or change as many formats as you wish.
5. When you have made all of your changes, click Done.
6. The Cross-Reference dialog box reappears. You can now insert or replace a cross-reference using your new formats.

Building Blocks:

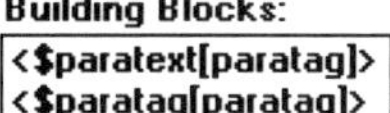
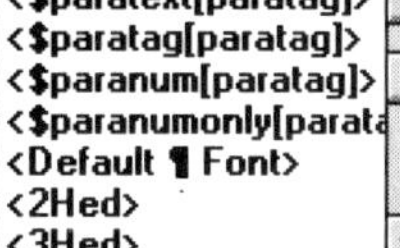

Choose a building block or a character format from the Building Blocks scroll list.

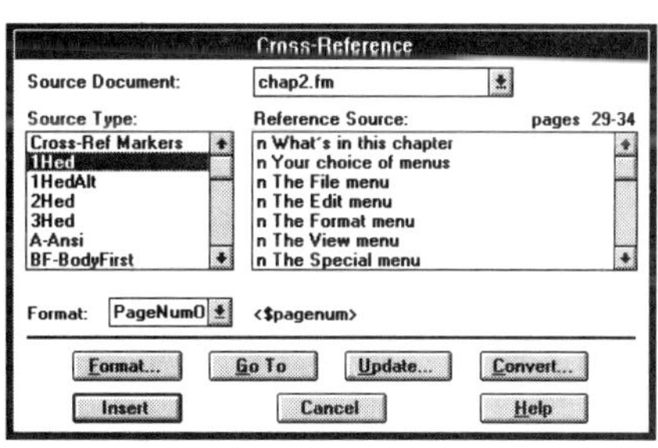

Adding a character from a symbol font

1. If you don't have one already, make a character format that calls the font you need (Zapf Dingbats, Symbol, or Wingdings, for example). There is an example of how to create such a format on page 79.
2. In the format definition text box, position the insertion point where you want the character. Click on the appropriate character format from the Building Blocks list.
3. Type the hex code for the character. See Appendix A for a list of hex codes.
4. If you want to return to regular text in the cross-reference, click on Default ¶ Font in the Building Blocks list. If the character is the last thing in the cross-reference, you don't have to change back to Default ¶ Font after it.

<Z-ZapfDing>s<Default ¶ Font>

*This produces this symbol, ▲, and returns to the default paragraph font. (**s** is the access character for ▲ in the Zapf Dingbats font.)*

Cross-references

Cross-reference samples

This definition	Gives you this cross-reference
page <$pagenum>	page 42
Chapter <$paranum>, \`<$paratext>\'	Chapter 6, "Design and Typography"
Chapter <$paranum>, <I-Italic><$paratext>	Chapter 6, *Design and Typography*
See \`<$paratext>\' on page <$pagenum> of <I-Italic><$paratext[T-Title]><Default ¶ Font>.	See "Units of Measurement" on page 107 of *Design and Typography.*

Updating cross-references

As you edit text, cross-references can become out of date. You can make sure that all cross-references are current and correct by Updating.

1. Display the Cross-Reference dialog box: double-click on any cross-reference, or choose **Special→Cross-References**. [Alt s c]
2. Click on Update. FrameMaker displays the Update Cross-References dialog box.
3. Choose whether you want to update references to the current document, all open documents, or all documents.
4. Click Update. FrameMaker updates the specified cross-references and then displays the Cross-References dialog box when it's finished. If there are unresolved cross-references, it displays the Unresolved Cross-References dialog box instead.

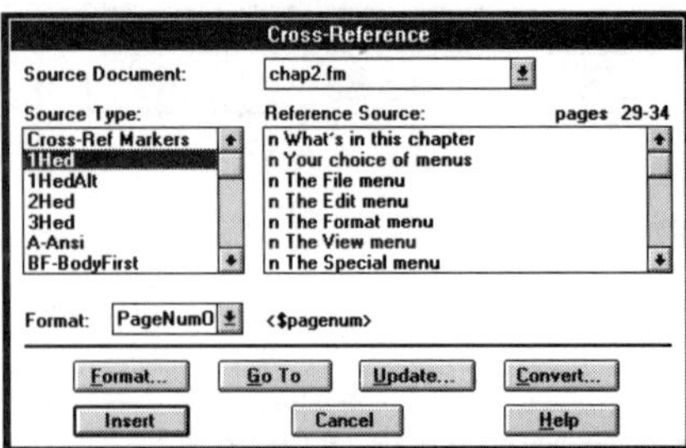

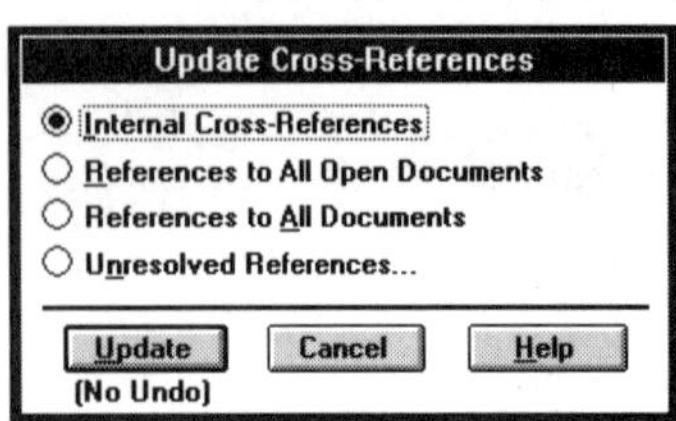

If you choose References to All Open Documents, the update process goes faster if you open all the files first. Better still, put all the files in a book, and Generate/Update the book.

Put the files in a book If you have several related files that reference each other, the easiest way to keep all the cross-references current is to put the files together in a FrameMaker book. You can Generate/Update the book to keep all cross-references current. See Chapter 13, "Books."

Unresolved cross-references

When you choose a source point for a cross-reference, FrameMaker places a cross-reference marker at that point. If you accidentally delete the marker in the course of editing, cross-references referring to that point are *unresolved*. Similarly, if you move or rename the source document containing the marker, you create unresolved cross-references.

If FrameMaker finds unresolved cross-references when you Update cross-references, it displays the Update Unresolved Cross-References dialog box.

Click on the old file name here.

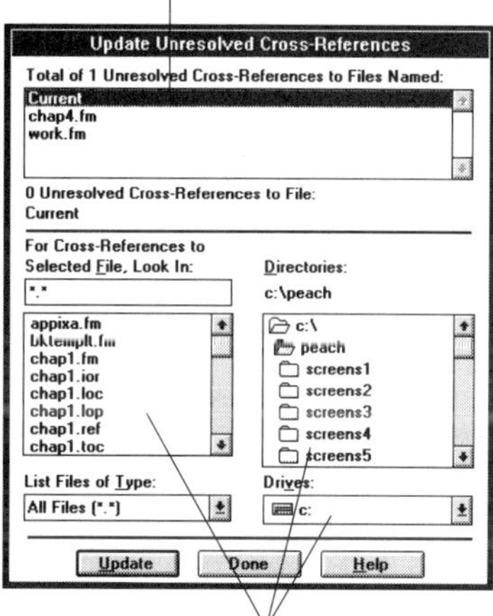

Choose the new drive, directory, and file name here.

If the source document has been renamed or removed

1. In the top list of the Update Unresolved Cross-References dialog box, click the original name of the file.
2. Choose the new drive, directory, and file name from the areas at the bottom of the dialog box.
3. Click Update.

If the source marker has accidentally been deleted

This is the most common kind of cross-reference problem. It's easy to delete a marker by accident as you edit text.

1. Display the Find window. [**Ctrl-f**]
2. From the Find pop-up, choose Unresolved Cross-Reference (page 172).
3. Click Find. FrameMaker highlights the first unresolved cross-reference it finds.
4. Double-click on the cross-reference to bring up the Cross-Reference dialog box.
5. Enter the new source point, just as you would to create a new cross-reference (page 150).
6. Click Replace.
7. Return to the Find window, and Find the next unresolved cross-reference. Continue until you have fixed them all.

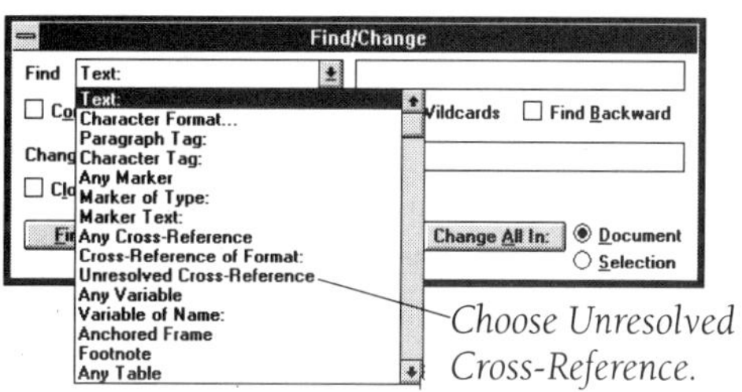

Choose Unresolved Cross-Reference.

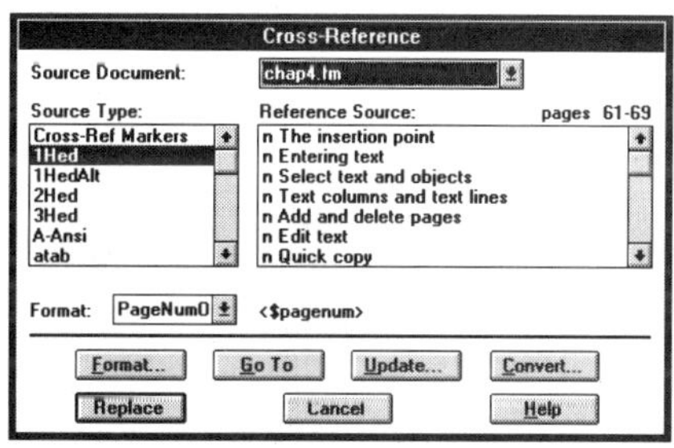

Note *When you copy and paste text that includes cross-reference markers, the markers are not copied with the text.*

Double-click on a cross-reference in text, or choose one here.

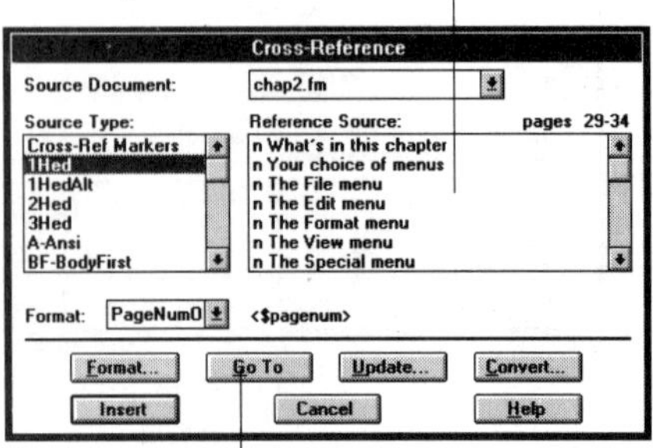

Click Go To to go directly to the source of the reference. If it is in an unopened document, FrameMaker asks you if it's okay to open the document.

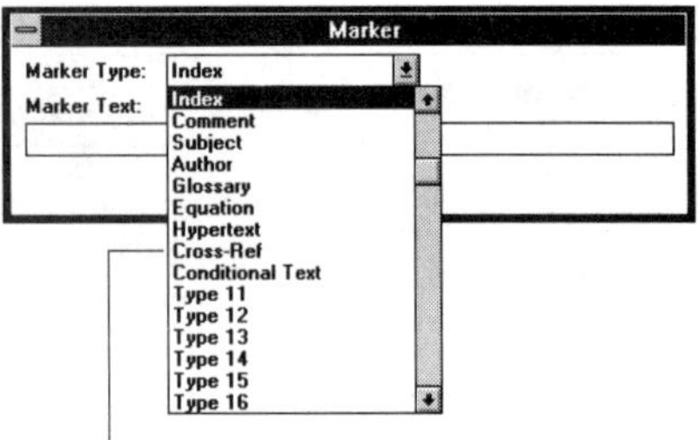

Choose Cross-Ref from the Marker Type list.

Choose Cross-Ref Markers to refer to a marker.

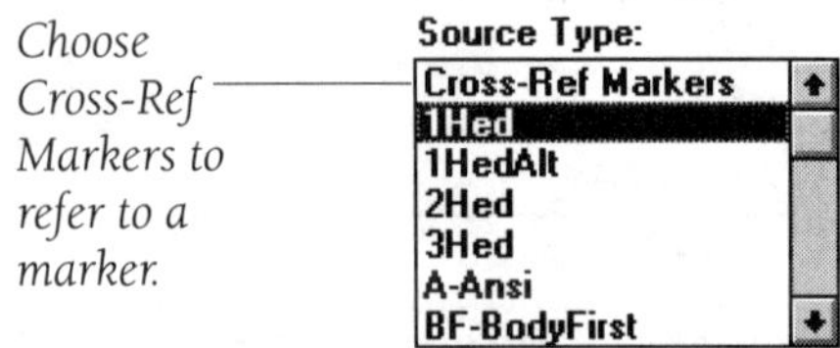

Deleting a cross-reference

1. Single-click on the cross-reference to select it.
2. Press Delete. FrameMaker deletes the cross-reference and its source marker.

Going to a cross-reference source

You can go directly to the source of a cross-reference with incredible ease.

1. Double-click on the cross-reference. FrameMaker displays the Cross-Reference dialog box.
2. Click on Go To.

Referring to a marker

When you choose a paragraph format as the source type, FrameMaker always refers to the page on which the paragraph *begins*. If you want to refer to a point later in a paragraph and have the page reference be correct even if the paragraph breaks across a page, you can place a Cross-Ref Marker at the right spot in the paragraph, and then refer to it by choosing Cross-Ref Marker as the Source Type. Here's how:

1. Place your insertion point at the exact point that you're referencing, and display the Marker dialog box: **Special→Marker** or **Alt s m**.
2. Choose Cross-Ref from the Marker Type pop-up.
3. Type some identifying text into the Marker Text box.
4. Click New Marker.
5. Place your insertion point where you want the cross-reference. Create the cross-reference as usual, but choose Cross-Ref Markers as the Source Type. You can refer to the page number of the marker, or the number or text of the surrounding paragraph, but you cannot refer to the marker text itself.

Converting a cross-reference to text

You can turn all or some of your cross-references into regular text.

1. If you want to convert the cross-references in a range of text, select that range. Otherwise, place your insertion point anywhere in the document.
2. Display the Cross-Reference dialog box [**Alt s c**], and click on Convert.
3. In the Convert Cross-References to Text dialog box, choose which cross-references to convert.
4. Click Convert.

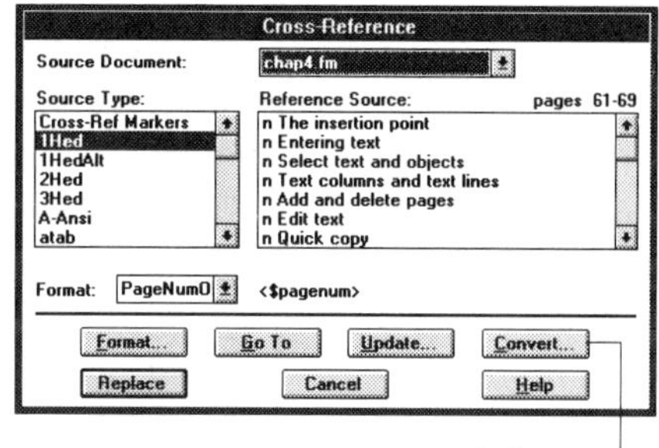

Click Convert.

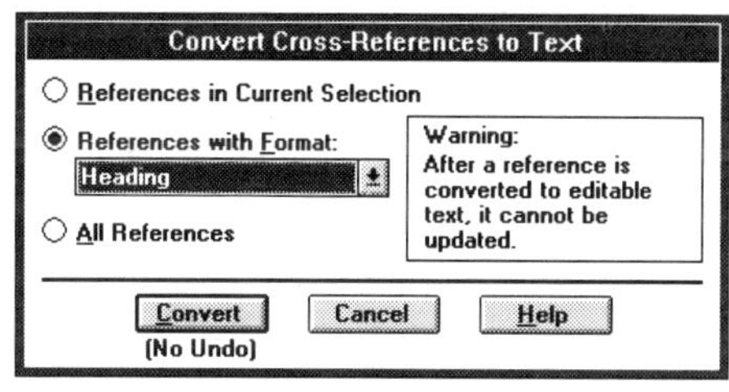

Choose what to convert and then click Convert.

■ Footnotes

Inserting a footnote

1. Place your insertion point at the place in the text where you want the footnote callout.
2. Choose **Special→Footnote**. [**Alt s f**] The footnote entry appears at the bottom of the page with your insertion point in position.
3. Type the text of the footnote. When you are finished, either click in the text where you want to resume working, or choose **Special→Footnote** again.

'Twas brillig and the
slithy[1] toves
Did gyre and gimble
in the wabe.[2] — *Callout*
All mimsy were the
borogroves
And the mome raths
outgrabe.

——————— — *Separator*

1. Lithe and slimy.
2. The grassy plot around a sundial.

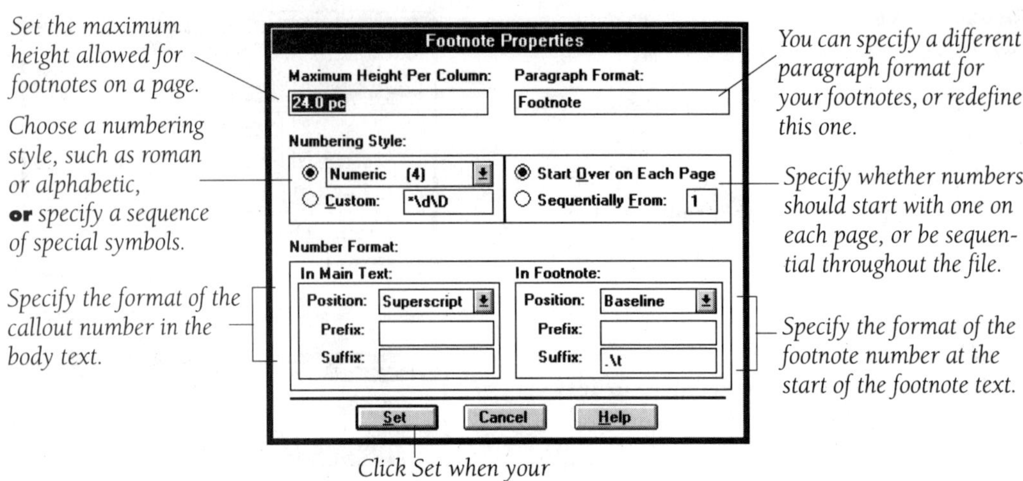

Formatting footnotes

FrameMaker allows two types of footnotes: text and table. You format each type separately.

1. To change the properties of text footnotes, place your insertion point in a text column. To format table footnotes, click in a table first. Display the Footnote Properties or Table Footnote Properties dialog box by choosing **Format→Footnote Properties.** [**Alt o o**] Make your settings and changes.
2. Click Set.

The footnote paragraph style

Every FrameMaker document has a Footnote format and a TableFootnote format in the paragraph catalog. Their properties probably don't quite match the style of your document, so feel free to change them if you want to. You can also type a different paragraph format tag name in the Paragraph Format box of the Footnote Properties dialog box (above).

Maximum Height Per Column

If the height of the footnotes plus the separator exceed the amount in this text box, FrameMaker moves the footnotes that don't fit to the bottom of the next column. You can change this number.

Numbering style

You can choose a style, such as numeric, roman, or alphabetic from the Numbering style pop-up. Or you can specify a sequence of symbols in the Custom text box.

You can pick a style from the pop-up or type a symbol sequence in the Custom text box.

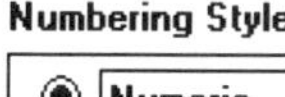

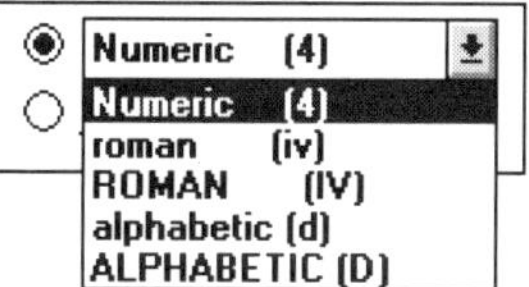

▲ For symbols, you must use either the Dialog Box code or the hex code. The symbol must be in the regular character set. There is no way to change fonts. There is a list of dialog box codes on page A-322.

▲ If you specify several characters, FrameMaker uses them in the order you specify, and then starts over again, using an additional symbol if there are more footnotes on the same page. In the example on the side, the sequence would be

*   †   ‡   **   ††   ... and so on.

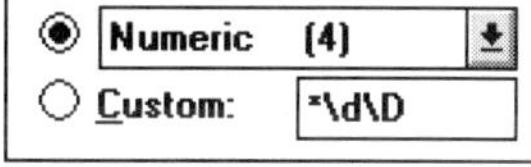

\d is a dagger and \D is a double dagger.

Numbering sequence

If you choose Start Over on Each Page, the footnotes for each page will begin with number one (or I, i, A, or a). If you choose Sequentially From, FrameMaker maintains a single sequence throughout the file. You can specify the first number of the sequence.

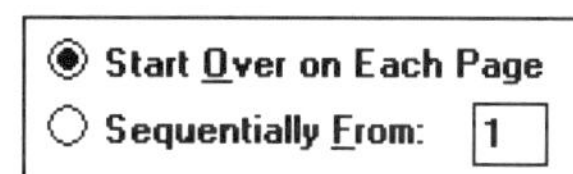

Number format

You can choose whether the number will be superscript, subscript, or baseline, both for the callout number in the body text, and for the footnote number itself. You can also specify whether any text or spacing accompanies the number, either before it (Prefix) or after it (Suffix). Use Dialog Box codes (page A-322) or hex numbers (page A-323). In the example, the footnote number is followed by a period and a tab.

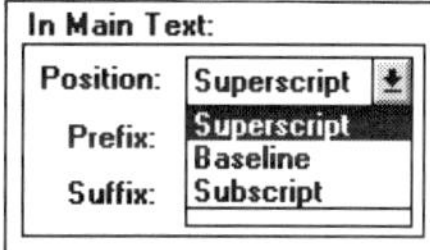

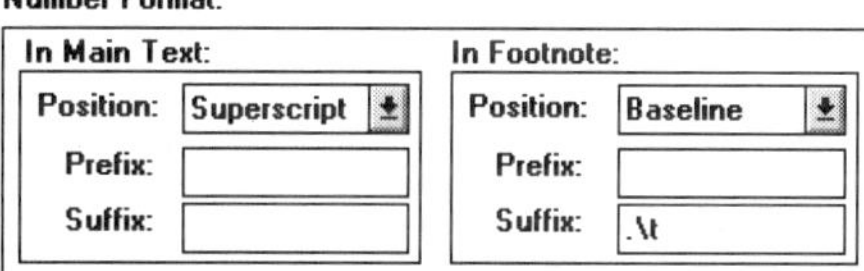

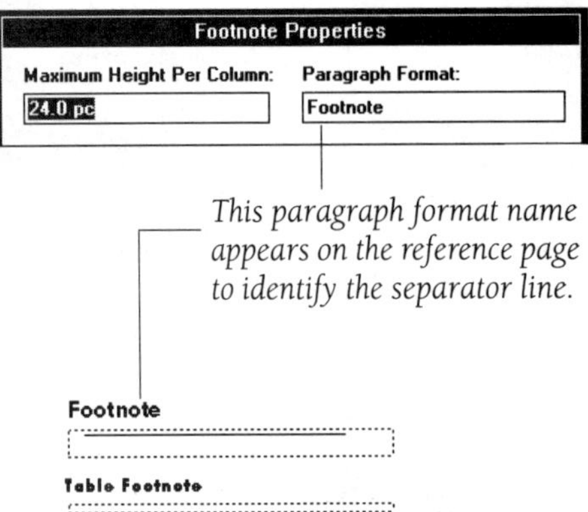

This paragraph format name appears on the reference page to identify the separator line.

On the reference page: the reference frames for footnotes and table footnotes. You can adjust the size of the frame, the size and thickness of the line itself, and the position of the line in the frame. You can put different text or graphics in the frame, as well.

The footnote separator

You can change the little line that separates the footnotes from the text. The line is stored on a reference page in a frame that has the same name as the Paragraph Format given in the Footnote Properties dialog box.

1. Display the reference page containing the Footnote frame. [**Alt v e**]
2. If you are using the Footnote paragraph format for your footnotes (see "The footnote paragraph style" on page 158), work with the Footnote reference frame.

   ▲ If you have specified a different paragraph format for your footnotes, you must either rename the Footnote frame to match your footnote paragraph format tag or create a new frame with a matching name. See "Frames on reference pages" on page 204.
3. You can resize the frame to adjust the distance between the footnotes and the text. You can reposition the line within the frame to adjust the position of the separator relative to the main text and the footnote text. Or you can put a different graphic or text in the frame. You can also delete the frame entirely.
4. When you have made your changes, return to the body pages. [**Alt v d**] Your changes are in effect. You do not need to add the frame as a Frame Above to the footnote paragraph definition.

▼

If you delete the Footnote frame from the reference page, you no longer have a separator, but you can adjust the space between the footnote and the text by specifying Space: Above for the footnote paragraph format (Basic page of the Paragraph Designer).

▲

Deleting or changing a footnote

To delete, copy, or move a footnote

1. Select the callout number in the main text.
2. Choose copy [**Ctrl-c**] or cut [**Ctrl-x**]. To delete, you can just press the Delete key.
3. To paste the footnote, place your insertion point in the body text where you want the new footnote and paste. [**Ctrl-v**]

▲ FrameMaker automatically renumbers your footnotes within the file when you copy, move, or delete them.

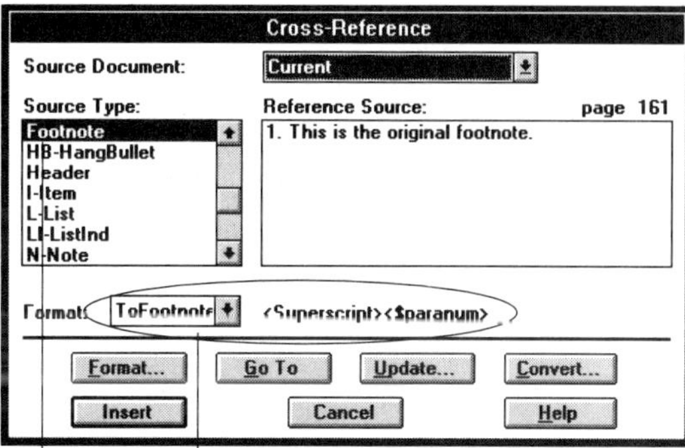

Refer to the paragraph format of your footnotes.

This format applies a character format named Superscript to the footnote number. (This assumes that your footnote callouts in text are superscript also.)

Additional references to a footnote

If you need to refer to the same footnote more than once, create the first reference as a normal footnote. Use cross-references to refer to the footnote after that. A footnote is autonumbered, so in your cross reference, refer to the <$paranum> of the footnote. In order to make the cross-reference numbers look like the footnote numbers in text, create a cross-reference format that matches your text footnote look.

Endnotes

1. Create an autonumbered paragraph format for your endnotes. Use the format to create the "look" you want for them.
2. Type your endnotes at the end of your file just as you would type any text. Use the autonumbered endnote format.
3. In your main text, place the insertion point where you want the first endnote reference.
4. Insert a cross-reference to the first endnote (page 150). [**Alt** s c] Refer to the <$paranum> of the note. Use or create a cross-reference format that produces a number in the format you want.
5. Continue the sequence—type the note in the endnote format, and then cross-reference it in text.

▲ This procedure is identical to "Additional references to a footnote," above, except that you refer to your endnote instead of a footnote.

Definition:

<Superscript><$paranum>

This is a cross-reference format you might use to refer to an endnote. It assumes that you want the callout to be superscript and that you have a character format named Superscript.

■ Variables

FrameMaker offers you two kinds of variables: user variables and system variables.

■ A **user variable** is user-defined. You can define a complex text sequence, complete with character formats, and then give it an easy-to-type name. Any often-used word or phrase that includes font changes or special characters is a good candidate to be a user variable.

■ A **system variable** picks up information such as date, time, filename, or page number from your system and inserts it into your document. System variables are provided by FrameMaker. You cannot create, delete or rename these variables, but you *can* redefine them.

User variables *provide an easy way to insert complex sequences, as well as an easy way to update elements that may change. When you change the definition of a user variable, FrameMaker automatically changes all the occurrences of that variable.*

Inserting a variable

The official way

This way you can see all your choices.

1. Position the insertion point where you want the variable to occur.
2. Display the Variable dialog box:
   Special→Variable or **Alt s v**.
3. Click on the variable you want to insert. Use the scroll bar or down arrow key to display the user variables at the bottom of the list.
4. Click Insert.

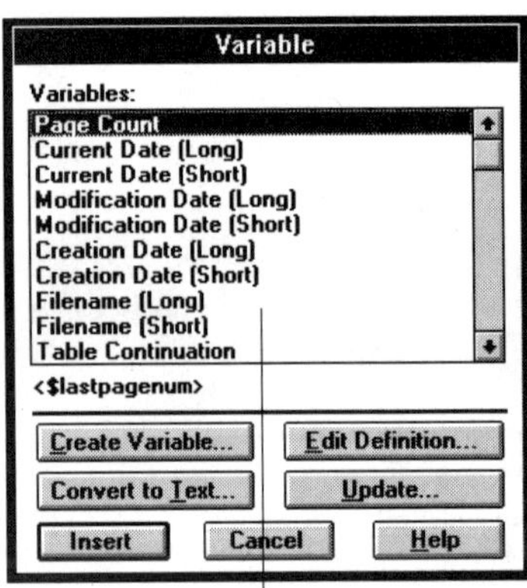

Your user variables are at the bottom of the list. You have to scroll to see them.

The quick and easy way

Look, Ma! No mouse!

1. Position the insertion point where you want the variable to occur.
2. Press **Ctrl-0** (*zero*) and begin typing the variable name. Look in the status bar; when the variable name you want appears, press Enter. You can also use the up and down arrow keys to scroll through the variable list, rather than typing the name.

V:Page Count

Variables from the keyboard *The Status bar in the lower left-hand corner of your document window shows what variable will be inserted if you press Enter.*

▲ You can insert most variables on either a body page or a master page. There are a few that can be used only on master pages. See "Using variables on master pages" on page 166.

Updating variables

FrameMaker automatically updates variables that are on master pages. You must update variables on body pages in order to keep system variables such as date and page count current. It's easy. Here's how:

1. Click anywhere in a text column to get an insertion point.
2. Display the Variable dialog box. [**Alt s v**]
3. Click Update. FrameMaker displays the "Okay to Update...?" box. Click OK.

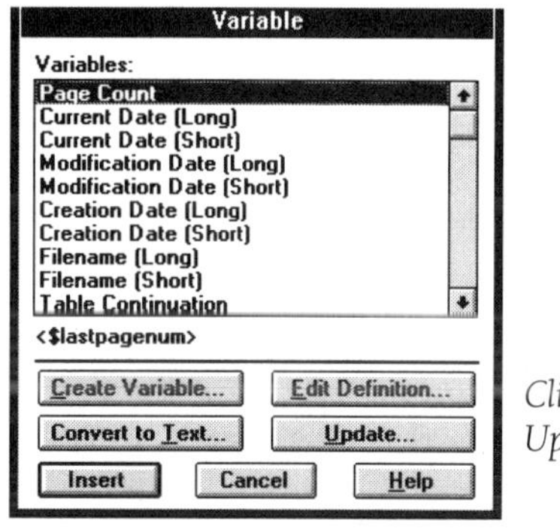

Click on Update.

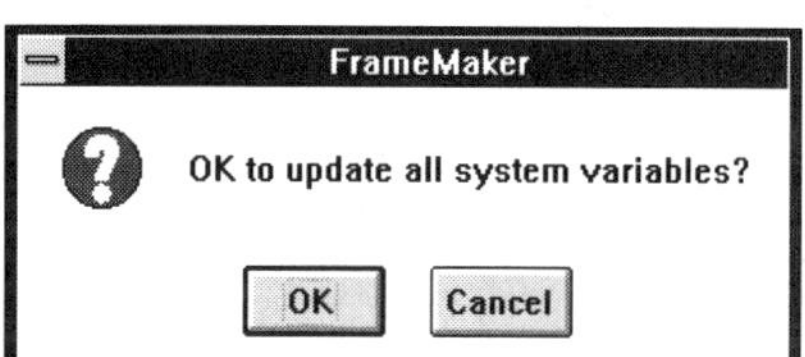

▲ Whenever you change the definition of a variable, FrameMaker automatically updates all variables on both master pages and body pages.

Copying, moving, and deleting variables

1. Click once on the variable to select it.

   ▲ If you don't see the variable you want, use Find. Choose Any Variable or Variable of Type from the Find list. Type the name in the text box and click Find. FrameMaker finds the variable and selects it. You can now move, delete, or copy the variable.
2. Copy it [**Ctrl-c**] or cut it [**Ctrl-x**]. To delete a selected variable, you can just press Delete.
3. To paste a variable, position your insertion point and choose **Edit→Paste**. [**Ctrl-v**]

Replacing a variable

1. Double-click on the variable you want to replace to display the Variable dialog box.
2. Choose the replacement variable from the scroll list.
3. Click on Replace.

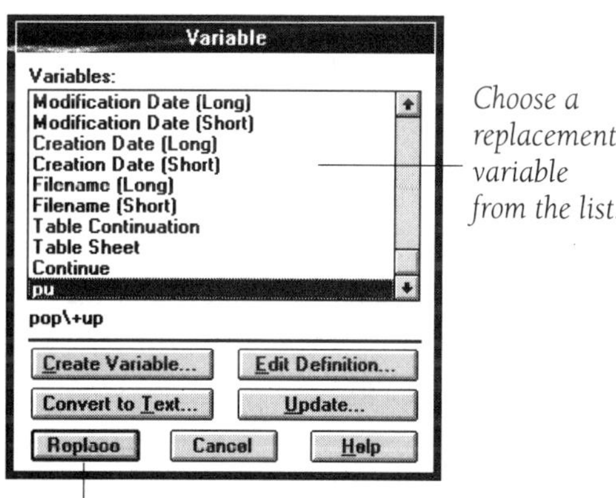

Choose a replacement variable from the list.

Click Replace.

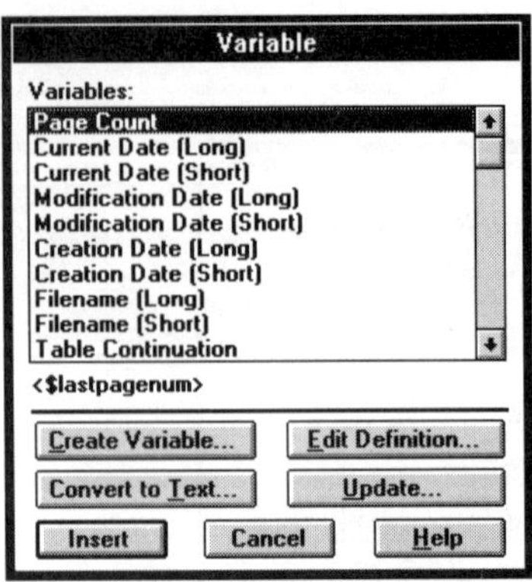

Choose a variable from the list and click Edit Definition **or** *click Create Variable.*

To edit or create a user variable

Give it a name and type in a definition.

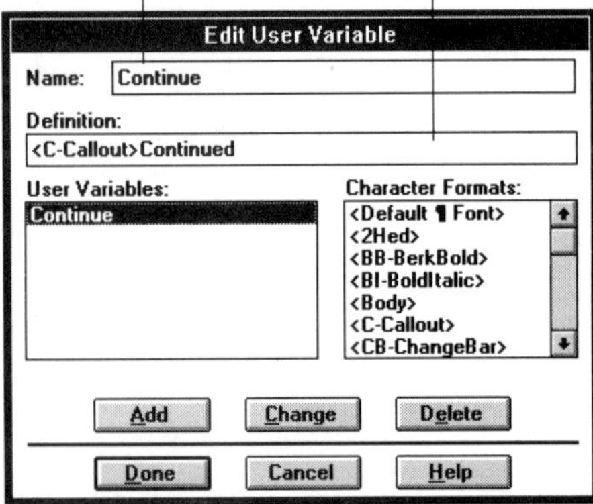

Click Add or Change. Your character formats are all available as building blocks.

To edit a system variable

Edit the definition of the variable here.

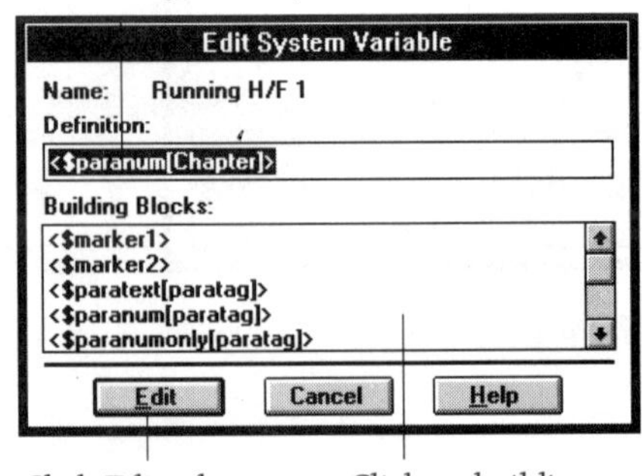

Click Edit when you're finished. *Click on building blocks in this list.*

Defining or editing a variable definition

1. Double-click on a variable to display the Variable dialog box, or choose **Special→Variable**. [Alt s v]
2. If you are editing an existing variable, click on the one you want to edit in the Variables scroll list if it is not already highlighted.
3. Click Edit Definition to edit either a user variable or a system variable. **Or** click Create Variable to create a new user variable. (You cannot create a new system variable, you can only redefine the ones you've got.)
4. In the Definition text box, add and delete text and building blocks.

   ▲ **To insert a building block**, position your insertion point in the Definition text box and click on the building block in the scroll list.

   ▲ **You get different building blocks** depending on which type of variable you're editing. User variables provide only the character formats as building blocks. System variables provide blocks that are appropriate to the type of variable.

   ▲ Your **character formats** are available as building blocks for all types of variables. For system variables, they are at the bottom of the list. Use Default ¶ Font to return to your regular font after changing formats within the variable definition.

   ▲ To use "<" or ">" as text characters, precede the character with a backslash.

   ▲ **For special characters**, use either the Dialog Box codes or the hex codes (Appendix A).
5. Click Edit or Create. The Variable box reappears. You can insert a variable, create or edit other variables, or click Done.

System variables

System variables are used to display information such as date, page number, or file name. They can also pick up the text or autonumber from a specified paragraph format. Here are the system variables you have available with their default definitions.

You can edit these

FrameMaker provides useful default definitions so that you don't have to edit them, but you are perfectly free to change them to suit yourself. This is particularly true of **Running H/F 1** *through* **4**, *that you use to reference text in your headers and footers.*

Variable	Default definition	Example
Page Count	<$lastpagenum>	224
Current Date (Long)	<$monthname> <$daynum>, <$year>	July 14, 1994
Current Date (Short)	<$monthnum>/<$daynum>/<$shortyear>	7/14/94
Modification Date (Long)	<$monthname <$daynum>, <$year> <$hour>:<$minute00> <$ampm>	July 14, 1994 10:24 am
Modification Date (Short)	<$monthnum>/<$daynum>/<$shortyear>	7/14/94
Creation Date (Long)	<$monthname <$daynum>, <$year>	July 14, 1994
Creation Date (Short)	<$monthnum>/<$daynum>/<$shortyear>	7/14/94
Filename (Long)	<$fullfilename>	c:\peach\work.fm
Filename (Short)	<$filename>	work.fm
Table Continuation	(Continued)	(Continued)
Table Sheet	(Sheet <$tblsheetnum> of <$tblsheetcount>)	(Sheet 6 of 8)
System variables available only on master pages		
Current Page #	<$curpagenum>	134
Running H/F 1	<$paratext[Title]>	FrameMaker 4 for Windows
Running H/F 2	<$paratext[Heading1]>	Design and Typography
Running H/F 3	<$Marker1>*	List of Variables
Running H/F 4	<$Marker2>*	Examples

**Although the default definition of Running H/F 3 and 4 is <$marker1> and <$marker2>, you can redefine them to pick up paragraph text, just as Running H/F 1 and 2 do. <$Marker1> displays the contents of a marker named "Header/Footer $1." <$Marker2> displays the contents of the Header/Footer $2 marker. This mechanism lets you use markers to provide header and footer contents that don't appear otherwise on the body pages.*

An empty header or footer column *Most FrameMaker master pages have columns for headers and footers already provided. If a master page column has no flow assigned it is a Background Text column. To check a column, select it (Ctrl-click) and press* **Alt o l** *(oh ell).*

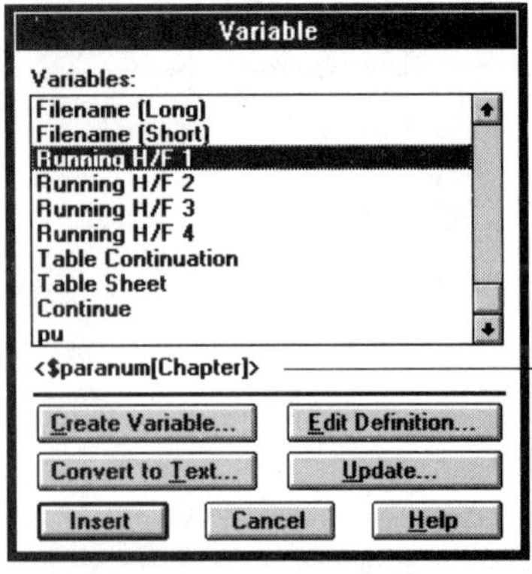

The definition of the highlighted variable appears here.

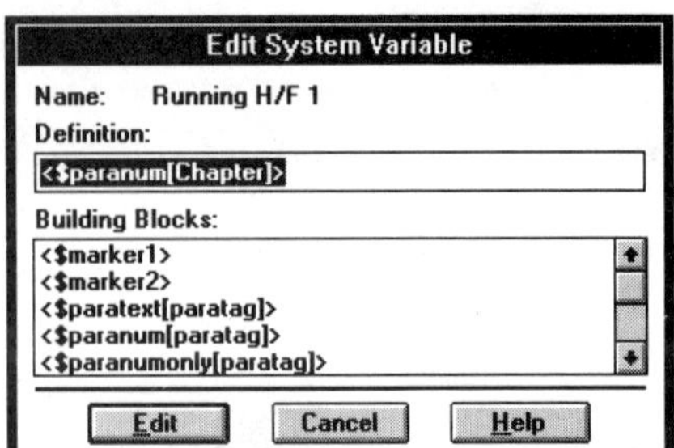

Using variables on master pages

- You can use any of the user or system variables on master pages. There are five system variables that are available *only* on master pages: Running H/F 1 through Running H/F 4, and Current Page #.
- Use Current Page # for numbering pages.
- Use Running H/F 1 through 4 to display the contents, tags, or autonumbers of selected text paragraphs. Common examples are displaying a document title, chapter title, or first-level head.

Using the Running H/F variables

1. On a master page, position your insertion point in a Background Text column where you want the variable.
2. Choose **Special→Variable**. [**Alt s v**]
3. In the Variable dialog box, choose one of the four Running H/F variables from the Variables list.
4. Click on Edit Definition.
5. To display the text of a paragraph, use the <$paratext[paratag]> building block. Replace "paratag" with the tag of the paragraph type whose text you wish to display. See "The Running H/F building blocks" on the next page for more options.
6. Include text and character formats to create the text and appearance you want. See "Defining or editing a variable definition" on page 164.
7. When the definition is complete, click Edit.
8. In the Variable dialog box, click Insert or Replace. (The button will say "Replace" if you have something selected. This is how you change a variable.)
9. Add other text and variables to the Background Text column and apply paragraph and character formats to create the appearance you want.

The Running H/F building blocks

Use any of the four Running H/F variables to display the text or autonumber of one or more chosen paragraph tags. Edit the definition of the variable, replacing "paratag" with your chosen paragraph tag names.

How they work On a body page that uses the master page you're creating, FrameMaker looks for the first occurrence of one of the tags in the square brackets. It then displays the text, the autonumber text, or the autonumber only of the found paragraph. If it doesn't find a matching paragraph tag on the current page, it looks backwards in the file until it finds a paragraph with a tag in the list. The text or autonumber of the found paragraph is then displayed on the current body page in the location and format specified by the variable on the master page.

Sample definition for Running H/F variables

<$paratext[T-Title,A-Appendix]>

This defintion would display the text of the first occurrence of a paragraph with either the T-Title paragraph tag, or the A-Appendix tag. If neither paragraph tag occurs on the current body page, FrameMaker looks backwards towards the front of the file until it finds an occurrence of one, and displays that text on the current page.

Variable definition	**Sample display**	**Explanation**
<$paratext[1Head]	Getting Started	Displays the text of a paragraph that has the tag **1Head**.
<$paranum[Section]>	Section 2	Displays the entire contents of the Autonumber Format text box of the appropriate paragraph that has the tag **Section**.
<$paranumonly[Section]>	2	Displays only the autonumber of the appropriate paragraph that has the tag **Section**.
<$paratext[T-Title, A-,Append]>	Character Sets	Displays the text of the first paragraph on the page that has either format tag; looks backward if necessary.
<$paratext[+,1Head]	A Final Word	Putting a plus and a comma before the tag name tells FrameMaker to refer to the *last* occurrence on the page instead of the first. This lets you create dictionary-style headers and footers.
<$paratag[Section]>	Section	I confess, it's not clear to me why anyone wants to display a paragraph tag.

Putting it all together

To show you all the parts of the system variables process, here are two examples from this book: the left-hand page header, which displays the chapter number, and the thumb tab, which displays the first-level heads.

The header on the master page for left-hand pages in this book

The background text column for the header looks like this:

Chapter Running H/F 1

Text. System variable.

I apply a paragraph format named Header to the header. It provides the 12-point Futura Light formatting.

This is the definition of Running H/F 1. *It picks up the autonumber from the most recent occurrence of a paragraph with a* C-ChapNum *tag.*

<$paranum[C-ChapNum]>

The chapter number for each chapter has a paragraph tag of C-ChapNum. *The Autonumber Format text box on the Pagination page of the* C-ChapNum *format looks like this: (<$paranum> can only pick up a value from an autonumbered paragraph.)*

☐ Autonumber Format

<n+>

And finally, this is the result of it all in Chapter 5:

Chapter 5

The thumb tab

Before I rotate it, the thumb tab looks like this on the master page.

Running H/F 3

A gray rectangle.

A background text column with the variable in it. A paragraph tag named Thumb has been applied to provide the right appearance.

This is the definition of Running H/F 3. *It picks up the paragraph text from the most recent occurrence of a paragraph with a* 1Head *tag.*

<$paratext[1Head]>

▼

This "last occurrence" option is necessary when you're creating a dictionary or glossary. Use this syntax to display the last item on the page in the running header or footer.

▲

Displaying the last occurrence of a tag

When you use a system variable that has the <$paratext[*paratag*]> syntax in a master page Background Text column, you display the text of the first *paratag* paragraph on the body page. To display the last occurrence of a paragraph format on a page, use this syntax: <$paratext[+,*paratag*]>.

Compound page numbers

Here's an example of how to create a compound page number that includes a chapter, part, or section number. In this example, the page number is in the footer and includes the chapter number. The chapter titles have an autonumbered format named C-ChapNum.

Text in the footer Background Text column on the master page:

Running H/F 1-#	*The hyphen is text that you type (because you want a hyphen in the page number). The pound sign is what you see on the master page when you insert the* Current Page # *variable.*
Definition of Running H/F 1	
<$paranum[C-ChapNum]>	*The first element in your page number will be the chapter number. The chapters are autonumbered, and FrameMaker will automatically include the current number—thanks to the* $paranum.
Definition of # (Current Page #)	
<$curpagenum>	*The final element is the current page number. Place your insertion point in the Background Text column where you're building the compound page number. Right after the* Running H/F 1 *variable and the hyphen, insert the variable* Current Page #.
Formatting	*Apply paragraph or character formatting to the assembled pieces on the master page to create the look you want.*
The result	
4-25	*A sample page number (page 25 of Chapter 4).*

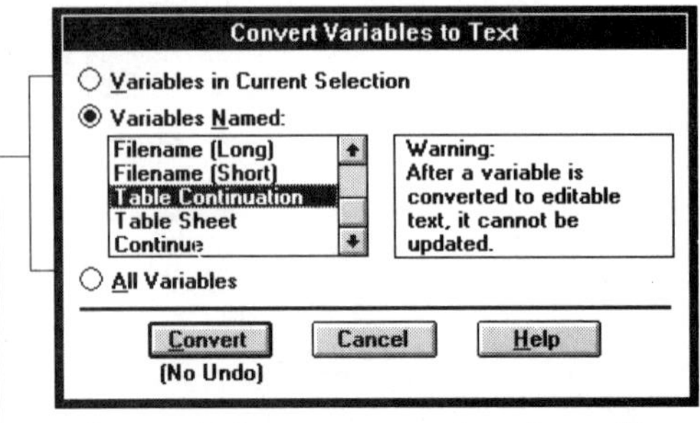

Choose whether to convert selected variables, a specific type of variable, or all variables.

Converting variables to text

If you're converting a FrameMaker file to another application, you might want to convert the variables and cross-references to text first. Most filters don't catch these.

1. If you are converting a single variable, or those in a range of text, select the variable or the range of text. If you are converting all variables, or variables of a certain type, click anywhere in your text.
2. Display the Variable dialog box: double click on a variable or choose **Special→Variable**. [**Alt s v**]
3. Click on Convert to Text. In the Convert Variables to Text dialog box, click a radio button to specify which variables to convert.
4. Click Convert.

Importing variable definitions

When you have defined some variables in a document (or someone else has), you can use those definitions in other documents. You don't have to repeat the work of defining them.

To import variable definitions from another document into your current document:

1. Open the document from which you are importing the variable definitions.
2. Place your insertion point in the document where you want the variable defintions.
3. Choose **File→Import→Formats**. [**Alt f i o**]
4. Turn on Variable Definitions and turn off all the other options (unless you intend to import other items as well).
5. Turn off Manual Page Breaks and Other Format/Layout Overrides, so that they are not removed.
6. Click Import.

Import Formats
Import from Document: work3.fm
Import and Update:
Paragraph Formats
Character Formats
Page Layouts
Table Formats
Color Definitions
Reference Pages
Variable Definitions
Cross-Reference Formats
Conditional Text Settings
Math Definitions
While Updating, Remove:
Manual Page Breaks
Other Format/Layout Overrides
Import
(No Undo)
Cancel
Help

Be aware
Format definitions in the source document overwrite definitions in your current document. when the format has the same name in both documents.

More Useful Tools

8

Finding and changing

FrameMaker lets you search for text and for many other elements. There is a complete list of what you can search for in the next section, "What you can look for" on page 173.

What's in this chapter? *Finding and changing, spell-checking, using the Thesaurus, the run-down on change bars, freezing pagination, and comparing two documents.*

Your Find/Change options

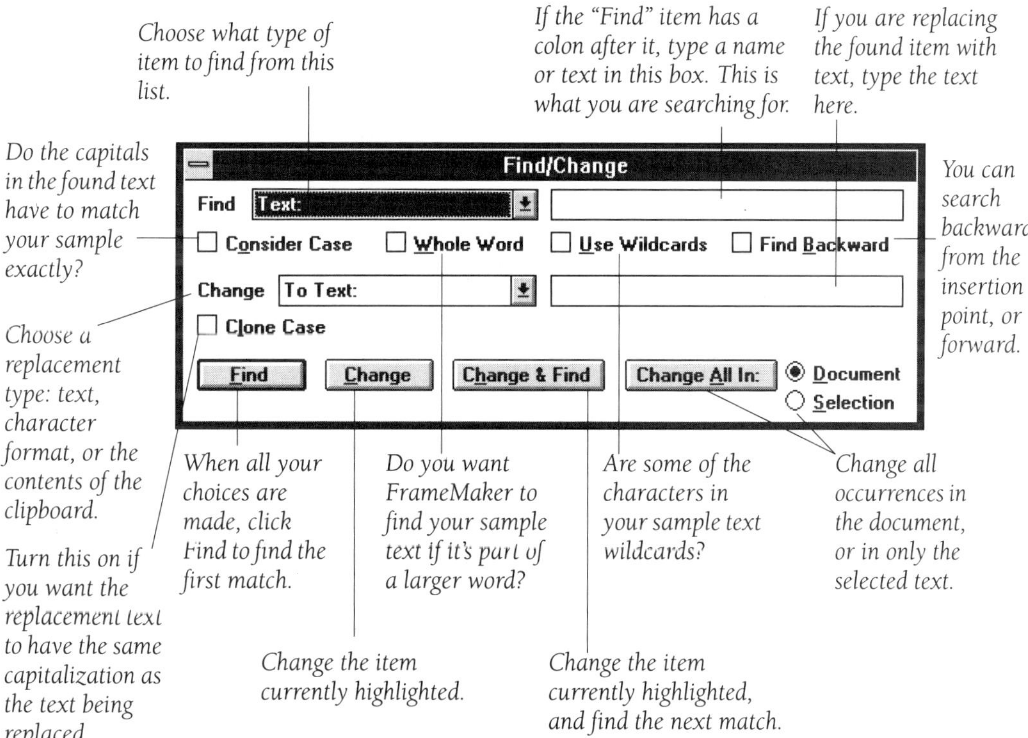

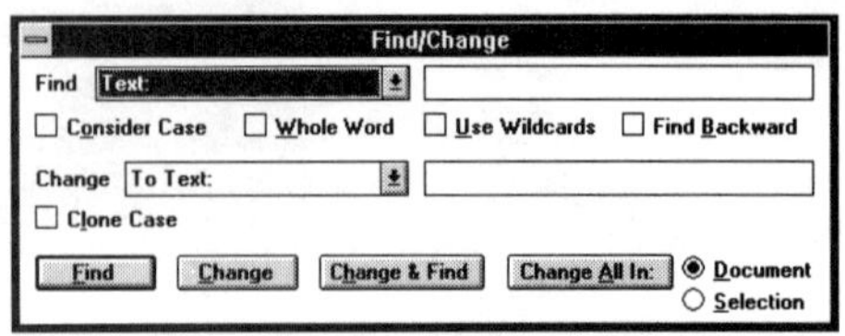

The basics of finding and changing

Here's the overview on finding and changing in FrameMaker.

1. Click in text to place your insertion point where you want the search to begin.
2. To display the Find/Change window, choose **Edit→Find/Change**. [**Ctrl-f**]
3. From the Find pop-up list, select the type of item you want to find.
4. If the item you choose in the Find list has a colon after it, you must type a name or text in the box to the right of the Find list.

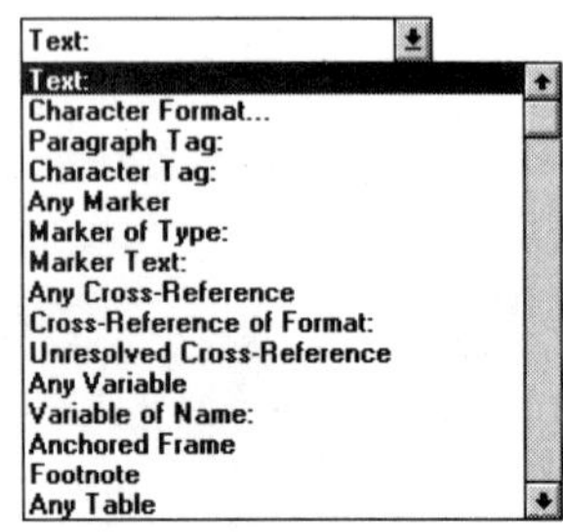

Choose the type of item you want to find from the Find pop-up list.

Find | Variable of Name: | PartName

5. If you are going to change what you find, choose the type of replacement from the Change pop-up list.
6. If your replacement is text, type the text in the box to right of the Change list.

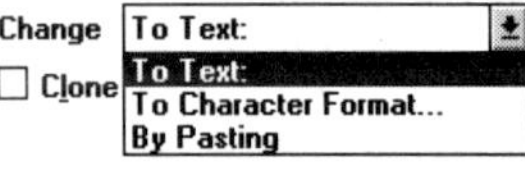

You can replace the items that you find with text, or with the contents of the clipboard (By Pasting). You can also apply a character format to the item.

Change | To Text: | NewText

7. Look over your other options. They are described in "Your Find/Change options" on page 171 and discussed on the next few pages.

8. When you have made all your choices, click Find. FrameMaker highlights the first occurrence of the item.
9. If you want to replace the highlighted item with whatever you specified in the Change box, click Change. Or click Change & Find to make the change and then automatically find the next item.

To search master pages or reference pages Place your insertion point on a master page or reference page before beginning the search.

What you can look for

Look at the pop-up Find list to see the amazing list of choices for what you can Find.

Type of item	Comments
Text:	Type the text you want to find in the box to the right.
Character format...	Displays a dialog box in which you specify the text properties to find.
Paragraph Tag:	Type the paragraph tag name you want to find in the box to the right.
Character Tag:	Type the character tag name you want to find in the box to the right.
Any Marker	To see the type and contents of the marker you find, look in the Marker window. [Alt s m]
Marker of Type:	Find occurrences of a particular type of marker.
Marker Text:	You can use wildcards to specify the text. To change marker text, use the Marker window (page 292), not the Find/Change window.
Any Cross-Reference	To go to the source of a cross-reference, double-click on it, and then click Go To in the Cross-Reference dialog box.
Cross-Reference of Format:	To see a list of defined cross-reference formats, click on the Format pop-up in the Cross-Reference dialog box. [Alt s c]
Unresolved Cross-Reference	Use this to find and fix cross-references whose sources have accidentally been deleted.
Any Variable	Find any user or system variable.
Variable of Name:	Type the variable name in the text box to the right.
Anchored Frame	Find any anchored frame.
Footnote	Find and select both the footnote and its callout.
Any Table	Find any table. FrameMaker highlights the table and its anchor point.
Table Tag	Find a table with the tag you type in the box at the right.
Conditional Text	Displays a dialog box in which you specify the conditional tag.
Automatic Hyphen	An easy way to check all FrameMaker's automatic hyphenations.

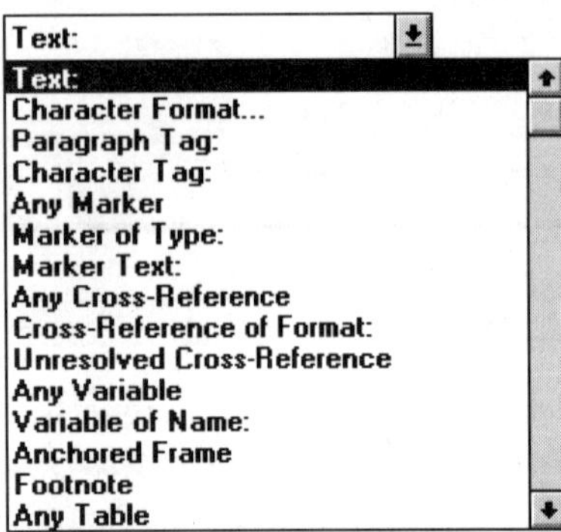

Using Find with move and copy

When FrameMaker Finds an item, it selects it. This means you can use Find to select any of the following types of items in order to delete, move, or copy them:

Marker	Variable
Footnote	Cross-Reference
Anchored Frame	Table

Finding and deleting

Be sure the Change To Text: text box is empty. Find the item. When you click Change, FrameMaker deletes it.

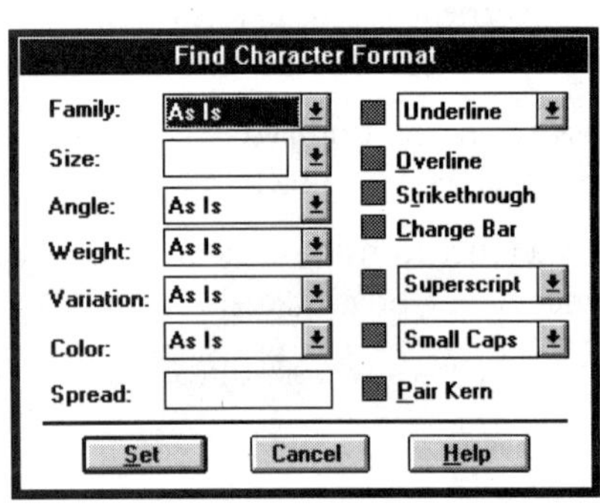

Finding certain properties

Choose Character Format from the Find list to display the Find Character Format dialog box. It displays the properties of the text containing your insertion point. Specify the format you want to find, and click Set. When your other Find choices are complete, click Find.

▲ To set the Find Character Format dialog box to As Is, click *outside* of all text columns before you choose Character Format from the Find list.

▲ To specify a new format to find, re-select Character Format from the Find list.

▲ If you are looking for text that has a particular character tag applied, select Character Tag from the Find list, rather than Character Format.

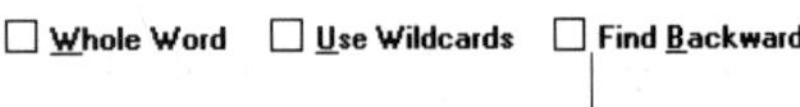

Change the direction of the search here.

Finding Backward

By default, FrameMaker searches from your insertion point toward the end of the document. If you turn on Find Backward, it searches toward the beginning of the document. In either case, the search wraps around the end until the entire document has been scanned.

Using wildcards

When you are searching for text, you can use any of the following wildcards to make your search both broad and precise. When you use any of the following wildcards, you must turn on Use Wildcards so that FrameMaker will give these characters their special meaning.

To search for one of the following wildcard symbols when you have Use Wildcards turned on, precede it with a backslash.

Type this	To find this	Example:
*****	Any amount of any character	**m*d** finds all words beginning with **m** and ending with **d**: e.g., **mad**, **mood**, **martyred**.
|	Any of the spaces and punctuation characters that end a word	**walk|** finds **walk**, **walk.**, **walk?**, and **walk:**, but not **walking** or **walks**.
?	Any single character, excluding spaces and punctuation	**w??k** finds any four-letter work that begins with **w** and ends with **k**: e.g., **walk**, **weak**, and **wick**.
[ab]	Any one of the characters between the brackets	**[cdlmr]ove** finds **cove**, **dove**, **love**, **move**, and **rove**.
[^ab]	Any character not between the brackets	**[^cd]love** finds **love**, **move**, and **rove**, but not **cove** or **dove**.
[a-f]	Any character in the range	**[a-l]ove** finds **cove**, **dove**, and **love**, but not **move** or **rove**.
^	The beginning of a line	**^[0-9]** finds lines beginning with a number.
$	The end of a line	**[^.]$** finds lines that don't end with a period.

Other options

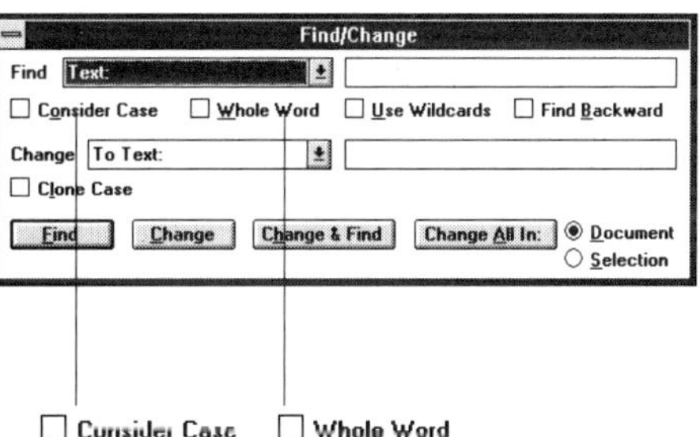

Whole word If you want to find only whole words, turn on the Whole Word option. If you do not turn this on, and you type "the" in the Find text box, FrameMaker will find "theater" as a match.

Consider case If you want to find only text with capitalization that matches your Find text exactly, turn this on.

Using special characters

Here is a list of special characters that are useful in searching. Use them in either the Find or Change text box.

▲ You can use any of the Dialog Box codes listed on page A-322. You can also search for any character using its hex code (Appendix A).

Type this	To find this
\t	tab
\r	forced return (shift-return)
\p	End of paragraph
\P	Start of paragraph
\f	End-of-flow symbol
\<	Start of word
\>	End of word
space	Nonbreaking space

Type this	To find this
\- *(hyphen)*	Discretionary hyphen
\+	Nonbreaking hyphen
_	Suppress hyphenation
\st	Thin space
\sn	En space
\sm	Em space
\s#	Numeric space

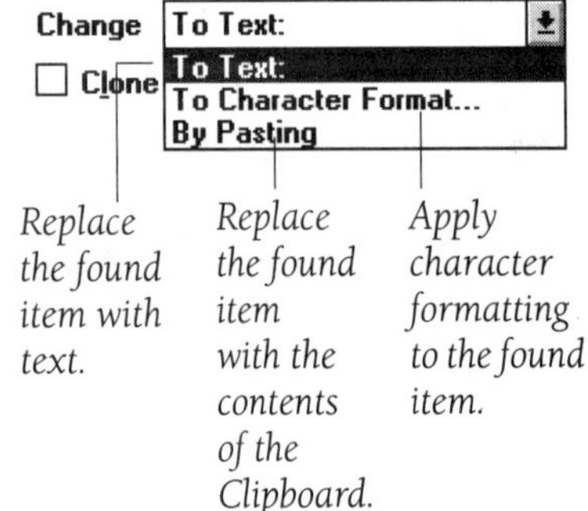

Changing what you find

Changing to text

Choose Change To Text: and type the replacement text in the box next to the right. When you want to change the currently selected item, click Change. To automatically search again after the change, click Change & Find, instead.

Replacing the found item with the contents of the Clipboard

Before you begin searching, create your replacement text, including character formatting and capitalization, and copy it to the Clipboard. [Ctrl-c] Then choose By Pasting from the Change pop-up list. When you choose Change, Frame-Maker replaces the found item with the contents of the Clipboard.

Applying a character format to your found item

Choose To Character Format from the Change pop-up list. In the Change to Character Format dialog box, choose the properties you want to apply. Set the others to As Is and click Set.

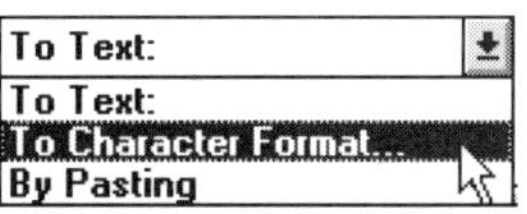

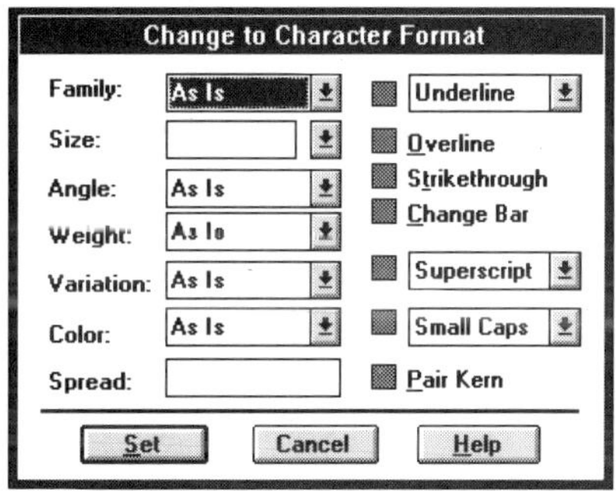

Cloning case

Turn this on to make the capitalization of the replacement text match that of the replaced text.

☐ Clone Case

Cancelling a search

Press Esc at any time to cancel a search that's in progress.

Finding and Changing from the keyboard

1. Type **Esc f i s** to display the Set Find/Change Parameters dialog box. It is the same as the regular Find/Change window, but without the Find and Change buttons.
2. Set up the conditions for Finding and Changing just as you would in the Find/Change window.
3. Click Set.
4. Use the following keystrokes to find and change:

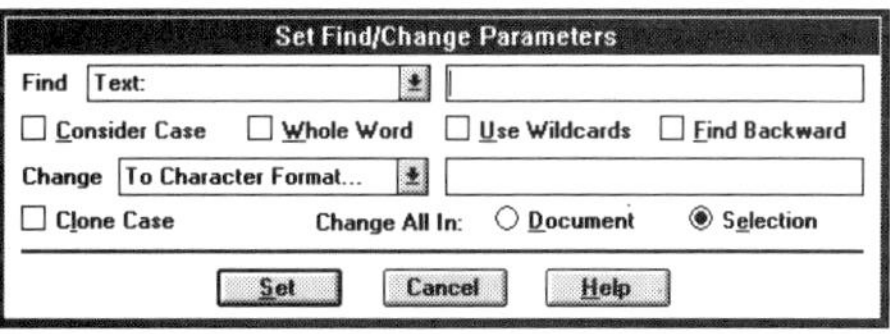

When you Find and Change from the keyboard, you don't have the Find window on top of your document all the time.

Type this	To do this
Ctrl-Shift-f or **Alt-Ctrl-s**	Search forward
Ctrl-Alt-f or **Alt-Ctrl-r**	Search backward
Esc r o	Change current selection
Esc r a	Change and search again
Esc r g	Change all occurrences in the file *(Be careful of this one!)*

▼

Making macros

You can use the Windows Recorder to make shorter key sequences for these.

▲

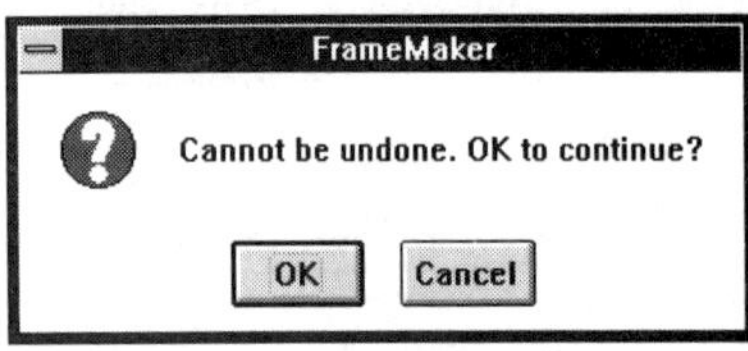

Changing automatically

You can tell FrameMaker to change all occurrences of your Find text in the whole file, or in a selected portion of the file.

1. Set up the Find and Change properties as you want them.
2. Click on Document or Selection to indicate the scope of the automatic change.
3. Click Change All In. FrameMaker posts a box warning you that this cannot be undone. Click OK.

Note Try finding and changing a few occurrences manually to be sure you are getting the effect you want before clicking Change All In. For example, if you're changing *old* to *previous*, you may change *told* to *tprevious* if you don't turn on Whole Word. FrameMaker's potent Find/Change feature gives you the power to wreak havoc as well as to perform miracles.

▲ If you save your document right before executing Change All In, you can use **File→Revert to Saved** if the wrong thing happens and you want your original document back.

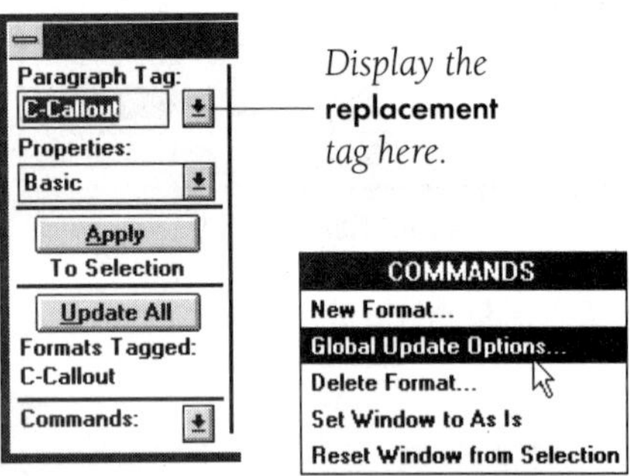

Display the **replacement** *tag here.*

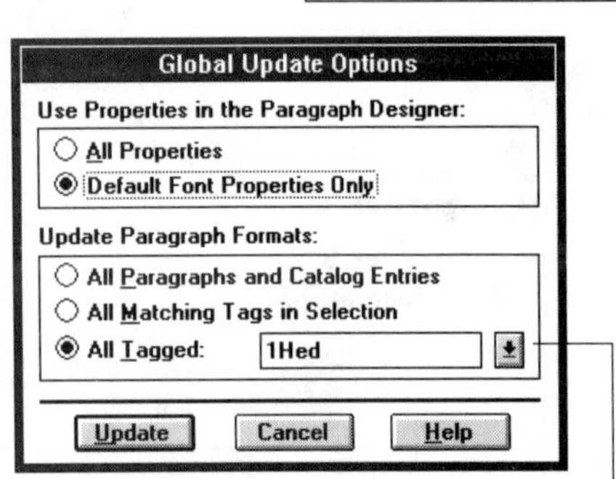

Display the tag **to replace** *here.*

Changing one format tag to another

To replace all occurrences of a particular paragraph or character tag with another tag, use the Paragraph Designer or the Character Designer.

1. Display the replacement tag in the Character Tag or Paragraph Tag box.
2. Click Commands. Click Global Update Options.
3. In the All Tagged pop-up list, choose the tag to be replaced.
4. Click Update.

▲ This procedure removes the replaced tag from the catalog as well as from the text.

■ Spell-checking

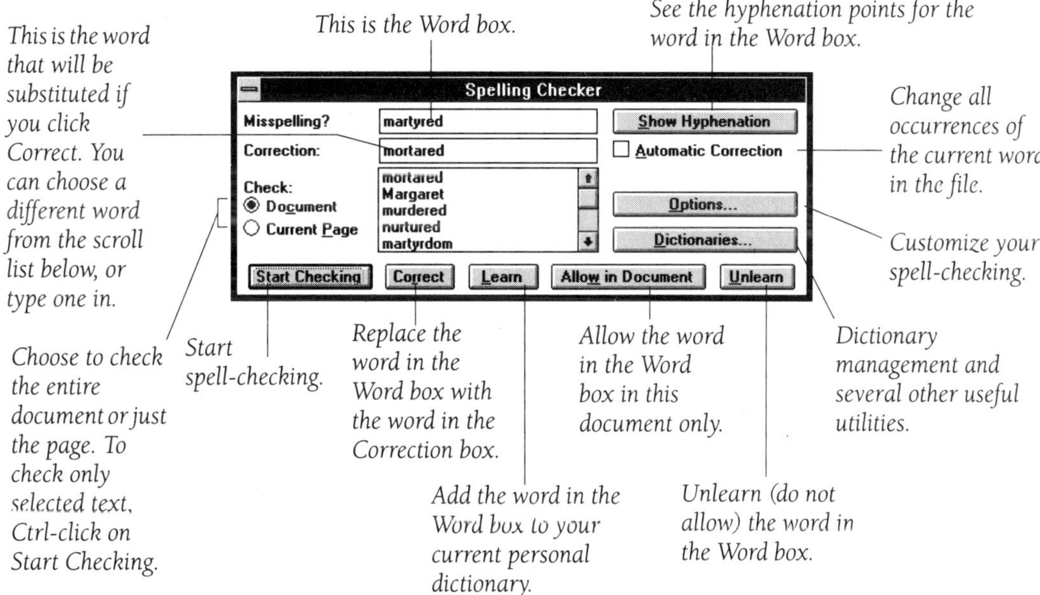

Basic spell-checking

1. Place your insertion point anywhere in text. Or select the portion of text you wish to check.
2. Display the Spelling Checker window: **Edit→Spelling Checker** or type **Alt e l** (*ell*).
3. Make any changes in the Options and Dictionaries dialog boxes.
4. Click Start Checking.

   ▲ **To check only the selected text**, hold down Ctrl when you click Start Checking.

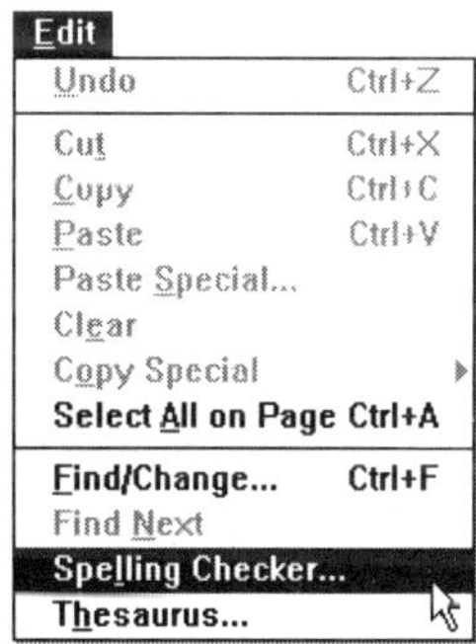

Spell-checking

Misspelling? dilog

Correction: dialog

Correction: dialog

dialog
deluge
dialed
dilate
dilute

Click on a word in the scroll list to make it appear in the Correction box.

To dismiss the Spelling Checker window *double-click in the upper left-hand corner.*

5. **Correct or confirm** When FrameMaker finds a word it questions, it displays it in the Word box with the query, "Misspelling?" You now have several choices:
   ▲ **Replace the found word with the word in the Correction box** Click Correct.
   ▲ **Choose a different correction** Click on a different word in the Correction list. Or type a different word into the Correction box. Click Correct.
   ▲ **Edit the text directly** You can make your changes directly in the text. Click Start Checking to resume spell-checking.
   ▲ **Allow the word in the document** Click Allow in Document to add the questioned word to the **document dictionary**. FrameMaker will not question the word again in this document.
   ▲ **Tell FrameMaker to learn the word** Click Learn to add the word to your **personal dictionary**. Now FrameMaker will not question the word in any document.
   ▲ **Do nothing** Click Start Checking. FrameMaker continues the spell check without making any changes.
6. When FrameMaker has scanned the entire document, it displays "Spelling OK" next to the Word box. If you left something uncorrected (the "Do Nothing" option), FrameMaker keeps finding it and questioning it instead of saying "Spelling OK." See "Skipping individual words" on page 182.

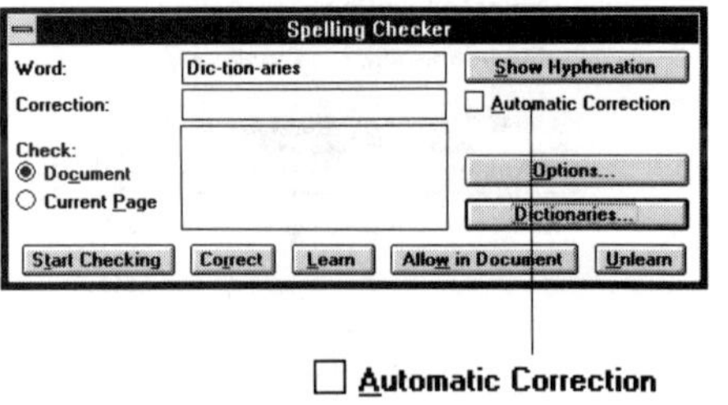

Automatic Correction

This is one more option for step 5, above. You can turn on Automatic Correction before you click Correct. FrameMaker will change all occurrences of the word in the Word box to the word in the Correction box. It will change them not only in the current file, but in all files you work in until you exit FrameMaker.

▲ **Beware** Automatic Correction is one of those options that gives you tremendous power. You could easily find FrameMaker changing things you didn't realize would be changed.

▲ **Clearing Automatic Corrections** If you change your mind and want FrameMaker to stop making an automatic correction:

1. Click on Dictionaries.
2. Click on Clear Automatic Corrections.
3. Click on OK.

FrameMaker will clear the entire Automatic Corrections list, but it cannot undo any of the changes it has already made.

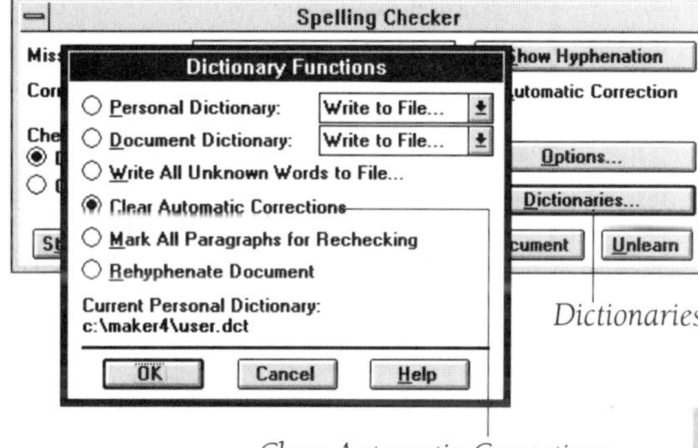

Dictionaries

Clear Automatic Corrections.

Using Options to customize your spell-check

Take a little time to look over the Options dialog box. It contains a list of things you can tell Frame-Maker to find, such as repeated words or straight quotes. There is another list of things to ignore, such as single-letter words, or roman numerals. Make your choices and then click Set.

Spelling Checker Options

Find:
☒ Repeated Words
☐ Unusual Hyphenation
☐ Unusual Capitalization
☒ Two in a Row: !,.:;?
☒ Straight Quotes (")
☒ Extra Spaces
☒ Space Before: !%),.:;?]}»\'\
☒ Space After: $([{«\`\(\.\g

Ignore:
☒ Single-Character Words
☒ Words That Are All Uppercase
☒ Words Containing: .
☐ Roman Numerals
☒ Words with Digits

Get Defaults

Set Cancel Help

This returns you to the settings that were in effect when you started FrameMaker. When you exit FrameMaker, the current settings become the new defaults.

This is where you "educate" FrameMaker's spelling checker. Tell it exactly what to find and what to ignore.

Spell-checking

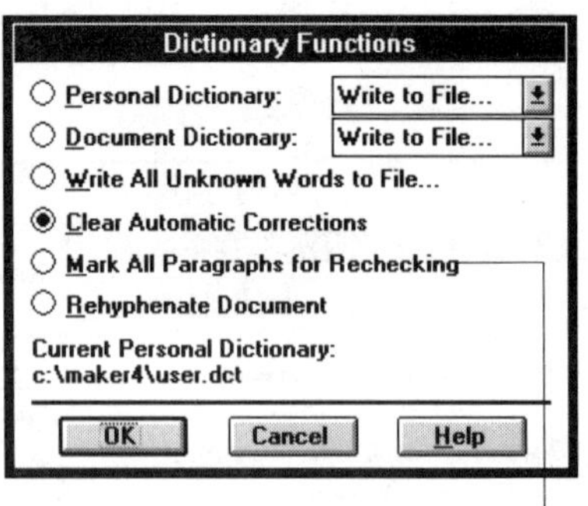

Recheck a document.

Rechecking a document

If you have changed any options or any dictionaries, you must take an extra step to recheck the document.

1. Click on Dictionaries.
2. Turn on Mark All Paragraphs for Rechecking.
3. Click on OK.
4. Click on Start Checking.

Skipping individual words

Usually, you can add a word to the document dictionary (All in Document) or to your personal dictionary (Learn), to avoid further questioning by the Spelling Checker. Sometimes you find an item that is allowable only in one place, but not in the rest of the document. Here's what to do:

1. Place your insertion point in the paragraph containing the special occurrence. Be sure that the whole paragraph is spelled correctly.
2. Display the Advanced page of the Paragraph Designer. In the Language pop-up menu, choose None.
3. Click Apply to Selection. FrameMaker does not spell-check or hyphenate any paragraph whose Language is set to None.

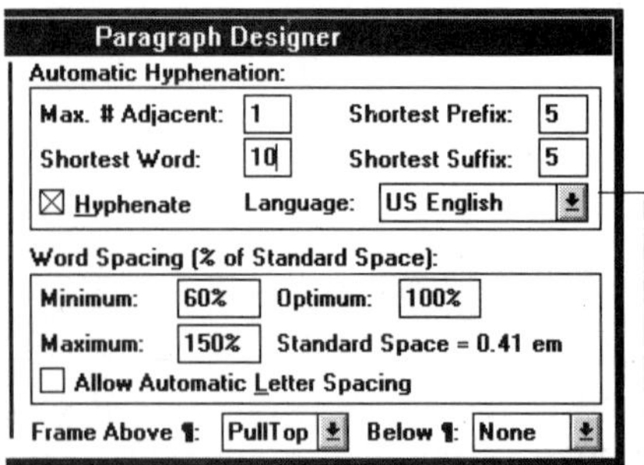

Set the language to None in this pop-up.

Skipping paragraphs

You may have certain types of paragraphs—computer code, for example—that should not be spell-checked. You can make FrameMaker skip such paragraphs during spell-checking by setting the Language for those paragraphs to None as part of the paragraph format definition. See steps 1–3 of "Skipping individual words," above, for how to do this on a case-by-case basis. See "Creating a new paragraph format" on page 93 for creating a format definition.

Changing the hyphenation of a word

You can permanently change the way FrameMaker hyphenates a word. The steps are described on page 74.

Rehyphenating a document

1. In the Spelling Checker window, click Dictionaries.
2. Turn on Rehyphenate Document.
3. Click OK. FrameMaker rehyphenates the document, incorporating any hyphenation changes you may have made to the dictionaries.

Managing your personal dictionaries

When you click Learn, you add words to the current personal dictionary. The default dictionary is USER.DCT in the FrameMaker 4 home directory (usually \MAKER4). You can see the name of the personal dictionary currently in use by clicking on Dictionaries in the Spelling Checker window.

Here's the overview of how to manage your personal dictionaries:

1. In the Spelling Checker window, click Dictionaries.
2. In the Personal Dictionary pop-up list, choose the operation you want: Write to File (clone the dictionary), Merge From File (add the contents of another dictionary to the current one), Change Dictionary (load a different dictionary), or Set to None (unload all personal dictionaries).
3. Click OK.
4. In the resulting dialog box, choose the file name and location to write to, merge, or load (Change Dictionary).
5. Click Merge, Save, or Use.

Type the word in here and click Show Hyphenation to see the current hyphenation.

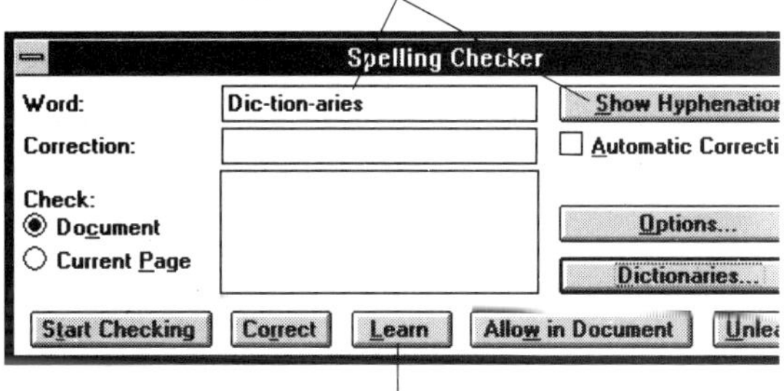

Correct the hyphenation in the Word box and click Learn.

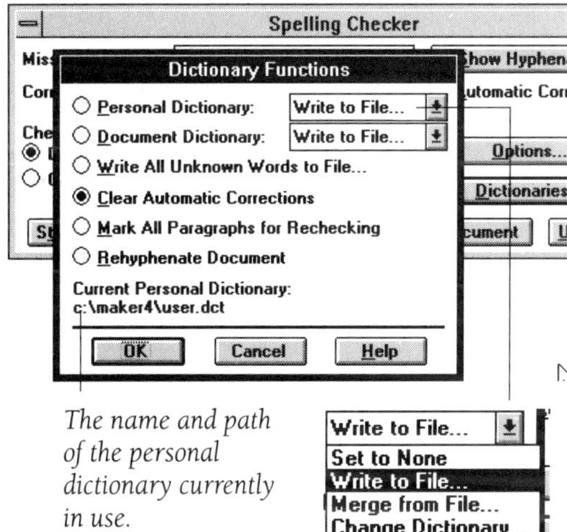

The name and path of the personal dictionary currently in use.

Change, save, or merge your personal dictionary.

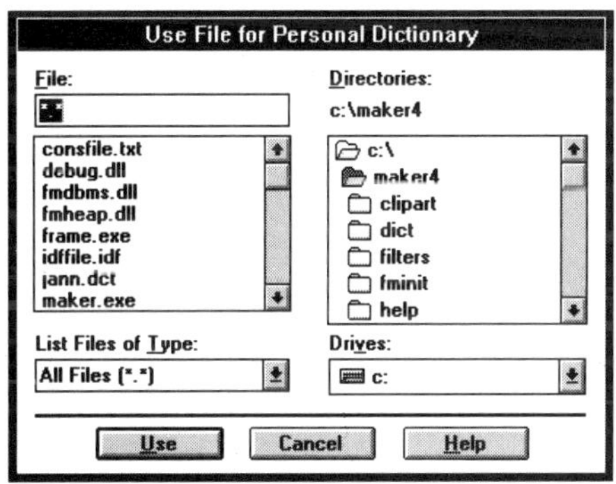

Spell-checking

Change the name of your personal dictionary by choosing Personal Dictionary: Write to File. Then load that dictionary by choosing Personal Dictionary: Change Dictionary. This allows each user to have a separate dictionary; or you can keep different dictionaries for different types of documents.

To save your document dictionary to an editable file, choose Write to File.

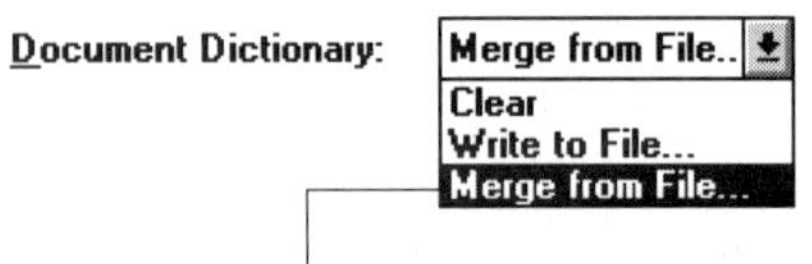

To merge your edited document dictionary back into the document, choose Write to File.

▲ A personal dictionary must begin with the line <MakerDictionary 2.0>. You can create a personal dictionary using a text editor, or you can create it in FrameMaker and then save it as text (page 50). You can clone your current dictionary (Write to File), edit it, and either merge with the current dictionary or load it in place of the current one. If you use FrameMaker to edit it, be sure to save it as text. See "Managing text files" on page 49.

Document dictionaries

A document dictionary is stored inside a document. It is the list of words for which you click Allow in Document when you Spell-Check.

Edit To edit a document dictionary, you must save it using Document Dictionary:Write to File. Edit your saved file using a text editor, or edit it using FrameMaker and save it as a text file ("Saving a file as text" on page 50).

Merge Add the contents of another file to the current document dictionary. You can merge a file that you saved using Write to File or a file that you created using Write All Unknown Words to File. You can create your own list. The file that you merge must be a text file, and must begin with the line <MakerDictionary 1.0>.

Clear If you have removed words from a document dictionary while editing it, and wish to load your changes, clear the old dictionary before merging the new one. Otherwise the words you removed will still be present, since they are still in the old dictionary.

■ Using the Thesaurus

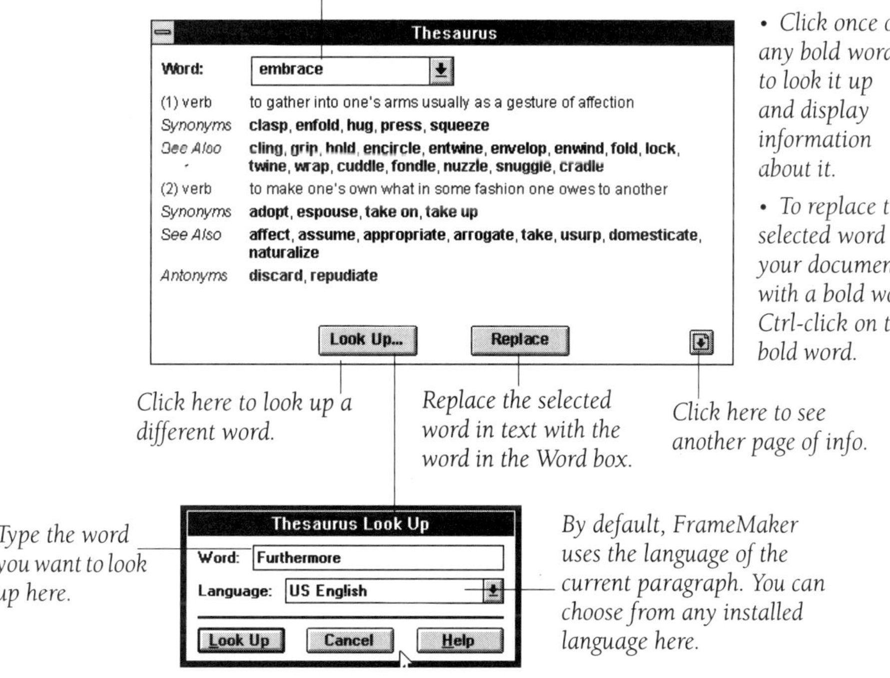

How to use the Thesaurus

To do this	Do this
Find a related or opposite word	Highlight the word in text and choose **Edit→Thesaurus** [**Alt e h**] **or** display the Thesaurus when you have no insertion point to get the Thesaurus Look Up dialog box.
Get more information on one of the bold words	Click on the bold word.
Go back to one of your last ten lookup words	Click on the Word pop-up list, and then click on the word you want to return to.
Replace the selected word in text with the word in the Word box	Click Replace. If you have an insertion point but no selected text, the word is inserted at the insertion point.
Replace the selected word in text with a bold word	Ctrl-click the bold word and click Replace.
To look up a phrase	Choose **Edit→Thesaurus** and type the phrase in the Word box, putting hyphens between the words.

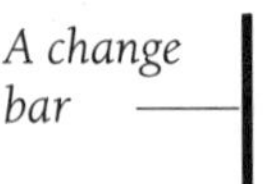

Document the vicissitudes of your document, if not your life, using FrameMaker's handy change bars.

■ Change bars

Change bars are vertical lines that appear just to the right or left of a text column to show where text has been changed. They make it easy to keep track of changes in an ongoing document.

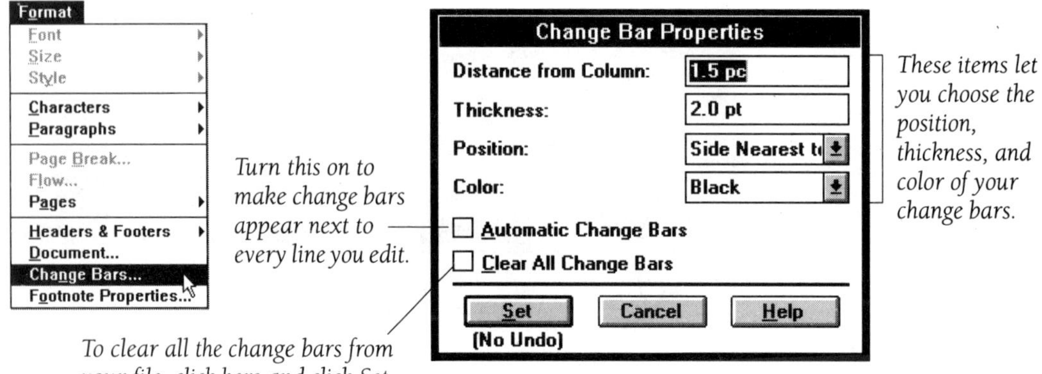

Change bar properties

You can determine the appearance and location of your change bars, make them automatic, and clear them from a whole file at once. Choose **Format→Change Bars** to display the Change Bar Properties dialog box. [**Alt o n**]

Turning on automatic change bars Click in the Automatic Change Bars box and then click Set. Now, every edit you make will automatically generate a change bar of the thickness, position, and color that you specify in this dialog box.

Clearing all change bars Click in the Clear All Change Bars box, and click Set. Your change bars are gone.

Formatting change bars Make whatever changes you want to the Distance, Position, Thickness, and Color items, and then click Set. The appearance that you select will affect both automatic and manual change bars throughout the file.

▼

Automatic Change Bars

When Automatic Change Bars are on, you get a change bar next to every line you make a change in. It doesn't matter whether Change Bars are turned on in the individual paragraph and character formats, or not.

▲ *When you turn Automatic Change Bars off, FrameMaker no longer generates them automatically, but the old ones stay in place until you Clear All Change Bars or remove them manually.*

▲

Manual change bars

- You can define character and paragraph formats that include change bars, so any text with those formats will be marked. Turn on Change Bar when you define the format.
- You can select text, and then turn on change bars and Apply to Selection to affect that text only.

Line-by-line Select some characters in the line, or select a few lines. In the Character Designer, turn on Change Bar, and then Apply to Selection.

Paragraph-by-paragraph Select one or more paragraphs. In the Default Font page of the Paragraph Designer, turn on Change Bar, and then Apply to Selection.

Removing change bars Select the paragraph or text whose change bars you wish to remove. Display the appropriate Designer (Character Designer if the change bar is applied to only part of a paragraph, Paragraph Designer if the bar is applied to the whole paragraph). Turn off Change Bar, and then Apply to Selection.

Here's where you turn Change Bars on and off in both the Character and Paragraph Designers.

Use the Paragraph and Character Designers to create change bars on a case-by-case basis, when Automatic Change Bars are turned off.

Freezing pagination

This feature is most often used for making corrections that have been marked on a draft copy. If you allow FrameMaker to adjust the pagination as usual, you soon find that the page numbers on your screen no longer match the page numbers in the draft copy, and it's hard to find where to make the corrections. To prevent this problem, you can "freeze" the page numbering. If FrameMaker needs extra pages for added material, it creates *point pages*. It numbers these pages by adding decimal numbers, letters, or roman numbers to the regular page numbers.

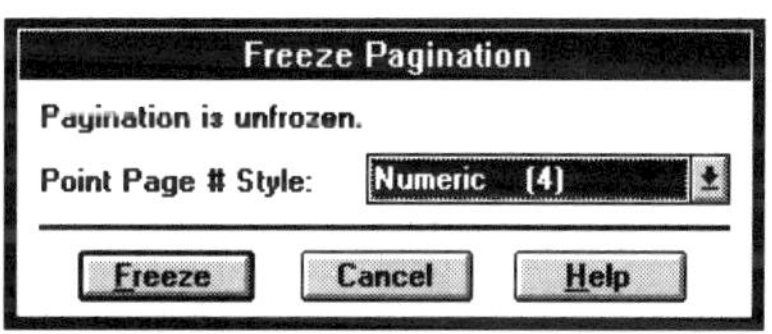

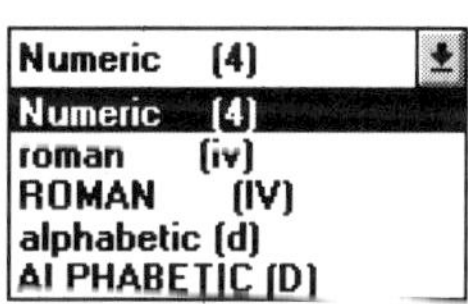

Point page numbering choices

After page 2, for example, you could have any of the following:

Numeric	2.3
roman	2.iii
ROMAN	2.III
alphabetic	2.c
ALPHABETIC	2.C

To freeze pagination

1. Type **Esc p z**. (There's no menu item for this—only the keyboard shortcut.)
2. From the pop-up, choose a numbering style for any added pages (point pages).
3. Click Freeze.

To unfreeze pagination

1. Type **Esc p z**.
2. Click Unfreeze.

Warning FrameMaker warns that freezing pagination may have "undesirable results" if you have multi-page tables in your document, or if you have anchored frames with "floating" turned on. Worse still, if a paragraph breaks between a regular page and a point page, it becomes two paragraphs, and does not rejoin when you unfreeze the pagination.

■ Comparing two documents

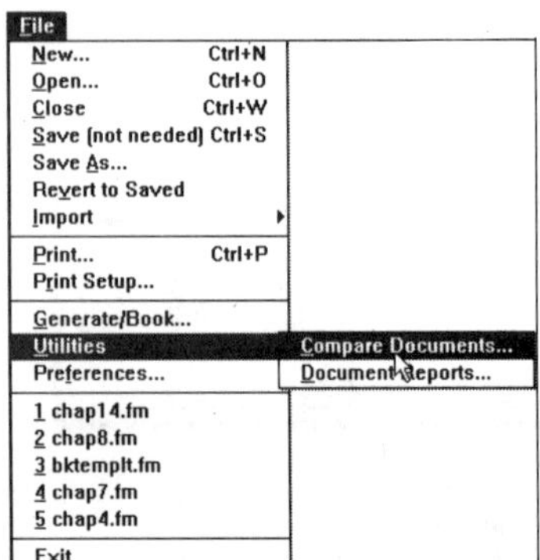

How many times have you looked at two different versions of a document listed in a directory and wondered just what the differences were between them, and which was the one you really wanted? FrameMaker has finally made it possible to compare two documents.

You can choose to generate both a composite document and a summary document, or a summary document only. The composite document uses conditional text to let you see the differences between the documents. The summary document lists the differences.

■ The composite document is described on page 190 and the summary document is described on page 191.

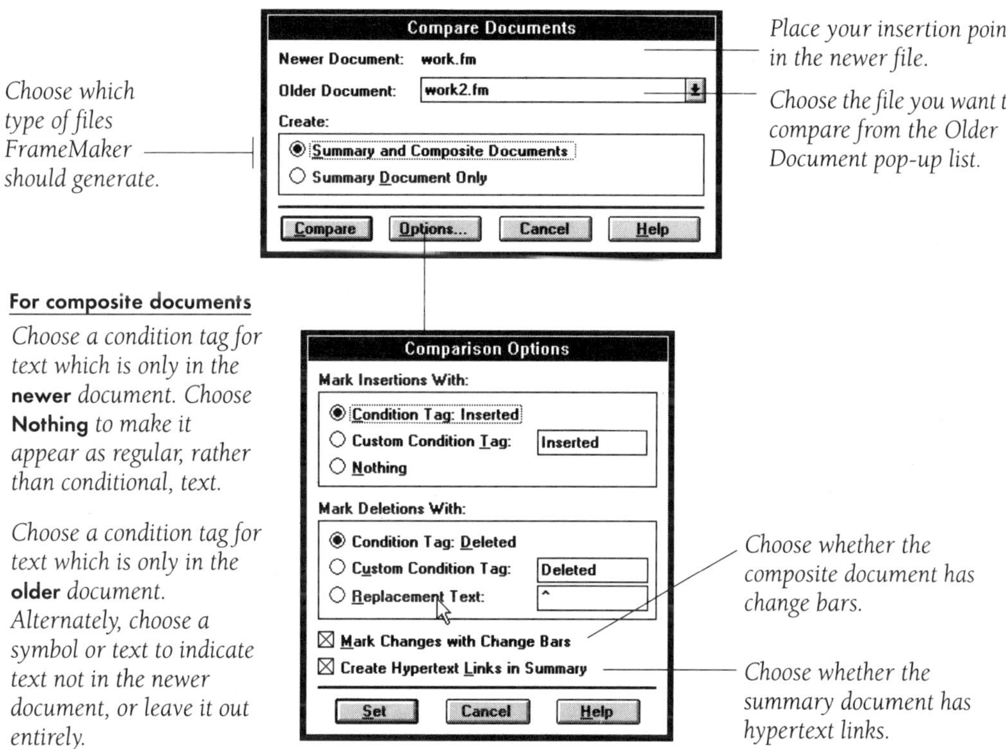

Creating the comparison

1. Open both documents.
2. Place your insertion point in the newer document, and choose **File→Utilities→Compare Documents**.
3. From the Older Document pop-up, choose the name of the document you want to compare. It must be open in order to appear in this list.
4. Choose whether you want to see both a summary and a composite document, or only a summary.
5. Click Options if you want to change any of the options. Make your choices in the Comparison Options dialog box and click Set.
6. Click Compare.

The following section is all in ~~WORK2.~~WORK.FM

Save a file in MIF

If you want to open a FrameMaker 4 file in FrameMaker3, you must save it in MIF. Then open the MIF file in FrameMaker 3.

1. Choose **File→Save As.**
2. In the Save Document dialog box, choose Interchange - MIF from the Formats pop-up.
3. Give the document a name that has a MIF extension in the Save in File text box.
4. Click Save.

~~This concludes the "MIF" section in WORK2.FM~~

This is the end of the mif section in WORK.FM

A composite document: text that is only in the older document has a strikethrough; text that is only in the newer document is underlined. All differences have a change bar. You can choose different treatments in the Comparison Options dialog box.

The composite document

This document considers the newer document—the one from which you generate the comparison—to be the base. If you understand the following two things, you can understand the comparison:

Deleted Material that is only in the older document (the base document) is viewed as being "deleted" from the newer one and appears in the composite document as conditional text with a "Deleted" condition tag.

Inserted Material that is only in the newer document is viewed as being "inserted" and appears in the composite document as conditional text with an "Inserted" condition tag.

▪ By default, text that has the Deleted conditional tag appears with a strikethrough property applied. Inserted text is underlined. You can change the appearance of either conditional tag; choose **Special→Conditional Text** and click Edit Condition Tag.

▪ In the Comparison Options dialog box, you can choose to see only deleted material, and not insertions (Mark Insertions With Nothing); you can choose to replace deleted text with a symbol or identifying text string (Mark Deletions with Replacement Text); or you can omit the older text altogether by choosing Replacement Text and leaving the text box blank.

The summary document

The Summary outlines all the differences between the versions, listing the page number in each of the two original documents and in the composite document for each insertion, deletion, or replacement.

▲ **Hypertext links** If you choose Create Hypertext Links in Summary from the Comparison Options dialog box, the page numbers in the Summary will be hypertext links. Click on one to go directly to that point in the document!

▲ **Naming** FrameMaker always names a summary document "Summary." If you want to have more than one in a directory, you must give the original one a new name using Save As before generating the next one.

▲ *If you are confused by the summary (I was!), remember that insertions and deletions are all relative to the newer document—the one from which you generated the summary. When you see "inserted" or "deleted," read it as "inserted into (or deleted from) the newer document."*

Document Comparison Summary

Documents

	Name	Modification Date
Newer Document:	work.fm	October 25, 1993 10:52 am
Older Document:	work2.fm	October 25, 1993 10:52 am

Number of Changes

Type	Insertions	Deletions	Changes
Text Content	1	1	5
Cross-Ref Formats	1	0	0

Flow A

Text Content Changes

Page Numbers

Composite	Newer	Older	Change	Text
1	1	1	Replaced:	"work2." With: "work."
1	1	1	Replaced:	"This concludes the" mif" section ..". With: "This is the end of ..".
2	2	1	Inserted:	"This text is common to ..".
3	3	2	Replaced:	"line " With: "material "
3	3	2	Replaced:	"two " With: "3 "
3	3	2	Replaced:	"the older work2.fm." With: "both documents."
4	3	3	Deleted:	"This material is on page ..".

Cross-Reference Format Changes

Name	Change
newInserted:"<Z-ZapfDing>¶"	

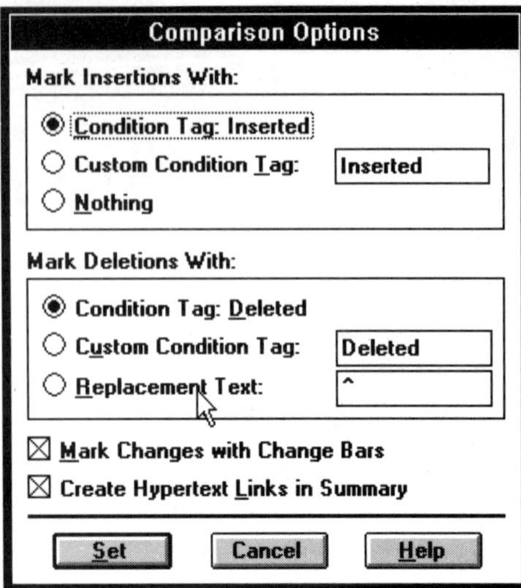

Generating change bars only

You can create a composite document that has only the text of the most recent document and that has change bars where text is missing from the older document.

1. In the Comparison dialog box, click on Options.
2. Choose Mark Insertions With: Nothing and Mark Deletions With: Replacement Text. Be sure the Replacement Text box is empty.
3. Turn on Mark Changes with Change Bars.
4. Click Set. Click Compare.

Formatting your comparisons

As a rule, your comparisons are not permanent documents: you are not likely to format them. But if you do need to do so, you need to change them from view-only to normal documents first.

Changing a view-only document to "normal"

1. Open the document to change.
2. Press **Esc F l k** (*capital F, lowercase ell k*).

▲ This key sequence toggles any document between view-only and normal.

Once the composite or summary is normal, rather than view-only, you can format it as you would any FrameMaker document.

What's not compared

There are a few things that are not compared between files: text tags and formatting, anchored frame position (anchored frame contents are carefully compared), footnote properties and numbers, table tags and formatting, graphic objects that are not in an anchored frame, and text that does not have a flow assigned and is not in an anchored frame. This sounds like a long list, but it's a lot shorter than the list of what *is* compared!

Frames

9

■ What's a frame for?

Think of a frame as a container—a sort of bag or box that you put text and graphics into. The big difference is that when you put objects into a box in the real world, they may rattle around and get disordered. When you put things into a Frame-Maker frame, they stay exactly where you put them. If the frame is an anchored frame—and most of them are—the frame will move along as you edit and retain its position flawlessly with respect to the text.

▼

I've seen applications where frames had a nasty way of sliding out of place when the document was re-worked. Not so in FrameMaker. You can count on frames to stay right where you want them, and their contents will be undisturbed as well.

▲

■ Most often, the frames you use will be anchored frames. An **anchored frame** is attached to a point in the text stream, and thus moves along with text as material is added and deleted. **Unanchored frames** are used on reference pages, to crop graphics, and to place fixed graphics on body pages.

▼

This side item is in an anchored frame

In this whole book, each page has a single text column next to the inner edge of the page. All the text and graphics that you see in the wide outer margin are in frames whose anchor position is "Side Farthest from Page Edge." (That means the side of the text column that's farthest from the page edge.)*

*Except Chapter 2.

▲

■ Anchored frame properties

This page illustrates the Anchoring Position choices that appear in the Anchored Frame dialog box. When you create or modify an anchored frame you pick one of these positions.

Anchoring Position: Below Current Line

(The largest gray rectangle is the anchored frame.)

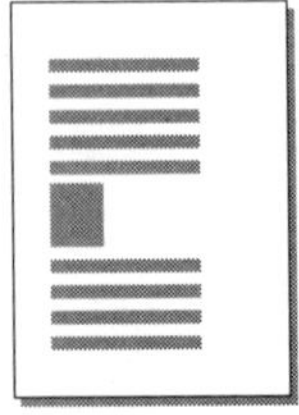

Alignment: Left

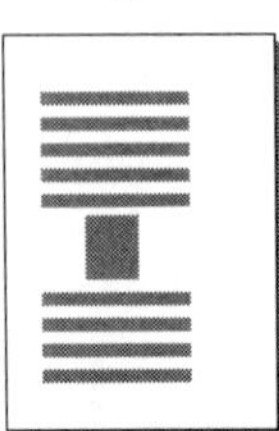

Alignment: Center

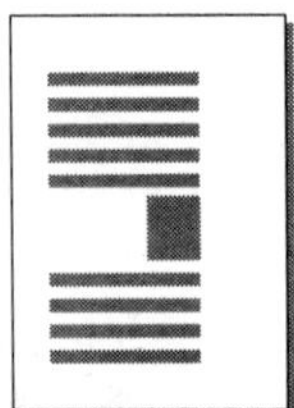

Alignment: Right

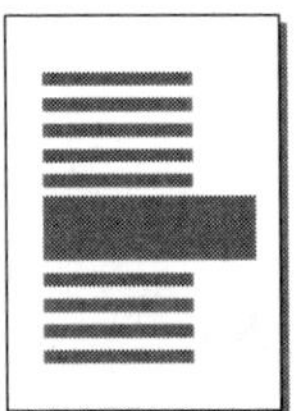

Alignment: Left *and* Cropped *off* *(page 195)*

Floating *off. Text does not "float" to fill up space.*

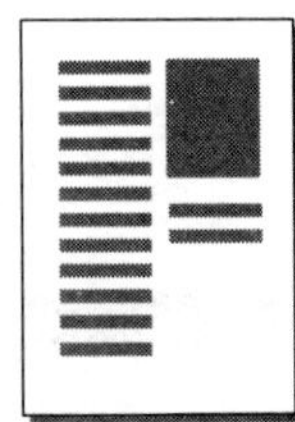

Floating *on. Text fills up the leftover space.*

Anchoring Position: At Insertion Point

In the following examples, I turned on the border of the frames, so that you could see their position with respect to the baseline of the type. By default, frame border pen is set to None.

The symbol is in a frame ▲ anchored at the insertion point.

Baseline Offset: 0

The symbol is in a frame ▲ anchored at the insertion point.

Baseline Offset: –3 points

The symbol is in a frame ▲ anchored at the insertion point.

Baseline Offset: +3 points

Anchoring Positions at the side

Left Side of Column

Right Side of Column

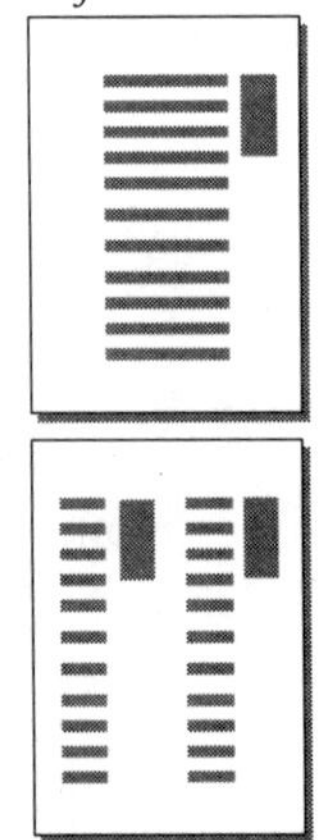

Side Closest to Page Edge

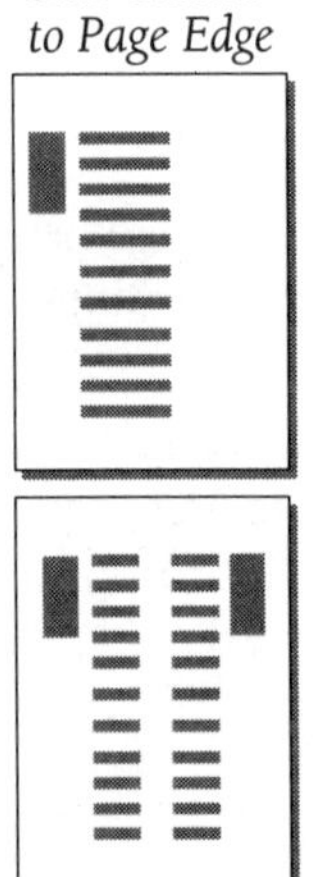

Side Farthest from Page Edge

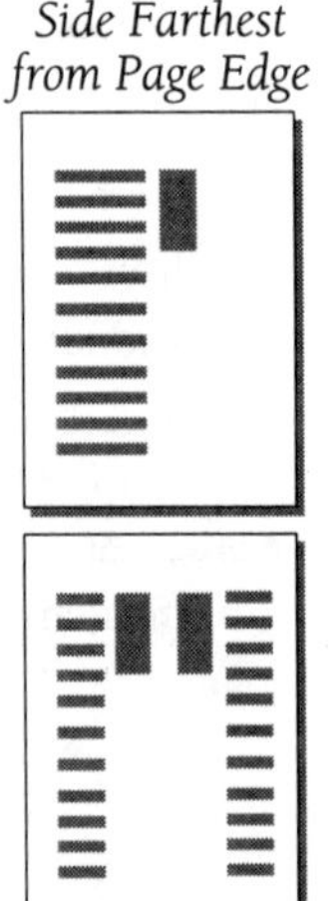

Creating an anchored frame

1. Place your insertion point in the paragraph that you want to anchor the frame to.

2. Choose **Special→Anchored Frame**. [**Alt s a**]

3. **To place the frame inside the text column**, choose Below Current Line, At Top of Column, or At Bottom of Column. (See step 4 if you want it at the insertion point.)

▲ Choose whether the frame will align with the left side or right side of the column, or be centered in it.

▲ If you turn on **Cropped**, the text column crops the frame: any part of the frame that extends beyond the column will be invisible. When you turn Cropped off, the frame can extend beyond the column width. If you are going to make the frame wider than the column, you can only extend it on a side it's *not* aligned with.

▲ If you turn on **Floating**, text that occurs after the line where the frame is anchored moves backward, if necessary, to fill up a space left behind the frame. (This occurs when the frame doesn't fit at the bottom of a column.) With floating off, the text retains its original relationship to the frame (i.e., before or after), even if space is left at the bottom of a column.

4. **To place a frame in the text line at the insertion point**, turn on At Insertion Point. Use the Baseline Offset to determine how the bottom of the frame is positioned relative to the baseline of the type. A negative Baseline Offset moves the bottom of the frame down, a positive number moves it up. Choose zero to put the bottom of the frame at the baseline of the type.

The top three are the "in-column" choices.

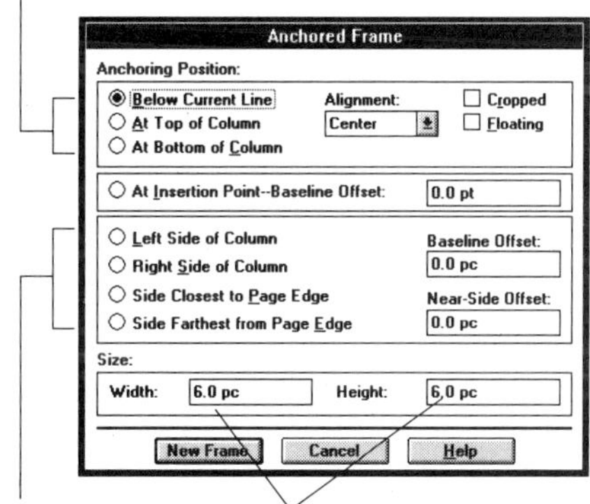

The bottom four are all outside the text column.

The size choices are for all types—inside or outside the column or at the insertion point.

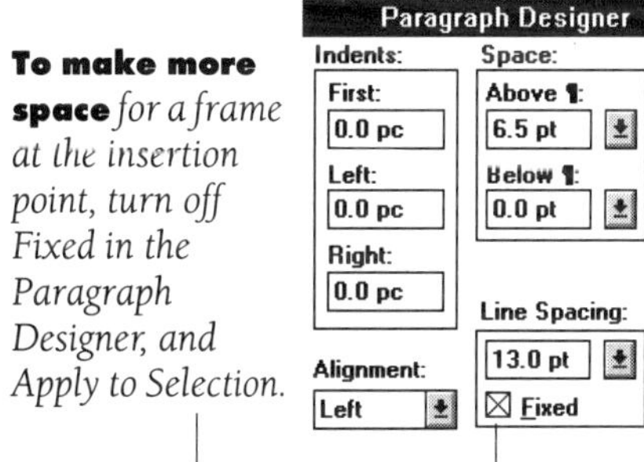

To make more space *for a frame at the insertion point, turn off Fixed in the Paragraph Designer, and Apply to Selection.*

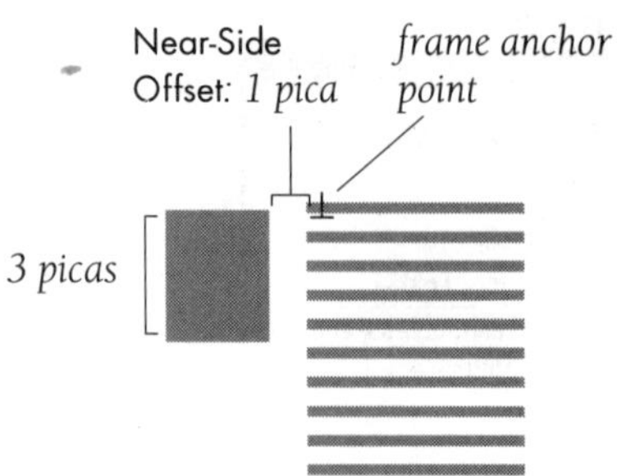

In this example, the height of the frame is 3 picas, and the Baseline Offset *of the frame is –3 picas, so the top of the rectangle is even with the baseline of the line containing the anchor point.*

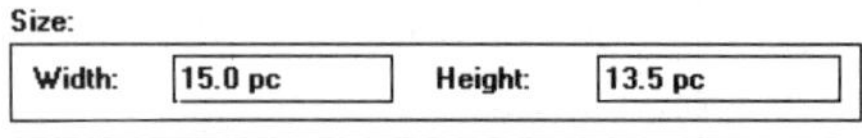

In the Anchored Frame dialog box, specify the size of the frame.

▼

What's a graphic object?

Graphic objects include imported graphics, graphics that you create with FrameMaker graphic tools, text columns, text lines, and frames. To select a text line as a graphic object, you must select it with Ctrl-click, rather than selecting its contents as text.

▲

5. **To place a frame in the margin**, choose one of the four "side" positions. They are illustrated at the bottom of page 194. The "side" referred to in all four of these choices is the side of the text column. "Side Farthest from Page Edge" puts the frame in the wider margin (on a single column page).

   ▲ **Baseline Offset** is the distance between the anchoring point and the bottom of the frame. A negative number is down.

   ▲ **Near-Side Offset** is the gap between the frame and the column.
6. Set the **size** of your frame. You're not stuck with anything you specify here. It's easy to resize frames after they're created.
7. Click New Frame.

   ▲ If you have a frame selected, the button says Edit Frame instead of New Frame. The properties you have specified in the dialog box will be applied to the selected frame. This is how you change a frame.

Automatic frames

When you paste a graphic object at an insertion point, FrameMaker creates a frame for you.

1. Select any graphic object.
2. Cut or copy the object.
3. Place your insertion point in text.
4. Paste. FrameMaker creates an anchored frame centered below the line containing the insertion point. The frame contains the graphic object you are pasting. You can now select this frame and change its properties, just as you would any other frame.

■ Moving and sizing frames

Moving an anchored frame

A frame **in the column** cannot be grabbed and dragged. You can, however, resize it and re-align it (see "Moving and sizing frames (continued)" on page 198). A frame **at the insertion point** can be moved vertically and resized. A frame **in the margin** can be dragged almost anywhere, but it won't go above or below the column containing its anchor point.

Grabbing frames

1. Click on the border of the frame to select it.
2. Place the pointer over an edge *but not over a resize handle*. The pointer should have a handle and be hollow.
3. Press the left mouse button and drag the frame to its new location.

Micropositioning frames

This is the perfect way to make delicate adjustments. You can use it to position a frame in the margin, or to move a frame at the insertion point in the vertical direction only. The "in-column" positions—Top of Column, Bottom of Column, and Below Current Line—must be moved using the Anchored Frame dialog box.

1. Click on the frame border to select the frame.
2. Hold down Alt and press any of the arrow keys to move the frame in really tiny increments. (The exact amount of motion depends on the zoom factor of the screen.)
3. Hold down Shift and Alt and press the arrow keys to move the frame in slightly larger increments.

▲ This micropositioning technique works on any selected graphic object or text.

Selecting an anchored frame

Position the pointer over the border of the frame and click.

Unselecting an anchored frame

Click anywhere outside the frame.

Note *You can only select one frame at a time.*

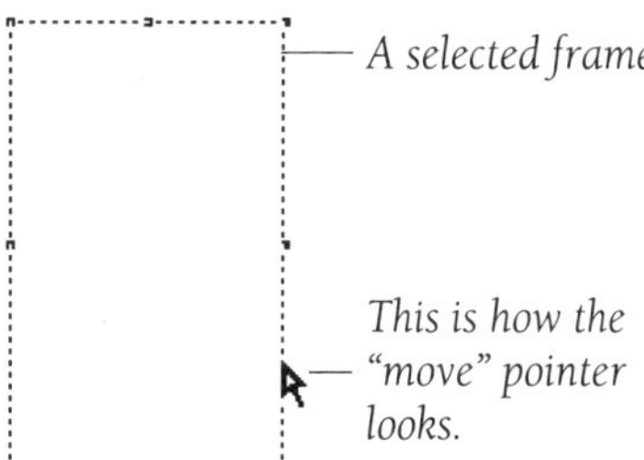

To see the anchor point

To see the anchor point of a frame, turn on Text Symbols: **View→Text Symbols** *or* **Alt v t**. *The anchor point looks like this:* ⊥ *.*

You can select the frame and its anchor point by choosing Anchored Frame from the Find list in the Find/Change window. You'll see a small black rectangle in the text where the anchor point is.

Moving and sizing frames

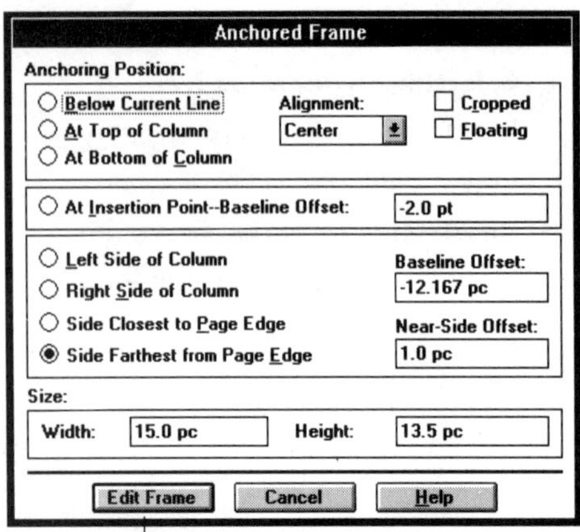

Click Edit Frame to apply new properties to a selected frame.

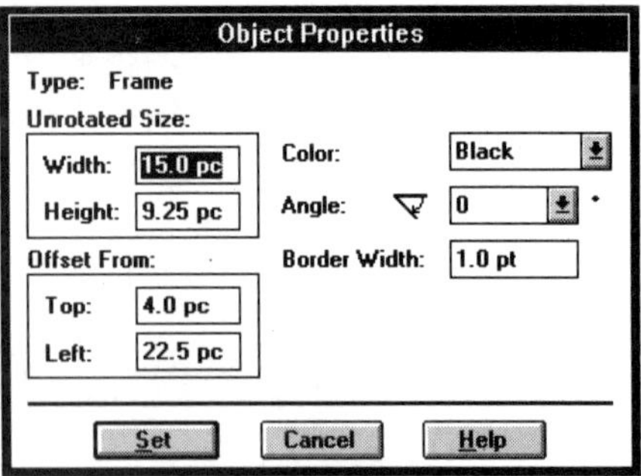

The Offset From is the distance from the top and left side of the frame containing the selected object. FrameMaker considers the page itself to be a frame.

Moving and sizing frames *(continued)*

Using the Anchored Frame dialog box

1. Select an anchored frame.
2. Choose **Special→Anchored Frame**. [**Alt s a**]
3. The Anchored Frame dialog box displays the properties of the selected frame. Make any changes you want to the properties, and then click Edit Frame. See "Creating an anchored frame," beginning on page 195, for lots more information about the choices in this dialog box.

Using the Object Properties dialog box

1. Click on the border of a frame to select it.
2. Display the Object Properties dialog box: **Graphics→Object Properties**, the button on the QuickAccess bar, or **Alt g p**.
3. Change Offset From to change the position of the frame.

   ▲ **Offset From** gives you the distance from the top and left side of the page *unless the frame is inside another frame*. Then it's giving the offset from the side and top of the containing frame. (FrameMaker is actually always giving you the offset from the top and left side of the containing frame. It's just that to Frame-Maker, the page is a frame.)
4. Click Set. FrameMaker applies the new properties to the selected frame.

A note on the Object Properties dialog box

You can use this dialog box to change the size of a frame, to position it, or to rotate it. You can change the border color and thickness, too, but nothing will happen until you go to the graphics palette and use the button to change the border from None to solid. See "Frame fill and borders" on page 201.

Moving and sizing frames *(continued)*

Cutting and pasting

You can move a frame to a new location with a new anchor point by cutting it and pasting it into a new location. See "To cut, copy, or paste the whole frame" on page 200.

Resizing a frame

Grabbing it

1. Click on the border of a frame to select it.
   ▲ **To see the border**, turn Borders on—**Alt v b**. Even when borders are off, you can tell when the pointer is over a border because the arrow turns hollow.
2. Place the pointer over a resize handle. The corner resize handles let you pull in any direction. The side handles let you change only one dimension at a time.
3. Press the left mouse button and drag the handle.

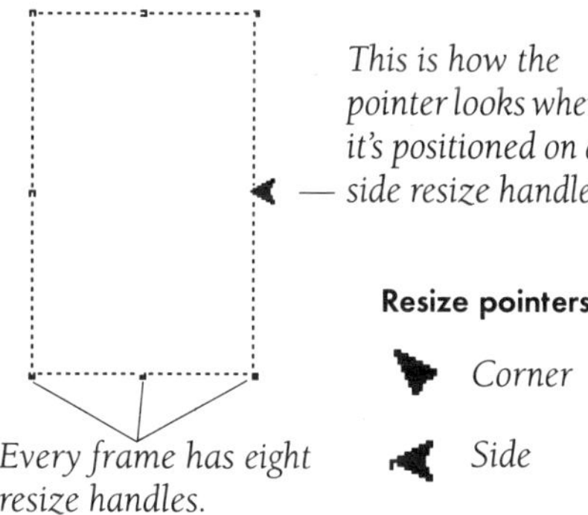

Using the Anchored Frame dialog box

1. Select an anchored frame.
2. Choose **Special→Anchored Frame**. [**Alt s a**]
3. The Anchored Frame dialog box displays the properties of the selected frame. Enter the new dimensions in the Width and Height boxes, and click Edit Frame.

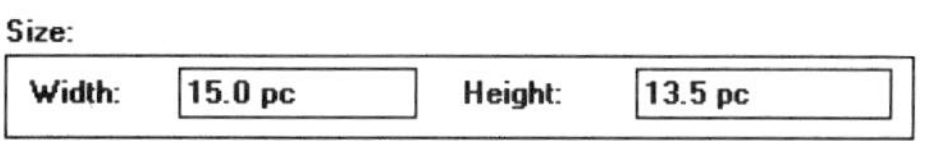

You can resize your frame in the Anchored Frame dialog box.

Using the Object Properties dialog box

1. Click on the border of a frame to select it.
2. Display the Object Properties dialog box: **Graphics→Object Properties**, the [x,y] button on the QuickAccess Bar, or **Alt g p**.
3. Enter the new dimensions in the Width and Height boxes.
4. Click Set. FrameMaker applies the new dimensions to the selected frame.

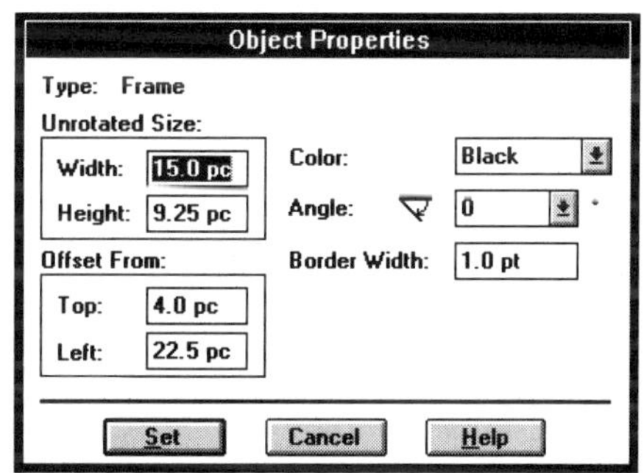

Specify new dimensions for the selected frame, or change any of the other displayed properties.

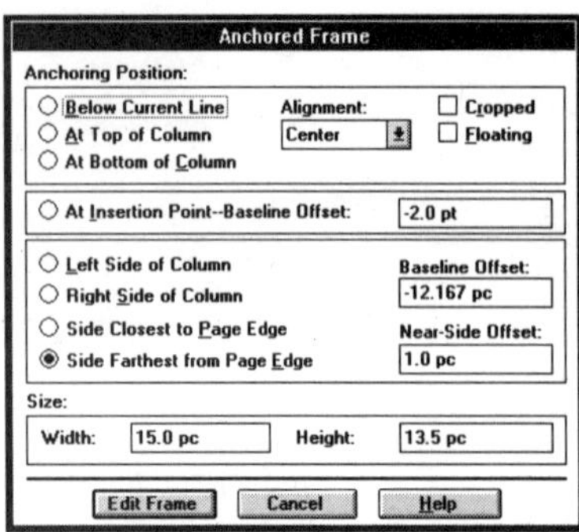

Click Edit Frame to apply new properties to a selected frame.

Finding out about the properties of a frame

■ *Select an anchored frame, and display the Anchored Frame dialog box.* [**Alt s a**] *The properties of the selected frame are displayed. You can change any of them and click Edit Frame to apply the changes.*

■ *Select any frame and display the Object Properties dialog box (page 198).* [**Alt g p**] *The properties of the selected frame are displayed. You can change any of them and click Set.*

■ Copying & pasting a frame or its contents

To cut, copy, or paste the whole frame

When you select a frame and then cut, copy, or paste it, you cut, copy, or paste all of its contents as well.

1. Click on the border of the frame to select it.
2. Cut or copy it: choose **Edit→Cut** or **Edit→Copy**. [**Ctrl-x** or **Ctrl-c**]
3. Place your insertion point where you want the new anchor point to be.
4. Paste: **Edit→Paste** or **Ctrl-v**.

▲ You must have an insertion point in order to paste an anchored frame.

▲ You can paste an unanchored frame anywhere.

To cut, copy, or paste the contents

1. To select everything in the frame, first select the frame by clicking on the border.
2. Choose **Edit→Select All in Frame**. [**Ctrl-a**]
3. Choose Cut, Copy, or Paste from the Edit menu, or use the keyboard shortcuts: **Ctrl-x**, **Ctrl-c**, and **Ctrl-v**.

To paste something inside a frame

1. Select the frame by clicking on its border.
2. Paste.

FrameMaker places the contents of the Clipboard into the frame.

▼

You can paste the contents of a frame anywhere; you do not have to have an insertion point. If the pasted items are not in an anchored frame, however, they will not move with the text.

▲ *If you paste the contents of a frame at an insertion point, FrameMaker automatically creates a frame at the insertion point to hold the pasted material. (See "Automatic frames" on page 196.)*

▲

■ Frame fill and borders

To see frame borders even when the pen is turned off (the default), choose **View➔Borders.** [**Alt v b**]

Frames are graphic objects. You can set their borders, fill, and color just as you would for any object. Here is a overview of the available graphic tools. See Chapter 12 for more on using the graphic tools palette.

To use any of these tools Select the frame. To apply the selected property, click on a button in the right-hand column. To choose a different property, click on a left-hand button, and then click on the property you want in the pop-up menu that is displayed.

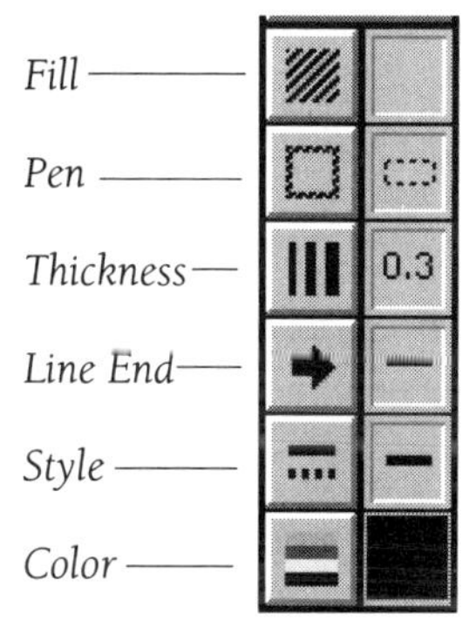

Placing a border on a frame *Click on the Pen tool and choose a pen pattern. (The default is None.) The most usual choice is solid. Then choose a thickness, style, and color.*

Placing a border around text

1. Draw a frame, or create an anchored frame.
2. Turn on the pen, and choose Thickness, Style, and Color. Add Fill if you like.
3. Draw a text column inside the frame, using the Text Column tool in the graphics palette. [**Esc 1** *(one)* **t c**]
4. Position the text column and type the text in it. Format the text as usual.

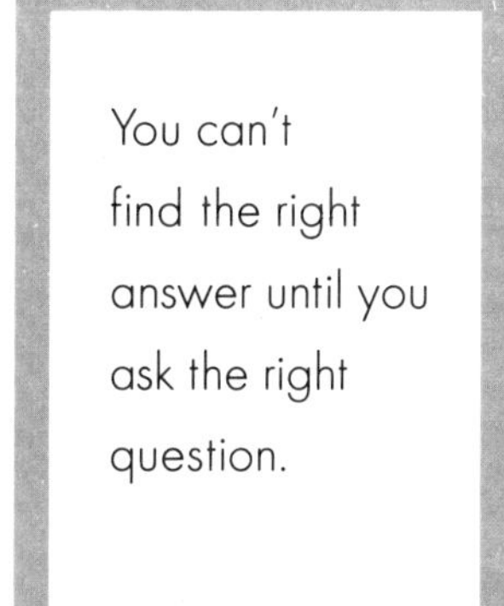

Other ways to do it

You can also put a border around text by typing the text in a single-celled table and turning the table edges on. Another way is to draw a rectangle, oval, or any graphic shape around the text column (page 267).

These are all frames with various fills and borders.

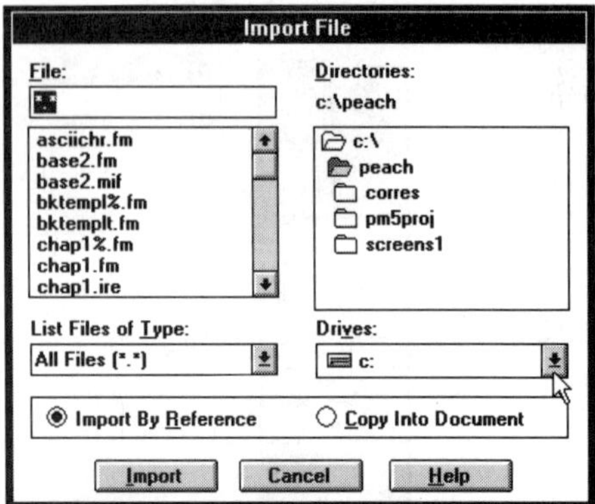

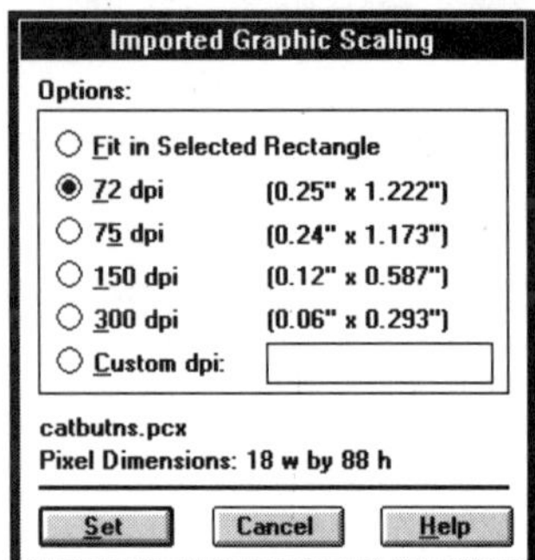

▼

More about Importing by Reference

When you import graphics by references, they remain as separate files. If you copy or move your FrameMaker file, you must remember to copy or move the graphics, too. You have to keep them in the same location relative to the FrameMaker file. You can't change the name or path of the graphics, but you are perfectly free to edit the graphics themselves.

▲

■ Putting text and graphics in frames

You have a variety of ways available to put text and graphics in frames.

Pasting See "To paste something inside a frame" on page 200.

Dragging Select any graphic object elsewhere on the page and drag it into the frame. In order to be contained in the frame, the object must be *entirely* inside the frame. If even one pixel is outside the frame, the object will not move with the frame.

▲ When you're dragging a graphic into a frame, the graphic will be outside the frame until the tip of the pointer moves into the frame. Then the graphic is inside.

Drawing objects directly in the frame

Look in Chapter 12 for a description of how to use FrameMaker's drawing tools.

Importing graphics into a frame

1. Select the frame.
2. Choose **File→Import→File**. [Alt f i f]
3. In the Import File dialog box, select the drive, display the directory containing the file, and select the filename to import.
4. Choose Import By Reference or Copy Into Document.

   ▲ I use Import By Reference a lot. It saves space because FrameMaker "points" to the graphic instead of copying it into the document. The effect is exactly the same as copying. It's displayed just the same, and you can do anything with a referenced graphic that you can do with a copied graphic.
5. Click Import.
6. In the Imported Graphic Scaling dialog box, select the size by selecting the dpi (dots per inch) of the graphic (page 268).
7. Click Set. The graphic appears in the frame.

Text in frames

Text lines

Click on the Text Line tool in the graphics palette. [**Esc 1** (*one*) **t l** (*ell*)] Click in the frame where you want the text to begin, and type. See page 68 for more on text lines. You can Ctrl-click on a a text line to select it, and the reposition it by dragging or micropositioning (page 197).

Text columns

Yes! You can draw one or more text columns inside a frame and type in them just as you would in any text column.

▲ In this book, all the italic text that you see accompanying the graphics in the wide margins is typed in little text columns. For each illustration, I created the anchored frame, imported the graphic, and then drew as many text columns as I needed, and typed the descriptive text in them.

▲ To draw a text column click on the Text Column tool in the graphics palette. [**Esc 1** (*one*) **t c**] Drag diagonally where you want the text column to be.

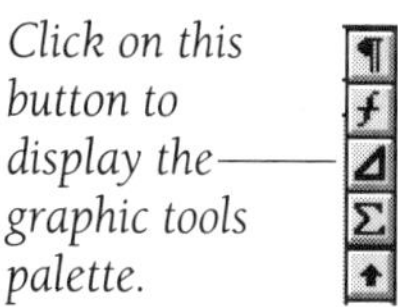

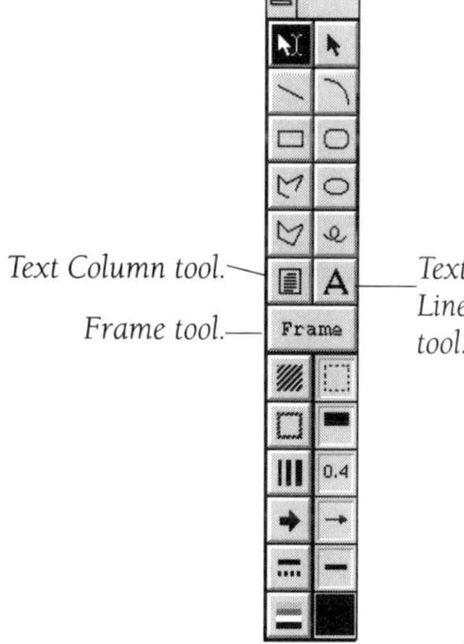

+ This pointer shows that a drawing tool is selected.

You can draw any graphic object directly in a frame. See Chapter 12 for more on drawing objects.

■ Drawing an unanchored frame

■ To draw an unanchored frame select the Frame tool from the graphics palette. [**Esc 1** (*one*) **m**] Position the pointer where one corner of the frame is to be, press and hold the left mouse button, and drag diagonally to define the size of the frame. Release the mouse button.

▲ Use unanchored frames to hold graphics and associated text on body pages when the frame is fixed—i.e., it will not need to move when the text changes.

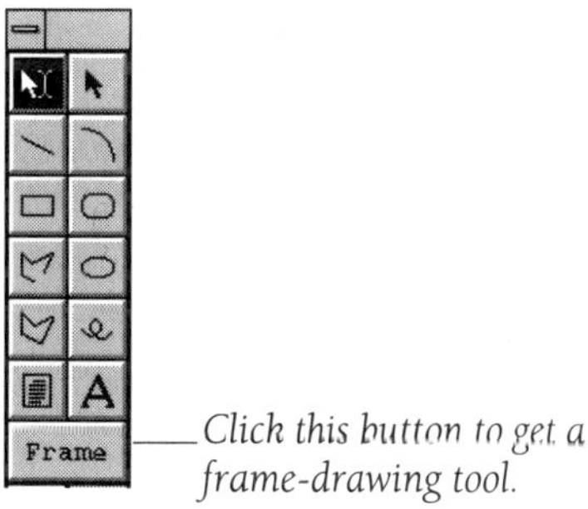

▲ Draw an unanchored frame on a reference page to hold text or graphics that go above or below a paragraph.

■ Frames on reference pages

When you draw a frame on a reference page, FrameMaker presents you with a dialog box asking for a name. This is because FrameMaker assumes that the frame is going to be used as a Frame Below or Frame Above in a paragraph definition, or as a footnote frame. These frames all need names so that they can be identified in the Paragraph Designer in the list of available frames.

Click on the Frame tool in the Graphic palette. Frame

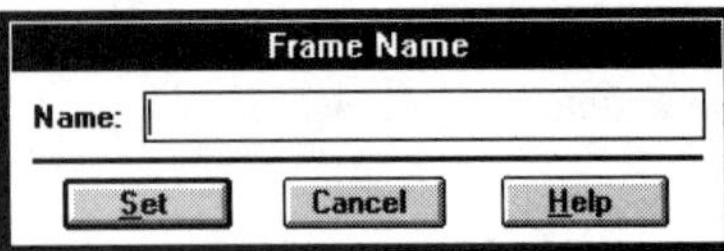

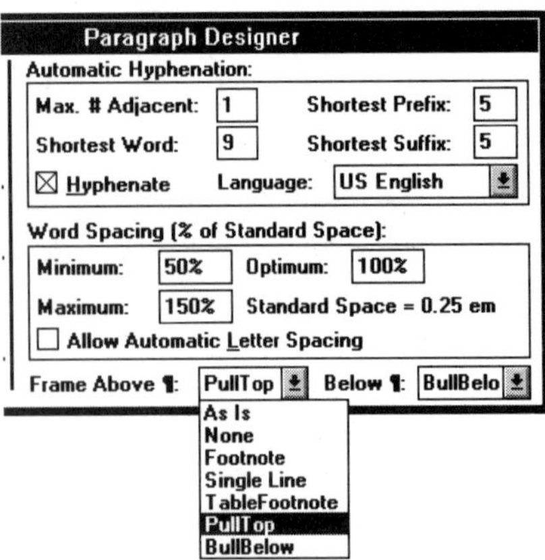

Frames on reference pages appear in the Frame Above and Frame Below pop-up lists. That's why you need to give each one a name when you create it.

Drawing a frame on a reference page

1. Choose the Frame tool from the graphics palette. [**Esc 1** (*one*) **m**]
2. Drag diagonally to create the frame.
3. Type a name in the Frame Name dialog box and click Set.
4. Choose the Text Line tool from the graphics palette. [**Esc 1** (*one*) **t l** (*ell*)] Type the *same name* above the frame. Now you and FrameMaker can both identify the frame.
   ▲ The text line you just typed is for you, the human, rather than for the computer. You can type a description as well as the name. It won't interfere with anything at all. You can also use a text column rather than a text line for the name.

Page Layout

10

■ What's in this chapter

Page layout in FrameMaker can be as simple as filling in a few items of information in the Normal Page Layout dialog box. FrameMaker will automatically add pages as you need them, using the Normal master pages. At the other end of the spectrum, you can create intricate page layouts to your exact specifications, working on master pages or on body pages.

■ This chapter covers the use of the Normal Page Layout dialog box, the creation and use of master pages, management of text columns on either master or body pages, the use of flow and Autoconnect to direct the flow of text, and techniques for drop caps and flowing text around graphics.

▼

How FrameMaker uses Normal Pages

FrameMaker uses a master page to provide the column layout of every body page. In a single-sided document, FrameMaker uses a master page named Right as the default master page. In a double-sided document, it uses two default master pages: Right and Left. These default master pages are called the Normal Page layouts.

▲

The Autoconnect concept

Autoconnect is a property of a text column. When the columns on a body page have Autoconnect turned on, FrameMaker will add new pages as the current ones fill up. This is the most common way of working in FrameMaker. See page 221 for more on Autoconnect.

The Flow concept

Think of a magazine, where an article begins on a page and then continues on a much later page. It shares both of these pages with other material. If you're laying out these pages, how do you tell the layout application (FrameMaker, for example) where everything goes? You assign each article a different **flow** *(page 220). The text columns have a flow, too. Text that has flow* **A** *assigned to it flows into columns with flow* **A** *assigned: exactly which column is determined by the order in which the columns are* **connected** *(page 218).*

■ *Most documents have only one flow, so you don't have to think about it.*

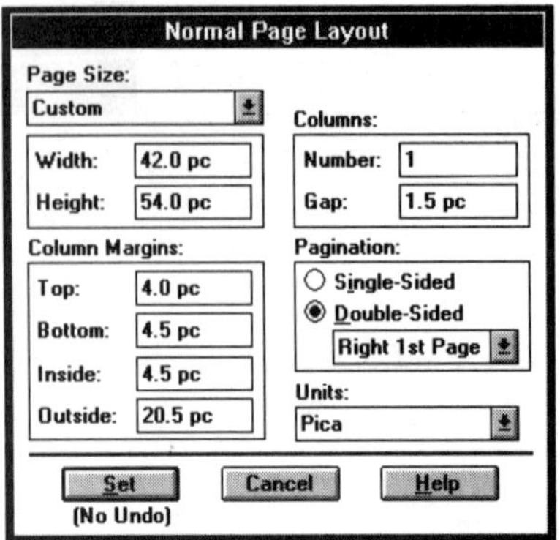

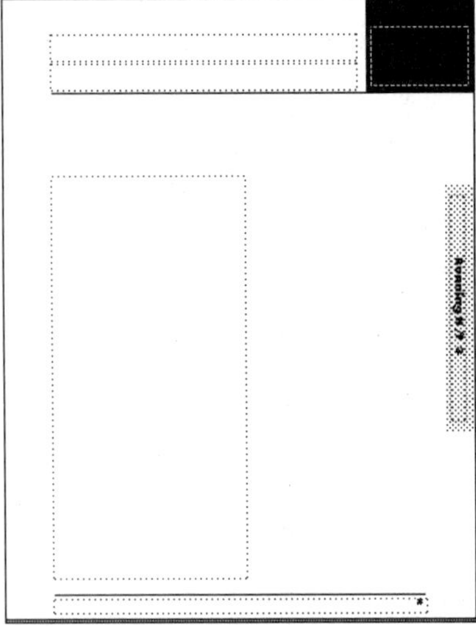

A master page used in this book.

■ Page layout: ways to do it

The Normal Page Layout dialog box

If your page layout is simple, you can enter all your page, column, and margin sizes in this dialog box. FrameMaker uses these figures to create the "Normal" master pages (page 209). You may need to customize the information in the header and footer of the Normal master pages, but all the other work is done. Enter your text: FrameMaker creates new pages for you as you go, using the specifications you provide here.

Work on master pages

You can always work directly on the master pages: you can work on the "normal" Right and Left master pages, and create as many new ones as you like. Add background text and graphics, and modify the text columns to your heart's content. FrameMaker applies the Right and Left master pages by default, but you can assign any master page to any body page. See "Applying master pages to body pages" on page 210.

Work on body pages

You can change the text column layout directly on a body page: add, delete, resize, move, combine, or split the columns, and change their flow or connections. See "Managing text columns" on page 215 and "Text alignment: feathering and synchronization" on page 222. You cannot edit headers or footers, or other background items on a body page.

Use a document template that has the page layout you want

You can use any document as a template. Choose one that has the page layout you want. Open it using **File→New** [**Ctrl-n**], and use **File→Save As** [**Alt f a**] to give it a new name. Select the old contents with **Ctrl-a** and delete them. See pages 45 and 48 if you need more details on this process.

■ The Layout palette

FrameMaker has collected all of its layout commands onto one palette that you can keep handy while you work. To display the Layout palette, choose **Format→Pages→Layout Commands**. [**Alt o a l** (*ell*)] Several of these commands are also available from **Format→Pages** or **Format→Flow** if you do not have the palette displayed.

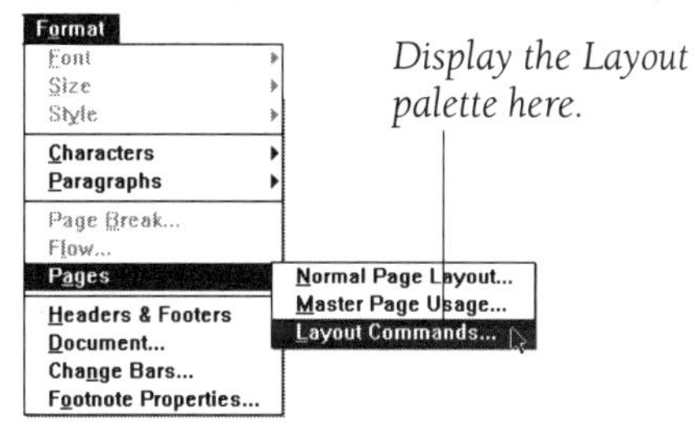

Display the Layout palette here.

Overview of FrameMaker's Layout palette

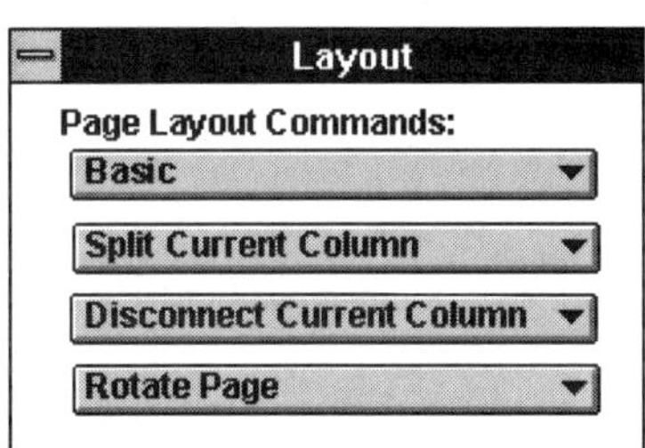

These four buttons produce the four menus below. The keyboard shortcuts are worth learning if you do much page layout, because they save you a **lot** *of mousing around.*

Three dots after a menu entry *mean that clicking on that entry displays a dialog box.*

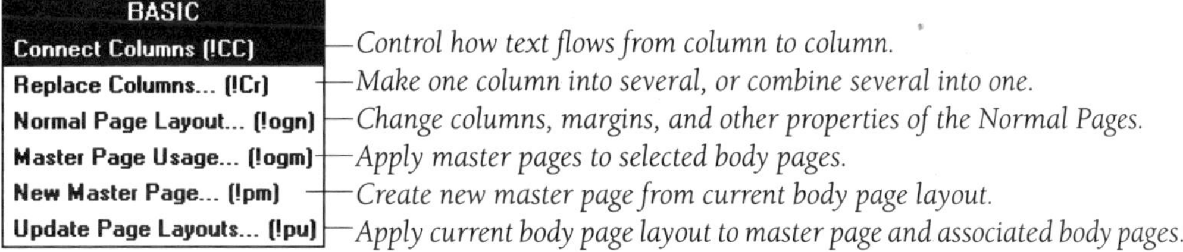

SPLIT CURRENT COLUMN
Below Selection (!CS)
Right of Selection (!CR)
Into Lines (!CL)

The three **Split Current Column** *commands are used by placing the cursor in text. You cannot use these commands on empty columns. Use these commands to create runarounds.*

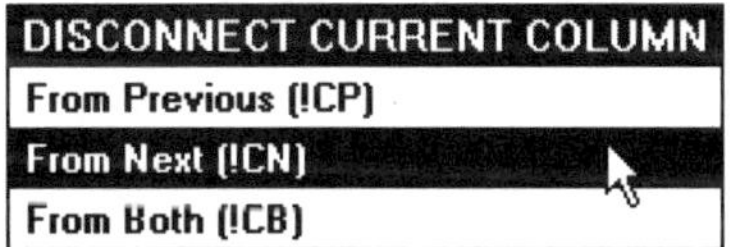

Use these commands to control how text flows from column to column. They are the opposite of the Connect Columns command in the Basic menu, above.

ROTATE PAGE
Clockwise (!pO)
Counterclockwise (!po)
Unrotate (!pU)

Use these commands to rotate a body page or a master page.

A note on the keyboard shortcuts: *The shortcuts displayed in the Layout palette begin with an exclamation point. This is shorthand for the Escape key. In this book, I use* **Esc** *instead of* **!** *when I give a shortcut.*

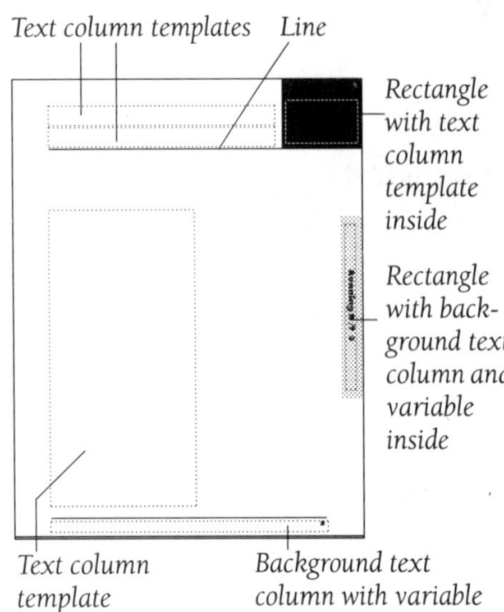

The master page for chapter openings in this book.

■ Managing master pages

FrameMaker's "Normal" master pages

In a single-sided document, FrameMaker automatically creates the Right master page. In a two-sided document, it creates Right and Left master pages. These are the "Normal" page layouts, used as the default master pages for new body pages.

■ You can change these Right and Left master pages by using the Normal Page Layout dialog box (page 209), or by working directly on the master pages, described throughout this chapter.

Your very own master pages

■ You can create master pages at will, and assign any master page to any body page.

What's on a master page?

There are three kinds of things on master pages: text column templates, background text columns (usually with text in them), and graphics.

Text column templates

■ These columns have a flow assigned and usually have autoconnect turned on.

■ They are templates for text columns on body pages. They appear on any body page that uses the master page they are on. You type in them on the body page

■ If you put text in a text column template *on a master page*, it will not appear on the body page. To put background text on a master page, put it in a *background text column.*

Background text columns

■ A master page text column that has no flow tag assigned is a background text column.

■ Any text that you put in a background text column appears on any body page that uses that master page. The column itself is not visible on the body page, only the contents.

■ Header and footer columns are the most common example of background text columns.

■ Background text is editable only on master pages. You can't touch it on a body page.

Graphics

Place graphics wherever you need them on a master page. You can draw graphics with Frame-Maker's drawing tools (page 255), or import them (page 84). They will appear on any body page that uses that master page. You can use Text Lines—they're a type of graphic object. Do not put text or graphics in a text column template if you want them to appear on body pages.

■ Normal page layout

Use the Normal Page Layout dialog box to modify the layout of the default master pages (Right and Left) only when their layout is fairly simple and does not include asymmetrical design, columns of unequal widths, rotated pages or other complexities. More elaborate layout should be done directly on the master pages.

1. Display the Normal Page Layout dialog box: either choose **Format→Pages→Normal Page Layout** or, if the Layout palette is displayed [**Alt o a l** (*ell*)], click on the Basic button and choose Normal Page Layout from the menu.
2. Make the changes you want and click Set. If FrameMaker detects layout overrides on individual pages that will be affected by your changes, it asks whether you want to retain the overrides.

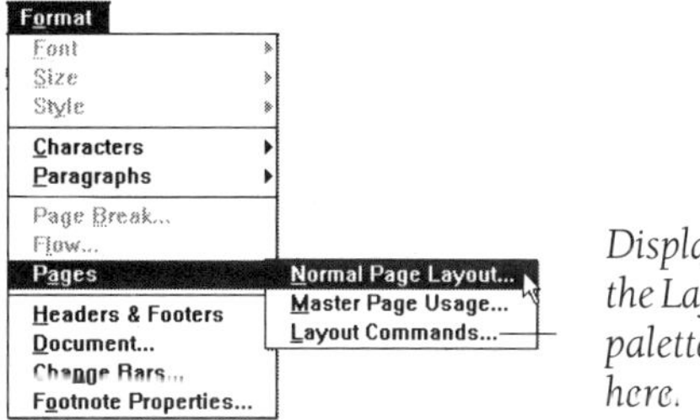

Display the Layout palette here.

Use either the Format menu (above) or the Layout palette (below) to display the Normal Page Layout dialog box (bottom of page).

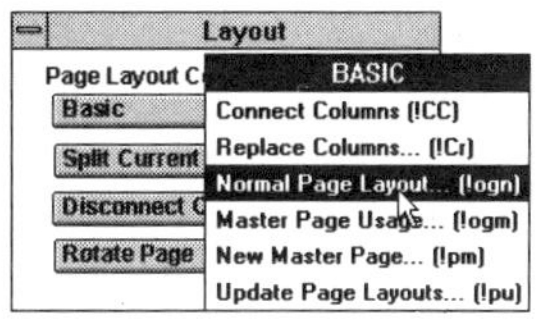

The "Normal" pages are the Right master page in a single-sided document, and the Right and Left master pages in a double-sided document.

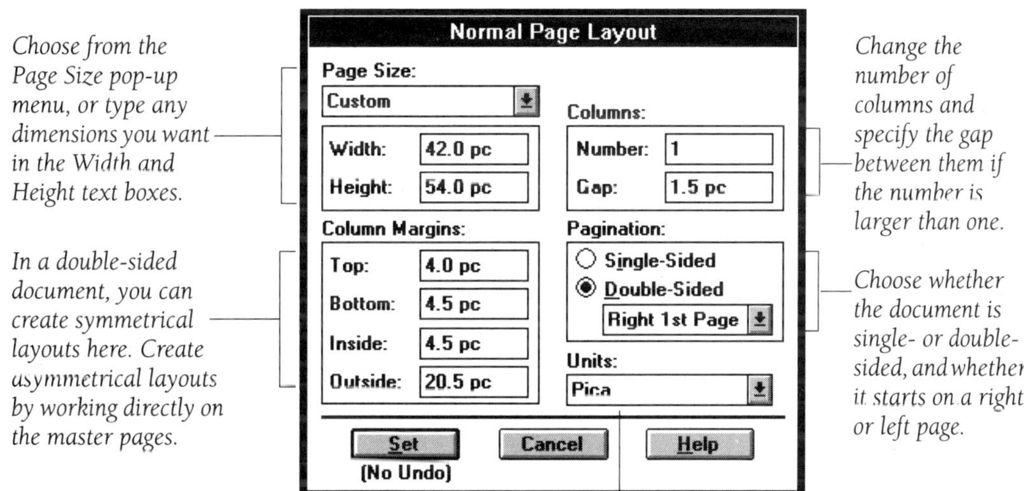

Choose from the Page Size pop-up menu, or type any dimensions you want in the Width and Height text boxes.

In a double-sided document, you can create symmetrical layouts here. Create asymmetrical layouts by working directly on the master pages.

Change the number of columns and specify the gap between them if the number is larger than one.

Choose whether the document is single- or double-sided, and whether it starts on a right or left page.

Change the display units for the document. You can also do this in **View→Options**.

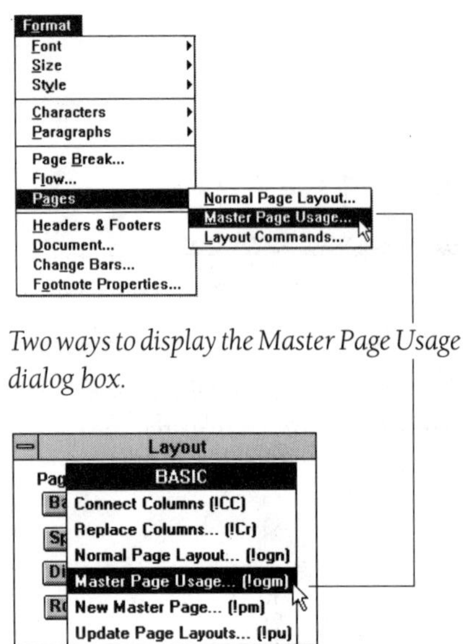

Two ways to display the Master Page Usage dialog box.

Applying master pages to body pages

You can apply any master page to any body page. The body page will then have

- the text columns that are created by the text column templates on the master page;
- text that is in background text columns on the master page, including text generated by variables;
- and any graphics present on the master page.

▲ If the body page has a flow that is not present on the new master page, FrameMaker leaves that flow's text columns in place, so you can decide what to do with them. You don't have to worry about text being destroyed when you apply a master page.

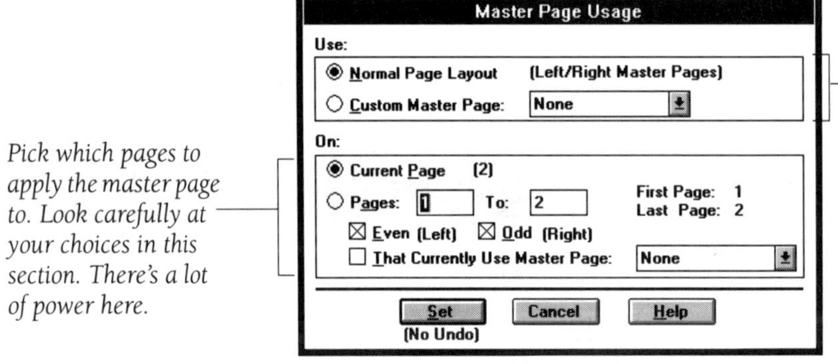

Pick which pages to apply the master page to. Look carefully at your choices in this section. There's a lot of power here.

Pick which master page to apply. Normal Page applies the Right master page in a single-sided document. It applies Right or Left appropriately in a double-sided document. The Custom Page pop-up lists all the available master pages.

Applying a master page to a range of body pages

Choose the range, and then choose whether to apply the master page to only the left pages in the range, only the right pages, or only to pages in the range with a particular type of master page.

- If you have a group of pages that need a special master page, you can create them all at once. Create several new pages by applying "Start: Top of Page" to several empty lines (page 134). Then apply the appropriate master page to the group by specifying the page numbers in the Master Page Usage dialog box.

Creating a custom master page

Many documents use a special layout for the first page. Sometimes they need special layouts for other pages as well. If a page layout is a one-time-only occurrence, you can just modify the body page (page 222). But if you might need to use a layout more than once, it's easy to create a master page and then apply it as needed to body pages.

1. Display master pages. [**Alt v m**]
2. Choose **Special→Add Master Page**. [**Alt s p**]
3. Turn on Copy from Master Page: and choose an existing master page that is similar to the one you want to create. Or choose Empty to begin with a blank page.
4. Type a name in the Name box and click Add. FrameMaker creates and displays the new master page.

▲ Make whatever modifications, additions, and deletions you wish. See "Managing text columns" on page 215 for more about adding text column templates and background text columns. See also "What's on a master page?" on page 208.

Creating a master page from a body page

1. Modify column layout directly on a body page. (You cannot change background text on a body page.)
2. Choose **Format→Pages→Layout Commands→Basic→New Master Page**. [**Esc p m**]
3. Type in a name for the new master page and click Create.

Updating a master page from a body page

1. Modify column layout directly on a body page. (You cannot change background text on a body page.)
2. Choose **Format→Pages→Layout Commands→Basic→Update Page Layouts**. [**Esc p u**]
3. In the Update Page Layouts dialog box, click Update.

Type a name for the new master page.

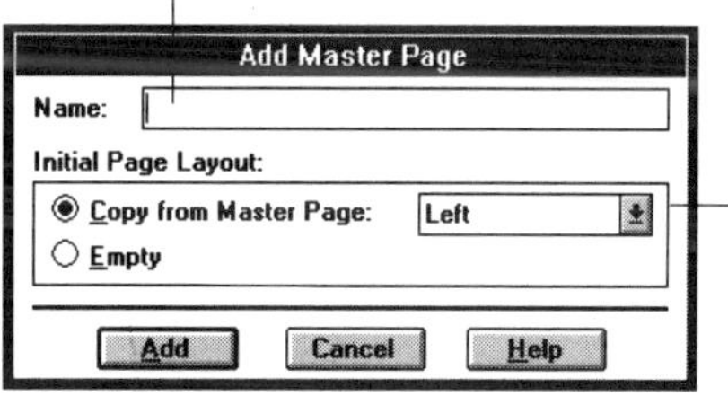

Choose to copy a similar master page to use as a starting point, or choose Empty to start with an empty page. Then click Add to create the page.

Create a master page from a body page.

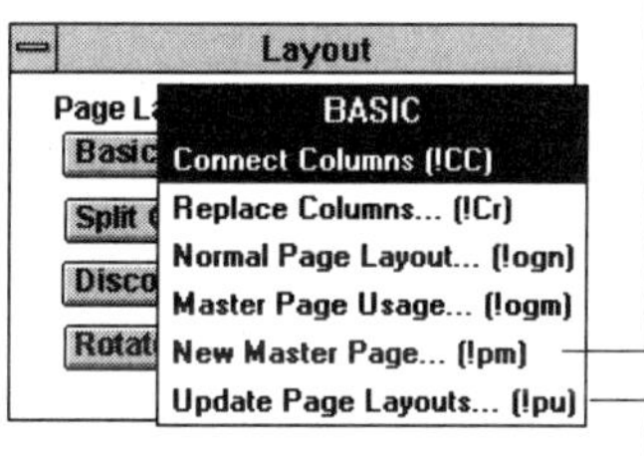

Update a master page and all associated body pages from a body page.

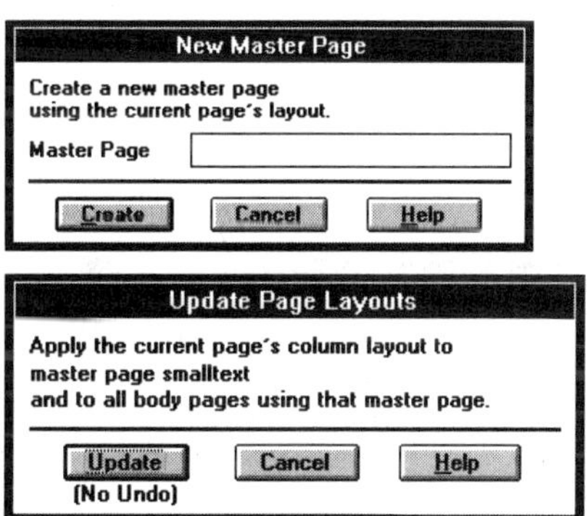

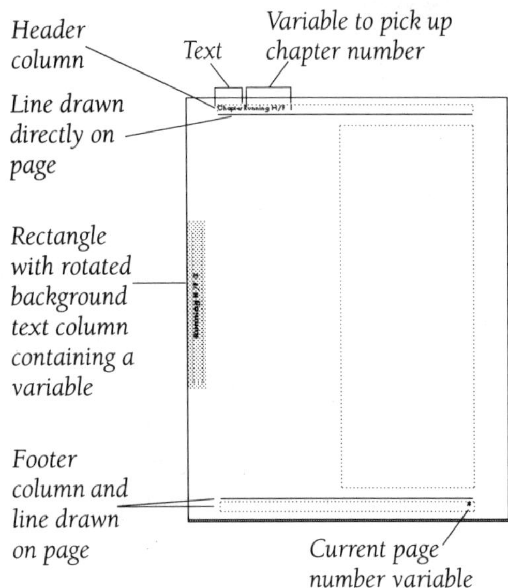

The Left master page from this book.

Insert variables to display

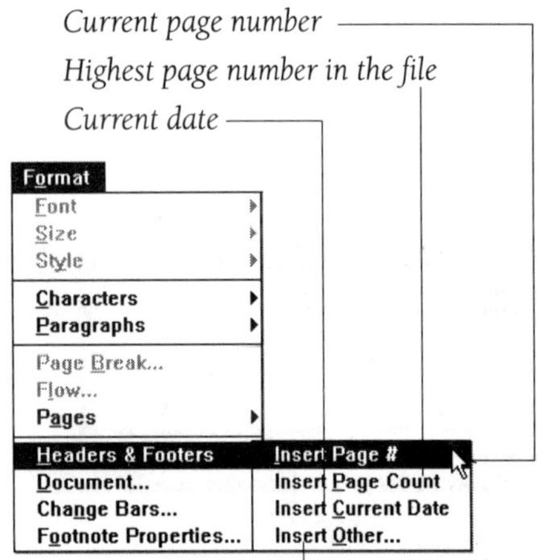

Headers and footers

Headers and footers are background text. They are typed in background text columns on master pages. FrameMaker provides columns for headers and footers in the master pages that it provides with templates and new documents.

- The header columns on FrameMaker's master pages contain an empty paragraph called Header. It has a centered tab in the middle and a flush right tab at the right edge. It determines the look of text that you type in the header column. You can modify this format just as you would any other paragraph format, to make your headers look the way you want them to. You can also apply a different paragraph format to the text in the header column. Similarly, the footer columns contain a paragraph with a format called Footer.
- In header or footer columns that you draw yourself, click in the column to place your insertion point, and then apply whatever paragraph format you want for your headers or other background text.

1. Type text in the header or footer column. Remember that there are tabs available.
2. Add variables for page numbers, paragraph text, dates, file names, or other system information that you want to display.

   ▲ Choose **Format➔Headers & Footers** to easily enter a variable for the page number, page count, or date, or click on Other to display the Variable dialog box.

   ▲ Alternately, you can insert any variable by displaying the Variable dialog box [**Alt s v**] or by using the keyboard [**Ctrl-0** (*zero*) plus letter] See pages 162 to 170 for more on variables.
3. Modify the Header paragraph format, or apply a different paragraph format. You can also use character formats where needed.

Page numbering style

Choose the Page # Style (arabic, roman, or alphabetic) from the Document Properties dialog box (page 23). [**Alt o d**] This specifies the page number style that the Current Page # variable displays.

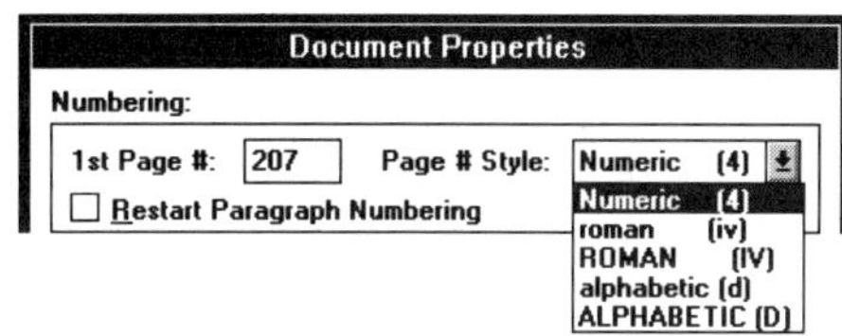

Other background text

Headers and footers aren't the only way you can use background text on master pages. Any time you need text to appear on body pages in a non-editable form, put it on the master page.

▪ Take a look at the **fax template** for a beautiful example of making good use of background text. Type **Ctrl-n** to display the New dialog box. Then click on Explore Standard Templates. Choose Fax from the Business group, and then click on Show Sample. Display the master page [**Alt v m**] and analyze what they've done (see below).

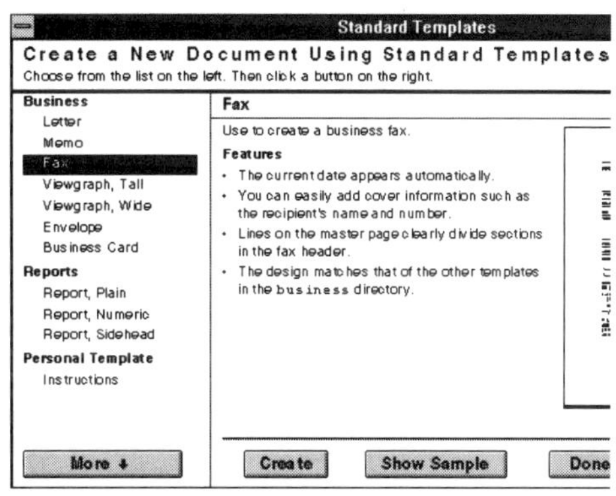

Choose Fax from the Business group, and click Show Sample.

The master page of FrameMaker's Fax template

(A master page example worth studying!)

FAX Transmittal

DATE: November 2, 1993
SENT BY:
TO:
COMPANY:
FAX NUMBER:
NUMBER OF PAGES (WITH COVER):
MESSAGE:

Select this text column and display its properties. [**Alt o l** *(oh ell)*] *It has no flow, so it is a* **background text column**. *The text in it appears on the body page, but is not editable there. The "Fax Transmittal" column is background text, too.*

This column has a flow assigned; it is a **text column template**. *Users type messages here on the body page.*

To examine this text column, you must first ungroup it (select it and press **Alt g u**). *Then select the larger column and look at its properties. It has a flow so it is a text column template. Users type in this area on the body page to fill out the form.*

The horizontal lines are drawn directly on the page with the Line tool. They appear on the body page, but are not editable there.

Rotating a master page

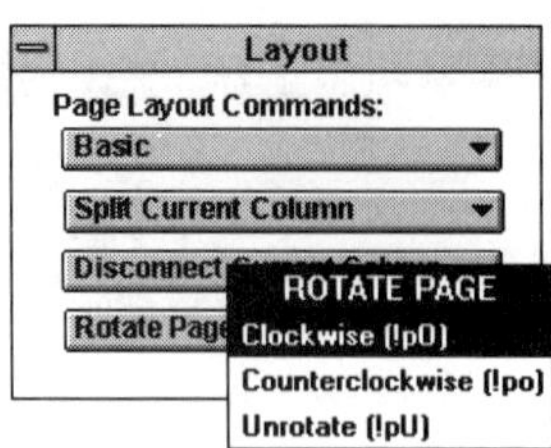

Create a rotated master page so that you can type rotated text in normal, horizontal position.

1. First create any columns or background text that will not appear rotated on the body page (headers and footers, for example).
2. Rotate the page by choosing **Format→Pages→Layout Commands→ Rotate Page**, and choosing Clockwise or Counterclockwise from the menu. [**Esc p O** or **Esc p o**]
3. Add text template columns for rotated text.

▲ This allows you to work on the rotated text in a normal, horizontal position. However, the page prints in its original, unrotated position, so that the text appears rotated.

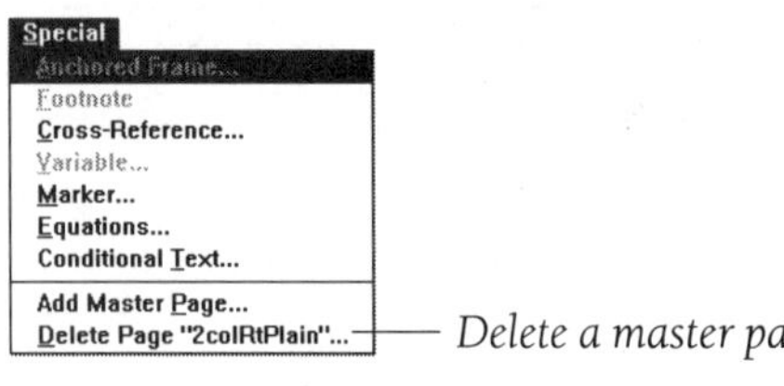

Delete a master page.

Deleting a master page

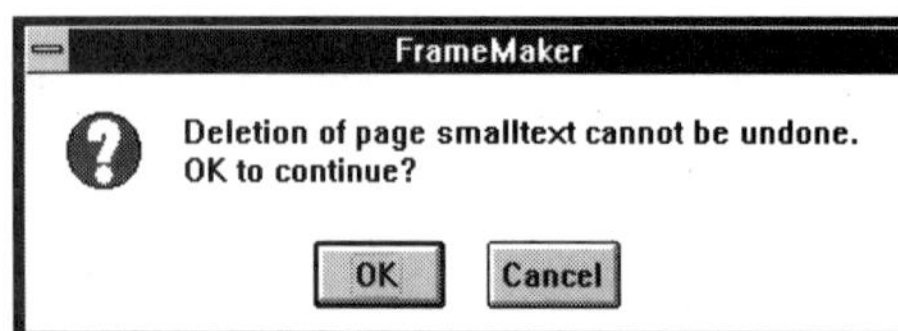

1. Display the master pages. [**Alt v m**]
2. Go to the page you want to delete. [**Ctrl-g** or PgUp and PgDn]
3. Choose **Special→Delete Pages**. [**Alt v m**]
4. In the warning window, click OK.

▲ You cannot delete a master page that is in use by body pages. If you try to do so, FrameMaker posts a message window telling you which body pages use that master page. You can then change the master page assignment.

Renaming a master page

Click on this area of the status bar to rename a master page.

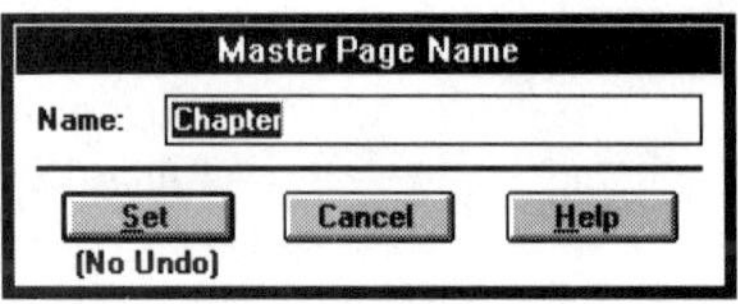

1. Display the master pages. [**Alt v m**]
2. Go to the page you want to rename. [**Ctrl-g** or PgUp and PgDn]
3. Click on the page name in the status bar.
4. Type a new name in the Master Page Name dialog box.
5. Click Set.

■ Managing text columns

Here are the basic manipulations. It doesn't matter whether you're working on a body page or a master page. These work anywhere.

Working with text columns

These techniques work on all text columns—template columns or background text columns.

Draw	Click on the [text column] button in the graphics palette. [**Esc 1** *(one)* **t c**] Drag diagonally where you want the text column to be, and then release the mouse button.
Move	Ctrl-click on the border of the text column to select it. Position the pointer over the border of the column *between the resize handles*. Drag the column to its new location (page 258). **Or** display the Object Properties dialog box [**Alt g p**] and change the top and left offset (page 262).
Resize	Ctrl-click on the border of the text column to select it. Position the pointer over one of the eight resize handles and drag the handle to a new position (page 264). **Or** display the Object Properties dialog box [**Alt g p**] and change the width or height (page 262).
Copy or cut	Ctrl-click on the border of the text column to select it. Choose **Edit→Copy** or **Edit→Cut**. [**Ctrl-c** or **Ctrl-x**]
Paste	Choose **Edit→Paste**. [**Ctrl-v**] (First click outside all text columns to be sure you don't have an insertion point at the time you paste—unless you really want FrameMaker to create an anchored frame and put the column in it.) **Paste in a frame** Click on the border of the frame to select it. Then paste. This guarantees that your pasted object will land inside the frame.

Drawing a text column on a master page

Draw the text column as always: select the [text column] button in the graphics palette and drag across the area where you want the column. FrameMaker then displays a dialog box in which you specify whether the column is a background text column or a text column template (page 208).

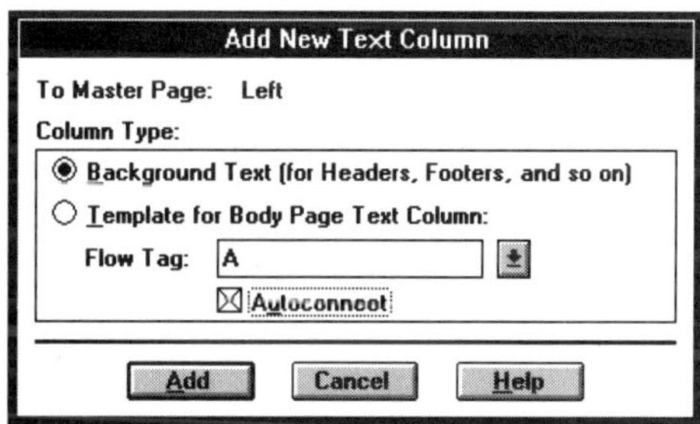

FrameMaker displays this automatically when you draw a text column on a master page.

Managing text columns

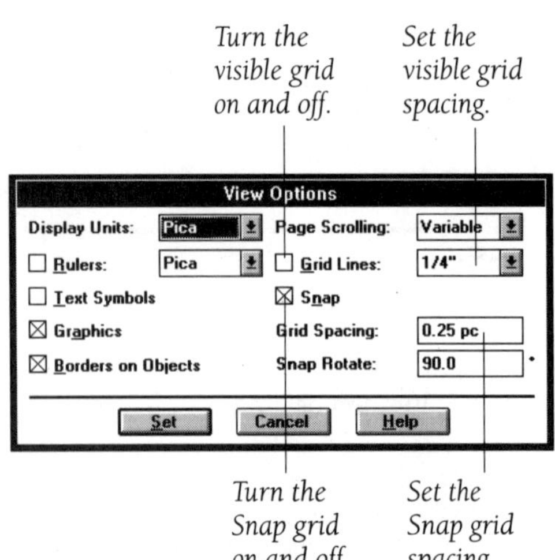

▲ *Turning either grid on or off from the View Options dialog box is exactly the same as using the menus.*

▼

To select a text column *Ctrl-click on its border. If the column contains text, you can ctrl-click anywhere in the text to select the column.* **To select another** *text column, Ctrl-click on it also.* **To unselect a text column** *click anywhere outside it, or Ctrl-click on its border again.*

▲

Positioning and aligning text columns

Snap grid: Graphics→Snap [Alt g n]

When Snap is on, things automatically position themselves on the invisible Snap grid as you move them. I usually keep this turned on as I work. It saves a lot of cleanup later. Sometimes you have to turn it off to move something to a position not on the grid.

Visible grid: View→Grid Lines [Alt v l]

Turning Grid Lines on displays a visible grid of lines. (I don't like the grid, personally, but many people do.)

The Object Properties dialog box

The Object Properties dialog box shows you the properties of the currently selected object, and lets you change those properties. It's handy when you need to work by the numbers, instead of just using your intuition as you drag things around.

1. Select the text column or other object.
2. To display the Object Properties dialog box, choose **Graphics→Object Properties**. [Alt g p]

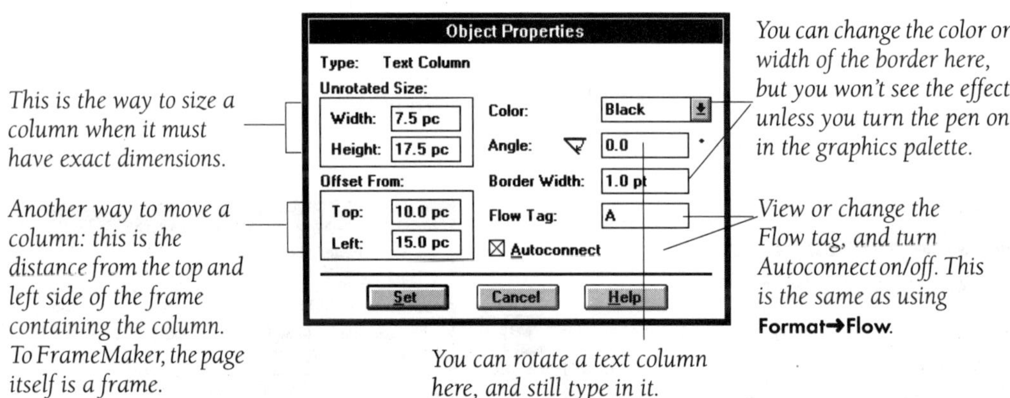

The Object Properties dialog box *shows you the properties of the selected object (a text column in this case). You can change any of the properties and click Set.*

Creating and combining multiple text columns

On the menu of the Basic button of the Layout palette, you will find the Replace Columns command. Use this command to perform a number of slick tricks with columns: you can replace one column with many, or many columns with one.

1. **To merge several columns into one column**, select all the columns to merge. The columns must all be on the same page or in the same frame; they must be connected, and they must not be Grouped. **Or, to split one column into several columns**, select the column.
2. In the Layout palette, click on Basic, and choose Replace Columns from the menu. [**Esc C r**]
3. In the Replace Selected Columns dialog box, fill in the number of columns you want and enter a gap width if you are creating multiple columns. The Column Margins are the distance from the outer boundaries of the whole group of columns to the edges of the containing frame. FrameMaker considers the page itself to be a frame.

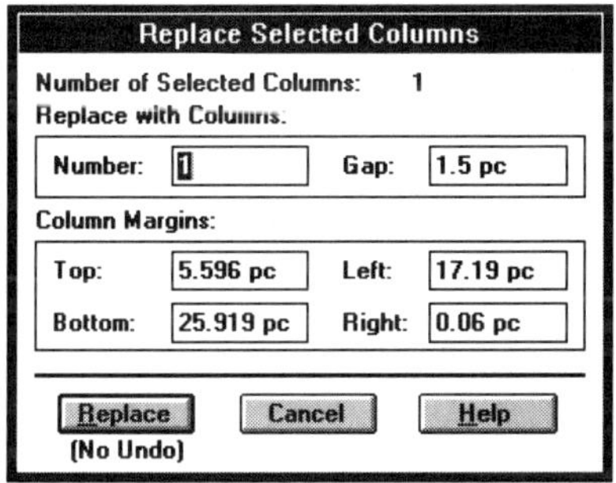

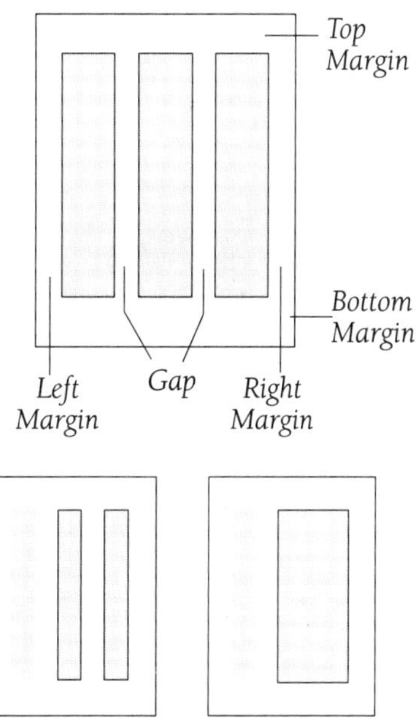

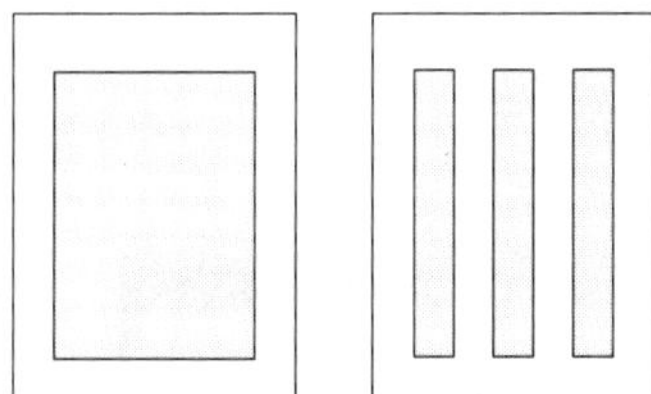

Select one column and Replace it with three.

Select two columns and Replace them with one.

▲ The easiest way to create evenly-spaced multiple columns of equal width is to draw a single column and then use Replace Columns to split it into the desired number of columns.

▲ You can use Replace Columns on empty columns or on columns with text in them.

Connecting and disconnecting columns

Flow You can think of the text columns in a FrameMaker document as a sort of riverbed: the text is the water flowing along its appointed course. The flow of text from one column to the next is determined by the column connections.

■ If you're using a template that has been properly designed, the text flow will happen automatically. When you're designing templates, though, or creating a complex layout (think of a newspaper or magazine, for example), you need to be able to tell FrameMaker where to "flow" the text.

Displaying the Layout palette

Choose **Format→Pages→Layout Commands** *to display the Layout palette.* [**Alt o a l** (*ell*)] *In the procedures in this section, I will assume that you are working in the Layout palette, and will describe the location of the commands on the palette without repeating the procedure for displaying it.*

Connecting two columns

The columns can contain text or be empty when you do this.

1. Select the columns in the order you want the text to flow. *The order in which you select the columns is crucial.* You can select columns that are on two different pages. To select the second column, Ctrl-click on its border, in exactly the same way you selected the first one.
2. In the Layout palette, click Basic, and choose Connect Columns. [**Esc C C**]

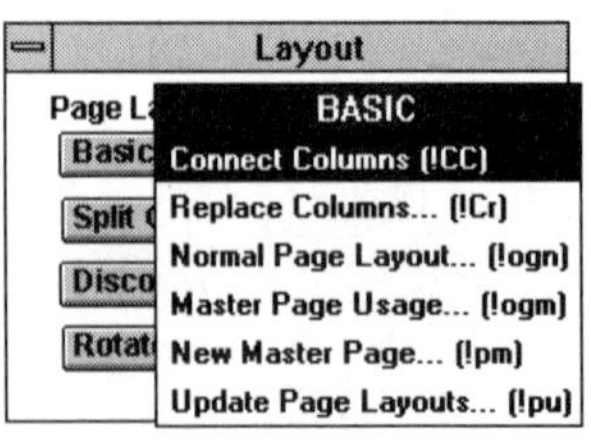

▲ If the columns are on two different pages, FrameMaker asks

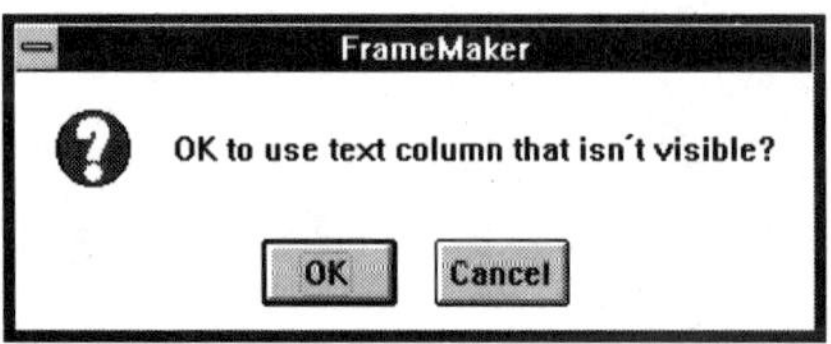

(...because the column on the first page is now invisible). Click OK.

▲ If the first of the two columns has a flow assigned, FrameMaker assigns that flow to the second column when it makes the connection. *All connected columns have the same flow.*

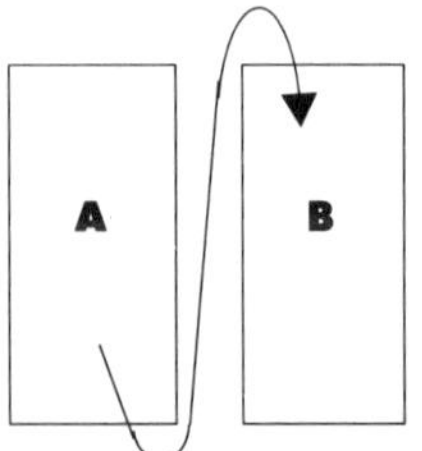

Suppose that originally, text flows from **A** *to* **B**.

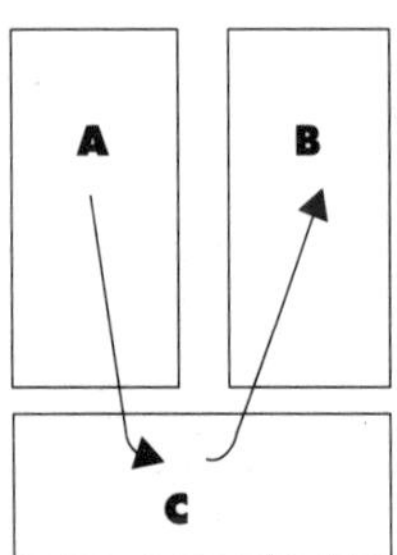

Connect **A** *to* **C** *(select them in that order). Now the text flow is* **A** *to* **C** *to* **B**.

Disconnecting a column

To disconnect two columns, you choose only one. Decide whether you want to disconnect it from the previous column, the next column, or both.

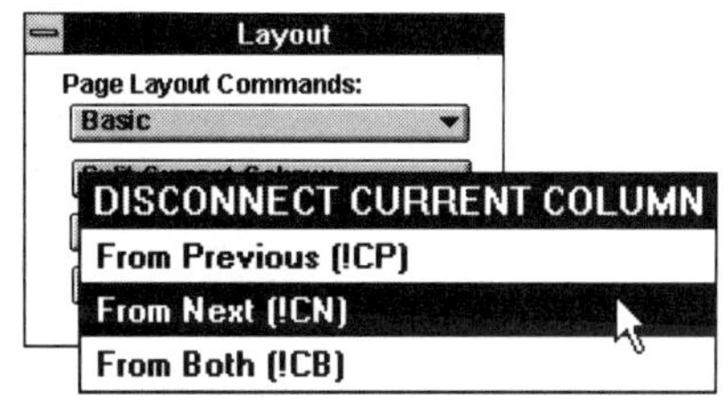

1. Select one column.
2. Click on the Disconnect Current Column button of the Layout palette, and then click on From Previous, From Next, or From Both [**Esc C P**, **Esc C N**, or **Esc C B**]

Removing a column from the middle of a flow

If you want text to skip over part of a column—so you can put a pull quote or graphic in it, for example—you don't have to disconnect anything. Instead, split the column up into pieces [**Esc C S**], and select the piece before and the piece after, and connect them to each other. [**Esc C C**]

Split the column at the arrows. [**Esc C S**]

Select the top column and the bottom column, and connect them. [**Esc C C**] *Now the text jumps over the disconnected middle column.*

See where text flows

In a complex multi-flow document, you can lose track of where a flow goes. Here's how to track a flow across several pages:

1. Zoom the document out to a small setting, such as 30 or 40 percent.
2. Set Page Scrolling to Variable in the **View→Options** dialog box, if it's not already.
3. Place your insertion point in the flow you want to track.
4. Choose **Edit→Select All in Flow**. [**Ctrl-a**] The selected flow will be highlighted. You can see its progress across the pages.

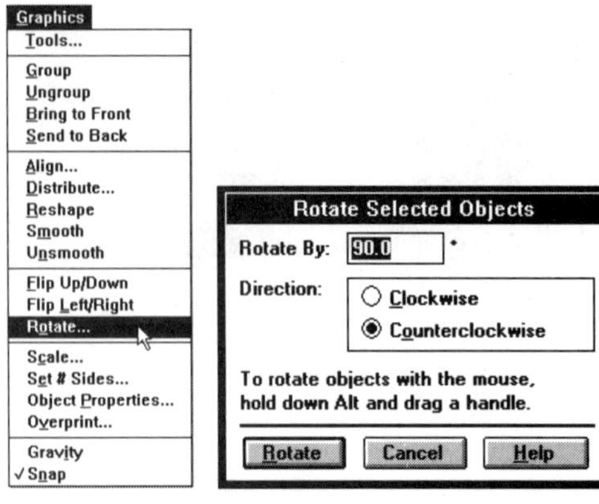

Rotating a column

1. Ctrl-click on the border of the column to select it.
2. Choose **Graphics→Rotate**. [**Alt g o**]
3. In the Rotate Selected Objects dialog box, fill in the number of degrees to rotate and choose a direction.
4. Click Rotate.

▲ Yes, you can also rotate the text column using the Object Properties dialog box [**Alt g p**], or by using Alt-drag (page 261).

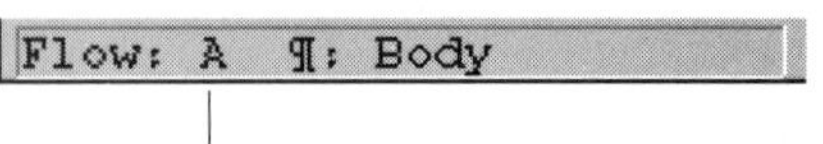

Look in the status bar at the bottom of your document window to see the flow tag of the text containing your insertion point.

Flow tags

Most FrameMaker documents have only one "flow" of text, named A by default. Place your insertion point anywhere in text and look at the status bar at the bottom of the window. The first item of information is the flow of the text.

■ Flow is a property of text and of text columns. The flow tag of a column is always the same as the flow tag of the text it contains. To change a flow tag, you can either select the column, or select the text flow by placing your insertion point in it.

Change the flow tag here.

Flow Properties
Flow Tag: A
☒ Autoconnect
☐ PostScript Code
☐ Baseline Synchronization:
Synchronize ¶'s with Line Spacing Of: 0.0 pt
First-Line Synchronization Limit: 0.0 pt
☐ Feather
Feathering Padding for All Document Flows:
Maximum Interline Padding: 0.0 pt
Maximum Inter-¶ Padding: 6.0 pt
Set Cancel Help

Assigning or changing a flow tag

1. Place your insertion point anywhere in the text flow you want to change. If you are assigning a flow tag to an empty column, select the column.
2. Choose **Format→Flow**. [**Alt o l** (*oh ell*)]
3. In the Flow Properties dialog box, type in the new flow tag. The tag is case-sensitive: **A** is not the same as **a**.
4. Make any other changes, such as changing Autoconnect, and then click Set.

■ When you change the flow tag of any part of a flow, you change the whole connected flow. FrameMaker also displays a dialog box, asking you if you want to change all occurrences of that flow tag.

How Autoconnect works

Autoconnect determines whether FrameMaker will automatically add a new page when the columns on the current available connected pages fill up. To have FrameMaker add pages automatically, turn Autoconnect on when you create the text column templates on the master pages.

1. Place your insertion point anywhere in the text flow you want to change. If you are changing the Autoconnect property of an empty column, select the column.
2. Choose **Format→Flow**. [**Alt o l** (*oh ell*)]
3. In the Flow Properties dialog box, turn autoconnect on or off, as you wish.
4. Make any other changes, such as changing the flow tag, and click Set.

■ When FrameMaker automatically adds a new page, it uses the appropriate Normal Page layout. In a single-sided document, this is always the Right master page. In a double-sided document it is either Right or Left, depending on whether the page number is odd or even.

Automatic custom master pages

■ There is one situation where FrameMaker automatically adds pages using custom master pages instead of the "normal" ones. If you are working on a body page that uses a custom master page whose columns have a different flow than the Normal Pages, FrameMaker will use the custom master page to continue text on that body page. You must have autoconnect turned on for the columns on both the master page and the body page.

Autonumbering and column connection

In order for autonumbering to continue between columns, those column *must be connected*. They don't necessarily have to have Autoconnect turned on: you can connect them by hand.

Turn Autoconnect on here.

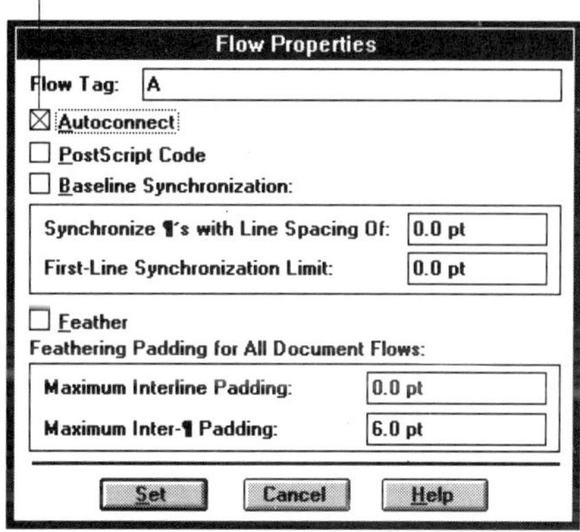

▼

If new pages aren't happening

If you find that new pages are not happening, and you think they should be, check to see whether Autoconnect is on. Select the column that should be right before the new page. Display the Flow Properties dialog box [**Alt o l** (*oh ell*)] *and make sure that Autoconnect is turned on.*

If Autoconnect is incorrectly turned off on your body page, you might want to check the master page also, and make sure that it is turned on there. Then newly-created body pages will automatically have the Autoconnect property turned on.

▲

▼

Autoconnect and flow

A flow that has Autoconnect turned on must have a flow tag assigned.

▲

Text alignment: feathering and synchronization

To specify feathering and synchronization, choose **Format→Flow** to display the Flow Properties dialog box.

When you turn **feathering** on, FrameMaker makes text line up at the bottom of columns as well as the top. It adds space between paragraphs up to a preset limit, and then, if necessary, adds space between lines up to another preset limit.

When you turn **baseline synchronization** on, FrameMaker tries to align the baselines of type in adjoining columns. It does this by placing the first line of each paragraph on an invisible grid.

- Feathering and synchronization properties apply to an entire flow.
- If FrameMaker cannot make text reach the bottom of a column by adding the maximum allowed interline and inter-paragraph space, it does not feather the column at all.
- For baseline synchronization to work properly, paragraph formats in the flow must have Fixed Line Spacing turned on.

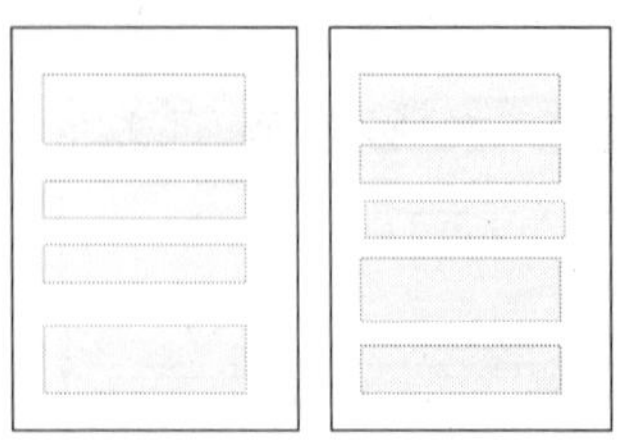

Feathering
The text lines up at the bottom of the text column.

Synchronizing
The baselines of text line up across pages and columns because they are positioned on an invisible grid.

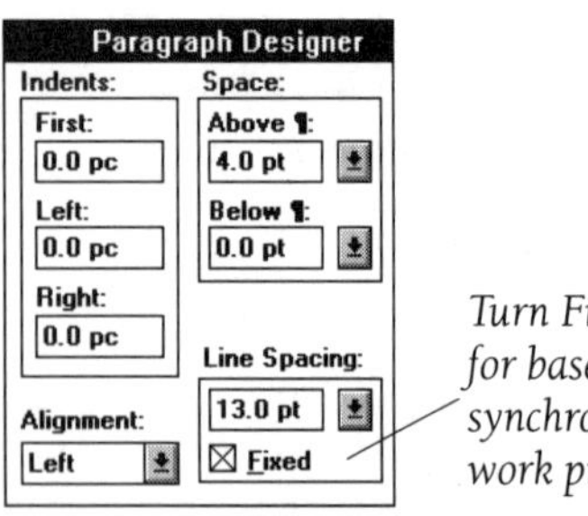

Turn Fixed on for baseline synchronization to work properly.

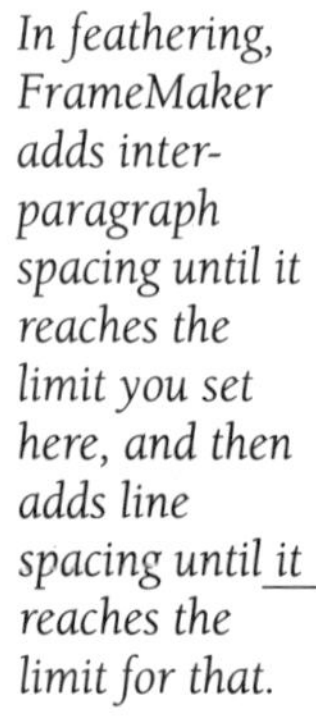

In feathering, FrameMaker adds inter-paragraph spacing until it reaches the limit you set here, and then adds line spacing until it reaches the limit for that.

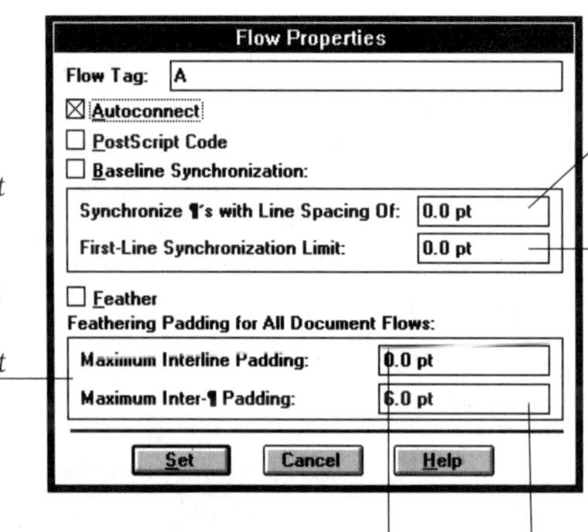

Type the line spacing for the invisible alignment grid.

Type the largest type size that FrameMaker should try to align to the invisible grid at the top of a column. This prevents FrameMaker from trying to align headline type to a text grid.

Type the largest amount of space that FrameMaker can add between paragraphs to make type go to the bottom of columns.

Type the largest amount of space that FrameMaker can add between lines to make type go to the bottom of columns.

■ Designing text on body pages

For one-time-only layout changes, you can work directly on the body pages.

■ All of the techniques discussed in "Managing text columns," pages 215 to 222, are available to you.

■ You must work directly on master pages to change background text and background graphics.

▼

In this section

"Designing text on body pages" describes a technique used only when designing layouts on body pages: splitting columns that have text in them. At the end of this section are three practical examples: a drop cap, a runaround, and a pull quote.

▲

Splitting columns

You have an additional tool available when you work in text columns on a body page: You can split a column below a text line, or to the right of the insertion point. In addition, you can split a selected column into individual lines in order to flow text around a graphic.

▲ Place the insertion point in text and specify which kind of split you want from the Split Current Column button of the Layout palette. This kind of splitting cannot be performed on empty columns.

■ The three column splits described in this section allow you to create drop caps and text that flows around graphics or pullouts.

■ When you have split a column, you can delete one of the resulting columns without losing text. The text that it contained flows into the next connected column.

Choose **Format➔Pages➔Layout Commands** *to display the Layout palette.*

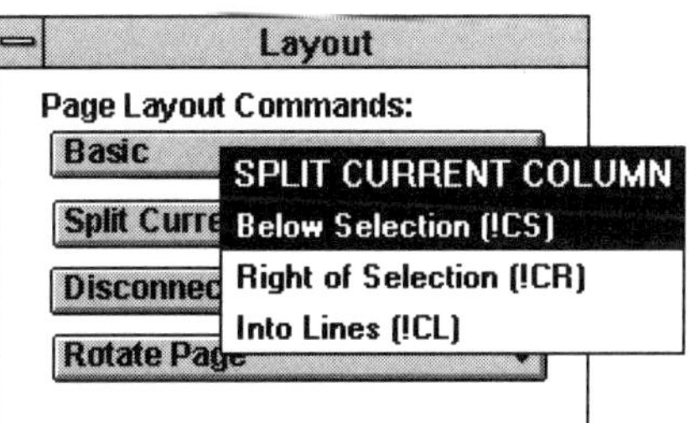

The choices in the Split Current Column menu let you create custom layouts on body pages.

▼

Working with layout

The Layout palette (page 207) is convenient if you are doing much layout work; the keyboard shortcuts are particularly useful here, too. They are listed on the Layout palette menus.

▲

"You are old, Father
William," the young man
said. "And your hair has
become very white."

This column was split horizontally (Below Selection) between the second and third lines.

"You are old, man said.
Father "And your
William," hair has
the young become very

This column was split vertically (Right of Selection) by placing the insertion point at the arrow.

"You are old, Father
William," the young man
said. "And your hair has
become very white."

This column was split into individual lines (Into Lines).

Splitting a column horizontally

1. Place your insertion point in the line above your desired split point.
2. In the Layout palette, choose Below Selection from the Split Current Column menu. [**Esc C S**] If you have Borders turned on [**Alt v b**], you will see the dotted lines of the column split appear below the current line. The two columns are connected.

Splitting a column vertically

1. Place your insertion point at the point in a line where you want the vertical split.
2. In the Layout palette, choose Right of Selection from the Split Current Column menu. [**Esc C R**]

Splitting a column into individual lines

This splits the selected column into individual lines. Each line is in its own connected text column. You can grab the end of each of these columns and resize it. The text flows through the columns as needed. I describe this process in more detail in "Making text flow around a graphic" on page 226.

1. Select the column that you want to split into individual lines.

   ▲ If you want to split only part of a column in this fashion, separate that part from the rest of the column by making horizontal splits above and below it first.
2. In the Layout palette, choose Into Lines from the Split Current Column menu. [**Esc C L**]

Drop caps

Here is a routine for creating a three-line drop cap. **Hint**: Before beginning, be sure that the Widow/Orphan lines of the drop cap paragraph are set to one in the Pagination page of the Paragraph Designer.

1. If the first line is not at the top of a column, split the column above the first line: place your insertion point in the line above and choose Below Selection from the Split Current Column menu in the Layout palette. [**Esc C S**]
2. Disconnect the drop cap column from the one above it. [**Esc C P**]
3. Place your insertion point in the third line of the drop cap column and once again Split Current Column Below Selection. [**Esc C S**]
4. Select the three-line column. Resize it, dragging the left side in to make room for the drop cap. Delete the first letter.

   ▲ **Or** to position individual lines: split this three-line column into three individual lines by choosing Split Current Column Into Lines. [**Esc C L**] After you have placed the drop cap (step five), adjust each line.
5. Select the Text Line tool [A] from the Graphics palette. [**Esc 1 t l** (*one tee ell*)] Click in the area where you want the drop cap and type the letter.
6. In the Character Designer, select the font properties for your drop cap. **Or** apply a character format with the properties you want.
7. Fine-tune the spacing. Select the drop cap by Ctrl-clicking on it, and microposition it (page 258). Adjust the edge of each column relative to the drop cap by dragging the resize handle.

▲ Some of you may wonder why I didn't recommend placing the drop cap first, and then making a vertical split in the column and deleting the left-hand portion. It's true. That works, too.

Place the insertion point in this line to make the first horizontal split (step one).

This is the last line before the drop cap.

Where the bee sucks, there suck I: In a cowslip's bell I lie; There I couch, when owls do cry: On the bat's back I do fly After summer merrily.

Place the insertion point in this line to make the second split (step three).

This is the last line before the drop cap.

W here the bee sucks, there suck I: In a cowslip's bell I lie; There I couch, when owls do cry: On the bat's back I do fly After summer merrily.

Here is the completed drop cap with Borders turned on, so you can see where the columns are. The **W** *is created with the Text Line tool, and is not in a column.*

This is the last line before the drop cap.

W here the bee sucks, there suck I: In a cowslip's bell I lie; There I couch, when owls do cry: On the bat's back I do fly After summer merrily.

Here is the alternate form of the drop cap: the three-line column was split into separate lines, which were then positioned individually.

Where the bee sucks, there suck I: In a c lie; There I c owls do cry: back I do fly A merrily. ❖ Wi SHAKESPEARE, *The Tempest*

Here is the graphic lying on top of the text. The text column has been split above and below the runaround area.

Where the bee sucks, there suck I: In a cows lie; There I co owls do cry: back I do fly A merrily. ❖ WILLIAM SHAKESPEARE, *The Tempest*

Now the text is lying on top of the graphic.

Where the bee sucks, there suck I: In a cow-slip's bell I lie; There I couch, when owls do cry: On the bat's back I do fly After summer merrily. ❖ WILLIAM SHAKESPEARE, *The Tempest*

The final product: the runaround has been split into lines, and the lines individually adjusted. (Also, Borders have been turned off.)

Making text flow around a graphic

There's nothing new on this page: it just shows you how to put the techniques on the previous few pages to work for you.

1. Place the graphic directly on the page. If it's in a frame, drag it out of the frame and delete the frame.
2. Position the graphic where you want it relative to the text: select it and drag it or microposition it. Put it right on top of the text.
3. Select the text column and bring it to the front [**Alt g b**]. Set the fill of the text column to None. [**Esc 9 f**]
4. Split the text above and below the part that will flow around the graphic, using the Split Current Column Below Selection. [**Esc C S**] **Note** First set the Widow/Orphan property of the paragraph to one.
5. The graphic is now lying beneath a separate column. Select this column and apply Split Current Column Into Lines from the Layout palette. [**Esc C L**]
6. Now select one single-line column at a time, and drag its left- or right-side resize handle so that the text is positioned where you want it with respect to the graphic. Do this with each line in turn until you have created the look you want. The text flows between columns as you resize them— you don't have to fuss with the line endings.

Hint If the vertical spacing between the lines of the runaround becomes uneven, do this: Position the top line of the runaround where you want it. Do the same with the bottom line. Now select all the lines of the runaround and choose **Graphics→ Distribute**. [**Alt g d**] In the Distribute dialog box, choose Horizontal Spacing: As Is and Vertical Spacing: Equidistant Edges. Click Distribute.

Adding a stationary graphic

Here's how to create an unmoving space in a column, where you can place something like a pull quote or a graphic. The text will flow past it as you edit, the graphic will stay put.

1. Place your insertion point in the text line right above the stationary area you are creating. Split the column horizontally. [**Esc C S**]
2. Place your insertion point in the line of text at the bottom of the area. Split the column horizontally. [**Esc C S**]
3. Select the column above the area and the column below the area, in that order.
4. Connect the two columns. [**Esc C C**]

▲ You now have a connected text flow that jumps over an empty, unconnected text column. You can delete the empty column and replace it with a graphic, or you can put special text such as a pull quote in it. As you edit the main flow of text, the text in the unconnected column will remain undisturbed.

Hint Any time you are splitting columns horizontally, it's a good idea to set the Widow/Orphan property of the paragraph to one, if it's not already. Otherwise, FrameMaker splits the lines in unexpected places in order to obey the Widow/Orphan property.

This is a column of text. We are going to place a pull quote
→ *in the middle of it. We don't want it to move with the text. It's easy to do using FrameMaker. The two*
→ *arrows at the left point to the two lines where I will place the insertion point and make a horizontal split.*

This is a column of text. We are going to place a pull quote in the middle of it. We don't

Nothing in this area will move with the text.

want it to move with the text. It's easy to do using FrameMaker. The two arrows at the left point to the two lines where I will place the insertion point and make a horizontal split.

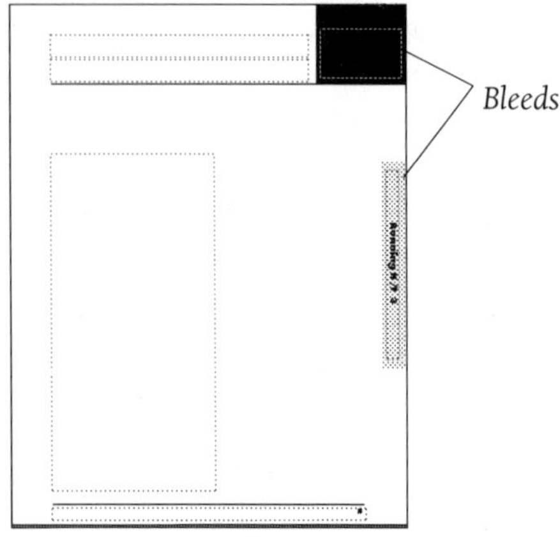

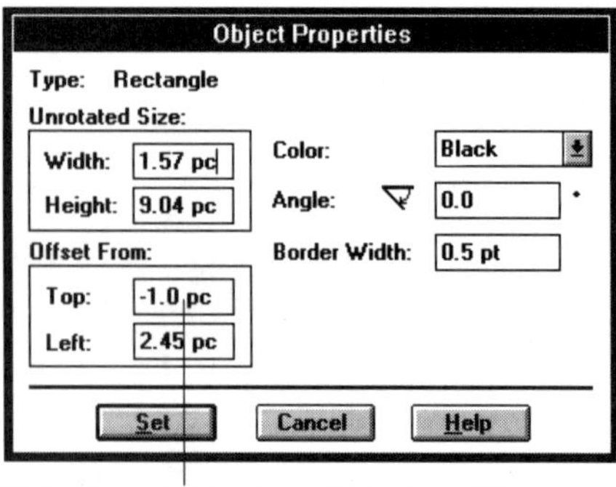

This object is bleeding off the top of the page.

■ Bleeds

When an object goes all the way to the edge of a page, it is called a "bleed." If your job is going to a printer, the printer will want the bleeds to go a little bit beyond the edge of the page because the page-trimming process is not absolutely perfect. If your object goes just to the edge and stops, there may be a thin white line at the edge after the printed pages are trimmed to size. You must create bleeds to prevent this.

Creating bleeds

1. On either a master page or a body page, select the object that you want to bleed.

2. Display the Object Properties dialog box. [**Alt g p**]

3. To bleed an object off the top or left side, put a negative value in the appropriate Offset From box.

3a. To bleed an object off the right side or bottom of the page, give it a size and offset that add up to a figure larger than the dimension of the page.

4. Click Set.

On the screen, it looks as though there's no bleed, because FrameMaker doesn't display anything beyond the edge of the page. When you print the page on paper larger than the page size, however, your bleed is there.

Tables

■ Inserting a table

Tables have formats, just as paragraphs do. When you insert a table, choose a format from the Table Format catalog in the Insert Table dialog box. If you are familiar with the formats in the list, pick one that's close to the properties you want. If you're not sure, you can just pick the default, Format A. You're never stuck with anything. Once you've inserted a table, you can modify everything about it. If you expect to create another, similar table, you can then save the format of your current table for future use.

1. Place your insertion point in the line of text where you want to anchor your table. (Tables have anchors, just like frames.)
2. Choose **Table→Insert Table**. [**Alt t i**] Or click on the table insert button on the QuickAccess bar.
3. In the Insert Table dialog box, choose a format from the Table Format list, and fill in the number of rows, columns, heading rows, and footing rows that you want your table to have.
4. Click Insert. FrameMaker inserts the table. Its position (indent, alignment, space above and below) is determined by the properties included in the format. You can change all of them and more using the Table Designer and the other tools described in this chapter.

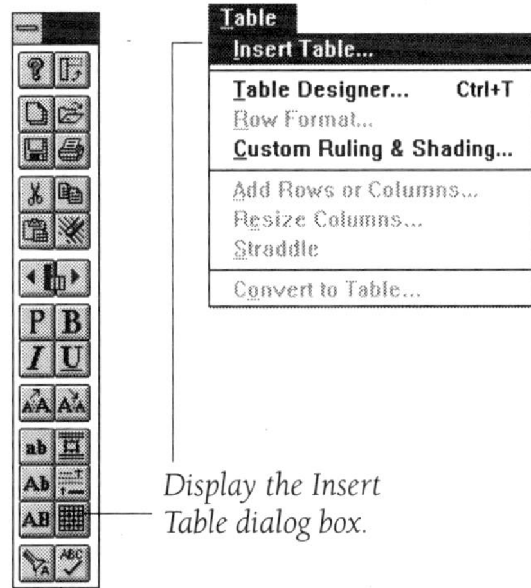

Display the Insert Table dialog box.

This shows the currently selected format.

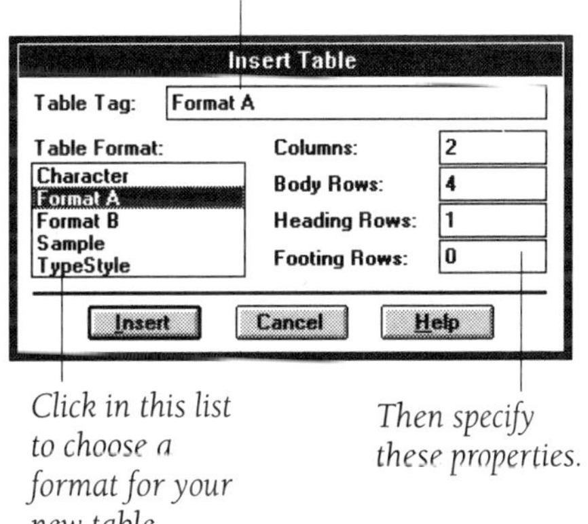

Click in this list to choose a format for your new table.

Then specify these properties.

■ Table basics

Moving around in a table

▼

Selecting in tables

Selecting text in a cell is different from selecting the cell itself. Select text in order to edit it within the cell. Select cells in order to copy, move, or delete the cells or their contents.

▲

- Click in any cell to select it and work in it.
- The keyboard shortcuts for moving around in a table are all rather long. You can make macros using Windows' Recorder or another macro application. Here are a few of the more useful ones. (There's a complete list in the FrameMaker *Quick Reference*, but many of them are more trouble than they're worth.)

Go to	Keystrokes
Rightmost cell in current row	**Esc t m e**
Leftmost cell in current row	**Esc t m o**
Top cell in current column	**Esc t m t**
Bottom cell in current column	**Esc t m b**
Top left cell	**Esc t m T**

Selecting text in cells

Select text in order to edit it, as you would any text in FrameMaker.

- Within a single cell, select text just as you would in any text column—a cell is really just a tiny text column.
- There are a few additional keyboard shortcuts:

Selection	Keystrokes
All text in the next cell	**Tab**
All text in the previous cell	**Shift-Tab**
All text in the cell below	**Alt-Ctrl-Tab**
All text in the cell above	**Alt-Ctrl-Shift-Tab**

- If you select just part of a row or column (all of the column except the header, for instance), FrameMaker will automatically cut, copy, delete, and paste the text only and not the row or column.

The QuickAccess bar, Level 4

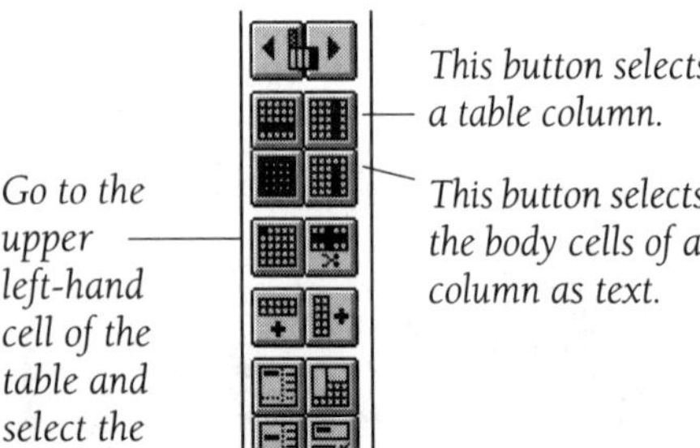

Selecting parts of a table

Selecting a cell Ctrl-click in it; **or** place your insertion point in the cell and drag the pointer over a cell boundary and then back into the cell.

Selecting a range of cells Drag across the range of cells; **or** Ctrl-click in the first cell, and then Ctrl-Shift-click in the last cell.

Selecting a column Drag from the header into the first cell to select a whole column; **or** Ctrl-double-click on a horizontal border in the column.

Selecting a row Drag across the whole row; **or** Ctrl-double-click on a vertical border in the row.

Selecting an entire table Drag diagonally across the table; **or** Ctrl-triple-click anywhere in the table; **or** Ctrl-click to select a cell and then press **Ctrl-a**.

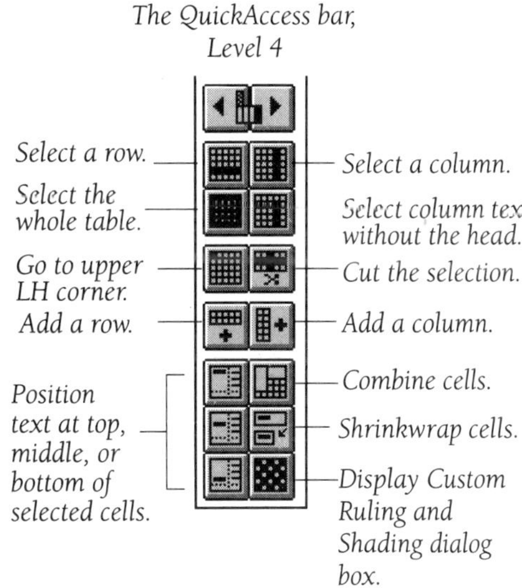

The QuickAccess bar, Level 4

Using the QuickAccess bar

The QuickAccess bar is particularly helpful for working with tables. The button, for example, is by far the easiest way to select all the text in a column without selecting the header as well.

I particularly like the table editing page of the QuickAccess bar. The selection buttons are by far the easiest way to select columns, rows, and whole columns without the head. You can select with a button and then Shift-click to extend your selection.

■ Entering text in a table

■ Within each cell, enter and format text just as you would elsewhere in FrameMaker. Apply paragraph and character formats as usual, or apply formatting in any of the normal ways. (See Chapters 5 and 6.)

Typing a tab in a table cell Type Esc Tab. (The Tab key by itself moves you to the next cell of a table.)

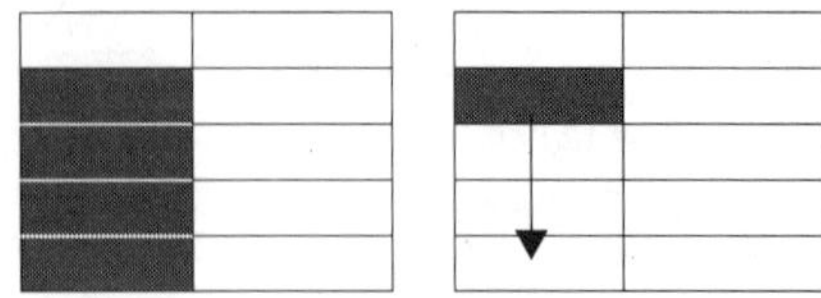

If you copy the contents of four cells, and select only one cell to paste into, FrameMaker will paste into four cells, not just one. Any previous contents are replaced.

Copying or moving text

FrameMaker distinguishes between a cell and the text *in* the cell.

1. Select text from one or more cells (page 230).
2. Copy or cut as usual. [Ctrl-c or Ctrl-x]
3. Select the cells to paste into. Paste. [Ctrl-v]

▲ If you select several cells to cut or copy, and then paste, FrameMaker pastes the text into that same number of cells, starting with the ones you choose.

▲ If you select multiple cells, this procedure copies cell formatting, such as rules and shading. If you select only the contents of a single cell, it copies only the contents. If you select the cell itself, FrameMaker copies the cell formatting and the contents. See page 230 for how to select text or cells.

The QuickAccess bar Level 4

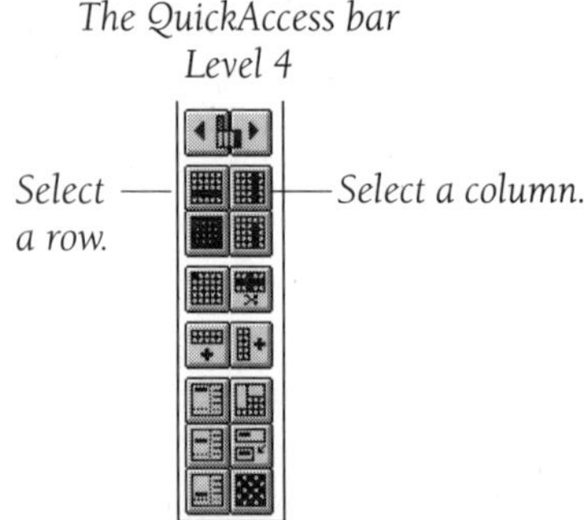

■ Rearranging tables

Copying a row or column of a table

1. Select one or more columns, or one or more rows. You must select at least one complete row or column. Otherwise, FrameMaker thinks you are just copying text, rather than a row or column.
2. Copy as usual. [Ctrl-c]
3. To replace a row or column with your selected material, place your insertion point in it. To insert your row or column, place the insertion point in a row or column adjacent to where you want the insertion.
4. Paste. [Ctrl-v] FrameMaker displays the Paste Columns or the Paste Rows dialog box. Choose the location for your new row or column and click Paste.

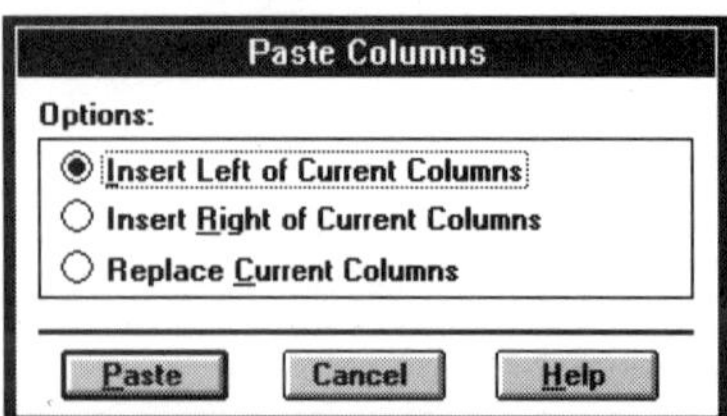

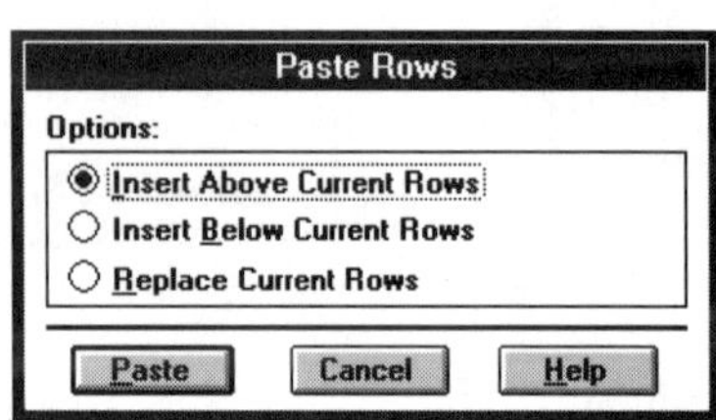

When you Paste, you get to choose the location of your new rows or columns.

Moving a row or column of a table

1. Select one or more columns, or one or more rows. You must select at least one complete row or column. Otherwise, FrameMaker moves the contents only, rather than a row or column itself.
2. Cut as usual. [Ctrl-x] FrameMaker displays a dialog box, asking whether you wish to cut only the text (leaving the empty cells), or whether you wish to remove the cells as well. Make your choice, and click Cut.
3. To replace a row or column with your selected material, place your insertion point in it. To insert your row or column, place the insertion point in a row or column adjacent to where you want the insertion.
4. Paste. [Ctrl-v] FrameMaker displays the Paste Columns or the Paste Rows dialog box. Choose the location for your new row or column and click Paste (illustrated on the previous page).

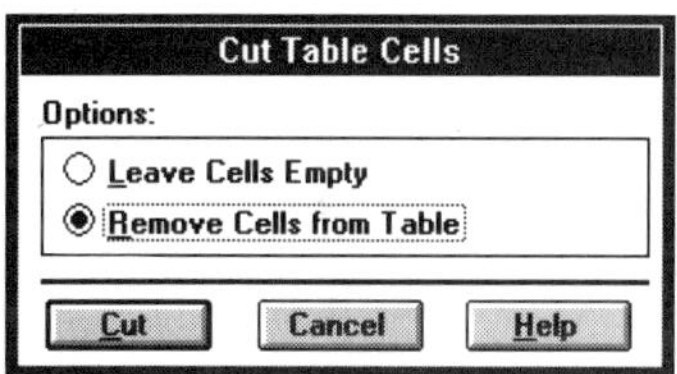

When you Cut, you get to choose whether to remove the rows or columns completely, or to leave them empty.

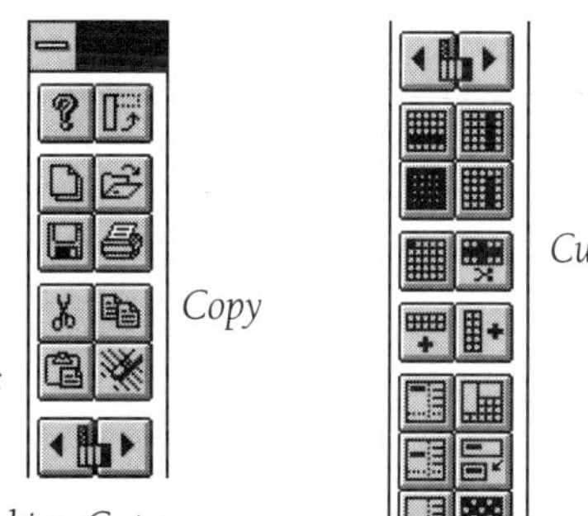

Clicking Cut on the top of QuickAccess bar displays the Cut Table Cells Options dialog box shown above.

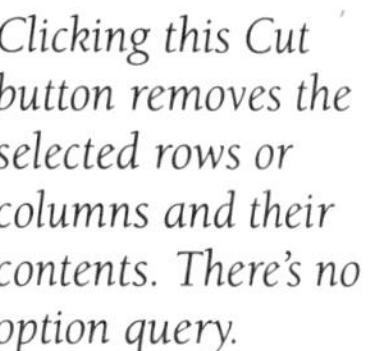

Clicking this Cut button removes the selected rows or columns and their contents. There's no option query.

Adding empty rows or columns

Using the Table menu

1. Place your insertion point in a row or column next to where you want the new row or column.
2. Choose **Table→Add Rows or Columns.** [Alt t a]
3. In the dialog box, choose how many rows or columns to add, and their position relative to the insertion point.
4. Click Add. The new rows or columns will have the same cell formats as the row or column containing your insertion point.

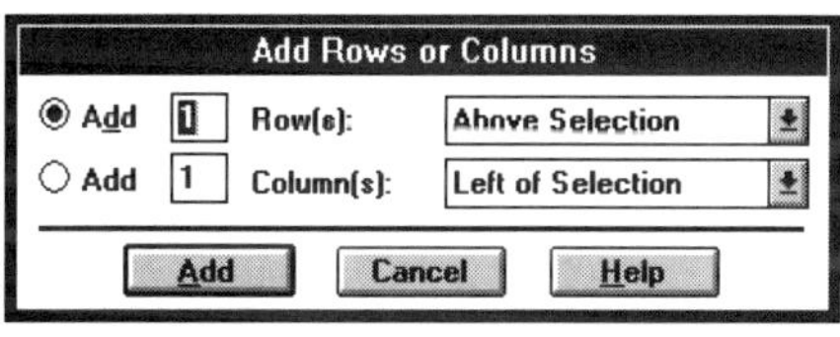

First choose the number of rows or columns to add. Then choose the position from the appropriate pop-up menu.

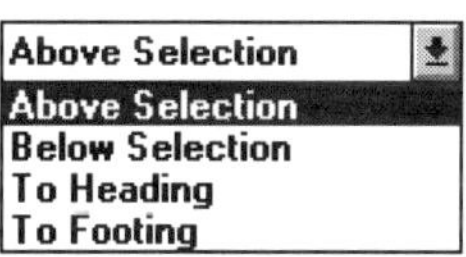

Position rows.

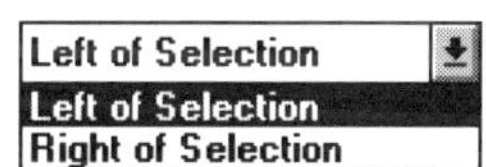

Position columns.

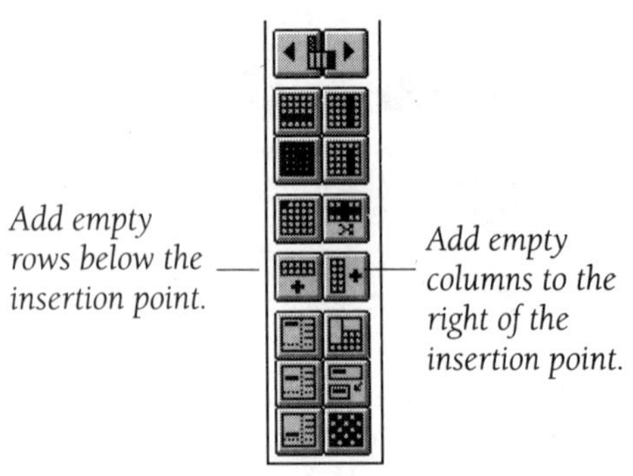

Select several rows or columns, and then click here to add a number equal to the number selected.

Adding empty rows or columns *(continued)*

Using the QuickAccess bar

1. Place your insertion point in a row or column adjacent to where the new row or column will be. To add several rows or columns, select a number equal to the number you want to add.
2. Click on the appropriate button in the QuickAccess bar. Depending on the button you chose, FrameMaker adds either one column to the right of your insertion point, or one row below the insertion point. There's no dialog box and no choices, but it's quick and easy. The new rows or columns will have the same cell formats as the row or column containing your insertion point.

Deleting or clearing rows and columns

You can delete rows or columns completely from a table, or you can clear old text out, leaving empty cells to work in.

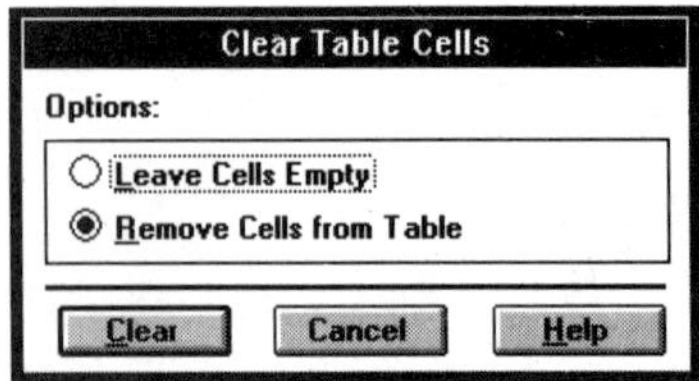

1. Select one or more columns, or one or more rows. You must select at least one complete row or column. Otherwise, FrameMaker deletes the text only, without asking you whether you want to delete the row or column itself.
2. Press Delete.
3. In the Clear Table Cells dialog box, choose whether you want to remove the cells completely, or whether you just want to remove the text in them.
4. Click Clear.

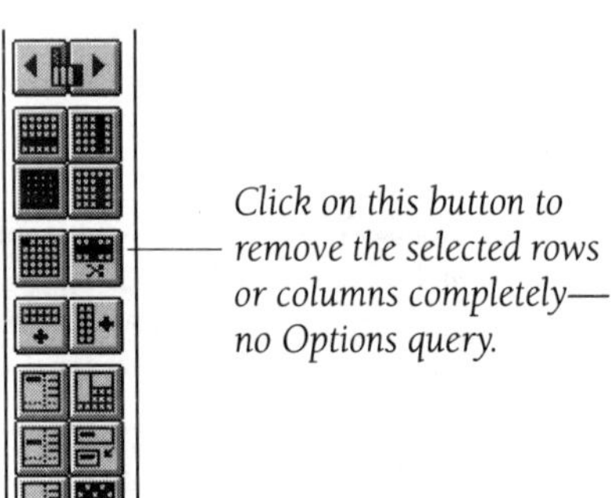

Using the QuickAccess bar

Select the rows or columns to delete and click on the Cut button in the QuickAccess bar. There is no dialog box. FrameMaker deletes the selected cells completely.

Resizing columns

You have many ways available to resize columns in a table.

▲ Begin by selecting one or more columns. For resizing columns (but not for copy, cut, or delete), you can select a column just by placing the insertion point in it.

▲ **Resize the entire table** by selecting all the columns.

▲ Choose **Table→Resize Columns** to display the Resize Selected Columns dialog box.

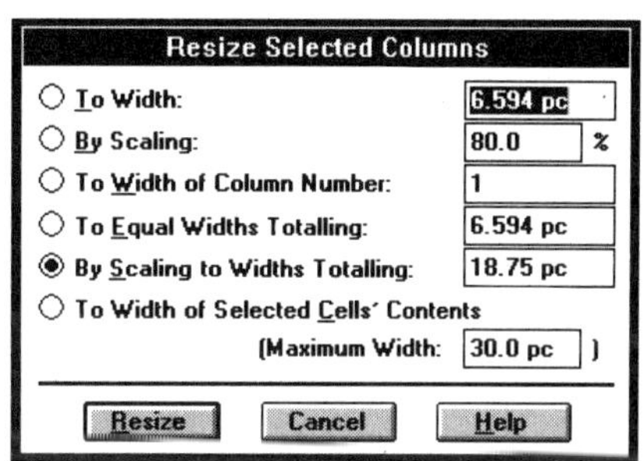

To do this	**Do this**
Resize columns visually	Select one or more columns so that the resize handles appear on the right of the selection (page 231). Drag a resize handle until the columns are the size you want. If you select more than one, FrameMaker resizes them proportionally.
Resize columns without changing the width of the table	Select one or more columns so that the resize handles appear on the right of the selection (page 231). Hold down Alt and drag a handle until the column is the size you want.
The following techniques use the Resize Selected Columns dialog box (see above). [**Alt t e**] *Make your settings and click Resize.*	
Make one column the same size as another	Select the columns. ▲ **Use the dialog box** Choose To Width of Column Number and type in the column number to match. Each selected column will have that width. ▲ **Or use Copy Special** Choose one column, and then choose **Edit→Copy Special→Table Column Width**. [**Alt e o w**] You have now copied the width of the column. Choose one or more other columns and paste. [**Ctrl-v**] Each column now has the width that you copied.
Resize a column to fit the contents of a selected cell, so that no line in the selection wraps ("shrinkwrap").	Select a cell or a column. If you select a column, FrameMaker resizes it so that no line in it wraps. Choose To Width of Selected Cells' Contents. You can limit the width by giving a maximum. By default, the maximum is the width of the table. [**Esc t w**] Or select and then click on the button in the QuickAccess bar.

Resizing columns *(continued)*

To do this	Do this
The following techniques use the Resize Selected Columns dialog box (see above). **[Alt t e]** *Make your settings and click Resize.*	
Make one or more columns (or the whole table) an exact width	Select the columns. ▲ **Equal-width columns of a specified size** Type the size for *each* column in the To Width text box. ▲ **Equal-width columns totalling a specified size** Type the total width you desire in the To Equal Widths Totalling text box. *Before you change it, this box shows the total width of the selection.* ▲ **Proportional columns totalling a specified size** Type the total width you desire in the By Scaling to Widths Totalling text box. The columns are resized in proportion to their original size. *Before you change it, this box shows the width of the text column containing the table.*
Resize by a percentage	Select one or more columns, and type the percent of change in the By Scaling text box.

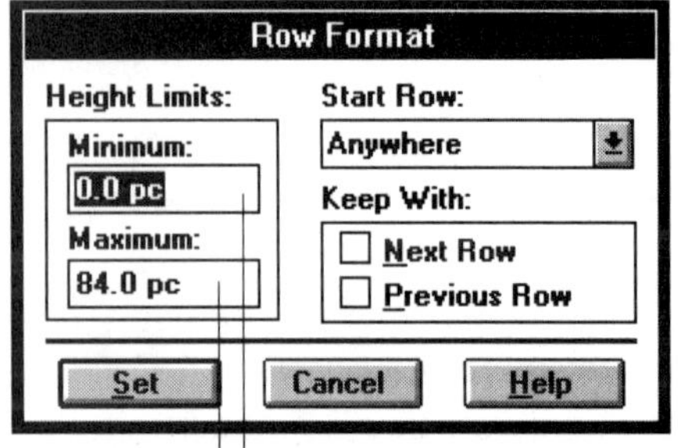

Specify a maximum or minimum height for your selected rows.

Limiting row height

As a rule, the height of a row in a table is whatever is necessary to accommodate the maximum number of lines occurring in a cell, plus the Top and Bottom Cell Margin specified in the table format (page 241). You can specify a maximum or minimum height for selected rows in your table.

1. Select one or more rows in a table.
2. Choose **Table→Row Format** to display the Row Format dialog box. **[Alt t r]**
3. Type a maximum and/or a minimum allowable height in the Height Limits text boxes.
4. Click Set. The limits you specified are applied to the selected rows.

Combining cells (straddling)

You can select several cells and combine them into one cell. The new cell can straddle rows, columns, or both.

1. Select the cells you want to combine.
2. Choose **Table→Straddle** **[Alt t s]** or click the button in the QuickAccess bar.

Unstraddling cells

1. Click in a cell that straddles rows or columns.
2. Choose **Table→Straddle** **[Alt t s]** or click the button in the QuickAccess bar. FrameMaker re-creates the original cells and puts all the text in the left-most or top-most cell.

Rotating cells

Using the Graphics menu

1. Select the cells you want to rotate.
2. Choose **Graphics→Rotate**. **[Alt g o]**
3. In the Rotate Table Cells dialog box, choose the orientation you want the type to have. Click Rotate.

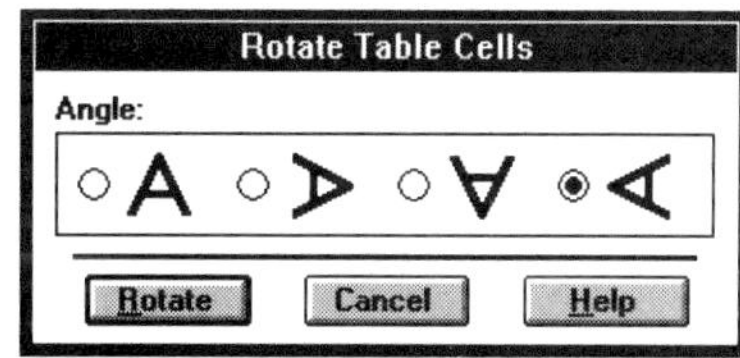

Choose the orientation for your rotated cells here.

Using the QuickAccess bar

1. Select the cells you want to rotate.
2. Click on one of the Rotate buttons in the QuickAccess bar, third page.

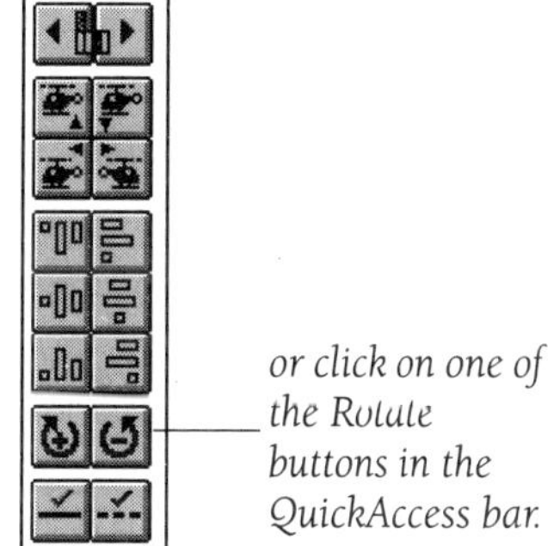

or click on one of the Rotate buttons in the QuickAccess bar.

▲ You can type in rotated cells.

▲ FrameMaker does not automatically break lines of type in rotated cells; it extends the length of the cells instead. You can specify a maximum height using the Row Format dialog box. Then it will break the lines when the cell reaches the maximum height.

▲ See "Positioning text in cells" on page 241 for information on positioning text in cells.

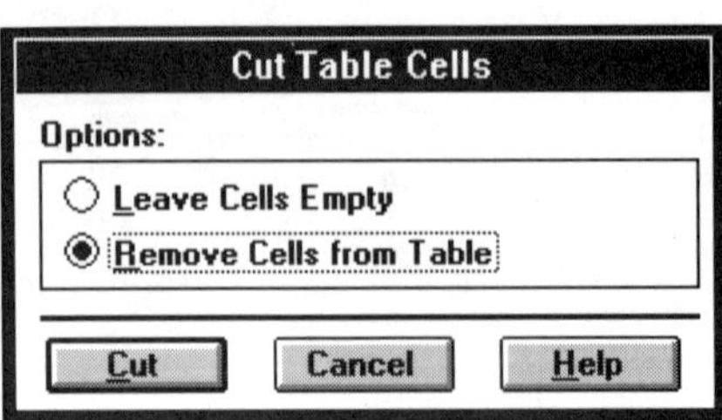

When you Cut or Delete rows or columns, you can choose whether to remove them completely, or to remove just the text and leave the cells empty.

■ Managing tables

Moving a table

1. Select the table and cut it. [Ctrl-x]
2. In the Cut Table Cells dialog box, choose Remove Cells from Table. Click Cut. [r c]
3. Place your insertion point where you want to anchor the new table and Paste. [Ctrl-v]

Copying a table

1. Select the table and copy it. [Ctrl-c]
2. Place your insertion point where you want to anchor the new table and Paste. [Ctrl-v]

Deleting a table

1. Select the table and press the Delete key.
2. In the Cut Table Cells dialog box, choose Remove Cells from Table. Click Cut. [r c]

Clearing the contents of a table

1. Select the table and cut it. [Ctrl-x]
2. In the Cut Table Cells dialog box, choose Leave Cells Empty. Click Cut. [l c]

Combining two tables

1. Select the one table and Cut it. [Ctrl-x]
2. Place the insertion point in a row above or below where the new rows will go. (FrameMaker considers the table to be a collection of rows.) Paste. [Ctrl-v]
3. In the Paste Rows dialog box, choose the location for the new rows. Click Paste.

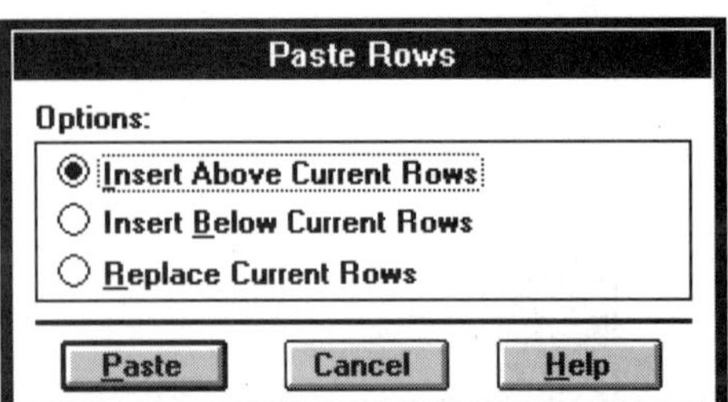

Choose whether the rows on the Clipboard will go above or below the selected row(s) in the new table, or whether they will replace the selection.

Splitting a table

1. Select the rows or columns you want to move and Cut them. [Ctrl-x]
2. Place your insertion point where you want to anchor the new table and Paste. [Ctrl-v]

Rotating a table

Placing it in an anchored frame

1. Create an anchored frame of a size and position to contain your rotated table (page195).
2. Draw a text column in the anchored frame (page 215).
3. Paste the table in (page 238).
4. Rotate the text column (page 220).

▲ You may need to select the text column and reposition it in the frame.

▲ You cannot edit a table that is rotated in this fashion. Rotate the text column back to its normal position to make changes in the table.

▲ This technique allows you to combine a rotated table and unrotated text on the same page.

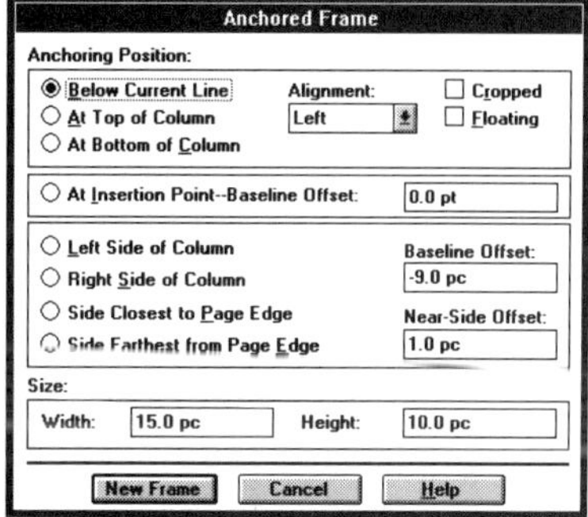

Create an anchored frame.

Choose the Text Column tool from the Graphics palette and draw a text column in the frame.

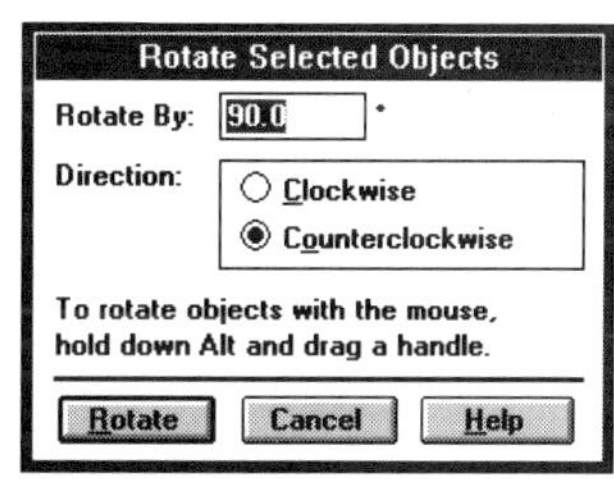

You can rotate the text column before or after you paste in the table.

Using a rotated master page

1. Create the table.
2. Create a rotated master page (page 214).
3. Apply the rotated master page to the page with the table (page 210).

▲ You cannot have unrotated body page text on the page with the table using this technique.

▲ You can edit the table "as is," since on the screen the text is horizontal and the rest of the page is sideways.

▲ If editing the document causes the table to move, you will have to apply a normal master page to its old location, and the rotated master page to its new location.

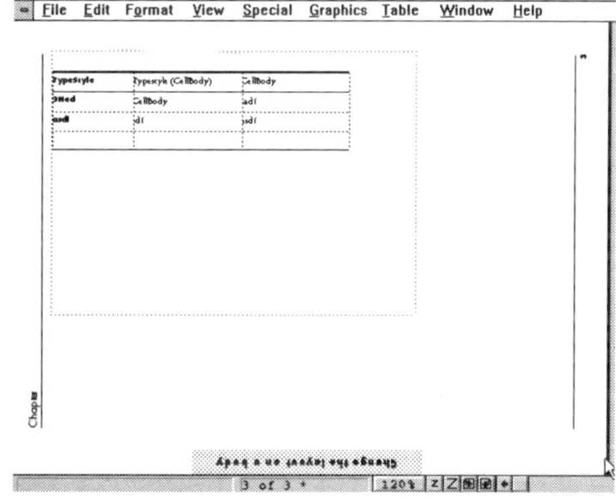

A table on a page using a rotated master page.

Positioning tables

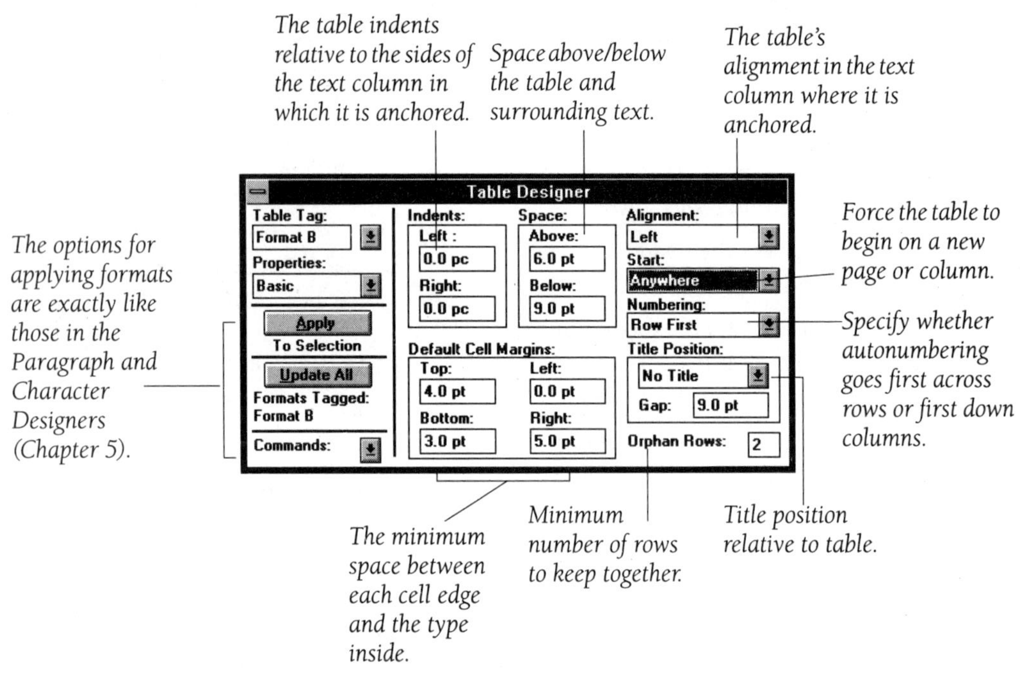

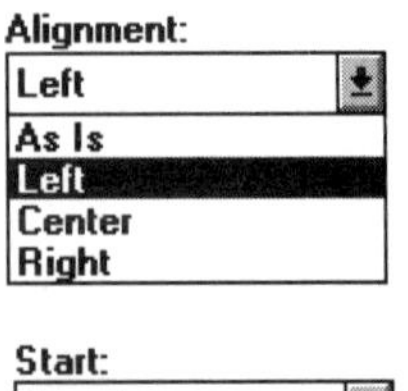

Choose the table alignment.

Choose the starting point for the table.

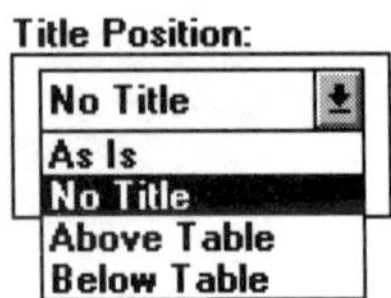

Choose the position for the table title, or turn off the title.

Notes on positioning tables

Alignment The table can be flush left, flush right, or centered in the text column. Use As Is when you want to create a format that affects other properties but leaves Alignment alone.

Starting position Force the table to be at the top of a new page, column, right page or left page. "Float" has the same meaning that is does for frames: text will move backwards to fill in empty spaces left where the table doesn't fit.

Title position You can place the title above or below the table, or eliminate a title entirely.

Autonumbering in tables Autonumbering can go across rows first and then down columns, or it can go first down columns and then across rows. The choice is yours.

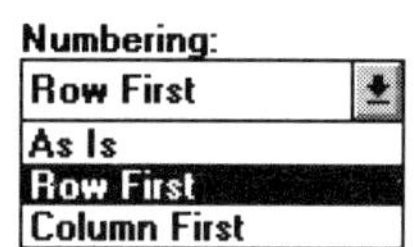

This choice is only meaningful if you are using autonumbered paragraphs in your table.

■ Positioning text in cells

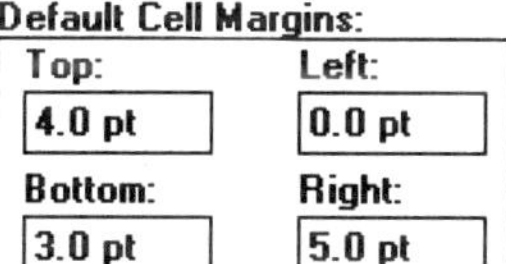

This is the area in the Table Designer where you set the default cell margins for the whole table.

Cell margins

Defaults

To position text horizontally and vertically in table cells, you first set defaults for the whole table using the Table Designer. Then you can alter the margins for selected cells using the Table page of the Paragraph Designer.

▲ The cell margins are the minimum distance between the contents of the cell and each edge of the cell.

▲ **To set cell margin defaults** Fill in the four Default Cell Margins text boxes in the Basic page of the Table Designer.

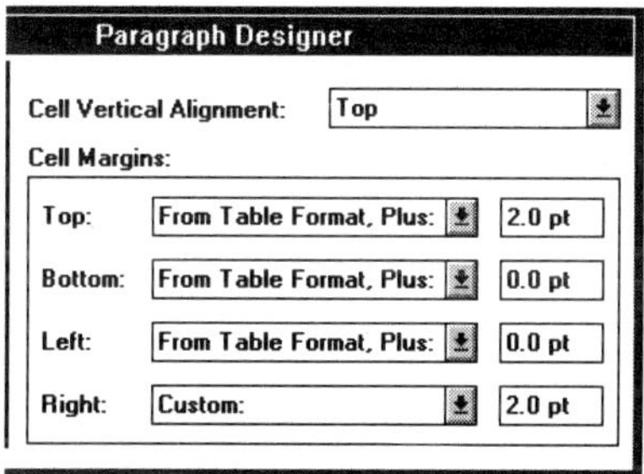

Alter the margins for selected table cells using this page of the Paragraph Designer.

Custom margins

Select the cells for which you want different margins and display the Table Cell page of the Paragraph Designer.

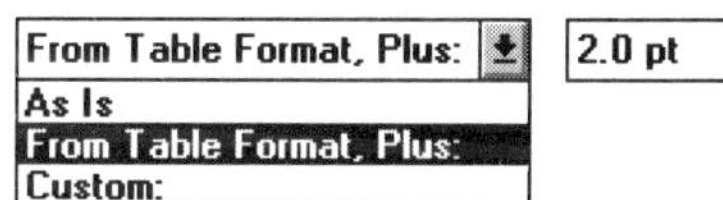

2.0 pt

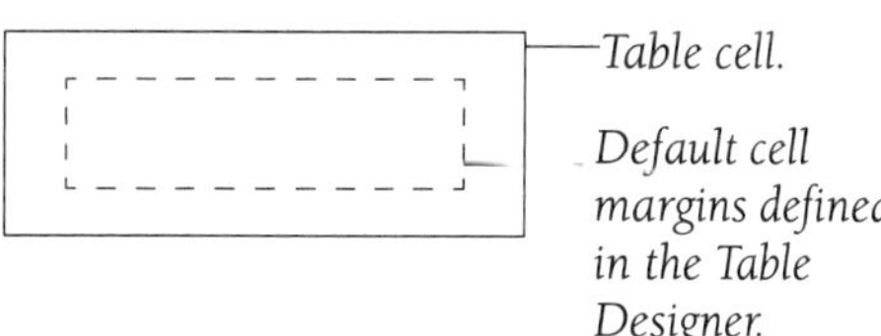

Add to the default margins by choosing From Table Format Plus and typing in an additional amount for the margin. **Override the default margins** by choosing Custom and typing in a total margin amount.

Use the Top, Bottom, Left, and Right Cell Margin properties to either add to these pre-defined boundaries (Table Format Plus), or override them (Custom). Text in cells will never get any closer to the cell edges than these margins.

Text in cells can be flush to the top or bottom of the cell, or centered vertically, but it will never get any closer to the cell edges than the amount of the custom or default cell margins.

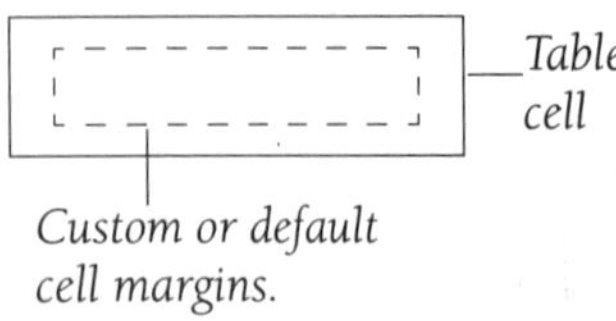

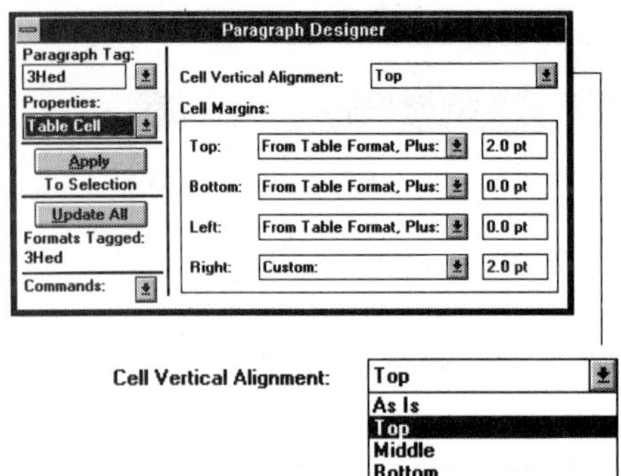

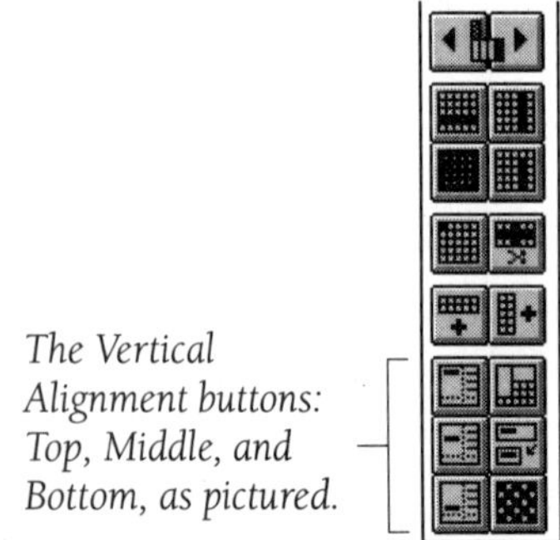

The Vertical Alignment buttons: Top, Middle, and Bottom, as pictured.

Vertical position of cell contents

The vertical position of type in a cell (top, middle, or bottom) is not specified in the Table Designer, but when you save a table format (Update All), FrameMaker saves the vertical position in the top header cells of each column, and in the top body cell for each column, and those become the defaults for tables using that format.

Using the Paragraph Designer

For selected cells To change the vertical alignment of selected text, select the cells, and then display the Table Cells page of the Paragraph Designer and choose Top, Middle, or Bottom from the Cell Vertical Alignment pop-up menu.

For a format Make the Cell Vertical Alignment part of the format definitions that you use in the tables.

Using the QuickAccess bar

Select the cells whose contents you want to align vertically, and click one of the three Cell Alignment buttons in the QuickAccess bar.

Using keyboard shortcuts

Use these keyboard shortcuts to align text to the top margin or the bottom margin of a cell, or to center it vertically between the margins.

Alignment	Keystroke
Top	Ctrl-F1
Middle	Ctrl-F2
Bottom	Ctrl-F3

Horizontal position of cell contents

The horizontal position of type in a cell (flush left, flush right, or centered) is specified in the paragraph formats that you use in table cells, rather than in the Table Designer itself. When you save a table format (Update All), FrameMaker saves the paragraph format in the top header cells of each column, and in the top body cell for each column, as defaults.

Type in cells can be flush left, flush right, centered, or justified, but it will never get any closer to the cell edges than the amount of the custom or default cell margins.

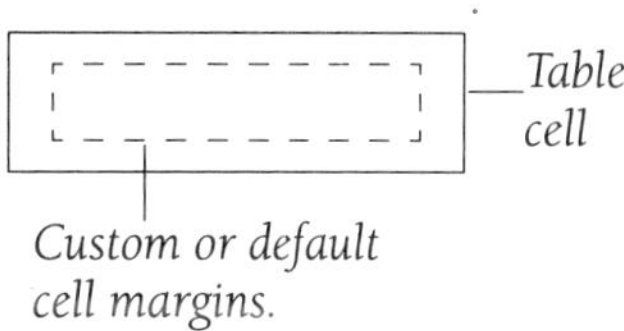

Using the Paragraph Designer

For selected cells To change the horizontal alignment of selected type, select the cells, and then display the Basic page of the Paragraph Designer and choose Left, Center, Right, or Justified from the Alignment pop-up menu.

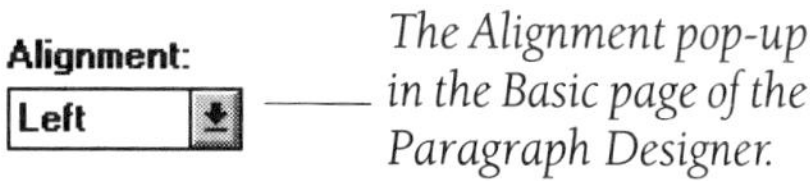

The Alignment pop-up in the Basic page of the Paragraph Designer.

For a format Make the Alignment you want part of the format definitions that you use in the tables.

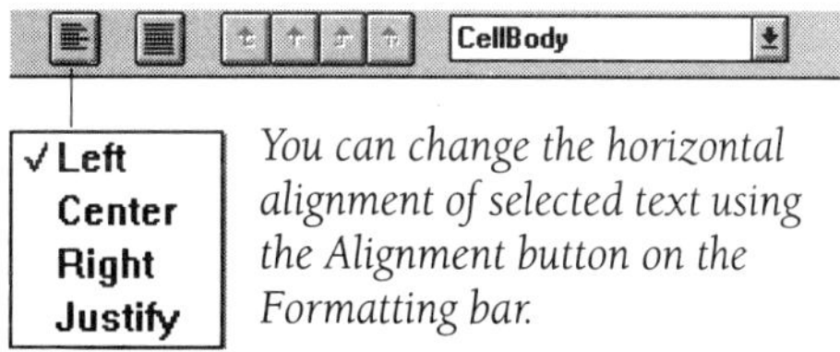

You can change the horizontal alignment of selected text using the Alignment button on the Formatting bar.

Using the QuickAccess bar

Select the cells to change, and click one of the three Cell Alignment buttons in the QuickAccess bar.

Using keyboard shortcuts

Use these keyboard shortcuts to align text to the top margin or the bottom margin of a cell, or to center it vertically between the margins.

Alignment	Keystroke
Left	Esc j l
Center	Esc j c
Right	Esc j r
Justify	Esc j f

▼

Indents

The horizontal position of text in a cell is also affected by the indent properties of the paragraph format you are using. Changing the indent may be easier in some cases than changing the cell margins or the text alignment. If text is not positioned where you expect it, the paragraph definition may have right or left indents that you've forgotten about.

▲

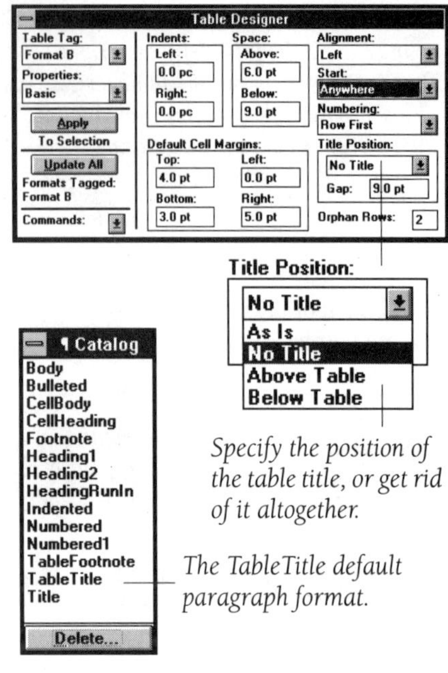

Specify the position of the table title, or get rid of it altogether.

The TableTitle default paragraph format.

■ Table titles

■ The table format definition includes the position of the title and the distance between the title and the rest of the table (the Gap).

■ By default, the table title text box contains a paragraph format named TableTitle. You can redefine this format any way you please. You can also apply a different paragraph format.

To have a different title paragraph format as part of the table definition Apply the new format to an existing table. In the Table Designer, click Update All. FrameMaker stores the new table title format as part of the table definition.

■ You can choose not to have a table title at all. In the Table Designer Basic page, choose No Title from the Title Position pop-up menu. Then click Update All to change the format definition or Apply to Selection to change only the selected table.

Autonumbering table titles The default title paragraph format, TableTitle, includes the word "Table" and an autonumber counter. You can modify this as you would modify any autonumber by displaying the Numbering page of the Paragraph Designer, displaying the format, and editing the Autonumber Format text box (page 141).

Compound autonumbers for your tables

Suppose you want your table title autonumber to include the chapter number: Table 4-3, for example. The process is described on page 143, but I have given an example in the margin here, too.

▲ If you need compound autonumbers for several series (e.g., tables, figures, and examples), see "A compound autonumber example" on page 144.

▼

Compound autonumbering

1. Suppose you want to include a chapter number in the table autonumber. The chapter is autonumbered, and its paragraph format tag is C-Chapter. Its autonumber format is
   A:Chapter <n+>
2. To create the table autonumber format, give it the same series tag as the chapter. Use the placeholder, <n>, to pick up the chapter number. Add text, such as a hyphen, as then the counter for the table number. The format would look like this:
   A:Table <n>-<n+>\sn
   The \sn puts an en space after the numbers. See pages 139 to 144 for much more on autonumbering.

▲

Ruling and shading

Default ruling

Use the Ruling page of the Table Designer to specify default ruling properties for a table or table format.

Column Ruling and Body Row Ruling:

Columns: Pick a single rule to be different from the others. Rows: Pick an interval at which the rules will be different.

Make these two the same if you want all the vertical or horizontal rules to be the same.

Choose a thickness for the "different" rules here.

Choose a thickness for the rest of the rules here.

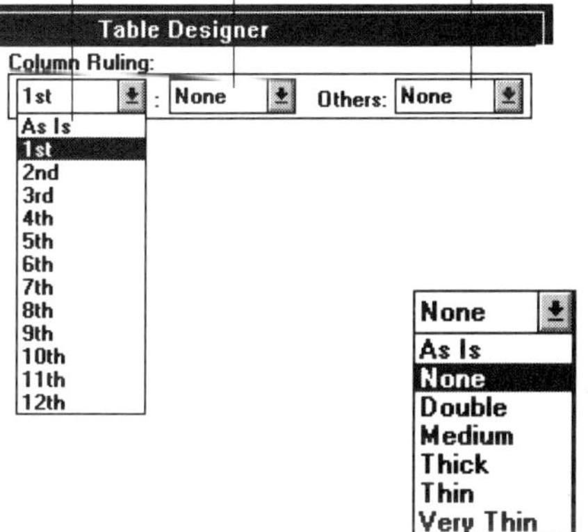

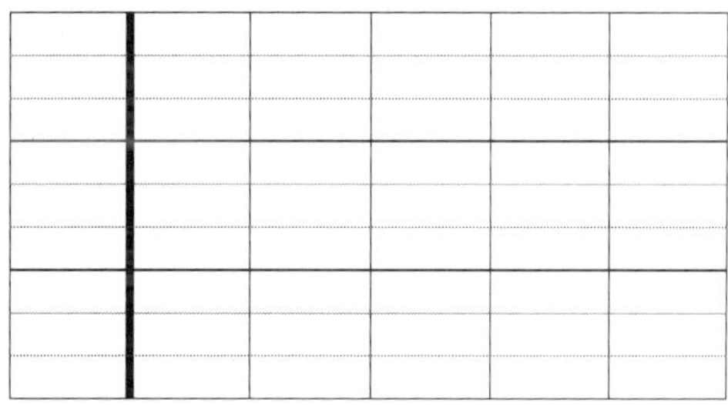

In the Ruling page of the Table Designer, the default ruling for this table is specified as:

- *Column Ruling: 1st: Medium, Others: Very Thin*
- *Body Row Ruling: Every 3rd: Thin, Others: Gray*

There is no custom ruling.

None
As Is
None
Double
Medium
Thick
Thin
Very Thin

The "thickness" pop-up menus all look like this. This is the default list that FrameMaker provides. You can define others; see the Edit Ruling Style dialog box illustrated in the lower left part of page 246.

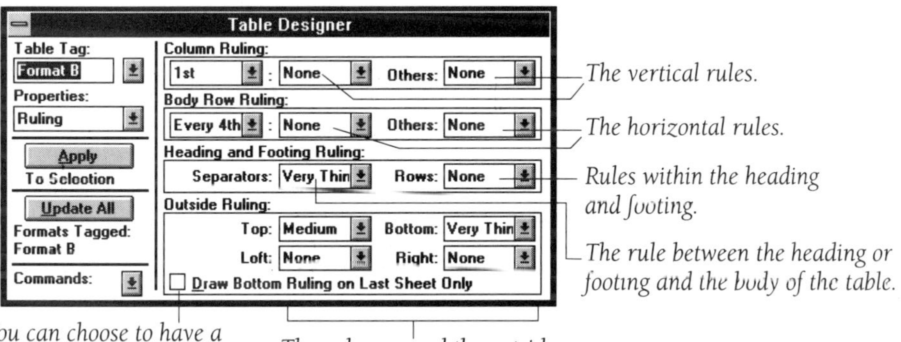

The vertical rules.

The horizontal rules.

Rules within the heading and footing.

The rule between the heading or footing and the body of the table.

You can choose to have a bottom rule on only the last page of a multi-page table.

The rules around the outside of the whole table.

Custom ruling and shading

1. Choose a group of table cells whose bounding rules, interior rules, or shading you want to change.
2. Display the Custom Ruling and Shading window.
3. Make your changes and click Apply.

Apply ruling one style at a time *Pick a ruling style from the scroll list and turn on the areas where you want to apply that ruling to the selected cells (top of selection, inside rows of selection, etc.). Turn off Custom Cell Shading unless you are also applying shading. Click Apply. Then choose the next ruling style to apply and repeat.*

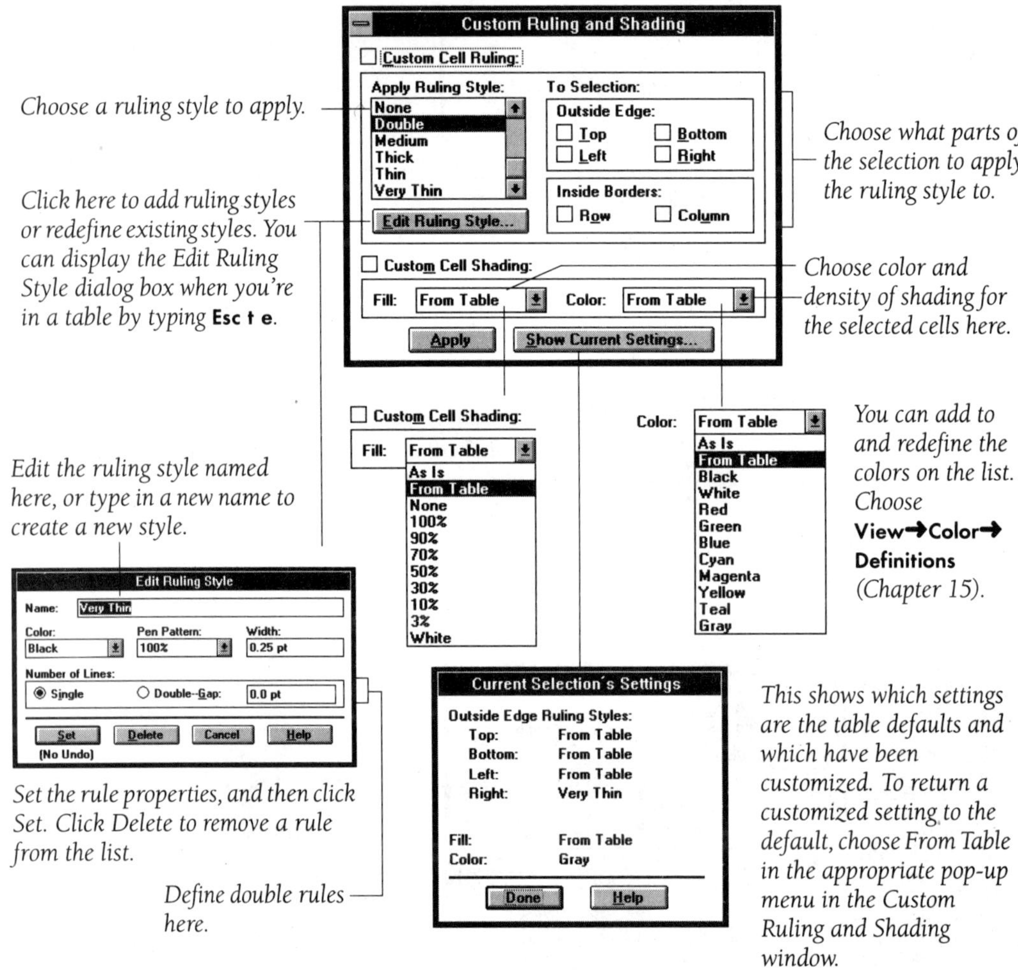

Default shading

Use the Shading page of the Table Designer to specify default ruling properties for a table or table format.

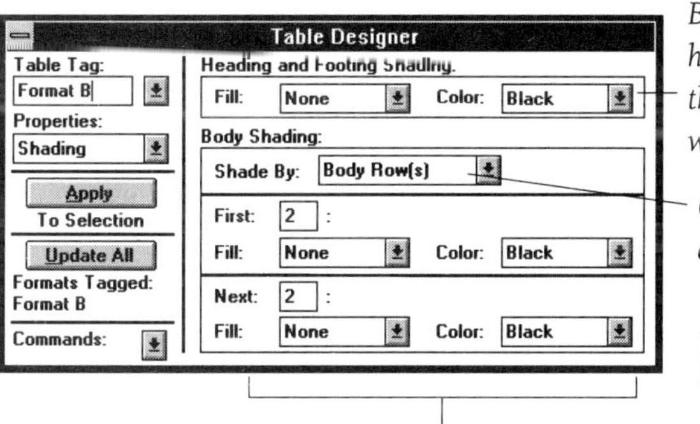

By default, the heading and footing rows have the same shading. You can change that using the Custom Ruling and Shading window.

Choose whether to shade rows or columns.

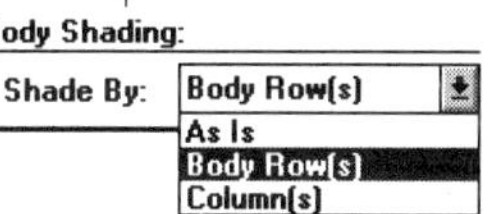

*"First **n** rows/columns" plus "Next **n** rows/columns" taken together form a repeating pattern of shading. For each, specify how many rows/columns are to be shaded. Then choose a color and a Fill density (%).*
*[**n** stands for the number you type in the box.]*

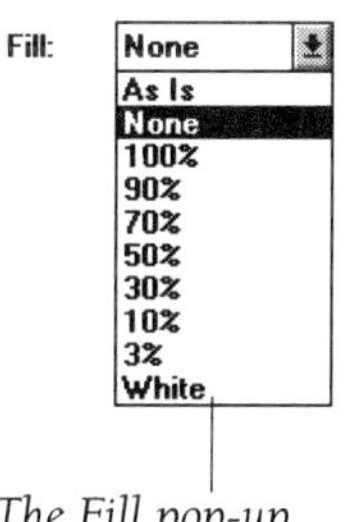

The Fill pop-up menus all look like this.

The Color pop-up menus all include FrameMaker's default colors plus whatever other colors you have defined, like Teal and Gray.

In the Shading page of the Table Designer, the default shading for this table is specified as:

- *Shade By Body Row(s)*
- *First* 1 *: Fill: 50%, Color: Black.*
- *Next* 2 *: Fill: None, Color: Black.*

There is no custom shading.

The application options in the Table Designer are exactly the same as those in the Paragraph and Character Designers. See Chapter 5, "Using the Designer Windows" starting on page 85.

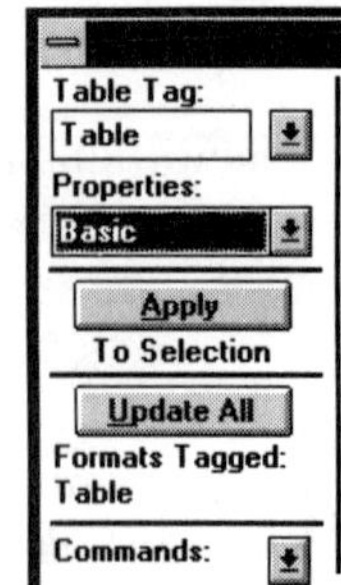

The paragraph formats in Head 1, Body 1, Body 2, Body 3, Foot 1, and the title column are stored as defaults for the table format when you Update All.

Head 1		
Body 1	Body 2	Body 3
Foot 1		

Table 11-1 Title.

■ Table formats

Defining and applying table formats, and working in the Table Designer, is exactly parallel to working in the Paragraph and Character Designers. Read Chapter 5 for more detailed descriptions of using the Designers.

What's in a table format

When you store a table format by clicking Update All, or by choosing New Format, just what table properties get stored? You store the following properties of the table that is selected when you choose Update All in the Table Designer:

- All the properties that you set from any of the three pages of the Table Designer;
- The number of heading, footing, and body rows;
- The number and widths of the columns;
- The paragraph format of the first title paragraph;
- The paragraph format of the first paragraph in each body column, in each heading column, and in each footing column. These paragraph formats will be the default paragraph formats for the heading, footing, and body cells of newly inserted paragraphs using the table format you are updating.

What's not stored

No custom settings are stored: cell margins, vertical alignment, ruling and shading, rotation, straddling, "keeps," or row heights.

■ Multi-page tables

Titles, headings, and footings

When a table is too long to fit on the current page, FrameMaker inserts a page break and repeats the title, heading rows, and footing rows on each new page of the table. You can only edit the title, header, and footer on the first page of the table.

Adding "(continued)" to a table's title

FrameMaker provides a variable that you can insert in the title, heading, or footing to cause the word "(continued)" to appear after the title on subsequent pages of a multi-page table.

1. Place your insertion point in the title, heading, or footing on the first page of the table. Use spaces or tabs to position it.
2. Choose **Special→Variable** to display the Variable dialog box. [**Alt s v**]
3. In the Variable scroll list, click on Table Continuation.
4. Click Insert.

▲ You can change the content or appearance of this variable just as you would any other variable; see "Defining or editing a variable definition" on page 164.

▲ There is another handy variable that you can add in exactly the same way: the **Table Sheet variable**. It gives the current sheet number and the total sheet count for the table (Sheet 3 of 4).

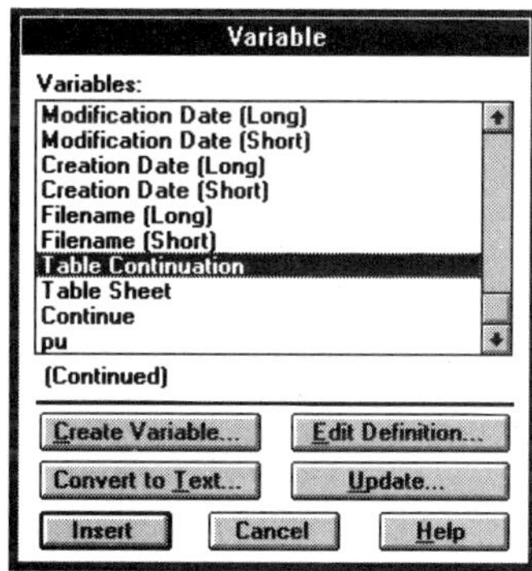

Insert the Table Continuation or Table Sheet variable into your table title. The default definitions are
- *Table Continuation = (Continued)*
- *Table Sheet = (Sheet 3 of 4)*

Setting the minimum number of rows per page

In the Basic page of the Table Designer, type in a number for Orphan Rows equal to the minimum number of rows that can be on a page. Orphan Rows: 3, for example, means that if only one row of a table doesn't fit on a page, FrameMaker still moves three rows to the next page.

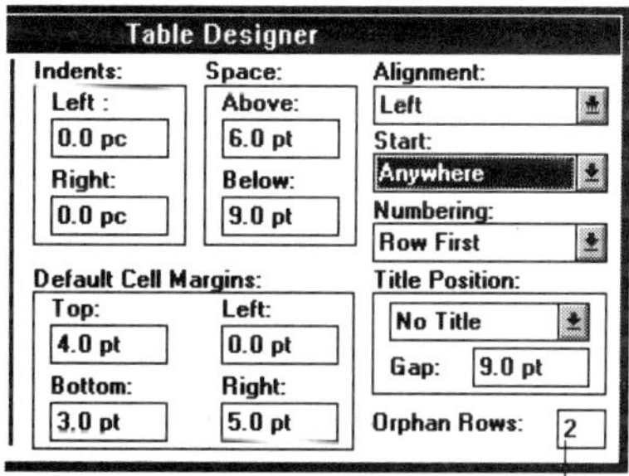

Set the minimum number of rows on a page here.

Forcing a break where you want it

1. Place your insertion point in the first row that should move to a new page or column.
2. Choose **Table➔Row Format**. [**Alt t r**]
3. In the Row Format dialog box, choose the page or column break you want from the Start Row pop-up menu.
4. Click Set.

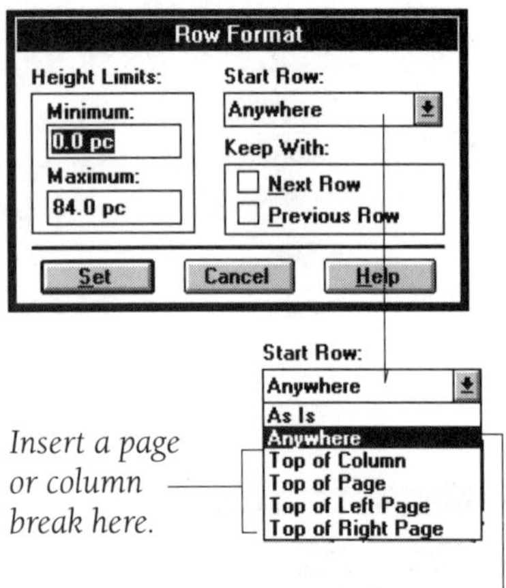

Insert a page or column break here.

Use this to remove an inserted page or column break.

Removing an inserted page break

1. Place your insertion point in the first row after the page break you are removing.
2. Choose **Table➔Row Format**. [**Alt t r**]
3. In the Row Format dialog box, choose Anywhere from the Start Row pop-up menu.
4. Click Set.

Keeping rows together

You can keep selected rows together. When you apply a "keep," FrameMaker cannot insert a page or column break within it.

1. Select all but the last row to keep together.
2. Choose **Table➔Row Format**. [**Alt t r**]
3. Turn on Keep With: Next Row.

▲ You can, of course, select all but the first row, and then turn on Keep With: Previous Row.

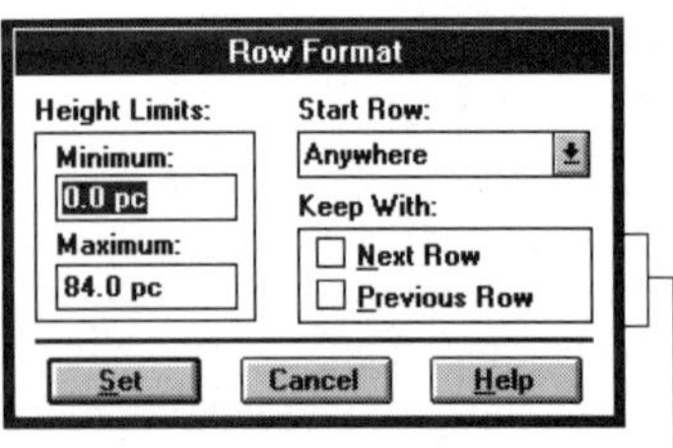

Keep rows together: FrameMaker cannot insert a page or column break in a group of rows with this property applied.

■ Placing a graphic in a table cell

1. Click in the cell where you want to insert the graphic.
2. Center the paragraph in the cell: use the Paragraph Designer to set the paragraph alignment to Center (page 243) and the vertical alignment to Middle (page 242). In the Line Spacing box, turn off Fixed.

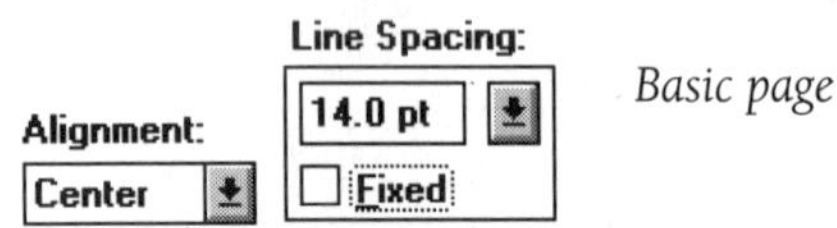

In the Paragraph Designer, set Alignment to Center, and turn off Fixed. Set vertical alignment to Middle.

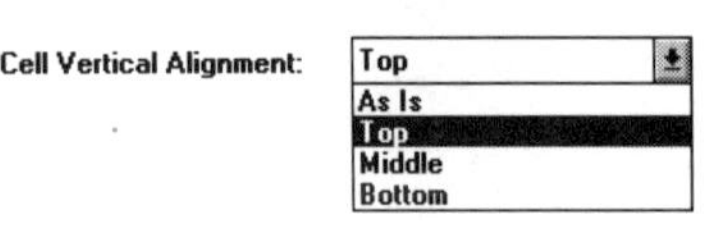

Table page

3. Create an anchored frame anchored at the insertion point in the cell (page 195). Make the frame large enough to contain your graphic. Widen the column if necessary (page 235).
4. Put the graphic in the frame (page 202).

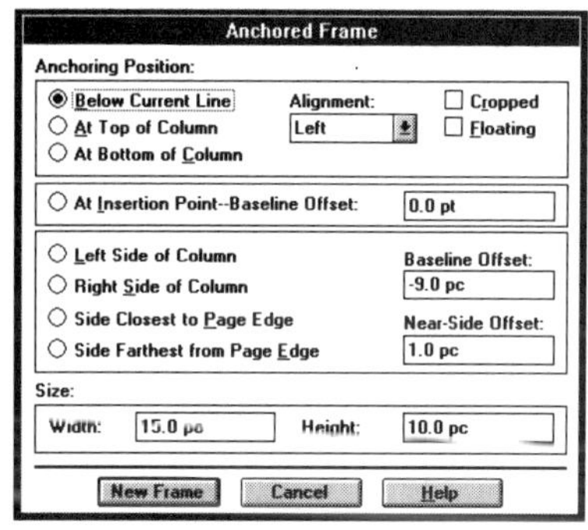

Anchor the frame At Insertion Point to put a graphic in a table cell. Anchor it Below Current Line to include a table in a table cell.

■ Placing a table in a table cell

1. Click in the cell where you want to insert the table.
2. Create an anchored frame anchored Below Current Line in the cell. Make the frame large enough to contain your inserted table. Widen the column if necessary to accommodate the frame.
3. Draw a text column in the frame.
4. Put the table in the text column.

■ Creating boxed text

There are several ways to create boxed text in FrameMaker. Page 201 describes how to do it using a frame and a text column.

■ You can also box text by created a single-celled table with no header, footer, or title. Turn on ruling around the outside of the table to create the border. Adjust the margins to position the text within the border.

This text is in a single-celled table.

The box around the text is the outer boundary of a one-celled table.

■ Importing table formats

To import only the table formats from another document, follow the instructions on page 107 for importing formats. In step 5, turn on only Table Formats in the Import Formats dialog box.

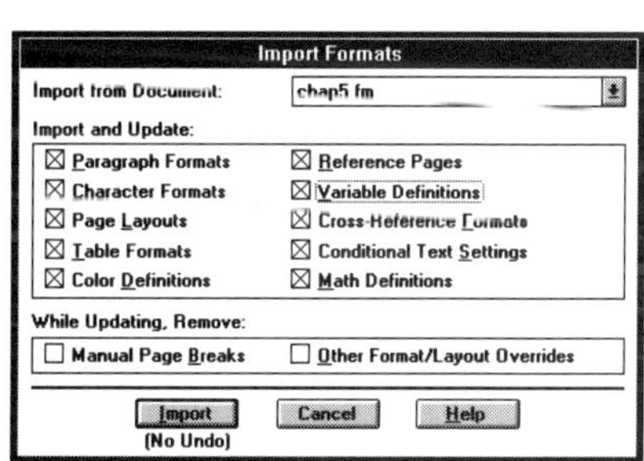

thing1;thing2;thing3
thing4;thing5;thing6
thing7;thing8;thing9

thing1	thing2	thing3
thing4	thing5	thing6
thing7	thing8	thing9

Table 11-2: Each paragraph become a row with cells separated by **;** .

The text at the top has three paragraphs with items separated by semicolons. In the Convert to Table dialog box, I used the following specifications to create the table:

- *Treat Each Paragraph As:*
- *A Row with Cells Separated By:*
- *Other:* **;** .

thing1
thing2
thing3
thing4
thing5
thing6
thing7
thing8
thing9
thing10

thing1	thing2
thing3	thing4
thing5	thing6
thing7	thing8
thing9	thing10

Table 11-3: Each paragraph becomes a cell.

This is an example of a conversion where each paragraph is a cell. The specifications are

- *Treat Each Paragraph As A Cell, and*
- *Number of Columns* 2.

■ Converting text to tables

1. Select the text to convert.
2. Choose **Table→Convert to Table**. **[Alt t o]**
3. In the Convert to Table dialog box, choose which of two ways to convert your text.
   - If each paragraph contains material for a whole row of cells, the contents for each cell must be separated by a consistent character or by spaces. If this is the case, choose Treat Each Paragraph As A Row with Cells Separated By: If the separator is a tab, check tab. If it's spaces, fill in the minimum number of spaces required to constitute a cell division. If it's another character, as in the example at the left, type that character in next to Other.
   - If each paragraph is the contents of one cell, choose Treat Each Paragraph As A Cell.
4. Choose a table format from the scroll list.
5. Fill in the number of heading rows you want. If you do not turn on Leave Heading Rows Empty, FrameMaker puts the first row(s) of text into the heading.
6. Click Convert.

Choose the table format to use.

Choose whether each paragraph is a row or a cell. If it's a row, designate the separator.

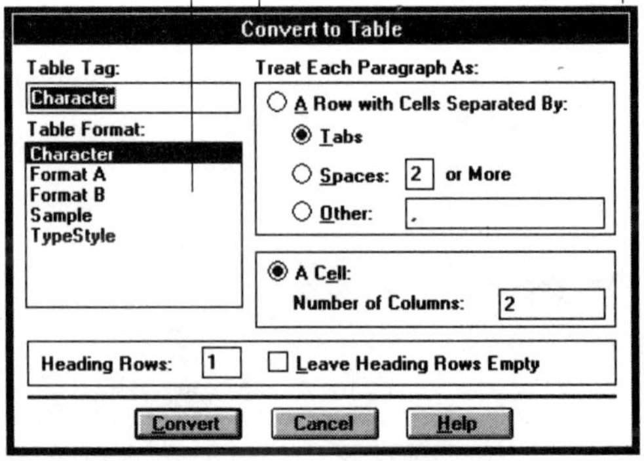

Choose the number of heading rows, and whether they should contain any of the selected text.

Graphics

■ What's in this chapter

FrameMaker has a really nice graphics module. It's not even "extra." It comes with the program. Overall, I find it intuitive and easy to use. I've used it a lot, and I like it a lot. There are a few details that you wouldn't necessarily guess right off the bat, though. This chapter is to guide you through the mechanics of FrameMaker graphics.

■ You can also import graphics from a wide variety of applications. FrameMaker supports OLE.

Elsewhere in this book

Graphics are discussed in connection with other topics in a few other chapters in this book:

Graphics and Frames

Graphics are typically contained in frames. A frame keeps all the pieces of a graphic and its labels and callouts together and undisturbed. Read Chapter 9 to learn about creating and using frames. There is a section about frames and graphics on pages 202 to 204 of that chapter.

Text columns and text lines

Text columns and text lines are special cases of graphic objects. Text columns are discussed in Chapter 10 on pages 215 to 222. Find out about text lines on page 67.

The QuickAccess bar is illustrated and described in detail on page 7. Here is a quick review of the two pages of it that are devoted to graphics operations.

Previous page	*Next page*
Group	*Ungroup*
Bring to front	*Send to back*
Distribute	*Reshape*
Smooth	*Unsmooth*
Flip up/down	*Flip right/left*
Scale	*Properties*
Snap	*Gravity*

Page 2 Graphics

Previous page	*Next page*
Move up 1 pt	*Move down 1 pt*
Move 1 pt left	*Move 1 pt right*
Top align	*Left align*
Vertical center align	*Horizontal center align*
Bottom align	*Right align*
Rotate clockwise	*Rotate counterclockwise*
Set line to solid	*Set line to dashed*

Page 3 Graphics editing

■ The Graphic Tools palette

The drawing pointer

When you click on one of the drawing tools, you get the drawing pointer: +

Hold down shift when you click a tool to keep it selected for more than one use. Click a Selection tool to finally unselect it.

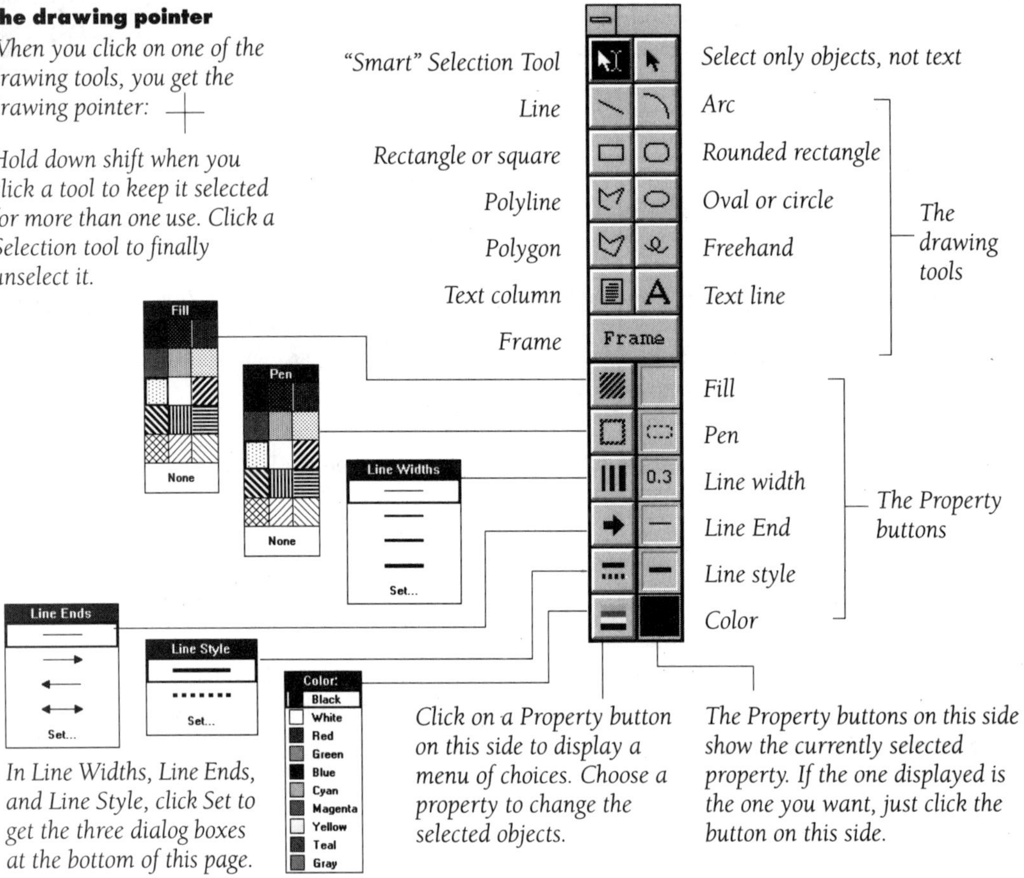

"Smart" Selection Tool — *Select only objects, not text*

Line — *Arc*

Rectangle or square — *Rounded rectangle*

Polyline — *Oval or circle*

Polygon — *Freehand*

Text column — *Text line*

Frame

The drawing tools

Frame

Fill

Pen

Line width

Line End

Line style

Color

The Property buttons

Fill

None

Pen

None

Line Widths

Set...

Line Ends

Set...

Line Style

Set...

Color:

Black

White

Red

Green

Blue

Cyan

Magenta

Yellow

Teal

Gray

In Line Widths, Line Ends, and Line Style, click Set to get the three dialog boxes at the bottom of this page.

Click on a Property button on this side to display a menu of choices. Choose a property to change the selected objects.

The Property buttons on this side show the currently selected property. If the one displayed is the one you want, just click the button on this side.

When you click Set in one of the menus above, you get the corresponding dialog box here:

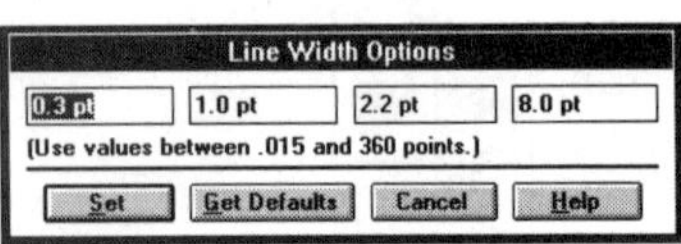

Line Widths Set *Define the four line widths that appears as choices in the Line Widths menu.*

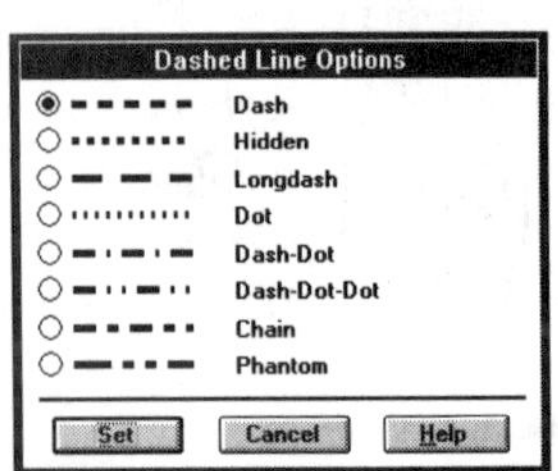

Line Style Set *Choose the type of dashed line you get when you choose Dashed from the Line Style menu.*

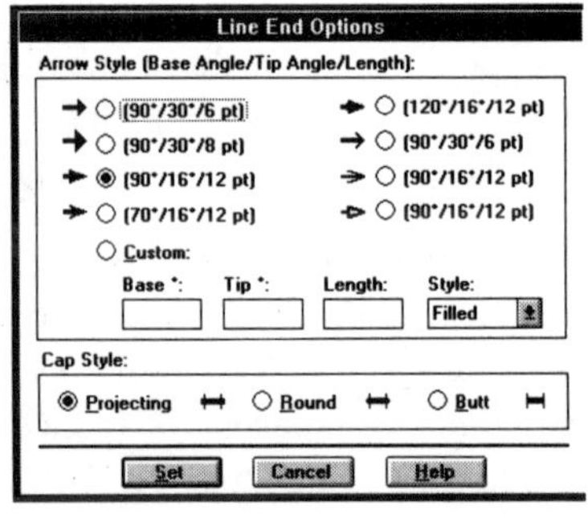

Line Ends Set *Choose a type of arrowhead or design your own.*

What's in this chapter

■ Drawing things

■ Click on a drawing tool and then drag the drawing pointer where you want the object. Release the mouse button when you're done.

To draw this		Click on the tool and...
	Line	drag from the beginning to the end of the line; or click at the beginning and again at the end. Hold down Shift to make the line exactly horizontal, vertical, or 45 degrees.
	Arc	drag along the path of the arc.
	Rectangle	drag diagonally across the rectangle; to **draw a square**: hold down Shift as you drag.
	Rounded rectangle	*(this is a rectangle with rounded corners)* drag diagonally across the rectangle; to **draw a square**: hold down Shift as you drag.
	Polyline	click at the beginning of the line; click at each point it changes directions; double-click or right-click at the end.
	Oval	drag diagonally across the oval; to **draw a circle**: hold down Shift as you drag.
	Polygon	click at each vertex; double-click or right-click at the last one.
	Freehand	drag along the path you want. You can also draw a polyline or polygon and Smooth it (page 266), to get a similar effect.
	Text column	drag diagonally across the column; see pages 215 to 221 for much more about text columns.
A	**Text line**	click where you want the text to begin, then type. See page 68.
Frame	**Frame**	drag diagonally across the frame to draw an unanchored frame.

Regular polygon

Set Number of Sides
Number of Sides: 3 (3 = Triangle)
Start Angle: 0 (0 = 12 o'clock) (90 = 3 o'clock)
Set Cancel Help

1. Draw a rectangle, an oval, a square, or a circle and select it.
2. Choose **Graphics→Set # Sides**.
3. In the Set Number of Sides dialog box, fill in the number of sides and the starting angle.

0° **45°**

Drawing things

Pointer	What it does
	Click to select an object **Drag** to move or resize an object
	Click to get an insertion point **Drag** to select text **Ctrl-click** to select an object
	Click to unselect everything **Drag** to create a selection border
	Drag to resize an object. You see here the horizontal and corner resize pointers.

Selecting things

The selection tools

When you use the **Smart Selection tool**, the pointer is an I-beam when it is over text. It's a hollow-headed arrow when it's in a position to select an object; it becomes a solid arrow when it's away from both text and objects.

When you use the **Object Selection tool**, the pointer is a hollow-headed arrow when it's in a position to select an object. It's a solid arrow the rest of the time. Anything you can do with the Object Selection tool you can also do by Ctrl-clicking with the Smart Selection tool.

Select by clicking

- Click on the first object, Shift-click on additional objects.
- To select an unfilled object, click on its border.
- Shift-click on a selected object to unselect it.
- Click in a blank area to unselect everything.

The selection border

- Position your pointer so that it's a solid arrow, and drag diagonally across an area you want to select. As you move the pointer you see a bounding box showing the selected area. When you release the mouse button, everything that is *completely inside* the box is selected.

A selection border tip In order to guarantee that you draw a border instead of accidentally selecting or moving something, hold down Ctrl-Shift as you begin to draw the border. You don't have to continue holding them down. Ctrl and the right mouse button does the same thing.

Uh-oh! If you're trying to draw a selection border and you accidentally move something instead, Undo immediately: **Ctrl-z**, **Edit→Undo**, or the  button on the QuickAccess bar.

More about selecting

- *To select everything in a frame, select the frame and then press* **Ctrl-a**.
- *To select everything on a page, unselect everything, be sure your pointer is a solid black arrow, and press* **Ctrl-a**.

(**Ctrl-a** *is* **Edit→Select All In.**)

Drag to draw a selection border around objects. Hold down Ctrl-Shift when you begin to make sure you don't move anything by mistake.

■ Grouping things

You can select two or more objects and Group them into a single object. You can do anything with a grouped object that you can do with a single object: move, resize, rotate, copy, etc. This is an incredibly handy feature.

Three objects, selected but ungrouped.

1. Select two or more objects.
2. Choose **Graphics➔Group** [**Alt g g**] or click [Group button] in the QuickAccess bar. The objects are now a single object.
3. You can select a grouped object and make it part of a still larger group. Build complex images up in logical, useful units in this way.

Hey presto! One object (still selected).

▲ Text lines and text columns are objects and can be grouped. To select a text line or text column as an object, Ctrl-click on its border, or choose it with the Object Selection pointer (page 254).

Group 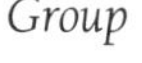 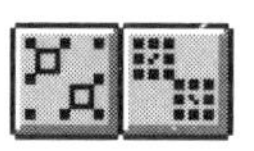 *Ungroup*

The Group and Ungroup buttons on the QuickAccess bar.

Ungroup

Select a grouped object and choose **Graphics➔ Ungroup** [**Alt g u**] or click [Ungroup button] in the QuickAccess bar.

■ Positioning things

Gravity and Snap

Gravity and Snap help you join and align objects. They are discussed on pages 26 to 28. I find Snap particularly useful. I leave it turned on most of the time. As I move things around, they always land on the nearest invisible Snap border. Things automatically line up with very little effort on my part.

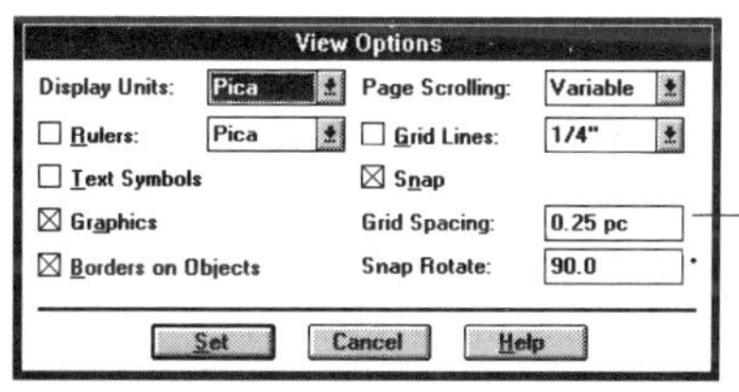

Adjust the size of the invisible Snap grid here.

A quick review

Turn Gravity and Snap on and off from the Graphics menu [**Alt g i** for gravity and **Alt g n** for Snap] Or use the buttons on the QuickAccess bar. Adjust the size of the Snap grid from the **View➔Options** dialog box.

Snap  *Gravity*

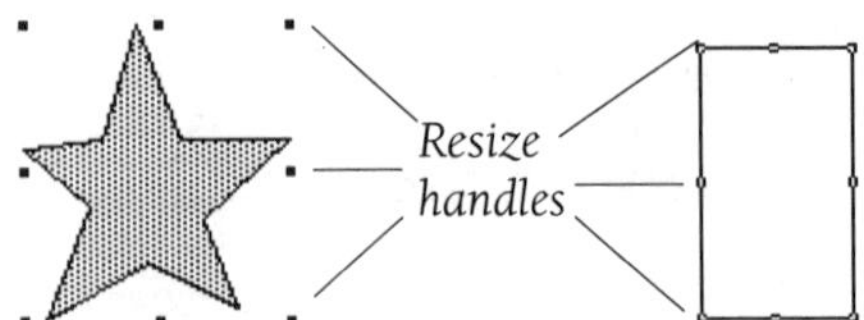

To move an object, moved the pointer over it, so that the pointer becomes a ↖ *. Press and drag. Do not place the pointer on a handle, or you will resize the object instead of moving it.*

Moving things

Dragging

■ Select an object and move it by placing the pointer anywhere on or near it. The pointer arrow must have a hollow head. Drag the object to the new location. **Warning** If your pointer is the triangle with no handle, it is over a resize handle. If you drag, you will resize, rather than move, the object.

■ Hold down Shift as you drag to constrain the movement to horizontally-only or vertically-only.

■ To move an object with no fill, place the pointer on the border of the object.

Micropositioning

1. Select one or more objects. *Optional*: Group them to ensure that they stay together. [**Alt g g**]
2. Hold down Alt and press the arrow keys to move the objects in tiny steps. (The amount of movement for each key press depends on the Zoom setting: it's one point at 100% zoom, and 0.5 point at 200% zoom.)
3. Hold down Shift-Alt to move in larger steps (six points at 100% zoom).

This is one of my favorites. I use it a *lot*.

The QuickAccess bar

The four helicopter buttons move selected objects 1 point in the indicated direction at 100% zoom.

On page three of the QuickAccess bar there are four buttons for moving selected objects. They move objects the same amount as Alt-arrow does when you're micropositioning (above).

The Object Properties dialog box

You can position an object very precisely by specifying the Offset in the Object Properties dialog box. See page 262, "Object properties."

Aligning

Select objects and then align them on the left, right, top, or bottom, or center them vertically or horizontally. Choose **Graphics➔Align** to display the Align dialog box. [**Alt g a**]

The "As Is" tells FrameMaker "leave this part alone."

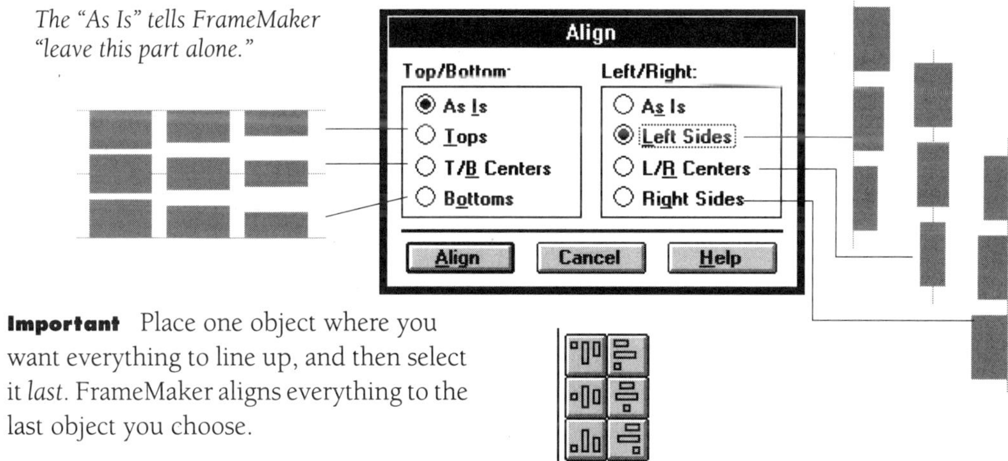

Important Place one object where you want everything to line up, and then select it *last*. FrameMaker aligns everything to the last object you choose.

The six QuickAccess Alignment buttons correspond exactly to the six choices in the Align dialog box. (You don't need "As Is" because the buttons are separate.)

Distributing

Use Distribute to position objects so that either their centers are equidistant, or their edges are equidistant. FrameMaker leaves the outermost objects in place and positions the ones in between evenly. If you specify an exact Edge Gap, FrameMaker leaves the left-hand or top item in place and positions the rest. To display this dialog box, choose **Graphics➔Distribute** [**Alt g d**] or click the button on the QuickAccess bar.

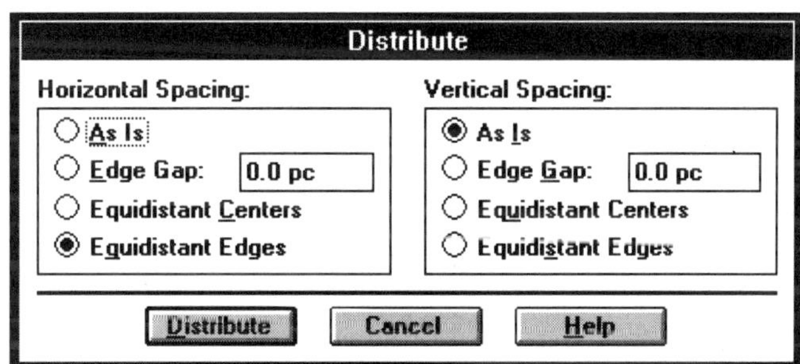

Select the objects to position and choose whether to space their centers or their edges evenly. If you are distributing only vertically, or only horizontally, set the spacing you're not using to As Is.

The original group.

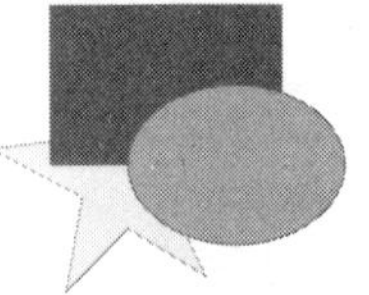

I selected the star and applied Send to Back.

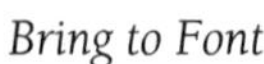

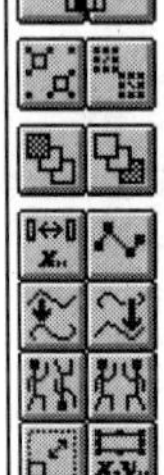

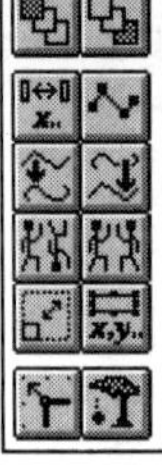

Bring to Font

Send to Back

Flip Up/Down

Flip Left/Right

Draw half the object.

Make a copy.

Flip the copy.

Move the second half into position.

Stacking objects

Control which object is on top of other objects by using Send to Back and Bring to Front from the Graphics menu.

1. Select an object to stack. If you select objects that are already stacked, FrameMaker selects only the topmost one. Grouped objects count as one object.
2. Choose **Graphics→Send to Back** or **Graphics→Bring to Front**. [**Alt g s** and **Alt g b**]

Flipping

1. Select the object.
2. Choose **Graphics→Flip Up/Down** [**Alt g f**] or **Graphics→Flip Left/Right**. [**Alt g l**]

Draw a symmetrical object

1. Draw half the object.
2. Turn on Gravity and Snap. [**Alt g i** and **Alt g n**]
3. Make a copy of the object. [**Ctrl-c** and **Ctrl-v**]
4. Select the copy and flip it.
5. Select one side and drag it so that it is joined to the other half. (That's where Gravity helps.)
6. Select both halves and Group them. [**Alt g g**]

▲ The QuickAccess bar has buttons for steps 2 through 6.

Rotating

▲ If you select several objects at once, each object rotates around its own center.

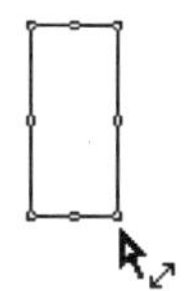

To rotate an object, hold down Alt, place the pointer on a handle, and drag. Notice the special Rotation pointer.

Dragging

1. Select one or more objects.
2. Hold down Alt, place the pointer over any handle and drag.

▲ If Snap is off, the objects turn smoothly. If Snap is on, the object snaps to preset intervals. Set this interval in the **View➔Options** menu (Snap Rotate). [**Alt v o**]

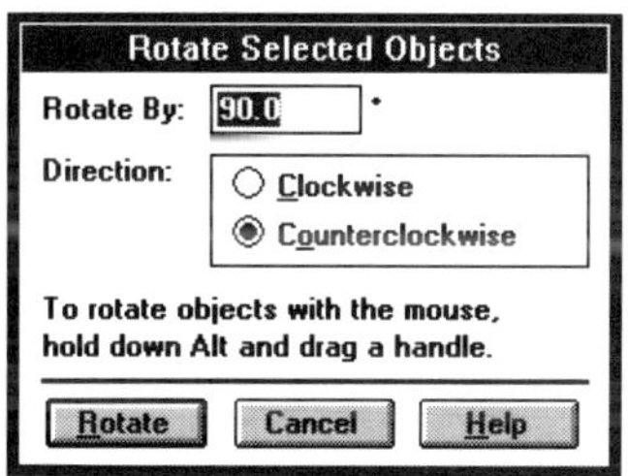

When you choose **Graphics➔Rotate**, *you get this dialog box for any object except a frame, a table cell, or an equation.*

Using the QuickAccess bar

1. Select one or more objects to rotate.
2. Click on one of the Rotate buttons on page three of the QuickAccess bar. The objects rotate 15 degrees in the indicated direction with each click.

The rotate buttons on the QuickAccess bar.

The Graphics➔Rotate dialog box

1. Select one or more objects to rotate.
2. Choose **Graphics➔Rotate** to display a dialog box. [**Alt g o**] For any object except a frame, a table cell, or an equation, you specify the amount of rotation *from the object's current position*, and the direction of rotation. For a frame, you pick one of four orientations.

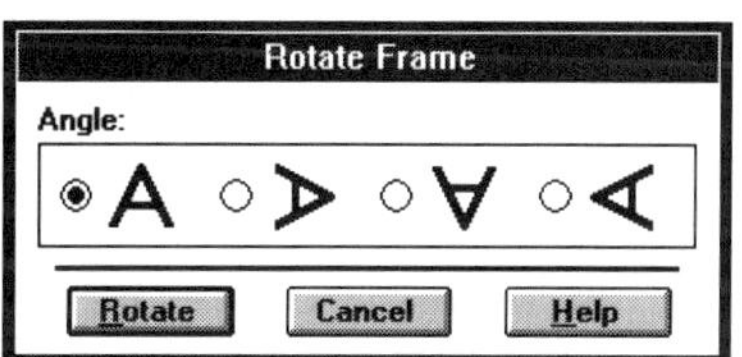

This is the **Graphics➔Rotate** *dialog box for a frame.*

Using the Object Properties dialog box

1. Select one or more objects to rotate.
2. Choose **Graphics➔Object Properties** to display the Object Properties dialog box. [**Alt g p**]
3. In the Angle text box, specify how many degrees *from their original, unrotated position* to rotate the objects.

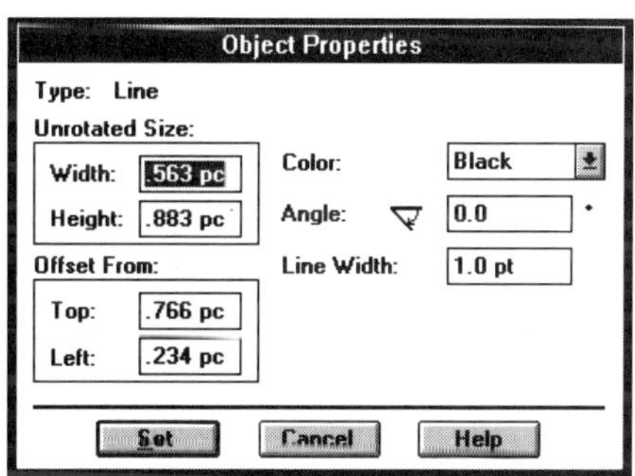

In the Angle text box, specify an angle relative to the object's original, unrotated position.

▲ **You can reset the original rotation angle!** You can specify that an object's current position is to be defined as 0 degrees: type **Esc g 9**.

Unrotate an object Type **Esc g 0** (*zero*).

Rerotate an object Type **Esc g 1** (*one*).

■ Object properties

Object Properties dialog box

■ Select an object and then choose **Graphics➔ Object Properties** or click the button to display the Object Properties dialog box.

Find out about an object's properties

This dialog box gives you information about the selected object. You see slightly different dialog boxes depending on whether you have selected a frame, a text column, a text line, or another type of object.

Hint In my version of FrameMaker 4, you frequently see just the last three decimal places of the various numbers. You can't see the beginning of the number. *Here's the fix*: Click in the box you want to read and press Home.

A note about Offset From The offsets given in the Object Properties dialog box are the distance from the top and left side of the frame containing the object. FrameMaker considers the page itself to be a frame, so there is always a frame to reference.

Change an object's properties This is a very precise way of positioning something when you know where you want it.

1. Select an object and display the Object Properties dialog box. [**Alt g p**]
2. Make whatever changes you want.
3. Click Set.

Display an object's properties in the Graphic Tools palette Select the object and hold down Shift as you choose **Graphics➔Pick Up Object Properties**. [**Esc g O** (*uppercase oh*)]

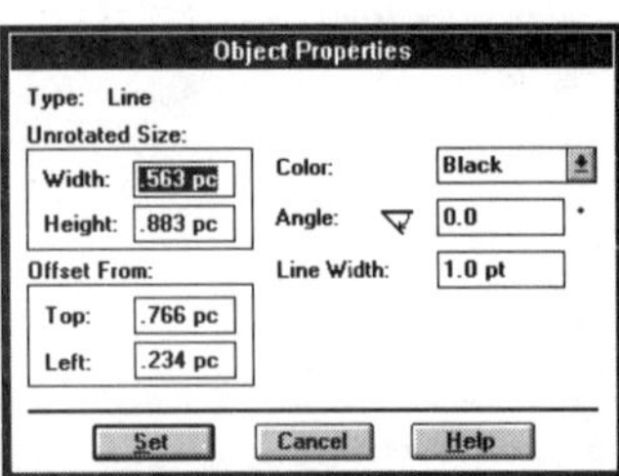

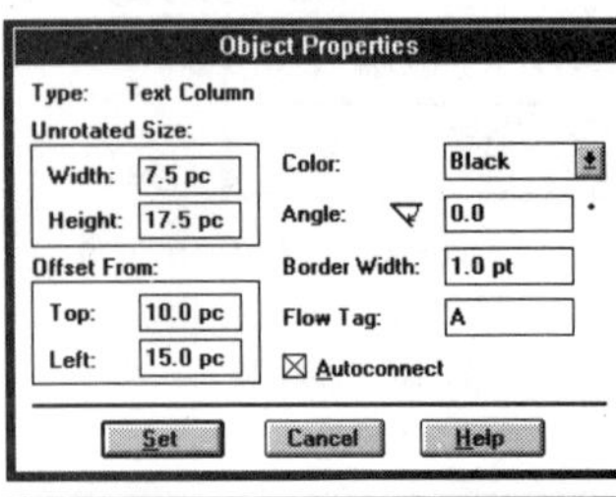

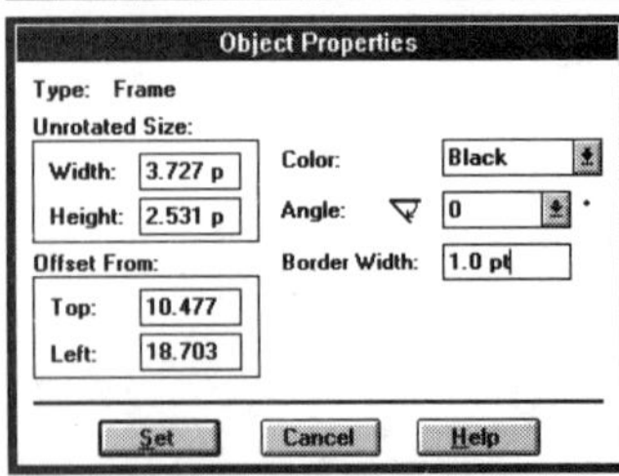

Did you ever wonder whether the object you just selected is a frame or a text column? The Object Properties dialog box will tell you. The object Type is always displayed in the upper left-hand corner.

View Graphics

You can speed up the page display by turning off graphics: choose **View➔Options** *and turn off Graphics.* **Warning**: *When you do this, all your graphics—FrameMaker and imported—are totally invisible and cannot be selected or edited.*

Status bar

See the size of an object

w: 15.0 pc h: 16.25 pc

When you position the pointer over a handle of a selected object and hold down the left mouse button, the object dimensions appear in the status bar.

You can see the size of a selected object displayed in the status bar at the bottom of the document window. Position the pointer over one of the object's handles and hold down the left mouse button. The dimensions appear in the status bar.

▲ The status bar also displays the size of an object as you draw it.

See the location of an object as it moves

As you drag a selected object, its **x** and **y** coordinates are displayed in the status bar.

Copying & pasting properties

You can apply the properties of one object to another object. You do this by displaying the first object's properties in the Graphic Tools palette and then applying them to the other object.

1. Select the object whose properties you want to copy.
2. Display the Graphic Tools palette and press **Alt g O** (*uppercase oh*). The object's properties are now displayed as settings in the Graphic Tools palette.
3. Select the second object, and click in the Graphic Tools palette to apply the properties you want from the first object.

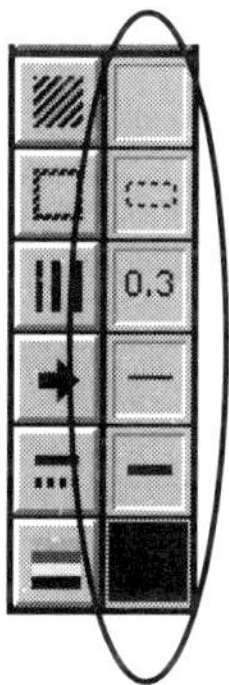

Select an object and press **Alt g O** *to display its properties in this part of the Graphic Tools palette. You can then apply these properties to other selected objects.*

Measuring things

Measure any object or any distance on the page by drawing a selection border either around the object or around the space you want to measure. Hold down Ctl-Shift at the beginning to be sure you don't move anything by accident.

This is a selection border being drawn to measure the space between the word **It** *and the triangle.*

As you draw the selection border, the status bar window shows the dimensions of the border and therefore of the space.

w: 15.0 pc h: 16.25 pc

Editing graphics

Create drop shadows

Draw the object.

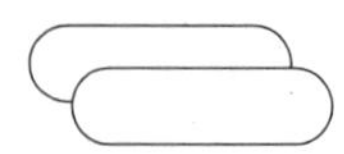

Copy and paste it or quick-copy it.

Change the fill to the shadow pattern.

Send the shadow to the back. [**Alt g s**]

To maintain the proportions of an object *you are resizing, hold down Shift as you drag the resize handle.*

Cutting, copying, & pasting

1. Select one or more objects using the techniques described on page 256.
2. Cut or copy the selection using any of the usual techniques: Edit menu, QuickAccess bar, or keyboard shortcuts. A copy of your selection is placed on the Clipboard.
3. Paste.

▲ If you have an insertion point in text at the time you paste, FrameMaker automatically creates an anchored frame to hold the pasted graphics.

▲ If you have a frame selected at the time you paste, FrameMaker places the pasted objects inside the frame.

Quick copy

1. Select one object.
2. Hold down Alt and drag. Be careful not to position your pointer over a handle. FrameMaker creates a copy of the object; that is what you are dragging.

▲ I really love this one. Who says there's no magic?

Resizing

Dragging a handle

1. Select an object.
2. Place the pointer over a handle. The pointer becomes a ◀ or a ◤, depending on whether you are over a side handle or a corner handle. (There's one for the top and bottom, too.)
3. Drag the handle. The side handles only let you change the width, and the top/bottom handles only let you change the height. You don't have to worry about changing a dimension accidentally. The corner handles let you change both dimensions at once.

Resizing *(continued)*

Using a Scale factor

1. Select the object.
2. Choose **Graphics→Scale** or click the button on the QuickAccess bar.
3. Type in either a percent by which to change the object's size, or type in the exact dimensions that you want the object to have
4. Click Scale.

▲ You can also specify exact dimensions for an object by using the Object Properties dialog box (page 262).

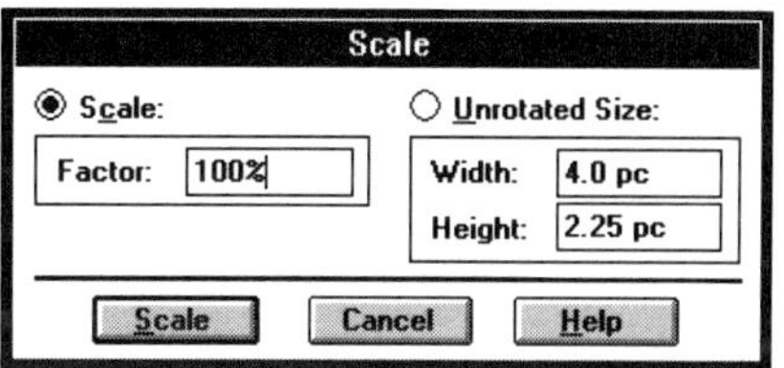

Change an object's size by a percentage, or specify the new size exactly.

Reshaping

Each type of graphic object can be reshaped as well as resized. The possibilities are different for different types of objects.

1. Select the object to reshape.
2. Choose **Graphics→Reshape** or click the button to display the object's reshape handles.
3. Drag any reshape handle to reshape the object.

This object has its **resize** *handles displayed.*

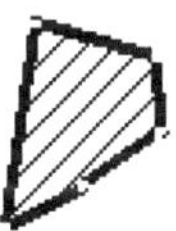

This object has its **reshape** *handles displayed.*

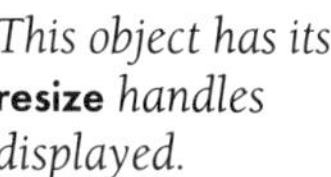

Reshape handles: adding, deleting, and moving

You can add, delete, and move reshape handles on polylines, polygons, and freehand curves.

- Ctrl-click on a border of an object that has reshape handles displayed. A new reshape handle appears where you click.
- Ctrl-click on a reshape handle to remove it.
- Drag any reshape handle to a new location.

Play around a little If you plan to use FrameMaker's graphics much, it is worthwhile to try out each type of object. Draw it, then select it and resize it by dragging the handles. Then choose Reshape and drag the reshape handles around. See what different things happen. Resize and Reshape frequently produce very different results.

Rounded rectangle corners

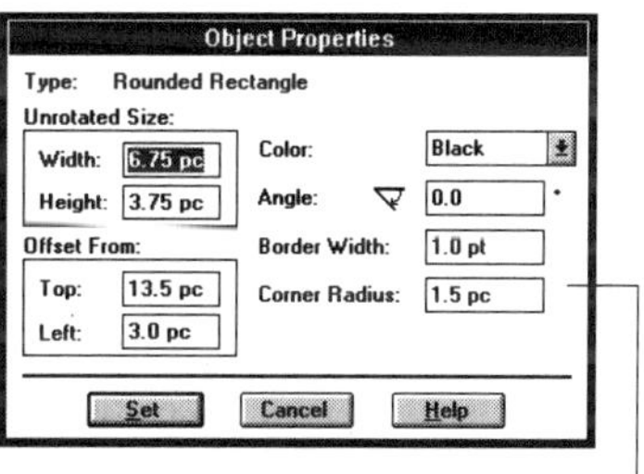

You can change the corner curve of a rounded rectangle here.

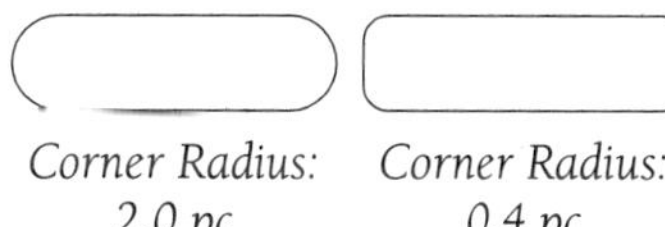

Corner Radius: 2.0 pc *Corner Radius: 0.4 pc*

At the top is the original graphic. I copied it and pasted it into a frame. Then I cropped it by moving it to one side. I turned on the border of the frame so you could see what's happening. (The graphic is FrameMaker clipart that comes with FrameMaker. Look for the DINGBATS *file in the* CLIPART *subdirectory of wherever FrameMaker is installed.)*

Overprinting

Normally, when one object overlaps another, FrameMaker does not print the invisible portion of the bottom object. In printing, a fine white line can result if the registration is not perfect. You can avoid this by turning on the Overprint property for the top object. If the top object is light and the bottom one is dark, however, you may not get complete coverage. You decide.

Turn on overprinting *Select the object and choose* **Graphics→Overprint**. **[Alt g v]** *Turn on Overprint and click Set.*

Cropping a graphic

There are two ways to crop objects in FrameMaker: put them in a frame or place white objects on top of unwanted portions of a graphic. These techniques can be used on either FrameMaker graphics, or imported graphics.

Using a frame

1. Draw an unanchored frame or create an anchored frame.
2. Place a graphic in the frame by pasting (page 264), dragging, or importing (page 202).
3. Resize the frame so that it cuts off unwanted portions of the graphic **or** move the graphic in the frame by dragging or micropositioning.

Pasting white objects

Block out parts of a graphic by creating any graphic object (a rectangle or a line, for example), and making the fill and border both white, or whatever color is appropriate.

Smooth and Unsmooth

Choose **Graphics→Smooth** or **Graphics→ Unsmooth** or click on the or button on the Quick-Access bar.

The best way to explain this feature is by example:

Original object.

The same object Smoothed.

Original object.

The same object Unsmoothed.

■ Boxing text

Here is a description of how to box text by putting a rectangle around a text column. Page 201 tells you how to do this by using a frame instead of a rectangle. You can also box text by putting it in a single-celled table that has no title.

1. Click on the Rectangle tool in the Graphic Tools palette. [**Esc 1** (*one*) **r**]
2. Draw diagonally across the area where you want the rectangle to be.
3. With the rectangle selected, use the Graphic Tools palette to apply Fill, Pen, Line Width, Line Style, and Color properties to the rectangle.
4. Click on the Text Column tool in the Graphic Tools palette.Draw a text column inside the rectangle. [**Esc 1** (*one*) **t c**]
5. Position the text column inside the rectangle. If you want it centered, select both objects and use the 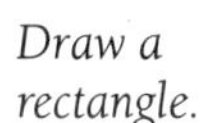 buttons in the Quick-Access bar. You can also select only the text column and microposition it using Alt, Shift, and the arrow keys (page 258). *Optional but recommended*: When the text column is in position, select the rectangle and the text column and Group them. [**Alt g g**]
6. Type or paste your text in the text column and format it as you would any text. The only restriction is that you cannot use an autonumber that is part of a series in the main text stream. You can get around this by putting the boxed text in a frame that is anchored to the main text flow.

▲ Place this whole thing in an anchored frame to make it move along with the text as the text is edited.

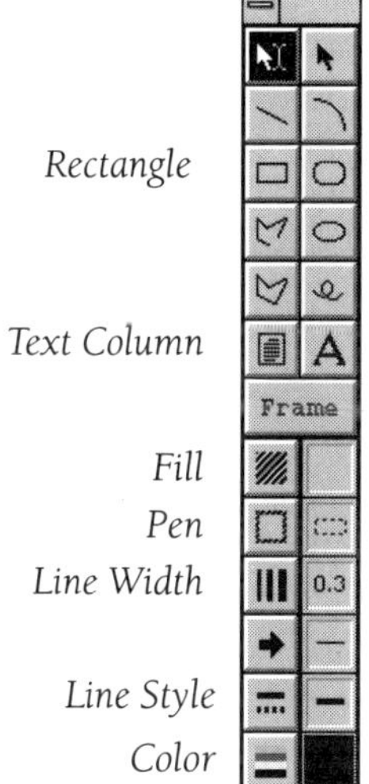

Here are the tools you use to put a border around text using a rectangle.

Draw a rectangle.

Adjust pen, fill, line width, line style, and color.

Draw a text column. It should have no fill and no pen. The border is turned on here so you can see.

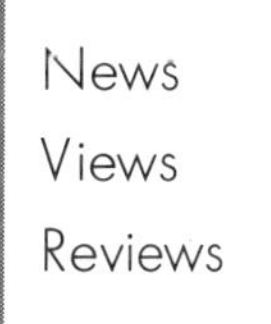

Add and format the text.

Help on graphic files

Look in the online manual "Using Frame Filters" for details about exactly what releases of each format are supported, and for other useful background information on importing graphics.

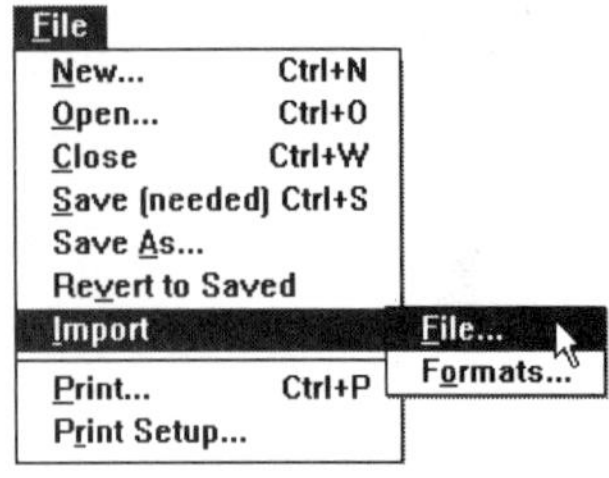

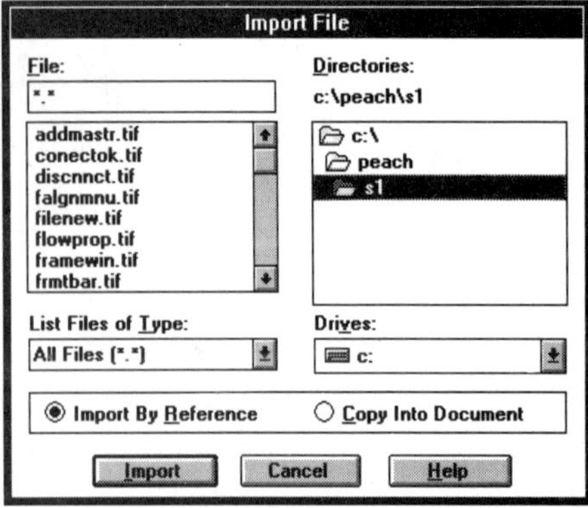

Import By Reference *maintains a link to the original file instead of copying it. You can have multiple links to a file. When you change the original graphic, all the occurrences of it in FrameMaker are updated as well.*

■ Importing a graphic file

You can import many graphics formats into FrameMaker:

BMP	EPSI	PICT
CDR	GEM	Sun Raster
CGM	GIF	TIFF
DRW	HPGL	WMF
DXF	IGES	WPG
EPS	MacPaint	XWD
EPSF	PCX	

1. Select where you want the graphic to appear:
   In a frame Select the frame by clicking on the border.
   Below a line of text Position the insertion point in text; the graphic will be imported into an automatically-created frame that is anchored to that point.
   Directly on the page Click on the page away from all graphics and text columns. After the graphic appears, you can drag it wherever you wish.
   Replace another graphic Select the graphic to replace.
   Fit into a rectangle Draw and select the rectangle (page 269).
2. Choose **File →Import →File** to display the Import File dialog box.
3. Choose **Import By Reference** or **Copy Into File**. If you import a file by reference, changes that you make to the graphic file in another application will appear in your FrameMaker document. This method also saves space, because no actual copy is made. If you copy the graphic into the file, a complete and independent copy of the graphic is stored inside your FrameMaker file.

4. Change the drive and directory to display the directory that includes your file. Type the file name into the File text box or choose it from the scroll list.
5. Click Import. The Imported Graphic Scaling dialog box appears.
6. Choose the dots per inch (dpi), or type a figure into the Custom box. The more dots per inch, the smaller the image.
   • It's a good idea to use a dpi figure that divides evenly into the dpi of the printer you'll be outputting on. (Most laser printers are 300 or 600 dpi. Imagesetters are 1200 or 2400 dpi.)
7. Click Set.

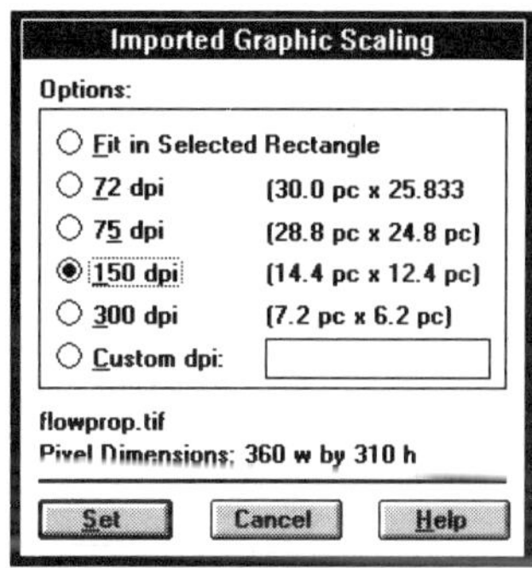

The dpi (dots per inch) setting determines the size of your graphic.

Import a graphic to a selected size

1. Draw a rectangle where you want the image.
2. Select the rectangle by clicking on the border.
3. Import the graphic as above, but in the Imported Graphic Scaling box, choose Fit in Selected Rectangle.
4. FrameMaker sizes your graphic so that none of it is outside the rectangle, but it does not change the proportions. If the rectangle has different proportions than the graphic, one part of it will be filled exactly, and one part will be partially filled. The rectangle disappears once the graphic is in place.

To fit an imported graphic to a designated space, define the space with a rectangle. Select the rectangle, import the graphic, and choose Fit in Selected Rectangle in the Imported Graphic Scaling dialog box.

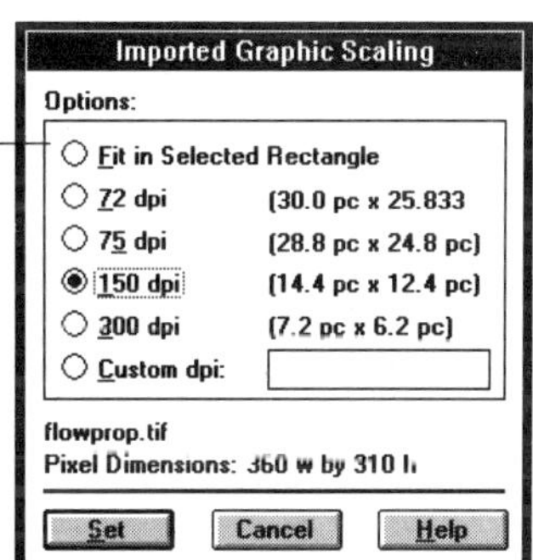

A note about Import By Reference

If you Import By Reference, you must remember to move and copy all referenced graphics files when you move or copy the main text file. The graphics file names cannot be changed (unless you re-import them with the new name) and the path from the main text file to the imported graphics must also remain the same after the move or copy.

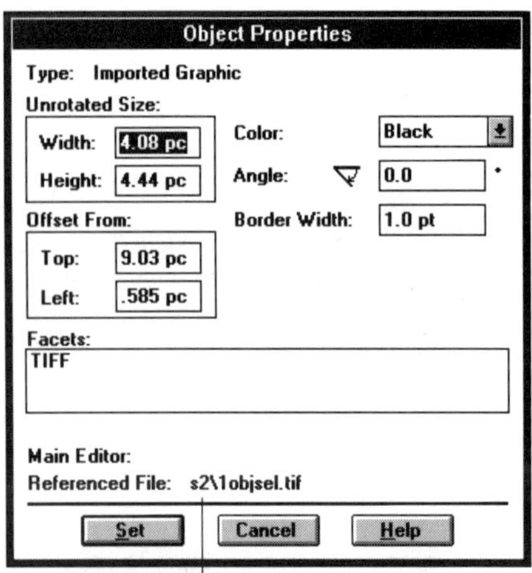

Select a file imported by reference and display the Object Properties dialog box to see. the file's name and path.

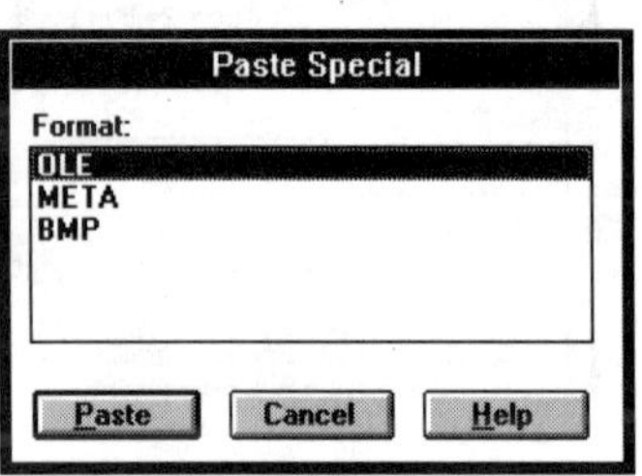

Replacing or modifying an imported graphic

Use this technique to replace an imported graphic with a different graphic, or to change the scale (dpi) of an imported graphic.

1. Click anywhere on the graphic to select it.
2. Follow steps 2 through 7 for importing a graphic, making whatever changes you want. To change the size of the graphic, choose a different number of dpi.

■ You can resize an imported graphic using any of the techniques described for FrameMaker's own graphics on pages 264 to 265.

Displaying the name of an imported graphic

To see the file name of a graphic that is imported by reference:

1. Click anywhere on the file whose name you want to see, to select it.
2. Choose **Graphics→Object Properties**. [**Alt g p**] The name of the referenced file is displayed in the Object Properties dialog box.

Embedding a graphic object

1. Create the graphic in any application that supports Object Linking and Embedding.
2. Copy the object.
3. In FrameMaker, indicate where you want to place the object. See step 1 of "Importing a graphic file."
4. Choose **Edit→Paste Special**. [**Alt e s**] In the Paste Special dialog box, choose OLE.
5. Click Paste. If you have selected an object to replace, click Replace instead.

Editing an embedded object

To edit an embedded graphic, double-click on it. A window opens in which you can edit the object in its native application.

Books

■ Why a book?

In FrameMaker, a book is a collection of related files. Here's what you can do with a book:

- Update page numbering and autonumbering for all files in the book.
- Update cross-references between all files in the book.
- Generate indexes, tables of contents, and lists of various kinds for the whole book.
- Open, close, and save all files in the book with a single command.
- Print selected files in the book.
- Import formats into selected files in the book.

Using the selection windows

Several of the dialog boxes that you see when you're working with books have a pair of selection windows in which you select which files to operate upon.

- *To move an item between the right and left columns, double-click it;* **or** *click once and click the appropriate arrow.*
- *To move everything at once, highlight one item and Shift-click the arrow.*

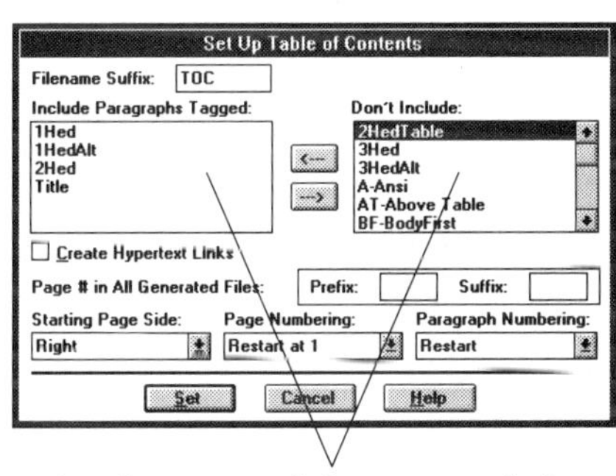

Select the paragraph formats to include in a table of contents.

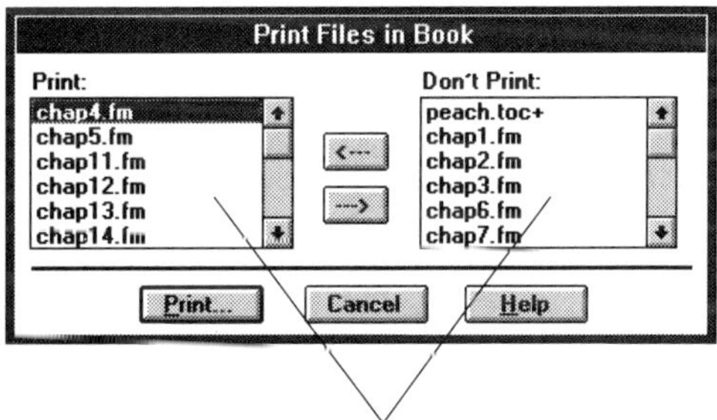

Select which files in a book to print.

Examples of selection windows

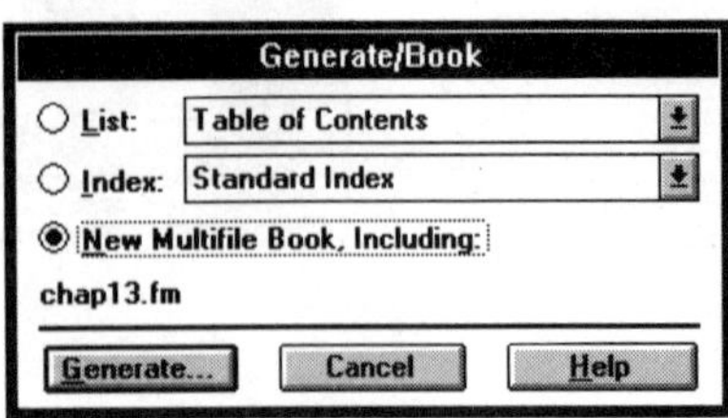

Click in any file that belongs in the book, and choose **File→Generate/Update;** *then choose New Multifile Book.*

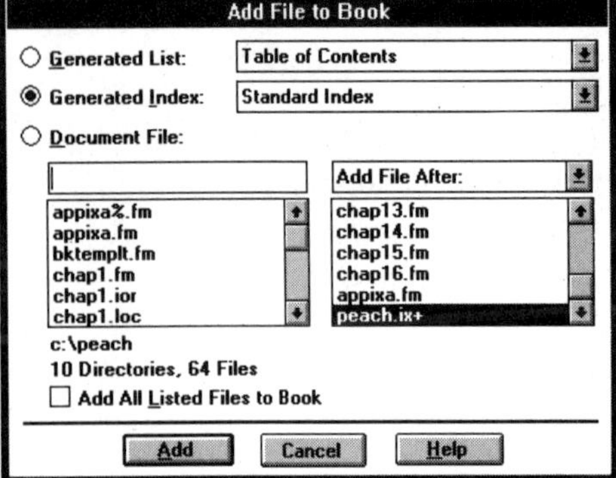

Add the document files to the book, singly or in a batch ("Add All Listed Files"). Then add the generated files, such as Table of Contents and Standard Index.

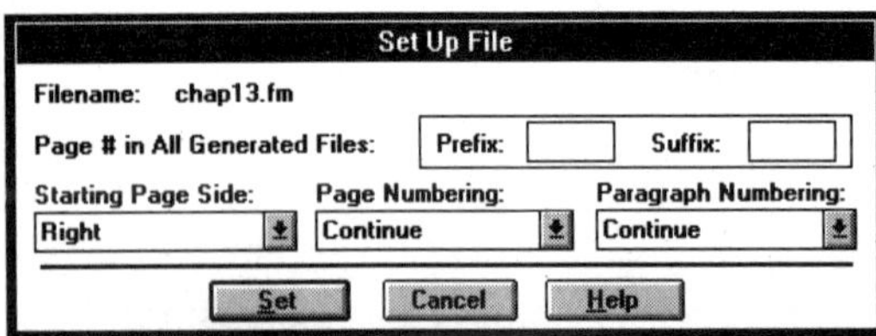

Specify pagination and numbering for each file.

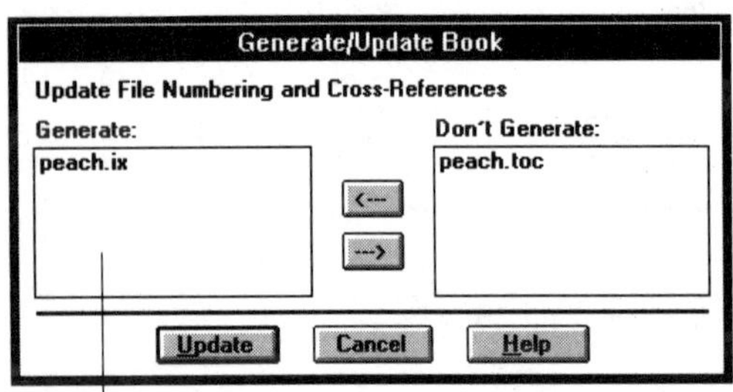

Request that files be generated as part of the update.

■ Steps to a book

The process of creating a book in FrameMaker has several steps. Here's a quick overview of them, before we get into the details.

1. **Create an empty book**. Click in any file that is to be part of the book, and generate an empty book by choosing **File→Generate/Book**, and then choosing New Multifile Book from the Generate/Book dialog box.
2. **Name the book and add files to it**. Use Save As to give the book the name you want it to have. Then use **File→Add File** in the book File menu to add the document files that belong in the book.
3. **Add generated files to the book**. Choose the generated files you want from the Generated List pop-up and the Generated Index pop-up. You have now told Frame-Maker that the generated files are to be part of the book. They are in the list of files, but they are empty; FrameMaker doesn't recognize them yet.
4. **Set up the pagination and numbering** for the files in the book. For each file, specify whether page numbering and autonumbering should continue in sequence from the previous file or start over; what page side the file should begin on; and whether any prefix or suffix should be added to its page numbers when its contents are referenced in generated files.
5. **Generate/Update the book**. Choose Generate/Update from the File menu in the book window. FrameMaker updates autonumbering, page numbering, and cross-references for all files in the book. If you request that files be generated, it also extracts the information you request from the book's documents into the generated files, such as the Table of Contents and Standard Index. Now your generated files are no longer empty.

■ Working with books

A book has its own window, just as a document does. The difference is that a document has text and graphics as its contents, but a book has files as its contents. A book can be opened, saved, copied, or Saved As, just as files can. By holding down Shift when you click on the File menu, you see a version of the file menu that lets you open, close, or save all the files in the book.

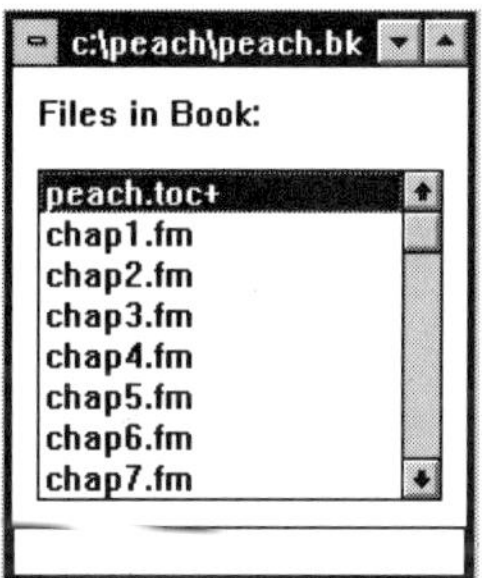

A book window.

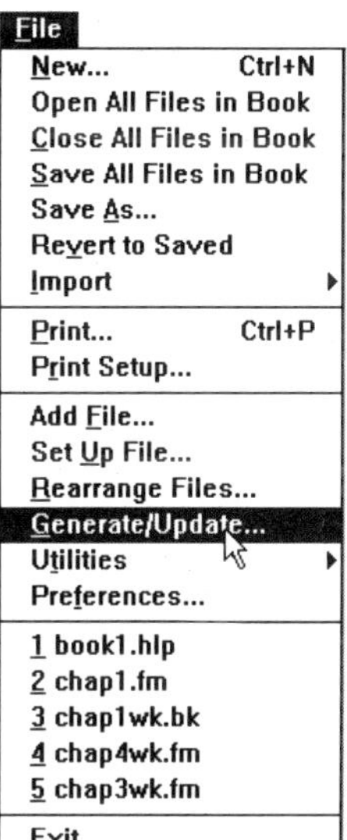

In a book file, Shift-click on File to get this menu.

Opening or displaying files

Opening or displaying one file In the book window, double-click on the file you want to open. FrameMaker opens the file if it is closed. If the file is already open, but iconized or buried, Frame-Maker displays it and makes the window active.

Opening all files in a book In the book window, hold down Shift as you click on File. Then choose Open All Files in Book.

Saving or closing

Save or close the book Choose **File➔Close Book** or **File➔Save** from the book window.

Save or close all files in the book In the book window, hold down Shift as you click on File. Then choose Save All Files in Book or Close All Files in Book.

Printing files in a book

1. In the book window, choose **File➔Print**. FrameMaker displays the Print Files in Book dialog box.
2. Move files so that the Print window contains the list of files you want to print. Double-click on a file to move it between columns, or Shift-click on an arrow to move all files.
3. Click Print. FrameMaker displays the Print Book dialog box. This is the same as the Print dialog box described on pages 51 to 54.

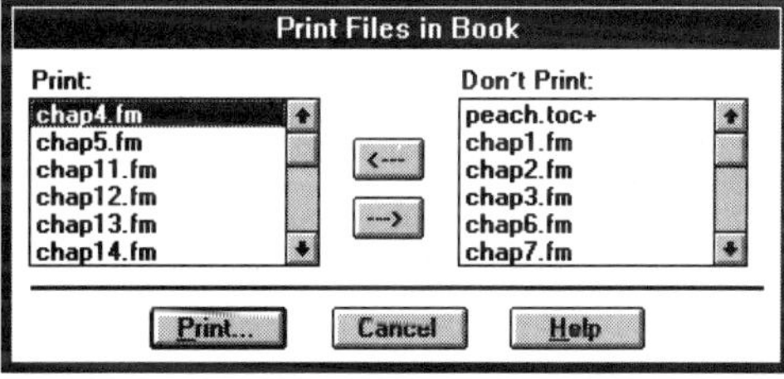

Double-click on a filename to move it from one column to the other. When the Print column contains the right files, click Print to display the Print Document dialog box.

Terminology:
"in the book window"

Throughout this chapter, when you see the instruction "In the book window, choose..." it means that you click on the top bar of the book window to make it active (if it isn't already), and then click on the menu item—usually File.

■ Creating an empty book

1. Open and display any one of the files that will be part of the book.
2. Choose **File➜Generate/Book**. [**Alt f g**] In the Generate/Book dialog box, click on New Multifile Book, Including. The name of the current file appears on the next line.

Create a new multifile book.

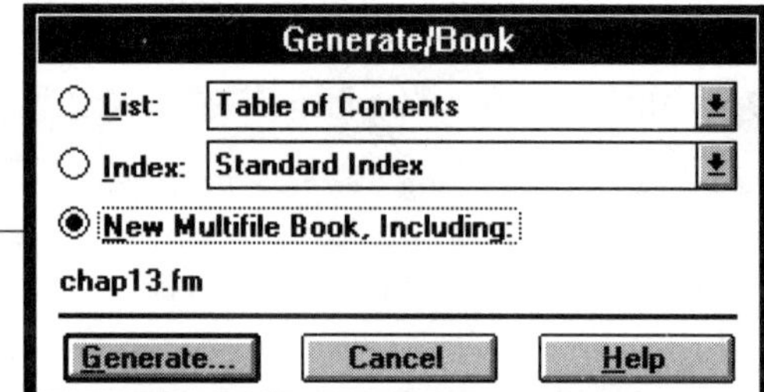

3. Click Generate. FrameMaker displays the new book window.

Saving and naming the book

FrameMaker gives the new book a name based on the name of the file you created it from. This probably isn't the name you want.

Type the new name here.

1. In the book window, choose **File➜Save As**.
2. In the Save Book dialog box, type the name you want in the Save in File text box; click Save.

Here's your new book window, new name and all, ready for you to add the rest of the files.

■ Adding files to a book

This is how to add a text file to a book. To add a generated file, such as an index or a table of contents, see page 276.

1. In the book window, choose **File➔Add File**.
2. In the Add File to Book dialog box, click on the filename you want to add.

   To add files from a different directory, scroll to the bottom of the file list. Other available drives and subdirectories are listed. To display the parent directory, click on the **[..]** symbol.
3. Choose Add File After or Add File Before and then choose a file from the list to specify a position for the new file. The position of the file in the book determines the autonumbering sequence if you choose to continue numbering between files (page 279).
4. Click Add.

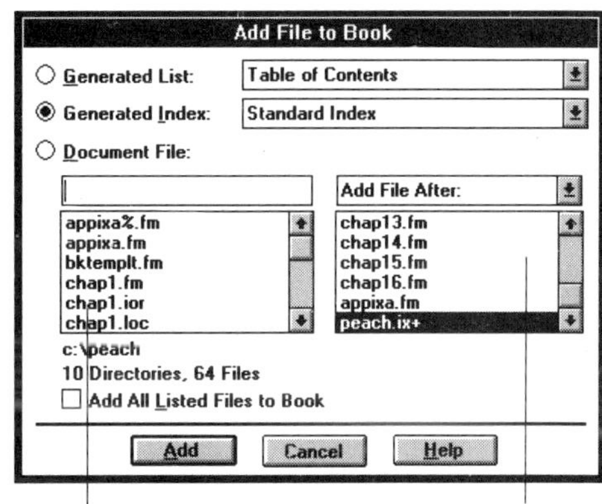

Choose the file to add. *Choose where to place the file in the book.*

c:\peach
10 Directories, 81 Files
☒ Add All Listed Files to Book

Add all the files displayed in the Document File scroll list at once by turning this on. Don't pick a location from the scroll list at the right, just click Add. You can restrict the display by typing a wildcard filespec in the Document File text box and pressing Enter. It's okay if some files in the list duplicate files already in the book. FrameMaker is smart. It doesn't add the files twice.

A shortcut

When you use the method above, you have to add each file individually. In a large book, that can be a long process. Here's a shortcut:

1. Display the Add File to Book dialog box.
2. In the Document File text box, type a wildcard spec that will, as nearly as possible, display the files you want in the book; press Enter to display only the specified files. If the spec includes a few extra files, that's okay. It's easier to remove files from a book than it is to add them.
3. Turn on Add All Listed Files to Book and click Add. FrameMaker adds all the files that you listed with your wildcards to the book. No files are added twice.
4. If the book now includes some files you don't want, remove them by choosing **File➔Rearrange Files** (page 277). Select a file to remove and click Delete.

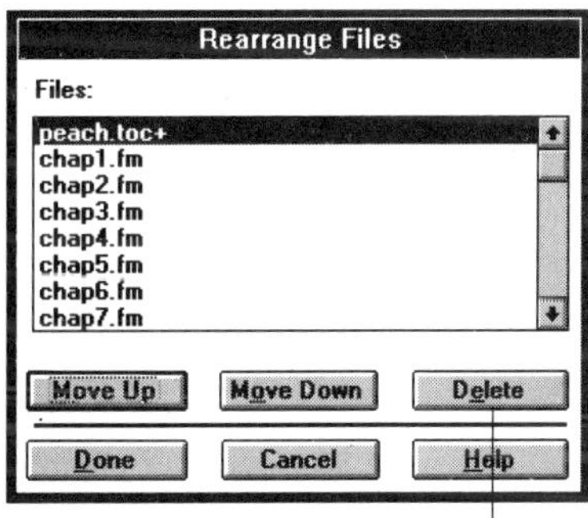

Delete files from a book—not from the disk—here.

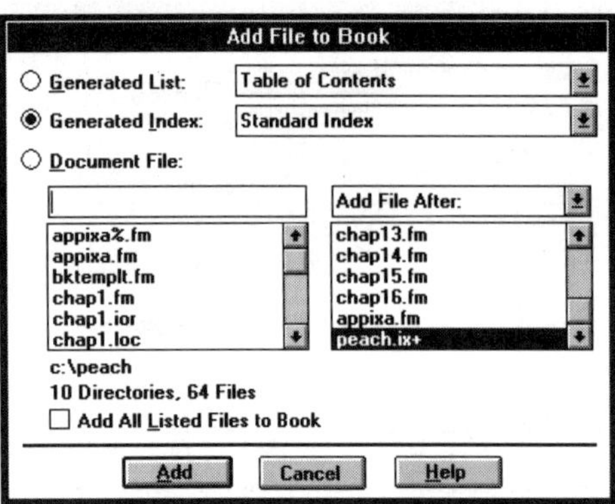

To add a generated file, click on Generated List or Generated Index, and choose a type of file from the pop-up. See page 278 for a list of choices. Click Add.

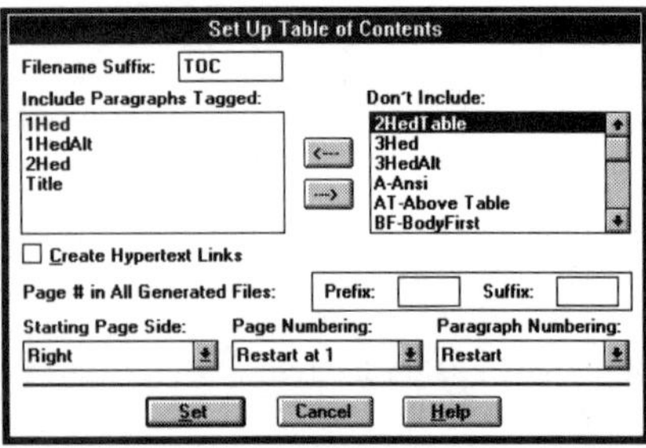

Move the paragraph formats or marker types that FrameMaker should include in the generated file into the Include window.

Generated files have the same name as the book, with an identifying extension to show the type. They are shown with a + after their name in the book window.

■ Adding generated files

Generated files are files that FrameMaker creates ("generates") for you from information contained in the document files. The most common generated files are Table of Contents, Index, List of Figures, and List of Tables. FrameMaker offers you many other options, as well.

Tell FrameMaker what generated files you want, and where they go in the book:

1. In the book window, choose **File→Add Files**.
2. Click the radio button next to Generated List or Generated Index, and then choose the type of list or index to add from the pop-up menu.
3. Click Add. FrameMaker displays the Set Up dialog box for the type of file you chose.
4. In the Set Up dialog box, specify the following properties for the new file:
   - What paragraph tags or marker types should be included in the generated file;
   - Whether the entries in the new file should have hypertext links to the document files;
   - What page side the file should start on;
   - Whether page number and autonumbering (Paragraph Numbering) should continue from the previous file in the book or start over at one;
   - Prefix and Suffix for page numbers. See "Pagination and numbering" on page 279.
5. Click Set. FrameMaker adds an empty file to the book. When you Generate/Update the book, FrameMaker extracts the contents of the paragraphs or markers that you specified in the Set Up dialog box, and places them in the generated file.

Generated file names

When you add a generated file to a book, FrameMaker uses the name of the book as the filename, but adds an identifying extension. TOC, for example, is table of contents. IX means the file is an index.

■ Rearranging files

You can change the order of files in the book or remove files.

1. In the book window, choose **File→Rearrange Files**.
2. Click on a file to select it.
3. Click on Move Up, Move Down, or Delete.
4. When your files are arranged to your satisfaction, click Done.

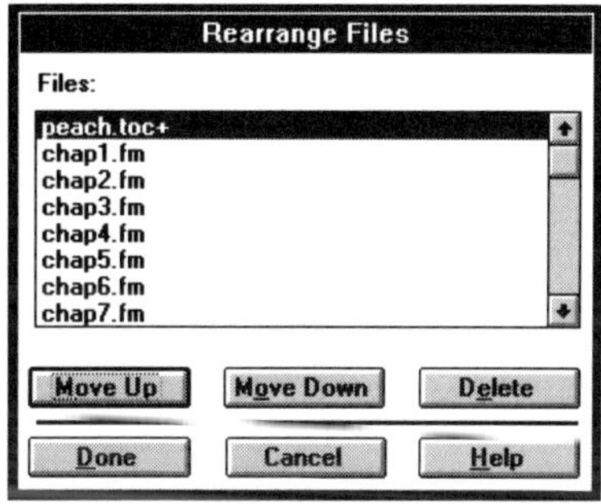

FrameMaker considers deleting a file from a book to be a form of rearranging it!

Hypertext links

When you add a generated file such as an index or table of contents to a book, one of the choices in the Set Up dialog box is Create Hypertext Links. If you turn this on, *the generated file will be a hypertext document*. Those who read it on-line can click on an item to go directly to the referenced point in the document file. In a table of contents, for example, they click on the entry they want to see, and FrameMaker displays the document page! This is one of FrameMaker's killer features.

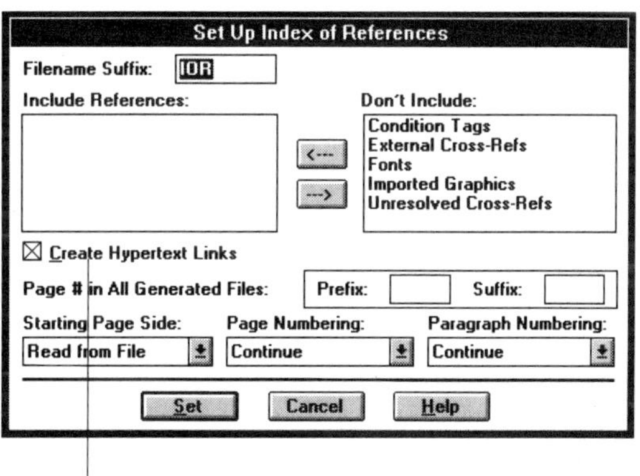

You find this option in the Set Up dialog boxes for generated files.

Using hypertext links

- In an *unlocked* (normal) document, Ctrl-Alt-click on the item you want to see.
- In a *locked* (view-only) document, click on the item.

Locking and unlocking a document

To toggle a document between locked and unlocked ("normal" and view-only):
Esc F l (*lowercase ell*) **k**. The **F** must be uppercase, the **l** and **k** are lowercase.

Turning hypertext on

1. In the book window, click on the generated file you want to change.
2. Choose **File→Set Up File**. [**Alt f u**]
3. In the Set Up dialog box, Turn Create Hypertext Links on or off.
4. Click Set.

Hypertext: What happens

The reader clicks on an area of interest. *FrameMaker displays the associated page.*

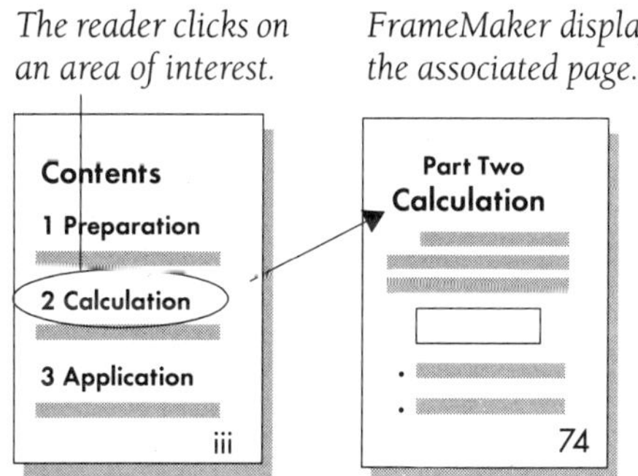

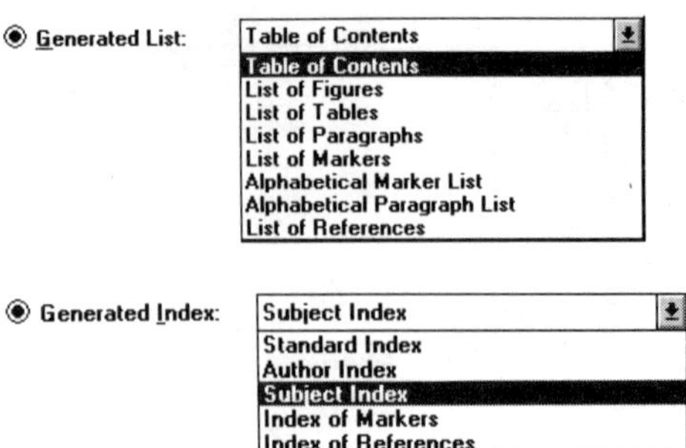

These are the types of lists and indexes you can generate.

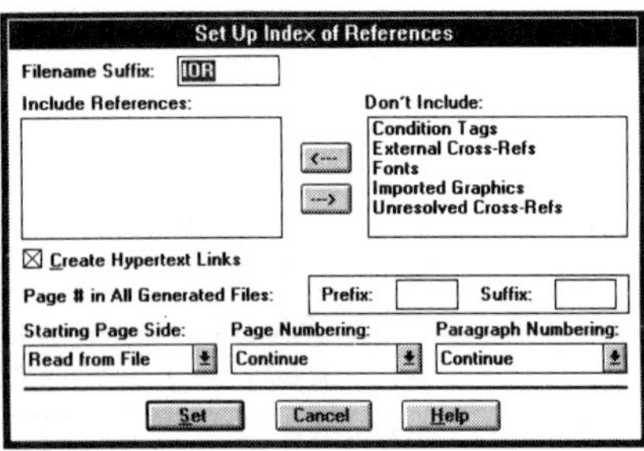

If you choose List of References or Index of References, you have this further list of choices.

Types of generated files

Lists and indexes

In the Add File dialog box, there are two pop-up menus: List and Index.

▪ In a **list**, an item is listed each time it occurs in the source file. Tables of contents and lists of figures are examples of lists. Your List choices are:

- Table of Contents
- List of Figures
- List of Tables
- List of Paragraphs
- List of Markers
- Alphabetical Markers List
- Alphabetical Paragraph List
- List of References

The four list types in the left column can be used for whatever paragraph types you choose. The names are only suggestions.

▪ In an **index**, each item appears only once, followed by all the page numbers on which it occurs in the source file. FrameMaker lets you generate four different types of indexes: standard, author, subject, and marker (they're all "marker," really). You can specify any type of marker for any type of index. The index offerings are:

- Standard Index
- Author Index
- Index of References
- Subject Index
- Index of Markers

References

If you choose **List of References**, or **Index of References**, you can choose to list or index the following items in the document:

- condition tags in use
- cross-references to other files
- fonts in use
- graphics imported by reference
- unresolved cross-references

In producing this book, I found it very useful to be able to list the graphics I imported by reference, and to check which fonts I used. This is a powerful and helpful feature tucked away at the bottom of the list. Check it out.

■ Pagination and numbering

After you add a document file to a book, select the file in the book window and choose **File➔Set Up File** to specify a number of things about pagination and numbering in the document:

▼

Setting up files

For each file in a book, highlight the file in the book and choose **File➔Set Up File**. *Check to make sure all settings are as you want them for each file and save the book.*

▲

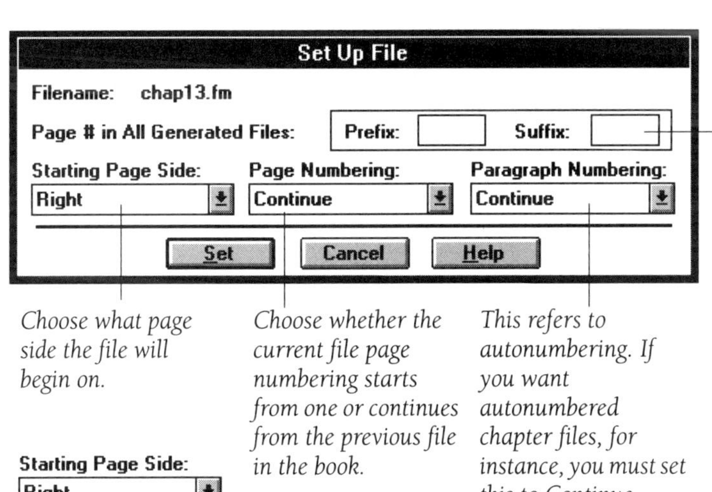

Add a Prefix or Suffix such as a chapter number; FrameMaker uses these when it references a page number from the current document in a generated file. What you type here does not affect running headers or footers.

Choose what page side the file will begin on.

Choose whether the current file page numbering starts from one or continues from the previous file in the book.

This refers to autonumbering. If you want autonumbered chapter files, for instance, you must set this to Continue.

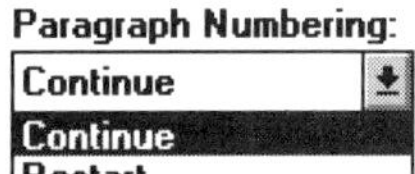

The Page Numbering and Paragraph Numbering pop-up both look like this.

Prefix and Suffix

These determine how the page number from the current file will appear in generated files. It does not have any effect on the page number in cross-references or running headers and footers.

To include a chapter or part number with the current page number Type the number plus any accompanying text, such as a hyphen, in the Prefix or Suffix text box. In Chapter 3, for example, you would type **3** in the Prefix text box to have page 6 appear as 3-6 in an index, table of contents, or other generated file. **Hint** Use a nonbreaking hyphen, \+, to keep FrameMaker from breaking a line at the hyphen.

Type this in the Set Up dialog box for a file

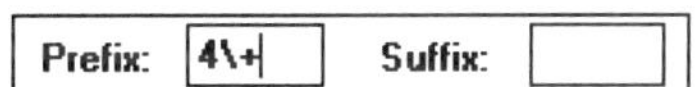

To get this kind of page number in a generated file such as an index or table of contents:

4-12

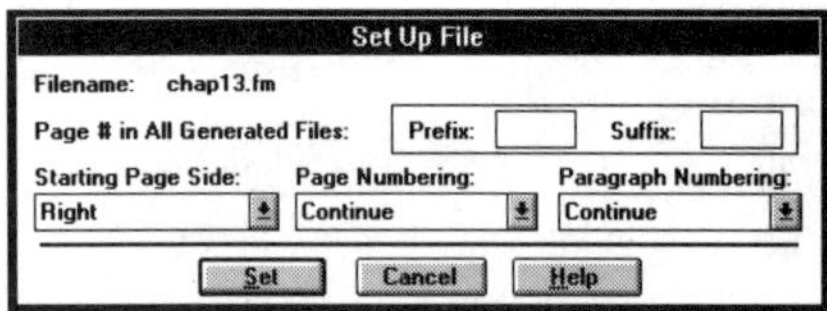

The Set Up dialog box for a document file.

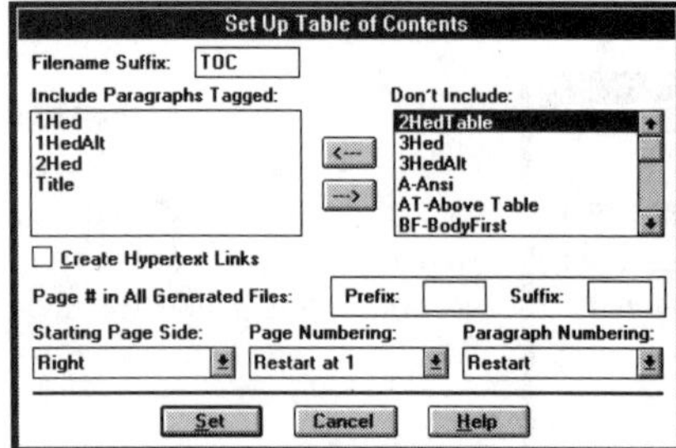

Each type of generated file has its own Set Up window. This Table of Contents Set Up window is typical.

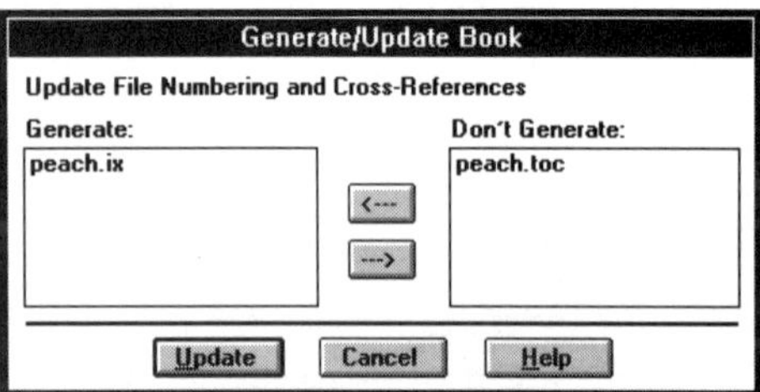

These windows list the generated files that you have added to the book. If you're just updating cross-references, you may not want to take the time to generate the index, for example. All document files are automatically updated every time, so you do not have to choose them.

Changing the setup

You can change your setup choices for both generated files and document files.

1. In the book window, click on the file you want to change.
2. Choose **File→Set Up File**.
3. In the Set Up dialog box, make the necessary changes, and click Set.

Starting page side This setting in the book set up overrides the Before Saving and Printing property that you set in the Document Properties dialog box (**Format→Document**, see page 25).

■ Generating and updating

When you have added all the files to the book, it is time to Generate/Update the book. Do this to accomplish the following things:

- Renumber all pages.
- Update all autonumbering.
- Update all cross-references
- Add empty pages where necessary to make each file begin on the specified page side.
- Create or update generated files, extracting the specified information from the updated document files.

Generate or Update a book

1. In the book window, choose **File→Generate/Update**.
2. In the Generate/Update Book dialog box, choose which generated files you actually want to generate this time. You may not need to take the time to generate the index and table of contents every time you update autonumbering and cross references, for example.
3. Click Update.

Speeding up the process The generate/update process goes considerably faster if you open all files in the book before you choose Generate/Update. If you don't do this, FrameMaker has to open each file not once, but twice, scan it, and close it again. On the other hand, if your book is too large to fit in memory all at once, you're still okay. Just leave the files closed, and wait a little longer for FrameMaker to update.

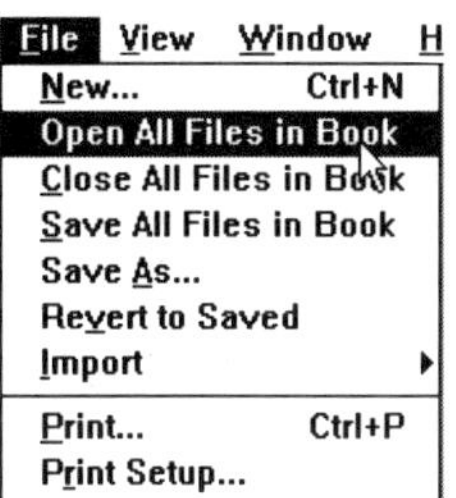

Shift-click the file menu in a book window to get options for opening, saving, or closing all the files in a book.

▲ If you open all the files before generating/updating the book, you must save them all when the updating is finished. FrameMaker automatically saves files that it had to open just for the update, but not files that are already open.

Unresolved cross-references

If FrameMaker finds a cross-reference whose reference point has been moved, removed, or renamed, it halts the Generate/Update process. It displays the book window with the file containing the unresolved cross-reference highlighted. There is a message in the bottom bar of the book window describing the problem.

When FrameMaker finds an unresolved cross-reference during a Generate/Update, it halts the process, displays a message at the bottom of the book window, and highlights the file containing the unresolved cross-reference.

1. In the book window, double-click on the file name to go to that file.
2. Display the Find/Change window, and choose Unresolved Cross-Reference from the Find pop-up. Click Find. FrameMaker highlights the first unresolved cross-reference.
3. Double-click the cross-reference to display the Cross-Reference dialog box. Complete all the specifications and click Replace.
   ▲ Continue this sequence until you have found and fixed all unresolved cross-references.
   ▲ See pages 149 to 157 for the full story on cross-references, and page 155 for the specifics on dealing with unresolved cross-references.
4. Generate/Update again.

When to generate/update your book

When you do any of the following things, Generate/Update your book to be sure all page numbers, autonumbers, cross-references, and generated files are current:

- Create a new book.
- Add, delete, or rearrange files in a book.
- Change the Setup of any file in the book.
- Edit the reference pages of any generated files.
- Edit any of the document files in ways that could change the page numbering, cross-references, autonumbering, or generated file contents.
- Change conditional text settings or overrides.

Formatting generated files

Generated files can be formatted just as any document file can. The reference pages of generated files provide some extra options as well. Chapter 14 discusses formatting generated files in detail on pages 286 to 292.

Generated Files

■ What's in this chapter

This chapter describes how to insert markers—used for creating indexes, among other things—and how to format generated files. There is also a description of how to generate files from a single document. The previous chapter discusses generating files that extract information from an entire book.

■ What you can create

Generated files

Generated files are made up of the contents of paragraphs with selected tags, or of the contents of markers of selected types. When you choose to generate a file, FrameMaker displays a dialog box in which you specify what paragraph tags or marker types are to be included in the generated file.

If you are generating a file which displays marker contents, such as an index, you must first insert the markers in the document file.

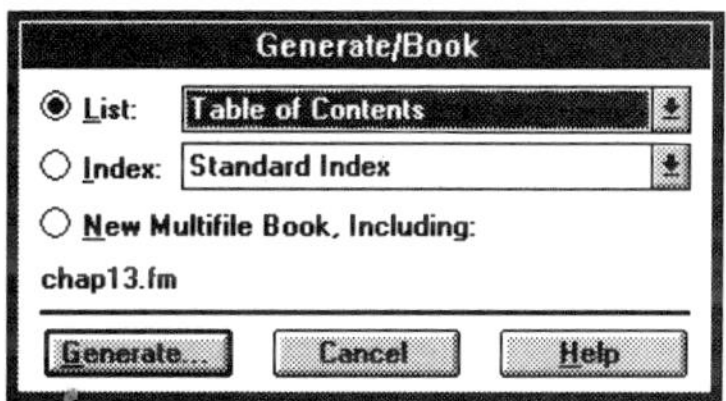

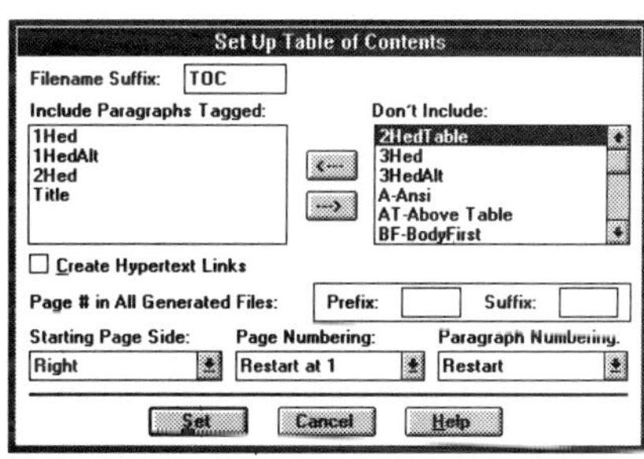

Each type of generated file has its own Set Up dialog box. This one is for a table of contents.

Lists and indexes

When you choose **File➜Generate** from either a document or a book, you see two pop-up menus in the dialog box: List and Index.

Types of lists

In a list, there is a separate entry for each occurrence of an item. The items occur in the list in the same order they occur in the source file, except for alphabetical lists. The most common form of list is a table of contents.

Types of lists:

- Table of Contents
- List of Figures
- List of Tables
- List of Paragraphs
- List of Markers
- Alphabetical Marker List
- Alphabetical Paragraph List
- List of References

Lists take their contents from specified paragraph tags except for List of Markers or Alphabetical Marker List.

Types of Indexes

In an index, each item occurs only once, in alphabetical order, followed by all the page numbers on which it occurs.

Types of indexes:

- Standard Index
- Author Index
- Subject Index
- Index of Markers
- Index of References

Indexes all take their contents from markers you insert.

List or Index of References

If you choose List of References or Index of References, you can choose to list or index the condition tags in use, cross-references to other files, fonts in use, graphics imported by reference, or unresolved cross-references.

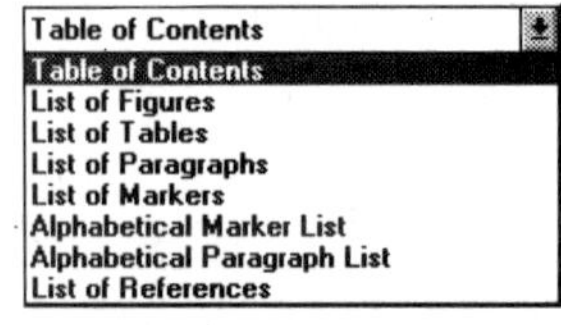

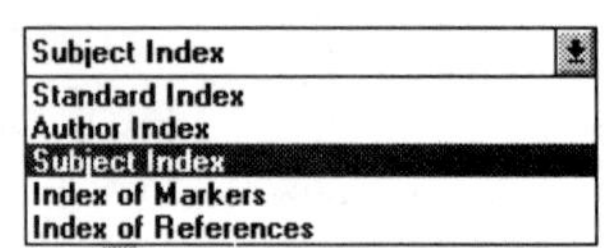

These are the types of lists and indexes you can generate.

■ Generating files

To create a generated file that extracts information from several related files, put the files in a book, and generate the lists and indexes from the book. This process is discussed in detail in Chapter 13.

■ The procedure for generating an index or list from a single document is essentially the same, and is listed on the next page.

■ To generate any kind of index, or a list of markers, you must first place the markers. You can choose from several types of markers and then specify which types are included in a particular type of index. Placing markers is discussed in detail beginning on page 292.

Generate files from a single document

You can generate any type of file from a single document that you can generate from a book. The only difference is that the Set Up dialog box doesn't ask you which page side to start on or whether the page and paragraph numbering continues from the previous document.

■ The generated file is always a separate document. You can copy and paste the generated file's contents back into your original document if you want to.

1. In a document window, choose **File➔Generate/Book**. [Alt f g]
2. In the Generate/Book dialog box, turn on either List or Index and choose a type of file from the pop-up menu.
3. Click Generate.
4. In the Set Up dialog box, choose which paragraph tags or marker types to include in your list or index.
5. Turn on Create Hypertext Link if you want the generated file to be an active hypertext document (page 277).
6. Click Generate.

▲ FrameMaker extracts the requested information (paragraph contents or marker contents) from the current document and places it in a separate file, which it then displays. Read pages 286 to 292 for how to format this file, and how to determine the form the information takes.

▲ Chapter One contains details on generating reference files (List of References or Index of References). See pages 55 to 56.

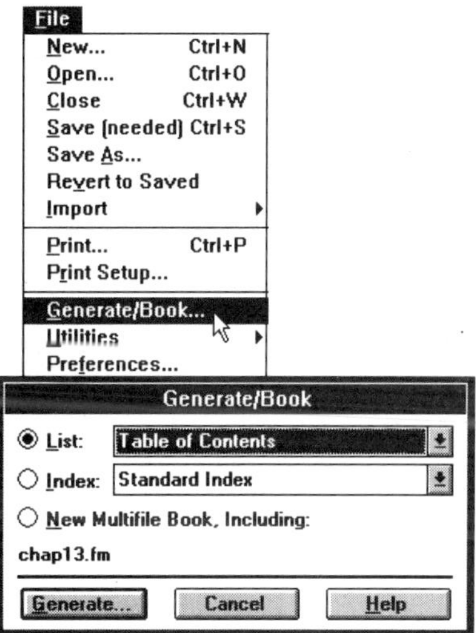

Choose the type of file you want to generate from the List pop-up or the Index pop-up.

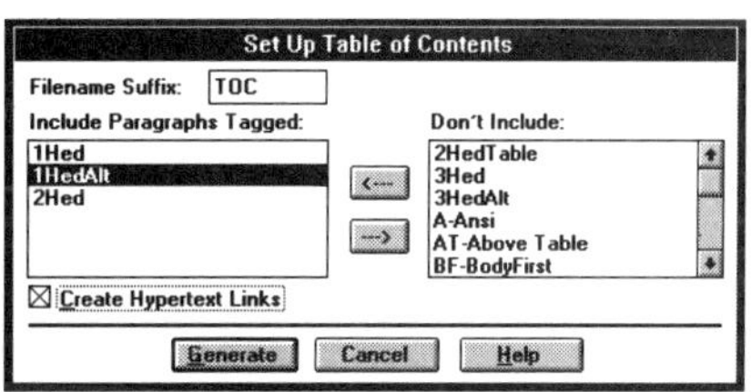

FrameMaker displays a Set Up dialog box appropriate to the type of generated file. Choose what paragraph tags or markers to include and whether the file should be hypertext.

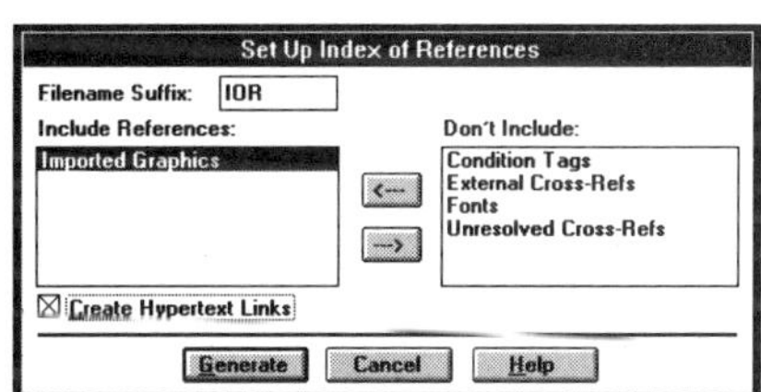

If you choose List or Index of References, you have these further choices. See pages 55 to 56 for generating reference files.

■ Formatting generated files

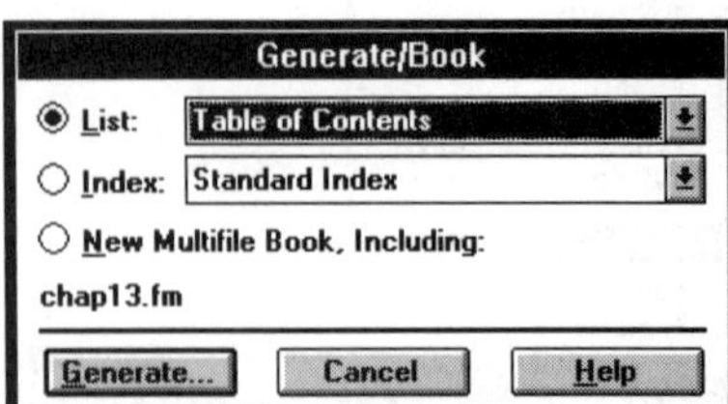

Formatting a list

The most common list is a table of contents. Other popular lists are lists of tables and lists of figures. You can also make a list of graphics included by reference, fonts in use, or other useful things by choosing List of References. For a complete list of possibilities see page 284.

1. Generate the list, either from a book (page 280), or from a single document (page 285).
2. In the generated file, you will find that each line has a paragraph tag named after the paragraph tag from which it was generated and the type of list it is in. For example, a line in a table of contents (TOC) file that was generated from a 1H-Hed1 paragraph tag will have a 1H-Hed1TOC paragraph tag in the generated file.
   ▲ Redefine each of these paragraph formats to create the "look" you want for your generated file (page 91).
   ▲ If you want a tab between the text and the page numbers, include the tab setting in the paragraph definition. Include a tab leader if you want one (page 113).
3. **Edit the reference pages** to determine the position and format of page and paragraph numbers. Display the reference page of the generated file [**Alt v e**], and PgDn until you see the first page that displays the formatting. It looks like this: <$paratext><$pagenum>. See page 287 for detailed information on editing reference pages for lists.
4. Generate the file again, exactly as you did the first time, to see your formatting changes.

The reference format page has entries like this:

<$paratext><$pagenum>

There is one such line for each paragraph type you choose to include in your generated list.

Editing reference pages for lists

Contents and order of information There are four building blocks available. Use these building blocks to specify the contents of the generated information (text, page number, etc.). The order in which you place the building blocks on the reference page determines the order of the information in the generated file.

This	Generates this
<$paratext>, <$markertext>, *or* <$referencename>	The text of the paragraph, contents of the marker, or item being referenced.
<$pagenum>	The page number on which it occurs.
<$paranum>	The entire contents of the Autonumber Format box for an autonumbered format.
<$paranumonly>	The value of the counter in the Autonumber Format box for an autonumbered format.

On the reference page, place the building blocks in the order you want information to appear in the generated file. If you want tabs between items, place your insertion point and press Tab.

- To keep items from separating, use nonbreaking spaces (Ctrl-space) or em (\sm) or en (\sn) spaces.
- You can add text around a building block.
- For example:

<$paranum>\sm <$paratext> > [<$pagenum>]

would produce a paragraph number, em space, paragraph text, tab, and the page number in square brackets.

▲ **Character formats** To make page or paragraph numbers appear in a different type style than that in the rest of the paragraph, create a character format (page106), and apply it to the appropriate building block (usually <$pagenum>) on the reference page.

<$paratext> <$pagenum>
<$paratext> <$pagenum>
<$paratext> <$pagenum>

On the second reference page of a generated list, there is one line like this for each paragraph tag you choose to include. These lines all say to generate the text of the paragraph followed by the page number.

Click in a line and look at the Status bar at the bottom of the window to see what tag the line is for. For example:

Flow: TOC ¶: 1HedTOC

Your insertion point is in the format line for 1Hed paragraphs. Edit the 1HedTOC paragraph tag to format these entries.

- *Edit the paragraph tag using the Paragraph Designer to get the look you want for that type of entry.*
- *On the reference page, apply a character format to the* <$pagenum> *to make the page number look different from the rest of the paragraph.*

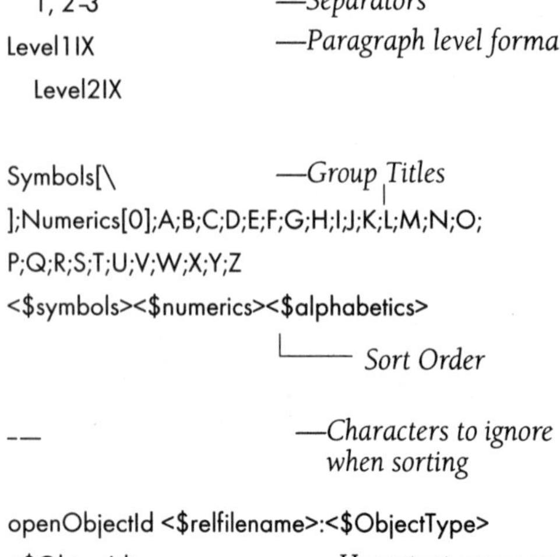

<$autorange><$pagenum> —*Marker format*

These are the things you will find on the reference pages of a generated index file.

`Flow: IX ¶: *IndexIX f: IX (2 of`

This Status Bar shows that the insertion point is in the format line for the Index marker.

Formatting an index

Read through the instructions for formatting a list. The only difference in formatting an index is the elements you find on the reference pages. Illustrated in the margin are the lines you typically find on the reference page of an index, identified by function. Below is a typical index segment:

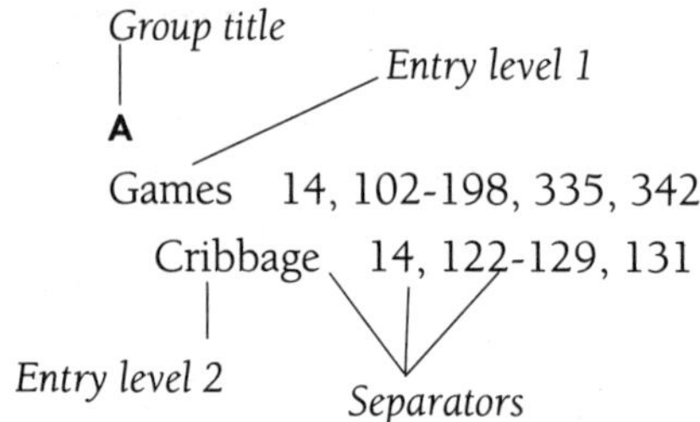

Formatting each entry level

Each level has its own paragraph format. Change the paragraph format definition, using the Paragraph Designer, to create the look you want. Include any desired tabs in the definition. To align numbers at the right of the column, for example, place a Right tab at the right side of the column in the paragraph definition for each level. Then add a tab to the Separator line on the reference page before the first number (place your insertion point and press the Tab key).

Formatting the page numbers

There is a <$pagenum> Marker format line on the reference page for each marker type you choose to include. To make the page numbers different from the rest of an entry, apply a character format to the Marker format line for each included marker type. If you want certain page numbers to look different from the other page numbers, use a different marker type for those items. Then apply a different character format to the different Marker format lines. Click in a Marker format line and then look in the Status Bar at the bottom of the document window to see which marker each format line is for.

Autorange

If you place the <$autorange> building block before the <$pagenum> building block in the Marker format line, FrameMaker will cite successive pages as a range: 16, 17, 18 becomes 16–18. (See the example on page 288.)

<$autorange><$pagenum>

When you want successive pages to be listed as a range (e.g., 4–7), add the Autorange building block to the Marker Format line.

Formatting the separators

Put a tab, nonbreaking space, or other special space or text here: whatever should appear between the entry and the number

1, 2-3

You can indicate a range by replacing the hyphen with the word "to", or anything else.

If you want entries separated by something other than a comma, replace this comma with the desired text or space.

Use \+ (a non-breaking hyphen) in place of the hyphen if you don't want lines to break at the hyphen.

Formatting the Group Titles

To change the appearance, change the definition of the GroupTitlesIX paragraph tag. To change the actual text of the titles, edit the GroupTitles paragraph on the reference pages. The square brackets specify where the title appears; the other material is the group title text itself. The semicolons separate the groups.

■ If you don't want a title before every letter, for example, you can specify groups. You can remove text, such as "Numerics" altogether. For example, the following Group Title entry

[\ ];1 to 9[0];A-C[A];D-G[D];H-P[H];Final Group[Q]

would produce the index headings in the example on the side. Notice that since no text was given for symbols, no text appears before them in the index.

@, meaning 4
†, meaning 12

1 to 9
2Head 33-38
12 gun salute 35

A-C
Autochthons 11
Bilberries 24, 26
Cartouches 18

D-G
Dogberries 48
Erasmus 8, 51
Falafel 4, 30

H-P
Harbingers 15
Inklings 27, 39
Japes 1, 42
Karma 44-46
Levant, the 2, 5
Mnemonics 16
Nits 21, 34
Ptarmigans 43

Final Group
Quests 3, 14
Riddles 25
Tarns 17
Weirs 17-19
Zymurgy 32

■ To create an index with space but no text above each group, edit the GroupTitles paragraph as follows:

[\ ];[0];[A];[B];[C];[D];[E];[F];[G];[H];[I];[J];[K];[L];[M];[N];[O];[P];[Q];[R];[S];[T];[U];[V];[W];[X];[Y];[Z]

■ To create an index with neither space nor text between the groups, delete all the text of the GroupTitles paragraph, but leave the paragraph ending.

Guidelines

To keep your generated files working properly, follow these guidelines:

- *Don't change the name of any generated file if you ever plan to update it by generating again.*
- *Don't change any of the paragraph tag names in the generated file. Redefine the properties as much as you like, but don't rename them.*
- *When you create and redefine formats in the generated file, be sure to Update All and to add them to the format catalogs.*

Changing the sort order of the index

By default, FrameMaker places entries beginning with nonalphanumeric characters (symbols) first, then those beginning with numbers, and finally, those beginning with letters. The order is determined by the line with the SortOrderIX tag:

<$symbols><$numerics><$alphabetics>

You can change the order of these three building blocks to change the order in which entries appear.

■ You can also specify the individual entries of a category, and can indicate that two characters are to be sorted as a single character by placing them in angle brackets. For example, to sort Spanish so that Ç follows C, and Ch follows Ç, write out the alphabetic characters, separating each group with a space, and type the "C" group as follows:

CÇcç<CH><Ch><ch>

Adding a title

To add a title to a generated file, place it before any of the generated entries, and give it a paragraph tag that does *not* end with FrameMaker's identifying file letters (TOC or IX, for example). Add the paragraph tag to the catalog.

Using a template

Once you've done all the work of creating a generated file that looks just the way you want it to, you can use that formatting in other generated files of the same type. There are two ways: rename a copy of the template file, and import formats from the template file. Renaming is easier.

The generated file template should use the same paragraph tags or marker types as the file you are formatting. If your current document uses paragraph tags, marker types, or index levels not in the template, you will have to define the paragraph formats for them.

Using another generated file as a template

The template must have the same paragraph formats as the generated file you are formatting.

1. Add the empty generated file to the book (page 276). Note the name that FrameMaker gives it.
2. Copy the file you are using as a template into the directory where the book is. Give the template the exact name that the generated file in the book has, not including the +. For example, if the book is named Cardinal.bk, then the index file is named Cardinal.IX. Name your template file Cardinal.IX.

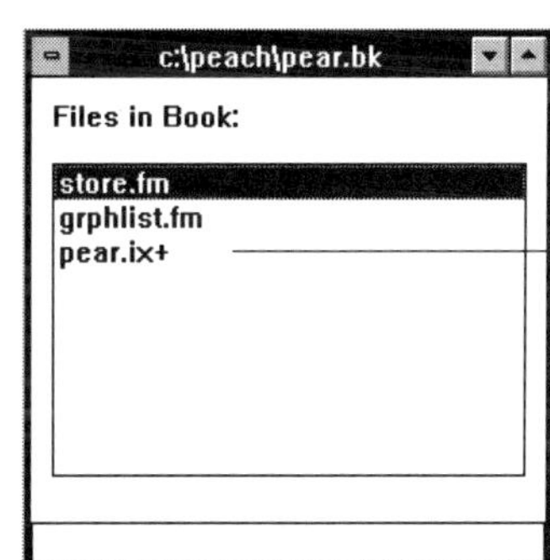

Add the generated file to the book and note the name that FrameMaker gives it. Copy your template file to this exact name (without the +).

Importing formats from another file

This is another way to use the formats from another file. You can import formats into a document or a generated file.

1. Add the empty generated file to the book (page 276).
2. Generate the book.
3. Open the template file.
4. In the book window, choose **File➔Import➔ Formats.** [**Alt f i o**]
5. In in Import Formats dialog box, choose the template file from the Import from Document pop-up menu. Turn on the things you want to import from the template. Move the files that are to receive the formats into the Update window and place the others in the Don't Update window. Click Import.
6. Generate the book again.

Select the template file from this pop-up menu.

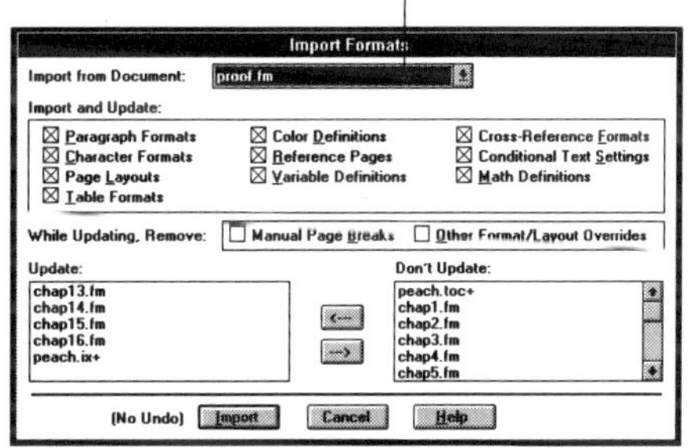

Move the files that need the new formats into the Update window.

▲ *See page 107 for more details on importing formats into a document.*

■ Placing markers

A marker is an invisible container holding text that will be referenced elsewhere: in an index or list of markers, in a cross-reference, or in a variable that is in a running header or footer.

Inserting a marker: the basics

1. Choose **Special→Marker** to display the marker window. [**Alt s m**]
2. Place your insertion point where you want the marker.
3. Type the marker text in the Marker window.
4. Click New Marker, or press return.

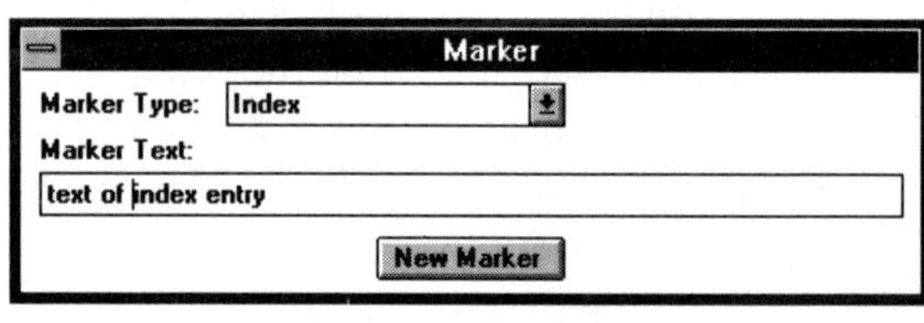

Header/Footer $1
Header/Footer $1
Header/Footer $2
Index
Comment
Subject
Author
Glossary
Equation
Hypertext
Cross-Ref
Conditional Text
Type 11
Type 12
Type 13
Type 14

Choose a type of marker. Do not use the Header/Footer markers for indexes. They are for displaying marker text in system variables (Running H/F 3 and 4). The Conditional Text, Hypertext, and Cross-Ref markers are also reserved and should not be used for indexes.

Editing marker text

1. Display the Marker window.
2. Select the marker you want to change.
   ▲ The easiest way to do this is to use Find: choose Any Marker, Marker of Type, or Marker Text from the Find pop-up menu. If you choose Marker of Type or Marker Text, enter the type of marker or the marker text you are looking for in the text box to the right of the Find pop-up. You can also select a marker by placing the insertion point to the left of it and holding down Shift as you press the right arrow. Turn on Text Symbols so you can see the marker symbol to select. [**Alt v t**]
   ▲ When you have selected the marker, the marker text appears in the Marker window.
3. Make your changes to the marker text in the Marker window and click Replace Marker.

T

Marker symbol.

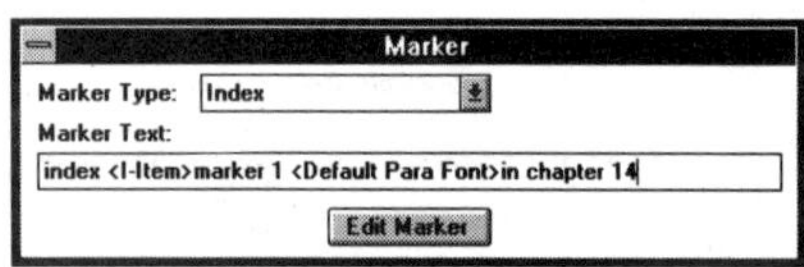

▼

To delete a marker

Select the marker, as described in "Editing marker text." Press Delete.

Hint *Be sure the focus is on the document window, not the marker window. If you just delete the text from the marker window, you leave an empty marker.*

Marker shortcuts and fancy stuff

Automatic text

- Place a marker at the beginning of a word and don't put any text in the box of the marker window. FrameMaker picks up the word as the marker text.
- Highlight some text and then insert a marker. The highlighted text is the marker text.

'Twas brillig and the slithy toves

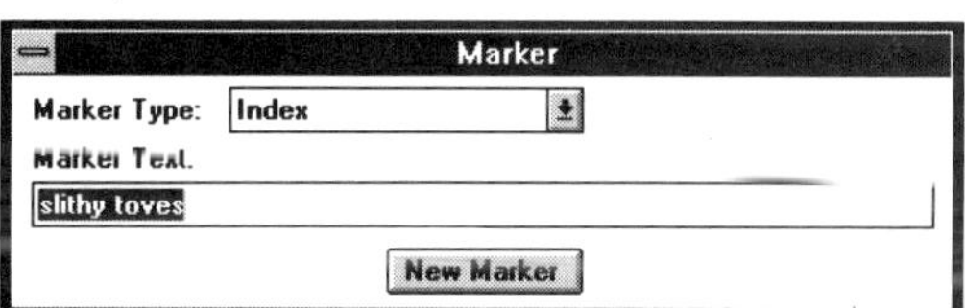

A highlighted phrase appears automatically in the Marker window.

Cutting and pasting

You can keep all your index entries in a separate work file. When you want to insert one as a marker, do this:

1. Copy the text you want from the work file into the Clipboard.
2. Place your insertion point where you want the marker.
3. Display the Marker window and paste the text into the Marker Text box.
4. Click New Marker. Works like a charm. This reduces the chance of inconsistencies in index entries.

Adding formats to markers

1. Create character formats for any special character formatting that you need within markers (page 106).
2. In the marker text box, place your insertion point where you need the format and type the format name enclosed in angle brackets. For example:
   <I-Italic>
3. If you need to return to the paragraph font in the marker, type
   <Default Para Font>
   The case and spaces must be exact.
   ▲ If the specially-formatted text is the last thing in the marker, you do not need to change back to Default Para Font at the end. FrameMaker does that automatically.

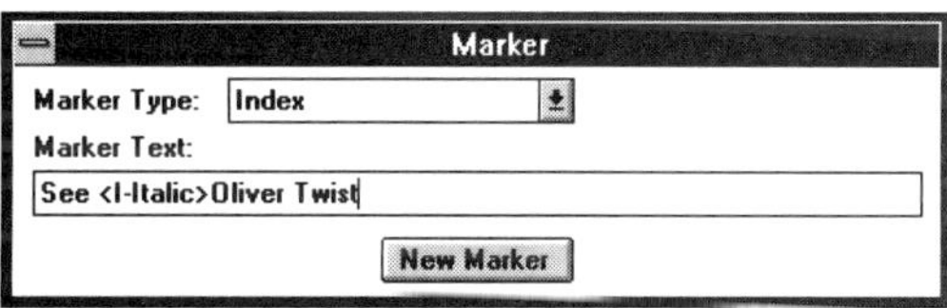

Include character formatting in generated text by typing the character format name in angle brackets into the Marker window.

<Z-ZapfDings>n<Default Para Font>

This code would produce a solid square box ■ from the Zapf Dingbats font and then return to the paragraph font. It assumes that you have created a character format named Z-ZapfDings to apply the Zapf Dingbats font.

Special characters in markers

You can have any character in a marker that you have available on a font. Use the hex code or the Dialog Box code listed in Appendix A. If the character is in a font other than the paragraph font, create a character format for the font wanted and then change the font by typing in the format name in angle brackets. See "Adding formats to markers," page 293.

Structuring index markers

Multi-level entries

Separate levels of index entries with a colon. For example

Level one text:Level two text

Multiple entries in one marker

Separate different entries with a semicolon.

Entry 1;Entry 2

Specifying a range of pages

To create an index entry that shows a range (like "4–5" or "4 to 5"), place a marker at the beginning of the range and another at the end. The first marker text must begin with <$startrange> and the second marker must begin with <$endrange>. The rest of the text *must be identical* in the two markers.

Entries with no page number

To create an entry with no page number, place <$nopage> at the beginning of the entry.

This marker text — <$nopage>Sylvan, <I-Italic>see<Default Para Font> Wooded

Produces this index entry. The page number of the marker is not given because it has been suppressed with the <$nopage> *code.* — Sylvan, *see* Wooded

To restore page numbers in multiple entries

If you have several index entries in a single marker, separated by semicolons, using <$nopage> will suppress the page number for all subsequent entries in the marker. Restore page numbering after it has been suppressed with <$nopage> by placing the <$singlepage> code at the beginning of an entry.

Changing the sort order of an index entry

If you want an entry to appear in a position other than its normal position, indicate the spelling that would place it in the desired position in square brackets.

Marker text	Index position
24-gun salute[twenty-four]	Tools 24 24-gun salute 18 Tyson, Rubert 33
Games:21 [Games:twenty-one]	Games Faro 21 Verity
Mountains:in Wittgenstein[Mountains:Wittgenstein]	Mountains Folklore Mining In Wittgenstein
<$nopage>Food:<I-Italic>See also <Default Para Font> Fishing[Food:zzz]	Food Gathering Varieties *See also* Fishing (The zzz causes the entry to be last in the group.)

■ Troubleshooting generated files

Fixing bad line breaks

Suppose you're including your first- and second-level heads in the Table of Contents. If you put a line break in one of these heads using the Return key, the line break appears in the Table of Contents. To fix these and other line breaks, try these methods:

■ In the occurrence in the document, remove all hard line breaks except the one at the very end. Then you have two choices:

▲ Change the right indent of the paragraph until you like the line breaks (page 112). For a centered heading, change both the right and left indents.

▲ Keep groups of words together with nonbreaking spaces (Ctrl-Space) instead of hard line endings.

Use hypertext to help you fix files

- *Turn on Create Hypertext Links when you Set Up your generated files (page 277).*
- *In the generated file, Ctrl-Alt-click on the problem entry to go directly to the source in the document file.*
- *If you are working with an index, display the Marker window. Then when you click on a hypertext entry, the marker text is displayed in the window, ready for editing.*

Missing entries

Go to the entry that did not get included and check its paragraph tag. Is the tag one of the ones in the Include list in the generated file Set Up dialog box? Either change the tag of the paragraph, or add the tag to the Include list.

To add a tag Click on the generated file in the book list. Choose **File→Set Up File**. In the Set Up dialog box, double-click on the tag name in the Don't Include list to move it to the Include list. Click Set.

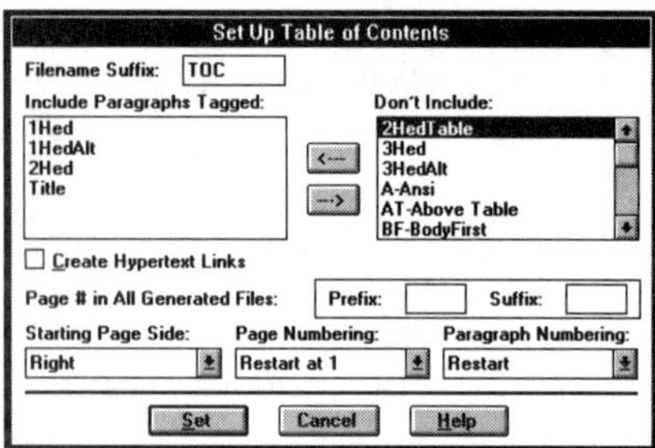

Is the paragraph tag or marker type of your missing entry on this list? If not, either change the list in this dialog box, or change the tag or type of the missing entry.

Empty lines

An empty entry in a generated file means you have an extra line return in the source file. The easiest way to find and fix these is to generate the file as a hypertext document. Then Ctrl-Alt-click on the empty entry to go directly to the extra line return.

Color

■ What's in this chapter

Add color to text, graphics, change bars, and tables; define new colors; select which colors to display on screen and print (views), and set up separations.

■ Applying color to text and graphics

A pop-up menu of available colors appears in several places: The Default Font page of the Paragraph Designer, the Character Designer, the Object Properties dialog box, the Graphic Tools palette, the Shading page of the Table Designer, the Custom Ruling and Shading dialog box for tables, and the Change Bar Properties dialog box.

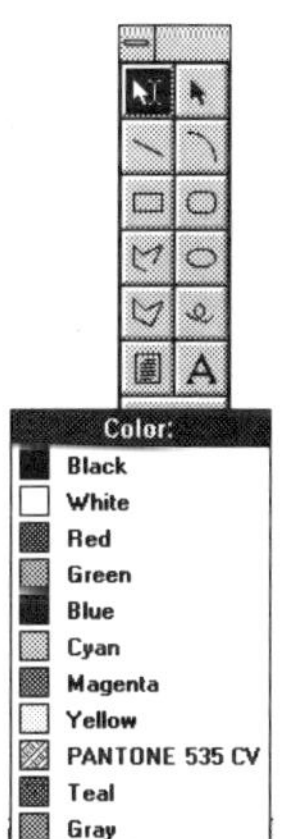

Apply color to graphic objects.

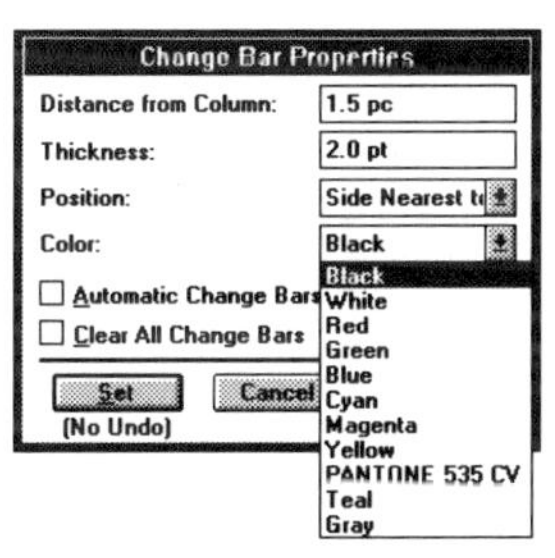

Have colorful change bars: **Alt o** *(oh)* **n** *displays the Change Bar Properties dialog box.*

Where to find color

Paragraph Designer

Family: Berkeley Boo | Underline
Size: 10.5 pt | Overline
Angle: Regular | Strikethrough
Weight: Regular | Change Bar
Variation: Regular | Superscript
Color: Black | Small Caps
Spread: | Pair Kern

As Is
Black
White
Red
Green
Blue
Cyan
Magenta
Yellow
PANTONE 535 CV
Teal
Gray

Apply color to paragraphs, including paragraphs in tables.

Character Designer

Family: Berkeley B | Underline
Size: 10.5 pt | Overline
Angle: Regular | Strikethrough
Weight: Regular | Change Bar
Variation: Regular | Superscript
Color: As Is | Small Caps
Spread: | Pair Kern

As Is
Black
White
Red
Green
Blue
Cyan
Magenta
Yellow
PANTONE 535 CV
Teal
Gray

Apply color to selected characters, including equations.

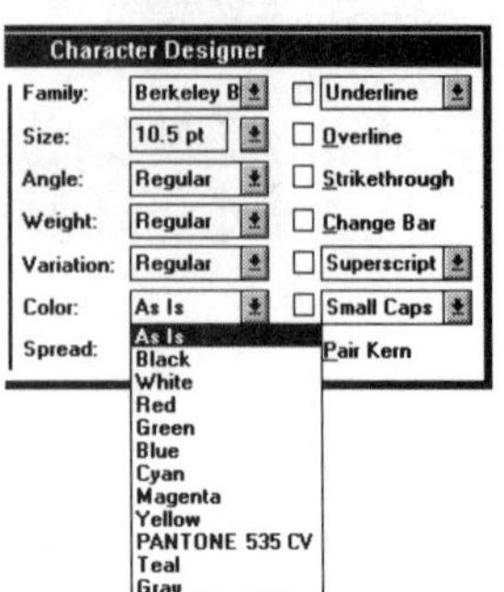

All default colors, plus any that you define, are available in both the Character and Paragraph Designers. See page 300 for how to define colors.

Applying color to text

Apply color to text as you would apply any other property from the Paragraph or Character Designers. See Chapter 5 for how to use the Designers.

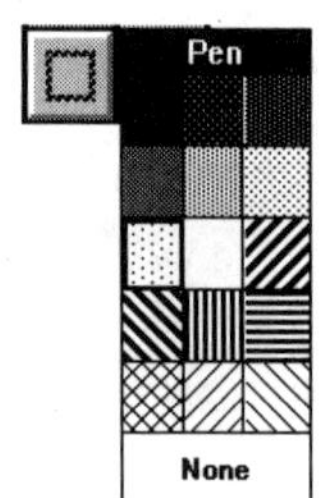

Choose a fill pattern and a pen pattern or choose None.

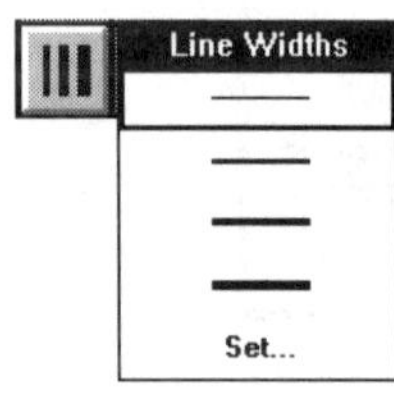

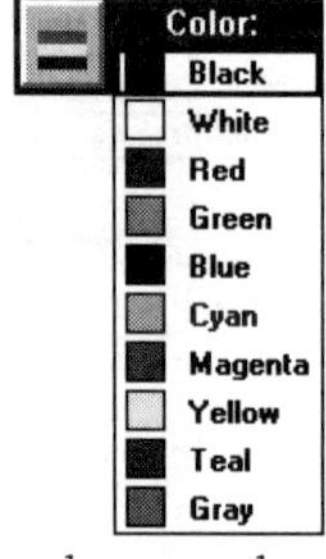

Set the pen width, and then choose a color.

Apply color to graphic objects using the Graphic Tools palette

Adding color to text and graphics

The colors on the list The colors in the color pop-ups are FrameMaker's default colors plus any additional ones you have defined. See "Defining colors" on page 300 for how to add colors to the list.

Applying color to selected characters
Select the characters, choose the color you want from the Character Designer, and click Apply to Selection. **Or** create a character format that has that color as one of its properties and apply the format.

Applying color to selected paragraphs
Select the paragraphs, choose the color you want from the Paragraph Designer, and click Apply to Selection. **Or** create a paragraph format that has that color as one of its properties and apply the format.

Apply color to graphic objects Select the object and click [icon] to display the Graphic Tools palette. Choose a fill pattern, a pen pattern, and a pen width, and then pick a color from the color pop-up menu. You can choose None for either the Pen or the Fill. The Pen and Fill are always the same color, but by varying the pattern, you can have one much darker than the other.

- **A text column is a graphic object** To give a text column a shaded and colored background, select the column (Ctrl-click) and apply a fill and color from the Graphic Tools palette. Another way to create a colored background for text is to draw a colored rectangle and place it behind the text column; use Group [**Alt g g**] to keep them together.

▲ Using the Object Properties dialog box

You can change the pen and fill color of a graphic object by selecting it and choosing a color from the Object Properties dialog box. [**Alt g p**] You cannot turn the fill or pen on or off from here, though.

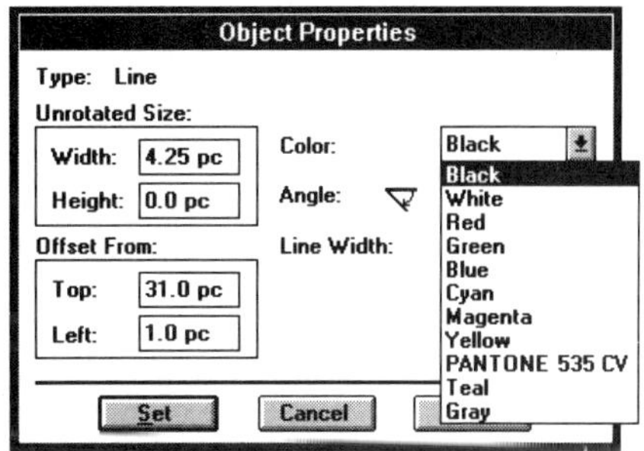

Use the Object Properties dialog box to change an object's color. This won't have any effect unless the pen and fill have already been turned on using the Graphic Tools palette.

Adding color to tables

Adding color to table text

Add color to text in tables as you would to any other text, by using the Paragraph and Character Designers.

Shading rows or columns with color

- To make the color shading part of the table definition, select a Fill and Color from the Shading page of the Table Designer.
- To add spot color to selected cells, select the cells and apply color from the Custom Ruling and Shading dialog box. [**Alt t c**]

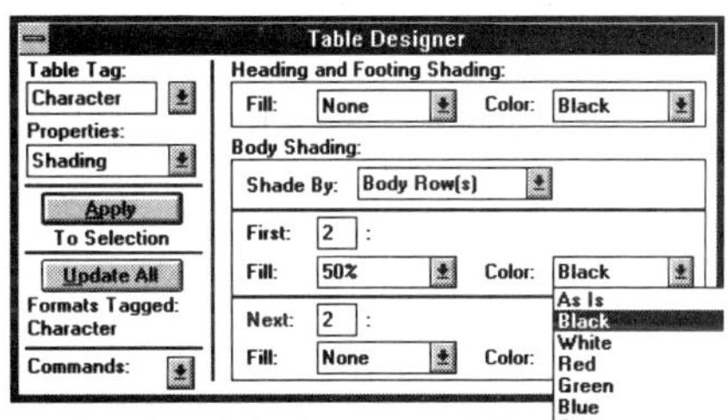

Add colored shading to a table definition; specify Fill as well as Color.

Adding colored ruling

- Define a ruling style with the color, pattern, and thickness you want.

1. Display the Custom Ruling and Shading dialog box. [**Alt t c**] If you are going to change an existing ruling style, click on that name in the Apply Ruling Style scroll box.
2. Click on Edit Ruling Style to display the Edit Ruling Style dialog box. Type in a new name if you're creating a new style.
3. Specify the ruling properties, including color, and click Set.

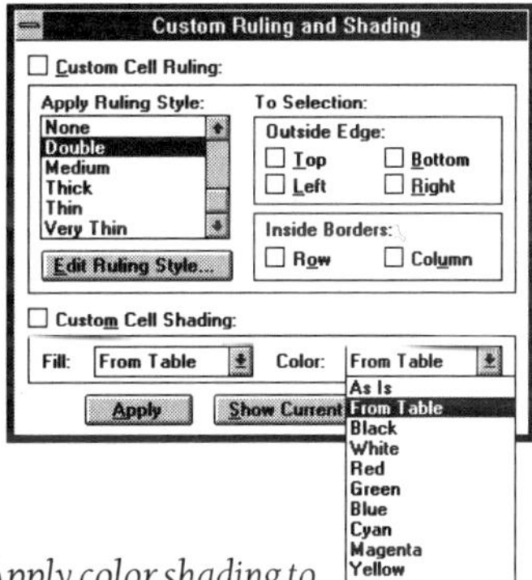

Apply color shading to selected table cells.

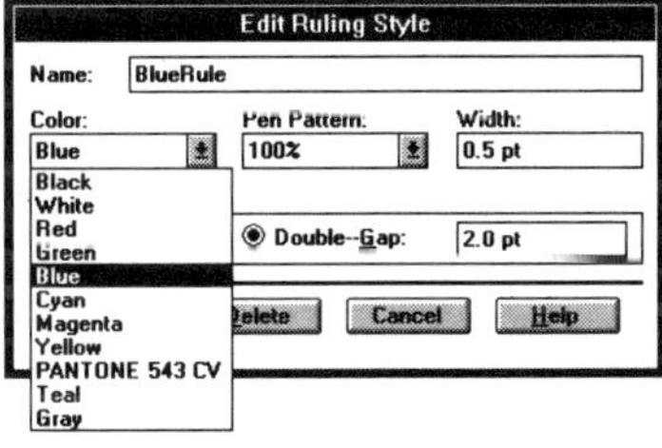

Define a table ruling style with the color you want.

When you have defined a ruling style, it is available in the pop-up menus on both the Table Designer Ruling page and the Custom Ruling and Shading dialog box.

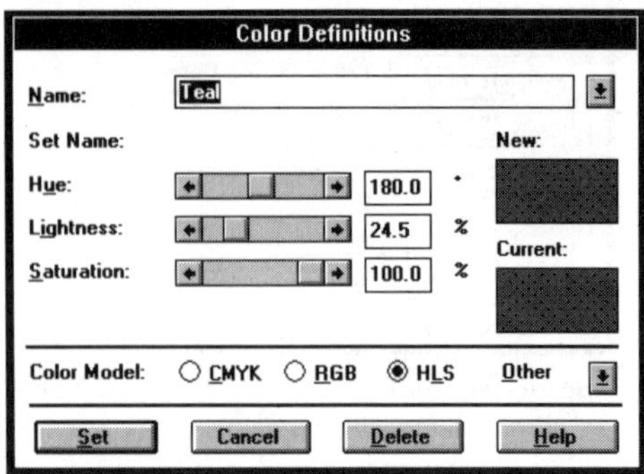

The HLS color definition dialog box.

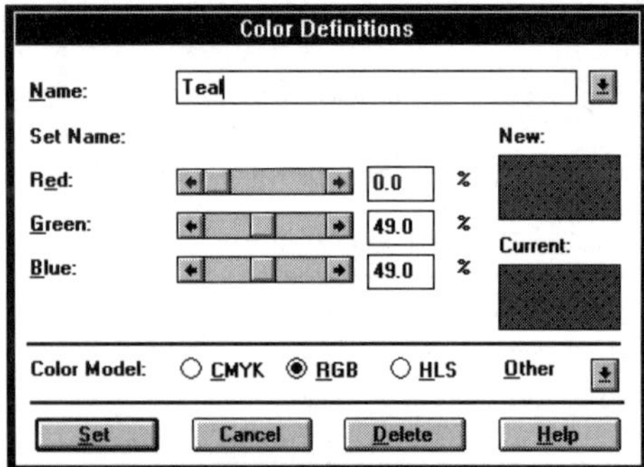

The RGB color definition dialog box.

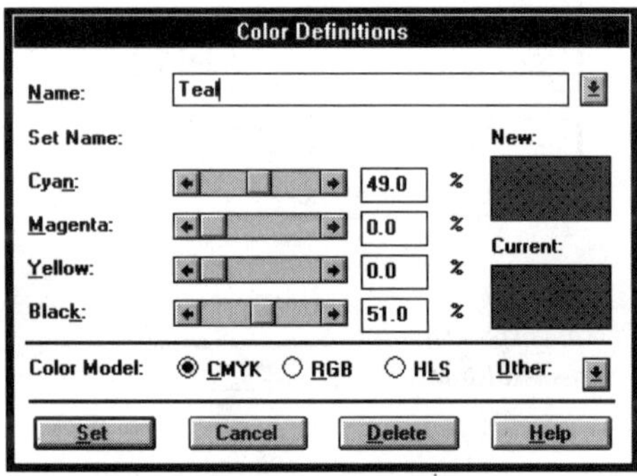

The CMYK color definition dialog box.

■ Defining colors

FrameMaker gives you five (yes, five!) ways to add new colors to the pop-up menu of colors. (See page 297 for all the places this menu occurs.)

- Use the CMYK model when you are going to create separations for four-color process printing.
- Use the PANTONE® colors to make it easy for printers to match spot colors exactly. The printed output may not match what you see on your screen (because of the screen's limitations), but it *will* match the PANTONE colors in the sample books. Get a sample book, locate the color you want, and add that color by number to the color menu in FrameMaker ("Add a Pantone color to the list" on page 301). Apply it where you want it, and you'll end up with the right thing.
- The RGB model is recommended for use in documents that are going to be viewed primarily on line.

Defining a new color

1. Choose **View→Color→Definitions**. [**Alt v c d**]
2. Type in a new name; if you want to add a Pantone color to the color menu using its Pantone name and number, leave New Color displayed.
3. Define your new color according to the following instructions and click Set. The new color now appears on all pop-up color menus.

Using the CMYK, RGB, and HLS models

Click on the color model you want to use. FrameMaker displays the appropriate set of slider bars. Drag the slider buttons, click on the arrow keys at the ends of the sliders, or type values directly into the text boxes next to the sliders.

Defining a new color *Continued*

Using the Common Color Picker

Click on the Other button in the Color Definition dialog box and choose Common Color Picker.

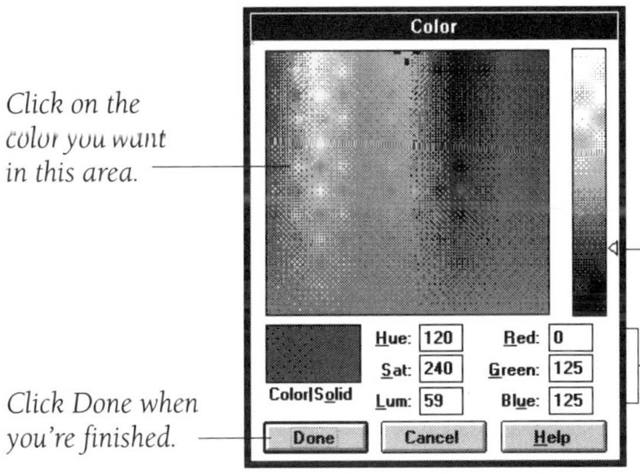

Click on the color you want in this area.

Click Done when you're finished.

Click in this column or drag the little white pointer to make the color brighter or darker.

These boxes show the numeric values for the current color. You can type directly into the boxes, but you would be doing the same thing as using the HLS or RGB model in the Color Definitions dialog box.

Add a Pantone color to the list

Type a color name in the Name box of the Color Definitions dialog box **or** choose New Color from the pop-up menu if you want to use the Pantone number as the color name. Click on the Other button in the Color Definition dialog box and choose PANTONE. Follow these instructions:

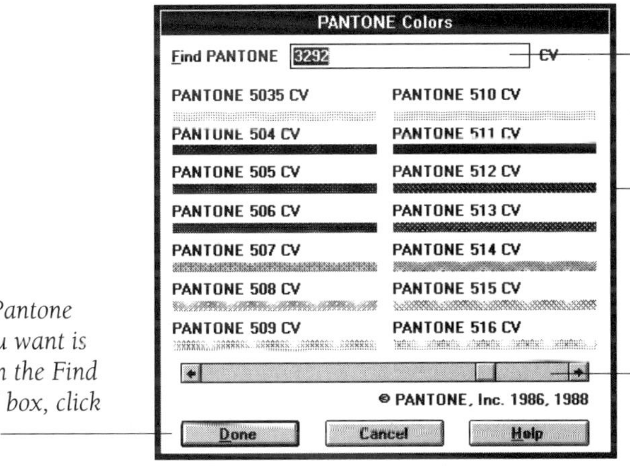

If you know the Pantone number of the color you want, type it in this box to display and select the color.

Click on a color to choose it.

When the Pantone number you want is displayed in the Find PANTONE box, click Done.

Drag the button or click on the arrows at the end to display more choices.

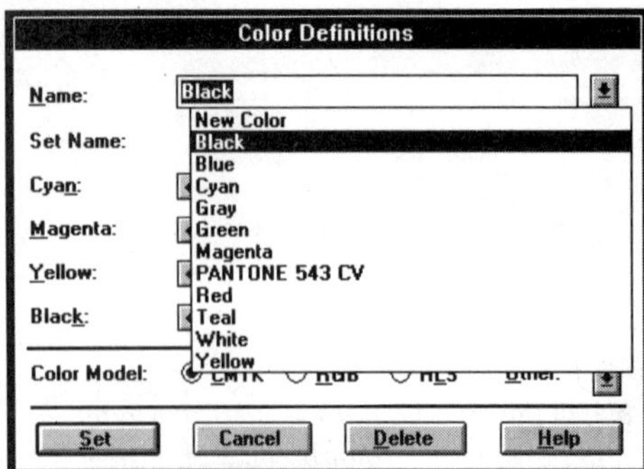

From the Name pop-up, choose the color to modify or delete.

Modify a color definition

1. Choose **View➔Color➔Definitions**.
   [Alt v c d]
2. From the Name pop-up menu, choose the color to modify.
3. Make changes to the color definition in the same way that you define new colors, using any of the color models, the Common Color Picker, or the Pantone color selection dialog box (pages 300 to 301).
4. Click Set when you have specified the definition you want for the displayed color name.

   ▲ You cannot change or delete the following colors: Red, Green, Blue, Cyan, Magenta, Yellow, Black, and White.

Delete a color

1. Choose **View➔Color➔Definitions**.
   [Alt v c d]
2. From the Name pop-up menu, choose the color to delete.
3. Click Delete. This removes the color from all the color pop-up menus.

   ▲ The instant you click Delete, your color is gone. Forever. I've clicked Delete at least once when I meant to click Cancel. Be careful.

■ Color views

You can choose to display certain colors by defining and displaying color views. A color that is not displayed does not print. Color views are helpful for making sure that the right things are the right color. They are also useful when working in color on a monochrome monitor. I have also seen this feature used for creating slightly different versions of a document for different audiences. It's an alternative to conditional text in some cases.

Warning Remember that when you display a view in which certain colors are in the Invisible column, all text and graphics in those colors are *completely invisible*. You can easily forget about the view and wonder what happened to your document.

Color views and conditional text

You can create different versions of a document by displaying different colors in different views. Conditional text also creates different versions of a document. The difference is that undisplayed conditional text doesn't occupy any space. Items in an undisplayed color still use up space, they're just not visible. You see blank space instead.

To display a view *Click on the radio button for the view you want and click Set.*

Define Color Views

Define Color Views
View 1 | View 2 | View 3 | View 4 | View 5 | View 6

Normal: Black, Red, Green, Blue, Cyan
Cutout: White
Invisible: Teal

<--- | ---> | Get Default

Set | Cancel | Help

To create or modify a view *Click on the view number. Then click on a color and click on an arrow to move the color to the box where you want it. To move all the colors from a box, click on one color and then Shift-click an arrow. When the colors are arranged the way you want them, click Set.*

Defaults are the settings in effect when you started FrameMaker. When you exit FrameMaker, the current settings become the new defaults. Clicking Get Defaults restores the default settings to the currently selected view.

Cutouts Objects that have a color in the Cutout column of the current view appear as white. When they overlap objects or text in a different color, their shape is cut out or "knocked out" of the other shape. (Printers call these cutouts "knockouts.")

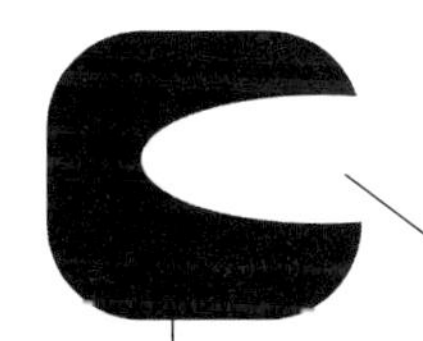

This Blue shape will print just as you see it, with the oval shape cut out of it.

This is a Red oval, but Red is in the Cutout column for this view, so you don't see it or anything under it.

■ Printing colors

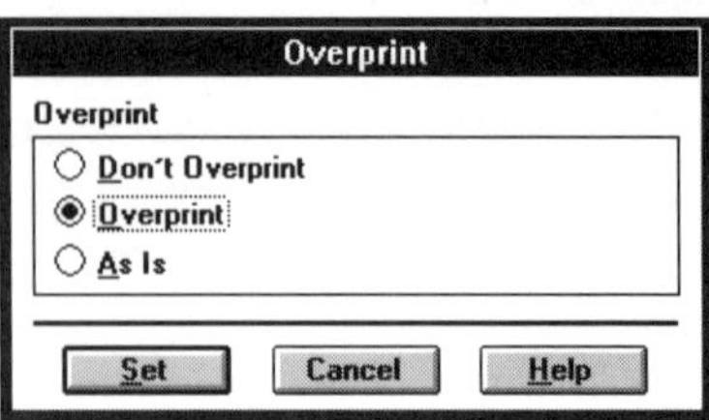

Overprinting

As you create your graphics, decide whether the ones on top should overprint (the hidden portion of the bottom object is still printed), or not (the hidden portion does not print). See page 266 for more on overprinting. Choose **Graphics→Overprint** *to display the Overprint dialog box.*

To print colored text as solid black, rather than shades of gray, turn on Spot Color As Black/White.

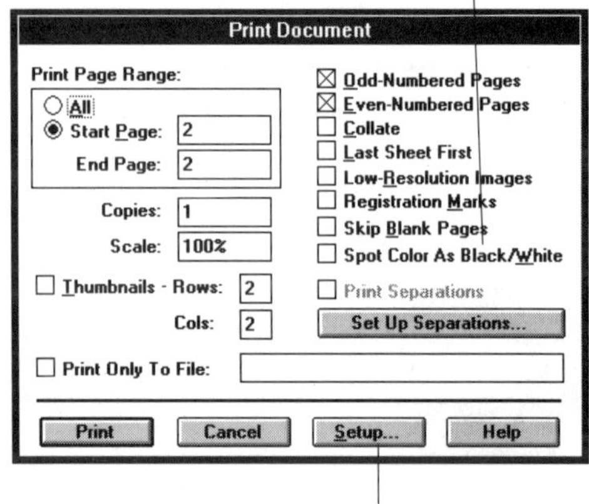

To print a composite document, turn off Print Separations.

Decide what you want

Colors can be printed as spot colors (the printer inks the press with that specific color) or as four color process (the printer uses Cyan, Magenta, Yellow, and Black to create all other colors). You need to know what your printer is going to do before you output your final work. Ultimately, if your work is going to be printed on paper, you will create a separate output page for each spot color and each process color you are using. This is called "printing separations." For on-screen viewing, and for output on a black-and-white printer, don't print separations: print everything together (composites).

Printing composites

To print all the colors in your document together on a single set of pages, leave Print Separations turned off. Follow the instructions on pages 51 to 54 for setting up print options. Your colors will print in color on a color printer. On a black and white printer, you can choose whether colors print as black or shades of gray.

Spot color text

In the Print Document window, turn on Spot Color as Black/White. Text with color applied will print as solid black rather than shades of gray. Graphics are not affected.

Graphics with color

From the Print Document dialog box, choose Setup. Click Options in the resulting dialog box; in the Options dialog box, click Advanced. To print all colors as solid black (including gray), turn on All Colors to Black.

Graphics settings

When you print a composite document, the graphics settings are in the Advanced Options box. (When you print separations, they are set in the Halftones Screens dialog box, page 306.)

▪ From the Print Document dialog box, choose Setup. Click Options in the resulting dialog box; in the Options dialog box, click Advanced.

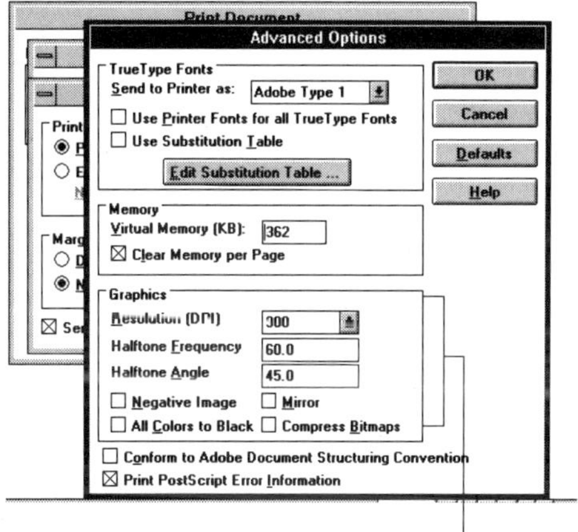

For a composite document, in which you print all colors together, set the graphics printing properties here.

▪ Printing separations

To print a separate page for each color, you must first tell FrameMaker which colors to print.

1. **Set up separations** Choose **File→Print** and click on Set Up Separations.
2. Click on a color and the click on an arrow until the color is in the correct column.

   ▲ To print a spot color as four color process, you must include each of its components (Cyan, Magenta, Yellow, Black) in the Print As Process column. Display the color definition using the CMYK model if you are not sure what colors are included in it. [**Alt v c d**]

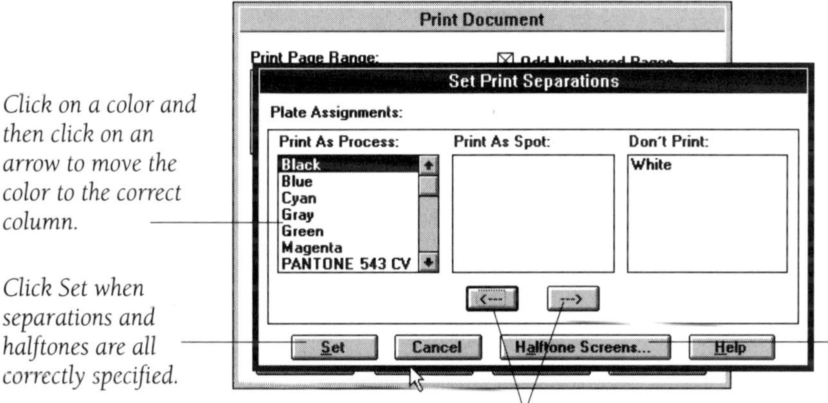

Click on a color and then click on an arrow to move the color to the correct column.

Click Set when separations and halftones are all correctly specified.

If you are using process color, click on Halftone Screens to specify halftone settings.

To move all colors together, click on one color in the column you want to move, and then Shift-click an arrow.

3. **Specify halftone settings** If you have halftones, click on Halftone Screens to specify halftone settings.

The Cyan, Magenta, Yellow, and Black settings affect only colors that you place in the Print As Process column of the Set Print Separations dialog box.

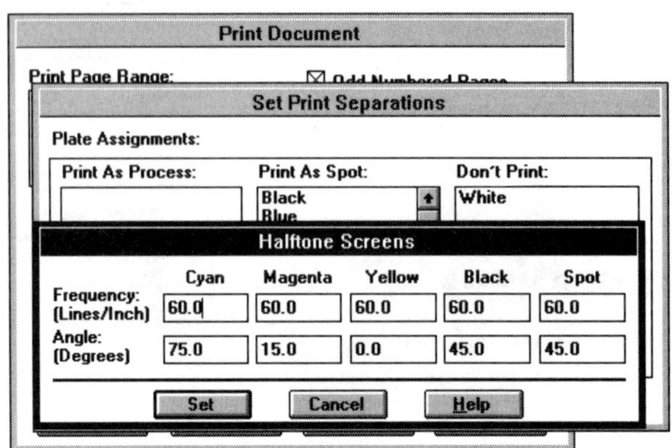

The Spot settings affect only colors that you place in the Print As Spot column of the Set Print Separations dialog box.

The Angle and Frequency settings depend on the exact device you're outputting on as well as the type of paper and press that will be used to print the document. Talk to your imagesetter and your printer to determine appropriate settings.

4. Click Set to return to the Set Print Separations dialog box. If that box is set correctly, click Set to return to the Print Document dialog box.
5. **Check other print settings**
   • If you are printing a proof, you may want to turn on Print Low Resolution images.
   • Skip Blank Pages is a good option when you are printing separations: then FrameMaker does not output a page when a particular color does not occur on it. Otherwise, you get a complete set of pages for each color you choose to print. At the imagesetter's, that can be costly.
   • Check the Setup, Options, and Advanced Options to make sure all settings are as you want them. The halftone settings that you made in the Set Print Separations/Halftone Screens dialog box override the ones in the Advanced Options dialog box.
6. Return to the Print Document box and click Print.

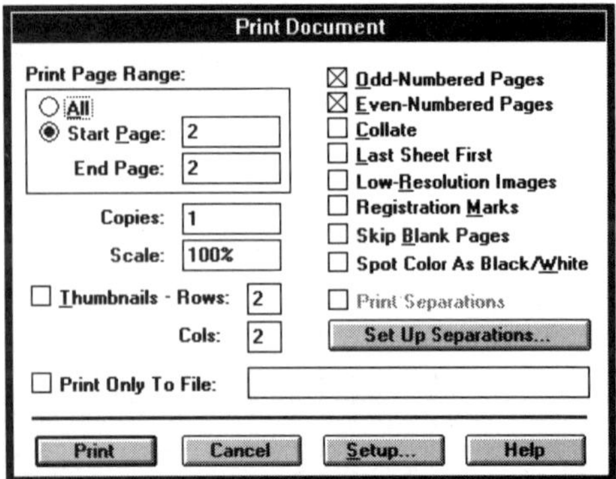

Pages 51 to 54 give more information on print setup.

Hypertext, Conditional Text, and Equations

16

■ What's in this chapter

Stuffed into this last chapter are quick introductions to three of FrameMaker's most powerful features:

Hypertext Create hypertext online documents.

Conditional text Create different versions of a document by choosing which text to display.

Equations Use FrameMaker to typeset the most complex mathematical equations and expressions; and that's not all—use FrameMaker to evaluate them, too!

Create online hypertext documents

FrameMaker gives you all the tools you need to create sophisticated online document systems, and interactive help and demonstrations. If your readers don't all have FrameMaker, you can provide FrameViewer with your document (for a price!).

■ Hypertext

Here is a sketch of the most basic kind of hypertext link and how it works.

What happens

The reader clicks on an area of interest.

FrameMaker displays a page with information about the topic.

How you make it happen

- *Define an active area by applying a character format*
- *Insert a hypertext marker that specifies an action (e.g.,* gotolink*) and a destination in the form of a link name (e.g.,* calculate*). If the link is in a different document, specify the document name as well (e.g.* PartTwo:calculate*).*

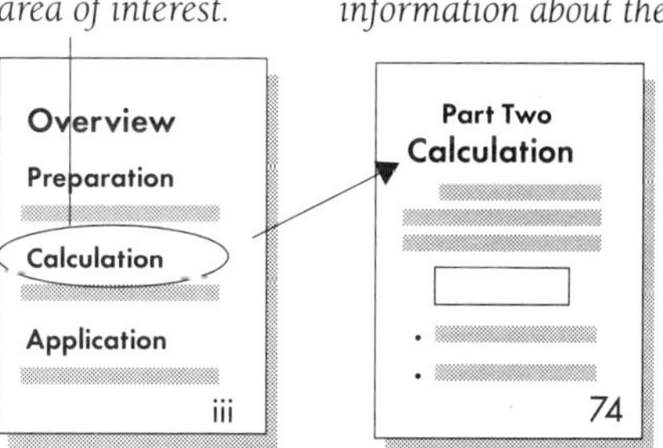

Make it happen, part two

At the destination (the place FrameMaker should go when the reader clicks), place the word newlink *and a matching link name (e.g.,* calculate*).*

Steps to hypertext

The first step, of course, is planning. Much has been written of late on both visual issues and structural approaches in the creation of online documentation. With careful planning on your part, your readers will be inspired and enlightened. A poorly-planned hypertext document will leave them bewildered and frustrated.

Active area An *active area* is an area that a reader can click on to active a hypertext command.

Destination The *destination* is what Frame-Maker displays when a reader clicks the active area.

Here are the steps:

1. **Create one or more character formats** to designate active hypertext areas. You may want more than one to signal different responses to your readers. For example, one color may indicate a pop-up menu, while another signals a move to another part of the same document, and a third signals that a new document will be opened.
   ▲ The character format can use color to signal the active area, or some other property such as underlining or bolding. You can also set all the properties of the format to As Is, so that the active area looks exactly like the surrounding text.
2. **Prepare an active area** by applying one of your hypertext character formats. The area included in the format tells FrameMaker what area is active.
   ▲ An active area cannot have any other character format changes within it.

Hypertext the easy way: Cross-references

In a view-only document, all cross-references become active hypertext areas. When a viewer clicks on any cross-reference, FrameMaker displays the source of the cross-reference. This provides you with a very easy way to create simple hypertext documents, but it can also be a hazard if you don't plan ahead.

Hypertext on master pages

When you want something to appear on every page, such as a navigation aid, place it on the master page. When you draw the text column, make it a background text column *(page 215).*

Overrides *You can override hypertext on a master page by placing a text column over that spot on the body page and placing a new hypertext command.*

3. Insert hypertext markers. Place one in the active area, one at the destination. Follow the instructions for inserting markers on pages 292 to 294. Choose Hypertext as the marker type for both markers.

The syntax of basic active area markers:

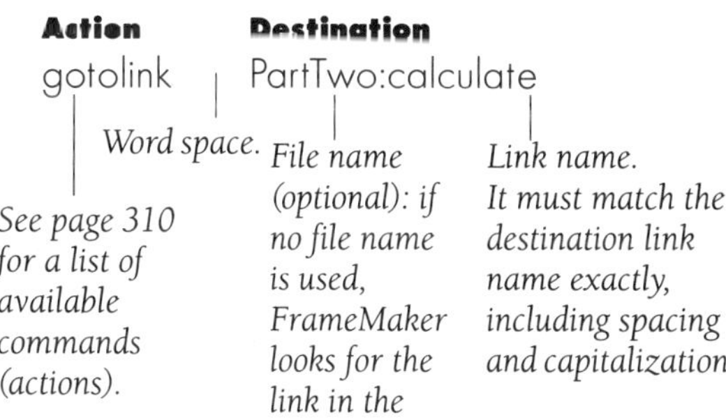

The syntax of destination markers:

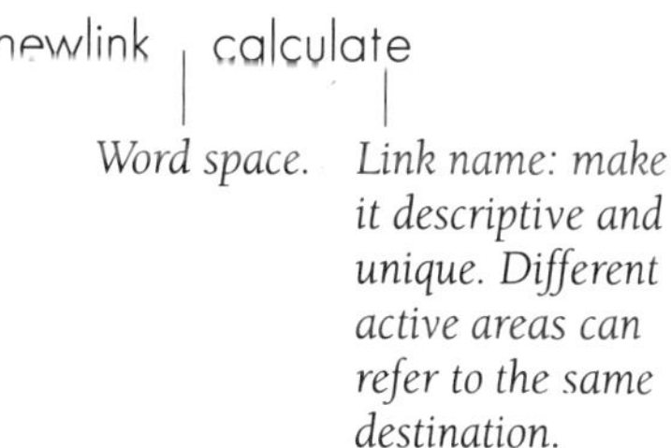

Typing hypertext commands Type the hypertext commands in all lower case. The link names and file names can be any case, but are case-sensitive. ▲ Type a colon between a file name and a link name. ▲ The file name is optional: use it only when the destination is in a different file than the active area. ▲ Be careful not to include a trailing space after a link name.

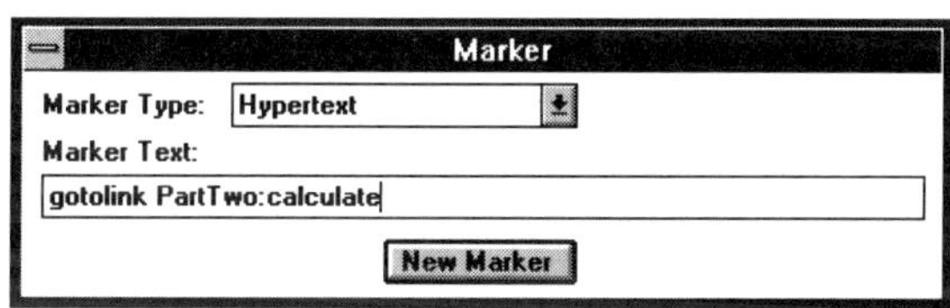

To insert a hypertext marker, place your insertion point in a prepared hypertext area; display the Marker window [**Alt s m**]; *type in the hypertext command and click New Marker.*

4. Make the document **view-only** before you distribute it to users. **Esc F l k** (*capital F, lowercase ell k*) toggles a document between view-only and the "normal," write/view states.

Editing or deleting hypertext commands

■ If the document is view-only, change it to normal. [**Esc F l k** (*capital F, lowercase ell k*)]

■ Follow the instructions on page 292 for editing and deleting markers. Check out the "browse" illustration on page 311, too; it's the same process.

▼

Using hypertext

■ *In a view-only document*, click on an active area.

■ *In a "normal," write/view document*, hold down Ctrl and Alt and click on an active area.

▲

In the commands below, omit filename *if the destination is in the current document.*

Hypertext commands

Here is a list of FrameMaker hypertext commands.

Hypertext command	**Function**
gotolink *filename*:*linkname*	*Displays the page containing the corresponding newlink command in the current window, closing the current document if the link is in a different document.*
gotolink *filename*:**firstpage** **gotolink** *filename*:**lastpage**	*Displays the first or last page in the current window, closing the current document.*
openlink *filename*:*linkname*	*Displays the page containing the corresponding newlink command in a new window if it is in a different document.*
newlink *linkname*	*Marks the location to be displayed by a* gotolink *or* openlink *command with a matching linkname.*
gotopage *filename*:*pagenum*	*Displays the specified page number in the current window.*
openpage *filename*:*pagenum*	*Displays the specified page number in a new window.*
previouslink	*Displays the location before the last "jump."*
previouspage **next page**	*Displays the previous or next page of the current document.*
quit **quitall**	*Closes the current document.* *Closes all view-only documents.*
alert *message*	*Displays a message up to 249 characters long in an Alert box.*
message system (or **message winexec**) *application pathname,windowstate*	*Start another application. Pathname is optional. Default windowstate is* SW_SHOWNORMAL. *Type the command, space, application name, space, pathname, comma, windowstate.*
openew *filename*	*Opens a new, unnamed file. This would let readers open a file from a custom template in a pop-up hypertext list, for example.*
popup *flowname*	*Displays a pop-up menu. Place the* popup *command on the body page. Create the menu of choices and hypertext commands on a reference page in a column of flow* flowname. *The first line is the menu title with no hypertext command in it. Each successive line is a single menu entry containing a single hypertext command.*
matrix *rows columns flowname*	A B C / D E F — *Allows multiple hypertext commands in a single graphic area. Define them on a reference page in a column of flow* flowname. *Each line in the reference page column is one cell. The order of lines is A, B, C, D, E, F.*

Hypertext

Hypertext graphics

You can provide graphics with hypertext functionality. Use this to create navigation buttons, for example, or interactive screen shots.

1. Create the graphic and draw a text column over it.
2. Give the text column a pen and fill of None.
3. Select the text column (Ctrl-click) and bring it to the front of everything. [**Alt g b**]
4. Insert a hypertext marker. The entire text column is now an active area.

Create a graphic.

Draw a text column over it.

Place a hypertext marker in the text column.

A hypertext tutorial

FrameMaker's online help system is an excellent example of real-world hypertext. To get a good look at how the experts create hypertext, do this:

1. Copy one or more help files from \MAKER4\HELP\MAKER to another directory.
2. Open one of the help files and change it from view-only to normal. [**Esc F l k** *(capital F, lowercase ell k)*]
3. Display the Marker window [**Alt s m**], and then use Find Marker of Type Hypertext to browse through the hypertext markers.

More about hypertext

Generate hypertext lists and indexes of information about your file *including lists or indexes of graphics imported by reference, fonts, external or unresolved cross-references, and condition tags; pages 55 and 56.*

Any generated file can be hypertext *Read all about it on pages 276 to 278 and elsewhere in Chapter 13.*

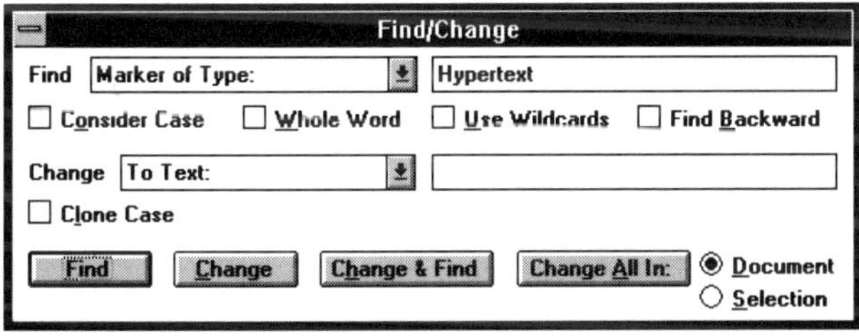

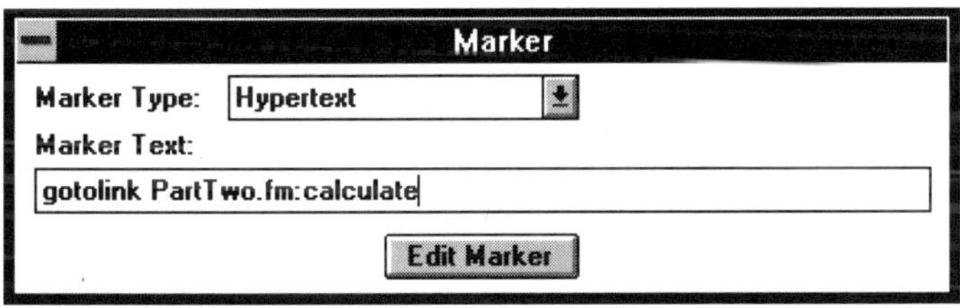

This sequence for browsing hypertext markers (Find Marker of Type Hypertext, look in the Marker window) is also how to edit hypertext commands. To edit a command, change the text in the marker window and click Edit Marker.

■ Conditional documents

When you have several similar documents, combining them into a single conditional document will simplify the task of maintenance. The common portions can be edited and updated only once, instead of having to make sure that a change has been made in several different documents.

What can you conditionalize?

You can select any of the following types of things and apply a condition tag:

- *Text*
- *Anchored frame*
- *All of a table or selected rows*
- *Cross-reference*
- *Variable*
- *Marker*
- *Footnote*

The elements of conditional text

■ **Create** a condition tag for each version of the document.

■ **Apply** appropriate condition tags to text that appears in only certain versions of the document. Text can have more than one condition tag applied to it.

■ Choose which conditions to **display and print**.

Creating a condition tag

1. *Choose* **Special→Conditional Text.**

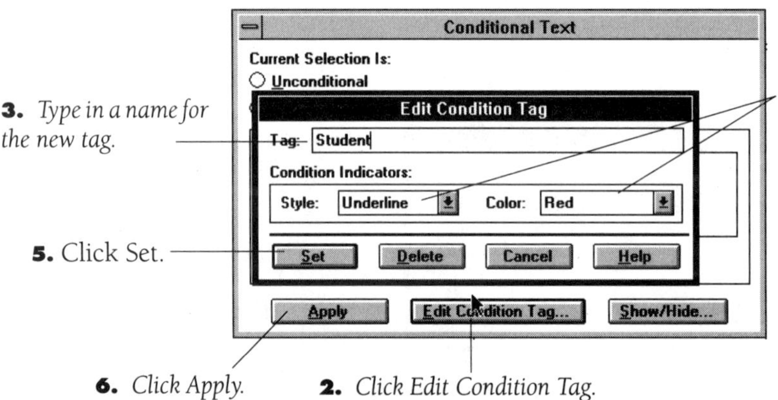

2. *Click Edit Condition Tag.*

3. *Type in a name for the new tag.*

4. *Choose a Style and Color as condition indicators to mark that tag while you're working on the document. You can turn these indicators off whenever you wish (page 314).*

5. Click Set.

6. *Click Apply.*

Editing a condition tag

Highlight the tag name to edit in the Conditional Text window, click Edit Condition Tag, make your changes, then click Set and Apply.

Applying a condition tag

You can apply a condition tag to text using any of three methods: the Conditional Text window, the keyboard, or by copying.

Applying a tag using the Conditional Text window

1. *Select the item to conditionalize.*
2. *Choose* **Special→Conditional Text**

Note *Using this method, you can apply more than one tag at a time.*

The settings in the window are for the currently selected text only. Click Show/Hide to specify what settings to display and print for the whole document.

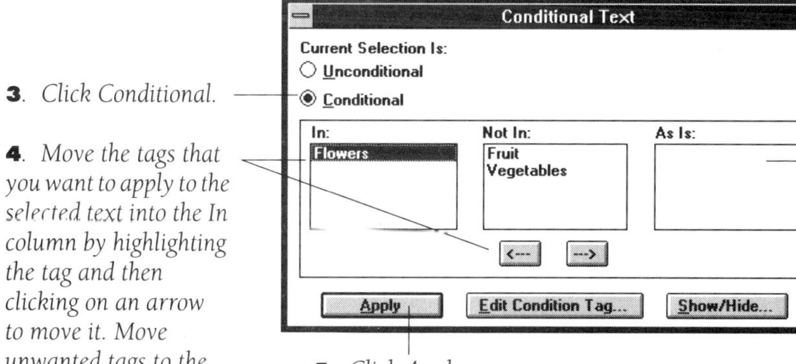

3. *Click Conditional.*
4. *Move the tags that you want to apply to the selected text into the In column by highlighting the tag and then clicking on an arrow to move it. Move unwanted tags to the Not In column.*
5. *Click Apply.*

When your selected text has more than one condition tag applied, all the tags contained in the selection are displayed in the As Is column.

Removing a condition tag from text
Select the text and move the tag to the Not In column. Click Apply.

Applying a tag using the keyboard

1. Select the text.
2. Press **Ctrl-4**. A question mark appears in the Status bar at the bottom of the document window. Begin typing the condition tag name or press the down arrow to scroll through your choices.
3. When the tag name you want to apply appears in the Status bar at the bottom of the document window, press Enter.

?:

Press Ctrl-4 and then watch the Status area at the bottom of the document window as you type the tag name or press the up and down arrow keys.

?:Flowers

When you see the tag name you want, press Enter.

Removing a tag from text using the keyboard Select the text and press Ctrl-5; follow the procedure above. **To remove all condition tags**, select the text and press Ctrl-6.

Deleting a condition tag from a document

- *In the Conditional Text window, highlight the tag to delete.*
- *Click Edit Condition Tag, and click Delete.*
- *Choose whether to delete text that has this tag applied, or to deconditionalize it. Click Set.*

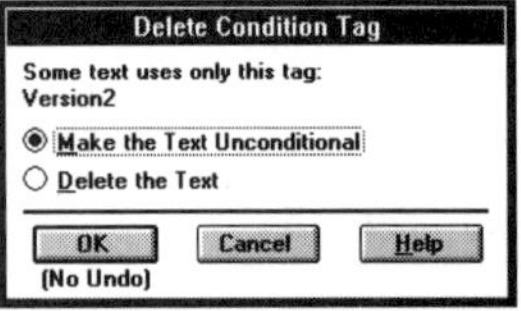

Using Copy Special to apply a condition tag

1. Select text that has the condition tag you want to copy.
2. Choose **Edit→Copy Special→Conditional Text Settings**. [**Alt e o t**]
3. Select the text you want to apply the tag to and paste. [**Ctrl-v**]

Viewing and printing conditional text

You can choose to display (show) as many or as few conditions at a time as you want. When you print, the conditions in the Show list are the ones that will print.

The condition indicators that you specified when you defined your condition tags are useful for editing. You probably want to turn them off when you're ready to print, so that conditional text is not distinguishable from regular text.

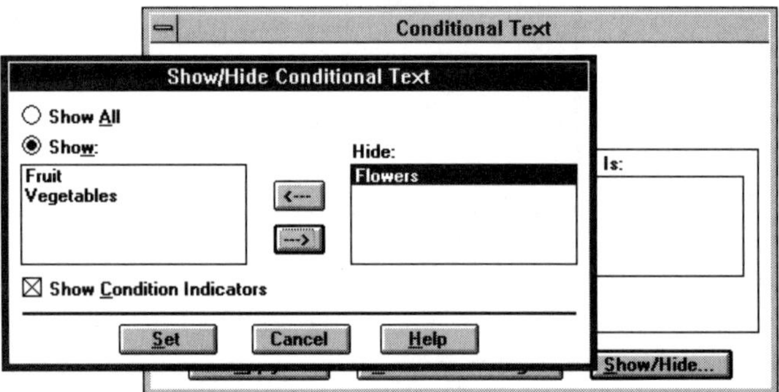

Click on a condition name to highlight it, and then click on an arrow to move the condition name to the appropriate column. When the Show column contains all and only the conditions you want to see and print, click Set.

Guidelines for creating conditional text

- Be consistent about including punctuation and spaces in conditionalized phrases.
- Enter text for different tags in the same sequence each time (e.g., first Vegetables, then Flowers), to make it easier to keep track.
- You can't conditionalize text lines (created with the A tool).
- Insert index markers in appropriate text.
- Both parts of a cross-reference—reference and source—must be in text with the same condition tag.
- FrameMaker places the marker for the source of a cross-reference next to the first word in the paragraph. If the first word is conditional, so is the source marker. You can select the marker and make it unconditional.

■ Equations

FrameMaker provides a *killer* equation feature. It takes my breath away. It's outside the scope of this book to go into detail about using this feature, but I will show you the tools you have to work with, and give you a couple of pointers.

The Equation help system

FrameMaker provides particularly complete online help for equations. Be sure to look it over if you're planning to work with this feature. You can access it from the regular help menu, or you can click the Help button on the Equations palette.

■ When you're looking at the online help, check out the keyboard shortcuts. The backslash codes are listed here; they are needed in working with equations and are not listed anywhere else.

Printing the help files To print a help file, you must copy it to a different directory first. You can then print it normally. *To change the zoom percent*, or reformat after you have copied a help file, you must change it from view-only to normal: **Esc F l k** (*Shift F, lowercase ell k*).

FrameMaker - Help

FRAMEMAKER HELP

Keyboard Shortcuts

Click a main topic in the menu below. Then click a subtopic in the list on the right.

Conventions and function keys | Documents | Windows and dialog boxes | Text | Text formats | Tables | Graphics

Color | Document design | Document utilities | Markers and variables | Conditional text | ▶ Equations

Equations pop-up menu | Symbols page | Operators page | Large page | Delimiters page | Relations page | Calculus page | Matrices page | Functions page | Positioning page | Navigating in an equation | Moving math elements

Index | Shortcuts | More | Done | Main Menu

To see the keyboard shortcuts and backslash codes for equations, choose Shortcut and then click Equations. Then click any item in the list on the right.

▼

The math help files

The help files are all in \MAKER4\HELP\MAKER if MAKER4 is your FrameMaker4 home directory. The keyboard shortcuts for math are in KMATH1.HLP and KMATH2.HLP and the general math help is in MATH1.HLP, MATH2.HLP, and MATH3.HLP.

▲

The Equations palette

To display the Equations palette, click the [Σ] button at the right of the document window, or choose **Special→Equations**. [**Alt s e**]

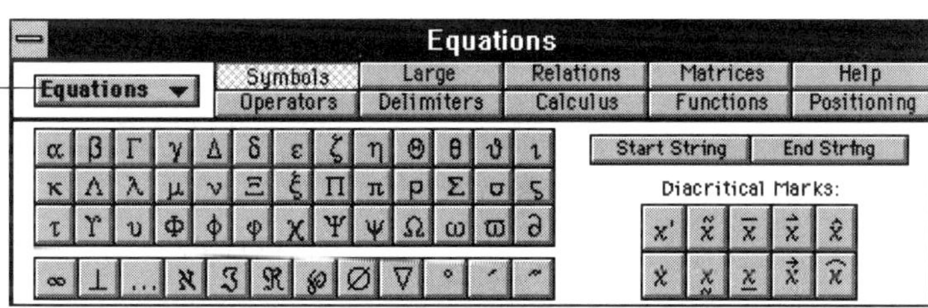

Click on Equations to display the Equations pop-up menu (page 318).

These nine buttons (all but the Help button) access the nine pages of the Equations palette.

Insert a character by clicking on it. Its position depends on what you have selected at the time you click (page 317). All characters in the Equations palette can also be inserted from the keyboard. See the online help for keyboard shortcuts for equations.

This: $x^2 + y^2 = z^2$ is an in-line equation.

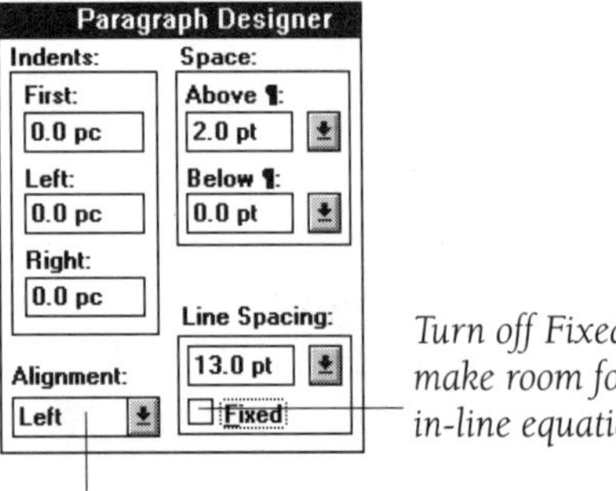

Turn off Fixed to make room for an in-line equation.

Specify the alignment for a display equation here.

Selecting an equation

Place the pointer on the equation and Ctrl-click. You can copy and paste the equation, and drag it around. To be sure you have selected the equation rather than its frame, press **Alt g p** *to display the object properties dialog box.*

Creating equations

1. Place the insertion point in a paragraph if you want an in-line equation. Place the insertion point in an empty paragraph if you want a display equation. Select a frame or an object in the frame to place the equation in a frame.
2. In the Equations palette, click Equations and choose one of the three New Equation items (Small, Medium, or Large). FrameMaker creates an anchored frame below the current line, with the first element highlighted.
3. Create the equation by inserting the math elements you want from the equation palette or the keyboard. See the Teeny-tiny tutorial, page 317.
4. Shrinkwrap the equation. Select the frame containing the equation and choose Shrink-Wrap Equations from the Equations pop-up menu. [**Esc m p**] This removes the extra spacing. If the equation is in a frame rather than a paragraph, you do not need this step.

▲ You may need to turn off Fixed Line Spacing to make room for an in-line equation.

▲ *Number display equations* by formatting the autonumber of the paragraph that contains the equation. If you want the equation number to be flush right and to include the text EQ plus the equation number, for example, set the autonumbering like this for the containing paragraph and set Position to End of Paragraph:

☒ **Autonumber Format:**

EQ <n+>

This would produce the following format:

$x^2 + y^2 = z^2$ EQ 2

Inserting math elements in an equation

- Every math element can be inserted from the equations palette or from the keyboard.
- You *must* select the appropriate part of the equation before inserting the new element. If you are inserting at the insertion point, look carefully at the size of the insertion point to determine the scope. The placement of your new element will depend on what is selected, or on the scope of the insertion point.

Using the Equations palette Display the proper page of the Equations palette by clicking on a button at the top of the palette. Select the appropriate part of the math expression and then click the element on the palette.

Using the keyboard The online help for math gives all the keyboard shortcuts. You can insert any element using the keyboard.

The insertion point

The size of the insertion point tells you where a new element will be inserted:

Insertion point	*What happens when you insert x*
$x^{2|} + ?$	$x^{2x} + ?$
$\frac{x^2 + y|}{x}$	$\frac{x^2 + yx}{x}$
$\frac{x^2 + y}{x}\Big|$	$\frac{x^2 + y}{x}x$

The teeny-tiny tutorial at the side hardly scratches the surface of FrameMaker math, but it will give you a feeling for how this feature works.

A teeny-tiny tutorial

1. *Insert new equation: select the equation object if it's not already highlighted:*

? — *This is an* **equation object**.

2. *Display the Operators page of the Equation palette and click the* ? + ? *button. You get*

$? + ?$

3. *With the first equation object highlighted (selected), type 3x from the keyboard:*

$3x + ?$

4. *Press Tab to select the next equation object* **or** *click next to the* **?** *to select it:*

$3x + ?$

5. *In the Operators page of the Equation palette, click the* $?^?$ *button to get this:*

$3x + ?^?$

6. *Type* **y** *and press Tab to get this:*

$3x + y^?$

7. *Type* **2** *to insert the exponent and then drag across the expression to get this:*

$3x + y^2$

8. *Type* **x** *to get this; notice that FrameMaker inserts the parentheses automatically:*

$(3x + y^2)x$

9. *Click anywhere in the expression and press the space bar until the whole expression is selected:*

$(3x + y^2)x$

10. *In the Operators page of the Equation palette, click the* $\frac{?}{?}$ *button to get this:*

$$\frac{(3x + y^2)x}{?}$$

Equations

The Equations menu

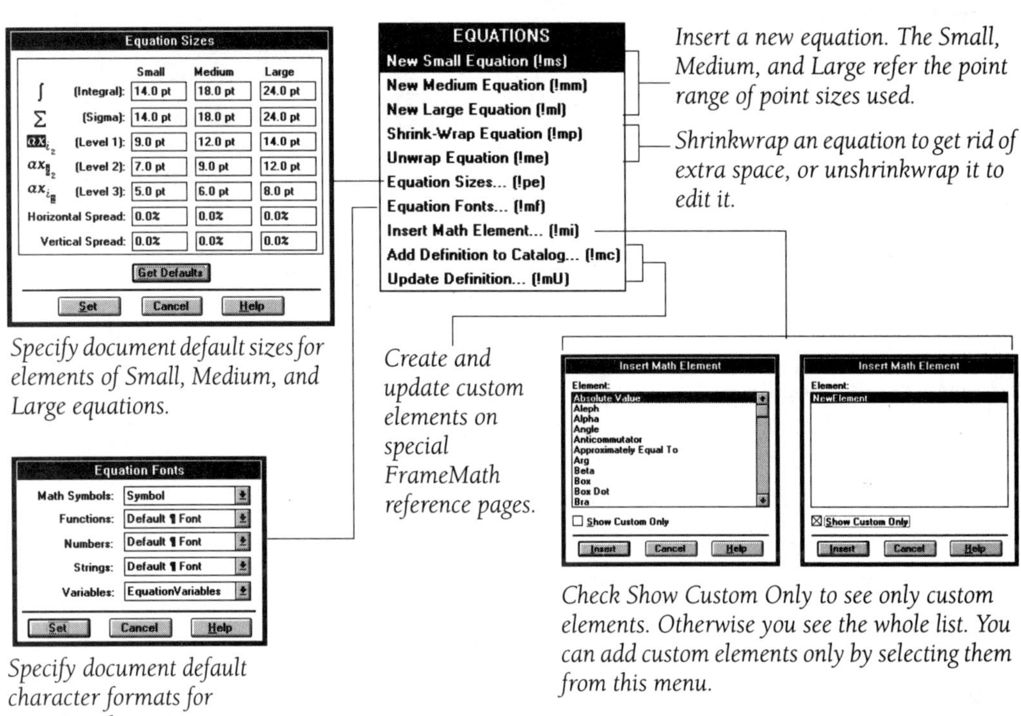

Insert a new equation. The Small, Medium, and Large refer the point range of point sizes used.

Shrinkwrap an equation to get rid of extra space, or unshrinkwrap it to edit it.

Specify document default sizes for elements of Small, Medium, and Large equations.

Create and update custom elements on special FrameMath reference pages.

Check Show Custom Only to see only custom elements. Otherwise you see the whole list. You can add custom elements only by selecting them from this menu.

Specify document default character formats for equation elements.

Equation palette highlights

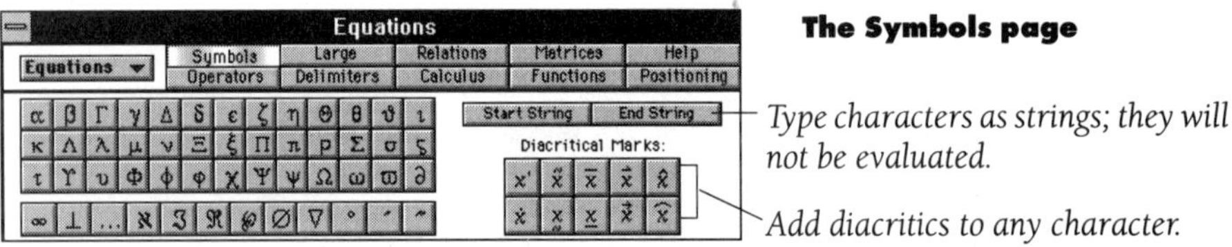

The Symbols page

Type characters as strings; they will not be evaluated.

Add diacritics to any character.

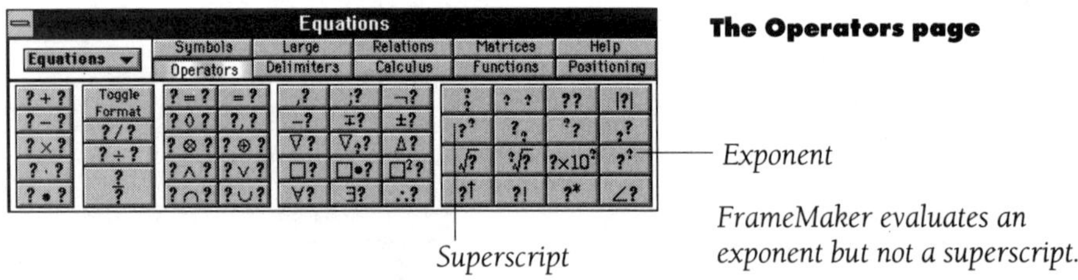

The Operators page

Exponent

FrameMaker evaluates an exponent but not a superscript.

Superscript

Equations palette highlights *continued*

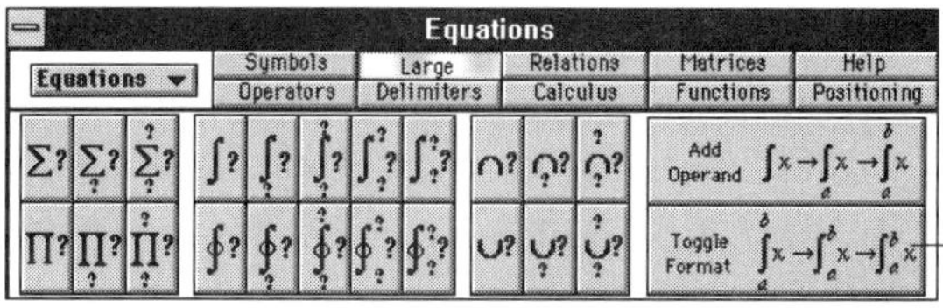

The Large page

Use this page to create things like this:

$$\sum_{x=0}^{x=12} x^2$$

Toggle the format with ease:

$$\sum\nolimits_{x=0}^{x=12} x^2$$

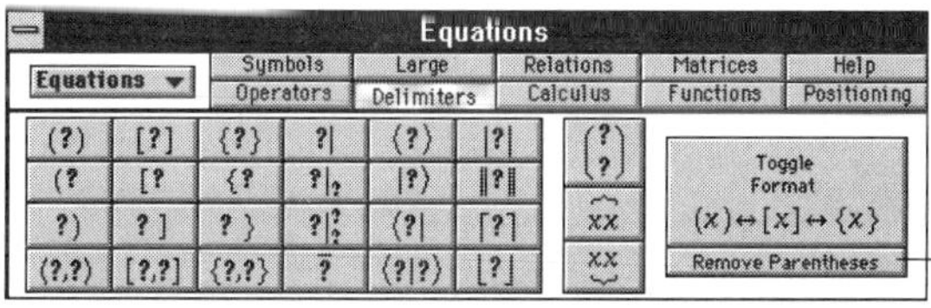

The Delimiters page

Remove parentheses from the selected expression here.

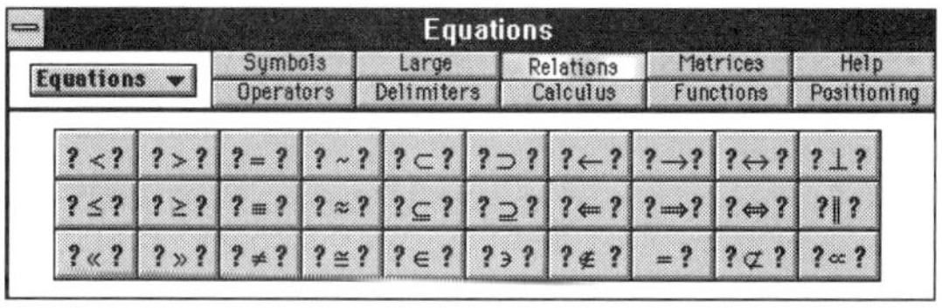

The Relations page

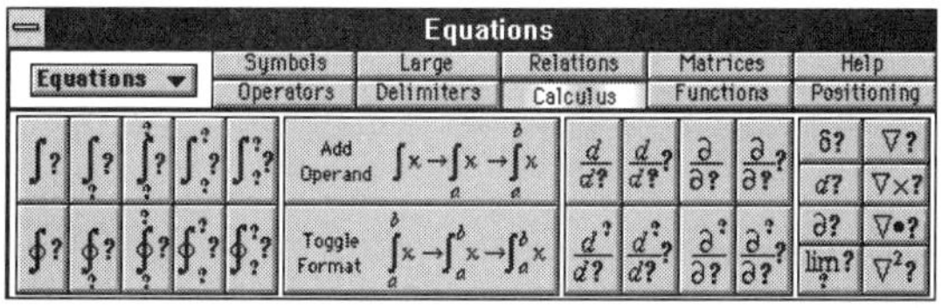

The Calculus page

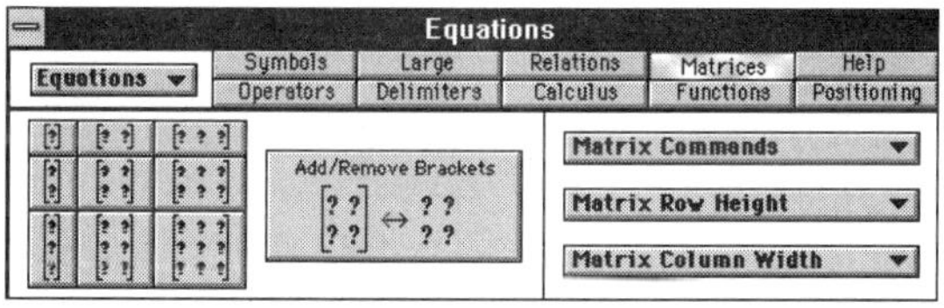

The Matrices page

Create and evaluate matrices.

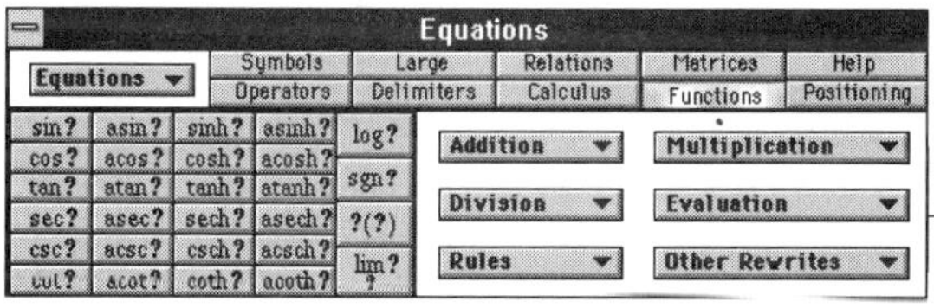

The Functions page

These buttons produce menus for a huge variety of ways to **evaluate equations.**

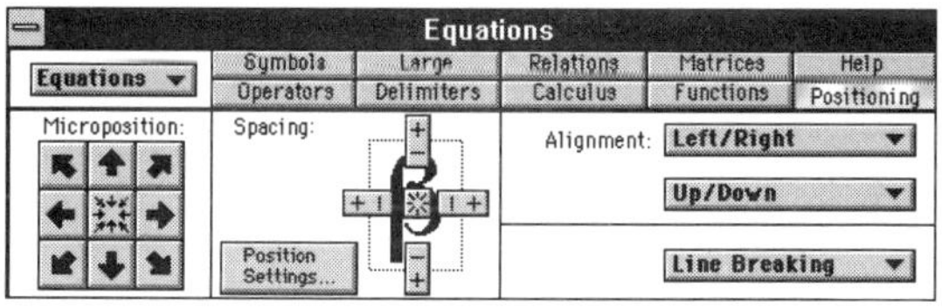

The Positioning page

If you don't like FrameMaker's original spacing and line breaks, you can improve on them here.

Equations

Evaluate equations

There are seven menus of commands available for evaluating mathematical expressions and equations. Six of them are accessed from the six buttons on the Functions page of the Equations palette. The seventh, Matrix Commands, is on the Matrices page.

This page simply shows the menus you have available.

The first six menus are all accessed from the six buttons on the Functions page of the Equations palette.

ADDITION
- Add Fractions (!maa)
- Order Sum (!mao)
- Order Sum Reverse (!maO)

DIVISION
- Long Division (!mdl)
- Remove Division (!mdd)
- Remove Division 1 Level (!mdD)
- Remove Negative Powers (!mdn)
- Remove Negative Powers 1 Level (!mdN)

RULES
- Enter Rule (!mre)
- Apply Rule (!mra)
- Designate Dummy (!mrd)

MULTIPLICATION
- Factor (!muf)
- Factor Some (!muF)
- Multiply Out (!mum)
- Multiply Out Once (!muM)
- Distribute (!mud)
- Distribute Over Equality (!muD)

EVALUATION
- Number Crunch (!mvn)
- Show All Digits (!mv.)
- Evaluate (!mve)
- Evaluate Substitution (!mvs)
- Evaluate Integrals (!mvi)
- Evaluate Derivatives (!mvd)
- Evaluate Derivatives 1 Level (!mvD)

OTHER REWRITES
- Simplify (!mos)
- Simplify Some (!moS)
- Isolate Term (!moi)
- Expand First Term (!moe)
- Expand All Terms (!moE)

MATRIX COMMANDS
- Create 1 x 1 Matrix (!xm)
- Add Row (!xr)
- Add Column (!xc)
- Matrix Transpose (!xt)
- Matrix Algebra (!xa)

Access the Matrix Commands menu from the Matrices page of the Equations palette.

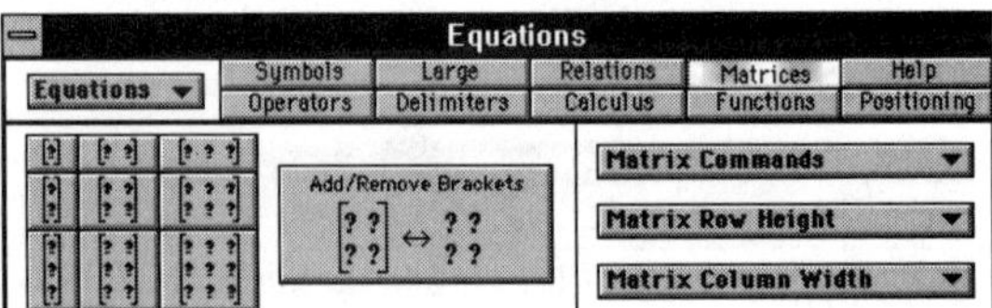

Accessing Special Characters

■ Special characters in text

In regular text, you can use either the ANSI numbers or the key sequence. The result is the same, but the technique is different.

The ANSI numbers

1. First change to the font that contains the character you want.
2. Turn on NumLock. Hold down the Alt key, and type the ANSI number on the numeric keypad. Always start with a zero.

The key sequence

1. Type the key sequence before you change fonts. Some of them don't work of you change to a symbol font before typing the sequence.
2. If the character you want is in a font other than your text font, select the character you just inserted in step one, and apply the necessary font. Use the Character Designer, or apply a character format that has the right font.

Note It's essential that you change the font first (or apply the font to a space or dummy character) if you're using the ANSI number. If you use a key sequence, it's equally essential that you type the key sequence before applying the font. Some of the key sequences won't work if you chanoge to a symbol font first.

Quotation marks

You type quotation marks differently depending on whether Smart Quotes are on or off (page 81).

Character	Smart Quotes on	Smart Quotes off
“	"	Ctrl-Alt-`
”	"	Ctrl-Alt-'
‘	'	`
’	'	'
'	Ctrl-'	Ctrl-'
"	Esc "	"

Typing accented characters

To type an accented character, type Esc plus one of the symbols in the table, plus the letter.

Type this	plus this	to get this	Example
Esc	' *Single quote*	´	Esc ' a = á
	`	`	Esc ` a = à
	^	ˆ	Esc ^ a = â
	~	˜	Esc ~ n = ñ
	%	¨	Esc % a = ä
	*	˚	Esc * a = å
	, *Comma*	¸ *Cedilla*	Esc , c = ç

Many accented characters can also be accessed using their ANSI character numbers.

Dialog box codes

- Type the hex code to insert any character in a dialog box; **or**
- Type the dialog box codes which are somewhat simpler and more mnemonic.

▲ To use either code, type all the characters, beginning with the backslash.

What's a dialog box?

FrameMaker calls these "dialog box codes," but they get used in some windows, as well. Examples of dialog boxes and windows where you might need special characters are: Find/Change, Autonumber Format, Spell Checking, editing user or system variables, editing cross-reference formats, and the Marker window.

Changing fonts in a dialog box

- To access characters that are in a font other than the default paragrpah font, create a character format that calls the font you need (page 79).
- In Autonumber Format, Edit Cross-Reference Format, Edit System Variable, and Edit User Variable, you can select the character format you need from a scroll menu. In the Marker window, you must type in the name of the format enclosed in angle brackets, like this: <C-Callout>. To change back to your text font, type: <Default Para Font>.

Find/change codes

The following codes are used only in the Find/Change window:

Type this	To find this
\<	start of word
\>	end of word
\P	beginning of paragraph
\p	end of paragraph

Dialog box codes

Type this	To get this	
\b	•	bullet
\t		tab
\d	†	dagger
\D	‡	double dagger
\e	...	ellipsis
\TM	™	trademark (serif)
\%	‰	perthousand
\-		discretionary hyphen
\+	-	nonbreaking hyphen
\m	—	em dash
\=	–	en dash
\sm		em space
\sn		en space
\st		thin space
\s#		numeric space
space		nonbreaking space
\r		line return *(does not work in Autonumber Formats)*
\`	“	left double quote
\'	”	right double quote
`	‘	left single quote
'	’	right single quote
\"	'	straight quote
"	"	straight double quote
V	¤	fraction
\F	*f*	florin
\(	‹	guilsinglleft
\)	›	guilsinglright
\, *(comma)*	,	quotesinglebase
\g	„	quotedblbase
\@	ˆ	circumflex
\{	`	grave
\&	2	hungarumlaut
\~	˜	tilde
\oe	œ	oe
\OE	Œ	OE

■ Standard character set

See pages A-321 and A-322 for more information about when and how to access characters using ANSI numbers, hex codes, and key sequences.

This first short table is a collection of special characters that have no ANSI numbers. Access them with the key sequence in text, and with the hex codes or dialog box codes in dialog boxes (page A-322).

Key sequence notation A hyphen means hold down both keys at once; a space means type them in sequence, without holding anything down.

Character	Hex	Key sequence
discretionary hyphen	\x04	Esc hyphen d *or* Ctrl-hyphen
suppress hyphenation	\x05	Esc n s
nonbreaking hyphen	\x15	Esc hyphen h
tab	\x08	Tab
forced return	\x09	Shift-Return
end of paragraph	\x0a	Return
numeric space	\x10	Esc space 1 *(one)*
nonbreaking space	\x11	Esc space h *or* Ctrl-space
thin space	\x12	Esc space t
en space	\x13	Esc space n *or* Ctrl-Alt-space
em space	\x14	Esc space m *or* Ctrl-Shift-space
single quote '	\x27	Ctrl-'
grave accent `	\x60	Ctrl-`
hungarian umlaut ˝	\xfd	Ctrl-q }
fraction bar	\xda	Ctrl-q Z

Starting with ANSI number 32, you can use either the ANSI number or the key sequence to place a character in regular text. Use the hex code in dialog boxes. For some characters, a special dialog box code is available (page A-322).

Char.	ANSI	Hex	Key sequence
space	032	\x20	*space*
!	033	\x21	!
"	034	\x22	*See page A-321*
#	035	\x23	#
$	036	\x24	$
%	037	\x25	%
&	038	\x26	&
(	040	\x28	(
)	041	\x29	)
*	042	\x2a	*
+	043	\x2b	+
,	044	\x2c	,
-	045	\x2d	-
.	046	\x2e	.
/	047	\x2f	/
0	048	\x30	0
1	049	\x31	1
2	050	\x32	2
3	051	\x33	3
4	052	\x34	4
5	053	\x35	5
6	054	\x36	6
7	055	\x37	7
8	056	\x38	8

Char.	ANSI	Hex	Key sequence
9	057	\x39	9
:	058	\x3a	:
;	059	\x3b	;
<	060	\x3c	<
=	061	\x3d	=
>	062	\x3e	>
?	063	\x3f	?
@	064	\x40	@
A	065	\x41	A
B	066	\x42	B
C	067	\x43	C
D	068	\x44	D
E	069	\x45	E
F	070	\x46	F
G	071	\x47	G
H	072	\x48	H
I	073	\x49	I
J	074	\x4a	J
K	075	\x4b	K
L	076	\x4c	L
M	077	\x4d	M
N	078	\x4e	N
O	079	\x4f	O
P	080	\x50	P
Q	081	\x51	Q
R	082	\x52	R
S	083	\x53	S
T	084	\x54	T
U	085	\x55	U
V	086	\x56	V
W	087	\x57	W
X	088	\x58	X
Y	089	\x59	Y

Char.	ANSI	Hex	Key sequence
Z	090	\x5a	Z
[	091	\x5b	[
\	092	\x5c	\
]	093	\x5d	]
^	094	\x5e	^
_	095	\x5f	_
a	097	\x61	a
b	098	\x62	b
c	099	\x63	c
d	0100	\x64	d
e	0101	\x65	e
f	0102	\x66	f
g	0103	\x67	g
h	0104	\x68	h
i	0105	\x69	i
j	0106	\x6a	j
k	0107	\x6b	k
l	0108	\x6c	l
m	0109	\x6d	m
n	0110	\x6e	n
o	0111	\x6f	o
p	0112	\x70	p
q	0113	\x71	q
r	0114	\x72	r
s	0115	\x73	s
t	0116	\x74	t
u	0117	\x75	u
v	0118	\x76	v
w	0119	\x77	w
x	0120	\x78	x
y	0121	\x79	y
z	0122	\x7a	z
{	0123	\x7b	{

Char.	ANSI	Hex	Key sequence
|	0124	\x7c	¦
}	0125	\x7d	}
~	0126	\x7e	~
‚	0130	\xe2	Ctrl-q b
ƒ	0131	\xc4	Ctrl-q D
„	0132	\xe3	Ctrl-q c
…	0133	\xc9	Ctrl-q I *(shift eye)*
†	0134	\xa0	Ctrl-q *space*
‡	0135	\xe0	Ctrl-q `
ˆ	0136	\xf6	Ctrl-q v
‰	0137	\xe4	Ctrl-q d
Š	0138	\xb3	Ctrl-q 3
‹	0139	\xdc	Ctrl-q \
Œ	0140	\xce	Ctrl-q N
‘ *(left quote)*	0145	\xd4	Ctrl-q T
’ *(right quote)*	0146	\xd5	Ctrl-q U
“	0147	\xd2	Ctrl-q R, Ctrl-Alt-`
”	0148	\xd3	Ctrl-q S, Ctrl-Alt-'
•	0149	\xa5	Ctrl-q %
– *(en dash)*	0150	\xd0	Ctrl-q P
— *(em dash)*	0151	\xd1	Ctrl-q Q
˜	0152	\xf7	Ctrl-q w
™	0153	\xaa	Ctrl-q *
š	0154	\xf0	*reserved*
›	0155	\xdd	Ctrl-q]
œ	0156	\xcf	Ctrl-q O *(shift oh)*
Ÿ	0159	\xd9	Esc % Y
¡	0161	\xc1	Ctrl-q A
¢	0162	\xa2	Ctrl-q "
£	0163	\xa3	Ctrl-q #
¤	0164	\xdb	Ctrl-q [
¥	0165	\xb4	Ctrl-q 4

Char.	ANSI	Hex	Key sequence
¦	0166	\xad	Ctrl-q - *(hyphen)*
§	0167	\xa4	Ctrl-q $
¨	0168	\xac	Ctrl-q , *(comma)*
©	0169	\xa9	Ctrl-q)
ª *(fem ord)*	0170	\xbb	Ctrl-q ; *(semicolon)*
«	0171	\xc7	Ctrl-q G
¬	0172	\xc2	Ctrl-q B
-	0173	\x2d	- *(hyphen)*
®	0174	\xa8	Ctrl-q (
¯ *(macron)*	0175	\xf8	Ctrl-q x
° *(ring)*	0176	\xfb	Ctrl-q {
±	0177	\xb1	Ctrl-q 1 *(one)*
²	0178	\xb7	Ctrl-q 7
³	0179	\xb8	Ctrl-q 8
´ *(acute)*	0180	\xab	Ctrl-q +
µ	0181	\xb5	Ctrl-q 5
¶	0182	\xa6	Ctrl-q &
·	0183	\xe1	Ctrl-q a
¸	0184	\xfc	Ctrl-q ¦ *(pipe)*
¹	0185	\xb6	Ctrl-q 6
º *(masc)*	0186	\xbc	Ctrl-q <
»	0187	\xc8	Ctrl-q H
¼	0188	\xb9	Ctrl-q 9
½	0189	\xba	Ctrl-q : *(colon)*
¾	0190	\xbd	Ctrl-q =
¿	0191	\xc0	Ctrl-q @
À	0192	\xcb	Esc ` A
Á	0193	\xe7	Esc ' A
Â	0194	\xe5	Esc ^ A
Ã	0195	\xcc	Esc ~ A
Ä	0196	\x80	Esc % A
Å	0197	\x81	Esc * A

Char.	ANSI	Hex	Key sequence
Æ	0198	\xae	Ctrl-q . *(period)*
Ç	0199	\x82	Esc comma C
È	0200	\xe9	Esc ` E
É	0201	\x83	Esc ' E
Ê	0202	\xe6	Esc ^ E
Ë	0203	\xe8	Esc % E
Ì	0204	\xed	Esc ` I *(shift eye)*
Í	0205	\xea	Esc ' I *(shift eye)*
Î	0206	\xeb	Esc ^ I *(shift eye)*
Ï	0207	\xec	Esc % I *(shift eye)*
Đ	0208	\xc3	Ctrl-q C
Ñ	0209	\x84	Esc ~ N
Ò	0210	\xf1	Esc ` O *(shift oh)*
Ó	0211	\xee	Esc ' O *(shift oh)*
Ô	0212	\xef	Esc ^ O *(shift oh)*
Õ	0213	\xcd	Esc ~ O *(shift oh)*
Ö	0214	\x85	Esc % O *(shift oh)*
×	0215	\xb0	Ctrl-q 0 *(zero)*
Ø	0216	\xaf	Ctrl-q /
Ù	0217	\xf4	Esc ` U
Ú	0218	\xf2	Esc ' U
Û	0219	\xf3	Esc ^ U
Ü	0220	\x86	Esc % U
Ý	0221	\xc5	Ctrl-q E
Þ	0222	\xd7	Ctrl-q W
ß	0223	\xa7	Ctrl-q '
à	0224	\x88	Esc ` a
á	0225	\x87	Esc ' a
â	0226	\x89	Esc ^ a
ã	0227	\x8b	Esc ~ a
ä	0228	\x8a	Esc % a
å	0229	\x8c	Esc * a
æ	0230	\xbe	Ctrl-q >

Char.	ANSI	Hex	Key sequence
ç	0231	\x8d	Esc comma c
è	0232	\x8f	Esc ` e
é	0233	\x8e	Esc ' e
ê	0234	\x90	Esc ^ e
ë	0235	\x91	Esc % e
ì	0236	\x93	Esc ` i *(unshift eye)*
í	0237	\x92	Esc ' i *(unshift eye)*
î	0238	\x94	Esc ^ i *(unshift eye)*
ï	0239	\x95	Esc % i *(unshift eye)*
ð	0240	\xb2	Ctrl-q 2
ñ	0241	\x96	Esc ~ n
ò	0242	\x98	Esc ` o *(unshift oh)*
ó	0243	\x97	Esc ' o *(unshift oh)*
ô	0244	\x99	Esc ^ o *(unshift oh)*
õ	0245	\x9b	Esc ~ o *(unshift oh)*
ö	0246	\x9a	Esc % o *(unshift oh)*
÷	0247	\xd6	Ctrl-q V
ø	0248	\xbf	Ctrl-q ?
ù	0249	\x9d	Esc ` u
ú	0250	\x9c	Esc ' u
û	0251	\x9e	Esc ^ u
ü	0252	\x9f	Esc % u
ý	0253	\xc6	Ctrl-q F
þ	0254	\xca	Ctrl-q J
ÿ	0255	\xd8	Esc % y

■ Zapf Dingbats

Char.	ANSI	Hex	Key sequence
✁	033	\x21	!
✂	034	\x22	" *(straight dbl quote)*
✃	035	\x23	#
✄	036	\x24	$
☎	037	\x25	%
✆	038	\x26	&
✇	*not used*	\x27	Ctrl-'
✈	040	\x28	(
✉	041	\x29	)
☛	042	\x2a	*
☞	043	\x2b	+
✌	044	\x2c	, *(comma)*
✍	045	\x2d	- *(hyphen)*
✎	046	\x2e	. *(period)*
✏	047	\x2f	/
✐	048	\x30	0
✑	049	\x31	1
✒	050	\x32	2
✓	051	\x33	3
✔	052	\x34	4
✕	053	\x35	5
✖	054	\x36	6
✗	055	\x37	7
✘	056	\x38	8
✙	057	\x39	9
✚	058	\x3a	: *(colon)*
✛	059	\x3b	; *(semicolon)*
✜	060	\x3c	<
✝	061	\x3d	=
✞	062	\x3e	>
✟	063	\x3f	?

Char.	ANSI	Hex	Key sequence
✠	064	\x40	@
✡	065	\x41	A
✢	066	\x42	B
✣	067	\x43	C
✤	068	\x44	D
✥	069	\x45	E
✦	070	\x46	F
✧	071	\x47	G
★	072	\x48	H
✩	073	\x49	I
✪	074	\x4a	J
✫	075	\x4b	K
✬	076	\x4c	L
✭	077	\x4d	M
✮	078	\x4e	N
✯	079	\x4f	O
✰	080	\x50	P
✱	081	\x51	Q
✲	082	\x52	R
✳	083	\x53	S
✴	084	\x54	T
✵	085	\x55	U
✶	086	\x56	V
✷	087	\x57	W
✸	088	\x58	X
✹	089	\x59	Y
✺	090	\x5a	Z
✻	091	\x5b	[
✼	092	\x5c	\
✽	093	\x5d	]
✾	094	\x5e	^

Char.	ANSI	Hex	Key sequence
✿	095	\x5f	_ *(underline)*
❀	*not used*	\x60	Ctrl-`
❁	097	\x61	a
❂	098	\x62	b
❃	099	\x63	c
❄	0100	\x64	d
❅	0101	\x65	e
❆	0102	\x66	f
❇	0103	\x67	g
❈	0104	\x68	h
❉	0105	\x69	i
❊	0106	\x6a	j
❋	0107	\x6b	k
●	0108	\x6c	l
❍	0109	\x6d	m
■	0110	\x6e	n
❏	0111	\x6f	o
❐	0112	\x70	p
❑	0113	\x71	q
❒	0114	\x72	r
▲	0115	\x73	s
▼	0116	\x74	t
◆	0117	\x75	u
❖	0118	\x76	v
◗	0119	\x77	w
❘	0120	\x78	x
❙	0121	\x79	y
❚	0122	\x7a	z
❛	0123	\x7b	{
❜	0124	\x7c	¦
❝	0125	\x7d	}
❞	0126	\x7e	~
❡	0161	\xa1	Ctrl-q !
❢	0162	\xa2	Ctrl-q "
❣	0163	\xa3	Ctrl-q #
❤	0164	\xa4	Ctrl-q $
❥	0165	\xa5	Ctrl-q %
❦	0166	\xa6	Ctrl-q &
❧	0167	\xa7	Ctrl-q '
♣	0168	\xa8	Ctrl-q (
♦	0169	\xa9	Ctrl-q)
♥	0170	\xaa	Ctrl-q *
♠	0171	\xab	Ctrl-q +
①	0172	\xac	Ctrl-q , *(comma)*
②	0173	\xad	Ctrl-q - *(hyphen)*
③	0174	\xae	Ctrl-q . *(period)*
④	0175	\xaf	Ctrl-q /
⑤	0176	\xb0	Ctrl-q 0
⑥	0177	\xb1	Ctrl-q 1
⑦	0178	\xb2	Ctrl-q 2
⑧	0179	\xb3	Ctrl-q 3
⑨	0180	\xb4	Ctrl-q 4
⑩	0181	\xb5	Ctrl-q 5
❶	0182	\xb6	Ctrl-q 6
❷	0183	\xb7	Ctrl-q 7
❸	0184	\xb8	Ctrl-q 8
❹	0185	\xb9	Ctrl-q 9
❺	0186	\xba	Ctrl-q : *(colon)*
❻	0187	\xbb	Ctrl-q ; *(semicolon)*
❼	0188	\xbc	Ctrl-q <
❽	0189	\xbd	Ctrl-q =
❾	0190	\xbe	Ctrl-q >
❿	0191	\xbf	Ctrl-q ?
➀	0192	\xc0	Ctrl-q @
➁	0193	\xc1	Ctrl-q A
➂	0194	\xc2	Ctrl-q B
➃	0195	\xc3	Ctrl-q C
➄	0196	\xc4	Ctrl-q D
➅	0197	\xc5	Ctrl-q E
➆	0198	\xc6	Ctrl-q F

Char.	ANSI	Hex	Key sequence
⑧	0199	\xc7	Ctrl-q G
⑨	0200	\xc8	Ctrl-q H
⑩	0201	\xc9	Ctrl-q I *(shift eye)*
❶	0202	\xca	Ctrl-q J
❷	0203	\xcb	Esc ` A
❸	0204	\xcc	Esc ~ A
❹	0205	\xcd	Esc ~ O *(shift oh)*
❺	0206	\xce	Ctrl-q N
❻	0207	\xcf	Ctrl-q O *(shift oh)*
❼	0208	\xd0	Ctrl-q P
❽	0209	\xd1	Ctrl-q Q
❾	0210	\xd2	Ctrl-q R
❿	0211	\xd3	Ctrl-q S
➔	0212	\xd4	Ctrl-q T
→	0213	\xd5	Ctrl-q U
↔	0214	\xd6	Ctrl-q V
↕	0215	\xd7	Ctrl-q W
➘	0216	\xd8	Esc % y
➙	0217	\xd9	Esc % Y
➚	0218	\xda	Ctrl-q Z
➛	0219	\xdb	Ctrl-q [
➜	0220	\xdc	Ctrl-q \
➝	0221	\xdd	Ctrl-q]
➞	0222	\xde	Ctrl-q ^
➟	0223	\xdf	Ctrl-q _ *(underline)*
➠	0224	\xe0	Ctrl-q `
➡	0225	\xe1	Ctrl-q a
➢	0226	\xe2	Ctrl-q b
➣	0227	\xe3	Ctrl-q c
➤	0228	\xe4	Ctrl-q d
➥	0229	\xe5	Esc ^ A
➦	0230	\xe6	Esc ^ E
➧	0231	\xe7	Esc ' A
➨	0232	\xe8	Esc % E
➩	0233	\xe9	Esc ` E
➪	0234	\xea	Esc ' I *(shift eye)*
➫	0235	\xeb	Esc ^ I *(shift eye)*
➬	0236	\x93	Esc % I *(shift eye)*
➭	0237	\xed	Esc `i *(unshift eye)*
➮	0238	\xee	Esc 'O *(shift oh)*
➯	0239	\xef	Esc ^ O *(shift oh)*
➱	0241	\xf1	Esc ` O *(shift oh)*
➲	0242	\xf2	Esc ' U
➳	0243	\xf3	Esc ^ U
➴	0244	\xf4	Esc ` U
➵	0245	\xf5	Ctrl-q u
➶	0246	\xf6	Ctrl-q v
➷	0247	\xf7	Ctrl-q w
➸	0248	\xf8	Ctrl-q x
➹	0249	\xf9	Ctrl-q y
➺	0250	\xfa	Ctrl-q z
➻	0251	\xfb	Ctrl-q {
➼	0252	\xfc	Ctrl-q ¦
➽	0253	\xfd	Ctrl-q }
➾	0254	\xfe	Ctrl-q ~

Symbols

Char.	ANSI	Hex	Key sequence
!	033	\x21	!
∀	034	\x22	" *(straight dbl quote)*
#	035	\x23	#
∃	036	\x24	$
%	037	\x25	%
&	038	\x26	&
∋	*not used*	\x27	Ctrl-'
(	040	\x28	(
)	041	\x29	)
∗	042	\x2a	*
+	043	\x2b	+
,	044	\x2c	, *(comma)*
− *(minus)*	045	\x2d	- *(hyphen)*
.	046	\x2e	. *(period)*
/	047	\x2f	/
0	048	\x30	0
1	049	\x31	1
2	050	\x32	2
3	051	\x33	3
4	052	\x34	4
5	053	\x35	5
6	054	\x36	6
7	055	\x37	7
8	056	\x38	8
9	057	\x39	9
:	058	\x3a	: *(colon)*
;	059	\x3b	; *(semicolon)*
<	060	\x3c	<
=	061	\x3d	=
>	062	\x3e	>
?	063	\x3f	?

Char.	ANSI	Hex	Key sequence
≅	064	\x40	@
Α	065	\x41	A
Β	066	\x42	B
Χ	067	\x43	C
Δ	068	\x44	D
Ε	069	\x45	E
Φ	070	\x46	F
Γ	071	\x47	G
Η	072	\x48	H
Ι	073	\x49	I
ϑ	074	\x4a	J
Κ	075	\x4b	K
Λ	076	\x4c	L
Μ	077	\x4d	M
Ν	078	\x4e	N
Ο	079	\x4f	O
Π	080	\x50	P
Θ	081	\x51	Q
Ρ	082	\x52	R
Σ	083	\x53	S
Τ	084	\x54	T
Υ	085	\x55	U
ς	086	\x56	V
Ω	087	\x57	W
Ξ	088	\x58	X
Ψ	089	\x59	Y
Ζ	090	\x5a	Z
[	091	\x5b	[
∴	092	\x5c	\
]	093	\x5d	]
⊥	094	\x5e	^

Char.	ANSI	Hex	Key sequence
_	095	\x5f	_ *(underline)*
α	097	\x61	a
β	098	\x62	b
χ	099	\x63	c
δ	0100	\x64	d
ε	0101	\x65	e
ϕ	0102	\x66	f
γ	0103	\x67	g
η	0104	\x68	h
ι	0105	\x69	i
φ	0106	\x6a	j
κ	0107	\x6b	k
λ	0108	\x6c	l
μ	0109	\x6d	m
ν	0110	\x6e	n
ο	0111	\x6f	o
π	0112	\x70	p
θ	0113	\x71	q
ρ	0114	\x72	r
σ	0115	\x73	s
τ	0116	\x74	t
υ	0117	\x75	u
ϖ	0118	\x76	v
ω	0119	\x77	w
ξ	0120	\x78	x
ψ	0121	\x79	y
ζ	0122	\x7a	z
{	0123	\x7b	{
|	0124	\x7c	¦
}	0125	\x7d	}
~	0126	\x7e	~
ϒ	0161	\xa1	Ctrl-q !
′	0162	\xa2	Ctrl-q "
≤	0163	\xa3	Ctrl-q #
⁄	0164	\xa4	Ctrl-q $
∞	0165	\xa5	Ctrl-q %
ƒ	0166	\xa6	Ctrl-q &
♣	0167	\xa7	Ctrl-q '
♦	0168	\xa8	Ctrl-q (
♥	0169	\xa9	Ctrl-q)
♠	0170	\xaa	Ctrl-q *
↔	0171	\xab	Ctrl-q +
←	0172	\xac	Ctrl-q , *(comma)*
↑	0173	\xad	Ctrl-q - *(hyphen)*
→	0174	\xae	Ctrl-q . *(period)*
↓	0175	\xaf	Ctrl-q /
°	0176	\xb0	Ctrl-q 0
±	0177	\xb1	Ctrl-q 1
″	0178	\xb2	Ctrl-q 2
≥	0179	\xb3	Ctrl-q 3
×	0180	\xb4	Ctrl-q 4
∝	0181	\xb5	Ctrl-q 5
∂	0182	\xb6	Ctrl-q 6
•	0183	\xb7	Ctrl-q 7
÷	0184	\xb8	Ctrl-q 8
≠	0185	\xb9	Ctrl-q 9
≡	0186	\xba	Ctrl-q : *(colon)*
≈	0187	\xbb	Ctrl-q ; *(semicolon)*
…	0188	\xbc	Ctrl-q <
|	0189	\xbd	Ctrl-q =
—	0190	\xbe	Ctrl-q >
↵	0191	\xbf	Ctrl-q ?
ℵ	0192	\xc0	Ctrl-q @
ℑ	0193	\xc1	Ctrl-q A
ℜ	0194	\xc2	Ctrl-q B
℘	0195	\xc3	Ctrl-q C
⊗	0196	\xc4	Ctrl-q D
⊕	0197	\xc5	Ctrl-q E
∅	0198	\xc6	Ctrl-q F
∩	0199	\xc7	Ctrl-q G

Char.	ANSI	Hex	Key sequence
∪	0200	\xc8	Ctrl-q H
⊃	0201	\xc9	Ctrl-q I *(shift eye)*
⊇	0202	\xca	Ctrl-q J
⊄	0203	\xcb	Esc ` A
⊂	0204	\xcc	Esc ~ A
⊆	0205	\xcd	Esc ~ O *(shift oh)*
∈	0206	\xce	Ctrl-q N
∉	0207	\xcf	Ctrl-q O *(shift oh)*
∠	0208	\xd0	Ctrl-q P
∇	0209	\xd1	Ctrl-q Q
®	0210	\xd2	Ctrl-q R
©	0211	\xd3	Ctrl-q S
™	0212	\xd4	Ctrl-q T
∏	0213	\xd5	Ctrl-q U
√	0214	\xd6	Ctrl-q V
·	0215	\xd7	Ctrl-q W
¬	0216	\xd8	Esc % y
∧	0217	\xd9	Esc % Y
∨	0218	\xda	Ctrl-q Z
⇔	0219	\xdb	Ctrl-q [
⇐	0220	\xdc	Ctrl-q \
⇑	0221	\xdd	Ctrl-q]
⇒	0222	\xde	Ctrl-q ^
⇓	0223	\xdf	Ctrl-q _ *(underline)*
◊	0224	\xe0	Ctrl-q `
〈	0225	\xe1	Ctrl-q a
®	0226	\xe2	Ctrl-q b
©	0227	\xe3	Ctrl-q c
™	0228	\xe4	Ctrl-q d
∑	0229	\xe5	Esc ^ A
⎛	0230	\xe6	Esv ^ E
⎜	0231	\xe7	Esc ' A
⎝	0232	\xe8	Esc % E
⎡	0233	\xe9	Esc ` E

Char.	ANSI	Hex	Key sequence
⎢	0234	\xea	Esc ' I *(shift eye)*
⎣	0235	\xeb	Esc ^ I *(shift eye)*
⎧	0236	\x93	Esc % I *(shift eye)*
⎨	0237	\xed	Esc `i *(unshift eye)*
⎩	0238	\xee	Esc 'O *(shift oh)*
⎪	0239	\xef	Esc ^ O *(shift oh)*
〉	0241	\xf1	Esc ` O *(shift oh)*
∫	0242	\xf2	Esc ' U
⌠	0243	\xf3	Esc ^ U
⎮	0244	\xf4	Esc ` U
⌡	0245	\xf5	Ctrl-q u
⎞	0246	\xf6	Ctrl-q v
⎟	0247	\xf7	Ctrl-q w
⎠	0248	\xf8	Ctrl-q x
⎤	0249	\xf9	Ctrl-q y
⎥	0250	\xfa	Ctrl-q z
⎦	0251	\xfb	Ctrl-q {
⎫	0252	\xfc	Ctrl-q ¦
⎬	0253	\xfd	Ctrl-q }
⎭	0254	\xfe	Ctrl-q ~

Index

Index

Index

Index

Acknowledgements

My heartfelt thanks to Jeremy Griffith of Omni Systems, without whom this book would not have happened, and to Ardis Waters and Stephen Pitcher for proofreading, editing, and moral support.

Thanks also to Ted Nace of Peachpit Press for believing in me, and to Roslyn Bullas for being a pleasure to work with.

Wayne Rainey and Kristin Vais of Frame Technology Corp. were tremendously supportive and encouraging of me, which I appreciate greatly, and the FrameMaker tech support people willingly provided me with a great deal of friendly and competent consultation. Thank you all.

More from Peachpit Press...

CorelDRAW 4: Visual QuickStart Guide
Webster & Associates
Our QuickStart guide on CorelDRAW 3 was so popular that we've put together a new edition covering CorelDRAW 4, the latest version of this versatile drawing program. Not only does it cover the basics and newest features of CorelDRAW, but it also incorporates features of CorelTRACE and CorelMOSAIC. *(350 pages)*

Desktop Publishing Secrets
Robert Eckhardt, Bob Weibel, and Ted Nace
This is a compilation of hundreds of the best desktop-publishing tips from five years of *Publish* magazine. It covers all the major graphics and layout programs on the PC and Macintosh platforms, and valuable tips on publishing as a business. *(550 pages)*

Dr. Daniel's Windows Diet
Daniel Will-Harris
Put Windows on a high-performance diet! This little book offers simple solutions to a universal problem—Windows can be slow. This set of easy-to-follow prescriptions covers the essentials of making Windows work faster—from autoexec.bat to virtual memory. It helps you work faster, too, with keyboard shortcuts, file tips and more. *(96 pages)*

Four Colors/One Image
Mattias Nyman
Step-by-step procedures for reproducing and manipulating color images using Photoshop, QuarkXPress and Cachet. Filled with before-and-after examples, this is an invaluable resource for those who need great color output. *(84 pages)*

Jargon
Robin Williams
Finally! A book that explains over 1200 of the most useful computer terms in a way that readers can understand. This straightforward guide not only defines computer-related terms but also explains how and why they are used. Covers both the Macintosh and PC worlds. *(688 pages)*

The Little PC Book
Larry Magid
Friendly advice on the basic concepts of operating a computer in non-technical, bite-size pieces. *The Little PC Book* won rave reviews for providing a painless way to become PC literate without being buried in details. Rather than covering a wide range of non-essential information, this book helps make a novice more comfortable with his or her PC. *(376 pages)*

And here's even more selections,

The Little Windows Book, 3.1 Edition
Kay Yarborough Nelson
This second edition of Peachpit's popular book explains the subtle and not-so-subtle changes in Windows 3.1 as it gives the essentials of getting started with Windows. Additionally, each chapter includes a handy summary chart of keyboard shortcuts and quick tips. *(144 pages)*

The Little WordPerfect for Windows Book
Kay Yarborough Nelson
This book gives you the basic skills you need in order to create simple documents and helps you become familiar with WordPerfect's new Windows interface. *(200 pages)*

Mastering CorelDRAW 3
Chris Dickman
Like its earlier versions, this terrific tutorial book is studded with tips and undocumented features, and covers topics such as service bureau output and default customizing. Includes two disks that contain utilities and 26 commercial-grade TrueType fonts. *(600 pages)*

The PC is not a typewriter
Robin Williams
PC users can now learn trade secrets from author Robin Williams, whose best-selling *The Mac is not a typewriter* introduced tens of thousands of Mac users to the secrets of creating beautiful type. Covers punctuation, leading, special characters, kerning, fonts, justification, and more. *(96 pages)*

Photoshop in Black and White
Jim Rich and Sandy Bozek
An illustrated guide to reproducing black and white images using Adobe Photoshop 2.5. Provides detailed information on how to adjust the tonal range of black and white images for optimum reproduction. *(489pages)*

Photoshop for Windows: Visual QuickStart Guide
Elaine Weinmann and Peter Lourekas
The author of our award-winning *QuarkXPress for Windows: Visual QuickStart Guide* does it again. An indispensable guide for Windows users who want to get started in Adobe Photoshop but who don't have a lot of time to read books. Covers how to use masks, filters, colors, tools, and more. *(264 pages)*

QuarkXPress for Windows: Visual QuickStart Guide
Elaine Weinmann
Take an easy, visual approach to learning the basics of QuarkXPress. This handy guide covers everyday features of one of the most popular and powerful desktop publishing programs. Put together in a concise, straightforward way so you'll be up and running in no time. *(224 pages)*

all available from Peachpit Press.

The QuarkXPress Book, Windows Edition
David Blatner and Bob Weibel
The Mac version of this book has been a bestseller for two years—so useful that Quark's own support staff uses it. It tells you everything you need to know about QuarkXPress—importing and modifying graphics, creating large documents, printing, and much more. *(542 pages)*

Real World Scanning and Halftones
David Blatner and Steve Roth
Master the digital halftone process—from scanning images to tweaking them on your Mac to imagesetting them. Learn about optical character recognition, gamma control, sharpening, PostScript halftones, Photo CD and popular image-manipulation software like Adobe Photoshop and PhotoStyler. *(296 pages)*

Windows 3.1 Font Book
David Angell and Brent Heslop
The first hands-on font guide for Windows users. This book explains managing, choosing, and using fonts, with instructions for working with TrueType and PostScript fonts. It also contains suggestions for building a font library, with a list of font vendors and over 100 font samples. *(184 pages)*

Word for Windows Essentials
Geoffrey Mandel
This book is a handy reference to Word for Windows 2.0, loaded with useful tips and tricks. It explains both basic and advanced features, and you'll learn how to customize your program and use the math and graphics features. Now you can master this popular and sophisticated word processing program! *(232 pages)*

WordPerfect: Desktop Publishing in Style, 2nd Edition
Daniel Will-Harris
This popular guide (over 90,000 in print) to producing documents with WordPerfect 5.0 or 5.1 opens with a tutorial and proceeds through 20 sample documents. Humorous and fun to read, this book is invaluable to people who desktop publish using WordPerfect. *(672 pages)*

WordPerfect for Windows with Style
Daniel Will-Harris
Gives step-by-step instructions for creating good-looking business documents using WordPerfect for Windows. Shows a variety of documents, provides insights into styles, graphics, fonts, tables, macros, clip art, printers, and utilities. Will Harris combines technical accuracy with detailed and easy-to-understand explanations. *(528 pages)*

Order Form

to order, call:

(800) 283-9444 or (510) 548-4393 or (510) 548-5991 (fax)

#	Title	Price	Total
	CorelDRAW 4: Visual QuickStart Guide	15.00	
	Desktop Publishing Secrets	27.95	
	Dr. Daniel's Windows Diet	8.95	
	Four Colors / One Image	18.00	
	FrameMaker 4 for Windows: Visual QuickStart Guide	17.95	
	The Little PC Book	17.95	
	The Little Windows Book, 3.1 Edition	12.95	
	The Little WordPerfect for Windows Book	12.95	
	Mastering Corel Draw 3 (with 2 disks)	38.00	
	The PC is not a typewriter	9.95	
	Photoshop in Black and White	18.00	
	Photoshop for Windows: Visual QuickStart Guide	18.95	
	QuarkXPress for Windows: Visual QuickStart Guide	15.00	
	The QuarkXPress Book, Windows Edition	28.00	
	Real World Scanning and Halftones	24.95	
	Windows 3.1 Font Book	12.95	
	Word for Windows Essentials	14.00	
	WordPerfect: Desktop Publishing in Style, 2nd Edition	23.95	

SHIPPING:	First Item	Each Additional
UPS Ground	$ 4	$ 1
UPS Blue	$ 8	$ 2
Canada	$ 6	$ 4
Overseas	$14	$14

Subtotal		
8.25% Tax (CA only)		
Shipping		
TOTAL		

Name

Company

Address

City　　State　　Zip

Phone　　Fax

❑ Check enclosed　　❑ Visa　　❑ MasterCard

Company purchase order #

Credit card #　　Expiration Date

Peachpit Press, Inc. • 2414 Sixth Street • Berkeley, CA • 94710

Your satisfaction is guaranteed or your money will be cheerfully refunded!